Professional
Rich Internet Applications:
AJAX and Beyond

Dana Moore

Raymond Budd

Edward Benson

Wiley Publishing, Inc

Professional Rich Internet Applications: AJAX and Beyond

Published by
Wiley Publishing, Inc.
10475 Crosspoint Boulevard
Indianapolis, IN 46256
www.wiley.com

ISBN: 978-0-470-08280-5

Manufactured in the United States of America

10 9 8 7 6 5 4 3 2 1

Library of Congress Cataloging-in-Publication Data is available from the publisher.

For general information on our other products and services please contact our Customer Care Department within the United States at (800) 762-2974, outside the United States at (317) 572-3993 or fax (317) 572-4002.

Wiley also publishes its books in a variety of electronic formats. Some content that appears in print may not be available in electronic books.

About the Authors

Dana Moore is a division scientist with BBN Technologies and is an acknowledged expert in the fields of peer-to-peer and collaborative computing, software agent frameworks, and assistive environments. Prior to joining BBN, Dana was chief scientist for Roku Technologies, and a Distinguished Member of Technical Staff at Bell Laboratories. Dana is a popular conference speaker, a university lecturer, and has published both articles for numerous computing publications, and books, including *Peer-to-Peer: Building Secure, Scalable, and Manageable Networks* and *Jabber Developer Handbook*. Dana holds a master of science degree in technology management from the University of Maryland, and a bachelor of science in industrial design, also from the University of Maryland.

Raymond Budd is a software engineer with BBN Technologies. He has designed, developed, and supported a variety of Web applications and other distributed systems in Java, Ruby, and Python. He has been published in several conference proceedings, such as the Eighteenth National Conference on Artificial Intelligence, and journals, including *Applied Intelligence*. Additional areas of interest include knowledge representations, knowledge engineering, and distributed planning and scheduling. He received a bachelor of science degree in computer science from the University of Pittsburgh.

Edward (Ted) Benson is a software engineer with BBN Technologies. His experience and interests include distributed programming frameworks, multi-agent systems, Web development, and knowledge representation. Ted has developed Web applications for several community groups and companies, and he has been published in IEEE conference proceedings on the subjects of distributed and multi-agent systems. He gradated *summa cum laude* from the University of Virginia with a bachelor of science degree in computer science.

Credits

Acquisitions Editor
Kit Kemper

Development Editor
Maureen Spears

Technical Editor
William Wright

Production Editor
William A. Barton

Copy Editor
Luann Rouff

Editorial Manager
Mary Beth Wakefield

Production Manager
Tim Tate

Vice President and Executive Group Publisher
Richard Swadley

Vice President and Executive Publisher
Joseph B. Wikert

Graphics and Production Specialists
Brooke Graczyk
Barbara Moore
Heather Ryan
Alicia B. South

Quality Control Technicians
John Greenough
Jessica Kramer
Brian H. Walls

Project Coordinator
Adrienne Martinez

Media Development Project Supervisor
Laura Carpenter Van Winkle

Media Development Specialists
Angie Penny
Kit Malone
Kate Jenkins
Steve Kudirka

Proofreading and Indexing
Aptara

Anniversary Logo Design
Richard Pacifico

Acknowledgments

The authors gratefully acknowledge the contributions of our friend and colleague William Wright, whom we cajoled into acting as the technical editor and all-around technical conscience of this book. Our warmest gratitude also to Maureen Spears, our English editor at Wiley, who put up with our terrible geek humor during conference calls and worked tirelessly to bring the quality of this book up to what you see before you.

We also appreciate the Web 2.0 luminaries who agreed to share their expertise and candid opinions with us, and our readers for the interviews scattered throughout the book. These include Dojo Toolkit's Alex Russell, Ruby on Rails' David Heinemeier Hansson, 37Signals' Jason Fried, and Second Life's Wagner James Au. We thank our BBN colleagues John Hebeler, for his entertaining sidebar comments, and Jonathan Nilsson, for his helpful comments.

Finally, and most important, we thank our friends, families, and significant others for their forbearance. Writing is a solitary activity that tends to exclude others, even those most important to us; and we appreciate all their support, and promise somehow to make up for the lost time and opportunities.

For Jane, who "walks in beauty, like the night of cloudless climes and starry skies; And all that's best of dark and bright meet in her aspect and her eyes," and for Caitlin, who, like the spring breeze, breathes new life to the suffocated hills, and comes as the herald of each new dawn's possibilities.

—DM

For Leah, with love. I am inspired by your intelligence, strength, and beauty, and am immensely grateful for the support and understanding you gave me as I wrote this. Also for my parents with appreciation for everything you've taught me throughout my life.

—RB

For Grace, her warm eyes, gentle wisdom, and wonderful laugh.

And for my four parents, who taught me all the important things I know in life.

—EB

Contents

Contents

Contents

Contents

Contents

Contents

Contents

Contents

Contents

Introduction

This introduction orients you to the rest of the book and takes you for a brief tour of its primary subject, Rich Internet Application (RIA) architecture and how it evolved. In looking at how we could best serve our readers, we tried to create a blend of three elements to accomplish the following:

- ❑ Give you a sense of how RIAs are different from the previous generation of Web applications and how this difference is important to you, whether you are a corporate or independent software developer

- ❑ Present significant supporting code examples, rich enough to be complete and nontrivial, but simple enough to present in a page or two of code

- ❑ Describe and demonstrate important frameworks and APIs

Who Is This Book For?

The authors make no assumptions about the background of the book's readers other than that you are working software developers interested in practical solutions to real-world problems. This book explains how to use enabling technologies to create new kinds of distributed systems with features rivaling desktop systems. Whether your skills are in Web development, server architectures, or agile languages, you should find value in this book.

Given the fact that the examples are written in Python, Java, and Ruby on Rails, it is best if you have some familiarity with one of these languages. We do assume you have some experience developing and deploying Web applications, and can read basic UML diagrams. Finally, you should be familiar with basic database management operations, although any required database administration steps are clearly outlined in each chapter.

What Is This Book's Focus?

Because the authors are professional corporate software developers, we know that the quickest road to understanding code and APIs is to review working code examples, but often books consist of a stream of didactic examples. Although this approach may reveal important points of a topic, it ultimately leaves you unfulfilled because the simple examples don't build anything compelling outside of the context of the point the author is trying to make. Thus, this book focuses on an interesting and feature-complete application that functions as a recurring theme holding the book together and helps you to gain a growing sense of mastery over RIA design, frameworks, and implementation.

Accordingly, you have the opportunity to build a *capstone* application, which we call *ideaStax*. IdeaStax is an idea capture tool that enables users, either singly or in community, to record, tag, search, organize, and present ideas. Ideas are the atomic units of ideaCards, and ideaCards are the building blocks of ideaStax. IdeaStax serves multiple other purposes too. For one thing, it serves to illustrate the notion of how applications might change in capability and character if they were built from the ground up to reflect RIA concepts and capabilities. In a sense, you might think of ideaStax as a re-envisioning of what a desktop application such as Microsoft's PowerPoint might be like if it had been designed to conform to the concepts of RIAs in the twenty-first century, instead of the rich client platform (RCP) of the twentieth.

In addition to getting the code for ideaStax from the Wrox publishing site (`www.wrox.com`), the authors are developing a site (`ideaStax.com`) where you can also contribute ideas and code, show off your skills, and participate in evolving the application and its capabilities in the best tradition of open-source software. If your contributions are worthwhile, you can become a committer to the project.

The Book's Topical Approach

For several decades now, developers have believed certain things to be objectively true, perhaps even indisputable. We consider ourselves members of a specific development and deployment "tribe." Rather than consider yourself a developer, you may consider yourself to be a "Java developer," or "Microsoft .Net developers," with the limitations and technology constraints implied by membership in the tribe. In the case of Java, this means "one language, many platforms," and in the case of Microsoft Windows 32 APIs, it means "a few languages, one platform." In any event, writing for a rich client platform traditionally means having developers make compromises, having end users manage installation and updates, and having the involvement of corporate IT departments. The economics and mechanics of selling and buying licensed software have created a heavy burden for everyone involved in the process.

It's hardly possible to have been a software developer for any length of time and not have written code using a rich client API for Windows, MAC OS/X, or Linux. Thus, we're all familiar with the rich client platform (RCP) model. Almost every application we've written, used, managed, or deployed over the last three decades on microcomputers adheres to RCP capabilities and limitations. When you think like an RCP developer, you may take for granted that the operating system, data access and storage, and the user's experience of the application are tightly bound. This accounts for the responsiveness of certain types of applications — word processors, for example.

Now this status quo is changing, and changing rapidly. By the end of 2005, a good deal of "buzz" was emerging over something called AJAX (asynchronous JavaScript and XML). AJAX, while simply an umbrella term for assembling applications by using several mature technologies already in common use, nevertheless seemed to evoke something more than the sum of its constituent parts. There's now growing recognition that a tectonic shift promises to change the very foundations of how we develop and deploy applications. The Web is undergoing a profound transformation from a collection of news articles, static forms, and bulletin boards to a location-agnostic computing platform in and of itself.

Together, we will explore the elements of this change in browser-based applications — from greater dynamism and responsiveness to faster development cycles to greater embrace of social networking. The phrase "programming above the platform level" has come to be closely associated with Rich Internet Applications. We didn't invent the phrase, but we will illustrate, in many working examples in multiple programming languages, the importance of this concept to Web 2.0 applications and even beyond.

Our objective is to prepare both the corporate and independent developer to take advantage of this new emerging landscape. As the world of shrink-wrapped boxes of client-side software begins to wane, a new ecology of Rich Internet Applications is emerging to bring both developers and end users new benefits that take full advantage of today's connected world. Developers who take advantage of this new ecology will prosper and stay at the front of their professional ranks.

Learning the technical approaches from this book, and understanding how and why Rich Internet Applications are different, will teach you to look at the world from a completely different point of view. For one thing, you will discover that most of the "action" of your applications actually takes place not on the user's desktop but on a server that may exist anywhere, and that what users see and experience through their browser is far more simplistic — mediated by the constraints of the browser.

RCP applications have a richness and responsiveness that has been generally impossible on the Web. Traditionally, the simplicity that enabled easy deployment to the Web has also brought with it a gap between the experiences you can provide and the experiences users can get from a desktop application. Now, for perhaps the first time since the inception of the Web, that gap may be closing. Emerging is a new generation of applications in which the line between rich client and rich Internet applications is blurring; and perhaps in the not too distant future it will disappear altogether.

Consider Google Suggest. Watch the way the suggested terms update as you type, almost instantly. Now look at Google Maps. Zoom in. Use your cursor to grab the map and scroll around a bit. Again, everything happens almost instantly, with no waiting for pages to reload. Google Suggest and Google Maps are two examples of a new approach to Web applications that use *AJAX* effectively, and each in its way represents a fundamental shift in what's possible on the Web.

Consider the various models for creating new applications or redesigning existing ones:

- ❏ **Desktop model** — In this model, the rich client platform (RCP) tool still "owns" your ability to manipulate the data model (i.e., the Word doc, the Excel spreadsheet, etc.). The desktop paradigm creates a "walled garden" by tightly integrating the operating system, the data format, and file system organization, which tends to constrain the user.

- ❏ **Web 1.0 or "old school" Web applications** — In this model, the user fills out a form, clicks and submits, and then waits nervously for a response, hoping that application integrity will not be broken. Developers have dealt with this level of Internet application brokenness for many years now by various improvisational means, including cookies for session robustness and hidden fields in form-based applications to orchestrate multi-step transaction-oriented applications.

- ❏ **RIA (Rich Internet Application) model** — In this new model, users walk up to a handy device, start a browser, and access their assets and applications. It doesn't matter what kind of machine it's on or what kind of browser they use — any modern browser will do. In the RIA model, users needn't lug anything from home to work to home again in order to be functional or productive. Often, the data assets the user creates are stored in an industry-standard format (HTML, XML). Users can leave them on the server in the Net, or make a local copy (to a host computer's hard disk or to a flash drive, for example).

What's key in the new generation of RIAs is the degree to which *partial page replacement* involves the server side of the application in maintaining application state and robustness. We will make the point more than once that the key to the liveliness of RIAs is this idea of partial page replacement. When the user doesn't have to wait for a server to serve up the entire page after every user interaction, a browser-based application can hardly help being perceived as delivering a better user experience. Not coincidentally, the developer experience becomes better as well, involving far less ad hoc code.

Consider, therefore, the direct consequences of creating new applications using RIAs, for yourself as a developer, for your users, and for your potential to leverage the climate for innovation. The RIA model directly and immediately threatens the hegemony over the user of such players as Microsoft. Currently, whoever owns the OS and the RCP tools controls the user. The more users who buy into a given platform and toolset (MS Windows and MS Office, for example), the higher the level of control over users. There is a so-called *network effect* that creates a value to a potential customer dependent on the number of customers already owning that tool. The RIA model creates a network effect as well, so a viral adoption menaces the status quo and creates new opportunity for you as a developer, writing for yourself or for the enterprise.

Frameworks and JavaScript Libraries

A number of incredible frameworks and JavaScript have emerged in the past few years, and we cover a number of these. The general philosophy behind current frameworks is that given current connection speeds, page composition and partial page replacement by the server becomes the norm, rather than the exception. The wide proliferation of broadband (over 70 million broadband connected computers in the U.S. alone) has opened up server interaction to a degree not possible before.

Thus, even though the XmlHttpRequest and response (about which we will be saying much more) has been available in modern browsers for several years, only recently have we seen applications such as Google Map pioneering its use, and making partial page replacement the rule rather than the exception. Consequently, we have seen a commensurate rise in simple Java, Python, and Ruby servers, and a decrease in complex and formal multi-tiered schemes such as WSDL. This book covers a few server frameworks, including Google Widget Toolkit (Java), TurboGears (Python), and Ruby on Rails (Ruby).

On the client side, dramatic changes are taking place as well. JavaScript has always been considered a painful fact of life for developers. A quirky language, never a developer favorite, and lacking a strong unifying open-source library layer, it now has a number of libraries, from MochiKit, whose mantra is that it "makes JavaScript suck less," to Prototype, the library of choice underlying so many Rails applications. You will examine both of these libraries.

The Hybrids and the Exotics

In addition to strictly browser-based RIAs, we also cover two other incarnations of networks-centric applications, the first exemplified by DashboardWidgets on Mac OS/X and Google Desktop Widgets on Windows, and Yahoo Widgets on both platforms. Widgets are rather like applications, each hosted in its own mini-browser environment. While such applications often have the same characteristics of native desktop applications, they are arguably easier to design and construct, built of HTML, stylesheets, and JavaScript (elements familiar to Web developers). We chose to cover Yahoo Widgets, owing to its presence on multiple operating systems.

A second, and even more groundbreaking network-centric, application paradigm is that of immersive 3D environments, exemplified in applications such as Second Life. Numerous past attempts have been made to create immersive environments, but they have all failed for various reasons — network and bandwidth issues or awkward user experiences, but now, perhaps for the first time, immersive environments are suddenly not only possible but also vibrant. Second Life gives developers a simple, yet complete scripting language and object building environment. We will cover this emerging phenomenon, and show you usable code for both "in-world" and network-connected objects.

What This Book Covers

This book explores a number of frameworks, in-browser APIs, and server code examples. It also presents a variety of implementation languages and illustrates implementations in code. To present the capstone, we had to choose whether to compose it from disparate frameworks and languages or choose a single implementation framework and (by extension) a single language and design for the application. After much experimentation and discussion, we decided to implement ideaStax in a specific framework, Ruby on Rails (usually referred to simply as "Rails"), primarily for its code compactness, its comprehensive set of capabilities, and its ability to produce something both useful and reasonably easy for you to understand, even if you have no Rails (or even Ruby) experience.

This is not to say that the other implementation frameworks we highlight in the book (e.g., TurboGears or the Google Widget Toolkit — GWT) are in any way inferior to Rails, because they certainly are not; and in fact if you prefer to work in another language (Python for TurboGears, or Java for GWT), then these are preferable options. We simply had to make a choice, and given the pace of advancement by the Rails community, it seemed to be a reasonable choice, but by no means the only one.

Although we chose to work in Rails for the capstone application, we didn't want to play favorites with languages or frameworks — after all, this book is about RIA, not Rails. We decided on a compromise we hope you will like: We use other languages to demonstrate code for key concepts such as mashups, client-side validation, and auto-completion; and social site concepts such as tagging. There should be plenty to hold your interest regardless of your language preference.

Many developer books have to decide between greater breadth of coverage versus greater depth. Because of the explosive growth of tools and libraries, we opted for breadth. Thus, we cover a significant amount of the RIA and Web 2.0 landscape, and accordingly we won't exhaustively cover any particular framework. We have, however, extracted the important concepts from each. Because the details of some frameworks are documented online (although there's a wide variance in the quality of online documentation), we have striven to give you the developer point of view, or the "inside scoop," for each of the frameworks.

Part I: An Introduction to RIAs

In this part, you're provided with the background you need to develop Rich Internet Applications. You learn what distinguishes Rich Internet Applications and how they work, you get a refresher on Web application concepts, and you get your feet wet by implementing a simple Hello World example RIA. Finally, you learn some tips for enhancing your productivity through an exploration of some common approaches and tools for JavaScript debugging.

❑ Chapter 1 explores several traits of Rich Internet Applications, and investigates what makes true RIAs so different from traditional Web applications. It explores the differences in development process, marketing, and philosophy used when developing traditional verses Rich Internet Applications.

❑ Chapter 2 provides you with the foundations in Web technologies that you'll need for the remainder of the book. It includes a refresher of the Extensible Markup Language (XML) and the document object model (DOM). Extensible Hypertext Markup Language (XHTML), Cascading Style Sheets (CSS), and JavaScript are reviewed next. Finally, all the reviewed technologies are brought together in a simple example.

❑ In Chapter 3, the mashup phenomenon common in RIAs is explored in detail. This chapter shows you what a mashup really is, and walks you through the steps necessary to write your own mashup. It also provides you with a detailed look at the XMLHttpObject and JavaScript Object Notation (JSON).

❑ Chapter 4 details RIA development with a Hello World example. In this chapter, the differences between AJAX applications and traditional Web applications are first explored in detail. Then the steps required to write a simple Hello World Web application are outlined. You also learn the steps necessary to make and respond to an asynchronous call in both Java and PHP. Finally, you learn how to implement and respond to an asynchronous request in a simple example in both Java and PHP.

❑ Issues related to debugging Web applications are explored in Chapter 5. This chapter provides a detailed survey of the language-independent debugging tools, and approaches available to the RIA developer. It looks at Firefox as a key test browser, and describes some of the common debugging plug-ins available for the tool. It also shows how to use a variety of debugging tools, including Venkman and FireBug. Finally, it examines the utility of logging, and outlines the steps necessary to develop a simple JavaScript logging tool.

Part II: RIAs Explored

Part II expands upon the technologies introduced in Part I and explains some of the higher-level themes and development packages that build on top of them.

❑ Chapter 6 discusses the Model-View-Controller (MVC) paradigm of design, possibly the most important concept to learn for developers of any platform. The MVC pattern represents a way to architect and organize modules of code so that concerns are separated between the domain information and business logic (Model), visualization of output to the user (View), and management of user input (Controller). This type of architecture is particularly important to RIA developers because the underlying client-server architecture upon which the Web is built makes RIAs a near-perfect medium for MVC design. Chapter 6 introduces the three server-side development packages highlighted by this book: Java, Ruby on Rails, and TurboGears. Each of these frameworks is explained in the common parlance of MVC terminology.

❑ Chapter 7 pits various JavaScript frameworks against each other so that you get a chance to learn which tool is right for which job. In traditional Web development, most of the programming work is done on the server, and the client-side tasks are primarily design-oriented. RIA programming can require just as much attention to client-side logic as the server side does, so choosing the right JavaScript library is an important task. This bake-off helps you learn where each framework excels and where each falls short.

❑ Chapter 8 enters the relatively new arena of compiled-to-JavaScript frameworks and outlines the two different approaches to this technique taken by Google and the Ruby on Rails team. These solutions replace JavaScript programming with higher-level languages that are easier to code, maintain, and debug. At some point before RIA pages are sent to the client, the higher-level code is machine-translated into JavaScript.

❑ Chapter 9 presents this book's capstone application, ideaStax. IdeaStax is a simple Web application that enables users to create and maintain stacks of note cards containing rich text and images. As the chapters of Part III explain various RIA interface techniques, ideaStax is used to frame the examples in a simple and consistent context. Chapter 9 outlines the goals and capabilities of the Stax concept, of which many are implemented in Part III.

When you have finished with this part, you will have a thorough understanding of the underlying design principles behind professional RIA development, and a solid knowledge of the various tools and frameworks that are available to accomplish your design goals.

Part III: RIA Development in Depth

In this part, you're provided with the tools necessary to develop RIAs in the real world. In this part, you explore common issues in Web applications, and how they can be solved or minimized when developing a RIA. You'll also see some new capabilities, such as drag and drop, and autocompletion of form fields with server data that are increasingly used in real-world RIAs. Throughout this part, you'll gain familiarity with several powerful JavaScript libraries, such as Dojo, script.aculo.us, and MochiKit.

These chapters contain a variety of examples that show you how to develop RIAs in three different languages: Java, Ruby, and Python. Regardless of your preferred language, you can always follow along with the intent of the example by noting whether the objects or functions appear in the model, view, or controller. Even if you're quite familiar with the example language, you may want to explore the capabilities of the other candidate languages. You can do this with a little work, by porting the example to the other language, if you pay attention to which objects are in the model, view, or controller. After you've finished, go to the book's Web site at www.wrox.com, which contains the examples implemented in each of the three reference languages. Recall from Chapter 6 the three alternative implementations and how they incorporate the MVC.

All of the chapters define capabilities that are incorporated into the capstone Stax application. You can see the full code for the capstone, and a working version, on the book's Web site. Also see Chapter 9 for an introduction to the application.

❑ Chapter 10 explores issues associated with form field validation in a Web application. The chapter explores the problem of form input data, and common approaches used to validate data. It includes client-side validation with the Dojo JavaScript library, server-side validation in Java, and server-side validation of a single field in Java with AJAX.

❑ Chapter 11 builds on the previous chapter, examining other issues in form usability. It includes an exploration of AJAX-based approaches to enhance a user's form interactions. It then builds on the example from Chapter 10 to incorporate several AJAX-based enhancements.

❑ Chapter 12 shows how to greatly increase RIA interactivity by adding drag and drop capabilities. This chapter defines the concept of drag and drop, and briefly explores how it works using the script.aculo.us library. It shows how to develop a RIA that has drag and drop capabilities with script.aculo.us and Ruby on Rails.

❏ Chapter 13 examines some of the ways in which subtle JavaScript effects can improve the usability of a RIA. It introduces the script.aculo.us Effects library and demonstrates several ways to bind these effects to events and actions on a RIAPage. Code examples are provided for several scenarios in which special effects are useful, including dynamic user notifications and full-screen previews.

❏ Chapter 14 looks at the concepts of tagging and rating in detail. It explains what tagging and rating are and shows why the capabilities are being incorporated in many new RIAs and other Web applications, and why they are gaining more and more popularity. It includes an example written in Python.

❏ Chapter 15 builds on the example introduced in Chapter 14, and explores implementing tagging and searching as one aspect of a larger RIA. This chapter shows you how to add tagging and searching to a more complex application through adding the capability to Stax, the capstone application. The Python implementation in Chapter 14 is replaced with an implementation in Ruby on Rails.

Part IV: Beyond the Web

Part IV examines the spread of Rich Internet Applications outside of the traditional Web browser. As RIA development becomes a more professional and capable process, their reach is slowly extending to all areas of computing, from operating systems to applications to games. Through the use of APIs, many RIAs now have tie-ins to desktop applications so that users can benefit from the best of both worlds. Online applications such as Yahoo's Flickr, for example, integrate seamlessly into Apple's iPhoto, enabling users to manage their photo albums locally but share their favorites with the world. The chapters in this part discuss how these combinations are possible and show examples of how they are being used today.

❏ Chapter 16 takes a brief look at the importance of the Application Programming Interface (API). Successful RIAs don't just present users with a polished Web interface; they also present developers with a capable programmatic interface. Access to an API is what makes mashups and desktop RIA extensions possible. This chapter explains how to develop, deploy, and control third-party access to your RIA.

❏ In Chapter 17, you are introduced to the concept of desktop widgets. Widgets are small applications that float on a user's desktop and provide access to a specific piece of information or functionality. This chapter demonstrates how Yahoo! Widgets are used to provide quick access to frequently needed RIA functions that are exposed through an API. The availability of such widgets allows for tie-ins to a user's desktop and relieves the user of the need to open a Web browser and log in to accomplish simple tasks.

❏ Chapter 18 explores the early stages of the migration out of the confines of the browser and into immersive virtual worlds, in the spirit of Neal Stephenson's novel *Snow Crash*. Immersive applications are socially rich environments populated and created by end users around the world. Chapter 18 takes you into a world called Second Life, presenting the technical approach and examples of how to allow this world to interact with the Web at large. Second Life presents its users ("residents") with a full-featured programming language to manipulate the world around them, and it is gaining support to access external services and display Web documents from within its 3D immersive environment. Real economies are springing up in this virtual space, and traditional companies are beginning to take note. Connecting one's RIA to virtual worlds such as Second Life puts your product in a cutting-edge environment that will one day be commonplace.

Part V: Appendix

The Appendix extends the discussion in Chapter 10 by discussing Dojo validation functions and flags.

What You Need to Run the Examples

Many books focus on a single technology or single language. It's easy to define, right up front, the needed support software or environment. This book covers a wide range of browser-side JavaScript libraries, multiple dynamic page generation frameworks, and multiple server-side implementation languages. Each chapter outlines its specific support and environmental requirements; just look for the heading "Getting Started." This will enumerate the support elements for the specific chapter. The authors' site, `RIABook.ideastax.com`, will also maintain links to the latest versions of supporting software and provide additional comments from the authors and other readers on supporting code. Of course, the code will be maintained on both the publisher's site (`www.wrox.com`) and the `RIABook.ideastax.com` site.

Conventions

To help you get the most from the text and keep track of what's happening, we've used a number of conventions throughout the book.

Code has several styles. When we're talking about a word in the text — for example, when discussing the `helloForm` — it appears in `this font`.

> In code examples we highlight new and important code with a gray background.
>
> The gray highlighting is not used for code that's less important in the present context, or has been shown before.

Note that most long blocks of code include listing numbers (for example, Listing 5-1). These listings contain code that have numbered lines so that the authors can more easily refer to specific lines during the discussions that generally follow the code block.

Listing 5-1: HelloWorld.html

```
1.  <html>
2.   <body>
3.    <form id="helloForm"><LABEL>Say Hello: </label>
4.     <select id="country">
5.      <option>France</option>
6.      <option>Germany</option>
7.      <option>Spain</option>
8.      <option>USA</option>
9.     </select>
10.   </form>
11.   <p/>
12.    <label id="messageLabel" style="border: thin solid"></label>
13.  </body>
14. </html>
```

Sometimes you will see a mixture of styles. For example, when certain sections of changed code are being discussed, they're presented in bold, as shown in Listing 18-1.

Listing 18-1: Default LSL script

```LSL
default
{
    state_entry()
    {
        llSay(0, "Hello, Avatar!");
    }

    touch_start(integer total_number)
    {
        llSay(0, "Touched.");
    }
}
```

> **Boxes like this one hold important, not-to-be forgotten information that is directly relevant to the surrounding text.**

Tips, hints, tricks, and asides to the current discussion are offset and placed in italics like this.

As for styles in the text:

❑ We *highlight* new terms and important words when we introduce them.

❑ We show filenames, URLs, and code within the text like so: index.html

Source Code

As you work through the examples in this book, you may choose either to type in all the code manually or to use the source code files that accompany the book. All of the source code used in this book is available for download at www.wrox.com. Once at the site, simply locate the book's title (either by using the Search box or by using one of the title lists) and click the Download Code link on the book's detail page to obtain all the source code for the book.

Because many books have similar titles, you may find it easiest to search by ISBN; this book's ISBN is 978-0-470-08280-5.

Once you download the code, just decompress it with your favorite compression tool. Alternately, you can go to the main Wrox code download page at www.wrox.com/dynamic/books/download.aspx to see the code available for this book and all other Wrox books.

Errata

We make every effort to ensure that there are no errors in the text or in the code. However, no one is perfect, and mistakes do occur. If you find an error in one of our books, such as a spelling mistake or faulty piece of code, we would be very grateful for your feedback. By sending in errata you may save another reader hours of frustration, and at the same time you will be helping us provide even higher quality information.

To find the errata page for this book, go to www.wrox.com and locate the title using the Search box or one of the title lists. Then, on the book details page, click the Book Errata link. On this page you can view all errata that has been submitted for this book and posted by Wrox editors. A complete book list, including links to each book's errata, is also available at www.wrox.com/misc-pages/booklist.shtml.

If you don't spot "your" error on the Book Errata page, go to www.wrox.com/contact/techsupport.shtml and complete the form there to send us the error you have found. We'll check the information and, if appropriate, post a message to the book's errata page and fix the problem in subsequent editions of the book.

p2p.wrox.com

For author and peer discussion, join the P2P forums at p2p.wrox.com. The forums are a Web-based system for you to post messages relating to Wrox books and related technologies and interact with other readers and technology users. The forums offer a subscription feature to e-mail you topics of interest of your choosing when new posts are made to the forums. Wrox authors, editors, other industry experts, and your fellow readers are present on these forums.

At p2p.wrox.com you will find a number of different forums that will help you not only as you read this book, but also as you develop your own applications. To join the forums, just follow these steps:

1. Go to p2p.wrox.com and click the Register link.
2. Read the terms of use and click Agree.
3. Complete the required information to join as well as any optional information you wish to provide and click Submit.
4. You will receive an e-mail with information describing how to verify your account and complete the joining process.

You can read messages in the forums without joining P2P but in order to post your own messages, you must join.

Once you join, you can post new messages and respond to messages other users post. You can read messages at any time on the Web. If you would like to have new messages from a particular forum e-mailed to you, click the Subscribe to this Forum icon by the forum name in the forum listing.

For more information about how to use the Wrox P2P, be sure to read the P2P FAQs for answers to questions about how the forum software works as well as many common questions specific to P2P and Wrox books. To read the FAQs, click the FAQ link on any P2P page.

In Our Opinion

This is an "opinionated book." The authors are all professional software developers who benefit daily from using agile languages and open-source frameworks. We think it's important to point out that our examples, our discussions, and our applications use (almost exclusively) frameworks, toolkits, and languages that are open source and available to all developers. This affords you, the reader, access to capabilities and tools that are within the means of even the smallest enterprise or individual.

One of the features of the book is the inclusion of interviews with opinionated figures in the RIA community. In our interview with David Heinemeier Hanson of 37Signals and innovator of Ruby on Rails, you'll learn why "small is better" in terms of both team structure and application functionality. In our interview with Alex Russell, innovator of Dojo Toolkit, you'll get an inside view of one of the most successful and comprehensive JavaScript libraries. In our final chapter, we present a conversation with Second Life's Official "Embedded Reporter," Wagner James Au.

An Invitation

We hope that after reading this introduction you cannot wait to begin digging into the rest of the book. At this point, we hope that you understand this book is dedicated to providing you with insightful examples and a good fundamental understanding of the available APIs. You should expect a lot of exploration of the important features of Rich Internet Applications. Finally, you will gain expertise and confidence from usable sample source code that functions as both interesting application and instructive example.

We hope — and endeavor — to exceed your expectations. Let us know if we succeeded.

— **Dana Moore** (dana.virtual@gmail.com)

— **Raymond Budd** (ray.budd@gmail.com)

— **Edward Benson** (edward.benson@gmail.com)

Part I
An Introduction to RIAs

What Characterizes Rich Internet Applications?

"Let me just say just one word to you, young man — plastics!"

— Older male character giving investment advice to Dustin Hoffman's character, Benjamin Braddock, in the 1964 film *The Graduate*

First things first. This is a book for software developers by software developers. As developers, we are inclined to jump to the technical detail immediately. When we learn a new language, for example, we probably want to understand concepts such as typing, declaration, variable assignment, containment, and control flow structures: iteration, test and branching, modularization, and so on. This chapter is going to be a little different, but no less valuable.

This chapter lays a foundation for why learning the RIA design approach is important. In that sense, this chapter is going to be more "philosophical" than any other chapters in this book. It has only a couple code examples, primarily explaining the software revolution under way, and helping you understand the nature of the revolution. The rest of the book discusses code and coding; here you discover what's different and how you can profit from it. The discussion tilts toward independent software writers, by explaining how the competitive landscape is changing; but developers within the enterprise will benefit from understanding how to make their company more competitive externally, by building more scalable and user-centric public user experiences; and more effective internally, by building better collaboration and coordination tools.

In that spirit, read on to find out what makes RIAs (Rich Internet Applications) something worth paying attention to.

Rich Internet Applications are "Plastic"

The reference to plastics from *The Graduate* at the beginning of the chapter suggests the most famous meaning of the word "plastic," a commodity material which is often used as a substitute for the real (usually more expensive) material. In the film, plastics were being touted to the character as a good investment for the future. When we, as developers, look back at the formative days of this period, the next incarnation of the Internet, we may think "plastic" as well—in the dictionary meaning of the word: "transforming; growing; changing; dynamic, developing."

Thus, a first characteristic of RIAs is *plasticity*. The new generation of Internet-platformed applications is extensible and able to be recomposed into many different "look and feel" models, sometimes with the swipe of a cascading style sheet (CSS) paintbrush. Web applications, and Web pages before them, have always been "skinnable," and a simple demonstration of applying a cascading style sheet (CSS) in an HTML page shows how plastic (dynamic) an ordinary Web page can become. If you are well versed in Web page plasticity, feel free to skip this section; otherwise, read on.

An Example of Plastic (Dynamic) Web Pages

First, a Web page with no formatting: boring and mundane. Figure 1-1 shows a Web page with no applied styles. The information is there, but the page is static and lifeless.

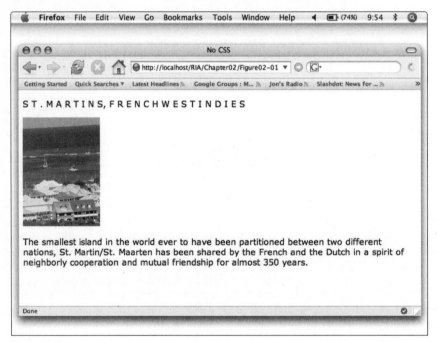

Figure 1-1

The following code creates the trivial Web page shown in Figure 1-1. The few DOM (document object model) elements are placed by default—a couple paragraphs identified by the <p> and </p> tag pairs and a JPEG image declared in the <img/> tag:

```html
<html>
<head>
    <title>No CSS</title>
</head>
<body>
<p>
ST.MARTINS, FRENCHWESTINDIES
</p>
<img src="images/Scenic.jpg"/>
<p>
The smallest island in the world ever to have been partitioned between two
different nations,
St. Martin/St. Maarten has been shared by the French and the Dutch in a spirit of
neighborly
cooperation and mutual friendship for almost 350 years.
</p>
</body>
</html>
```

In contrast, applying a style sheet to the identical DOM dramatically changes the page to give it style and appeal, as Figure 1-2 shows.

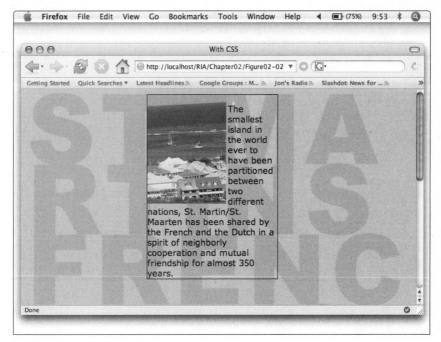

Figure 1-2

As the following HTML code shows, none of the DOM elements have changed, but a little style has been added to the page. The information content of the Web page is identical to that of Figure 2-1, but now the content stands out:

```html
<html>
  <head>
    <title>With CSS</title>
    <style>
      #sxm {
        position: absolute;
        left: 10px;
        top: 1px;
        font-family:'Arial Black';
        font-size:180px;
        line-height:130px;
        color:rgb(173,181,184);
        word-spacing:-50px;
        margin:0;
        padding:2px;
        z-index:1;
      }
      #stm {
        position: absolute;
        left: 240px;
        border:1px solid #000;
        top: 10px;
        width: 248px;
        height: 340px;
        z-index:2;
      }
    </style>
  </head>
  <body style="background-color:rgb(194,203,207); margin:0; padding:0;">
    <div id="sxm">
     S T . M A R T I N S F R E N C H W E S T I N D I E S
    </div>
    <div id="stm">
      <img src="images/Scenic.jpg" align="LEFT">
      <p>
      The smallest island in the world ever to have been partitioned between
      two different nations, St. Martin/St. Maarten has been shared by the
      French and the Dutch in a spirit of neighborly
      cooperation and mutual friendship for almost 350 years.
      </p>
    </div>
  </body>
</html>
```

How Style Sheets Create a Better Page

You find the first secret to the improved page between the `<style>` ... `</style>` tag pair, where two styles, named #sxm and #stm, have been created. Additionally, now the informational elements of the page are set into their own divisions, demarked by `<div>` ... `</div>` tag pairs. In these two examples showing a traditional use of the Web page, specific divisions are used (among other things) to show the browser where to apply styles. This is a simple but effective demonstration of the inherent plasticity you can take advantage of when writing the new style of applications, which you'll find in later chapters.

Divisions become even more important in designing RIAs, where they delineate segments of the page that modern browsers can dynamically update without a total page refresh. Throughout the book, and especially in Chapter 10, which describes the capstone application, you'll see many examples where dynamic partial page refresh creates a critical bond between the user and the application, and avoids the total page refresh, which made older-style applications seem static and more like filling out a form than working with an interactive desktop application.

This section showed a trivial example of page plasticity in Web 1.0 pages. To get a flavor of just how far designers can take pages, look at CSSZenGarden's page at www.csszengarden.com, *for some really fun examples of plasticity using only CSS overlay for the identical content.*

To run either of the two example pages in this section, one easy method is to create a folder somewhere on your PC, edit each of the examples into its own HTML file, and then (assuming you have Python on your system, which Mac OS/X and Linux users do by default) start a Web server in the same folder with the following:

```
python -m SimpleHTTPServer
```

This starts a Web server capable of serving any pages in the same folder or child folders. If you don't have Python 2.4 or 2.5 on your system, you can download it from several sources, including www.activestate.com. *Use*

```
http://localhost:8000/<name of the HTML file>
```

as the URL for the page. For example, if the name of the page without a stylesheet is "noStyle.html", then point the browser at

```
http://localhost:8000/noStyle.html
```

We demonstrated plasticity in an old-style Web page to make the point that some level of dynamism has always been a possibility in the Web. Interactivity was another matter. Prior to the emergence of the Rich Internet, it was never that easy to provide interactivity, but Web 2.0 applications take basic elements of the traditional W3C specification of HTML and repurpose them to serve a far more interactive style of application construction.

A more dramatic, exciting, and compelling style of plasticity is accomplished by interfacing the APIs of various service-oriented applications to "mash up" your own application. Mashups take the idea of plasticity to a much higher level, as shown in the next chapter.

RIAs also differ from the traditional Web in many important ways, and before looking at more code, let's talk more about these.

Rich Internet Applications: The Web Is Disruptive (Finally)

Often, disruptive technologies such as RIAs appear to emerge suddenly, almost at the speed of thought, with no obvious evolution. You could argue that in reality it's only notice by the popular press and a set of descriptive buzzwords that have sprung up in short order. The technologies behind Rich Internet Applications have been growing and maturing since even before the original Internet bubble.

Consider the enablers required for your new Web 2.0 applications to work at all. For one thing, in order for RIAs to exhibit the same level of responsiveness as their Rich Client Platform (RCP) ancestors, high-speed Internet access must be near ubiquitous. You can't offer a seamless user experience or convincingly separate the browser-resident user view and the server-resident model and controller logic without broadband, and when the Web was a toddler in the 1990s, such was not the case. Try using Google Maps over a 56 Kbps modem connection and you will understand the problem. Fortunately, you now have nearly ubiquitous broadband in the market, as well as customers who are your likely targets. Broadband is available almost everywhere in the U.S. At least 73 million Americans had high-speed Internet access as of April 2006.

Additionally, as mentioned earlier, the fundamentals of Web design have changed. Originally, design was about making pretty pages or replacements for magazines. Now design is slanted toward making things look like actual applications. Web design has become application design, and CSS have been repurposed to enhance the user experience, rather than the layout of the content.

Technology development takes longer than most of us think, with gradual changes that result in a perceivable difference taking years. The reasons for this are beyond the scope of this book, but gradual evolution, from the adoption of the lowly paper clip to the emergence of Rich Internet Application design and implementation techniques, can take decades. In truth, the underlying technologies that support RIAs have been around in one form or another for quite some time. In some ways, RIA development is a modern updating of the client-server model. The profound difference is the number of possible clients, given the explosion of wireless telephony-enabled devices, laptop portability, the proliferation of WiFi, and the next generation of PDA descendents.

From a very high altitude, you can view another RIA enabler, AJAX in the browser, as a simple trick by which round-trips to the server, as users input data that affects other fields/data on the page, implement "partial page refreshes." As mentioned earlier, modern browsers can refresh certain segments of the page (delineated by `<div>`...`</div>` tag pairs) without doing an entire page refresh. Partial refresh significantly improves the user experience by making application responses appear more seamless.

Neither of these technologies, whether in isolation or paired as they are in RIA, may seem like the basis for a revolution in application design and delivery, but consider some examples of how small changes conspire to promote dramatic change. E-mail and instant messaging (IM) are extremely similar in some respects. Both are essentially store-and-forward messaging strategies, after all. Both require a network to operate. In some cases, an e-mail and an IM sent at the same time to the same recipient can arrive at their destination nearly simultaneously, yet the end user perceives them as very different applications. Indeed, although they may share design characteristics, they have evolved to become very different applications with rather different monetization profiles and developer communities (if in fact e-mail can still be said to have much of a developer community). Looking at the difference between e-mail and IM is instructive if you consider the new generation of applications you can deliver as RIAs, and how they are different from what came before them. Consider Table 1-1, which shows that two different software platforms may share similar design centers, but be very different due to the community that forms around them.

Table 1-1: Differences Between Instant Messaging and E-mail

Characteristic	E-mail	IM
Usage pattern	A formal enterprise communication mechanism	A convenient way to communicate whenever you need to say something to someone, usually in real time, and usually something immediate and possibly pithy
What it displaces	The business letter and formal corporate communications	The telephone, or even face-to-face communication
Ease of use	Requires a formal setup and system administration	Is always "on" with no effort on your part. You talk about "checking for e-mail," but you never say, "I am checking for IMs."
Immediacy	Slower and more ponderous; formal thought is required to compose a communication before you send it	Immediate, conversational, and social. You say what you need to say, when you need to say it. Although both platforms use a store and forward protocol, changing the speed of IM interchange creates a change in experience.
Application continuity	Episodic, with formal give and take and formal presentation or argumentation	Continuous, with the exchange of ideas just "happening"
Administrative burden to the user	You often feel the need to folderize and categorize e-mail for future reference.	You don't often review IM communication streams, although you could use search tools to review logged conversations. This distinction may be ending due to migrate-to-Web e-mail tools such as Gmail, or a RIA, where searching has replaced folder navigation.

You could argue that the differences between these two applications, which have similar technical underpinnings, are the differences between old school RCP or Web 1.0 applications and RIAs. RIAs offer invisibility, immediacy, a continuous streamed user experience, and "ad hoc-rity" (a lack of formal setup requirements). These are the disruptive qualities of Rich Internet Applications, each of which is explained in the rest of this chapter.

Rich Internet Applications Are Invisible

You are a software developer, yes, but at times you're also an end user, and as an end user of desktop applications, you are used to acquiring (sometimes even purchasing), installing, and maintaining applications, You look after their well-being, contributing a lot of unpaid labor to do the necessary "yak shaving" (see the sidebar in this chapter) to get applications into the necessary state to "serve your needs." Figure 1-3 shows Google, a prime example of the invisible application. It's taken for granted, but it's never far from the end user's reach.

Figure 1-3

Invisibility of Google

Google is a prime example of the invisible application few can live without. Google's developers have deliberately made their software more valuable and more invisible by embedding its simple type-in box into the toolbar of modern browsers, and into the Windows System Tray for desktop search (Google Desktop), as shown in Figure 1-4. More than any other application, Google, has insinuated itself into the browsing experience so deeply that many users unconsciously invoke it almost as a reflex action. Unconscious use is the highest compliment users can pay to any product or service.

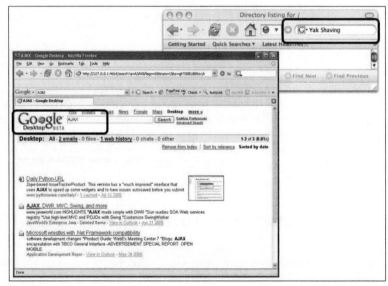

Figure 1-4

Traditional applications are a lot like a high-maintenance relationship in that they deliver value, but not necessarily in portion to the equity you invest. The more we experiment with this new paradigm, the more the kinds of applications we used to write begin to look clunky and primitive to us.

The more you use RIAs as an end user, the less you notice the fact that they are just "there," that they somehow disappear into the background. As a developer, you may remember the epiphany that occurred the first time you got facile with the many "applications" on the Linux (or if you're old enough, UNIX) command line. Although you rarely thought of them as such, `find`, `grep`, `ps`, `ls`, and `gcc` were indeed applications, and a shell "incantation" such as

```
$ ls -lat | grep html | wc -l
```

to count the number of possible HTML files in a folder was an early example of chaining applications in UNIX to create a mashup, or composite, application. After a while, though, you probably just forgot about them, used them to perform your work, and didn't even recognize them as software anymore.

Focusing Your RIAs

As you survey the universe of Web 2.0 applications, you'll possibly notice that individual applications don't (as yet) suffer from the bloat of native tools. They seem to focus on doing one thing and doing it solidly.

That's not to say it's impossible for you to write really bad RIAs, or that an escalation to bloated Web-based applications with needless baggage won't happen as a response to market pressure. It may. It's just that what has currently garnered the most mindshare and jumps out from the pack is notable for its simplicity. For an industry perspective on what it takes to fight bloat, see the sidebar "An Interview with 37Signals."

Two things may mitigate bloat and bad design, though:

❏   Bloated software won't be as quick to load or as responsive to use.

❏   Users will find switching costs much lower.

The advice often repeated in this book, and hopefully emphasized in the example code, is to design with a single feature in mind, and with the understanding that users do not want to "train up" on Web-based software. An important dictum to remember is that on the Web, user experience is paramount.

Eating Our Own Dog Food

One decision the authors made early on in the writing of this book was to use an AJAX word processor rather than a desktop tool, not just to "eat our own dog food" as we used to say during the dotcom era, but because we often needed to collaborate at a moment's notice, regardless of location, regardless of what operating system that was at hand. That way, we found that we didn't have to worry about having the "correct" software installed, or where precisely the content we needed to work with resided. Striving to make your software something that a large number of users take for granted only serves to increase your reputation and value. (See the section "How Am I Going to Make Money from RIAs?" later in the chapter for more information.)

Another reason why the transition between "applications" seems, from a user standpoint, so easy, natural, and seamless really has little to do with RIAs directly, but is worth mentioning: Tabbed browsers are most likely the desktop you always wanted but never got.

Users have settled for the chaotic Windows environment as though it were a fundamental law of nature. Developers went right along with this, "compounding the felony," as it were, but think for a moment: The windowed world of the traditional desktop is chaotic and switching from one application's space to another entails some pain because you're constantly searching, dragging windows around, and manipulating the file systems to get content into the right place for the benefit of the application.

Rich Internet Applications Break Down Walled Gardens

Platforms currently in use tend to control and channel intellectual property into a "walled garden." When you create a document with an RCP document creator, although you are the author, you don't own the content independently of the tool you use to create it. You can't write or read Microsoft Word documents without something that works remarkably like Microsoft Word. In fact, Word's vendor would rather you didn't use *anything* other than Word to interact with what should be "your" information. To take this logic even a step further, they really *insist* you use the operating system(s) that they will happily sell you to run the application that they also sell you, all to get at the information that really should be your information.

In the ideal world (from the *traditional desktop era software vendor's* standpoint):

❑ Content cannot exist without the mediating application. Vendors sell applications and store the content model in a format that prevents anyone from easily usurping their dominance over the user. The vendor decides when, if, and how bugs are addressed. Vendors need to create massive distribution systems that rely on end-user sweat equity to keep applications as up-to-date as the vendor decides they ought to be.

❑ Applications cannot exist independently of the specific operating system. The vendor will publish as much or as little of the system call stack as they deem sufficient to encourage independent software developers to develop the kinds of applications they want to support on their operating system. Generally, they will "bless" a certain few languages and dissuade others.

❑ Both the operating system and the application are tightly bound so that, at the vendor's discretion, both can be rendered obsolete. Vendors will do this ostensibly in the name of operating efficiency, but it also means that they can (and do) feel free to break the Model-View-Controller paradigm or inject other undocumented efficiencies into "house" code. It also means that the inner mechanism of the OS or application becomes arcane, brittle, and opaque to independent software vendors and developers (ISVs) outside of the organization. External developers thus struggle to come up with competing benchmark applications in addition to those they internally produce. Dominant vendors thereby protect their hegemony over the "cash cow" applications responsible for their revenue stream.

❑ Each tool creates an "island of automation," with its own data model, its own controller, and a view dependent on the OS and tool as platform. Because vendors are stuck in our worldview, they will have a hard time developing (for example) applications that are net-centric, collaboration-rich, OS neutral, or extensible—either by the end user or by other software developers.

❑ In marketing, developer conferences, and other interactions, vendors tend to convince both ISVs and end users that the trades-offs for these annoyances will result in assurance of (generally) seamless and smooth interaction (for the users), and protection and a ready market (for the ISV). They thus ensure a barrier to entry that keeps software prices artificially high and difficult to replicate.

It would be surprising if anything on this list is a revelation to you, either as a software developer or in your other role as an end user. These are the basic tenets of software, as it has existed for over three decades. In writing this book and asking you to look at new techniques, ask yourself whether the state of the world must be this way for some fundamental unalterable reason, or whether it simply has become a staid custom that limits our innovation and spirit of adventure.

In the traditional software world — the one that should be left behind — tools and applications have become traps for both the creator and potential consumers because they imprison content and intellectual property. A few words of caution, though: Just because you learn to write extensible, re-mixable, software-as-service applications in this book doesn't make you immune to the imposition of other forces just as inimical to open software as the old school OS and software vendors were. See the sections "Rich Internet Applications Are Network-Centric" and "Rich Internet Applications Are Browser-Centric" later in the chapter for more information.

> *Ironically, although consumer put up with walled gardens, software developers don't much care for them. Consider the wide variety of ways in which you can create and manipulate your Java/Python/ Ruby code. VI, Eclipse, Netbeans, EMACS, and note padding applications (which exist seemingly beyond number) will do just fine. When you need a code viewer, open a terminal window, cat mycode.py, and you're done. One reason why you can operate in such an unfettered atmosphere is that ASCII is ASCII all over the world, and no single vendor can imprison the format. As long as you can create ASCII, you can program.*

Rich Internet Applications Create New (Unwalled?) Gardens

The aim of this book is to motivate developers to write new generations of applications that create a different kind of garden. In this garden, the richness of the application is set free in order for content creators and consumers to interact with far less interference and human investment in acquiring and maintaining tools than the previous generations of "walled garden" applications. If the first incarnation of the Internet was about serving and presenting hyperlinked information, and the second was about submitting personal information to complete transactions, then the third is surely about creating, consuming, and manipulating content *in a social or collaborative setting*. Specifically, a generation of applications have emerged that are "us" powered.

The desktop generation of applications enabled end users to write, draw, print, and circulate their creations to a relatively limited circle of consumers, but today's content is potentially open to unlimited numbers of consumers, raters, taggers, and bloggers, who have raised the rate of content creation, consumption, and the potential for debate and discourse to new highs. Whole businesses are being created over the ranking of content by the "wisdom of crowds." Consider, for example, how difficult it would have been to create del.icio.us, Slashdot.org or dig.com in the desktop generation.

Constraints in the Unwalled Garden

The community of developers working with this new architecture (and you either are or soon will be a member of that community) has converged on a couple of critical concepts about how to create value with RIAs. Whether you build an application to create, store, and share content (too many to mention, but think Flickr), comment on content (e.g., Slashdot), collaborate on content (think Writely and this book's capstone application, "ideaStax"), or to remix content (again, too many to mention, but consider Google Map mashups, Apple or Yahoo! desktop widgets), the architect/developer chain of reasoning forces some interesting design constraints on new-style applications:

❑ Shareable content and dynamic content publishing are a foundational element of this new Internet age.

❑ You have less impedance to content creation and publishing than in past. To some extent, blogs replace magazines and books. At the very least, they expand publishing options.

❑ More shareable is better than less shareable and may even be monetizable.

❑ High-speed networks are pretty ubiquitous in the user community that consumes new-style applications.

❑ Given the ability to create a large community around specific content categories, there is a need for applications to reach large numbers of end users.

❑ An application has to resemble a radio or television network in its dynamics — except, of course, that those sorts of networks are "consume only." They don't permit the kinds of rich interactions that this new kind of network encourages.

❑ The end user will largely use a browser to reach an application.

❑ There is no monopoly on browsers. Browsers are supported practically everywhere (desktops, mobile phones, and various handheld incarnations); therefore, a new application doesn't have to write a vendor-specific API. In fact, it wastes developer cycles to write to specific client-side APIs, and it may sub-optimize the value of a new application to both the developer and potential end users.

❑ There is an industry-wide data transport API (HTTP), and an industry-wide display standard (HTML) for the client side.

❑ The application creator can still hold real value on the server side in the data model and the data manipulation logic (which need not be exposed to the application's user).

No formal committee sat down somewhere in Silicon Valley and decided that these principles would be the foundation for RIAs. There is no list like the preceding one formally stated anywhere in the literature, but the logic does seem both sound and fairly bulletproof when you consider the following:

❑ This book comes out at a time when it makes sense for developers to both write and read it.

❑ The characteristics for most RIAs observed "in the wild."

Some of these notions just evolved as a result of the availability of enabling technologies. Since the first Internet bubble burst, software developers went back to the drawing board with a strong understanding of the architectural possibilities. Innovators bootstrapped the current Internet "boom" by creating value around ideas and applications that would not have been possible before. The existence of this new architecture for applications creates a large "surface area" for content that was difficult to achieve in the desktop era.

Technically, the seamless experience of using Internet-based tools is one pillar of the next generation of applications. The ubiquity of broadband is one reason you can write distributed applications and not worry (as much) about responsiveness, as you did with desktop generation applications. The availability of unencumbered browsers is a ready-made outer container for applications.

However, there's more to RIA than simply moving traditional desktop productivity applications to a new venue. If you want to succeed at creating the next "must-have" application, you should keep the vision just laid out for you in mind: Expose the surface area of content-based applications to the largest number of "us" that you can. This, more than anything else, is your new design center.

At the time of writing, there were about 1 billion online content creators and consumers. These are the new end users; and if you make it easy for them, they will provide untold wealth in shared wisdom, social networks, personal perspectives, and a willingness to collaborate, all of which can be applied to your application. It's suddenly possible (maybe even for the first time in recorded history) to experience the massive cooperation referred to as the "gift economy" if you write applications that enable small contributions.

Understanding the Counter-Manifesto

The new kind of garden that you, the RIA developer, and by extension your end users, create can be stated in a kind of "counter-manifesto" that is used as the design center for the code example and the capstone application worked toward in this book. This counter-manifesto sounds remarkably different to the one described earlier for the desktop era developer. We present them as a set of application-level design patterns, which we enumerate in the next few sections.

Pattern 1: Expose (at least some of) the Remote API

RIA developers should create content in such a way that other mediating applications that other developers or end users might dream up can interact with it, display it, or repurpose its content.

> You'll read more about this topic in Chapter 3, where you create mashups. Mashups and remixes occur when new applications (originally unintended) are constructed from data and services originally intended for some other purpose.

> For some interesting GoogleMaps mashups, check out www.housingmaps.com (houses to let) and www.mywikimap.com (cheap gas finder)

Pattern 2: Use a Common Data Format

A different (but similar) pattern suggests that RIA developers create data models underlying the service-based applications so that they or another developer can leverage them. While the backend server may store the data model in whatever form that's convenient (whether that's a SQLite relational DB, an NFS mounted flat file system, or an XML data store is irrelevant), the output to the user view is expressed as something that any number of readers/parsers can handle.

> It's cheating just a tiny bit to call this a "design pattern" and then suggest that you support it. Chapters 10 and 11 show that output to the browser really must be either XML or JavaScript Object Notation (JSON). Like the speed of light, this is not just a good idea; it's the law, duly enforced by all browsers.

Pattern 3: The Browser Creates the User Experience

The only real limiting factor on application capabilities is the limitations of common commercially available browsers. You, the developer, can deal with this limitation because, as a trade-off, it's a lot better than the tall stack of entry limitations and barriers that drove you crazy during the previous software epoch.

If you need visual sophistication beyond the capability of the modern browser, you can use other browser pluggable alternatives, such as Flash. Additionally, in extreme situations, you can employ launchers for external application engines, although this may create a jarring discontinuity in the user's experience. One somewhat successful application-level pattern for doing this is Java Web Start, whereby the user navigates to a URL, which contains JavaScript for launching an application.

Pattern 4: Applications Are Always Services

Applications are part of a service-oriented architecture (SOA) in which applications are services, created from scratch or as artifacts from recombining other application facets. Subject to limitations (such as the availability of some other service on which your application may depend), SOA will create the software equivalent of evolutionary adaptation. Remarkably, no "protocol stack by committee" of desktop vendors was required to create this pattern. Further, unlike the UDDI/WDSL stack, the Web 2.0 SOA is simple and almost intuitive.

Pattern 5: Enable User Agnosticism

RIAs won't force the user to worry about operating systems or browsers. As long as the browser supports scripting in the browser, applications "just work." Developers could choose to take advantage of "secret handshakes" or other backend implementations that assure vendor or OS lockdown (and you can probably think of one browser and one OS vendor that does this), but the downside of making such a devil's bargain is that ultimately you, as a developer, will wind up expending more cycles when, after getting some user traction on a specific platform, you find that your best interests are served by extending you application to every other platform. It's better not to support vendors with their own backend implementation agenda, and to design from the start to avoid the slippery slope that leads to the trap of another walled garden. Thus, it's best to design to steer clear of OS and native library dependencies. If you do this, you can safely ignore much of the annoying Byzantine detail of writing applications, and specifically the parts that tend to make applications most brittle. Instead, you can concentrate on the logic of what it is that you're trying to accomplish for the user.

Pattern 6: The Network Is the Computer

Originally a Sun Microsystems marketing slogan from the 1980s, this bromide goes in and out of vogue. Java Applets exemplified it with the X11/Motif distributed model in the 1990s. Both those models ultimately failed, on infrastructural weaknesses. X11 failed because it exacted a huge performance cost on the expensive "workstation" CPUs of the era, and because its network model couldn't extend beyond the LAN with the broadband era still a decade or so away. Java Applets failed because of their size (long load time) and sluggish performance — again, broadband was a few years away.

This time, broadband is near ubiquitous in much of the cyber landscape. In addition, because the current RIA user experience is small and fits comfortably within the memory footprint of the modern browser, failure seems far less likely. Thus, the "operating system" for this new generation of applications is not a single specific OS at all, but rather the Internet as a whole. Accordingly, you can develop to the separation of concerns afforded by the Model-View-Controller paradigm, while ignoring (for the most part) the network in the middle of the application. There still remain some real concerns about the network in the middle, and you do need to code to protect the user experience, given this reality. Many of these issues are covered in Part III.

Pattern 7: Web 2.0 Is a Cultural Phenomenon

Except for the earliest days of personal computing, when the almost exclusively male Homebrew Computer Club, which gave birth to the first Apple, defined the culture of hackerdom, the PC desktop has never been a cultural phenomenon. In contrast, Web 2.0 has never *not* been about the culture. End users rally around "affinity-content." Community is everywhere in the culture of Web 2.0. craigslist, Digg, and Slashdot exist as aggregation points for user commentary. Narrow-focus podcasts replace broadcast TV and radio. Blogging replaces other publishing formats and mass distribution formats. Remixing and mashups are enabled by the fact that data models, normally closed or proprietary, are exposed by service APIs, but they also wouldn't exist without end user passion and sweat equity. Some enterprising developers (e.g., Ning at ning.com) have even managed to monetize this culture, offering a framework for creative *hobbyists* who create social applications based on existing APIs. Chapter 3, which is about mashups and remixes, gives you a feel for what end users can do with the Web as platform, and modest programming skills.

When you create an application, you should consider the social culture that may arise to embrace your application. You can likely build in collaborative and social capabilities (e.g., co-editing, social tagging) pretty easily; if there's a downside to having an application exist only "in the cloud," the best upside is that a networked application also obeys the power law of networks: The application's value increases as a log function of the number of users. Most RIAs in the wild have many or all of these characteristics.

Consider the elder statesman of content-sharing applications, the blog, and its close relative, the wiki. Many blogs approach or exceed print journalism in their reader penetration, and wikis are far more flexible than their power-hungry desktop predecessors (such as Groove, for example) in supporting multiuser coordination and collaboration.

Rich Internet Applications Are Always Up-to-Date

A big reason for the lowered barriers to use (the "yak shaving" factor, as we call it) is that something rather dramatic, and at the same time something taken for granted, happened when end users began to seriously use invisible and pervasive applications — software upgrades, patches, security fixes, and massive distributions of service packs just stopped; suddenly they seemed an artifact of a bygone era. The reason for this major end user shift seems so simple now, somehow obviously "right."

As a developer, you can understand the profound and yet simple explanation in a way that end users perhaps can't: Because RIAs deliver a fresh instance of the application into the browser on reload, the end user always receives the latest version, with all fixes and updates, automatically, even if you just finished making the fixes last night. No massive distribution headaches; no complicated patches in the lethal grip of the end user.

Yak Shaving, and the Traditional Desktop versus RIA Development Styles

A huge plus for every end user situation you can contemplate involves lowering the barriers to use. A lot of traditional RCP application development as we have come to know it involves a great deal of what is now called *yak shaving*. According to Wikipedia, the term may have been coined at MIT's CSAIL. In any case, it refers to any seemingly pointless activity that is actually necessary to solve a problem that solves a problem, which, several levels of recursion later, solves the real problem you're working on.

A posting at `http://projects.csail.mit.edu/gsl/gsb-archive/gsb2000-02-11.html` gives another definition and an example:

. . . yak shaving is what you are doing when you're doing some stupid, fiddly little task that bears no obvious relationship to what you're supposed to be working on, but yet a chain of twelve causal relations links what you're doing to the original meta-task.

Here's an example:

"I was working on my thesis and realized I needed a reference. I'd seen a post on comp.arch recently that cited a paper, so I fired up gnus. While I was searching for the post, I came across another post whose MIME encoding screwed up my ancient version of gnus, so I stopped and downloaded the latest version of gnus.

"Unfortunately, the new version of gnus didn't work with emacs 18, so I downloaded and built emacs 20. Of course, then I had to install updated versions of a half-dozen other packages to keep other users from hurting me. When I finally tried to use the new gnus, it kept crapping out on my old configuration. And that's why I'm deep in the gnus info pages and my .emacs file — and yet it's all part of working on my thesis."

And that, my friends, is yak shaving.

You will probably find that developing RIAs involves a lot less yak shaving, or at least is replaced by a more satisfying activity — perhaps wool gathering about how you can make your application more "trick." Or maybe just sheep shearing, because 1) the technologies tend not to be as reliant on secret handshake system calls, 2) the objectives of most RIAs are more focused and less feature laden and therefore quicker to conceive and deliver, and 3) the code, test, observe, refactor cycle seems (to us anyway) to be shorter and iterate more quickly toward a finished product.

In addition, as a developer, when you tweak the server side of the application, you spend late nights fixing the data model or converting from one database to another. The end user is totally unaffected. Native desktop software never looks as appealing again and end user expectations are permanently altered.

Finally, as a developer, your expectations are altered as well. Because you don't have to concentrate on side issues such as distributing and maintaining multiple versions, you can concentrate on useful refactoring, or creating the follow-up project.

Rich Internet Applications Are OS Killers

Software has been tied to given operating systems since the beginning of computing. Originally, software was offered almost as a loss leader for a vendor to assure loyalty to mainframe hardware. In the age of the personal computer, users still could not buy just any personal computer to operate a given application, for even after some vendors mastered the art of selling software as a standalone product, application users were required to buy the supporting operating system and the approved PC architecture. If automobiles worked this way, an automotive application — say, getting from Washington to Baltimore — would require the purchase of a specific brand of car, perhaps with specific tires, and the car would run only on roads paved with asphalt, and this would be the only way to achieve the application's goal of making that trip.

Web 2.0 Layering

Thankfully, neither the transport system nor Web 2.0 applications have such rigid constraints. As shown in the graphic in Figure 1-5, RIA solutions are not quite so overconstrained. The natural layering of Web 2.0–networked applications has positive indications for developers — forcing good development discipline through separation of concerns; and positive indications for the growth and evolution of the network itself — it becomes much easier to insert new (as yet unanticipated) layers, and ultimately adds scalability, as pointed out in the "Interview with Industry Leaders" section at the end of the chapter.

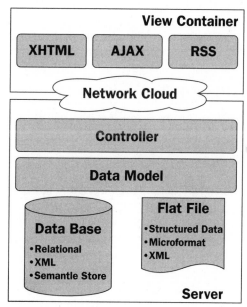

Figure 1-5

Thus, because RIAs use the Web itself as their platform, in the end it won't matter whether a user is running Windows, Linux, Mac OS/X, or something else. That's huge news for you as a developer. The design center of Web 2.0 requires the developer to deliver the application through a URL, via XHTML (the standards-based version of "good old HTML") into a browser. The Document Object Model (DOM) is used for dynamic display and interactivity without complete browser refresh. The developer embeds JavaScript inside the XHTML; that's the user experience side.

Cascading Style Sheets

The look and feel of the user experience is tailored through cascading style sheets (commonly CSS specifications in the XHTML.) The JavaScript logic in the browser uses a convenient feature built into all modern browsers as a way of making remote method calls (it's called an XMLHttpRequest, and is explained in detail in Chapter 3). The application's logic and the data model are often written in a popular framework (frameworks in Python, Ruby, and Java are covered), but a framework just buys you more productivity and less coding. There is no requirement to write to a framework — PHP, for example, is just fine. That's about all there is to it.

Leaving the Desktop Behind

In the desktop world, dealing with certain annoyances has become so ingrained in your life that you either hardly notice them or assume they are basic laws of the universe. Many of these seemingly immutable laws are part and parcel of the pain of working with applications in a native OS: compulsively hitting Save every few minutes as a safeguard against your word processor crashing; obsessively rearranging folder hierarchies; nervously running a virus checker a few times a day. RIAs embody a cultural shift for users, as well as a technological one.

In the event that users need to take smaller steps in leaving the desktop era behind, though, there is at least one effort to code an entire desktop in AJAX: AJAXOS (see www.michaelrobertson.com/ajaxos/. The differentiator for AJAXOS is that it assumes a network cloud, even for files on the computer platform on which AJAXOS runs. One might think of it as intentionally blurring the line between "local" and "in the cloud," in the belief that these options should always be a user choice. Everything, from the file system to the MP3 player, works this way in AJAXOS.

Is Java a Winner or Loser?

One question the authors of this book have been asked is whether Java is a winner or a loser in RIA, which is both a technological and cultural shift. We don't know the answer, but can hazard guesses; most developers would agree that delivering applications in Java on the browser side is a dead issue and has been for a long time now. As a comparison, run an RIA word processor such as Writely (docs.google.com) against a Java-in-the-browser applet version of Thinkfree (thinkfree.com). Although Thinkfree may, in the long run, offer similar features and responsiveness, in the end, the convenience of not having to deal with desktop issues wins the day for the RIA. It may be tragically ironic that Java, which in so many ways strives to be its own platform and manages nicely to be OS agnostic, and sparked the original move of applications from the desktop to the network, fails to be a significant technology of the future.

On the server side, it's another matter. Java is just as compelling as it is in the desktop application context. Additionally, Sun Microsystems, Java's inventor, may be one of the big winners in the cultural shift implied by the move to RIAs, simply because it's a server-class hardware vendor. For an additional perspective on Java versus agile languages on the server side, read the comments in the sidebar "An Interview with 37 Signals."

Finally, understand that AJAX brings it own brand of challenges: managing asynchronous operations and event-driven programming, especially if there's a need for multiple threads of control; network latency for these async requests; and coordination of multiple tasks on the Web interface, to cite but a few. You can read more about these and other challenges in Chapter 15. In summary though, RIAs are going to dampen future interest in both operating systems and "office suites."

Rich Internet Applications Are Browser Centric

The browser has evolved from an information-connecting appliance, to a modest application appliance (in Web 1.0), to a full blown application-hosting appliance in Web 2.0. And that's going to force us to think beyond the desktop. Whereas previously you only needed to test applications inside a software monoculture (for the most part), as a part of your development discipline, you now have to test with all major browsers, and at least the current and upcoming version of each.

Browsers are the "game changer" in the evolution of Web 2.0 applications, and you can highly leverage their native capabilities. As numerous code examples in succeeding chapters show, the simple ability to make remote procedure invocations using the built-in XMLHttpRequest from JavaScript has already changed so much of the "game." Consider how small a matter it would be for any modern browser to "up the ante" by incorporating work-alikes for the Microsoft Office, OpenOffice, Mac iWork suites. Already there are rich content editors — such as FCKEditor (www.fckeditor.net) and Tiny MCE (tinymce.moxiecode.com) — written completely in JavaScript and directly embeddable in the browser. In our capstone application, we will demonstrate an application similar to presentation composers.

Once content escapes the desktop and exists in the Internet "cloud," connected to the end user by wireless or broadband, the game has finally changed for good. TVs, phones, handheld devices, and devices yet to be conceived, are on an equal footing with the traditional PC or laptop. At this writing, most devices on the consumer market can host a browser. One operating system, Damn Small Linux, (www.damnsmalllinux.org), can boot from a USB thumb drive and host a full-featured browser.

Of course, you will still want to test every new application you write for browser compatibility. Some code for testing and working around browser peculiarities in various code snippets is available to you. The truth is that issues with browsers will likely decrease as AJAX development tools encapsulate the browser at a higher level of abstraction. Further, even mobile phone vendors (notably Nokia) are beginning to support AJAX-compliant browsers on their gear. Increased platform agnosticism will help bring your application to many more people globally than you would ever have attracted in the age of what has been called the software/hardware "monoculture."

Rich Internet Applications Are Network Centric

This is an additional reason why, as stated in the last section, RIAs work to deprecate the OS. Many end users are multi-locational and don't stop working just because they move from work to home. Nor do they set aside personal business when they move from home to work. There is no clear boundary between activities done in one location or another. As a result, end users spend huge amounts of time attempting to synchronize their home and work computers with both their content and the software that manipulates the content. The end value you create in the RIA space, whether it's the next great word processor or the next great personal information manager, enables your application user to access your software, and all their content, and is always available via a URL. Because of net centricity, sharing is easier as well. Consider all the end user tricks and accommodations that overcome distance and multiple computers: copying files to thumb drives, e-mailing content to Web mail accounts; using ponderous and sluggish synchronizer applications (Groove, for example). All these activities still require intentional and conscious planning and forethought about just what content you need to copy for availability in multiple locations.

Rich client platform application advocates hold fast to the argument that the downside of RIAs is that if the network is broken for a particular user, then their application is broken too. It's certainly true, just as it is true that a virus-compromised computer loses its utility. At the end of the day, however, the network is far more robust and better maintained than the average end user's PC. Consider, too, all the net-centric applications we use and rely upon without giving them a second thought — satellite or FM radio, mobile telephony, and television. The end user base for Internet applications is already familiar with and comfortable with networked applications and devices. In addition, considering the number of U.S. cities that have already deployed or are contemplating municipal WiFi, there is a growing understanding that network ubiquity is a necessity of modern society.

An issue of apparent concern (for end users anyway) related to net centricity is the oft-heard comment, "I am concerned that all my documents are no longer on my own PC. They're up there in the Internet cloud. They're on the network, and that feels really dangerous to me."

Is this really true? In many situations, having one's "stuff" close at hand is a really bad idea: end users probably don't hoard their life savings under the mattress, or insist on squirreling away their chest X-rays in the hall closet. Nonetheless, PCs often give users a false sense of security and trust despite the fact that large numbers of laptops are stolen in a given year.

When end users raise this particular bogeyman, it's worthwhile to point out that tangibility is difficult to access. A user may well have content secure on my laptop, which (alas) has a bad power supply, bad disk drive, failed motherboard, or software virus. Their content is therefore tangible and even close at hand, but not accessible without the painful "yak shaving" required to resuscitate the PC.

One need only ask how many of them have lost valuable content to PC hard disks, or given complete access rights to indexers such as Google Desktop, or loaded "phone home" programs such as certain tax preparation software, or allowed a clandestine spybot such as the Sony/BMG rootkit to insinuate its way onto their PCs. Most end users would be far better off letting a high-security data center host their digital content, but the road to end user buy-in is long and only time will make a difference. The best advice here is to push end user education.

A final note on the topic of net-centricity and you, as a developer, is that you shouldn't assume that simply by moving applications to an RIA architecture that you are going to bulletproof your work and create a garden of delights, rather than a walled garden. In the U.S. in particular, end users may be trading one kind of walled garden for another.

As of this writing, much attention is being paid to the concept of a two-tiered Internet whereby ISPs would charge premiums for better quality of service and throughput. Certainly, the Internet is not, by its nature, immune to walled gardens. If an ISP can get its users (either by government regulation, by economic inducement, or maybe by mass hypnosis) to agree to let them mediate their browsing experience, then they can shape their users' perceptions, prop up political agendas, or sell users things of interest (to the ISP).

By way of example, consider that in 2006 the Chinese government hobbled searches and political discourse by tightly regulating ISPs. And the Digital Millennium Copyright Act in the U.S. exemplifies walled gardens that service either political or commercial agendas. Thus, the global development community's best intentions are undone by circumstances beyond its control. The best advice is to become engaged in affecting change in your country.

Political regimes are not the only ones seeking to create walled gardens around the users' experiences of the Internet. America Online was the earliest example of an ISP placing users in a walled garden. They remain one of the few that still does so.

Rich Internet Applications Are Mind-Altering

You can assert this statement in two different ways. First consider how your mind is altered as a software developer and a system architect, and then as an end user.

Observations from a Developer's Altered Mind

Most developers, especially those of us who have been cutting code for a while, have had the experience of mastering a new computer language and suddenly having our worldview significantly shift. When developers discovered C, they found that they could manipulate a computer's internal system state at a much less primitive level than before.

When Smalltalk came along, savvy programmers found that they could think in a message-oriented way—applications were "conversations" whereby messages were created and consumed. When Visual Basic was promoted to service the needs of the desktop era, it introduced the document as a visual container for the application, and many coders found it useful to think in document-oriented metaphors. When C++ and, more important, Java came into common use, an entire generation of software architects and developers suddenly started thinking in a more model-oriented way (one in which documents were but one of a host of models for architecting an application).

More recently, a small but significant number of developers started writing serious applications with dynamic languages such as Python and Ruby, and that introduced many independent and a few in-house corporate developers to agile programming practice. At every waypoint in the odyssey, software creators gained new perspectives that helped them design and write code differently, and write different code as well.

Now, suddenly, fueled by dynamic behaviors in the browser and agile languages on the server side, the wheel has turned again, giving developers yet another new perspective. The landscape that developers seem to see from this altered mindset is an impressive list of modern application design attributes. In this section, we present some observations on ways in which our perspectives have been altered. How many of these are exemplary of your Web 2.0 development or end user creative experiences?

Some Observations from Our Altered Minds

The first observation we offer to you is that the current perspective shift you may be experiencing is not due to the introduction of a new language, but of an entire platform. Python advanced a fresh philosophy of *creating general applications*. Those of you who know about the "Zen of Python" know this concept; and for those of you who don't, try invoking the Python interpreter and type in **import this** at the Python prompt to expose the interesting little "Easter Egg" shown in the left screen in Figure 1-6. In contrast to the "zen" of any specific language, we suggest on the right screen in the same figure that RIAs advance a new philosophy of *what applications are*; these observations are discussed in the following sections.

Figure 1-6

Rich Internet Applications Are Software as Service

Applications, according to our unofficial "Zen of RIAs" are first and foremost services. This means that they are invoked by URL navigation, rather than by installation, preparation, and configuration on a specific compute platform. If a RIA fails to just "be there," then you failed as a developer, and potential end users will toss it aside. Software as service in this case also implies open APIs, which in turn implies remixing and mashups. Mashups and remixes are made possible because many RIA developers have opened their APIs specifically to allow for remixing. In truth, they can hardly prevent it, as in general, server method invocations are exposed in the browser's JavaScript. Many vendors ask a developer to "apply" for an API key to pass along with a service invocation to authenticate the invoking application. You can think of this as a way for the original software's creator to keep score of the remixes and mashups using their API.

Rich Internet Applications Are User Centered

RIAs are user centered in two different ways, and you should design with each of these aspects in mind. First, they are user centered because they operate at a level above the operating system. This is important, because traditionally, a lot of technology products start with the internals and wrap the user experience around the technology. For example, most OSs have a lot of scaffolding that revolves around manipulating the file system, (there have only been a handful that don't, such as General Magic's Magic Cap). Most technologists start with an interesting architecture and build outward from that toward something that the user eventually sees, the user experience.

A really bad example of something like this might be a command-line interface for controlling MP3 playback. Typically, no one has put any thought into the interface, or because it was built from the technology "out," it's so rooted in the inner workings of the system that the only person who really knows how to use it is the person who built it.

In contrast, the only contact point the user has with a RIA is the user experience, so it's designed with this in mind. Notice, for example, how although Writely creates documents, there is no explicit need to save a document. Ideally, a user should just be able to move from one functional context to another in a completely modeless fashion.

> *For a perspective on starting with the user experience and moving inward toward the working mechanism, read the sidebar "An Interview with 37 Signals" later in the chapter. Modeless operation explains a little of Google's success in becoming indispensable to the end user. The Internet is far bigger than any individual's file system; hence, searching and tagging become the evolutionary replacements for folder navigation and folder management.*

Whereas Web 1.0 sites sought to look and feel like magazines, Web 2.0 sites all seem to have a different (but common) look and feel — big bold buttons and operable fixtures are the order of the day. That's because they are emphatically *not* books on the screen. Developers are not HTML publishers putting up their political rants or the next Great American Novel for people to read; they're putting up full-featured applications.

End users, for their part, seem to have become comfortable with composing their own swivel chair integration point. They inherently "grok" that browsers offer topical separation of concerns/interests that can be accessed or set aside at the click of a tab. The Web 2.0 "power user" doesn't boast Excel proficiency. Instead, a user controls three or four browser instances, each with multiple tabs, and boasts the ability to manage a score of RSS feeds.

Rich Internet Applications Are Inherently Collaborative

RIAs are also user centered in that communities of people participate in elaborating the creations of others. Whether it's commenting a blog, tagging a news story, adding metadata to a digital photo, or creating a local marketplace with craigslist, people are forming communities around Web applications, and many notable Web 2.0 applications are focused on community service in some way.

Although the authors' parent company, BBN Technologies, is a large-scale player in developing the formalisms of the semantic Web through our work in OWL, the semantic Web language, we have been terrifically impressed with "folksonomy," a simpler kind of tagging that seems to work wonderfully well, despite its simplicity and idiosyncratic nature. As Wikipedia explains it:

> A "folksonomy" is a collaboratively generated, open-ended labeling system that enables Internet users to categorize content such as web pages, online photographs, and web links. The freely chosen labels–called tags–help to improve a search engine's effectiveness because content is categorized using a familiar, accessible, and shared vocabulary. The labeling process is called tagging.

Collaboration via the Web creates a new kind of participation, a new kind of information experience in which a potentially world-spanning user community has the ability to modify their own online experience, and contribute to shaping that of others. In the capstone application developed in this book, we provide a framework for multiple people to collaborate to create content with content locking. Interestingly, this is still something that absolutely eludes even the best-known desktop applications (e.g., collaborative real-time word processing has never been done well outside one or two exceptional efforts, notably SubEthaEdit on the Macintosh; real time multi-participant coding hasn't either outside Netbeans Java IDE).

Rich Internet Applications: Small and Agile Development

The next generation of Web development is still an unfolding story as we write this, so it's difficult to support some of the contentions we would argue in this section; however, we can use studies of agile language development (e.g., projects developed in Ruby and Python) as a yardstick, first of all because the pre-eminent frameworks for Web 2.0 development implement applications in these languages.

Studies involving agile languages (see, for example, Lutz Prechelt's "An empirical comparison of seven programming languages." *IEEE Computer* 33(10):23–29, October 2000) show that developers write less code overall in agile languages and achieve results faster. The power of the individual developer or the small team seems to be amplified. In many cases that researchers have looked at, teams are smaller and more agile for whatever reason. It appears that using the frameworks we cover here, teams can be smaller and get things done faster: Writely, acquired by Google in 2006, consisted at the time of three engineers (the three co-founders). 37Signals, inventors and heavy users of the Ruby on Rails framework, consisted of four or five in 2006.

Rich Internet Applications Are Bound to Change

At this writing, new versions of all major browsers are in the works. The Web 2.0 revolution appears headed for a tipping point regarding numbers of applications converted from the desktop, in terms of both user base and number of deployment platforms. The shortcomings of the current generation of browsers and new feature requirements for the next will become apparent. This simply means that your knowledge and competence will have to evolve as well. Whatever changes are in store for browsers, they will certainly evolve to become even more general-application platforms than they are currently.

How Do I Change the Way I Develop Applications?

You may well be thinking that if, as we have implied, the application world around us is in the midst of changing dramatically, whether that implies you are going to have to change your current development practice to fit this new world. What are best current practices for the new generation of applications? Clearly, something is happening: Applications are "in beta" for longer than many formal versions of traditional software. Extreme programming and continuous integration, so recently avant garde, now seem possibly a little shopworn. In our survey of successful Web 2.0 efforts, there is a marked difference between traditional development styles, with formal release cycles and technology focus, and the new motif of continually evolving applications and customer focus. The following list describes some of the manifestations of this change:

- ❑ **All applications are betas** — It's not clear where this trend started, but as in so many other areas, Google may have led the way. From the end user standpoint, it really doesn't matter. If the utility of the application is sufficiently compelling, the end user really doesn't care about labels. Betas set positive user expectations and enable developers to take risks and sometimes even fail. Private betas and limited betas are part of an older style of cyclical develop and release events. Applications with cycles also imply an end to the support of a previous release of an application, and a not-so-subtle, implicit message to the end user that the developer desires to end the relationship with the user community.

- ❑ **Versions and bugs** — Just because "it's all betaware" doesn't mean you can somehow get away with shoddy implementation, however. The betaware strategy allows you to add features of an application when they're ready, and not tie new features to a largely artificial version rollout system. It's as important as ever to maintain good (CVS or SVN) versioning, building (Ant, Cruise Control) and bug-tracking (Bugzilla) systems, but considering what we just said above, you will have to set internal release milestones. Like a shark, you always need to be moving forward. It's not important what bugs were reported by users last week or last month; if a bug can't be reproduced against the live code, then you can safely kick it to the curb. One problem you can't afford to ignore, and which you have to design and plan for, is that while you *can* roll back code, you *can't* roll back user-contributed content. Finally, whether you provide the back-end server or use one of myriad servers for hire, you can't afford to let server-side bugs take down your site, so think about this nonfunctional aspect as much as you do about the functional capabilities of your application. You want users to think of your site and your application(s) like a utility — always on, always operating, just like a light switch. (Remember the invisibility thing?)

- ❑ **Test-driven development** — Test drive development becomes especially important because of distributed development teams, miniscule staffs and limited QA budgets, Unit, and Subsystem tests.

- ❑ **A RIA is a living lab** — The numbers of unique users that RIA sites attract often shock the novice developer or entrepreneur. RIAs can grow from no users to hundreds of thousands exponentially. Even a small sampling of users can be a large actual number. Your application is your creation. You should feel free to change features and arrangements of controls and find out directly how well users react. Building in click counters to understand how users navigate your application, which features they use, which features they understand, and how they navigate the application can all be done at a fraction of the cost of traditional usability testing.

❏   **Don't write one application, write two** — As explained in the next section, there are many
paths to monetization, but understanding the community that accumulates around your application is one of the surest ways. Certainly, companies have attempted to categorize the people
buying their applications in an effort to ensure repeat business or new product lines. The effectiveness of their intrusive market research styles — such as user surveys packaged with product
registration — is debatable. Even in Web 1.0 applications, traffic monitors and other ways of
"slicing and dicing" the user populations are generally ineffectual. In contrast, consider the Web
2.0 "connected culture." Users themselves identify their social networks and invite new users to
share and otherwise become a part of the application's world. Flickr and YouTube are examples
of applications in which the community and the application become indistinguishable. The
kinds of user metadata that are useful to you in building value around your applications will
certainly vary according to application and end user community, and you need to apply as
much ingenuity to this aspect as the application itself.

How Am I Going to Make Money from RIAs?

If you're an enterprise applications developer, perhaps this is not a particularly relevant issue for you.
For others, however, the question hinges on more than idle curiosity. At first glance, one might think that
there is considerable exposure of intellectual property for your crafty rivals to inspect and emulate. After
all, the user experience of a RIA (the "view" portion of the application), including the HTML, inline
CSSs, and inline JavaScript, is available in clear text in the browser via any browser's "View Source"
capability.

Certainly, it is very hard to violate the basic separation of an application's basic wiring diagram (the
Model-View-Controller pattern) with RIAs. Remember, though, that the real intellectual content of an
Internet application is secure within the server. How much of your service interface you choose to
expose is up to you. As we will show in the next chapter, several "big name" providers expose a remarkable amount of their service call interfaces through external APIs. We will show you how to leverage
exposed APIs to create applications that are mashups composed from parts of other applications.

As far as your own viability is concerned, consider that economic models are changing rapidly. First, the
costs of production are really low. We have made a point in this book of demonstrating only frameworks
that are available and support open source. Second, server costs are really low. In the United States, ISP
costs continue to fall relentlessly. Further, when you begin to understand that with RIAs your application becomes a service, significant (nonfunctional) parts of your offering — storage, security, and always-
on availability — are no or low-cost value adds.

According to Michael Robertson, the creative force behind ajaxWrite (one of the RIA word processors),
millions of documents have been served to tens of thousands of end users. It seems clear that as more
content manipulation capability moves "into the cloud," the days of the $400 "Office" suite are num-
bered. Further, it also seems clear that as a result of the "gift" or sharing economy that seems to be an
emergent feature of the Web 2.0 culture, much of the content of new applications comes from end users.
The value of Flickr or YouTube is not so much that end users can put their pictures or videos on the
Internet cloud, but that they can publish their content to share with potentially millions of consumers.
What the developers behind Flickr and Writely have done is simply to provide a framework to load,
store, and tag content.

Although all sorts of models exist for creating value in return for compensation, the observation to readers is this: Don't use Microsoft as a reference point. The timeworn models from the desktop era may well be on their way to the dustheap of history. Further, build different things—things that play to the inherent advantage offered by the fact that you are building a networked application, one that provides a framework for multi-user contribution and collaboration. Remember that you may well want your application to be "invisible," enabling user content creation but building an air of indispensability around your application.

How much value is there to becoming so indispensable that you are taken for granted? As pointed out earlier in the chapter, the one application most end users take for granted, and consider to be a part of the essential fabric of the Internet, is Google search. Google's market cap in April 2006 was $128 billion USD.

Google's approach is that while they help end users locate content of interest, they also help advertisers locate "eyeballs" of interest, by assuming that an end user's search *might* be a search for goods and services. Most often it isn't, but Google doesn't need to be right much of the time, even most of the time. In 2005, advertisers sent $9 billion USD with the U.S. broadcast networks, where almost all their message was irrelevant to almost everyone. Google's AdSense capability can at least make a somewhat educated estimation of consumer interest. Perhaps even the advertising community is catching on—during 2005, Internet advertising revenues increased 28%.

The message here is that powerful things can happen if you build a target community around an application. Consider, for example, the potential for an application built as a volleyball-centric website—supporting league scheduling, result reporting, team statistics, and so on. Such a site, even with a relatively small user community, would be extremely valuable to equipment producers. Other Internet communities (e.g., del.icio.us, ClipMarks) create data sources that appear only on the Internet; the value of those data sources is currently underexploited, but you should recognize that there is value.

Rich Internet Applications Are Seductive

For end users, RIAs are certainly seductive, given the mashup capability for so many applications. Further, as suggested previously, they are seductively easy to use. Here, though, what we really mean is that they are seductive to us as developers. It seems much easier to get from thought to working application. Online tutorials for TurboGears and Ruby on Rails show a developer how to get a better than Hello, World quality Web 2.0 application coded and running in pretty short order, and that can be enough to show a novice developer the overall structure of these really fine frameworks. In truth, there's much more involved in doing nontrivial works, but the initial "seduction" provides a real "developer rush."

> *Ruby on Rails' captivating screencast boasts of "Creating a weblog in 15 minutes" (www.rubyonrails .org/screencasts); TurboGears' equivalent is "The 20-Minute Wiki" (www.turbogears.org/docs/wiki20)*

Because RIA development is most often associated with agile languages whereby often a small amount of code pays bigger dividends, milestones seem to happen faster. Those of us in the agile languages camp think we know why this is so. Agile language developers have always been a little suspicious of the *BIG DESIGN* waterfall method. That's the technical approach that always seems to produce a lot more UML than code. It always seems to such developers that having a well-defined application description in mind, plus the time-honored extreme programming approach of "design a little aspect, code a little, test a little, refactor, and repeat," yields better and faster results than endless agonizing over decomposing the big system picture.

In our experience, Web 2.0 design seems to strike the right balance between doing some up-front planning and modifying applications as experience moderates both the goals and the approach. Further, the frameworks that we cover in this book (Ruby on Rails, TurboGears, Django) make it eminently possible to do just that—incrementally design and deliver. That's not to say that *some* planning is a bad thing. The practices developers use commonly—separation of concerns, decomposition of the problem into object, and so on—still apply, and we will follow those precepts throughout the book (and, we hope, succeed).

Even when used for creating OS-bound applications, RIA standards may be easier to write for than desktop APIs. Slowly, the Macintosh Dashboard and Yahoo Widgets, the great-grandchildren of the old terminate-and-stay resident (TSR) applications (like the venerable DOS SideKick) are starting to gain some developer notice, and one reason is because, having mastered the skills and adopted the RIA mindset, it's hard to return to the bad old days of boring code. We cover desktop RIAs beginning in Chapter 17.

Interviews with Industry Leaders: Jason Fried and David Heinemeier Hansson of 37Signals

This chapter makes a number of assertions regarding the Web's future shape and potential beyond its first incarnation, and you may agree or disagree with at least a few of them. We drew many of our conclusions from listening carefully to industry leaders and revolutionary thinkers. From time to time throughout the book, we'll bring you insights from authoritative voices themselves. We interviewed Jason Fried and David Heinemeier Hansson of 37Signals, (37Signals.com), leaders in creating value in the Web's next generation.

On Being an Early Web 2.0 Innovator

Q: You started out as a Web design company. Now you are delivering the Web as an application platform. When did you realize that things were changing on the Web from a hyperlink information browser to the application framework we are beginning to have today? Was there ever an "Aha!" moment or was this just a natural progression from Web design to application design?

37Signals co-founder, Jason Fried: I don't think there was ever an "Aha!" moment, really. We needed to build a product for ourselves. Basecamp was built for ourselves originally. We decided that we needed to put it on the Web because we knew it needed to be centralized. Desktop software wasn't something we knew how to write, and desktop software really doesn't work well for centralized information. We felt that the Web was what we know best. It wasn't that we had a long-term vision, where we thought everything was going to the Web. It was just something we did out of necessity, and also we knew how to write Web-based software. We lucked into doing the easiest things for us and that happened to be doing Web stuff at the time.

Q: Have the other projects emerged out of Basecamp or are those projects that you thought would be relevant to your own company and then you started to expose those as external services as well?

Jason: Everything we built we built for ourselves first. We always filled a need that we had and we realized, as we like to say, "We are not unique snowflakes." If we need a tool, then so do hundreds of thousands of other companies just like us. There is nothing special about us that would only make a certain tool only relevant to us. So we say, let's put our own time into building this, and perhaps let's turn it into a product because other people need it as well and let's generate some revenue off of it.

On Managing to Make the Software Subscription Model

Q: You seem to have hit a golden mean in which people don't give a second thought to using your software through subscription, and yet one of the world's largest software vendors has tried that and broken their pick on it for more than a decade. Why do you think you're succeeding?

Jason: I think it's because our value proposition is significantly different . . . and that is fair pricing and good products—products that don't do a lot of [unneeded] "stuff"; products that just do a few things well and then get out of your way. That's what's compelling about what we are doing for people. If you look at a lot of other software companies—they are in the "software business," so they think they need to build more and more software that does more and more things to justify their cost and justify the belief they are the greatest software company in the world. More features doesn't mean that they deliver what people need. They really need to focus on simpler things that enable people to work better. We don't worry about what everyone else is doing and we make the pricing fair. For example, the entire software industry prices everything by seat, or by user. If one person uses it, it's X dollars, but if 10 people use it it's 10 times X dollars. Instead, we say, "Look, have as many people use it for the same price.

We don't exact what we call "a participation tax," which is what just about every other software company does. When you start doing that you are discouraging more people from using your product. All those things coming together is giving us a nice head start on the software subscription model.

On Maintaining Focus

Q: It seems like one of the common threads in interviews with 37Signals is to keep it simple, don't bother the user. Now that some of your products have been out on the Web for a while and you've gained more users, you've probably gotten a lot of feedback. Do you have to actively fight the urge to "feature creep" your applications.

Jason: It's certainly a challenge and takes a lot of discipline to say no, but we have it in our heads to say no to everything, including our own ideas, first. That's not to say that people won't say yes later, but initially we say no by default to every new idea, and that allows us to be selective and keep listening and hearing more requests; and if we keep hearing that from a large number of users, we'll say yes ultimately. We don't react to one person's request, not even our own. When you have hundreds of thousands of users, you can't respond to a single request.

It definitely requires a good bit of discipline to keep things simple, and the software industry, in general, doesn't have much [self] discipline. As products mature they get more and more complex for most companies. I don't feel that is the right trajectory. We are learning all the time.

On the Role of Agile Languages in Rich Internet Applications

Q: How did you guys come across Ruby? It would not have been the first choice on most peoples' lists a few years ago even if they were agile language savvy. Something that bothered people awhile back was that Ruby didn't have a native way to deliver user experience. Java has Swing. Python has TK, Wx, PythonCard, and a ton of other UIs. TCL has libraries, but Ruby had nothing but the Web. So how did you decide on Ruby?

Ruby on Rails creator, and 37Signaller, David Heinemeier Hansson: Ruby is a language for writing beautiful code. Beautiful code is code that makes the developer happy, and when a developer is happy they are more productive. Ruby is unique in the way it lets you express something briefly, succinctly, and beautifully, whereas both PHP and Java are either verbose or ugly in their structure and the way they structure code.

On the Role of Frameworks in Rich Internet Applications

Q: Have you seen the Java framework from Google (http://code.google.com/webtoolkit/)? Do you have an opinion about that? Have your looked at TurboGears (www.turbogears.org) or Django (www.djangoproject.com/)?

David: Yes. First, the Google stuff is still Java, so it's basically uninteresting to me in its raw form. The approach they are using is something that we've been championing for about a year now, which is to write JavaScript in another programming language other than JavaScript itself. We have in Rails something called RJS. We write JavaScript in Ruby and that gets compiled at runtime to JavaScript. It's great to see Google follow through on that.

As far as TurboGears and Django go, both are simply interesting frameworks. They have not been out as long as Rails and definitely don't have the same momentum as Rails, and also they are written in Python, which is a great language (but isn't Ruby). On the scale of things, it's much closer to Java than PHP. I'd rather be writing in Python than Java or PHP.

Django seems more interesting. TurboGears is basically a "glue" stack which takes existing components and "glues" them together in a way that will fit a solution. A big part of the success of Rails is that it is not a glue stack. All the components are developed knowing each other, and that's the big pain we are alleviating from the Java world where everything is a glue stack. You have to go out and hunt to get a ton of different frameworks and try and glue them together. I think that the Python frameworks are following the same approach we are, which is that if you use a consistently productive language, you can make everything yourself, and you'll be better for it.

On Agile Languages and Scalability

Q: With your selection of Ruby do you have concerns about scalability at all?

David: That's an easy answer, because it's exactly the same as other open-source languages. It follows what we'll call a *shared nothing architecture*. This means we split everything across three layers: Web, Application, and Database. Then make sure you don't keep state in your Web layer or in the Application layer. When you do that [adhere to these conventions—ed.] you get the wonderful benefit of being able to add unlimited Web servers, and unlimited application servers because all the state is being pushed down either to a DB, a shared memory layer, or NFS storage, so it's not your problem anymore.
That is basically the solution we picked. Scalability on data is hard. We don't want that problem. There are people out there that solved that problem long ago. Database folks are some of these people. So, scalability—it doesn't have any issues at all with respect to agile language. It's infinitely scalable at the Web and application layer—just add more servers.
The [Ruby] language itself is slightly slower than some other languages. It's in the same ballpark as Perl, PHP, and Python. Sure, you can hand-tune some Java code or write something in C or C++ that is faster. That's great, but it doesn't matter too much. We are in a time where CPU cycles are getting cheaper by the day, but programmer cycles are not getting cheaper and haven't gotten cheaper for a long, long time. The parameter you should be optimizing for is to get more programming cycles out of the development team. Using a more productive language and framework is the correct way to do that.
Just as a performance metric, we know that we are processing millions of requests a day. We're doing very well at that and plenty of other sites out there are supporting hundreds of thousands of users.

On Creating a New Rich Application Development Environment

Q: What are the general guidelines you use to determine whether a new feature or concept makes it into Rails' core? Is it a benevolent dictatorship like Linux? Or a group decision?

David: It's a group decision, but there's always a shadow of a benevolent dictator, me. If it's something I don't like, it's not going in. It's a simple as that. Most of the time, after using Rails for some time, they get the culture and they understand the motivation and what matures and tends to lead to patches in line with that vision.
Q: Where do you see Rails going as it evolves?

David: It continues to be a collection of solutions to problems encountered by the contributors. We don't have a road map. We don't intend to make a road map. We don't develop features for other people. The only features we develop are the ones we need ourselves. That is the only way to get an effective framework. If you try to imagine what some other programmer might need someday you are treading on thin ice.

On Working from the User Experience as a Functional Specification

Q: We've heard it said that it's a 37Signals philosophy to start from the user experience and, using that as a functional spec, turn traditional application design on its head. Spending 80% of the time working on the UI seems counterintuitive. Was that a personal sensibility or did you arrive at that because you stated out as a Web design firm?

David: Yes, that definitely helped. Once we started not trying to live up to other people's expectations of how you are supposed to do things, we got more things done and we got more right things done. That grew of practicing these things.

On Mashups

Q: *Something that amazes people new to Web 2.0 is the ease of doing mashups. You seem to be somewhat against exposing too much of your API so that other people can do mashups.*

David: Most of our products have exposed APIs, but there is a lot more "talk" than "walk." We haven't seen a large number of mashups that have been terribly useful rather than just cool. On the grand scale, exposed APIs don't matter as much yet as people would like us to believe. Our direction with Rails is to make it easier to do APIs right out of the box.

2

RIA Foundations

"The difficulty of literature is not to write, but to write what you mean."

— **Robert Louis Stevenson**

This chapter is your crash course in all of the languages necessary to convey your intentions to a Web browser. Most skilled computer professionals will attest to the belief that if you have learned one computer language, you have learned them all, or at least that learning your second is only a few days of effort away. Like the languages we speak, however, this maxim isn't really true for all computer languages, but rather just for those within the same family. Just as English speakers readily learn Spanish but struggle with Japanese, individuals whose entire programming experience has been in the family of procedural and object-oriented languages (such as Java and C++) sometimes break into a cold sweat at the thought of programming for the Web. This chapter shows you that you've probably already tackled the hardest language family there is to learn; the languages used on the Web are amazingly simple.

Writing an application for the Web is fundamentally different from writing an application for the computer desktop. A Rich Internet Application might look and perform exactly the same as a desktop equivalent, but the implementation is assuredly and wildly different under the hood. This difference stems from two separate worldviews. Desktop programming is *process focused* and *computer focused*, so languages in this world focus on controlling the hardware of a computer. Web programming, on the other hand, is *document focused* and *human focused* — its roots lie in the organization and presentation of structured information for human consumption.

The following pages introduce three markup languages and one scripting language that manipulate the objects described by documents written in those markup languages:

- ❑   **XML** — The eXtensible Markup Language is a meta-language that defines a common grammar with which to create topic-specific languages, which in turn create documents of meaningful data.

❑   **XHTML**—Defined under the rules of XML, the eXtensible HyperText Markup Language provides the concepts necessary to describe a document for publication on the World Wide Web.

❑   **CSS**—Cascading Style Sheets provide a way to create an aesthetic specification describing the way (X)HTML documents should be presented to the user.

❑   **JavaScript**—This is a scripting language that enables you to bring Web pages to life by interacting with both the user and a remote Web server to create real-time documents.

XML: The Lingua Franca of the Internet

Remember the bone song we all learned in second grade? "The hip bone's connected to the leg bone; the leg bone's connected to the . . ." and so on. If you are reading this book, you've likely heard of XML, and maybe already know all about it (feel free to skip a few pages ahead!). Regardless of your experience, however, we're here to tell you a secret that will allay any anxieties you might have about working with this buzzword technology: XML is really no more complicated than the hip-bone song.

First, some context. With the technology boom of the late 1990s, it became clear that the Internet, for better or worse, was around to stay as a major piece of our economic infrastructure. For reasons of either virtue or just pure profit, anyone with a computer and an idea could reach and be heard by the entire world. More than just human-to-human interaction, this infrastructure allowed for automated computer-to-computer interaction as well, which is what any operation on the Internet eventually boils down to at some point anyway.

Although networking has been around for some 30 years, the explosion in networked applications that occurred in the 90s revealed a serious problem: Few computer programs had any way of communicating with each other! For years, computer programs were written for specific purposes and for small, often academic, sets of customers. This environment did not require much investment in standardized data representation. With the boom of the late 90s, every grandma and grandpa in America was suddenly purchasing a computer to exchange baby pictures of their grandkids. Imagine taking isolated tribes that have spent 30 years developing their own languages and suddenly throwing them into a room together to have a chat!

XML was created to be the one data format to bind them all—a self-describing way of storing data that is simple in design but endless in possibility. If data is presented in XML, any computer in the world can read it and display its basic structure and contents, even if the program does not know exactly what to do with the data after that. For this reason, the few simple rules of XML are among the most basic and important that any Web application developer must learn, and they are the foundation upon which all Rich Internet Applications (RIAs) are based.

Back to the Hip-Bone Song—XML Fundamentals

Just as the hip-bone song describes how body parts are connected to each other, an XML document describes how objects are contained within other objects. You can put just about any conceivable description of the world in terms of containment: a room has tables, chairs, people, and so on. A person has a name, an address, a face, and a torso. This manner of describing objects is central to XML.

An XML document is composed of a series of *tags*. A tag is a marker that delineates one region in the document for another. You can embed regions in other regions any number of times, until eventually you hit an end and find just plain data. Tags almost always come in pairs: one to start the region and one to end the region. The combination of a start tag, end tag, and contents is called an *element*. The format of an element is listed in Listing 2-1.

Listing 2-1: An XML Tag

XML

```
<TAGTYPE attribute1="value1" attribute2="value2">Contents</ TAGTYPE>
```

The opening tag begins with a less-than (<) sign, which people often call an *opening bracket,* and is followed immediately by a word representing the type of tag. Any number of attributes come after the tag type, and then the tag ends with a greater-than (>) sign (commonly called a *closing bracket*).

The contents of the element come after the opening tag and are eventually followed by a closing tag, which looks just like the opening tag but contains no properties and has a forward slash immediately following the opening bracket. This tag pair is the fundamental construct of XML upon which any Rich Web Application, no matter how complex, is built. There are actually two types of XML tags — a tag pair and a lone-wolf — but you'll get to the second type in a moment.

As stated earlier, the contents of the region that a pair of tags defines can be anything, and, most significant, can be more XML nodes. The physical <TAGTYPE>-style text in an XML document is often called a *tag,* but the object that the tag represents is usually called a *node* or an *element*. Listing 2-2 shows one possible XML document.

Listing 2-2: A person described in XML

XML

```
<PERSON>
  <NAME>Blackbeard The Pirate</NAME>
  <PHOTO url="http://www.blackbeard.com/mugshot.jpg" />
  <ADDRESS type="home">
    <STREET>3 Davy Jone's Locker</STREET>
    <ZIP>08404</ZIP>
    <CITY>Atlantic City</CITY>
    <STATE>New Jersey</STATE>
  </ADDRESS>
</PERSON>
```

The XML in Listing 2-2 shows one possible way you could arrange contact information using XML. The top-most element is of type PERSON. This element contains two others, one called NAME and one called ADDRESS. The NAME element contains a literal string value, while the ADDRESS element contains still more elements, which eventually lead to raw data such as "Atlantic City" and "08404."

This example leads to two interesting observations:

❑ First, the zip code tag appears out of the order you would normally expect it to in the flow of an American address. Despite the fact that we, as humans, read an XML document from top to bottom, the XML language assigns absolutely no meaning or importance to the order in which tags in the same container appear.

❑   Second, notice that the Photo element is not a member of a tag pair. While most XML tags you encounter come in pairs, occasionally you will run into a situation in which the road stops and you do not need to contain anything else within an element. In these situations, you collapse the two tags into one by placing both the tag name and the forward slash (which signifies the close of an element) within the same tag, as shown in Listing 2-3. The forward slash always appears at the very end of the tag.

Listing 2-3

XML
```
<TAGTYPE property1="value1" property2="value2" />
```

Using Attributes

Notice that the address tag in Listing 2-2 contains an attribute called `type` with the value set to `home`. This attribute could have just as legitimately been coded as an element within the address element, as depicted in Listing 2-4.

Listing 2-4

XML
```
<ADDRESS>
  <TYPE>home</TYPE>
  . . .
</ADDRESS>
```

The choice between describing something as an attribute inside the opening tag of an element and describing it as an element contained within another is up to the reader, but much of this decision should be based upon the envisioned use of your particular data structure.

If the particular item you are trying to describe is complex and likely to contain a breakdown of more categories, then you have little choice but to encode this item as an element itself, such as the address element in Listing 2-2. If the item is an elemental data type — a string or integer, for example — then the possibility of using an attribute arises. The generally accepted wisdom regarding how to choose between the two in this circumstance is based on what that information is describing.

If the item in question is an interesting piece of data in and of itself, such as a zip code or a book title, then it is probably best to model that item as a full-blown element, such as the following:

```
<BOOK><TITLE>XML Haiku Anthology</TITLE></BOOK>
```

If the purpose of the item in question is solely to provide better context through which to understand the containing element, however, then encoding that item attribute is likely the route to go. In Listing 2-2, the `address` type was written as an attribute because the value `home` serves only to clarify the semantics of how the address element should be interpreted. For the preceding book example, a fine example attribute might be as follows:

```
<BOOK language="English"><TITLE>XML Haiku Anthology</TITLE></BOOK>
```

By itself, the `language="English"` statement has little meaning in the physical world. It only acquires meaning when used to express the greater context in which to judge the `BOOK` element.

One final concern that might affect whether a particular piece of data is an element or an attribute is the expected contents that the data member might hold. Some types of data encoding (such as long segments of binary data or text sequences with a lot of < or & characters) cannot be stored inside of an attribute or even a regular XML tag. This data must be placed in a special type of container called `CDATA`. CDATA regions start with `<![CDATA[` and end with `]]>`. These regions contain data that is left completely unparsed by the XML interpreter — usually binary data that does not conveniently fit an XML representation and certainly cannot be modeled as an element attribute.

The DOM Tree

You have now learned the basics of writing an XML document — namely, the following:

- ❑   XML documents contain an orderless set of elements.

- ❑   Elements can contain other elements, a text element, or nothing at all.

- ❑   Elements that contain further content are expressed as a pair of tags.

- ❑   Elements with no further content are expressed as a single tag.

- ❑   Attributes are used to provide greater context through which to understand the meaning of an element.

If XML were read in linear fashion, you would not be able to visualize a document's structure very easily once the document's size grew to be a few pages long. To remedy this, developers usually think of an XML document in terms of a large tree of information called the *Document Object Model*, or just the *DOM tree*. The DOM tree is nothing new in addition to what you have already learned; it is just a different way to talk about XML documents, using the vocabulary of a hierarchical lineage rather than containment.

Remember that XML is not so much a language itself; it is a method for creating your own vocabulary with which to express documents. As long as you follow the proper syntax, a computer program can interpret any conceivable XML document as a complex series of containments. Once parsed into the control of a programming environment, the XML document is modeled as a tree structure in which each XML element represents a tree node that has a parent (except for the root) and zero or more children. When an XML document is modeled this way, it becomes a tangible structure that you can mold and mix, break apart, and recombine. This is the DOM tree.

While the semantics in English are a bit different, the functional meaning of a tree of data is really the same as a series of containments. Think of the Russian dolls that you may have had in your house in your youth: Each larger doll could be opened to reveal a successively smaller one inside. Now imagine that you expressed the containment relationships of these dolls by arranging them onto an organizational ladder whereby big dolls were the superiors (or parents) of smaller, inferior (or child) dolls. This parent-child relationship is exactly how the DOM tree presents access to the information contained within an XML document. Each time an element has one or more elements within it, the tree grows a bit longer and branches a new sprout for each contained element.

Listing 2-5 shows a hypothetical XML document that might be in a book publisher's database.

Listing 2-5

XML

```
<Document language="en">
 <Author>Lieutenant Smee</Author>
 <Publisher>Pirate Publishing House</Publisher>
 <Title>Plank Safety Regulations</Title>
 <Chapter number="1">
        <Title>Washing the Plank</Title>
        <Paragraph number="1">
              When the plank isn't being walked, it is being washed...
        </Paragraph>
        <Paragraph number="2">
              Pickled herring poses the biggest safety hazard for...
        </Paragraph>
 </Chapter>
</Document>
```

Figure 2-1 illustrates the containment-based picture that this XML document represents — a page element containing a header and body element, and so on.

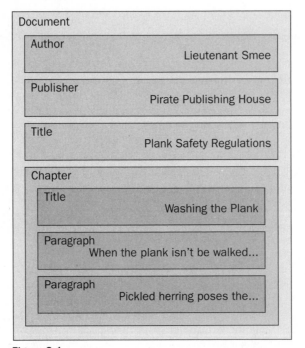

Figure 2-1

Figure 2-2 shows this XML document expressed as a tree. The Document node is the root of the tree, with each successive level of containment shown as a deeper layer in the tree. Notice that Figure 2-2 contains no more and no less information than Figure 2-1 — it is simply a different way of looking at it.

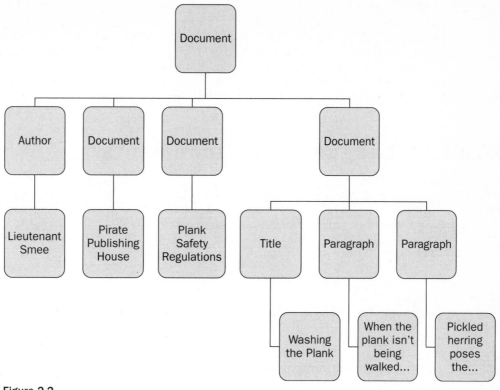

Figure 2-2

As you can probably see from these figures, the DOM tree provides some exciting features:

❑   The beauty of the DOM tree elements is that, like the ornaments on a Christmas tree, you can pluck the elements on it from one spot and place them in another. For example, you could swap the Title element directly under the Document element with the Title element beneath the first Chapter element. This might not seem very exciting now, but later you'll learn that when writing a Web page in XHTML, the XML-compliant variant of HTML, moving an element from one location to another can have serious effects on the way a Web page is displayed. Interactively manipulating the elements of the DOM tree that represents a Web page is in fact the fundamental operation that makes Rich Internet Applications different from regular Web pages, so if you understand the tree interpretation of an XML document, then you already understand the types of operations you'll perform on your Web page to create a rich user experience.

❑   The DOM tree makes it visually obvious that, just like man, no element is an island. An element's relationship to other elements is as important to understanding the element as the element's attributes. For example, by themselves, you cannot differentiate the two Title elements in Listing 2-5 from each other. However, you should treat the document title entirely differently than a mere chapter title — it should be on the book's cover, in gold print, and listed in the bookstore database, for example. Just as you clearly see from the DOM tree in Figure 2-2 which element is the document title and which the chapter title, the XML parser notices and reacts to this difference. This type of context comes in handy with cascading style sheets (CSS) documents you create to spice up Web pages later in the chapter.

❑ The DOM tree provides an easy abstraction for working with the data contained in XML documents. Because you treat elements as objects, rather than text on a page, the programmer can ask for a list of references to all children of an element, or a list of references to all elements within the tree that share a certain attribute. The simplicity of the XML specification makes it straightforward to map any conceivable element to a common object representation in your language of choice, which means that once parsing is complete, programmers do not have to learn anything new and exotic to work with XML immediately.

XHTML: A Language for Documents

Until this point, you've learned that XML is a meta-language that helps create topic-specific languages to describe structured data of that topic. XHTML, however, is a topic-specific XML-based language that describes the contents of a Web page. XHTML started out as HTML, the HyperText Markup Language — a way to publish digital documents containing in-text references to each other. After the introduction of XML as a standardized way to create documents, HTML passed the torch to XHTML, the XML-compliant version of HTML.

Modern Web browsers will parse either, and valid XHTML is always valid HTML, so this book tries to adhere strictly to the XHTML standard because of its more precise syntactical requirements. For nostalgia's sake, the book uses the XHTML and HTML terms interchangeably. The most visible differences between the two languages is the way in which you write tags without contents. XHTML tags always end with a forward slash before the closing bracket — for example, `<TAG property1="value1" />` — while HTML browsers will accept the tag without a forward slash, making the distinction between the opening tag of a pair and a lone-wolf tag ambiguous.

XHTML is an XML-based language to describe documents. Documents have a title and a header, a body with sections, headings, paragraphs, and tables. Documents contain such items as images, links to other documents, and bulleted lists. Conceptually, XHTML is very nontechnical. Where technical expertise is required is in the task of defining your Web documents so that you can easily manipulate them to interact with both your user and a remote Web server.

Without further ado, let's look at the specific XML elements that comprise an XHTML Web page. You may find it easiest to think of XHTML elements as falling into five main categories:

❑ Document structure

❑ Text structure

❑ Text type

❑ In-text objects (such as images and links)

❑ Document setup

This section attempts to provide a brief reference to some of the most common XHTML elements in each of these categories. There are still many more elements waiting for you to use, so anyone new to XHTML or just looking to freshen up should visit the World Wide Web Consortium's excellent Web site at www.w3.org. *This site contains the official XML, HTML, and XHTML specifications, as well as links to tutorials and slides on these languages*

Origins of XHTML

Sir Tim Berners-Lee developed HTML and HTTP (the HyperText Transfer Protocol) as a way to publish documents at CERN long before XML existed. HTML was specified using XML's parent meta-language, the Standard Generalized Markup Language (SGML). SGML further dates back to GML, developed by IBM researchers in the late 1960s. Like XML, SGML and GML are meta-languages — they do not define any particular elements or fixed document structure itself, but rather specify a standard grammar through which you can define your own language. HTML is an example of a language defined with SGML grammar.

Computer languages never really die completely; as time passes, they simply migrate from older to newer variants. As SGML was phased out in favor of the newer and simpler XML, the HTML that we have all come to recognize was transitioned into XHTML, an XML-compliant version.

Document Structure

If you only pay attention to one of the groupings of XHTML elements presented in this section about XHTML, pay attention to this one. Table 2-1 contains the XHTML elements that specify the overall structure of a document. The elements in this category range from the most mundane but important within XHTML — html, head, title, and body — to the most exciting and flexible elements in the eyes of a rich Web application developer, div and span.

Table 2-1: XHTML Elements for Document Structure

Element Name	Meaning
html	The root element for HTML and XHTML documents. All content within the Web page traces its containment lineage back to this element.
head	The head section of the Web page, which contains metadata about the Web page and instructions for additional files necessary to display the page properly
title	The title of the Web page to be displayed in the title bar of the Web browser
body	The body of the Web page. All content that you intend for the user to see is placed within this element.
div	Marks off a logical division within a document. You might group a title-section, login box, chat window, or comment box in a div element. Above all elements in the world of RIA, this element is your best friend.
span	Exactly the same as the div element except it is intended for in-line text only. Whereas a div marks off a region on the page, a span element marks off regions of text in mid-sentence or mid-paragraph.

As your development grows from dabbling with various Web techniques to creating full-fledged Web applications, you'll both want and need to design your Web page so that certain elements can be identified easily in the DOM tree. Using the `div` and `span` elements enables you to create as many layers of containment (branches in the DOM tree) as you want so that you can easily and precisely modify, add to, and remove regions of the Web page using JavaScript. The `div` and `span` elements are truly the bread and butter of Rich Internet Applications.

The `div` and `span` elements also provide a way for developers to use the DOM tree to provide context to elements that affects their presentation and behavior. Because XHTML does not allow custom tag types, creating XHTML that looks like the Address Book example in Listing 2-2 is not possible. The `div` and `span` elements step in to fill this void in flexibility. Listing 2-6 shows the XML in Listing 2-2 translated into a likely XHTML document describing the same data.

Listing 2-6

XHTML

```
<div id="person_342" class="person">
  <div class="name">Blackbeard The Pirate</div>
  <img id="person_342_photo" src="http://www.blackbeard.com/mugshot.jpg" />
    <div id="person_342_address" class="address home">
    <span class="street">3 Davy Jone's Locker</span>
    <span class="city">Atlantic City</span>
    <span class="state">New Jersey</span>
    <span class="zip">08404</span>
  </div>
</div>
```

The document in Listing 2-6 maps to a DOM tree of exactly the same shape as the XML document in Figure 2-2, but it uses only element types from the set defined in the XHTML language. Only three types of tags — `div`, `span`, and `img` — are used in Listing 2-6. Because XHTML does not allow arbitrary tag names, attributes become the only avenue through which to provide custom structure to your data, but attributes too are constrained by the XHTML specification.

Also notice how the order in which the address elements appear is what a U.S. citizen would expect, while in Listing 2-2 it was purposefully out of order. While it is possible to create a style sheet that orders XHTML elements properly no matter what order they come in, most Web developers exploit the fact that Web browsers default to displaying information in the order in which it is written. Whenever you have the option of placing something in an order that makes sense without any special formatting instructions, run with it.

Text Structure

The elements contained in Table 2-1 will get you started with some of the ways in which XHTML enables you to insert highly structured text into your document. To be specific, Table 2-2 samples tags that you can use to describe paragraphs, tables, and lists of items.

Table 2-2: XHTML Elements for Text Structure

Element Name	Meaning
p	A paragraph of text
table	A table of structured text
tr	A table row element
td	A table cell element. Table cells always come inside of table rows.
ol	An ordered list of items (1, 2, 3, and so on)
ul	An unordered list of items (called out by bullet points)
li	An item in either an ordered or unordered list

Because you can place data into structures that carry spatial relationships with each other, this grouping of XHTML elements is very important to Rich Internet Application developers. You can sort photos for display in a slide show by combining JavaScript with an ordered list. You can also use a table to provide a rough grid into which you can drop elements, or an unordered list as a region of the page that acts as a shopping cart, enabling users to drop items for purchase inside of it. Many real-life examples of these elements will appear in the rest of this book, so the elements are provided here without accompanying examples.

Describing Text Type

One of the most basic sets of elements is one that describes a certain kind of text. The elements in Table 2-3 help you capture different types of text, whether it is headings for regions in your document, a famous quote, or information that deserves emphasis. These elements are just a small subset of the elements available for this purpose, but enough to get you almost all of the way through this book.

Table 2-3: XHTML Elements for Text Type

Element Name	Meaning
em	*Emphasized* text
strong	**Strongly Emphasized** text
blockquote	A block of quoted text attributed to a different source
h1, h2, h3, h4, h5	First through fifth-level headers. For example, you might use Header 1 as a page title, Header 2 as a page subtitle, and Header 3 as a topic title.

Listing 2-7 and the accompanying rendering in Figure 2-3 show how you might organize text using a few of these elements and how a Web browser would visually interpret this markup if you specify no other visual guidelines. While you should not think of XHTML elements as carrying any particular visual meaning by themselves, all Web browsers contain a default set of visual interpretations for each element. You discover how to override these defaults using CSS in the next section.

Listing 2-7

XHTML

```
<h2>Chapter 2</h2>
<h3>Different Types of Text</h3>
Some text is <em>emphasized</em>,
while other text is <strong>STRONG!</strong>
<blockquote>
Don't worry about how it looks right now --

        CSS will help you specify

                        exactly how to display each kind!
</blockquote>
```

Different Types of Text

Some text is *emphasized*, while other text is **STRONG!**
    Don't worry about how it looks right now – CSS will help you specify exactly how to display each kind!

Figure 2-3

Notice the following observations concerning Listing 2-7:

❑ Recall that the elements contained in an XML document have no order, despite the fact that they must appear in a particular order in the XML document because of a document's inherently linear nature. Looking at the HTML and its rendered output, it is clear that order most definitely matters to a Web browser. Unless you use CSS to override the visual positioning of XHTML elements, the Web browser, by default, displays them in the exact order in which they were encountered in the XHTML document.

❑ Some text occurs outside of any XHTML elements. In a real XHTML document, fragments like the one in Listing 2-7 are not allowed. You, at the very least, enclose every piece of text between the HTML and body elements. Even so, you see natural language text intermingling with in-line XHTML elements. In these cases, the XTML parser built into the Web browser creates a hidden "Text Element" to wrap around the natural language text for you, so that your XHTML document remains a tree of elements and all natural text exists at the leaves of the tree.

❑ White space (the spaces, tabs, and newline characters) in the HTML do not seem to match up with the spaces in Figure 2-3. Because HTML is structured text, not styled text, the parser collapses any white space more than one space wide into a single space character on your Web page. New lines on a rendered Web page also have nothing to do with the newline characters in your HTML document. Instead, they are a function of the CSS properties applied to each element.

In-text Objects

The elements in Table 2-4 describe just a few of the nontext elements common to Web pages that you might want to insert into your document. These elements often appear as a single tag, rather than a pair, and often require a large number of attributes to provide information about how to display the in-text object.

Table 2-4: XHTML Elements for In-text Objects

Element Name	Meaning
img	An image. The address to the image file and other options are specified as attributes.
a	A link to another Web page. You specify the link's address as an attribute, and the displayed link text as the element's contents.
input	An input element on the Web page, such as a text box, radio button, or Submit button. You specify the type of input element as an attribute.
label	The label for another element on the page

Listing 2-8 shows an example of an image and link element in use.

Listing 2-8

XHTML

```
<img src="http....">
<a href="http://www.blar.com">Blar's</a> Logo.
```

Document Setup

The final elements in this section define information for the sake of the Web browser attempting to interpret the document, rather than for the user who will view it. As with previous element groups, the three items in Table 2-5 do not include all possible elements that fit this description, but you will use them in almost every rich Web application you ever write. There is little to no variation in the way you use these elements, so they are presented without an accompanying example.

Where Did the Boldface (`<b>`) Element Go?

Developers who have been writing HTML for years might scratch their heads at the conspicuous absence of several of the most common elements from this chapter. These elements are intentionally left out of this brief HTML reference in hopes that you never learn to use them! While HTML is a language that describes documents, XHTML should describe only a document's structure.

Many traditional HTML elements (and attributes) exist only to control the appearance of text: `<b>`, `<i>`, `<u>`, `<br>`, and `<font>`, to name a few. These elements are still valid XHTML, but you should avoid them at all costs. A general rule of thumb for any XML document is that if a tag name is not a noun, then it probably doesn't fit into the spirit of XML. Using only those XHTML elements that are nouns enables a developer to maintain the trinity of separation between a Web document's structure, presentation, and interaction that this chapter attempts to illustrate. When these three concerns are divided strictly between XHTML, CSS, and JavaScript, respectively, your life as a Rich Internet Application developer becomes much easier.

Table 2-5: XHTML Elements for Document Setup

Element Name	Meaning
!DOCTYPE	Appears at the beginning of an XML document to specify the particular XML-based language contained within the document. A link to a DTD file is included in this tag to provide parsers with a specification against which to check the validity of the rest of the document.
link	This element specifies a reference to another document, just like the a element, except it may only occur with the head element. The most common use of this element is to link an XHTML document to a cascading style sheet.
script	This element specifies a region within the XHTML document that should be interpreted as a scripting language. You can use this element both to include JavaScript files and to enclose in-page JavaScript.

CSS: A Language for Style

Now that you are comfortable with the concepts of XML and the vocabulary of XHTML, you can structure your information so that it can be read in by a Web browser. But let's face it: Very few people want to view a Web site that looks like a word processing document. They want the content accompanied by crisp logos, interesting design, and clever typesetting. Regardless of the geek factor, designing a Web application is every bit as artistically demanding as creating and managing the visual design of a magazine.

No matter what your medium, all visual design tasks on the Web fall into just two categories: describing where things are and describing how they look. In the early and even the recent days of the Web, HTML not only described a document's structure, but also specified these visual design properties. Objects were positioned on the page with endless nested `<table>` elements that created a nightmare of grids within grids. A mixture of HTML tags and tag attributes controlled how each of these objects appeared: `<b>` for boldface, `<font>` for text size and style, `background-color` and `color` as styling attributes, and so on. These constructs provided a way to beautifully style a Web page, but at the cost of cluttering an HTML document beyond recognition.

Computer programmers from all backgrounds know that one of the primary characteristics of any good software design is separation of concerns — the segmentation of an application into discrete units that you can test, reuse, and improve independently of other units. Programming this way simply leads to better, more understandable, and more maintainable code. As you have seen from the previous sections in this chapter, modern Web sites no longer encode visual specifications in XHTML. This concern is separated out into a separate file called a cascading style sheet (CSS). Using CSS to specify your Web site's look and feel has a number of benefits:

❑ **Visual properties are specified once and only once** — If you coded an element's look into the HTML document as attributes and helper elements, changes to that element only affect that element. Consider the impact on an online newspaper. If the editor decides to underline article titles in blue, someone would have to edit every single article on the Web site and manually update the title element. If, instead, the news organization uses CSS to describe how XHTML files display, updating the CSS file with the new look immediately changes how every article on the whole site is displayed.

❑ **Artistic design is completely separate from content development**—Often, the group who writes the Web page content is different from the group who programs the underlying structure of the Web page. By separating the visual formatting guidelines into a separate set of files, CSS enables developers to keep the task of programming a Web application completely separate from making that application look good. This results in a huge productivity boost because it makes each part of the code easier to understand and enables separate teams to work on their own parts simultaneously without stepping on each other's toes.

❑ **Artistic design is not bound by page structure**—If you structure the elements of your Web pages well, you can perform a complete overhaul of a site's visual appearance without touching anything other than the site's CSS file. You can even define the images on your site with CSS, so the number of possible ways to display the same DOM tree can be striking. To see just how flexible CSS-driven Web sites can be, visit the CSS Zen Garden at www.csszengarden.com. Graphic artists from all over the world have contributed hundreds of CSS files to the CSS Zen Garden, all of which can be applied to the main page as a demonstration of the flexibility benefits of good Web design.

❑ **Artistic intent is clearly stated**—When visual layout is embedded in HTML, looking at a raw HTML file is a bit like looking at the electrical wiring in a mad scientist's invention — it is almost impossible to get a picture of the overall themes and structures amidst the noise. Because CSS is a language that specifies visual styles and visual styles only, it has a clear and simple look that anyone without prior experience can understand. If you design the DOM tree with good ID and class names, anyone can easily pick up a CSS file, know immediately what the designer was thinking, and make changes.

XHTML in Rich Internet Applications

If a developer's objective is to simply create the electronic version of a beautifully typed page, then he or she need not pay much attention to the X in XHTML; any combination of elements that results in an aesthetically pleasing page suffices. However, Rich Internet Application developers are different. Their goal is not just to create a Web page that is attractive to look at, but to create the next killer application inside the Web browser. With this in mind, remembering the XML roots of XHTML is of utmost importance.

XHTML documents not only contain structure for the sake of reproducing the real-life objects they represent, they are also the living interface to your Web application, and, as such, they must be designed so that they are easily manipulated by computer code. The treelike structure of XHTML enables regions of the document to be easily styled and manipulated. Clever manipulation of the DOM tree through JavaScript is the defining characteristic common to all Rich Internet Applications.

Because XHTML limits your ability to use any tag type you want, to preserve meaning of custom tags in your DOM tree, you must extensively use the id and class attributes. Recall that when the XML of Listing 2-2 was transformed into XHTML in Listing 2-6, the descriptive tag types disappeared and were replaced by just div and span elements. To preserve the amount of information in the original XML text, the information encoded in those lost tag types was stashed in the id and class attributes of the new div and span elements. You will see just how important the class tag is when you learn to write visual specifications for your XHTML text with CSS in the next section, and you will grow to appreciate the id tag when you begin manipulating the structure of the DOM tree with JavaScript.

Because the CSS specification is large, it makes no sense to capture pieces of it here, but new CSS developers are in luck for three reasons. First, CSS is easy to understand when you see it, so continuing without reading an entire book on the subject should pose very little problem understanding the text. Second, the examples in this section show enough of the basic syntax that all you have left to learn is the breadth of the CSS vocabulary. Finally, the W3C Web site has links to numerous CSS references and tutorials (visit www.w3c.org).

In lieu of enumerating all the possible visual style properties and the arguments that they take, this section introduces how you can apply CSS to DOM elements, how the browser decides which styles to apply to an element, and how CSS can make RIA development fun.

Attaching CSS to a Web Page

There are three ways to attach cascading style sheets to a Web page: from an external file, in the Web page header, and in the attributes of an element. Which one you choose depends on what you want to accomplish at the time you are working on the document. Because one of CSS's great strengths is separating visual specification from content specification, all Web developers should ideally store their CSS within separate files, and link to those files from XHTML documents. If you want to debug a problem on a particular page and need to override some of your existing CSS properties, though, you might want to write your CSS directly into the XHTML document itself.

Attaching CSS code as an external sheet is accomplished with a `link` element inside the `head`. Listing 2-9 shows a link to an external CSS file.

Listing 2-9

XHTML
```
<link rel="stylesheet" href="http://www.ideastax.com/stylesheets/stax.css">
```

To place CSS instructions inside the header of an XHTML document in an inline fashion, use a `style` tag in the `head` element that contains the CSS within it, as shown in Listing 2-10.

Listing 2-10

XHTML / CSS
```
<head>
 <style type="text/css">
 p { margin-left: 10px; }
 body { background-color: blue; }
 </style>
</head>
```

CSS attached to an XHTML document as in Listing 2-10 will affect the entire contents of that document, but no other documents. To override the styling of an individual element within your XHTML, add the overriding CSS code to the `style` attribute of that element, as shown in Listing 2-11. This, too, is a useful debugging trick because any properties specified here will override other CSS styles that have been applied.

Listing 2-11

XHTML / CSS

```
<p style="background: blue; width: 90%; margin-left: 15px;">
This is a paragraph
</p>
```

Painting By Numbers

A CSS file is a list of elements and the contexts in which they might occur on a Web site and how those situations should be handled visually. There are four different ways that CSS can affect an element's styling: based on the tag type, based on the element's ID, based on the element's class, and based on the element's ancestry.

Styling Based on Tag Type

The most basic way CSS can specify a visual style is by overriding the default style of a valid XHTML tag type. Listings 2-12 and 2-13 show some examples. Listing 2-12 has an h1 (first-level header) element, with default font-weight, size, and bottom margin properties overridden by a CSS specification.

Listing 2-12

CSS

```
h1 {
  font-weight: bold;
  size: x-large;
  margin-bottom: 2px;
}
```

Listing 2-13 shows one way a Web site might display each paragraph. This example defines a top and bottom margin of 2 pixels, and a left and right margin of 5 pixels around each paragraph. The first line is indented by an extra 5 pixels, and the font is the default size, but is green and of typeface Veranda.

Listing 2-13

CSS

```
p {
  margin: 2px 5px 2px 5px;
  padding: 0px 0px 0px 0px;
  indent: 5px;
  font: Veranda;
  color: #00FF00;
}
```

While Listings 2-12 and 2-13 are useful, they only show you how to change the look of the built-in set of XHTML tags. Often you don't want to change the look of *all* header elements, but just a particular element. For that you need to create a style specific to a particular element ID.

Styling Based on Element ID

The second way to change the look of elements on a Web page is to apply a style to an element with a particular ID. You accomplish this by substituting the element ID for the tag name and preceding it with a hash (#) sign. Listing 2-14 demonstrates how to override the DOM element with the ID of `titlebar`. This element stretches horizontally across its container, is 100 pixels tall, and has white text on a navy-blue background. The ID-based method of specifying styles is good for elements that appear on every single page, such as a title, a footer, and possibly a sidebar or navigation menu.

Listing 2-14

CSS

```css
#titlebar {
  width: 100%;
  height: 100px;
  background-color: #000066;
  color: #FFFFFF;
}
```

Styling Based on Element Class

A class-based method of specifying look and feel provides the most flexible option. You can create a general style that you can then apply to any element in the DOM tree. Windows, doors, and submarine hatches are completely different objects, and each instance has a different ID, but they are all entrances. Class-based styles enable you to specify that all entrances have a transparent center and a border around the edge. As long as you make sure to specify in your element attributes that window, door, and hatch elements share the class `entrance`, then they will all be affected by that style guideline. Listing 2-15 shows an example of a class-based style. As you can see, it looks the same as an ID-based style except a period is used instead of a hash sign. This style specifies a warning class that you can apply to any element in the DOM tree. When an element has the word "warning" inside the class attribute, the text inside that element will be red and emboldened against a light-gray background.

Listing 2-15

CSS

```css
.warning {
  font-weight: bold;
  color: #CC0000;
  background: #EEEEEE;
}
```

DOM elements can have multiple classes if you separate the class names with a space. Listing 2-16 shows a `div` element that might show up in an online address book. This element has three different applied styles: one for the class `address`, one for `home_address`, and one for `outdated`. The Web browser evaluates these styles in the order in which they are listed, so latter classes may override properties that earlier classes set.

Listing 2-16

XHTML

```xhtml
<div id="person_23_address" class="address home_address outdated">
  ... (content goes here) ...
</div>
```

Styling Based on an Element's Ancestry

You can combine the last three methods of defining styles to create very specific styles dependent on an element's location in the DOM tree, as well as its name, ID, and attributes. Listing 2-17 shows a style that only applies to elements that have the class title and are the descendent of a DIV element with the class buddy_list. By placing ancestral constraints on your styles, you can create powerful context-sensitive styling guidelines without compromising the cleanliness of your XHTML document structure.

Listing 2-17

CSS

```css
div.buddy_list .title {
  border-color: #0000AA;
}
```

The CSS Cascade Shimmy

You should keep three separate rules in mind that dictate how CSS applies to your XHTML documents:

❑   They are applied in the order in which they appear in the CSS document, so if you accidentally define and then later redefine the h1 element, the latter definition is dominant for any properties of the two definitions that conflict.

❑   For all properties of the parent that can be applied to the child, each DOM element is styled in the manner of its parent.

❑   Properties defined for a child element override properties inherited from the parent element.

The XHTML and CSS code in Listing 2-18 and Listing 2-19 show combined examples of all of the CSS concepts presented thus far. Rendered in a Web page, this code displays the word "CASCADING" in small red print, with a line beneath stretching across the page. The word is red because the coloring on the element with ID foo cascades down to its h1 descendant. The word is underlined because it is contained within a descendant of ID foo with class bar. Finally, the element is extra-small because all h1 elements are overridden to be that size.

Listing 2-18

XHTML

```xhtml
<div id="foo">
  <div class="bar">
    <h1>CASCADING</h1>
  </div>
</div>
```

Listing 2-19

CSS

```css
#foo      { color: red; }
#foo div.bar     { border-bottom: 1px solid black; }
h1        { font-size: x-small; }
```

Taking Full Advantage of CSS in Your RIA

If you have a computer nearby and made a quick visit to the CSS Zen Garden while reading this, then it is safe to assume you don't need any more convincing as to the benefits of creating a well thought-out DOM tree and clean CSS code to match it. Here, then, are some general CSS development tips that will lead to a beautiful site design:

❑ **CSS classes should reflect their use, not their look** — One of the most common mistakes that both beginners and experts make is naming CSS classes after the visual style that the designer originally intended for members of that class. Although names such as `red` and `left_column` may indicate your initial intent, they do not give you the flexibility to easily change looks when you overhaul your Web site. Always name your CSS classes after their intended meaning, letting the properties within the class speak for themselves. If your CSS file has names such as `warning`, `important`, `main_content`, and `secondary_content`, this is a good indication that you are creating class names to stand the test of time.

❑ **Keep your CSS clean, commented, and separated into sections** — As you develop more sophisticated Rich Internet Applications, your CSS file may grow to be very large. From the start, use comments in your CSS files to describe how the trickier CSS wizardry works, or note how a class is intended to be used. Separate blocks of CSS in a way that makes sense for your application. This may mean grouping CSS pertaining to elements in certain regions of the page together. Or you could group together elements based on which XHTML element they override. No matter what your organizational needs, down the road, you'll be glad that you took the time to organize.

❑ **Remember that CSS is your RIA interface, too** — Just as the XHTML DOM tree structures the interface to a Web application, CSS provides the makeup for this interface. Because Web applications use XHTML as interactive interfaces instead of just static documents, CSS is your vehicle for describing visual feedback to a user as certain events on the Web page occur. A zip code text box might turn red if its contents are not a valid zip code, or a region of the page might turn orange to indicate that you have a new message available.

❑ **Class-based styles are a RIA developer's best friend** — Because of the need to apply and later remove styles to elements on the DOM tree, the class-based method of applying styles to an object is a closely guarded tool in the RIA developer's chest. The next section shows how JavaScript enables you to add and remove attributes from an object in response to a user's actions on the Web page. If a piece of JavaScript code modifies the class attribute of a DOM element, the Web browser immediately recomputes the visual styling on that element based on the new CSS classes that should be applied.

JavaScript: A Language for Action

You have learned how to structure a Web document with XHTML and how to make this document look good with CSS. With those skills alone, you can reproduce the static content and visual feel of just about any Web site out there, but stopping here limits your Web creation to a mere digital magazine; and if you have a copy of this book in your hands, then it is a safe bet that you want to create something more than that. JavaScript opens the door for you to take static Web pages and make them come alive with responsive, real-time interaction that approaches the quality of traditional desktop applications.

JavaScript is an object-oriented scripting language that enables you, the Web developer, to place code inside a Web document for client-side execution. Contrary to what its name suggests, JavaScript is not a derivative of Java, although many control structures are similar to any Java (or any procedural language) programmer. Although you can use JavaScript in many places—not just the Web browser—it's useful to Rich Internet Application developers because JavaScript interpreters and DOM APIs are built in to all modern Web browsers.

Like all programming languages, the possible statements and structures in JavaScript are immense. Whole series of books are devoted to the topic. This primer assumes that the reader is familiar with the concepts of object-oriented programming, and has some experience in the flexible, somewhat anarchistic, world of scripting languages. Given this, you can infer most of the semantics and control structures of JavaScript by looking at the examples provided in this book.

This section shows you how to attach JavaScript code to an XHTML page, and then outlines some the ways in which you can use JavaScript to manipulate the DOM tree. Just as the saying goes about all roads leading to Rome, all Web programming eventually must lead to the modification of the DOM tree displayed in the browser, so if you know how to do this in JavaScript, the Web applications you can build are limited only by your creativity.

Attaching JavaScript to a Web Page

You can attach JavaScript code to your Web page in the same manner as CSS—either inline within a special element or as a separate file. Many developers may find it useful to use inline JavaScript when starting out or testing a new function, but keep JavaScript relegated to its own file as much as possible for the sake of cleanliness, reusability, and maintainability.

Attaching Inline JavaScript

You place inline JavaScript into the HTML document as if it were ordinary text—anywhere within the head or body elements on your page, though you might choose which of these two elements to use as your container based upon what your JavaScript code does. In either case, the script code is executed as it is parsed by the Web browser. Listing 2-20 shows an example of inline JavaScript.

Listing 2-20

XHTML
```
<script type="text/JavaScript">
 // Your Code Here
</script>
```

Scripts located in the head are executed as soon as the page loads, so this location is best for defining functions that elements within the body will use, that a callback of sort some will trigger, or that need to perform some action before the page loads. Scripts you place in the body are executed when that portion of the page loads, so this is an ideal location to place scripts that fill in some element of the page body with content. Listing 2-21 shows a complete XHTML document containing inline JavaScript that causes a pop-up window to appear before the rest of the Web page is loaded.

Listing 2-21

XHTML
```
<html>
  <head>
    <title>Alert Page</title>
    <script type="text/JavaScript">
    alert("This is an alert!");
    </script>
  <head>
  <body>
    <p>You should see an alert before this loads!</p>
  </body>
</html>
```

Attaching JavaScript as a Separate File

To attach JavaScript to a Web page as a separate file, use the exact same script element, but make sure it is in the head element and apply a src attribute to it. Listings 2-22 and 2-23 show the alert box example using an attached JavaScript file. Note that the alert.js file shown in Listing 2-24 does not require any script tags and chooses to specify the alert code as a function called when the body of the HTML file loads.

Listings 2-22 and 2-23 also demonstrate the difference between executing the JavaScript in the head element and in the body element. In Listing 2-21, the alert code executes in the head element, which prevents the body of the Web page from loading until the JavaScript finishes executing (which means the user won't load the page until he or she clicks the OK button on the alert box). For the separate-file example, the JavaScript alert function loads in the head element, but doesn't execute until the body element loads (using the onload attribute). This latter method causes the Web page's body to load while the JavaScript executes, not after. If you try the two examples out for yourself, the differences are easy to see.

Listing 2-22

XHTML
```
<html>
  <head>
        <title>Alert Page</title>
        <script type="text/JavaScript" src="alert.js" />
  <head>
  <body onload="showalert()">
        <p>You should see an alert before this loads!</p>
  </body>
</html>
```

Listing 2-23: "alert.js"

JavaScript
```
function showalert() {
 alert("This is an alert!");
}
```

Binding JavaScript to User Actions

Most JavaScript scripts must be bound to actions on elements in the DOM tree in order to have the desired effect. Before you learn about DOM tree manipulations, it's important that you see some toy examples that demonstrate the various ways in which you can cause JavaScript to execute on a page. This way, you can easily create your own practice pages to test and demonstrate the JavaScript techniques you learn. There are three basic ways to cause the execution of JavaScript code within your Web page:

- ❑ Raw, in-line JavaScript
- ❑ Page lifecycle events
- ❑ User-driven events

In-line JavaScript

In-line JavaScript executes as soon as a Web browser encounters it. Although it's rare to use this style of code, because it doesn't offer much control over when and how the code executes, it is useful for testing code, initializing variables, or setting up a timer event. Listing 2-23 showed an example of in-line JavaScript being executed as the head element of the HTML document is parsed.

Page Lifecycle Events

The attributes in Table 2-6 enable you to bind JavaScript to different states in the lifecycle of a Web page. When these attributes are set from within an XHTML document, the camel case (e.g., onLoad) version is acceptable, but when overriding these attributes from within JavaScript, always remember to use the lowercase version.

Table 2-6: JavaScript Page Lifecycle Events

Attribute Name	Meaning
onLoad	When the browser has finished loading the page
onError	When an error occurs in the loading of the specified element or JavaScript
onAbort	When the user cancels the loading of the specified element before it is complete by clicking the browser's Stop button or by clicking another link
onUnload	When the user travels away from the page by clicking a link

Listing 2-24 shows how to use the onLoad and onUnload attributes in a Web page. Both are attached to the body element, which is the common place to find these two attributes. Notice that the onLoad attribute contains a function call, whereas the onUnload attribute contains a single JavaScript statement. You can actually put as much JavaScript as you want in these attributes' values, each statement separated by a semicolon, but most users find their needs best served by defining the JavaScript to be called elsewhere as a function and then calling this function from within the proper event on your body element.

Listing 2-24

XHTML
```
<body onLoad="loadComments()" onUnload="alert('Thanks for coming!');">
```

User-Driven Events

User driven events are those events that occur because the viewer of the Web page has performed some action with the mouse or the keyboard. These are the events that fuel the rich interaction between a user and your Web site, as you can use them to get real-time feedback about which elements the mouse is hovering over and when the user presses a key. Building off of these events, Chapter 5 demonstrates how to build Web applications that include Web content that enables rich interaction such as drag-and-drop or image resizing. Table 2-7 lists some of the most common user-driven events that can be attached, or bound, to DOM elements.

Table 2-7: Some JavaScript User Driven Events

Element Name	Meaning
onClick	When the user single-clicks on the element
onDblClick	When the user double-clicks on the element
onFocus onBlur	When the element gains focus or loses focus, respectively
onChange	When the contents of the element has changed, such as the contents of a text box being updated by the user
onMouseOver onMouseMove onMouseOut	When the mouse enters, moves within, and exits an element's region, respectively
onMouseDown onMouseUp	When the user depresses and releases the mouse button over an element, respectively

Listings 2-25 and 2-26 show two examples of user-driven events binding to elements on a Web page. In Listing 2-25, a function called addNumbers() executes when a user clicks the link.

Listing 2-25

XHTML
```
<a href="#" onClick="addNumbers()">Add The Numbers</A>
```

In Listing 2-26, the validatePhoneNumber() function is called each time focus is taken away from the phone number text box.

Listing 2-26

XHTML
```
<input type="text" name="phone" onBlur="validatePhoneNumber()"></input>
```

You can place these two events on more than just input elements and links — you can use them to control how images, regular text, or even `div` and `span` elements behave. This section is just to whet your appetite — the rest of the book includes plenty of examples of the preceding bindings, as well as more complex abstractions built on top of them.

Removing and Adding from the DOM Tree

When this chapter introduced XML, it presented the DOM tree as a way to visualize an XML document. The World Wide Web Consortium (the wizards who create and standardize everything that makes this book possible) actually defines the DOM tree not just as a convenient way to visualize XML, but also as an application programming interface (API) through which to access it. JavaScript gives you direct access to the DOM tree as an API through a built-in object called `document`. The `document` object provides read and write access to the hierarchy of the DOM tree elements so that you can manipulate them from within JavaScript.

The `document` object is always available from within your JavaScript code and references whichever XHTML document to which the code has been attached. See the methods in Table 2-8 for some of the ways you retrieve DOM elements off of the DOM tree using the `document` object. In Chapter 4, you can walk through using some of these methods as you create your first Rich Internet Application.

Table 2-8: Locating Elements in the DOM Tree

Method	Use
.getElementById(String)	Returns the element with the specified ID
.getElementsByName(String)	Returns a collection of elements with the specified name
.getElementsByTagName(String)	Returns a collection of elements with the specified tag name

Sometimes modifying an element currently on the DOM tree isn't enough. You have to create a whole new element for insertion. In a RIA, this scenario arises many times when you want the user to load content into certain regions on the Web page based on actions taking place somewhere else on the Web page. A RIA photo album, for example, might provide thumbnail previews of the owner's photos in a strip at the top of the page, and could dynamically load them into a box in the center as the user selects them. Google's Gmail users have undoubtedly seen its real-time chat feature. When a new chat message arrives and appears on your screen, the odds are good that the XHTML to contain and display that message are created with the functions in Table 2-9. You learn more about how to use these elements in Chapter 4.

Table 2-9: Creating New Elements to Insert into the DOM Tree

Method	Use
.createElement()	Creates and returns a new element
.createTextNode()	Creates and returns a new text node. A text node is the element that automatically is placed around text in your document when a browser parses an XHTML file. In JavaScript, you must create this element by hand.

Table continued on following page

Method	Use
.createEvent()	Creates and returns an event. The programmer can then set the details on this event and dispatch it as if it arose as the result of some other circumstance.
.createRange()	Creates and returns a range spanning multiple elements
.createAttribute()	Creates and returns an attribute. The programmer can then attach this attribute to a node.

Inspecting and Setting an Element's Contents

You can retrieve and insert DOM elements into the DOM tree all you want, but unless they contain attributes and content, from the viewer's point of view nothing ever changes. Not all DOM elements share the same set of methods and properties, but many are common to all. The number of possible methods and attributes common to most elements is far too expansive to cover here, but Table 2-10 and Table 2-11 get you started. As with the previous methods, seeing them here does not teach you nearly as much as reading through the examples in the following chapters, so take the time now to browse some of the simple method calls you will soon be weaving into a Web application.

Table 2-10: Useful DOM Element Properties

Property	Use
.childNodes	Returns an ordered collection of child elements to the given element
.attributes	Returns a collection of the attribute objects attached to the given element
.nodeName	Returns the name of the given element
.nodeValue	Returns the value of the given element
.tagName	Returns the tag name of the given element
.parentNode	Returns the parent node of the given element

Table 2-11: Useful DOM Element Methods

Property	Use
.appendChild(element)	Appends the given element as a child
.getAttribute(string)	Returns the value of the given attribute
.removeChild(element)	Removes the given element as a child

Property	Use
.removeAttribute(string)	Removes the given attribute
.setAttribute(string1, string2)	Sets the value of the attribute with name string1 to a value of string2
.parentNode	Returns the parent node of the given element

To demonstrate some of the properties and methods in Tables 2-10 and 2-11, you can walk through preparing the JavaScript file that is used as the example at the end of this chapter. The task involves taking text entered into a `textarea` element on the Web page and transferring it to a list item elsewhere on the page. To do this, follow these steps:

1. Retrieve the value inside the textbox and store it in a variable named `orderText`:

```
var orderTextBox = document.getElementById('order');
var orderText = orderTextBox.value;
```

2. Reset the contents of the textbox to an empty string, clearing out its contents. Because the variable `orderTextBox` is a reference to a text box element in the DOM tree, changing this property has an immediate effect on what the user viewing the Web page sees:

```
orderTextBox.value = "";
```

3. Before you can insert `orderText` as a list item, you must first create a new `li` node and add the text to it. Remember that all text in XHTML is actually treated as being inside special text elements, even if those elements are not explicitly created in the XHTML document. In JavaScript you must take the extra step of creating the `TextNode` to store your text before you can add it to the `li` element:

```
var newOrder = document.createElement('li');
var newOrderText = document.createTextNode(orderText);
newOrder.appendChild(newOrderText);
```

4. Finally, locate the `ol` element that represents the list into which you want to insert `orderText`, and append the new `li` element as a child:

```
var orderList = document.getElementById('order_list');
orderList.appendChild(newOrder);
```

With just these simple steps using the methods and attributes outlined in this section, you can transfer text from a `textarea` input box in one region of the page into an ordered list elsewhere, all without any page reloading.

A Concluding Example — Angela's Ristorante

Welcome to Angela's Ristorante, or at least its imaginary wait-staff portal. Listings 2-27, 2-28, and 2-29 present you with a final example to tie everything in this chapter together. This Web site is a simple two-column layout with a narrow "potpourri" column on the side for performing account actions and entering orders. The large main column in the center displays open orders. As with any Web page, the first step that you, as a developer, should take doesn't begin with a computer, but with a pencil and paper. Take some time to sit down and sketch out a few different possibilities for how you want your Web page to look. Your friends might laugh at you if they catch you on a Tuscan hill drawing sketches of a Web page, but this is one step you don't want to ignore because it is the only stage in the process where you can let your creative juices flow unhindered by technical hoops and hurdles.

After you have a good idea of how you want your Web site to feel, translate your sketch into a slightly less artistic containment diagram like the one shown in Figure 2-4. Even if you end up changing everything by the time you code your site, this diagram will serve as an anchoring guide that structures your work. It will also keep you thinking in terms of the DOM tree from the start, which isn't always an easy thing to do because ugly, poorly structured HTML can be so easy and tempting. You should always run your XHTML code through the W3C's Markup Validation Service at `validator.w3.org` to find any errors and ensure that you have succeeded in producing valid XHTML.

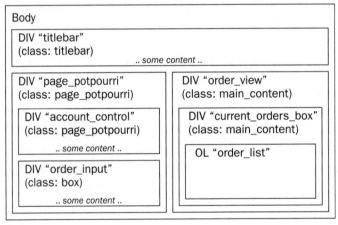

Figure 2-4

Finally, translate the containment diagram in Figure 2-4 into XHTML code. Listing 2-27 contains a complete XHTML document describing the page shown in Figure 2-4. It also makes references to two external files that will be developed next.

Listing 2-27

XHTML
```xhtml
<!DOCTYPE html PUBLIC "-//W3C//DTD XHTML 1.0 Strict//EN"
  "http://www.w3.org/TR/xhtml1/DTD/xhtml1-strict.dtd">
<html xmlns="http://www.w3.org/1999/xhtml" lang="en" xml:lang="en">
  <head>
    <title>Angela's Ristorante</title>
    <link rel="stylesheet" type="text/css"  href="FinalExample.css" />
    <script src="FinalExample.js" type="text/javascript" />
  </head>
  <body>
    <div id="titlebar">
      <h1>Angela's Ristorante</h1>
    </div>
    <div id="page_potpourri">
      <div id="account_control" class="box">
        <h1>Account</h1>
        <ul>
          <li><a href="#">Log Out</a></li>
          <li><a href="#">Change Password</a></li>
        </ul>
      </div>
      <div id="order_input" class="box">
        <h1>Add an Order</h1>
        <textarea id="order" name="order" cols="17" rows="3">
        </textarea>
        <input type="submit" value="Add Order" onclick="addOrder()" />
      </div>
    </div>
    <div id="main_content" >
      <div id="current_orders_box   " class="box">
        <h1>Order Summary</h1>
        <ol id="order_list">
          <li>Spaghetti a la Angela</li>
        </ol>
      </div>
    </div>
  </body>
</html>
```

Notice that there is not a single piece of code in the entire HTML file that specifies how something should look. Separating the display code from your document structure not only keeps your HTML document short and sweet, it also causes it to degrade properly for text-only browsers. If you try viewing the HTML document without any CSS file attached, you see what is shown in Figure 2-5.

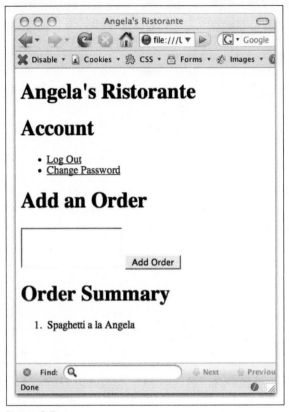

Figure 2-5

Listing 2-28 adds a CSS file to make the XHTML a little more pleasing to the eye. Place this code in the `FinalExample.css` file referenced from the XHTML document.

Listing 2-28

CSS

```
/* ----  The Page   ---- */

body {
 margin:    0px;  /* No Margin Outside the Object */
 padding:   0px;  /* No Padding Inside the Object */
 font-family:   Veranda, Arial, Tahoma, sans-serif;
}

#titlebar {
 width:   100%;  /* Stretch to 100% of the container width */
 height:   75px;
 margin:   0px 0px 10px 0px;  /* Bottom margin: 10px */
 background-color:   #444444;
 color:   #FFFFFF;  /* White text */
 text-align:   center;
```

```
}

#page_potpourri {
 width:   20%;
 float:   left;
}

#main_content {
 width:   80%;
 float:   left;
 position:   relative;
}

/*  ----    Box     ----  */

.box {
 border:   1px solid;
 padding:   0px 0px 0px 0px;
 margin:   5px 5px 5px 10px;
 width:   90%;
 overflow:   hidden;  /* Hide overflowing content */ }

#page_potpourri .box {
 border-color:   #0000AA;  /* Blue border */
}

#main_content .box {
 border-color:   #5500AA;
}

/*  ---- H1 ----  */

#titlebar h1 {
 margin:  0px;
 padding:  px;
}

/* The first will affect all box H1 elements */
.box h1 {
 width:   100%;
 color:   #FFFFFF;
 background-color:   #0000CC;
 padding:    2px 2px 2px 5px;
 margin:   0px 0px 5px 0px;
}

#page_potpourri .box h1 {
 font-size:   medium;
}

#main_content .box h1 {
 font-size:   large;
 background-color:   #7700CC;
```

(continued)

Listing 2-28: *(continued)*

```
}

/*  ----  Input Elements  ----  */

.box input {
  margin:    5px 5px 5px 10px;
}

.box textarea {
  margin:     5px 5px 5px 10px;
  background-color:    #FFFFCC;
}
```

Notice that CSS styles are defined by both element ID and element class. For elements that exist only once and on every page, an ID-based style is used. For objects that might exist many times per page, class-based styles are used. Neither extreme of the spectrum is correct, but if you have to err on one side, then choosing the class-based approach is a more flexible one than the ID-based approach. Also notice that Listing 2-28 names CSS classes after their functions, rather than their appearance.

Once you apply the CSS to the HTML, it changes from a bland black-and-white document into a decent-looking portal, as shown in Figure 2-6.

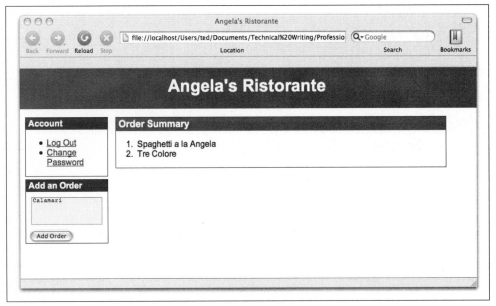

Figure 2-6

Finally, let's add the JavaScript prepared at the end of the JavaScript section. This function is executed whenever the user clicks the Add Order button below the text area. Place this code in a file named `FinalExample.js` as referenced from the XHTML file.

Listing 2-29

JavaScript
```javascript
function addOrder() {
  var orderTextBox = document.getElementById('order');
  var orderText = orderTextBox.value;
  orderTextBox.value = "";

  var newOrder = document.createElement('li');
  var newOrderText = document.createTextNode(orderText);
  newOrder.appendChild(newOrderText);

  var orderList = document.getElementById('order_list');
  orderList.appendChild(newOrder);
}
```

Voila! You have a simple Web portal that allows users to enter orders in the column on the right and transfer them over to the permanent list of orders in the center. Of course, this Web page does not hook up to any server, so entering these orders does not mean anything at this point. In the next chapter you will take your first steps in creating a true end-to-end RIA that includes both client and server participation.

Summary

This chapter presented a basic refresher course in the four main technologies that provide the foundation for all Rich Internet Applications. XML and XHTML are languages that provide structure to documents. CSS provides aesthetic guidelines for the display of XHTML documents, and JavaScript is a scripting language that makes XHTML documents interactive. These four languages fuel nearly all Web development, and knowledge of them is a required prerequisite for any serious RIA developer. The remainder of this book builds upon the foundation provided by these languages to explore the techniques of the Rich Internet Applications that are slowly taking over the desktop world.

The Programmable Web: The Mashup Ecosystem

"I was working in the lab late one night, when my eyes beheld an eerie sight
For my monster from his slab began to rise, and suddenly to my surprise:
He did the mash
He did the monster mash
He did the mash
It caught on in a flash . . ."

—**From the 1962 song "Monster Mash"**
by one-hit-wonder Bobby "Boris" Pickett

In current parlance, *mashup* is an overloaded term with two meanings. It can mean a multimedia composition having content from a variety of sources (see `http://eyespot.com` for a really good RIA tool that enables users to mashup video elements), or it can have a meaning more appropriate to this book — that is, creating applications from components whose APIs are offered as a public interface.

At the pinnacle of Visual Basic's success, literally hundreds of boutique suppliers made rough livings creating customer libraries that enabled the VB desktop developer to simply drop in a needed capability. In short order, the supporting elements of a more complex application were composed — components that encapsulated the Windows APIs at a more convenient level for the VB developer. In the rich client era, this was the essence of using the operating system as a platform. In much the same way, the various APIs to Web-resident services encapsulate the services in a way convenient to you for developing browser-based client-side applications. In the RIA era, this is the essence of using the net as a platform, also referred to as the *programmable Web*.

This chapter shows some sample applications that make use of one or more server-side capabilities that (and this is the good part) you don't have to write. Combining features that one or more pre-existing Web services support to derive a new, often narrowly focused, application is called *creating a mashup*. The essence of mashup creation goes like this:

1. You create the client user experience via style sheets, HTML, and JavaScript (or a variant such as Flash or Actionscript).

2. You make XMLHTTPRequest calls to one or more services.

3. The invoked service(s) return data in XML, plain text, or JavaScript Object Notation (JSON). Sometimes, the services require an identifying token from your Web site (as a way of "keeping score" for example), but most often, the call costs you or your site's user nothing—free, as in beer.

The result is a composite application that combines capabilities from the services invoked, plus your ingenuity in application design. As of this writing, MashupFeed (http://mashupfeed.com), a mashup advertisement and aggregation site, is adding more than two new mashups a day from contributors— some incredibly cool, some inane, some destined to become winners in the Web 2.0 space, and some losers. Often mashups use one or two external services, but Figure 3-1, shows a selection from MashupFeed that combines an amazing seven services. Mashups have become an extremely popular way for developers to access and play in the Rich Internet Application world. As developers combine existing services with user experiences of their own design, entirely new applications emerge.

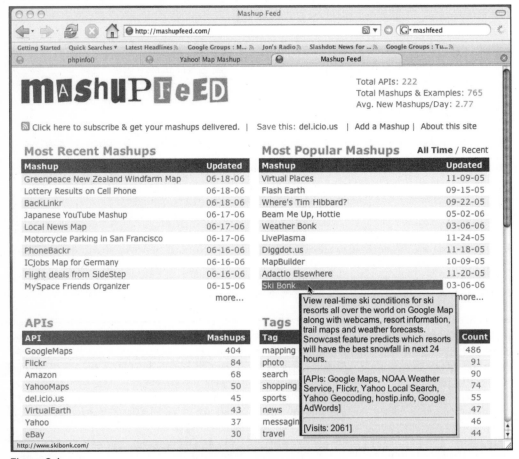

Figure 3-1

Getting Ready to Mash

As always, to try out these samples, to extend them, or to develop and test your own applications, you need to do a little prep work. Effectively developing and testing your own RIAs requires a few fundamental tools:

- ❑ **Your favorite integrated development environment or simple code editor** — Anything from Emacs to Eclipse will serve, although such features as syntax highlighting and integrated debuggers are worth more in this environment because certain server languages (for example, PHP) are notoriously difficult to debug.

- ❑ **A Web server of some sort** — You can take advantage of the myriad inexpensive commercial services available. An ideal ISP would support LAMP (Linux O/S, Apache Web server, MySQL database management, and PERL/PHP/Python for server side logic). Alternatively, you can fire up a Web server to test and develop on your own machine. Apache (`apache.org`) and Lighttpd (`www.lighttpd.net`) are excellent choices for Web servers that you can install on a PC class machine.

- ❑ **Runtime environments for some or all of these** — PHP, Python, Ruby, and Java. You may have several of these already on your system. If not, these are openly available on the Web.

- ❑ **A browser with good debugging capabilities** — Good choices are Firefox, Mozilla, Safari, or Opera (basically anything with console output and/or an integrated or plug-in debugger).

The Big Picture

Using AJAX (Asynchronous JavaScript and XML) to perform partial page refreshes is covered more fully in Chapter 4. For the moment, this chapter focuses on getting you up and running to do some experimentation on your own system, thus increasing your working confidence. This section begins by discussing how you communicate back and forth between the browser and what the response data will look like.

The execution environment for anything you write involves a Web server and HTML-based containers. As mentioned in Chapter 1, Web pages are one of the primary delivery platforms for creating full applications and hosting the user experience (others, such as desktop widgets, are shown in later chapters). Because RIA Web pages are significantly different from their forebears, this book uses the neologism *RIAPage* to remind you of the difference between modern, traditional Web pages, with the style of application they supported, and Rich Internet Applications.

To create mashups contained in RIAPages, you write pages that incorporate traditional Web elements: HTML layout markup to define the container and control structure for the application, cascading style sheets (CSSs) for tailoring the look and feel of the application, JavaScript to control the in-browser logic, including the invocation of remote services, and the implementation of event-driven callbacks.

Using this chapter's examples, you'll soon understand how to create an `XMLHttpRequest` object, how to open a connection to a local proxy that acts as a forwarding agent for the application, how to send requests to existing services, and how to use the response data provided by external service(s). Additionally, by the end of the chapter, you'll understand why a local proxy is necessary. Finally, you'll create a mashup that uses the Yahoo Geocoding API, the Yahoo Traffic API, and Google Maps to locate an address on a map and annotate it with useful traffic information.

XmlHttpRequest Object

The control path between the RIAPage and the invoked service is an object called the *XMLHttpRequest* (in Microsoft's Internet Explorer, it's called XMLHTTP, but it's the same thing). When you need to access the data model (i.e., the service portion) for your application, you make a network call to the service in the background using an XMLHttpRequest as the carrier object for the call. As the name XMLHttpRequest implies, the carrier protocol for the request is simply good old HTTP, so all the return codes that you may already know are relevant here and returned with the response to the request.

The XMLHttpRequest keeps alive a potentially two-way connection between the server and the browser, which erases the biggest drawback in traditional Web applications — namely, that the connection is closed after each call from the browser. Note that the network connects independently of the HTTP browser request that loads the page, and can happen asynchronously (you can set the call to be asynchronous or not, depending on how you establish the connection — see the method call signature for XMLHttpRequest in Table 3.1), so the user can continue to interact with other aspects of your application for the duration of the request and response. Traditional Web applications would return HTML (i.e., a new page) as a response to an HTTP request, which the browser would dutifully render. Rich Internet Applications, on the other hand, are interested in the data returned from the response to the request, which can be plain text, a stanza of XML, or JavaScript Object Notation (JSON).

> *Although the acronym AJAX explicitly acknowledges the role of XML, JSON is an important alternative data representation, but the acronym AJAJ wouldn't be as clever sounding.*

On receipt of the response, a RIA uses JavaScript and DHTML to redraw only the affected portion of the existing page, without issuing a new HTTP request that renders a whole new page. In fact, there may be no need to reload or redraw the page in its totality until an entirely new facet of the application is needed. If you design so that data returned from each external request is relatively small, given a broadband connection, the responsiveness of a RIA is very close to that of an RCP application.

A quick reference for the JavaScript API for XMLHttpRequest is shown in Tables 3-1 and 3-2.

Table 3-1: The XMLHttpRequest Object: Properties

Properties	Description
Onreadystatechange	Specifies an event handler called every time the state of the XMLHttpRequest object changes. The valid states are enumerated for the `readyState` property, shown next.
readyState	Returns the state of the XMLHttpRequest object, which can have the following values: 0=uninitialized, 1=open, 2=sent, 3=receiving, or 4=loaded. When a complete response to the call is received, the state should equal 4, and the status (see the `Status` property below) should be 200.
responseText	Returns the response as a string. Note that the content of the text can possibly be well-formed XML, plain text, or JavaScript Object Notation, or JSON (explained below). JavaScript in the browser is responsible for parsing and making sense of the returned data.

Properties	Description
responseXML	Returns the response as XML. This property returns an XML document object, if your application "knows" the expected structure of the returned XML, regular expression, or string operations. A better way is to use XML document object model (DOM) methods to extract the objects in the data. JavaScript methods are available to parse XML.
Status	Returns the numeric HTTP status (e.g., 404 for "Not Found" and 200 for "OK")
statusText	Returns the description associated with the HTTP status as a string (e.g., "Not Found" or "OK")

Table 3-2: The XMLHttpRequest Object: Methods

Method	Description
abort()	Cancels the current request
getAllResponseHeaders()	Returns the complete set of HTTP headers as a string
getResponseHeader(headerName)	Returns the value of the specified HTTP header
open(method, URL)	Specifies the method, URL, and other optional attributes of a request.
open(method, URL, async)	The `method` parameter can have a value of "GET", "POST", or "PUT" (use "GET" when requesting data and "POST" when sending data, especially if the length of the data is greater than 512 bytes).
open(method, URL, async, userName)	The `URL` parameter may be either a relative or complete URL.
open(method, URL, async, userName, password)	The `async` parameter specifies whether the request should be handled asynchronously — `true` means that script processing carries on after the `send()` method, without waiting for a response, and `false` means that the script waits for a response before continuing script processing.
send(content)	Sends the request
setRequestHeader(label, value)	Adds a label/value pair to the HTTP header to be sent

A Simple First Mashup

This first exercise invokes a service that Yahoo! provides. This service is an image search; and using this capability, you can build a simple but useful image search-and-display capability with a minimum of effort:

1. Invoke the service by pointing your browser to `http://RIABook.ideastax.com/RIA/XMLQueryExample.html`.

2. Enter a search term and click the Image Search Term button. An image responding to the search term will replace the bottom portion of the page.

3. Note that the code itself is available at `http://RIABook.ideastax.com/Chapter04.zip`. You can unzip the code into a convenient directory and try it out on your computer or on your ISP-hosted site. If you use the code on your host, you'll need to start a Web server and point to the HTML file.

The main point of this particular exercise is to convince you that first, it's easy to mashup, and second, you can flex your parsing muscles sufficiently to work with either XML or JSON (JavaScript Object Notation) returned from the server side.

Working with XML Output

In Chapter 1, you read a relatively formal explanation about working with XML. This section shows a practical example of working with XML returned from a server query.

Specifying an HTTP Request

In mashing up results from a service you invoke, one possible way the response data could appear is as a stanza of XML. The following exhibit shows an example of the way the data is returned. Although in the normal case you invoke a service from the JavaScript code running within your browser, you can simply make an HTTP request (remembering that the carrier protocol is just HTTP). Yahoo's Image Search Service is one of myriad such services. Let's do an HTTP request and see what the response looks like. Here's a sample query:

```
http://api.search.yahoo.com/ImageSearchService/V1/imageSearch?appid=YahooDemo&query
=Rose&results=1&output=xml
```

The elements of this service invocation may be old hat and patently obvious to you, but in case you don't often work with HTTP, or it has been a while, the salient parts of the call are as follows:

❑ `http://api.search.yahoo.com/ImageSearchService/V1/imageSearch` is the basic URL of the service.

❑ `?` is the required separator that signals the start of the arguments passing as input into the services. You need to know the legal input arguments to the service. In the case of your own service, you know what you're expecting. In the case of mashing up, you can look for the published API to the service. These are often published, and are easily found for the most popular, such as those from Yahoo! or Google.

❑ `appid=YahooDemo` is the first argument and value pair. As mentioned earlier, mashable services often require some sort of identifying information to understand what applications use their capabilities. For Yahoo!, an `appid` of `YahooDemo` is one offered to developers to try out their code, and limits the number of calls per day from a given calling URL.

❑ & separates the remaining arguments into argument and value pairs.

❑ query=Rose is the query that the service is to process.

❑ results=1 tells the service the maximum size of the result set returned.

❑ output=xml tells the service to encode the result data as XML.

Specifying a JSON Request

Watch what happens in Listing 3-1 when you specify output=json as the output format.

Listing 3-1: XMLXttpRequest data returned as XML

XML

```xml
<?xml version="1.0" encoding="UTF-8"?>
<ResultSet xmlns:xsi="http://www.w3.org/2001/XMLSchema-instance"
xmlns="urn:yahoo:srchmi" xsi:schemaLocation="urn:yahoo:srchmi
http://api.search.yahoo.com/ImageSearchService/V1/ImageSearchResponse.xsd"
totalResultsAvailable="4136737" totalResultsReturned="1" firstResultPosition="1">
 <Result>
        <Title>rose.jpg</Title>
        <Summary>
ou une rose ( fleur qu'on remarque ) pas une violette
        </Summary>
   <Url>
http://www.etfassociation.org/etf/home.nsf/public/⤴
9CE70C04703EBA7785256826001DFDB7/$file/rose.jpg
    </Url>
    <ClickUrl>
http://www.etfassociation.org/etf/home.nsf/public/⤴
9CE70C04703EBA7785256826001DFDB7/$file/rose.jpg
    </ClickUrl>
    <RefererUrl>http://misschahrazedbouteffel.myblogsite.com/blog
    </RefererUrl>
        <FileSize>37731</FileSize>
        <FileFormat>jpeg</FileFormat>
        <Height>600</Height>
        <Width>382</Width>
    <Thumbnail>
     <Url>
        http://mud.mm-a5.yimg.com/image/2044511447
        </Url>
        <Height>145</Height>
        <Width>92</Width>
       </Thumbnail>
  </Result>
</ResultSet>
```

The XML stanza shown has well-defined elements contained within the <ResultSet></ResultSet> tag pair and you can use the method discussed next to parse the result out of the XML.

Specifying an RIAPage Request

You can tease out the "stuff" that you're interested in by using string manipulation, as shown in Listing 3-2. Your code needs to know the explicit format of the data string returned in the XMLHttpRequest .responseText. If the information provider changes this format, obviously your mashup will break, and you'll need to rewrite code. Figure 3-2, which is a sample RIAPage, shows the RIAPage that was constructed from the code in Listing 3-2.

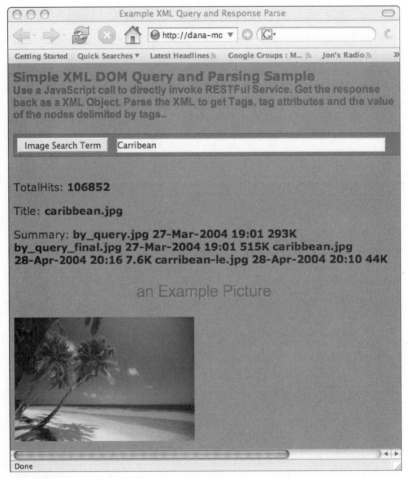

Figure 3-2

Listing 3-2: XMLQueryExample.html

XHTML

```
1 <!DOCTYPE html PUBLIC "-//W3C//DTD XHTML 1.0 Strict//EN"
  "http://www.w3.org/TR/xhtml1/DTD/xhtml1-strict.dtd">
2 <html xmlns="http://www.w3.org/1999/xhtml"
  xmlns:v="urn:schemas-microsoft-com:vml">
```

```
 3   <head>
 4    <meta http-equiv="Content-Type" content="text/html; ↵
      charset=utf-8"/>
 5
 6    <title>Example XML Query and Response Parse</title>
 7    <link rel=StyleSheet href= ↵
      "../stylesheets/RIAStyle1.css" TYPE="text/css">
 8    <script src="../scripts/xmlw3cdom.js"↵
      type="text/javascript"> </script>
 9    <script src="../scripts/xmlsax.js" ↵
    type="text/javascript"> </script>
10
11   <script type="text/javascript">
12   //<![CDATA[
13
14   var xmlhttp = false;
15
16     function queryHandler(target) {
17       try {
18         netscape.security.PrivilegeManager.enablePrivilege ↵
          ("UniversalBrowserRead");
19       } catch (e) {
20       }
21       if(target !== ""){
22         var url = '../phpscripts/xmlQuery.php?' +↵
                      target;
23         xmlhttp.open('GET', url, true);
24         xmlhttp.onreadystatechange = function() {
25          if(xmlhttp.readyState == 4 && ↵
            xmlhttp.status == 200) {
26            document.getElementById('Result'). ↵
              innerHTML = '';
27             var cleanXMLText = ↵
              cleanupResponseString(xmlhttp.responseText);
28            parseResult(cleanXMLText);
29          } else {
30            document.getElementById('State'). ↵
              innerHTML = "Loading...";
31          }
32         };
33         xmlhttp.send(null);
34       }
35     }
36
37
38   function cleanupResponseString(response){
39       return response.slice(response.indexOf("<"),↵
          response.lastIndexOf(">")+1);
40   }
41
42     function parseResult(xml) {
43       //instantiate the W3C DOM Parser
```

(continued)

Listing 3-2: *(continued)*

```
44        var parser = new DOMImplementation();
45     //load the XML into the parser and get the DOMDocumen
46        var domDoc = parser.loadXML(xml);
47     //get the root node (in this case, it is ResultSet)
48        var docRoot = domDoc.getDocumentElement();
49     //display the data
50     document.getElementById("Title").innerHTML =
   docRoot.getElementsByTagName("Title").item(0).
   getFirstChild().getNodeValue();
51       if (docRoot.getElementsByTagName("Summary").
     item(0).getFirstChild()
     != null){
52       document.getElementById("Summary").innerHTML =
53       docRoot.getElementsByTagName("Summary").item(0).
     getFirstChild().getNodeValue();
54     } else {
55       document.getElementById("Summary").innerHTML = "No Summary";
56     }
57 // here we are getting an attribute of ResultSet, not a node;
  // thus a somewhat different strategy ...
58       var totalHits =
docRoot.getAttributeNode("totalResultsAvailable").getNodeValue()
59
60     document.getElementById("TotalHits").innerHTML =
          totalHits;
61     document.getElementById("PictureHeader").innerHTML =
   "<p>an Example Picture</p>";
62     document.getElementById("PictureURL").innerHTML =
63       "<img src=\""+
64       docRoot.getElementsByTagName("ClickUrl").item(0)
     .getFirstChild().getNodeValue() +
65       "\" alt=\""+
66       docRoot.getElementsByTagName("ClickUrl").item(0).
     getFirstChild().getNodeValue() +
67       "\"/>"
68       ;
69       document.getElementById("State").innerHTML = "";
70     } // end function parseResult
71
72   function onLoad() {
73
74     if (window.XMLHttpRequest) {
75     xmlhttp = new XMLHttpRequest();
76     xmlhttp.overrideMimeType('text/xml');
77     } else if (window.ActiveXObject) {
78     xmlhttp = new ActiveXObject("Microsoft.XMLHTTP");
79     }
80     }
81
82
83   function doQuery() {
84     var query = document.getElementById("imageQuery").value;
85     var uri =
```

```
     "http://api.search.yahoo.com/ImageSearchService/V1/⤳
     imageSearch?appid=YahooDemo&query="+query⤳
     +"&results=1&output=xml";
86    queryHandler(uri);
87   }
88
89   //]]>
90   </script>
91
92  </head>
93  <body onload="onLoad()">
94   <div id="header">
95   <h1>Simple XML DOM Query and Parsing Sample </h1>
96   <h2>
97   Use a JavaScript call to directly invoke RESTFul Service.
98   Get the response back as a XML Object. Parse the XML to get
    Tags, tag attributes
99   and the value of the nodes delimited by tags..
100   </h2>
101
102  </div>
103
104  <br />
105
106  <div class="inputelement"><button onClick="doQuery()">⤳
    Image Search Term</button> 
107     <input id="imageQuery" value="Rose" size="50"></input>
108  </div>
109  <br />
110
111  <div id="State"></div>
112  <div id="Result"></div>
113  <p>TotalHits: <span id="TotalHits" ⤳
     style="font-weight:bold"></span> </p>
114  <p>Title: <span id="Title" style="font-weight:bold">⤳
    </span> </p>
115  <p>Summary: <span id="Summary" ⤳
    style="font-weight:bold"></span> </p>
116  <span id="PictureHeader" class="pictureHeader"></span>
117  <span id="PictureURL"></span>
118  </body>
119 </html>
```

The following sections discuss different lines of Listing 3-2:

General Things to Remember

Remember that you should place all scripting code in the page's HEAD section, defined by the <head> </head> tag pair along with other page-wide scoped items such as the age, title, and include files.

On line 7, the style sheet for the page is imported. You can specify style sheets externally, using the LINK directive, defined by the <link/> tag placed in the document HEAD section. The TYPE attribute for the LINK tag is optional, but a good idea. It specifies a media type—text/css for a cascading style sheet (by convention contained in a .css file) —allowing browsers to ignore style sheet types if they do not support them.

CSS files should never contain HTML tags, and specifically should not contain `<style></style>` pairs. The style sheet should consist of style rules or statements. A typical style rule might specify a certain color for the body of a RIAPage, as shown here:

```
body { background-color: #FF0000;}
```

Styling Issues

As long as the content of an external CSS rule file is contained in a STYLE directive, the browser understands the intent and the syntax of rules. You can combine several style sheets to customize a page or an entire Web site down to very fine grained detail, but note that the order in which the style sheets appear in the Web page is important in determining which rule prevails. As you might expect, the latest mention of a rule "wins."

You can also embed styles creating a STYLE section in a RIAPage, between a `<style></style>` pair. This increases the Web page's wordiness and decreases its readability, which is why the LINK directive is used on line 7 instead.

> *You can find a reasonable backgrounder with a bit more depth on CSS at* www.htmlhelp.com/ reference/css/style-html.html.

JavaScript Coding

Lines 8 and 9 include external JavaScript code in SCRIPT directives, contained within `<script></script>` pairs. By convention, external JavaScript code is contained in .js files, but there is no constraint requiring the JS naming convention. The JS file is referred to by the required href attribute. You use the optional src attribute when you import a script from an external source into the page. The type attribute is required, however, and may consist of the following:

```
text/ecmascript
text/javascript
text/jscript
text/vbscript
text/vbs
text/xml
```

Because the focus in this book is only on JavaScript as a scripting tool, none of the example code uses other scripting languages. Included are a set of functions contained in a pair of standard XML parser JavaScript collections available as open source (from xmljs.sourceforge.net), because although modern browsers include browser capability, different browsers may implement XML parsing differently — possibly correctly, but using browser-specific syntax. You want to test for browser type as few times as possible. The authors have chosen to ensure consistent parsing functionality by supplying the page with our own parsers. Note that the xmlw3cdom parser is a DOM parser, but it depends on the SAX parsing functions defined in xmlsax.js. You can include these in any order in your documents. The externally defined functions are here to implement the parseResult() function, beginning on line 42.

Lines 11–90 could have coded the JavaScript functions as an external JS file, but for discussion purposes, the critical working logic of the page was made visible. The browser-executable code is contained in a SCRIPT section; furthermore, there are some interesting delimiters on line 12 and on its paired closure on line 89. These ensure that the browser doesn't try to interpret characters within your JavaScript code that might ordinarily be mistaken for HTML formatting directives (e.g., angle brackets and forward slashes). These also allow you to insert code without having to escape any characters that might otherwise be mistaken for ordinary HTML. Often, you may compose some dynamic HTML for eventual output within JavaScript code, and you certainly don't want the browser to interpret that on initially loading the page. Many modern browsers are clever enough to skip over anything beginning at a <script> tag until they encounter its closing </script> tag, but it never hurts to err on the side of caution.

The critical JavaScript code here is all event driven. There are three events that can potentially happen in this simple mashup, as shown in Figure 3-3. An event fires when the page is initially loaded, when the user presses the Query button, and when the XMLHttpRequest completes, returning its payload. As Figure 3-3 suggests, the user can't do much in this simple mashup — simply type in a search term and press a button.

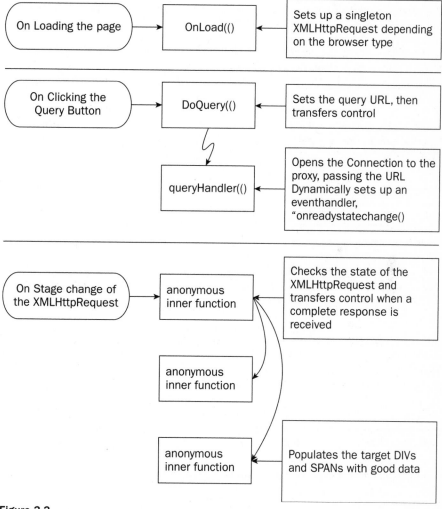

Figure 3-3

readyState, cleanupResponseString and parseResult Functions

In the anonymous inner function, on line 25, only the `readyState` and `status`, being tested in conjunction, are the "sunny day" state in which the request has been successfully completed and a "normal" HTTP completion status (200) is detected. You may want to probe for other conditions or keep the user updated, especially if the server side is slow or the data is complex or time-consuming. A possible strategy is posting a progress bar or other informative data. Because this doesn't involve a complete page refresh, it's trivial to post some sort of user information. Line 30 shows a trivial attempt to keep the user in the loop. If you insert an alert in between lines 24 and 25, something like `alert("xmlhttp.readyState:"`
`+xmlhttp.readyState);`, for example, the XMLHttpRequest is fairly chatty, reporting its change of state throughout the life span of the request connection. Thus, you have ample opportunity to interpose informational messaging. Another nuance is the `cleanupResponseString` function written to cleanse the response from the server. Whether it happens as a function of the browser or errors on the server side, you may often notice a fair bit of "cruft" in the form of stray characters tacked onto the response text. You should be prepared to assure your parser function(s) of a well formed string. One solution is to employ a function such as `cleanupResponseString`.

The `cleanupResponseString` function (line 38) chops off any stray characters in front of and after the good XML. It's always possible that some junk characters might be tacked onto the XML stream. This process is insurance to guard against "slop" characters.

Finally, `parseResult` teases the content from the XML stream and sets elements of the page. The root node of the page in this case is the ResultSet tag, so the first thing you should do after constructing the parse (line 44) and loading the result string into it (line 46) is to point at the root node of the document tree (line 48).

The DOM tree

After populating a DOM tree structure on line 46, you create a pointer to the root node. The document object model is discussed in Chapter 2, but for this example it's useful to remember that you need to extract both the content of nodes in the DOM tree and information from tag attributes. This example purposely extracts both types, to give you some feel for the necessary processing. Looking at the complexity of the accessor, you may conclude that it's slightly painful to find what you need in an XML DOM tree. What is all this `item(0), getFirstChild(), getNodeValue()` stuff anyway? Walking the document tree is somewhat tedious, but it will yield all the answers.

The document root node is the parent to all other nodes. When you request getElementsByTagName ("Title"), you get back a list of `TITLE` elements. Taking `item(0)` from the list of titles gets you the first node in the document tree. You already know the structure of the XML in the response (from Listing 3-1). Therefore, you know that there's a single `TITLE` element, so that's the one you want. If there had been a second `TITLE` element, you would have taken `item(1)` from the list, and so on. The `TITLE` element you now have a pointer to (...`getElementsByTagName("Title").item(0)`...) includes a pair of `TITLE` tags and the ordinary data captured between the opening and closing `TITLE` tags. It also includes any attributes (name-value pairs) stuck in with the opening `TITLE` tag itself; in this case, there are none.

The final step is to extract the characters belonging to the `TITLE` element you chose and assign that to the place in the document (a `SPAN` called "Title") where you want the characters to appear. You need to go through a similar process with other elements of interest, such as the `TITLE` element, and the picture itself.

Notice that the document itself is structured via a DOM. Notice, too, that you're setting a property called the `innerHTML` of a segment of the document. `InnerHTML` is a way of delimiting any well-formed element (i.e., it must have an opening and closing tag). The element must also have a name; therefore, notice that in the example, significant document elements (e.g., `DIV`s and `SPAN`s) have IDs, beginning at line 111, for example, so that you can later refer to them. As long as an element can be uniquely identified, you can get or set its content. An example of setting the `innerHTML` content using this technique is shown on line 50. An example of getting content is shown on line 84.

You could, for example make any entire document's visible content "disappear" with the following:

```
document.body.innerHTML = "";
```

This replaces the document body's content with an empty string, and it works because the body is uniquely identifiable. Try this little trick to amuse your friends: Type the following into the address bar:

```
Javascript:document.body.innerHTML = '';
```

Voila! No more document.

Extracting Attribute Information

The process changes slightly when you need to extract some attribute information. First, point to the node in which you're interested; in this case it's the `DOCROOT` node itself on line 57. Then `getAttributeNode ("totalResultsAvailable")` points toward the attribute of interest, and as before, `getNodeValue()` gets the character string.

Next, construct all the dynamic HTML around the image itself. Remember that the `<![CDATA[` before the start of the functional code up to the `//]]>` at its end "escapes" any embedded tags that the browser might otherwise (and mistakenly) interpret while loading the page.

You may have noticed and wondered why, in lines 27-28, `cleanXMLText`, consisting of the `XMLHttpResponse.responseText`, was passed to `parseResult()` rather than the `responseXML`. One reason is because is in general, a service must always return text, but is under no constraint to pass back XML, and in fact doing so simply makes the response longer. You may prefer to work with the XML, but it may also be more cumbersome to do so. Working with the XML rather than the text is really a matter of preference. You could certainly have coded `parseResult()` as something like the following:

```
function parseResult(req){
        var docRoot = req.responseXML.documentElement;
                document.getElementById("Title").innerHTML =
    docRoot.getElementsByTagName('Title')[0].firstChild.data;
   etc.
}
```

The page's action begins in `onLoad()`, which is invoked when the page is loaded (line 93, `<body onload="onLoad()>"`) instructs the browser to do this. `onLoad` creates a new `XMLHttpRequest`, customizing the request for the browser running the page.

When the page's only button (line 106) is pressed, the action shifts to the `doQuery` function.

`doQuery` forms the query by concatenating the user-entered text as arguments with the service URL, and shifts the procedural focus to the `queryHandler()` method. This reacts to the asynchronous state changes embodied in the `XMLHttpRequest`. The handler technical approach is more completely discussed in Chapter 4. Here, when the request is complete, the result is returned as the JSON textString, which is parsed, and the appropriate page divisions or spans are refreshed with the appropriate textual or image data without an entire page refresh.

The `onLoad` function creates an `XMLHttpRequest` object. Lines 74-79 test to determine whether the Web application is running in a browser that supports the native `XMLHttpRequest` object, or a version of Internet Explorer; when the browser is Internet Explorer, `XMLHttpRequest` is implemented as an ActiveX object (`XMLHTTP`). Although it's annoying to have to code around Microsoft, rest assured that the resulting object behaves properly in either case. It's acceptable for this didactic example to construct the `XMLHttpRequest` when the page is loaded, but it might be preferable in a more professional application context to delegate management of the object to a utility function.

Page Layout

Line 92 begins the layout portions of the page. This probably resembles traditional HTML, but one note of caution that you should observe is that you can't be sloppy when you lay out a page. You need to ensure that all tags are properly paired. You'll notice, for example, that all paragraphs are marked with opening and closing tags. That's the meaning of line 1 of the listing; it specifies strict enforcement of this rule:

```
<!DOCTYPE html PUBLIC "-//W3C//DTD XHTML 1.0 Strict//EN"
"http://www.w3.org/TR/xhtml1/DTD/xhtml1-strict.dtd">
```

> **Failing to create a properly tagged document causes serious problems and it's highly unlikely that your code will work at all in a document with construction flaws.**

There it is — a simple mashup for the investment of a little time writing HTML and JavaScript code. You can make other refinements to turn it into a more professional application. For example, you can write an event handler to recognize that the Return or Enter key had been pressed to launch the query, in addition to the button push.

One additional point before you leave this example behind. Notice that the signature of the URL itself is modified before it's passed the `XMLHttpRequest`. Line 22 of Listing 3-2 prepends the string "../phpscripts/xmlQuery.php?" to the URL before passing it as the argument to the request. The URL for Yahoo's image search capability is a valid one, which you can verify by entering it in the address window of a browser:

```
http://api.search.yahoo.com/ImageSearchService/V1/imageSearch?appid=
YahooDemo&query=rose&results=1&output=xml.
```

This will output a page resembling Figure 3-4.

Clearly, the URL is valid. Unfortunately, if you pass this URL unmodified, the browser doesn't permit a call to this URL through the Web server serving up the base page making the `XMLHttpRequest`. Why not? The section "What's a Proxy and Why Do I Need One?" later in this chapter explains the issue and how to resolve it.

You can see the browser's complaint by opening the JavaScript console. This window records any error output, so you should keep it open and use it as your handy debugger. Figure 3-5 shows a JavaScript console displaying the error.

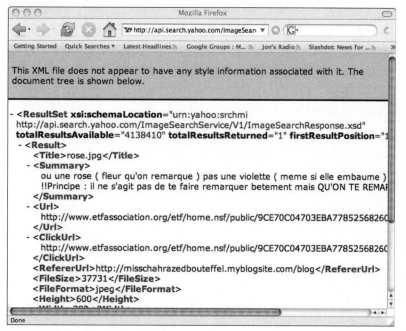

Figure 3-4

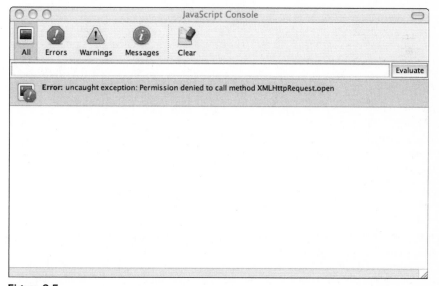

Figure 3-5

Working with JSON Output

An alternative to requesting that a server return its output in XML is requesting it in JavaScript Object Notation (JSON) format. In this section, JSON is presented as a viable alternative to XML as a data format, and it has several advantages and at least one major concern. In general, JSON is much easier to work with, as the next example will show; and if a service provides JSON, you may prefer to implement RIAPages.

You can call on the very same service, only varying the output format specification like this:

```
http://api.search.yahoo.com/ImageSearchService/V1/imageSearch?appid=⊃
YahooDemo&query=Rose&results=1&output=json
```

The only difference is the `output=json` qualifier, and now you will notice that the data is the same, but the representation has changed significantly, as shown in Listing 3-3.

Listing 3-3: XMLXttpRequest data returned as JSON

JSON

```
 1{
 2 "ResultSet":{
 3 "totalResultsAvailable":"4136737",
 4 "totalResultsReturned":1,
 5 "firstResultPosition":1,
 6 "Result":[
 7  {
 8    "Title":"rose.jpg",
 9    "Summary":"ou une rose ( fleur qu'on remarque ) pas une violette,
10    "Url":"http:\/\/www.etfassociation.org\/etf\/home.nsf\/public\/9CE70C0⊃
4703EBA7785256826001DFDB7\/$file\/rose.jpg",
11    "ClickUrl":"http:\/\/www.etfassociation.org\/etf\/home.nsf\/public\/9CE⊃
70C04703EBA7785256826001DFDB7\/$file\/rose.jpg",
12    "RefererUrl":"http:\/\/misschahrazedbouteffel.myblogsite.com\/blog",
13    "FileSize":"37731",
14    "FileFormat":"jpeg",
15    "Height":"600",
16    "Width":"382",
17    "Thumbnail":{
18     "Url":"http:\/\/mud.mm-a5.yimg.com\/image\/2044511447",
19     "Height":"145",
20     "Width":"92"
21    }
22   }
23  ]
24 }
25}
```

The output now conforms to the JSON standard. JSON is lightweight, and like other structured representation specifications (e.g., YAML), you could conceivably use it as a data-representation and interchange format even outside its primary use in Web applications. It's arguably easier for a human to understand than XML, and is easy both to emit from the server and to parse in any number of languages (see a representative list at `http://json.org`).

It's easy to pick out specific values from ResultSet via the JavaScript within the RIAPage, because what's contained in the XMLHttpRequest.responseText returned by the remote service is actually proper JavaScript code. You can assign it to an automatic variable like this:

```
var JSONObject = eval('(' + XMLHttpRequest.responseText + ')');
```

The JavaScript eval method takes an arbitrary string and converts it into what is commonly called *JavaScript object literal notation*. Object literal notation is JavaScript's way of defining an object dynamically, including its properties and even its functions, although no functions are defined in the preceding output. In the line of code above, JSONObject on the left hand side of the statement is constructed from the object literal definition on the right side.

JSON Constructs

JSON really only has two constructs, but these should be enough to compose any arbitrary object:

❑ First, there's the dictionary or associative array. In JSON, properties are declared and defined on the left side of a colon separator, and values are on the right.

❑ Second, there is the ordered list or array. A pair of curly braces delimit an object, and a pair of square brackets denote an array. Thus, in the preceding example, ResultSet is the *name* or label of the response data, and everything to the right of the ":" delimiter is the *value*. The value of ResultSet is an object that contains name/value pairs, one of which ("Result") is an array (whose extent is delimited by the brackets in line 5 in Listing 3-3). Each element in the Result array contains a number of name/value pairs, beginning with a Title, and on down to Thumbnail, which is also an object within the Result array, contained within the curly braces in line 16 of Listing 3-3.

Tacking on the leading and trailing parentheses ensures proper string closure for eval.

Referencing Fields

Once the text has been converted to a JavaScript object, you can refer to fields within it conveniently. Fields can be referenced by dot notation, subscripting, or a combination of the two. In the preceding example, JSONObject.ResultSet.totalResultsReturned yields the string "1".

JSONObject.ResultSet.Result[0].Thumbnail.Height yields the string "145". Why Result[0]? Remember that you limited the service invocation to return at most one result ("&results=1"). If you had widened that limit, the Result array could have had several objects, each of which is delimited by curly braces. The curly braces for the single Result object in Listing 3-3 are in line 16. The single object in the result array is at position 0, and referred to by Result[0].

It is convenient that you knew the particular structure of eval's production. That's because you knew in advance what it would look like in this particular case. If you didn't know in advance, you could have simply tried out the API, gotten the returned data, and printed it to understand the structure. Again, this is one reason why services often document their APIs. They might as well! Consider that no single provider can control all aspects of a distributed application based in a Web browser, all the way from the view through the controller to the model and back. Ultimately, whatever the service returns must be converted to a form capable of being consumed by one of many existing browsers. Once the data is at the browser, it is visible to anyone capable of inspecting it (a software developer like you, for example).

If you don't know a JavaScript object's structure *a priori*, just remember that all objects are simply hash tables, and can be introspected (although JavaScript's capacity to do this is fairly weak). You can get at all members of an array (such as the `Result` array in the previous example) by simple iteration, as shown in the following example:

```
for (i=0;i< JSONObject.ResultSet.Result.length;i++){
... do something with JSONObject.ResultSet.Result[1]; ...
}
```

Deconstructing a JSON Example

Let's deconstruct an end-to-end example using JSON with the API cited.

Figure 3-6 shows what the resulting Web page should look like, after a successful query.

Figure 3-6

Because the only significant differences between the JSON example and the XMLQuery example are the parsing approach, only relevant code differences are commented in Listing 3-4.

Listing 3-4: JSONQueryExample.html

HTML

```
1 <!DOCTYPE html PUBLIC "-//W3C//DTD XHTML 1.0 Strict//EN" ⤸
"http://www.w3.org/TR/xhtml1/DTD/xhtml1-strict.dtd">
2 <html xmlns="http://www.w3.org/1999/xhtml" ⤸
 xmlns:v="urn:schemas-microsoft-com:vml">
3  <head>
4   <meta http-equiv="Content-Type" content="text/html; ⤸
      charset=utf-8"/>
5
6   <title>Example JSON Query and Response Parse</title>
7   <link rel=StyleSheet
  href="../stylesheets/RIAStyle1.css"⤸
    TYPE="text/css">
8   <script
9   src="../scripts/json.js"
10   type="text/javascript">
11   </script>
12   <script type="text/javascript">
13   //<![CDATA[
14
15   var xmlhttp = false;
16
17     function queryHandler(target) {
18       if(target !== ""){
19         var url = '../phpscripts/json.php?' + ⤸
          encodeURL(target);
20         xmlhttp.open('GET', url, true);
21         xmlhttp.onreadystatechange = function() {
22          if(xmlhttp.readyState == 4 && ⤸
          xmlhttp.status == 200) {
23            document.getElementById('Result') ⤸
                   .innerHTML = '';
24            parseResult(xmlhttp.responseText);
25          } else {
26            document.getElementById('State'). ⤸
          innerHTML = "Loading...";
27          }
28         };
29         xmlhttp.send(null);
30       }
31     }
32
33   function cleanupResponseString(response){
34       return response.slice(response.indexOf("{"),
          response.lastIndexOf("}")+1);
35   }
36
```

(continued)

Listing 3-4: *(continued)*

```
37   function parseResult(result){
38    var resultString = cleanupResponseString(result);
39    var JSON_object = eval("(" + resultString + ")");
40
41    document.getElementById("TotalHits").innerHTML = ⤵
      JSON_object.ResultSet.totalResultsAvailable;
42    document.getElementById("Title").innerHTML = ⤵
      JSON_object.ResultSet.Result[0].Title;
43    document.getElementById("Summary").innerHTML = ⤵
        JSON_object.ResultSet.Result[0].Summary;
44    document.getElementById("PictureHeader").innerHTML = ⤵
      "<p>an Example Picture</p>";
45    document.getElementById("PictureURL").innerHTML =
46     "<img src=\""+JSON_object.ResultSet.Result[0].ClickUrl+ "\" alt=\""+
47     JSON_object.ResultSet.Result[0].ClickUrl +
48     "\"/>"
49     ;
50    document.getElementById("State").innerHTML = "Search complete";
51   }
52   function onLoad() {
53    //TODO Lock HTTP requests against each other...
54    if (window.XMLHttpRequest) {
55     xmlhttp = new XMLHttpRequest();
56     xmlhttp.overrideMimeType('text/xml');
57    } else if (window.ActiveXObject) {
58     xmlhttp = new ActiveXObject("Microsoft.XMLHTTP");
59    }
60   }
61
62
63   function doQuery() {
64    var query = document.getElementById("imageQuery").value;
65    var uri = ⤵
      "http://api.search.yahoo.com/ImageSearchService/V1/imageSearch⤵
         ?appid=YahooDemo&query="+query+"&results=1&output=json";
66    queryHandler(uri);
67   }
68
69   //]]>
70   </script>
71
72  </head>
73  <body onload="onLoad()">
74  <div id="header">
75  <h1>Simple JSON Query and Parsing Sample </h1>
76  <h2>
77  Use a JavaScript call to directly invoke RESTFul Service.
78  Get the response back as a JSON Object. Use the contents as ⤵
     JavaScript Objects.
79  </h2>
80
81  </div>
82
```

```
83  <br />
84
85  <div class="inputelement"><button onClick="doQuery()">↺
    Image Search Term</button> 
86   <input id="imageQuery" value="Rose" size="50"></input>
87  </div>
88  <br />
89
90  <div id="State"></div>
91  <div id="Result"></div>
92  <p>TotalHits: <span id="TotalHits" style="font-weight:bold"></span> </p>
93  <p>Title: <span id="Title" style="font-weight:bold"></span> </p>
94  <p>Summary: <span id="Summary" style="font-weight:bold"></span> </p>
95  <span id="PictureHeader" class="pictureHeader"></span>
96  <span id="PictureURL"></span>
97  </body>
98  </html>
```

Note the following things about this code:

❑   The JSONparser (from http://json.org) is imported on line 9 for later use in the
    parseResult() function. Using encodeURL() ensures that characters which might prove
    problematic (e.g., spaces or double quotes in the search term) are properly dealt with before
    transmission.

❑   Because a properly terminated JSON string is bounded by curly braces, you find them and trim
    anything outside those delimiters, on line 34.

❑   Now you're ready to parse the JSON. As explained above, the simplest way to turn any string
    into executable JavaScript code is to use JavaScript's built-in eval function, shown on line 39.
    Be nice and set "state" to something informative (line 50).

❑   Note that the small difference in the URI declaration is that you request JSON as the output for-
    mat. Not every site outputs JSON, so you have to test the waters with your mashup to ensure
    that the service in which you're interested does in fact.

❑   One additional thing worth mentioning is what happens on XMLHttpRequest.
    onreadystatechange. If you insert an alert just after line 26 in Listing 3-4, to print out the
    XMLHttpRequest.readyState, you may find that the alert fires as many as four times.

*Remember that all JavaScript code must appear within the HEAD section, and all of the relevant appli-
cation layout directives must appear in the BODY section.*

Relocating the Inner Function

The onreadystatechange function from Listing 3-4 is shown in the snippet that follows:

```
xmlhttp.onreadystatechange = function() {
 if(xmlhttp.readyState == 4 && xmlhttp.status == 200) {
  document.getElementById('Result').innerHTML = '';
  parseResult(xmlhttp.responseText);
 } else {
  document.getElementById('State').innerHTML = "Loading...";
 }
};
```

This implements the callback code as a closure, or an anonymous inner function, whichever terminology you prefer. However, the callback handler could certainly have been coded as a separate function and simply referred to in like this:

```
xmlhttp.onreadystatechange = stateChangeHandler;
```

And then, somewhere else in the code, you could have created the `stateChangeHandler` function:

```
function stateChangeHandler() {
  if(xmlhttp.readyState == 4 && xmlhttp.status == 200) {
   document.getElementById('Result').innerHTML = '';
   parseResult(xmlhttp.responseText);
  } else {
   document.getElementById('State').innerHTML = "Loading...";
  }
}
```

The use of an anonymous inner function is probably more a matter of personal preference than anything. If the handler is fairly simple, as it was in Listing 3-4, then an inner function is probably the best route.

The eval Function and Security

A note of caution about the use of `eval`: The built-in `eval` function is very useful in JavaScript, just as it is in other languages such as Python and Ruby. However, just as in Python, it can be dangerous. Remember that in whatever interpreted language you choose to think about, `eval` will compile *and immediately execute* arbitrary code, so there could potentially be security issues. As explained earlier, object literal notation offers a complete capability for dynamic JavaScript object creation, both properties *and* methods. Nothing would prevent a site from returning JSON that contains executable code. It is fine to use `eval` as shown on line 40 of Listing 4-3 because the service endpoint was known beforehand and considered secure. Additionally, the outbound request was passed through a proxy that tested to ensure that the URL was legitimate (explained below). An untrusted source is another matter, however. Certainly in the case of an application where both the Web server and the base page generating the JSON have been written by you, using `eval` is just fine.

If you are concerned over security, there's always the option of using a JSON parser. This approach is well assured, because a properly written parser will, like `eval`, produce JSON objects, but doesn't execute the object's code immediately. You can find a reasonable JavaScript parser at `http://json.org/json.js`. It implements only three methods to a Web page's JavaScript, but they are useful ones. In Listing 3-4, you could have replaced the `eval` call on line 39 with

```
39      var JSON_object = resultString.parseJSON();
```

and then proceeded just as before in lines 41-50.

What's a Proxy and Why Do I Need One?

Originally, browsers were the equivalent of the printing press in that the user instantiated a browser and typed in a URL, resulting in the end-to-end connection shown in Figure 3-7.

Page served from HERE

WEB Server

Figure 3-7

You could even serve out Web pages from your own host to test your HTML or your server logic. Typically, in the Web 1.0 era, you could create a one-line browser in Python:

```
python -m SimpleHTTPServer 8080 # for Python 2.4
```

or

```
python -c "from SimpleHTTPServer import test; test()" # Python 2.3, 2.2
```

or write a Ruby Web server, like this:

```ruby
#!/usr/bin/ruby
require 'webrick' ; include WEBrick
s = HTTPServer.new(:Port => 8000, :DocumentRoot => "/Users/danamoore/tmp")
trap ("INT") {s.shutdown}
s.startv
```

You then executed that file from the command line, and served out the pages from the folder for which the Web server was started — by accessing localhost:8080 in the Python example, or from DocumentRoot by browsing to localhost:8000 in the Ruby example, as shown in Figure 3-8.

Page served from HERE

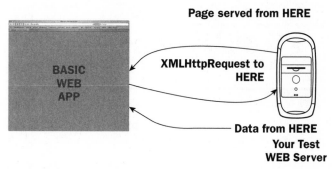

XMLHttpRequest to HERE

Data from HERE
Your Test
WEB Server

Figure 3-8

What you could not do is what you see in Figure 3-9 — that is, route a request to the Web server that is serving up the page, to pass the request to some other Web server and have *that* Web server return the page. Most browsers simply do not let the HTML page served from one domain open a network connection of any kind to domains other than the one that served up the HTML page.

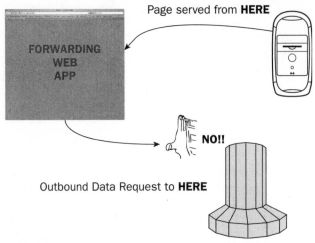

Page served from **HERE**

Outbound Data Request to **HERE**

Figure 3-9

Working with a Proxy

There are a couple of mechanisms for working around this issue. The first method interposes a small bit of code to act as a local "gatekeeper," as documented in the next two listings; the second method works directly with the JSON returned by the external site (see the next section, "Working without a Proxy"). The one in Listings 3-5 and 3-6 implements the approach illustrated in Figure 3-10, which shows a Web proxy forwarding a request to another domain.

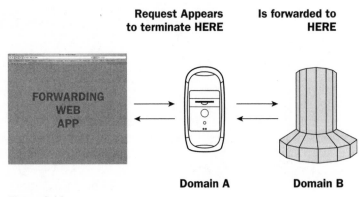

Request Appears to terminate HERE   **Is forwarded to HERE**

Domain A   **Domain B**

Figure 3-10

Listing 3-5 shows PHP code for managing the proxy for the XMLQueryExample.html (Listing 3-2) example above.

Listing 3-5: xmlQuery.php

PHP

```php
1  <?php
2  header("Content-type: text/xml");
3  $url = $_SERVER['QUERY_STRING'];
4  if ( strpos($url,"http://api.search.yahoo.com/") === 0)
5  {
6    $ch = curl_init();
7    curl_setopt($ch, CURLOPT_URL,$url);
8    $xml = curl_exec($ch);
9    curl_close($ch);
10   echo $xml;
11 }
12 ?>
```

Notice that you specify to the browser a return type of text/xml for the content.

Listing 3-6 is the PHP code for managing the proxy for the JSONQueryExample.html example above.

Listing 3-6: json.php

PHP

```php
1  <?php
2  header("Content-type: text/plain");
3  $url = $_SERVER['QUERY_STRING'];
4  if ( strpos($url,"http://api.search.yahoo.com/") === 0)
5  {
6    $ch = curl_init();
7    curl_setopt($ch, CURLOPT_URL,$url);
8    $json = curl_exec($ch);
9    curl_close($ch);
10   echo $json;
11 }
12 ?>
```

Here you specify a return type of text/plain for the JSON content. Otherwise, the PHP is identical. Here, the URL the Web application calls terminates in the current domain. Recall that the actual URL passed to the XMLHttpRequest's open method terminates in the same Web server as the Web application — here are lines 22–23 of Listing 3-2:

```
22         var url = '../phpscripts/xmlQuery.php?' + target;
23         xmlhttp.open('GET', url, true);
```

and lines 24–25 in Listing 3-4:

```
24         var url = '../phpscripts/json.php?' + target;
25         xmlhttp.open('GET', url, true);
```

In each case, the application appends an argument onto the URL; the argument representing the *actual* termination point of the request and the provider of the data. Thus, as far as the Web application is concerned, the PHP proxy terminates the request. In actual fact, the PHP code relays your application's request to another domain, in this case:

```
http://api.search.yahoo.com/ImageSearchService/V1/imageSearch.
```

Additionally, the proxy simply passes the additional arguments you constructed to the external domain, in this example:

```
?appid=YahooDemo&query=rose&results=1&output=xml.
```

A proxy makes the operation easy to shuttle requests to and from other domains. In fact, it may make things too easy. Make no mistake: A proxy has the potential to create a gaping security hole. However, you can mitigate this potential by rigorously constraining the potential forwarding domains. In Listing 3-5, for example, the first operation sets $url from $_SERVER, which is a PHP dictionary that the Web server itself creates. The 'QUERY_STRING' slot has as its value everything that the Web server passed to the PHP code (i.e., the actual URL and its arguments). The PHP checks the actual destination domain at Listing 3-5, line 4.

If the domain is acceptable, it passes the request along, or else it does nothing. Here, the PHP 5 CURL convenience library opens the connection and invokes the foreign server. The only significant difference between Listings 3-5 and 3-6 is that one sets the return header to be XML and the other to be JSON.

Working without a Proxy

Proxies are slightly painful to set up, and even when you use one you still have to exercise some care about what sites you permit to return data back to your Web page-as-application. Consider the following scenario: Your application makes an outbound call, specifying the returned data representation as JSON. Your callback does an immediate eval of the JSON, and in it there's a nefarious method that reads your cookies and does a subsequent HTTP POST to a rogue Web site. Now your system is possibly compromised. Although this is an extreme case, *perhaps* it could happen, although the odds seem acceptably low given that you have given thought to the validity of the data source you're choosing to mashup, and your application is source-aware.

Is working without a proxy really like a circus high-wire performer working without a net? Opinions are somewhat mixed, but given careful consideration, mashups can be (and have been) written that use an approach to get around the problem altogether. This is discussed in this chapter's capstone application in the section "The Yahoo and Google Traffic Mashup."

XML or JSON

As mentioned earlier, many sites produce output either in XML or in JSON. Given a choice, which should you prefer? This is mostly a matter of personal style for many developers; certainly both representations have a variety of advocates, and libraries abound for both. One consideration that helps tip the scales is that JSON is already expressed as a native object in your application's implementation language, and therefore is most easily consumed by your application code. Additionally, the json.js parser and string creation code is pretty compact overall—about 1K after being passed through JSMin (see www.crockford.com/javascript/jsmin.html), a nice open-source code compacter that eliminates spaces and other visual aids to code inspection (and as a side effect acts as a sort of minimal code obfuscator).

The Yahoo and Google Traffic Mashup

In previous examples seen in Figures 3-2 and 3-6, you invoked one service to add a simple image search-and-retrieval capability to your page-based application. Now you can combine more than one service into a composite application that none of the specific services provides, and that's the objective of this chapter's capstone application, which might be deemed the "Find a Location, Map It, and Tell Me about Traffic Alerts" application.

The capstone application for the chapter mashes up the following:

❑   The Google Maps dynamically produce a map and add it to the calling page.

❑   Yahoo's geocoding produces a set of latitude and longitude coordinates from a location.

❑   Yahoo's traffic alert annotates the map with relevant traffic information — at least for any urban U.S. area covered by the service.

Each of the constituent segments is partially shown, followed by the composite application. Not only is this a practical learning application, but it also is helpful in daily use. The application uses Yahoo's geocoder to convert a location description into latitude/longitude pairs. This is necessary because Google will *only* accept a latitude/longitude pair to create the contents of a map; thus, the services complement each other in a way that the individual API creators had not envisioned — the perfect definition of a mashup.

Getting a Geocode

Having worked through previous example mashups in the chapter you are familiar with the code strategy by now:

1.   Find an interesting and useful API.

2.   Determine the data representation it returns.

3.   Code a proxy to access it.

4.   Create an XMLHttpRequest as a transport mechanism.

5.   Attach a callback function to the request.

6.   Parse the results and populate DIV or SPAN sections of the document appropriately

This is precisely what you do in the next listing, which shows the functionality of first third of the ultimate mashup. Again, you can download the code from `http://RIABook.ideastax.com/Chapter03.zip`.

The application is shown in Figure 3-11. The user enters location information (in this case the address of Fenway Park) and in return gets a latitude/longitude pair. You can try this out at `http://RIABook.ideastax.com/RIA/GeoCodeProxy.html`, which is created from the code shown in Listing 3-7.

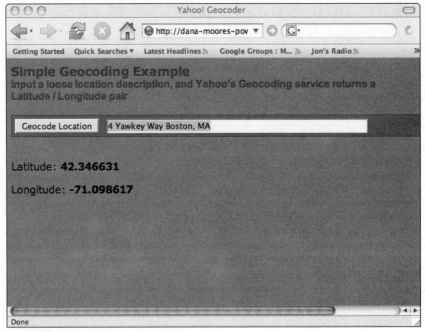

Figure 3-11

Listing 3-7: GeocodeProxy.html

HTML

```
 1 <!DOCTYPE html PUBLIC "-//W3C//DTD XHTML 1.0 Strict//EN"
      "http://www.w3.org/TR/xhtml1/DTD/xhtml1-strict.dtd">
 2 <html xmlns="http://www.w3.org/1999/xhtml" xmlns:v="urn:schemas-microsoft-
com:vml">
 3  <head>
 4   <meta http-equiv="Content-Type" content="text/html; charset=utf-8"/>
 5
 6   <title>Yahoo! Geocoder</title>
 7   <link rel=StyleSheet href="../../stylesheets/RIAStyle1.css" TYPE="text/css">
 8   <script src="../../scripts/createXMLHttpRequest.js"
      type="text/javascript"></script>
 9
10   <script type="text/javascript">
11   //<![CDATA[
12   var __xmlhttp = false;
13   var __appid = "YahooDemo";
14
15     function callWS(target) {
16        if(target !== ""){
17        var url = '../../phpscripts/geocoder.php?' + encodeURI(target);
18        __xmlhttp.open('GET', url, true);
19        __xmlhttp.onreadystatechange = function() {
20        if(__xmlhttp.readyState == 4 && __xmlhttp.status == 200) {
21        document.getElementById('Result').innerHTML = '';
22        getLatLon(__xmlhttp.responseText);
```

```
23            } else {
24              document.getElementById('State').innerHTML = "Loading...";
25            }
26          };
27          __xmlhttp.send(null);
28        }
29      }
30    function getLatLon(result){
31      var start = (result.search(/<Latitude>/) +10 );
32      var end = result.search(/<\/Latitude>/);
33      var lat = result.substr(start, (end -start) );
34
35      start = (result.search(/<Longitude>/) +11 );
36      end = result.search(/<\/Longitude>/);
37      var lon = result.substr(start, (end -start) );
38
39      document.getElementById("Latitude").innerHTML = lat;
40      document.getElementById("Longitude").innerHTML = lon;
41      document.getElementById("State").innerHTML = "";
42    }
43
44    function onLoad() {
45        __xmlhttp = createXMLHttpRequest();
46    }
47    function callGeocode() {
48     var query = document.getElementById("geoquery").value;
49     var uri = ⤸
       http://api.local.yahoo.com/MapsService/V1/geocode?appid=
       +__appid+"&location=" + query;
50     callWS(uri);
51    }
52    //]]>
53    </script>
54  </head>
55
56  <body onload="onLoad()">
57    <div id="header">
58    <h1>Simple Geocoding Example </h1>
59    <h2>Input a loose location description, and Yahoo's Geocoding service ⤸
        returns a Latitude / Longitude pair</h2>
60
61    </div>
62    <br />
63    <div class="inputelement"><button onClick="callGeocode()">⤸
       Geocode Location</button> 
64      <input id="geoquery" value="1300 N. 17th St, Arlington VA" ⤸
       size="50"></input>
65    </div>
66    <br />
67
68    <div id="State"></div>
69    <div id="Result"></div>
70    <p>Latitude: <span id="Latitude" style="font-weight:bold"></span> </p>
71    <p>Longitude: <span id="Longitude" style="font-weight:bold"></span> </p>
72  </body>
73 </html>
```

The code for the little request creator is now in a separate file and is included on line 8. At the end of the chapter is a general utility function that handles request creation and posting and getting requests. This is used frequently in subsequent chapters.

Again (on line 17), the URI string attached to the proxy (geocoder.php) is encoded to deal with any potentially troublesome characters, using the browser's built-in encoder. The `getLatLon()` function (beginning on Line 30) is an variant, designed to demonstrate to you that there are many ways to extract the returned data.

When you explore this service, hand-coding a URL (for example: `http://api.local.yahoo.com/MapsService/V1/geocode?appid=YahooDemo&location=4%20Yawkey%20Way%20Boston,%20MA`), you discover that just as in previous examples, the returned data representation is string data representing XML. An example of the data returned from a direct invocation is shown in Figure 3-12.

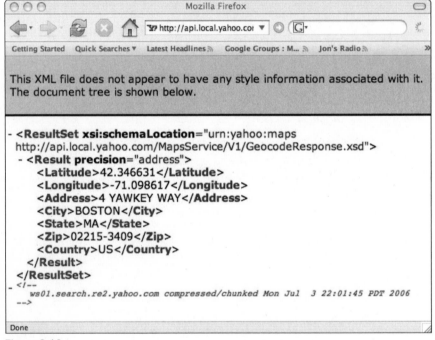

Figure 3-12

You can, as before, create a DOM parser, load the XML, and extract data that way. Alternatively, knowing that a string is a string, you can just use built-in JavaScript string manipulation methods. That's what lines 31–37 in `getLatLon()` do. You already know what you're looking for: normally tagged NODEs; extracting them can be a simple matter.

That completes the first part of the mashup. Now it's time to examine Google's Map API. The code shown in Listing 3-8 produces the application shown in Figure 3-13.

Listing 3-8: geocoder.php

PHP

```php
<?php
header("Content-type: text/xml");
$url = $_SERVER['QUERY_STRING'];
if ( strpos($url,"http://api.local.yahoo.com /") === 0)
{
 $ch = curl_init();
 curl_setopt($ch, CURLOPT_URL,$url);
 $xml = curl_exec($ch);
 curl_close($ch);
 echo $xml;
}
?>
```

You now have a way to convert a location described in free text into a geographic coordinate. Turning next to an example showing how you can get traffic for the location reveals something interesting.

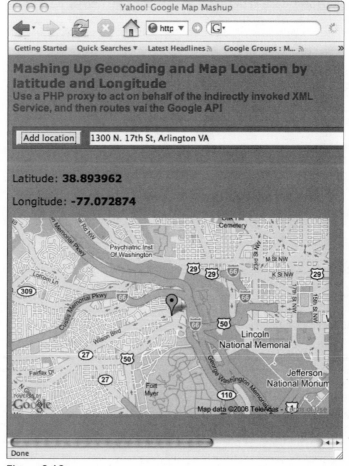

Figure 3-13

Getting the Traffic Report

Figure 3-14 shows a simple application that serves as the basis for the traffic data portion of the chapter's capstone mashup. In the figure, the user enters a location into the input box and the mashup retrieves the current traffic information.

Figure 3-14

As mentioned in the section "Working without a Proxy," you can work more directly with the data provider, without writing and deploying a proxy, without making an XMLHttpRequest, and without having to work with XML. If all this is not sufficient inducement, a final "sweetener" is that application performance is better as well.

The code for the application is shown in Listing 3-8, and it presents a completely new way to interact with a data source, and at the same time dynamically direct the script logic. By now, you should be comfortable with the concept that you can replace segments of a RIAPage's document object model (DOM) tree without having to re-fetch and re-render the entire application container. That's a fundamental *AJAXism*. The fuller implications may not have hit you yet, but they are about to. You may also have noticed that some elements in the RIAPage's DOM have the quality that they are "execute immediate": On encountering them, the browser deals with them immediately, substituting the data resulting from acting on the directive instead of the directive itself. You saw this effect in Listing 3-2, when you used the URI of the image retrieved by the search to construct an IMG tag:

```
62      document.getElementById("PictureURL").innerHTML =
63       "<img src=\""+
64       docRoot.getElementsByTagName("ClickUrl").item(0)⤸
         .getFirstChild().getNodeValue() +
65       "\" alt=\""+
66       docRoot.getElementsByTagName("ClickUrl").item(0).⤸
        getFirstChild().getNodeValue() +
67       "\"/>"
68       ;
```

The resulting `"PictureURL"` span tag (line 117 of Listing 3-2) didn't show the IMG tag constructed on lines 62–68; rather, it populates with the *result* of the browser's having parsed and satisfied the directive contained in the tag—a nice picture of some parakeets. Furthermore, this happened dynamically, as a side effect of your overwriting a node in your RIAPage's DOM tree. The fact that browsers do this "execute immediate" trick has been true ever since the first browser.

Every modern browser understands that it should do the same thing with elements in the HEAD, such as LINK tags, which include a `href="URI"` attribute for specifying cascading style sheets to import, and SCRIPT tags, where the `src="URI"` tag attribute is used. In both cases, the browser dutifully fetches the content of the URI and places it into the browser. It's effectively like the `#include` statement in C and C++, or the `import` statement in Java or Python.

What may not have occurred to you (and here comes the "magic" part), is that you can *dynamically* add to, replace, and remove elements of the DOM tree that are child nodes of the HEAD tag. Thus, you can add a SCRIPT node and the browser includes the properties defined in the JavaScript (and technically, any methods as well). This is rather like adding a new method to a running Java program (and is rather slick indeed).

Imagine that you could code in the `src` attribute a URI that would do the following:

1. Return the data result set for the query

2. Return it in JSON (making it very easy to work with)

3. Specify a callback method as a receiver for the data

You needn't just imagine this, however; it's what you're going to accomplish in Listing 3-9.

Dynamically Injecting a SCRIPT Tag into the HEAD

This script tag has as its SRC attribute the URL of the remote service being invoked. Normally this is a JavaScript file, but in this case it's JSON, which you can then reference directly by the callback associated with the data fetched from the URL. In summary, the design strategy goes like this:

❑   Add a new SCRIPT tag dynamically to the DOM tree of the browser, as a child of the HEAD tag.

❑   Specify the URL for the data directly. (Instead of pointing to a JavaScript library, the URL points to a Web service.)

❑   Add that the output should be JSON.

❑   Add the callback method (which must exist at the time of the dynamic execution of the SCRIPT directive).

The "callback" parameter is not a Web standard; and at the time of this writing, not a lot of Web services support it in their APIs. Before you mash up a given service, check what your target server does! Because the capability is so attractive and simple to implement, it is documented in the belief that it will become much more common.

To explore the Yahoo Traffic result set, try making the call directly, by typing the following into the address window of a browser:

```
http://api.local.yahoo.com/MapsService/V1/trafficData?appid=YahooDemo&location=
4%20Yawkey%20Way%20Boston,%20MA&output=json.
```

The format of the result set can be discerned from the return to the query:

```
 1 {"ResultSet":
 2  {
 3   "LastUpdateDate":"1152157153",
 4    "Result":
 5    [
 6
 7       {"type":"incident",
 8        "Title":"Slow traffic, on ONEILL TUNL NB at ⤴
         BANKNORTH GARDEN",
 9        "Description":"CONCERT:MADONNA;EXPECT DELAYS.",
10        "Latitude":"42.366000",
11        "Longitude":"-71.060300",
12        "Direction":"NB",
13        "Severity":2,
14        "ReportDate":1152228600,
15        "UpdateDate":1152142612,
16        "EndDate":1152239400
17        }
18 ... followed by more results
19    ]
20  }
21 }
```

The JSON contains several elements that will be useful in the chapter capstone. The `Result` array includes several incident reports containing latitude/longitude coordinates and an incident description. Next, Listing 3-9 uses this URI signature and adds a callback parameter to demonstrate the end-to-end application.

Listing 3-9: DynamicScripting.html

HTML

```
1 <!DOCTYPE html PUBLIC "-//W3C//DTD XHTML 1.0 Strict//EN" ⤴
     "http://www.w3.org/TR/xhtml1/DTD/xhtml1-strict.dtd">
2 <html xmlns="http://www.w3.org/1999/xhtml" xmlns:v="urn:schemas-microsoft-
com:vml">
3  <head>
4   <meta http-equiv="Content-Type" content="text/html; charset=utf-8"/>
5   <title>Yahoo!Traffic API Call. JSON. No Proxy</title>
6    <script type="text/javascript" src="../../scripts/jsr_class.js"></script>
7   <script type="text/javascript">
```

```
8    //<![CDATA[
9      var __appid = "YahooDemo";
10     var __location = null;
11     var __server = "http://api.local.yahoo.com/MapsService/V1/trafficData";
12     var __req = null;
13
14     function getTraffic(jData) {
15      if (jData.ResultSet.Result.length ==0){
16        document.getElementById('result').innerHTML = "No Traffic Data";
17        return;
18      }
19      var lat = jData.ResultSet.Result[0].Latitude;
20      var lon = jData.ResultSet.Result[0].Longitude;
21      var title = jData.ResultSet.Result[0].Title;
22      var descr = jData.ResultSet.Result[0].Description;
23      var severity = jData.ResultSet.Result[0].Severity;
24      var type = jData.ResultSet.Result[0].type;
25      var report = "<h2>" + title + "</h2><br /><hr/>"
26      + "Lat/Lon: " + lat + "/"+ lon + "<br/>"
27      + "Type: " + type + "<br/>"
28      + "Severity: " + severity + "<br />"
29      + "Details:" + descr;
30      document.getElementById('result').innerHTML = report;
31     }
32
33     function getTrafficReport(){
34      if (__req != null){
35        aObj.removeScriptTag(); // clean up the DOM
36      }
37      var __req = __server + "?appid=" + __appid
38      + "&location="+document.getElementById("location").value
39      + "&output=json&callback=getTraffic";
40      aObj = new JSONscriptRequest( encodeURI(__req));
41      aObj.buildScriptTag();
42      aObj.addScriptTag();
43     }
44   //]]>
45   </script>
46   </head>
47   <body>
48   <div id="header">
49      <h1>JSON Dynamic Script Approach for Web Service Requests</h1>
50      <h2>a SCRIPT section is dynamically injected into the ⤶
     page-as-application's HEAD'</h2>
51   </div>
52   <div class="inputelement">
53      <button onClick="getTrafficReport()">Get Traffic Report</button>
54      <input id="location" value="1300 N. 17th St., Arlington, VA 22209"⤶
             size="50"></input>
55   </div>
56   <br />
57   <div id="result"></div>
58   </body>
59   </html>
```

105

Note the following about Listing 3-9:

❑ The RIAPage imports an open-source JavaScript class (jsr_class.js), attributed to Jason Levitt and available from `www.decafbad.com/trac/browser/trunk/FeedMagick/js/jsr_class.js`. This utility does the heavy lifting of constructing the dynamic SCRIPT element and inserting it into the documents DOM within the HEAD element, where it's executed upon insertion.

❑ The function `getTraffic` is specified as the receiver for the returned JSON, which you can use directly because the object has been fully constructed by the mashup's service provider. For this simple example, only the first element in the `Result` array was chosen.

❑ On line 33, you remove any existing DOM element to avoid the piling up of SCRIPT elements.

❑ Lines 40–42 handle the mechanics of creating a valid custom SCRIPT tag encoding the URI with the location entered by the user. The jsr_class (see the URL above) is worth study for its simplicity and elegance.

In the interests of simplifying the application, your traffic reporter is limited to reporting the first incident, but this is enhanced in the next segment.

Thus far in the capstone mashup, you have a way to turn a location into map coordinates (the utility of which becomes obvious shortly), and you have a way of retrieving traffic data from location input as well. What's needed is a stunning visual element. You'll see that next.

Putting Together the Final Mashup

The final, and potentially most interesting, element in the mashup is the map display on which you post traffic information, given location input from the end user. Google Maps have proved interesting and exciting and exhibit exemplary use of AJAX concepts. When a user scrolls around the map, or zooms in or out, a new map tiles into a container (normally a `DIV`) on the RIAPage without a page refresh. With a sufficient broadband connection, the difference between Google Map in a browser versus a geospatial client application is imperceptible. Of course, no free desktop geospatial client with the wide range of Google Maps features and programmability exists, so the comparison is merely hypothetical. Of the huge number of mashups available at MashupFeed, the majority (by far) are map-based. Google Maps has a rich and well-documented API and encourages mashing up.

You can find interesting tutorials at `www.google.com/apis/maps/documentation/`.

Using the Map API

Typically, the way you use the Map API is to specify the container in its constructor, center the map at a specific geographic point, and set one or more listeners for events. Here's a trivial example showing the constructor, using a `GMap2` function, and finally adding a listener for click events:

```
...
var myMap = new GMap2(document.getElementById("someDiv"));
map.setCenter(new GLatLng(38.893813, -77.073733), 13);
GEvent.addListener
(
  myMap, "click", function() {alert("You clicked the map.");}
);
...
```

One slight problem with Google Maps is that the Map API doesn't include a geocoding capability. Google advances an explanation on their FAQ (www.google.com/apis/maps/documentation/), but some users have argued that the license arrangement for map data allows only *their* servers access to the geocoding data. The reason for Google's prohibition really doesn't matter, however, because given a location, you now know how to incorporate a geocoder into a RIA, right?

Before finishing the application, Figure 3-15 shows a RIAPage that explores some of the features of the Google Map API. In this RIAPage, a map is drawn about a fixed point and indicated by a marker that responds to an event handler associated with a click event (on the marker, and not on the map *per se,* as above).

Figure 3-15

Egregious Hacks or Must-Have Technical Approach?

The authors endeavored to inject a proper note of caution regarding the approaches shared in this chapter. The major issue is that modern browsers forbid data accesses to domains other than the one serving the page. The need to access data across domains is quite real in mashups, and it forces some uncomfortable design and implementation compromises on you, the developer.

The chapter shows code for two popular approaches:

❏ **Application proxies** — Proxies were shown in PHP, though practically any popular language works. Simply write a proxy in your favorite programming language and install it relative to your RIAPage on your server, and it enables your mashup to do the following:

    ❏ Respond to XMLHttpRequests from users

    ❏ Terminate a Web service call as though it were a browser endpoint, and return the data to the RIAPage

The essential concept of using a proxy is that you trick the Web browser into believing the service call terminates in the same domain as the Web page. The "downside" of this approach is in the effort required to create a robust, scalable proxy service, and the intricacies of parsing the XML data returned.

❏ **Dynamic scripting** — In this approach, you compose an HTML SCRIPT tag to make a request to an application proxy that returns your XML data wrapped in JavaScript. It's also possible, when a Web service returns JSON, to directly access the service and designate a callback function to directly use the JSON object returned. As long as you can certify the invoked service, this approach is as safe as using a proxy. It doesn't use the XMLHttpRequest, which many developers feel is a plus.

A technique that wasn't covered in this chapter is using the Apache configuration (assuming that your development server is Apache or that you have configuration capability for purchased space on a commercial server). You can configure your Web server to forward calls across domains seamlessly. This technique is more fully described at `http://httpd.apache.org/docs/2.0/programs/configure.html`.

Whichever approach you take should bring the following into the decision process:

❏ The reliability and reputation of the service being accessed

❏ The convenience of working directly with objects, rather than parsing XML

❏ Access to the server's configuration

In any case, there are cogent reasons why requests across domains are restricted. Allowing free requests across domains from within a RIAPage could expose your application's user to potential security exploits.

You may notice the absence of a proxy in this example. This is because the Google Map API uses a dynamic JavaScript callback strategy, as explained above and shown in Listing 3-10.

Listing 3-10: A Google Map API example

HTML

```
1  <!DOCTYPE html PUBLIC "-//W3C//DTD XHTML 1.0 Strict//EN"
2   "http://www.w3.org/TR/xhtml1/DTD/xhtml1-strict.dtd">
3   <html xmlns="http://www.w3.org/1999/xhtml">
4   <head>
5    <meta http-equiv="content-type" content="text/html; charset=utf-8"/>
6    <title>Google Maps JavaScript API Example</title>
7    <script
8     src="http://maps.google.com/maps?file=api&amp;v=2&amp;key=APIKEY"
9     type="text/javascript">
10   </script>
11   <script type="text/javascript">
12   //<![CDATA[
13   function load() {
14       if (GBrowserIsCompatible()) {
15        var map = new GMap2(document.getElementById("map"));
16        map.setCenter(new GLatLng(38.893813, -77.073733), 13);
17       }
18    // Create a base icon for all of our markers that specifies the
19    // shadow, icon dimensions, etc.
20    var baseIcon = new GIcon();
21    baseIcon.shadow = "http://www.google.com/mapfiles/shadow50.png";
22    baseIcon.iconSize = new GSize(20, 34);
23    baseIcon.shadowSize = new GSize(37, 34);
24    baseIcon.iconAnchor = new GPoint(9, 34);
25    baseIcon.infoWindowAnchor = new GPoint(9, 2);
26    baseIcon.infoShadowAnchor = new GPoint(18, 25);
27
28      // Creates a marker whose icon is an image and whose.
29
30      function createMarker(point, index) {
31       var icon = new GIcon(baseIcon);
32       var imageAddr = "../../images/1300N17TH.jpg";
33       icon.image = imageAddr;
34       var marker = new GMarker(point, icon);
35
36       GEvent.addListener(marker, "click",
37           function() {
38            marker.openInfoWindowHtml(
39            "<img src="+imageAddr+" \"width=125\" height=\"150\" />"
40            );
41           }
42       );
43       return marker;
44      }
45      var point = map.getCenter();
46      map.addOverlay(createMarker(point, 0));
47 }
48   //]]>
49   </script>
```

(continued)

Listing 3-10: *(continued)*

```
50  </head>
51  <body onload="load()" onunload="GUnload()">
52    <div id="map" style="width: 500px; height: 600px"></div>
53  </body>
54  </html>
```

Note the following about Listing 3-10:

❑ The SCRIPT tag asks for something called an APIKEY in the URL. Google demands you include this in your calls, perhaps as a way of keeping track of developers. It's not an onerous requirement, and you simply sign up for a key at `www.google.com/apis/maps/signup.html`. Make certain you do this step if you download the code to try it out.

❑ Once you import the JavaScript for the Map control, you can check for any browser incompatibilities that prevent using the API. Remember, there are inconsistencies among browsers and JavaScript is often broken, but broken in different ways on different browsers. The `load` function constructs the map and makes a persistent asynchronous connection to the map server. The next several steps create an icon that displays on the map marker for the center point of the loaded map.

❑ The `createMarker` function is contained within the `load` function. This may be unfamiliar to you and seem to contravene common sense, but it's perfectly allowable in JavaScript. It does contain variable scope and is simply a convenience.

❑ Again, the technique of setting up an anonymous inner function (line 36) handles opening the marker whenever a user clicks the marker created in the code.

❑ Having created the marker, you next add the marker as an overlay plane (lines 45–46). You can do a practically unlimited number of overlay planes onto a Google map, making it an ideal information presentation tool for geospatial data.

❑ Notice the approach on line 51 to ensuring that memory leaks (if any) are addressed. The `GUnload` function frees up any browser memory allocated by the map components.

The point about loading and unloading capabilities brings up a potentially interesting question: If a RIAPage is an application, and more than simply a Web page, does dynamically loading and unloading JavaScript amount to creating self-modifying code? Technically, you might think so. For example, it's certainly possible to dynamically compose a custom string (constituting some arbitrary JavaScript code), return it from a server, and have the RIAPage immediately execute it. Although that is not customary current usage, it is not far from it — consider that every call made from your user's input in Listing 3-8 returns custom data; but, again, there's no reason why the returned JSON cannot conceivably contain code as well.

Combining the Application Mashup

Finally, you can turn to the matter of the composite application mashup. Having experimented with the three elements of the mashup independently, you now combine them in Listing 3-11 to create an application that resembles the following figures. Figure 3-16 shows that you can type a location and click the Location button to reveal the traffic tie-ups for the location. Figure 3-17 shows that you can click the marker to reveal the centering location.

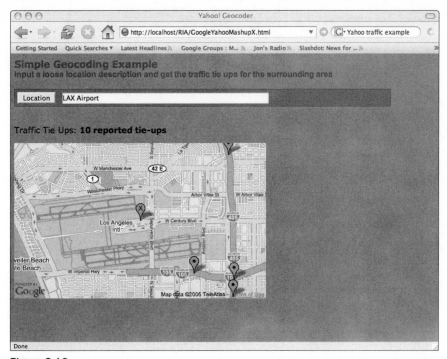

Figure 3-16

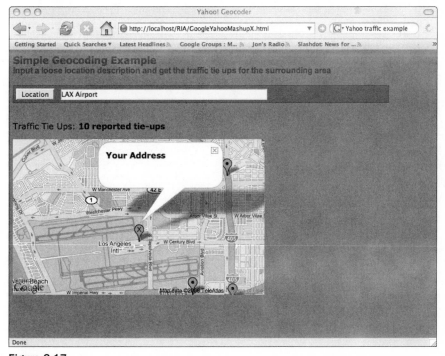

Figure 3-17

Listing 3-11: GoogleYahooMashup.html example

HTML

```
 1 <!DOCTYPE html PUBLIC "-//W3C//DTD XHTML 1.0 Strict//EN" "http://www.w3.org/
TR/xhtml1/DTD/xhtml1-strict.dtd">
 2 <html xmlns="http://www.w3.org/1999/xhtml" xmlns:v="urn:schemas-microsoft-
com:vml">
 3  <head>
 4   <meta http-equiv="Content-Type" content="text/html; charset=utf-8"/>
 5
 6   <title>Yahoo! Geocoder</title>
 7   <link rel=StyleSheet href="../../stylesheets/RIAStyle1.css" TYPE="text/css">
 8   <script src="../../scripts/createXMLHttpRequest.js"
type="text/javascript"></script>
 9    <script type="text/javascript" src="../../scripts/jsr_class.js"></script>
10   <script
src="http://maps.google.com/maps?file=api&amp;v=2&amp;key=ABQIAAAA-
j4r1Ft3AXUvtHpmQed5QBT2yXp_ZAY8_ufC3CFXhHIE1NvwkxT3MTfjNOb50deF4pcXwWhT9dALu    Q"
11   type="text/javascript">
12   </script>
13   <script "text/javascript">
14   // global vars
15   var __xmlhttp = false;
16   var __lat = null;
17   var __lon = null;
18   var __appid = "YahooDemo";
19   var __location = null;
20   var __geocoderURI = "http://api.local.yahoo.com/MapsService/V1/
geocode?appid="+__appid+"&output=xml";
21   var __geocoderProxy = "../../phpscripts/geocoder.php?";
22   var __trafficServer = "http://api.local.yahoo.com/MapsService/V1/
trafficData?appid="+__appid;
23   var __trafficReq = null;
24   var __map = null;
25 // Geocoding and application control
26   function callGeocode() {
27    __location = document.getElementById("geoquery").value;
28    var uri = __geocoderURI+"&location=" + __location;
29    callWS(uri);
30   }
31   function callWS(target){
32    if(target !== ""){
33     if (!__xmlhttp) {__xmlhttp = createXMLHttpRequest();}
34     var url = __geocoderProxy + target;
35     __xmlhttp.open('GET', url, true);
36     __xmlhttp.onreadystatechange = function() {
37      if(__xmlhttp.readyState == 4 && __xmlhttp.status == 200) {
38       document.getElementById('Result').innerHTML = '';
39       document.getElementById('State').innerHTML = 'Done.';
40       getLatLon(__xmlhttp.responseText);
41       loadMap();
42       getTrafficReport();
43      } else {
```

```
44        document.getElementById('State').innerHTML = "Working...";
45      }
46    };
47    __xmlhttp.send(null);
48    }
49  }
50  function getLatLon(result){
51   var start = (result.search(/<Latitude>/) +10 );
52   var end = result.search(/<\/Latitude>/);
53   __lat = result.substr(start, (end -start) );
54   start = (result.search(/<Longitude>/) +11 );
55   end = result.search(/<\/Longitude>/);
56   __lon = result.substr(start, (end -start) );
57   document.getElementById("State").innerHTML = "";
58   __xmlhttp = false;
59  }
60 // Mapping and associated functions
61  function loadMap() {
62    if (GBrowserIsCompatible()) {
63     __map = new GMap2(document.getElementById("map"));
64     __map.setCenter(new GLatLng(__lat.toString(), __lon.toString()), 13);
65    }
66   var marker = hereMarker(__map.getCenter());
67   __map.addOverlay(marker);
68  }
69
70  function createMarker(point, report) {
71   var marker = new GMarker(point);
72   GEvent.addListener(marker, "click",
73    function() {
74     marker.openInfoWindowHtml( report );
75    }
76   );
77   return marker;
78  }
79
80
81  function hereMarker(point){
82   var letter = null;
83   var marker = null;
84   var baseIcon = new GIcon();
85   baseIcon.shadow = "http://www.google.com/mapfiles/shadow50.png";
86   baseIcon.iconSize = new GSize(20, 34);
87   baseIcon.shadowSize = new GSize(37, 34);
88   baseIcon.iconAnchor = new GPoint(9, 34);
89   baseIcon.infoWindowAnchor = new GPoint(9, 2);
90   baseIcon.infoShadowAnchor = new GPoint(18, 25);
91   icon = new GIcon(baseIcon);
92   icon.image = "http://www.google.com/mapfiles/markerX.png";
93   marker = new GMarker(point, icon);
94   GEvent.addListener(marker, "click",
95    function() {
96     marker.openInfoWindowHtml("<b>Your Address</b>");
```

(continued)

Listing 3-11: *(continued)*

```
 97     }
 98     );
 99     return marker;
100     }
101
102  // Traffic Data and associated functions
103     function getTrafficReport(){
104     if (__trafficReq != null){
105      aObj.removeScriptTag(); // clean up the DOM
106     }
107     var __trafficReq =__trafficServer + "&location="+__location ⤶
+ "&output=json&callback=getTrafficData";
108      aObj = new JSONscriptRequest( encodeURI(__trafficReq));
109      aObj.buildScriptTag();
110      aObj.addScriptTag();
111     }
112     function getTrafficData(jData) {
113     if (jData.ResultSet.Result.length ==0){
114      document.getElementById('TrafficResults').innerHTML = "No reported ⤶
tie-ups";
115      return;
116     }
117      document.getElementById('TrafficResults').innerHTML = jData.ResultSet.⤶
Result.length+ " reported tie-ups";
118      for (var i = 0; i < jData.ResultSet.Result.length; i++){
119      var lat = jData.ResultSet.Result[i].Latitude;
120     var lon = jData.ResultSet.Result[i].Longitude;
121      var title = jData.ResultSet.Result[i].Title;
122      var descr = jData.ResultSet.Result[i].Description;
123      var severity = jData.ResultSet.Result[i].Severity;
124      var type = jData.ResultSet.Result[i].type;
125      var report = "<h2>" + title + "</h2><br /><hr/>"
126      + "Lat/Lon: " + lat + "/"+ lon + "<br/>"
127      + "Type: " + type + "<br/>"
128      + "Severity: " + severity + "<br />"
129      + "Details:" + descr;
130      __map.addOverlay(createMarker( new GLatLng(lat, lon), report));
131     }
132     }
133
134     //]]>
135     </script>
136
137     </head>
138
139     <body onunload="GUnload()">
140      <div id="header">
141      <h1>Simple Geocoding Example </h1>
```

```
142    <h2>Input a loose location description and get the traffic tie ups ⤺
for the surrounding area</h2>
143
144    </div>
145    <br />
146    <div class="inputelement"><button onClick="callGeocode()"⤺
>Location</button> 
147
148        <input id="geoquery" value="1300 N. 17th St, Arlington VA"
size="50"></input>
149    </div>
150    <br />
151
152    <div id="State"></div>
153    <div id="Result"></div>
154    <p>Traffic Tie Ups: <span id="TrafficResults" style="font-weight:bold">⤺
</span> </p>
155    <div id="map" style="width: 500px; height: 300px"></div>
156  </body>
157 </html>
```

You've already seen the code in lines 26–44. As before, it manages the service query; in this case, it's invoked from the callGeocode function after the user enters a location and clicks the Location button. This sets off a chain of events that includes first translating the location represented by the contents of the query textbox into a latitude/longitude pair, on line 35, attaching an array of traffic data to the map (line 37), and finally loading a Google map (line 41). Note the following about Listing 3-11:

❑   The getLatLon function uses a brute-force parse to extract the latitude and longitude from the returned data, and resets the XMLHttpRequest. It's the brute-force parse approach used in Listing 4-7. This function sets up a dynamic JavaScript element as a SCRIPT tag as before and executes the connection to the Yahoo Traffic Service, getting back a JSON object that's directly usable to the getTrafficData function.

❑   The getTrafficData function sets a DIV with the number of reported tie-ups and then constructs the set of markers, overlaying them onto the map (line 130).

❑   Markers can contain any reasonable HTML, in this case composing the report as micro-content, and then using the addOverlay function of the Map object. Map is constructed in the loadMap function. Here, you use GMarker, available as a result of loading the Map API on line 10. The anonymous inner function (or closure, if you prefer) adds a click handler for each marker such that when the user clicks anywhere within the marker's image, the informational window opens, exposing the traffic information, as shown in Figure 3-18.

   Here, you load the map and add a marker (hereMarker) to indicate the center latitude/longitude, lines 85–91. This is by far the most verbose function on the RIAPage—a lot of customization. To understand it at a detailed level, refer to the Google Map API (currently at www.google.com/apis/maps/documentation/).

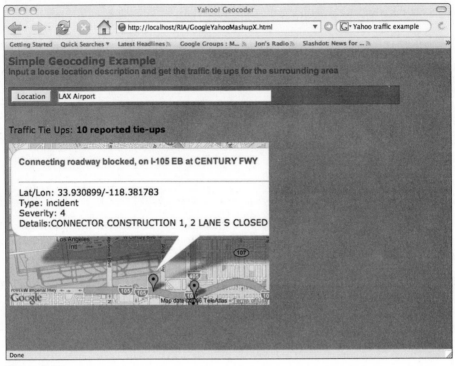

Figure 3-18

Summary

In this chapter, you explored techniques for creating new applications by seamlessly knitting together components. In the capstone application, you created a useful RIAPage that provides data conversion (location to geocodes), data (traffic data for a location), and perhaps most excitingly, a geospatial presentation backdrop. There are several other elements of mashups that couldn't be demonstrated due to space considerations, such as RSS feeds, audio, flash, and scalable vector graphics. The authors could have gone in several directions to make the point that mashups are only limited by the availability of open services on the Web.

4

Getting Started: Creating Your First RIA

"I learned more from the one restaurant that didn't work than from all the ones that were successes."

— Wolfgang Puck

Chapter 2 introduced the foundations of Web programming, including basic CSS, JavaScript, and DOM operations. This chapter builds on that introduction by outlining the components that make up AJAX, and explores the common aspects of AJAX Web applications. The chapter starts by exploring the differences between synchronous and asynchronous Web applications in a little more detail, and then prepares you for the example by examining how typical AJAX Web applications work. After that, the chapter jumps into the code and introduces the Hello World application, a simple AJAX Web application that says "hello world" in multiple languages. This example walks you through the setup of the client side of an AJAX application, including the use of JavaScript for event handling and callback specification. You are introduced to the indispensable `XMLHttpRequest` object, which enables the asynchronous behavior. You also learn how you can use the DOM introduced in the previous chapter to dynamically manipulate a Web page. After exploring the client side, the chapter runs through the steps necessary to enhance the initial application to include more interesting server-side logic in both PHP and Java.

Two Scenarios: If Restaurants Were Run Like Web Apps

Before jumping into the details of the Hello World example, let's explore some of the differences between Web applications that utilize AJAX versus the more traditional Web applications. It may be easier to use a couple of scenarios to explain this comparison.

The Unusual Restaurant

Imagine that you decide to go out to a restaurant for dinner. The host shows you to a table that is initially void of any setting, but the waiter quickly approaches with a complete table setting: tablecloth, centerpiece, napkin, silverware, plate, and bread basket. You wait patiently as he sets the table and then finally hands you the menu. You take your time perusing the menu and nibbling on a piece of bread, you settle on a drink, and give your beverage order to the waiter, who proceeds to pick up the entire table setting—tablecloth, centerpiece, napkin, silverware, plate, menu—in short, everything, including the piece of bread from your hand! He then walks off toward the bar area with the tablecloth bundle. Five minutes go by as you sit and wait. Unfortunately, you can't decide what you want to eat because he's taken the menu! Finally, the waiter returns with your drink in hand, as well as the same table setting he had just toted away. He takes a moment to lay out the tablecloth and set the table for you. He sets down your drink, gives you back your bread—no noticeable or unwanted bites missing—and hands you the menu again.

Once more, you look over the menu with the server at your side ready to take your order. You're quite hungry, so you decide to get some soup, a big plate of pasta, and a salad. However, you follow a strictly regimented diet due to food allergies—nobody said you were an easy customer—and you list several ingredients that the chef should not include in the salad. The waiter writes down your detailed order and accompanying instructions, sweeps up everything he set down at your table just a moment ago—including your hard-earned drink and now nearly stale bread—and disappears *again*, this time through the swinging door into the kitchen. Sigh. You drum your fingers on the bare table and wait.

After a few minutes the waiter comes back, of course, with the same table setting, your drink, and the bread. And, of course, you wait while he sets everything out for you again—but there's a new twist. The waiter informs you that the chef has rejected your order because you forgot to say what type of salad dressing you want. The tireless server hands you the menu again and politely asks you for a new order, this time with a salad dressing choice. At this point, you're probably sorely tempted to walk away and find a different restaurant with a simpler ordering process, but you stay and give things another shot because you're already at this restaurant. (You also promise yourself that you'll never eat here again.) You once again tell the waiter that you would like some soup, a big plate of pasta, and a salad, this time noting that you would like blue cheese dressing, on the side. Again, you give the waiter the same detailed instructions about the salad. The waiter writes all this down exactly as before, with the addition of the salad dressing, picks everything up off the table, and returns to the kitchen.

Unfortunately, the server does not immediately return with the table setting, drink, and food. (The ice must have completely melted in your drink by now.) Your guess is that he's waiting for the chef to make your food, but you have no idea when he's going to come back. After thirty minutes, the waiter comes out of the kitchen and proceeds to repeat the now very familiar process of laying out the table, setting down your drink, and handing you the bread. This time, however, he also has your soup, salad (with dressing), and pasta. Of course, you must wait for a few minutes while he performs these tasks. (If you're anything like the authors, you'd be quite thirsty, bored, and angry at this point!) But when he's finished you can at last take a drink and eat your meal. Of course, your pasta gets a little cold while you eat your soup and salad, but at this point you'll take what you can get.

An Alternative Experience

Now consider an alternative scenario. You go out for dinner the next night to a different restaurant. As in the first restaurant, you are seated at an empty table where the waiter brings the full place setting — tablecloth, centerpiece, napkin, silverware, and plate — sets the table, and hands you a menu. He leaves you with the menu for a moment and disappears into the kitchen. While you look over the menu, he brings some bread. When you order a drink, he leaves everything on the table, gives your drink order to the bartender, and after a few seconds returns to your table, ready to take your order. In the meantime, you can look over the menu, and may not notice he's gone. You decide on soup, a plate of pasta, and a salad. While you're describing your allergies to your server, another waiter appears — perhaps an assistant of sorts, because he looks much less experienced than your waiter — carrying the drink you ordered. He hands this off to the waiter, and then quietly stands by his side. The waiter turns his attention from you for a split second when he takes the drink, but you don't mind because you appreciate receiving the beverage you ordered.

After you've finished describing your allergies, the waiter and his assistant disappear into the kitchen, fortunately leaving everything on the table so you can eat some bread and take a few sips of your beverage. The waiter, gone for a few seconds, returns to ask if you want a drink refill or more bread. You decline, and he continues to stand unobtrusively by the table. After another moment, the assistant returns and whispers something to the waiter, who tells you that you've forgotten to order salad dressing. Rather than replace your entire order, you just provide the missing salad dressing choice. The waiter and assistant go back to the kitchen to update your order. The waiter quickly returns with your soup! Apparently, even though the chef couldn't make your entire order at once, he could at least get started on your soup while the waiter updated your salad order. The waiter whisks away your dirty bread plate from the table and replaces it with the soup. Of course, everything else on the table remains untouched. What a nice surprise. You don't even feel like you've been waiting, and you hungrily tuck into your first course.

While you devour your soup, the waiter stands by to refill your drink. Meanwhile, the chef prepares the rest of your dinner. As soon as your salad is ready, the chef gives it to the waiter's assistant, and starts on the pasta. The assistant takes the salad out to the waiter and disappears back into the kitchen. The waiter takes your finished soup bowl and replaces it with your salad plate. Again, he leaves everything else on your table untouched.

After you finish your salad, the waiter clears away your plate. You wait for just a few minutes, admiring the centerpiece, before the assistant reappears with your pasta. Without even realizing it, you were eating and drinking for the entire thirty minutes the chef needed to prepare your pasta. Your pasta is piping hot and you can get started on it now, before it gets too cold. It didn't feel like you waited around all night for your meal, or that you were forced to sit at an empty table. The waiter also didn't need to waste time setting up and removing everything from your table. On the whole, it was a much more rewarding experience than your previous night's experience, and one that you're likely to repeat.

How Does This Relate to My Web App?

Does the first scenario sound familiar? Maybe not at a restaurant, but this happens in many Web applications today. How many times have you filled out a long form, submitted it, had it rejected by the server, and had to fill in everything again? How many times have you clicked a button on a Web application and waited for a response, not knowing when it would come? You're tempted to reselect, but are unsure if this will duplicate the number of entries in your shopping cart, or worse yet, cause your credit card to be charged twice. These are some of the main frustrations of trying to deal with the Web.

What about the second scenario? It goes without saying that a less frustrating, and more interactive, Web site will be more successful than a frustrating one. Just like at a restaurant, if the customer leaves happy, he will be much more likely to return than if he was disappointed. When applying these scenarios to Web applications, think of the waiter as the Web application, the kitchen and bar as the server, and the assistant as an AJAX callback.

The waiter in the first scenario acts much like traditional Web applications. He synchronously satisfies requests. When the diner wants a drink, the waiter goes to the bar, waits as long as is necessary for the drink to be prepared, and only returns when it's ready. When a user fills in a form, he selects Submit and waits until the database is updated, and the server sends a new page to the Web application.

In the second scenario, the waiter and his assistant are like an AJAX Web application. When the diner wants a drink, the waiter goes into the bar and tells the bartender to make it. The waiter then leaves his assistant to bring the drink out when it's ready, and returns to see if the diner needs anything else in the meantime. In a Web application, you, the user, can fill in an element on the form, and a request is made to the server. While the server processes the request, you're free to fill out other elements on the form. When the request is satisfied, the page updates to contain the results.

Another difference between the scenarios involves the table setting. In first the restaurant, each time the diner requested something, the waiter would take everything from the table, even elements like the tablecloth that never changed throughout the entire meal, and replace it when he returned. In a traditional Web application, even static elements of the page are redrawn as the new page is served. In the second restaurant, the waiter initially set the table, and then left all the same pieces there throughout the duration of the meal. For example, the tablecloth didn't change so the waiter left it on the table. He only removed or added elements as required during the meal, such as the bowl of soup or the dirty bread plate. In a similar fashion, a Web application with AJAX only changes the parts of the page that need to be redrawn. The banner at the top of the page or the table on the side of the page doesn't need to be drawn with each request. This can cause a lot less overhead in refreshing the display.

AJAX versus the Traditional Approach

Now that you've got a basic understanding of the difference between AJAX and traditional Web applications, it's time to get into a bit more of the nuts and bolts of what makes a Web application a RIA — specifically, the main differences between a Web application that uses AJAX and the more traditional Web paradigm. The key to the main differences is in the name AJAX — Asynchronous JavaScript and XML. First, the fact that you make asynchronous requests to the server is critical in providing more interactive applications. These asynchronous calls enable the user to continue interacting with the Web application while data is being transferred. In most cases, the user doesn't even realize he's made a request. The second and third pieces of the name aren't new, but the way they're used is. In AJAX, JavaScript makes the asynchronous call, and with XML manipulates a portion of the currently viewed page. This avoids the traditional problem of forwarding to a new page with each request.

Understanding the Traditional Web Application

Before exploring a Web application that uses AJAX, let's examine the sequence of events that occur in a traditional Web application. The sequence diagram in Figure 4-1 outlines the interactions between a user, Web browser, and Web client using the traditional Web model. The diagram also includes the page the user is interacting with on the vertical bar on the left. This shows that the user initially interacts with the first page of the Web application. The dotted blocks indicate that the user is waiting for a response from the Web server, or a page to be redrawn, and cannot view or interact with any page in the Web application. After the response from the server is received, the first page is removed from the user's display (blocks in X hatch marks), and the user begins interacting with the second and completely new page (indicated with dotted lines, --). Any pertinent elements from page one are duplicated in the server response that contains the definition of page two.

> Note that the times of interaction are not intended to be proportional to each other. They are primarily an indicator of what the user is interacting with at each point in the process.

At first glance, you'll no doubt notice that the traditional Web application model is synchronous and thus very disconnected. The numbered list below outlines its various steps:

1. The user initially enters a URL into a Web browser to go to the Web application.

2. This results in a call to the server . . .

3. . . . as well as a server lookup.

4. Finally, after the HTTP response . . .

5. . . . an HTML document, page 1, is returned and presented to the user.

   At this point, the user can interact with the piece of the Web application displayed in the current HTML document. For example, if the returned page contains a form to be filled in, the user can fill it in and submit it, triggering JavaScript events that cause some client-side processing, or the user may select a link or button, which references a piece of the Web application not in the current page (i.e., page two).

6. When the user submits the form or selects the link, she makes another request to the server.

7. The user's request is sent to the server via a synchronous call. This call blocks the user from interacting with the Web application until a response is received.

8. In the meantime, server-side processing is performed.

9. . . . and after another HTTP response.

10. A completely new HTML document, page 2, is returned and presented to the user. After this page is presented, the user is finally free to interact with the new page.

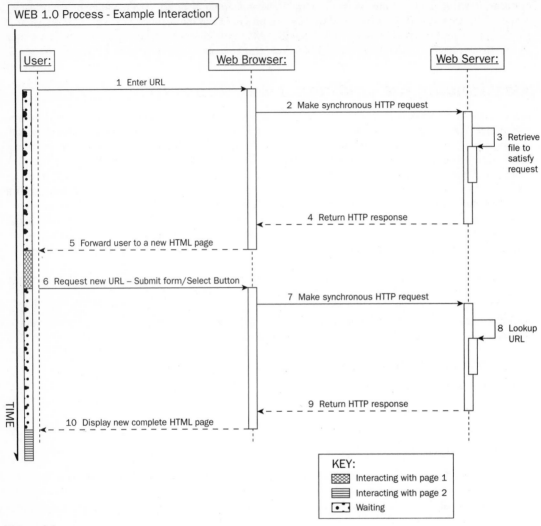

Figure 4-1

Limitations of the Traditional Web Application

There are several obvious limitations to this type of interaction:

❏ The synchronous nature of the request forces the user to wait while the Web server fulfills the request. She is not free to interact with any other piece of the Web application, or even scroll around on the original page. This can cause a great deal of user frustration, especially when the user must wait for large data sets, and frequently redundant information.

❑ The server returns a completely new HTML document after processing the user's request (see step 3 above). This greatly limits the interactivity of Web applications by forcing the Web browser to completely redraw the page (usually a long process with any nontrivial amount of data). This is further magnified by the fact that for most Web applications the page refreshed includes several pieces of primarily, if not completely, static information. For example, consider common Web application headers and footers such as menus, copyrights, login information, and version information.

❑ The state of the old page is lost, and you can only handle this by either saving parts of the state on the client machine as cookies, or forwarding parts of the state to the server as request parameters. To do this you need to explicitly note the parts of the state to retain; and some elements of the state, such as manually repositioned scrollbars, are difficult, if not impossible, to retain.

Historically, several approaches have been taken to reduce the effect of these limitations, with minimal success. Frames or IFrames are frequently used to isolate aspects of the Web application that don't frequently change, such as menus or toolbars. The limitation of frames is that the frame structure easily becomes quite complex. Frames also require the definition of separate HTML documents; this makes interactions between frames difficult to manage, and frequently results in the development of convoluted JavaScript libraries to manage these interactions. Complex JavaScript is also often developed to perform server-side tasks, such as data validation. This generally results in an ill-understood Web of JavaScript, which few can decipher as required for enhancements or debugging.

Understanding the Web Application That Uses AJAX

Now consider the AJAX approach, shown in Figure 4-2. The initial steps are the same:

1. The user enters the URL of the Web application in the Web browser.

2. Just like before, a call is made to the server . . .

3. . . . and a server lookup is performed.

4. The HTML document, page one, is then returned . . .

5. . . . and presented to the user. At this point you can see the difference between the two Web applications and the real power of an AJAX-enabled Web application.

6. The user starts interacting with the page. She may fill in a form element, tab off a field, or mouse over a particular area of the screen.

7. This causes a request to the server, similar to the request in message 7 in Figure 4-1.

   There is a significant difference in the types of requests made, though. In the traditional model, a synchronous request is made. This forces the Web browser to block until the server completes processing the request and returns a response. In the AJAX Web application, the request is asynchronous. This means that the Web browser makes the request to the server, which includes a callback function, and immediately returns control to the user without waiting for a server response.

8. Once the request is made, the server starts processing . . .

9. . . . but the user is still free to interact with the Web application. Many AJAX Web applications are structured in such a way that the user doesn't even realize she made the request.

10. After the server completes processing it invokes the callback. A callback is a bit of client code in JavaScript that executes on the Web browser, usually making use of the request results. This brings in the final aspect of the process.

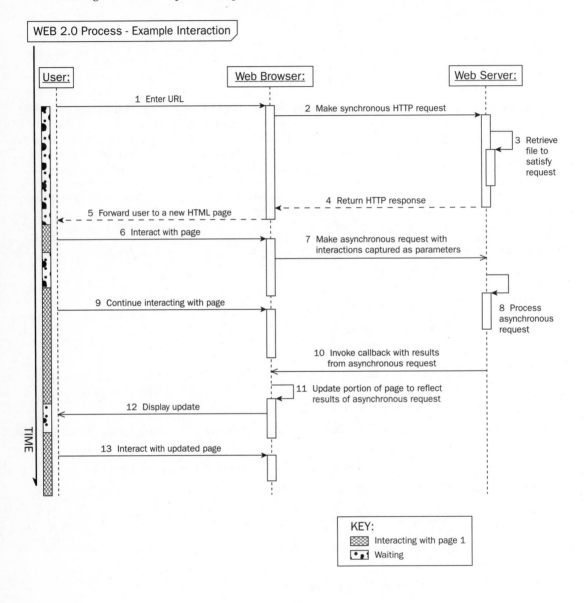

Figure 4-2

11. The update to the page is based on the results of the request. Chapter 2 outlines the details of the DOM, and shows how you can manipulate it via JavaScript. When the document is manipulated within a callback, you can replace a portion of the currently viewed page based on the results of the asynchronous request. For example, the page can be updated to show a server-side error message, the results of validating a form entry, or the results of a database lookup based on the selection of a data row key.

12. The display is updated after the callback, typically a quick operation, completes.

13. The user is again free to interact with the updated page. At this point, note the bar on the left of Figure 4-2 above. The user is always interacting with page 1; no other pages are ever requested from the server.

Advantages of Using AJAX over the Traditional Approach

The operation of an AJAX Web application offers many obvious advantages over the traditional model. In general, the user of a Web application written with AJAX instantly feels enhanced interactivity. For example, consider the ability to drag the mouse to move the map around in Google Maps (http://maps.google.com) or in the recent versions of the MapQuest site (www.mapquest.com). Compare this to the more traditional model, which requires you to select a link and wait for a page to reload with the updated map. This traditional approach was originally used by MapQuest and can still be seen when you visit the site with JavaScript turned off in your Web browser. The mapping sites can provide increased interactivity by using asynchronous requests, as described earlier, to keep the user from sitting around waiting for the server. Imagine an e-commerce site that doesn't require the user to wait for several database operations to finish before her shopping cart can be updated.

Interactivity is further increased when the DOM is used to update just a portion of the page based on the results of the asynchronous request. This means that the user doesn't need to wait for a page to be completely redrawn with each update. Using the same e-commerce example, imagine an inventory list that doesn't have to be completely redrawn as the user adds an element to her shopping cart. The partial page update is also beneficial because the client state is not lost when updating only a portion of the page.

AJAX also saves Web applications from using the various tricks commonly performed in traditional Web applications. You've probably tried to navigate overly complex JavaScript that performs tasks better suited to the server, or to debug a Web application with convoluted state passthrough, or tricky frame declarations. The result is simpler, more maintainable code. Of course, all of this assumes that the application is designed to maximize the effect the asynchronous operation, a topic covered in later chapters.

AJAX Components

The key components that make this possible have all existed since the beginning of Web applications, and most have been used in Web applications. The main addition is the use of the asynchronous request (XMLHttpRequest):

❑ **JavaScript event handling** — Enables capturing of the user interaction. Used throughout the history of Web applications.

❑ **XMLHttpRequest** — Allows the client to make an asynchronous request to the server

❑ **Document Object Model** — Allows JavaScript to be developed to manipulate a portion of the overall page

Development Environment Setup

Now that you've seen how the process works, you're ready to write your first RIA! Before you get started, you need the following;

❑ You need to set up a development environment that you can use to deploy and run the Hello World Web application. Of course, you'll need a Web client installed on your machine. The authors are using Firefox v1.5.0, but any modern Web client (e.g., Firefox, Opera, or Safari) will work, with one exception — for the purposes of this example, you cannot use Internet Explorer. This is because AJAX support is slightly different in Internet Explorer.

Chapter 7 shows you how to create an asynchronous request that supports IE as well as other Web clients. See the section "Why Use JavaScript Libraries?" For detailed Firefox download and installation instructions, see www.mozilla.com/firefox.

❑ You also need a Web server to serve your Web application. There are many potential configurations for the server side, so we'll just indicate the configuration that we're using, and won't go into the installation and configuration details here. You can use the link provided for each component that follows to download the software, which includes detailed installation instructions:

  ❑ **http://httpd.apache.org** — For the initial example, which uses only HTML and text files, you can use any desired Web server (e.g., Apache, Tomcat, or Jigsaw). The authors are using Apache v2.2 installed under `c:\Apache2.2` on a system running Windows XP.

  ❑ **http://www.php.net** — For the extensions introduced in the section "Programming the Server Side PHP," you need a PHP-capable Web server installed. For this section, we are using PHP 5.1.3, installed as a module in Apache2.2.

  ❑ **http://tomcat.apache.org** — To make the Java extensions described under "Programming the Java Servlet," you need a Web server that is capable of handling Java Servlets. We're using Jakarta Tomcat v5.5 installed under `c:\Tomcat`.

Your First RIA: Hello World

Now that you've set up a development environment, you're ready to get started with the application. For your first Rich Internet Application, you will implement a simple Hello World. When you're finished, you will have a RIA that contains a single drop-down list with a set of language names. Each time the user selects a language from the list, an asynchronous request is made to the Web server. After the request is processed, the Web page will update to display the results of this request, the words "Hello World" in the selected language. It may seem simple, but remember that the Web page remains the same and only the piece of the page that displays the text file is modified. In addition, it isn't obvious in this simple example, but keep in mind that the request is asynchronous. As soon as the request is made, the user is free to continue interacting with the Web application.

Creating HelloWorldv1.html

To get started, create the document that will contain the drop-down list with the various languages. Type the HTML described in Listing 4-1, which follows, and save it to a location that can be served

from your Web server. For example, using the apache installation described above, save this file to
`c:\Apache2.2\htdocs\HelloWorld\HelloWorldv1.html`.

Listing 4-1: HelloWorldv1.html

```
1.  <html>
2.  <body>
3.   <form id="helloForm"><LABEL>Say Hello: </label>
4.    <select id="country">
5.     <option>France</option>
6.     <option>Germany</option>
7.     <option>Spain</option>
8.     <option>USA</option>
9.    </select>
10.  </form>
11.  <p/>
12.   <label id="messageLabel" style="border: thin solid"></label>
13.  </body>
14. </html>
```

This is a simple document that creates a form `helloForm` (line 3), which contains the single drop-down list (line 4), with several elements denoting our languages (lines 5–8). In addition, an empty label with a thin, solid border is created and given an id of `messageLabel` (line 12). If you start the Web server and browse to `http://localhost/HelloWorld/HelloWorldv1.html`, you'll see the initial HelloWorld page, shown in Figure 4-3.

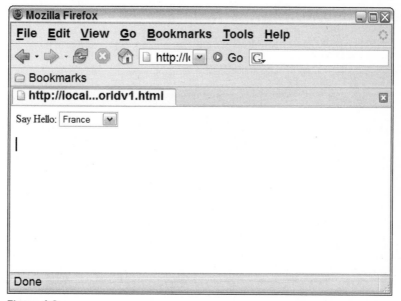

Figure 4-3

Adding a JavaScript Event Handler

Of course, this isn't a very interactive application right now. Nothing happens when you select a new language. You can fix that by adding a JavaScript event handler to respond to the user. First, open `HelloWorldv2.html` and modify the `select` element to contain the `onchange` and `onkeyup` event handler by modifying line 4 of Listing 4-1 as follows:

```
<select id="country" onkeyup="handleCountryChange()"
onchange="handleCountryChange()">
```

This tells the JavaScript interpreter to invoke the method `handleCountryChange` when the user chooses a new value in the `country` drop-down list by pressing the up/down arrows or using the mouse.

Defining the JavaScript Body

Next, you need to define the new `handleCountryChange` method that is invoked. First, insert the `head` and `script` open and close tags after line 1 to demarcate the beginning and end of the JavaScript code:

```
<html>
  <head>
    <script type="text/javascript">
    </script>
  </head>
  <body>
```

Creating the Asynchronous Request

Start defining the script by creating a global `XMLHttpRequest` object, as shown here:

```
<script type="text/javascript">
  var xmlRequest = new XMLHttpRequest()
</script>
```

As described above, the `XMLHttpRequest` is the component that allows you to make the asynchronous request, immediately return control to the user, and update the Web page in a callback after the server is finished processing the request. You'll notice that you're defining the variable outside of any function on the page. This causes the creation of a global variable that is accessible from within all the functions defined on your page. You'll see later that this is necessary to ensure that you can reference the `xmlRequest` variable in both your event handler function and the callback function that you're going to write.

Defining the Event Handler Function

After creating the `xmlRequest` variable, you're ready to define the event handler function. This function retrieves the value that the user selected from the list, generates the asynchronous request based on this value, and sends it to the server. See the specification (lines 4–10) as follows:

```
1.   <script type="text/javascript">
2.     var xmlRequest = new XMLHttpRequest();
3.
4.     function handleCountryChange() {
5.       var countryValue = document.getElementById("country").value;
6.       var uri = "helloFiles/" + countryValue + ".txt";
7.       xmlRequest.open("GET", uri, true);
8.       xmlRequest.onreadystatechange = helloCallback;
9.       xmlRequest.send(null);
10.    }
11.  </script>
```

Take a closer look at what's happing in the function you just added:

1. First, you need to get the value that the user selected in the drop-down list, which you accomplish by using a handy JavaScript function, `getElementById`. This function is extremely useful in many situations. It's used above to get the value entered in a form, but it's not limited to reading form elements. You can use it to select and manipulate any element on an HTML page that has an identifier. Using the function in this way becomes important when you write the callback function. See Chapter 2 for more detail on `getElementById` and related similar methods.

2. Once you use `getElementById` to get the `country` form element, you access the `value` property to get the latest value selected by the user. You read this into the variable `countryValue` (line 5), which you then use to construct a URI relative to the index URL (line 6). This URI is the name and relative location of the remote file that you want to retrieve and display. The URI you construct references a text file with the same name as the value selected in the drop-down list, in the relative path `"helloFiles/"`. For example, when the user selects Spain, you build the URI `"helloFiles/Spain.txt"`.

3. The next step is to use the `xmlRequest` to tell the Web server to give the file to the client (lines 7–9). First, you call `open` on the `xmlRequest` (line 7). This method effectively defines the details of the request you want to make, and usually takes three arguments:

   ❑ The initial argument is the method of the request. This should be one of `GET`, `POST`, or `HEAD`, and it establishes the method used when making the request.

   ❑ You provide the URI that you just created as the next argument to establish the location that you're requesting from the Web server.

   ❑ The third argument is the asynchronous flag that you've set to `true`. This argument determines whether the request made should be asynchronous (`true`) or synchronous (`false`). All the examples in this book use `true` for this flag because it's focusing on the AJAX paradigm. In practice, you'll almost always want this to be `true` anyway. As noted above, using synchronous calls isn't preferred because it locks the page until the server returns a response.

   Finally, note that there are two more optional arguments to `open` that we haven't included here: user and password. These can be used to handle any authentication required by the server, and are examined in more detail in later chapters.

4. After line 7, you set up the method and URI for the `xmlRequest`. The next step is to specify the callback function. Line 8 does this by setting the `onreadystatechange` property to the function `helloCallback` that you will define later. This property establishes the function that is invoked after the server finishes generating a response. Actually, this function is executed every time the `readyState` property of the `xmlRequest` changes, but more on that later.

5. At this point, your `XMLHttpRequest` object has been fully initialized, and you're ready to send the request (line 9). The `send` method takes a `Document` or a DOM string, but because you have no data to send with the request, you can just send `null`. When line 9 is executed, an asynchronous request is made to the server asking for the URI. When the server has processed the URI, and the request is fulfilled, the callback function is executed.

Defining the Callback Function

Now that you've set up your request, you need to define the callback function `helloCallback`. For now, just display a JavaScript alert to indicate that the callback function was actually called. See the method implementation in Listing 4-2, which follows. This is pretty simple right now, but you may want to look at line 13 for a moment. This line examines the state of the XML request and makes sure that the response has been completely generated before displaying the alert. Remember from the previous section that this method is invoked each time the ready state changes. This state can actually change several times before the request has completed. Because you only want your callback to display the alert after you know the request has been completed, the callback function's first step is to make sure that the value of the `readyState` property is 4. Initially, you don't have to worry too much about the details of the ready state, but just note that the ready state is set to 4 after the data transfer from the server has been completed. On the other hand, if you're really keen to get into the nuts and bolts of the ready state, you can find a detailed description of the `XMLHttpRequest` in Chapter 1.

Listing 4-2: The JavaScript in HelloWorldv2.html after the first helloCallback implementation

```
1.    <script type="text/javascript">
2.    var xmlRequest = new XMLHttpRequest();
3.
4.      function handleCountryChange() {
5.      var countryValue = document.getElementById("country").value;
6.      var uri = "helloFiles/" + countryValue + ".txt";
7.      xmlRequest.open("GET", uri, true);
8.      xmlRequest.onreadystatechange = helloCallback;
9.      xmlRequest.send(null);
10.     }
11.
12.     function helloCallback() {
13.       if (xmlRequest.readyState == 4) {
14.        alert("Hello callback was invoked!");
15.       }
16.     }
17.   </script>
```

At this point, if you save `HelloWorldv2.html` and reload the page in your Web client, you get a new page that displays the JavaScript alert each time you select a new value in the drop-down list (see Figure 4-4). Congratulations! You've just made your first asynchronous call, one of the key components of AJAX. It must be important if it's in the name, right?

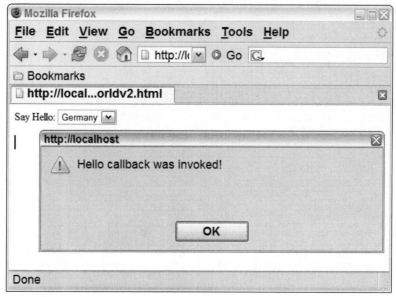

Figure 4-4

Processing the Server's Response

Of course, you want to process the server's response as a part of your callback, rather than simply display an alert. To do this, you use the remaining key component of AJAX: the document object model (DOM). As outlined in Chapter 2, the DOM is a model that describes a structured document. This can actually be any type of document, but in this case it's an HTML document. In general, the DOM provides a mechanism for programmatically exploring, modifying, and otherwise interacting with the structure, content, and style of the document. The structure is the composition of the document, or the location of elements in the document. For example, it includes any tables defined, where they are in the document, and the rows in each table. The content is the actual data in the document (e.g., the data in the tables). Finally, the style consists of presentation details for the data. For example, it outlines the font to use when displaying table row data. To get started, let's modify the callback function in `HelloWorldv3.html` to use the DOM to get the empty label you've defined in your HTML page and modify its content. Following is the new `helloCallback` implementation:

```
1.   function helloCallback() {
2.     if (xmlRequest.readyState == 4) {
3.       var messageL = document.getElementById("messageLabel")
4.       if (xmlRequest.status == 200) {
5.         messageL.innerHTML = xmlRequest.responseText
6.       } else {
7.         messageL.innerHTML = "Page Not Found"
8.       }
9.     }
10.  }
```

Take a look at what you've added:

1. As in Listing 4-2, you should continue to check the value of the `readyState` property of the `xmlRequest` (line 2) to ensure that you only do anything in the callback if the data transfer has been completed.

2. After you check the ready state, you use `getElementById` again on line 3 to initialize a new variable `messageL`. The variable is set to the label object that has the id of `"messageLabel"` defined in our HTML document. This is the portion of the document that you want to update to contain the results of our server call.

3. Now you examine the status of the request in line 4. As a Web programmer you're probably already familiar with the HTTP status code. The `status` property is just the HTTP status code of the request you just made. You look for a status of 200, which is the server response meaning OK. It indicates that no condition was encountered that caused the request to fail. For example, a common status code most everyone is familiar with is the 404, or Not Found, code.

4. If the URI you requested was found, you proceed to line 5 and update the page to contain the new data that you retrieved from the Web server. To perform the update, you reference a special property of the `LABEL` element called `innerHTML`. You can use this property to replace the contents of an element in the document.

*Note that using the `innerHTML` property in this example is a bit of a shortcut. What you should actually do is manipulate the DOM to add the new elements necessary to hold the label text. The `innerHTML` property is quite controversial because it's proprietary and not officially part of the W3C's DOM specification. This means that **not all browsers may support it**. The property has, however, been widely adopted by developers, and is supported in many modern browsers. Of course, it's also the source of much ongoing controversy on the net.*

The other aspect of line 5 that is of interest is that we use the request's `responseText` property to get the body of the data returned by the server. Note that the property returns the value as text here, but you can also get the response as XML. Since you're initially dealing with a completely text response, the `responseText` property will work without any problems. The final section of the listing, lines 6–8, is included to provide some basic error handling. If the asynchronous request was not successful for any reason, the label text is set to `'Page Not Found'`.

The Complete HelloWorldv3.html file

At this point, you're finished with the specification of our `HelloWorldv3.html` file. Listing 4-3 shows the complete version of the file.

Listing 4-3: Complete HelloWorldv3.html

```
1.  <html>
2.   <head>
3.    <script type="text/javascript">
4.     var xmlRequest = new XMLHttpRequest();
5.
6.     function handleCountryChange() {
7.       var countryValue = document.getElementById("country").value;
8.       var uri = "helloFiles/" + countryValue + ".txt";
9.       xmlRequest.open("GET", uri, true);
```

```
10.      xmlRequest.onreadystatechange = helloCallback;
11.      xmlRequest.send(null);
12.    }
13.
14.    function helloCallback() {
15.     if (xmlRequest.readyState == 4) {
16.      var messageL = document.getElementById("messageLabel")
17.      if (xmlRequest.status == 200) {
18.       messageL.innerHTML = xmlRequest.responseText
19.      } else {
20.       messageL.innerHTML = "Page Not Found"
21.      }
22.     }
23.    }
24.  </script>
25.  </head>
26.  <body>
27.   <form id="helloForm"><label>Say Hello: </label>
28.    <select id="country" onkeyup="handleCountryChange()"
29.        onchange="handleCountryChange()">
30.     <option>France</option>
31.     <option>Germany</option>
32.     <option>Spain</option>
33.     <option>USA</option>
34.    </select>
35.   </form>
36.   <p/>
37.    <label id="messageLabel" style="border: thin solid"></label>
38.  </body>
40. </html>
```

Creating the helloFiles Directory

You're almost ready to run our completed RIA, but you have one final step. On line 8 of Listing 4-3, a URI, referencing a text file under the "helloFiles" directory, is constructed. Now you need to create this directory and the files to be returned by the server when the asynchronous request is made. First, create the directory that will hold the text files, under the directory containing your HelloWorldv3.html file. In our environment, we use "c:\Apache2.2\htdocs\HelloWorld\helloFiles". Then, create the set of files as described in Table 4-1. There is one file for each option in your drop-down list. The name of the file is based on the option value.

Table 4-1: The Set of Hello Files and Their Contents

Hello File	Content
France.txt	Bonjour Monde!
USA.txt	Hello World!
Germany.txt	Hallo Walt!
Spain.txt	Hola Mundo!

Once all this is completed you're ready to reload and run your first complete RIA (shown in Figure 4-5A). As you select an element in the drop-down list (see Figure 4-5B), you should see the corresponding hello world message appear in your browser (see Figure 4-5C).

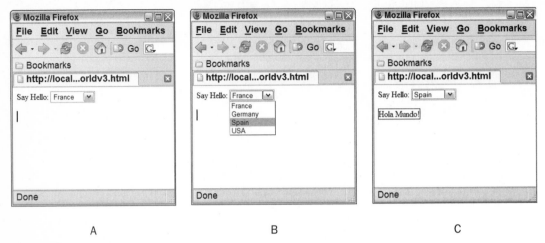

A   B   C

Figure 4-5

Of course, this may not look too exciting, but you need to keep in mind what's going on behind the scenes. The page is being dynamically modified with data asynchronously requested and returned by the server after the page has been loaded. The potential of this type of interaction, given thoughtful application design, is hugely significant.

Consider the following example issue, common in many Web applications. You want to allow the user to view a large list of basic data, such as CD titles. When the user selects a given title, you want to display the details of the data, such as the artist, year, and list of songs. In non-AJAX-enabled Web applications you have two basic options. The simplest approach is to go to a completely new page with the details of the CD when a title is selected, but this has a couple of drawbacks. The user can't see the title list and the details of a title at the same time. You will also most likely need to keep reloading the page containing the CD titles as the user decides to view the details of different titles. Alternatively, you can use two separate frames. The first frame contains a page with the list of CD titles. The second frame, updated each time a title is selected, holds the details of the most recently selected title. This fixes the problems with the original approach, but can quickly lead to Web applications with complex framesets or require large pieces of static information to be repeatedly refreshed.

Consider the addition of a mostly static menu, title, shopping cart, or status bar to the Web application. In the AJAX world, you have a single frame with a single page. The same page contains a section for the title list, and another section for the CD details. When the user selects a title, you simply update the section of the current page to hold the details of the CD. Only the portion containing the CD details is updated as the user selects a new title. The Web application is greatly simplified because there is no need to manage the interaction between two separate pages, each with its own state. The user also experiences a much more interactive environment because you're not redrawing static information, or requiring them to go back to the page containing the titles. Another contributor to the interactivity is the asynchronous call, which avoids blocking the user during the detail lookup.

Adding the Server Side

Now that you've explored the client side of AJAX in detail, it's time to explore how the server responds to asynchronous requests. Currently, the server generates the simplest possible response body when it responds to the request. The complete body consists of the text file contents, which varies depending on the request (e.g., the body of the response is "Bonjour Monde!" when the user selects France). The client-side handling of the response is quite basic too. The HTML value of the label is set to the entire body of the response (e.g., the label is set to the full body "Bonjour Monde!"). This simple handling is undesirable for a couple of reasons. First, you want to avoid creating a new file for each country that you add to the list. For example, if you want to add Italy, you need to create a file named "Italy.txt" with the phrase "Ciao Mondo!" as the file contents. The second problem is that you may need to return additional information with the response. For example, you may want a response that includes who the hello world message is from, but you may not want to display it in the same label.

In this section, you create two alternate server-side components that address the preceding issues. These components are basically the same, and generate the same response. The section "Programming the Server-Side PHP" walks you through the process of creating the new response using PHP, while the section "Programming the Java Servlet" shows the same component as a Java Servlet. Feel free to only work through the example that uses the language you're more comfortable with. The final part of this section describes some enhancements to the client side of the original RIA to make use of your new server-side components. Regardless of which server-side language you choose, you'll want to look at this part because it shows you how to update the URI of the asynchronous request and send the country as an argument, as well as how to modify the handling of the response to use the DOM to parse the new XML response.

Programming the Server-Side PHP

This section explores how to generate a response from a PHP page, assuming that you have PHP installed and loaded into your Apache Web server, as described earlier in the section "Development Environment Setup." Because you're building on the original Hello World, you'll want to keep working out of the same directory (c:\Apache2.2\htdocs\HelloWorld) that you used earlier in the chapter.

The first step in implementing our server side is to define the new PHP page named "helloResponsev1 .php" and described in Listing 4-4. First, you just replace your initial approach, which uses text files, with a PHP version that generates the same result. Later, you can enhance the format of the response.

Listing 4-4: Initial version of helloResponsev1.php

```
 1. <?php
 2. function lookupMessage($mCountry)
 3. {
 4.   if ($mCountry == "France")
 5.     return 'Bonjour Monde!';
 6.   else if ($mCountry == "Germany")
 7.     return 'Hallo Welt!';
 8.   else if ($mCountry == "Spain")
 9.     return 'Hola Mundo!';
10.   else if ($mCountry == "USA")
11.     return 'Hello World!';
12.   else
```

(continued)

Listing 4-4: *(continued)*

```
13.     return 'Unknown Message!';
14.  }
15. ?>
16. <?php echo lookupMessage($_GET['country'])?>
```

The initial script is pretty simple:

1. Lines 2–14 define the function `lookupMessage` that returns the hello message as a string depending on the value of the `mCountry` argument.

2. On line 16, you actually create the content of the response. You do this by calling `lookupMessage` with the value of the request parameter named `country`.

3. Save this file under `c:\Apache2.2\htdocs\HelloWorld`, start your Web server, and browse to `http://localhost/HelloWorld/helloResponsev1.php`. You initially see a page that says "Unknown Message!", but when you provide a country parameter you get a more reasonable response. For example, when you browse to `http://localhost/HelloWorld/helloResponsev1.php?country=Germany`, you get a page that says "Hallo Welt!"

The next step is to incorporate the new script into our Web application by making a small modification to `HelloWorldv4.html`. Simply replace the URI provided in the asynchronous request. Originally you constructed a URI that pointed to a text file based on the selected country using the following (from line 8 in Listing 4-3):

```
var uri = "helloFiles/" + countryValue + ".txt";
```

You need to replace this URI with a reference to the new PHP file and add a country parameter to the request as follows:

```
var uri = "helloResponsev1.php?country=" + countryValue;
```

After making this change you should be able run the application and get the results shown in Figure 4-5. Now that you're using the new PHP, you can enhance it to provide a more sophisticated response. In Listing 4-5, which follows, `helloResponsev2.php` has been updated to format the response as XML, and includes the sender with the hello message.

Note that you need to update the URI in the HelloWorld html file again to reference `helloResponsev2.php`.

Listing 4-5: Revised version of helloResponsev2.php

```
1. <?php
2. header('Content-Type: text/xml');
3.
4. function lookupMessage($mCountry)
5. {
6.    if ($mCountry == "France")
7.     return 'Bonjour Monde!';
8.    else if ($mCountry == "Germany")
9.     return 'Hallo Welt!';
```

```
10.    else if ($mCountry == "Spain")
11.      return 'Hola Mundo!';
12.    else if ($mCountry == "USA")
13.      return 'Hello World!';
14.    else
15.      return 'Unknown Message!';
16. }
17.
18. function lookupSender($mCountry)
19. {
20.    if ($mCountry == "France")
21.      return 'Dana';
22.    else if ($mCountry == "Germany")
23.      return 'Ray';
24.    else if ($mCountry == "Spain")
25.      return 'Ted';
26.    else if ($mCountry == "USA")
27.      return 'Jonathan';
28.    else
29.      return 'Unknown Sender!';
30. }
31. ?>
32. <?xml version="1.0" encoding="UTF-8"?>
33. <response>
34.   <sender><?php echo lookupSender($_GET['country'])?></sender>
35.   <message><?php echo lookupMessage($_GET['country'])?></message>
36. </response>
```

Note the following things about Listing 4-5:

1.   The first change is to modify the header of the response to indicate that you are sending a response body formatted as XML. This is done on line 2 with a call to the `header` function, to specify a new content type of `text/xml`.

2.   The next step is to add a new function that will figure out who the sender is based on the country. This is defined in a new function (lines 18–30), `lookupSender`, which is quite similar to the original `lookupMessage` function.

3.   Now that you've updated your header and functions, all that's left to do is enhance the way the content is created (lines 32–36). These lines create an XML-formatted response that includes a `response` tag containing a `sender` tag with some value, and a `message` tag with some value.

If you browse to your updated `helloResponsev2.php`, you should get a new XML-formatted error message.

To see the full, unformatted XML you can view the source by right-clicking on the page and selecting view source in Firefox. It should look similar to the following:

```
<?xml version="1.0" encoding="UTF-8"?>
<response>
 <sender>Unknown Sender!</sender>
 <message>Unknown Country!</message>
</response>
```

When you provide a country parameter you get the response for that country. For example, when you enter "http://localhost/HelloWorld/helloResponsev2.php?country=Spain", you should get the following result:

```
<?xml version="1.0" encoding="UTF-8"?>
<response>
 <sender>Ted</sender>
 <message>Hola Mundo!</message>
</response>
```

That's all there is too it! Now your server-side PHP script is ready. In the section "Enhancing the Client Application" later in the chapter, you can see how to enhance the Web application to use the new XML-formatted response. Feel free to skip to this section now, or continue on to the next section to see how to develop a Java-based version of the server side.

Programming the Java Servlet

This section discusses the development of a Java Servlet that produces the correct hello world message formatted in an XML document, given the selected country. The assumption as you work through this example is that you have a version of Apache Tomcat (the example uses v 5.5) installed under c:\Tomcat.

Before you jump into the code, you need to take care of a bit of administration necessary to create your new Web application. For more detailed information about setting up Web applications, refer to your Web server's documentation:

1. Create a location for the new Servlet. Create a directory "HelloWorld" under c:\Tomcat\ webapps.

2. You also need to create the standard WEB-INF directory at c:\Tomcat\webapps\HelloWorld\ WEB-INF, and a new directory that will contain the Servlet code and class files at c:\Tomcat\ webapps\HelloWorld\WEB-INF\classes.

3. Define the file for the Web application that will reference the Servlet. It should be similar to the one defined in Listing 4-6 and saved as c:\Tomcat\webapps\HelloWorld\WEB-INF\web.xml.

Listing 4-6: Hello World's web.xml

```
<?xml version="1.0"?>
<web-app xmlns="http://java.sun.com/xml/ns/j2ee"
   xmlns:xsi="http://www.w3.org/2001/XMLSchema-instance"
   xsi:schemaLocation="http://java.sun.com/xml/ns/j2ee
   http://java.sun.com/xml/ns/j2ee/web-app_2_4.xsd"
   version="2.4">

   <servlet>
     <servlet-name>HelloResponseServletv1</servlet-name>
     <servlet-class>HelloResponseServletv1</servlet-class>
   </servlet>

   <servlet-mapping>
     <servlet-name>HelloResponseServletv1</servlet-name>
     <url-pattern>/helloResponsev1</url-pattern>
   </servlet-mapping>
</web-app>
```

4. Finally, you're ready to write the Servlet! See Listing 4-7 for the initial version of the `HelloResponseServlet`. This version returns a message similar to that returned by the original approach that generated the response from separate text files. Create and save this under `c:\Tomcat\webapps\HelloWorld\WEB-INF\classes\HelloResponseServletv1.java`. After exploring this initial version, you will extend it to send a response formatted as XML.

Listing 4-7: Initial version of HelloResponseServletv1.java

```
1. import java.io.*;
2. import javax.servlet.*;
3. import javax.servlet.http.*;
4.
5. public class HelloResponseServletv1 extends HttpServlet {
6.
7.   public void doGet(HttpServletRequest req, HttpServletResponse resp)
8.     throws IOException, ServletException {
9.
10.    String country = "Unknown";
11.
12.    if ((req.getParameterValues("country") != null)&&
13.       (req.getParameterValues("country").length > 0)) {
14.     country = req.getParameterValues("country")[0];
15.    }
16.
17.    resp.getWriter().write(getMessage(country));
18.  }
19.
20.  private String getMessage(String country) {
21.    if (country.equals("France")) {
22.     return "Bonjour Monde!";
23.    } else if (country.equals("Germany")) {
24.     return "Hallo Welt!";
25.    } else if (country.equals("Spain")) {
26.     return "Hola Mundo!";
27.    } else if (country.equals("USA")) {
28.     return "Hello World!";
29.    } else {
30.     return "Unknown Message!";
31.    }
32.  }
33.
34. }
```

Note the following about Listing 4-7:

1. The majority of the initial Servlet code is boilerplate for any Java HttpServlet. This Servlet extends the `HttpServlet` base class (line 5), and overrides the `doGet` method (line 7) so that you can provide an implementation that returns the necessary data.

2. You can create a local variable and store the value of the country parameter when provided (lines 10–15). On lines 20–32, you define a private method, which returns the hello message for a given country.

3. On line 17, you generate a response consisting entirely of the string returned by the `getMessage` method.

You can compile your new Servlet with a command similar to the following:

```
C:\Tomcat>javac -classpath common\lib\servlet-api.jar webapps\HelloWorld\
WEB-INF\classes\HelloResponseServletv1.java
```

After compiling, you can test your Servlet by starting Tomcat and browsing to `http://localhost:8080/HelloWorld/helloResponsev1`. You will initially get a page with the error handler message "Unknown Message!" This will be replaced by an actual message if you provide a country parameter. For example, browsing to `http://localhost:8080/HelloWorld/helloResponsev1?country=Germany` will display the message "Hallo Welt!"

The next step is to update the HelloWorld HTML file to use the new Servlet when it makes the asynchronous request. First, make sure there's a copy of the original `HelloWorldv3.html` from Listing 4-3 saved as `HelloWorldv4.html` under `C:\Tomcat\webapps\HelloWorld`. Next, update the original URI construction code from line 8 in Listing 4-3:

```
var uri = "helloFiles/" + countryValue + ".txt";
```

This originally referenced a text file based on the selected country. The updated version should reference the new Servlet, and add a parameter for the selected country as follows:

```
var uri = "helloResponsev1?country=" + countryValue;
```

After making this change, if you browse to the new HTML page at `http://localhost:8080/HelloWorld/HelloWorldv4.html`, you will get a Web application that looks and behaves like the original shown in Figure 4-5. Now you're ready to extend the initial Servlet implementation to include a more interesting response. In this update, you add a sender of the hello message, and wrap the message as an XML document. The updated Servlet implementation follows in Listing 4-8.

Listing 4-8: HelloResponseServletv2.java

```
1.  import java.io.*;
2.  import javax.servlet.*;
3.  import javax.servlet.http.*;
4.
5.  public class HelloResponseServletv2 extends HttpServlet {
6.
7.    public void doGet(HttpServletRequest req, HttpServletResponse resp)
8.      throws IOException, ServletException {
9.
10.    String country = "Unknown";
11.
12.    if ((req.getParameterValues("country") != null)&&
13.      (req.getParameterValues("country").length > 0)) {
14.     country = req.getParameterValues("country")[0];
15.    }
16.
17.    resp.setContentType("text/xml");
18.    resp.setHeader("Cache-Control", "no-cache");
19.
20.    resp.getWriter().write("<?xml version='1.0' encoding='UTF-8'?>\n");
```

```
21.    resp.getWriter().write("<response>\n");
22.    resp.getWriter().write(" <sender>"+ getSender(country) +"</sender>\n");
23.    resp.getWriter().write(" <message>"+ getMessage(country)+"</message>\n");
24.    resp.getWriter().write("</response>\n");
25.  }
26.
27.  private String getMessage(String country) {
28.    if (country.equals("France")) {
29.     return "Bonjour Monde!";
30.    } else if (country.equals("Germany")) {
31.     return "Hallo Welt!";
32.    } else if (country.equals("Spain")) {
33.     return "Hola Mundo!";
34.    } else if (country.equals("USA")) {
35.     return "Hello World!";
36.    } else {
37.     return "Unknown Message!";
38.    }
39.  }
40.
41.  private String getSender(String country) {
42.    if (country.equals("France")) {
43.     return "Dana";
44.    } else if (country.equals("Germany")) {
45.     return "Ray";
46.    } else if (country.equals("Spain")) {
47.     return "Ted";
48.    } else if (country.equals("USA")) {
49.     return "Jonathan";
50.    } else {
51.     return "Unknown Sender!";
52.    }
53.  }
54.
55. }
```

Note the following about this listing:

1. The first addition to note is the new private method that calculates a sender based on the country (lines 41–53). This is pretty straightforward and looks quite similar to the getMessage method.

2. Next, turn your attention to the doGet method, because it contains the other major modification. It has been updated to generate our response as XML. Because you're sending your response as XML, the addition (line 17) is the specification of a content type for the response. This causes the header of the response to indicate that the response body will be in XML (text/xml) instead of plain text (text/plain) or HTML (text/html). Note that it is important to use the content type of text/xml instead of other commonly used types such as text/html because the XMLHttpRequest is only capable of handling a response of type text/xml.

3. You also need to specify that no caching is performed in the browser or proxy. You do this on line 18 by setting the cache-control portion of the header to no-cache. Lines 20–24 create the XML-formatted data stream to be sent to the client.

After recompiling and adding the new Servlet to the `web.xml` file, start Tomcat and browse to `http://localhost:8080/HelloWorld/helloResponsev2`. As above, you'll initially get an XML document with the error responses because you haven't specified a country argument. To see the full, unformatted XML, you can view the source by right-clicking on the page and selecting `"View Page Source"` in Firefox. It should look similar to the following:

```
<?xml version="1.0" encoding="UTF-8"?>
<response>
  <sender>Unknown Sender!</sender>
  <message>Unknown Message!</message>
</response>
```

When you specify a country argument you will get the hello world message and sender for that country. For example, when you enter `http://localhost:8080/HelloWorld/helloResponsev2?country=Spain`, you should get the following result:

```
<?xml version="1.0" encoding="UTF-8"?>
<response>
  <sender>Ted</sender>
  <message>Hola Mundo!</message>
</response>
```

If everything works as specified above, you've successfully finished your new Java Servlet! Now you're ready to enhance the client piece of the Web application to use the new XML-formatted response.

Enhancing the Client Application

Now that you've written your new server-side components that format a response as XML, you need to fix up the HelloWorld HTML file to make use of this formatted response. First, let's look at the problem with the current implementation of `HelloWorldv5.html`. To see the issue, point your browser to the current `HelloWorldv5.html` that uses your new server-side component, select Spain from the list, and take a look at the results. It should look similar to what is shown in Figure 4-6.

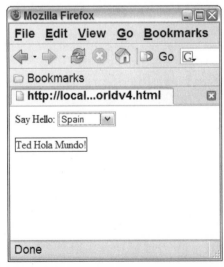

Figure 4-6

Notice that the contents of both the sender and message elements are displayed inside the border around the messageLabel label. This is due to a limitation in our implementation of the callback. In the original version, we set the contents of the label to the value of the request's responseText property (Listing 4-3, line 18) as follows:

```
messageL.innerHTML = xmlRequest.responseText
```

This is probably a good time to get into some detail about the response properties of the XMLHttpRequest. You can use two properties to get the server response to a request: responseText and responseXML. The property that you use depends on the format of the expected response. If you know you're dealing with an XML response (as you are when you make a request to the PHP or Servlet component), you should use the responseXML property. This property returns the response encoded as a Document object, which you can manipulate like any other document. This is handy because you can immediately call DOM methods such as getElementById on the object, but it will return null, or an empty document, if you're response is not valid XML.

Use the alternative, the responseText property, when you're dealing with a non-XML response. Of course, if you can't depend on the format of the response for some reason, you can always look at the document header to determine the type of response. Recall that you set it as text/xml in your server component implementation.

Because you're now working with an XML document, you can modify your callback in HelloWorldv6 .html to work with the response as a Document object. You can then easily replace the contents of the label with the contents of the message element. Here is the new implementation:

```
1. var responseDoc = xmlRequest.responseXML;
2. var messageElt = responseDoc.getElementsByTagName("message")[0];
3. var messageTxt = messageElt.childNodes[0].nodeValue;
4. messageL.innerHTML = messageTxt;
```

Notice the following about this code:

1. You first get the document as responseDoc (line 1).

2. The next step is to get a reference to the message element (line 2). You use the Document method getElementsByTagName to get an array of all message elements. Because you only have one element in your response that has the name "message," you can just get the 0th instance with [0].

3. Now that you have the element, you can get the actual text (line 3). Remember from the DOM discussion in Chapter 2 that you need to do a bit of work to get the CDATA of an element. Specifically, you need to get the nodeValue of the first childNode.

4. Now you can finally replace the contents of the label (line 4).

5. After making the modifications, reload HelloWorldv6.html and notice that the sender is missing from the page. The page once again looks like what is displayed in Figure 4-5.

This may seem like a lot of work with little benefit, but consider the possibilities. Your response can now have several distinct parts encoded in an XML document. On the client side, you can use the DOM to analyze the response, and quickly navigate to relevant portions of the response. The next enhancement shows how easy it is to retrieve the sender portion of the response and display it in a second label. Listing 4-9 shows the final version of HelloWorldv6.html, which creates a new label, senderLabel, to hold the sender details.

Listing 4-9: The final version, HelloWorldv6.html

```
1.   <html>
2.    <head>
3.     <script type="text/javascript">
4.      var xmlRequest = new XMLHttpRequest();
5.
6.      function handleCountryChange() {
7.       var countryValue = document.getElementById("country").value;
8.       var uri = "helloResponsev2?country=" + countryValue;
9.       xmlRequest.open("GET", uri, true);
10.      xmlRequest.onreadystatechange = helloCallback;
11.      xmlRequest.send(null);
12.      }
13.
14.     function helloCallback() {
15.      if (xmlRequest.readyState == 4) {
16.       var messageL = document.getElementById("messageLabel")
17.       var senderL = document.getElementById("senderLabel")
18.       if (xmlRequest.status == 200) {
19.        var responseDoc = xmlRequest.responseXML;
20.
21.        var messageElt = responseDoc.getElementsByTagName("message")[0];
22.        var messageTxt = messageElt.childNodes[0].nodeValue;
23.        messageL.innerHTML = messageTxt;
24.
25.        var senderElt = responseDoc.getElementsByTagName("sender")[0];
26.        var senderTxt = senderElt.childNodes[0].nodeValue + " says ";
27.        senderL.innerHTML = senderTxt;
28.       } else {
29.        messageL.innerHTML = "Page Not Found"
30.       }
31.      }
32.     }
33.    </script>
34.   </head>
35.   <body>
36.    <form id="helloForm"><LABEL>Say Hello: </label>
37.     <select id="country" onkeyup="handleCountryChange()"
38.         onchange="handleCountryChange()">
39.      <option>France</option>
40.      <option>Germany</option>
41.      <option>Spain</option>
42.      <option>USA</option>
43.     </select>
44.    </form>
45.    <p>
46.     <label id="senderLabel"></label>
47.     <label id="messageLabel" style="border: thin solid"></label>
48.   </body>
49.   </html>
```

Notice that this uses the Java Servlet for the URI (line 8). If you're working with PHP, you need to make sure that the URI references the PHP page:

1. The first change is the addition of the new label before the `messageLabel` label (line 46). This gives you a new location on the page to which you can add the sender details.

2. Add a lookup of the sender label (line 17).

3. Finally, update the sender label based on the server's response (lines 25–27).

After making the preceding modifications, reload `HelloWorldv6.html`. You will get an updated Web application that displays both the sender and message portions of the response, in different labels, each with different styles. See Figure 4-7 for an example of the final Hello World Web application after the selection of the France option. Note that the sender label consists of the text "Dana says" and has no border, while the message label is surrounded by the thin black border.

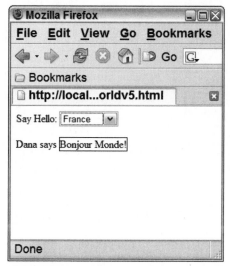

Figure 4-7

Summary

You've finally completed your first Rich Internet Application! This example has walked you through the way AJAX enables you to make Web pages much more interactive through asynchronous requests. It's remarkable how such simple concepts of asynchronous calls and the document object model (DOM) can have such a dramatic effect on the future of Web applications. These simple concepts can be (and have been) used to make the highly interactive and complex Web applications discussed in the previous chapters, and more are being developed every day. Though this example was quite simple, it should lay a foundation that will be built on throughout the remainder of the book in discussing more interactive and complex RIAs. The next chapter gets you started by providing a more realistic example. You'll apply AJAX to a requirement common in many Web applications: specification of user login information.

Part II

RIAs Explored

5

Debugging the Client Side

As soon as we started programming, we found to our surprise that it wasn't as easy to get programs right as we had thought. Debugging had to be discovered. I can remember the exact instant when I realized that a large part of my life from then on was going to be spent in finding mistakes in my own programs.

— Maurice Wilkes, 1949

Now that you have read Chapter 4 and developed your first AJAX application, you are probably rearing to get started and develop the next Gmail, but hold on to your horses — we've still got a ways to go. This chapter introduces some of the tools you will find invaluable when something goes awry — and you can trust that things *will* go awry! Whether it is a misapplied cascading style or an incorrectly inserted DOM element, tools such as JavaScript debuggers, browser consoles, and DOM Inspectors help you determine where the problem is, what the problem is, and sometimes even how to fix it.

Debugging has traditionally been one of the great difficulties of Web development. Whereas desktop application programmers have had a myriad of debugging tools and environments from which to choose, until recently Web developers had few offerings in this department, leaving Web debugging a mysterious and difficult topic. To make matters worse, RIA programming is also an inherently distributed undertaking, making debugging more complex. Often, you can't separate the execution of a RIA page from the execution of the backend server code and the asynchronous transmissions between them.

Today's RIA developers have a definite one-up on their predecessors of even just a few years ago. As JavaScript-based development has grown in popularity, the void that once existed in the area of RIA developer tools has begun to fill, and today these tools are beginning to approach their desktop counterparts in functionality. This chapter introduces two areas — debugging tools and logging — which together are absolutely essential for any sizable RIA project to succeed smoothly.

Debugging Tools

Debugging tools exist to answer two questions:

❑   What just went wrong?

❑   What is going on?

And usually in that order. In an environment as complex as Web development, divining the source of an error can often be a guessing game. Was the problem the result of malformed XHTML? Of misapplied CSS styles? Perhaps a JavaScript bug? The tools and techniques presented here make the process of identifying a problem and then determining its cause easy. Making the problem easy to fix, of course, is up to The Fates.

Most of the popular debugging tools are produced by the Mozilla Foundation, a nonprofit organization responsible for maintaining the well-known Mozilla, Firefox, and Thunderbird programs, among others. The Mozilla suite of debugging tools — Firefox, DOM Inspector, JavaScript console, and Venkman — are essential elements of all RIA designer's toolkits. This chapter also introduces FireBug, an amazingly useful Firefox plug-in by Joe Hewitt that integrates directly into the browser window to provide additional debugging functionality.

Firefox

Before this chapter continues any further, mull over for a moment this well-accepted bit of wisdom:

> *Always develop using Firefox first, and then adjust your code appropriately to work with other browsers.*

Let's get the issue of browser holy wars behind us. They exist. This maxim has nothing to do with them. The diversity of browsers on the market is beneficial to all, and each browser certainly excels in features that are all its own.

One of the features in which Firefox excels is standards compliance, which makes it an excellent risk reducer from a project management point of view. Firefox is about as correct an implementation of the W3C standards as you are going to be able to find. This means that if you program according to the XHTML, CSS, and JavaScript specifications, Firefox is as good a browser as any to check your work. Firefox cannot be guaranteed to always get it right, but if something looks odd, there's a good chance you have an error somewhere in your code.

Developing with strict adherence to the W3C standards will nearly always leave you with a RIA that only works in a small minority of browsers. To be more explicit, your RIA will probably not work perfectly as planned in Internet Explorer. Internet Explorer's implementation of the W3C specifications is a bit lackluster in places, causing it to have some nonstandard quirks and bugs that prevent it from interpreting XHTML and CSS as it should in all circumstances. CSS styles sometimes are not applied correctly, and some JavaScript commands do not operate as advertised — both requiring special fixes so that this segment of your audience can view the RIA page you intended. Though IE has long been the cause of Rube Goldbergeqsue CSS workarounds, it appears that Microsoft has listened and responded to its customers. Toward the end of 2006, Microsoft released Internet Explorer 7, which, while still having the occasional issue, is giant strides ahead of its predecessors in W3C compliance.

For any RIA to achieve a large audience, it must function properly within all of the major browsers on the market, and because Internet Explorer is the most frequently used browser on the Internet, it, and all of its quirks, simply cannot be ignored. For the most part, the display bugs of Internet Explorer are well documented on the Internet, and a quick search turns up a wealth of examples and workarounds. From a software architect's point of view, it is always easier and safer to write code based on the standard first and add on any required platform-specific code that breaks the rules as a later option. It is a bit like learning to speak a foreign language politely first before delving into the regional dialects and slang. In the near future, the number of workarounds required should drop dramatically. Internet Explorer 7 was released as a "critical update" to Windows, which means that it should not be long before a majority of Web users are using this new, much improved version.

A second feature in which Firefox excels is its plug-in architecture. Other browsers have similar plug-in capabilities, but the breadth of development aids that have been created as Firefox plug-ins is too rich to turn away from. Some of these tools are provided by the Mozilla Foundation, but many are created by individuals and simply hosted on Mozilla's plug-in site. All of these tools transform Firefox from an excellent standards-based browser into a full development and debugging platform in its own right.

The Mozilla DOM Inspector

Because of the precision with which you must manipulate the DOM tree to provide a RIA interface, the odds are good that you, the RIA developer, will nearly always write XHTML and CSS by hand, rather than use one of the various WYSIWYG editors available on the market (which are splendid but often do not provide the level of control over the DOM tree necessary for RIA development). As these files grow, maintaining a mental image of the DOM tree and of the cascade of CSS styles applied to each DOM element can become increasingly difficult; the document structure is simply too complex to hold in memory at one time. Introduce AJAX and dynamic DOM manipulation to the mix, and keeping track of the DOM tree while debugging becomes an impossible task.

The Mozilla DOM Inspector is one utility included in the Mozilla browser that relieves developers of the need to visualize their Web documents by opening up the raw source code in an editor. The DOM Inspector takes the DOM tree of whatever Web page is loaded into the browser and loads it into a GUI Widget that everyone is familiar with — the Tree Widget. This tree view permits the user to expand, collapse, explore, and modify the DOM tree of any Web page that can be viewed through the browser. Figure 5-1 shows a screenshot of the DOM Inspector's interface.

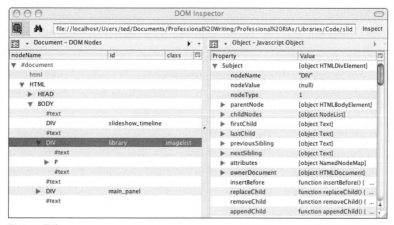

Figure 5-1

The left pane of the DOM Inspector provides a hierarchical tree interface to the elements of the DOM tree, and the right pane displays all of the available properties for the element selected in the left pane. Options also permit you to browse the CSS styles applied to the Web page and any JavaScript objects in memory. Debugging aside, the DOM Inspector is useful just as a JavaScript reference. To see what properties and methods are available on the JavaScript Document object, for example, simply switch to the JavaScript Object view and then select the #document node in the tree browser on the left pane. The Inspector's right pane will fill with the available methods and objects available for the Document type. To see the same reference for an Element object, simply select an element from the tree view at left.

The DOM Inspector, like many of the tools by the Mozilla Foundation, is included with the Mozilla Web browser by default, but you may have to go out of your way to select it as an install option for Firefox, depending on the platform and version of Firefox.

The JavaScript Console

Firefox's JavaScript console is the third tool in the Mozilla quartet of RIA development tools. Java or C# programmers are used to descriptive stack dumps when an error is encountered in a program. Developers new to JavaScript will be surprised to find that a JavaScript error simply causes the script execution to halt, sometimes without any apparent notification that something has gone wrong. This state of affairs can leave developers scratching their heads trying to decide what has gone wrong, and, more important, where something has gone wrong.

The JavaScript console provides a running list of all errors that Mozilla's JavaScript engine has encountered while processing the JavaScript attached to a Web page. This output comes in three levels of severity: errors, warnings, and messages:

❑   **Errors** — These are the result of either malformed JavaScript code or code that attempts to perform an action that is not possible.

❑   **Warnings** — These are usually situations in which the code encountered will work, but the interpreter suspects that the programmer might have been using a code feature in a nonrecommended way.

❑   **Messages** — Purely informational, low-priority notifications of some characteristic of the environment or state of the code. Developers often trigger output of this priority to preemptively debug their programs before anything goes wrong.

Generally, the JavaScript console will contain mostly errors or nothing at all. If something happens unexpectedly or goes wrong while testing a RIA component within Firefox, the JavaScript console should be the first place to investigate. As shown in Figure 5-2, it provides a complete time line of all the errors it encounters, complete with the source file, the line number, and an easy to understand description of what went wrong. Clicking the link in the error message opens a new window to the problematic file, with the offending line highlighted.

Venkman

Sometimes you cannot easily match a RIA error with the particular line in JavaScript that caused it. Maybe the error shown in the console is an attempt to access an uninitialized variable that should have been set at one of a handful of points earlier in the program. Or perhaps the JavaScript console shows no error at all, but from the output on the page, it's clear that a logic error exists somewhere in the code. For these particularly elusive errors, stepping through your code line by line is often the only way to find the source of the problem. In these cases, a tool called Venkman is of great help.

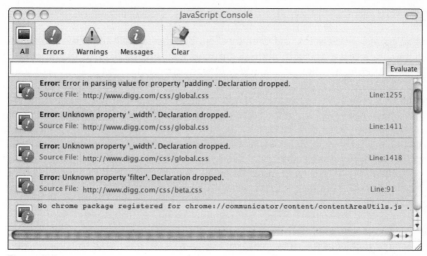

Figure 5-2

Venkman is a full-blown JavaScript debugging environment that comes in a number of different packages for Mozilla-based browsers (the authors of this book are using it as a Firefox plug-in). Venkman offers all of the capabilities a Java or C++ developer would expect in a debugger: breakpoints, code stepping, a view of the call stack, and variable monitoring, to name a few. An interactive JavaScript console also provides the developer access to the current in-memory objects. Using Venkman, it's easy to slowly step through the execution of your RIA line by line while monitoring its variables to identify where a problem's source is. Figure 5-3 shows Venkman just after starting up.

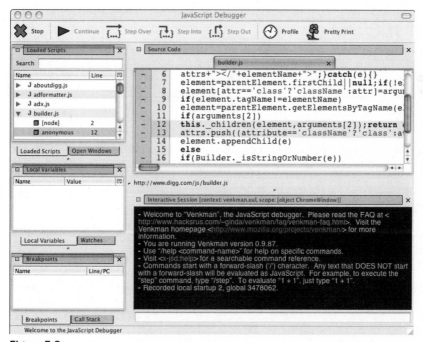

Figure 5-3

FireBug

FireBug is an extension to Firefox that combines many of the capabilities of the Mozilla developer tools, and more, into one panel at the bottom of the browser window. While it is still under development, the value added by FireBug is well worth the occasional bug.

FireBug contains advanced features such as a JavaScript debugger, but one of its most useful features is the way in which it enables users to interactively inspect DOM elements from within the Web page. Using the Inspector, the user selects the type of information to inspect (source, style, layout, etc.) and then hovers the mouse over an item of interest on the page. A blue box follows the mouse arrow, surrounding and highlighting whichever DOM element FireBug is currently displaying information for. This very intuitive way of retrieving information about an element makes it both quick and easy to find out what settings an element has, which is very useful in debugging cascaded CSS styles that seem to be affecting an element in the wrong way.

Figure 5-4 shows an action shot of FireBug in Layout Inspector mode in the process of inspecting CSS styles on a RIA page. Notice the rectangle stretching across the top of the page below the logo — this is blue on a Web page. This rectangle follows the mouse pointer, highlighting various DOM elements, as the FireBug user searches for an element to inspect. Clicking in this rectangle (after triggering it with the Inspect button at the bottom of the page) causes FireBug to load the CSS properties of the highlighted element in the view below.

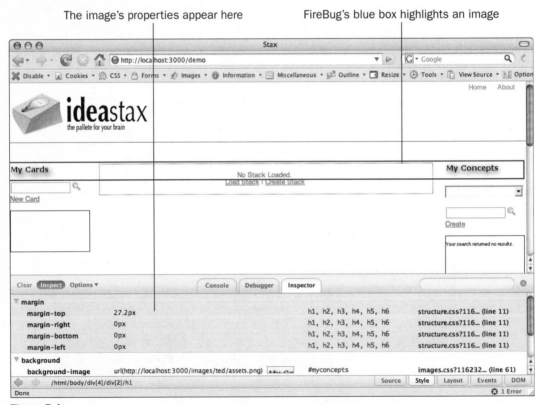

Figure 5-4

Learn Layout Tricks Like the Pros Using FireBug

Picasso once said that good artists borrow, but great artists steal. Although it's every Web developer's responsibility to respect another designer's property, you can still learn a great deal about Web development by examining how admired Web sites are engineered. FireBug's easy-to-use inspector superbly answers the question "How did they do *that?!*" for all those Web pages that seem to pull off feats of layout magic.

Luckily for you (and perhaps unluckily for big corporations), all of the client-side code in a RIA is interpreted, rather than compiled, which means that it is visible for all to see. Some RIA developers, such as Google (look at the Gmail source as an example), guard their secrets closely and go to great lengths to prevent others from understanding the XHTML, CSS, and JavaScript code that comprises their RIA pages. Many companies run their JavaScript code through obfuscators to render them completely incomprehensible to the human eye.

While FireBug cannot make obfuscated JavaScript any easier to read, it can provide an excellent way to navigate and examine the XHTML and CSS driving a page. With its intuitive interface, it is easy to discover the layout tricks of the pros. Just hover your mouse over an element and watch FireBug's inspector pick apart the various DOM element properties and CSS class hierarchies that control how a page appears.

In addition to the novel user interface FireBug provides, FireBug also automatically logs all AJAX requests between the Web browser and remote servers. To inspect the request object that was sent or the response as it came back, the developer need only switch to FireBug's console view and filter the console for AJAX communications.

The console view in FireBug provides the same functionality as Firefox's JavaScript console, except it can also serve as a general-purpose logging system for developers. In the next part of this chapter, you learn how to implement some simple logging capabilities throughout your RIA so that helpful debugging messages are recorded for reviewing. More advanced logging systems can send logging messages directly to the FireBug console.

Markup Validation

A final tool that is too useful not to mention here is the W3C's validation service. Have you ever seen at the bottom of a Web page a small icon that says "This Page is Valid XHTML 1.0 Strict"? Sometimes instead of text, the icon in Figure 5-5 is shown.

Figure 5-5

This message or icon informs users that the structure of the document adheres exactly to the rules outlined by the W3C specifications. At various intervals during the development of your RIA, it's a good idea to run your code through the W3C's validation service, available at validator.w3.org to see if what you've produced so far conforms to the XHTML 1.0 specification. If this is something you have never done before, you may be surprised to find out just how strict the specification actually is! Uppercase XHTML tag names, such as `<P>` or `<HTML>`, for example, are technically not allowed. The W3C also provides validation services for CSS and RSS files.

Validating your RIA serves both to keep your code in good shape so that it is easy to modify later as well as to let your users know that the site they are visiting was crafted with fine attention to detail. If you are experiencing a mysterious problem with your RIA and the tools described earlier have not been of any help, validation can sometimes provide a last-resort sanity check that may uncover XHTML-related errors.

But Wait, There's More!

These five tools — Firefox, the DOM Inspector, the JavaScript console, Venkman, and FireBug — provide you with a powerful start in the fight against software bugs, but there is a whole world of plug-ins and extensions available if these do not meet your needs. The best place to start is on the Mozilla Add-ons page at `addons.mozilla.org`. Here you can find a catalogue of extensions and plug-ins for all of the Mozilla products.

Logging

Picture yourself for a moment as a desktop application programmer. This is where most RIA developers started out, in fact, so the image is not far-fetched. When something goes wrong in a desktop development environment, the first action most programmers take is to insert console output immediately preceding the line on which the error behavior occurred. Though computer science professors are forced by their field to grumble at this primitive type of debugging, the usefulness of printing statements to a console is undeniable.

Logging is the more sophisticated variant of console output; and while console output is generally a temporary investigative tool, logging frameworks are often permanently built into the code of a production system. Logging is a virtually necessary and ubiquitous component of any enterprise application, in fact. A logger, such as Log4j if you come from the Java world, is an object accessible from any part of a computer program that accepts messages about what is going on. These messages are usually flagged as being one of various predefined levels of severity. The logger accepts these messages and either saves them to a file for later viewing or makes them immediately available to a log viewer or output console. In a production system, the logger is generally disabled completely, but if something begins to go awry, a developer need only enable the logger to begin viewing the pre-placed notifications throughout the code.

Proponents of logging, and that is nearly everyone, argue that logging should always be integrated into an application from the very beginning to minimize developmental risk. At first glance, however, it appears that Web developers are left stranded when it comes to console output and logging. This is quickly becoming not the case for three reasons:

❑ **Adding simple logging support to a Web application that amounts to console output involves little effort at all.** A logging console element is simple to append to the very end of a page template in such a way that removing it is a quick and fail-safe operation. This chapter demonstrates how to add such a capability.

❑ **Many browsers are beginning to add logging console support into their infrastructure.** The Opera browser and Apple's Safari already have console support, and FireBug adds this capability to Firefox. The upcoming version of Internet Explorer is also reported to include a logging console. This support builds the capability to capture debugging messages directly into the platform and relieves the need to build extra code to support logging.

❑ **Many JavaScript libraries provide built-in logging features similar to the logging packages of other development environment.** These loggers, such as the MochiKit logger, even go so far as to automatically detect whether a browser console is available and they either send output to the console or spawn a new browser window to serve as a console, depending on the features of the particular browser in use. Figure 5-6 shows the results of the MochiKit logger sending information to FireBug's console. Chapter 10 demonstrates library-based logging further, with examples from the Dojo Toolkit.

Figure 5-6

Taking advantage of native console support, when it's available, gives developers the best of both worlds. It enables developers to put extensive logging in their RIAs during development time while still having the log browser and code as a separate entity from the actual RIA page, as shown in Figure 5-6. If you do not have native console support available, or if you do not have access to a ready-made JavaScript logger, the following sections walk you through developing your own logging system.

The Alert Function

When you truly need a quick investigation—say, to verify what a particular variable's value is at a certain point in the code—the `alert(String)` function is a handy tool. Simply pass it a string, which could be composed in-line, as follows:

```
alert("The value of i is: " + i);
```

The browser's JavaScript engine executes this line as soon as it is reached in the program flow and triggers a pop-up window to appear, as shown in Figure 5-7.

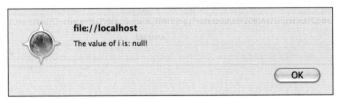

file://localhost
The value of i is: null!

OK

Figure 5-7

Although the `alert` function is a handy tool for quickly examining the value of a variable, be careful not to overuse this function because this can lead to more confusion than had you never used it at all. Too many `alert` commands placed all over a Web page will bombard the user with so many dialog boxes that it hinders testing. Because dialog boxes both block page execution and execute in a one-at-a-time fashion, they are not an effective strategy to debug problems that require the reporting of more than a handful of variables. Often developers need to not only view several lines of debugging output at once, but also continue using the page while they debug. These desires require a more sophisticated method of debugging output.

A Very Simple Logger

If you find yourself without a library-based logging package or a browser console, you can avoid having to use the `alert` function by creating your own in-page logger in a `div` element at the bottom of the page. Listing 5-1 contains a relatively empty XHTML document with the shell of an in-page logging console at the bottom. As your code outputs log messages, they will be appended as items in the ordered list with ID `debugging_messages`.

Listing 5-1: A simple logging region

XHTML

```
<html>
    <head><title>A Simple Logger</title></head>
    <body>
        <p>Insert Web Page Here!</p>
        <p>And then at the very bottom, put your debugging panel:</p>
        <div id="debugging_output"
                style="width: 100%; border: 1px solid black;">
          <h1>Debugging Output</h1>
          <ol id="debugging_messages">
          </ol>
        </div>
    </body>
</html>
```

Listing 5-2 contains the code necessary to add a message to the log. The `log` function takes in a string of text as the `message` variable and appends this text to the ordered list. First the function retrieves a reference to the `debugging_messages` ordered list. Then it creates the DOM elements necessary to enclose the contents of the `message` variable within a list item. Finally, it appends the new list item to the message list before exiting.

Listing 5-2: A simple log function

JavaScript

```javascript
function log(message) {
  message_list = document.getElementById("debugging_messages");
  log_message = document.createTextNode(message);
  log_list_item = document.createElement('li');
  log_list_item.appendChild(log_message);
  message_list.appendChild(log_list_item);
}
```

You can place the code in Listing 5-2 in a small JavaScript file and include it in pages during development time. Once included, the `log` function is accessible from any other JavaScript code within. Just call the `log` function in the same way you would have called `alert`, and your messages will be appended at the bottom of the page:

```javascript
log("The user's first name is: " + first_name);
```

This `log` function looks like the `alert` function but has significant advantages over it. Messages sent to the log occur without interrupting the user, they do not block the program flow, and they are stored side by side in the `debugging_messages` ordered list so that all of them can be examined at once.

Listing 5-3 shows a very simple page that makes use of the preceding logging code. In this example, the `log` function is assumed to be in the file `log.js`, which is included in the `head` element. The example sets up a text box and Submit button with a log `div` element below. The user can append text to the log via the textbox, and a few additional page events trigger log messages. A JavaScript function called `sendMessage` has also been defined inline to retrieve the text from the textbox, pass it to the `log` function, and then clear the textbox contents.

Listing 5-3: A sample page with logging

XHTML, JavaScript

```html
<html>
<head>
  <title>A Simple Logging Example</title>
  <script type="text/javascript" src="log.js">
</head>
  <body id="console" onLoad="log('The body has been loaded!')">
    <div id="main">
      <script type="text/javascript" charset="utf-8">
        function sendMessage() {
          textbox = document.getElementById('log_message');
          message = textbox.value;
          textbox.value = "";
          log(message);
        }
```

(continued)

Listing 5-3: *(continued)*

```
        </script>

        <input type="text" name="log_message" value="" id="log_message" />
        <input type="submit" name="submit_button"
           value="Append Message!"
           id="submit_button"
           onClick="log('Submit Clicked'); sendMessage();"/>
      </div>

      <div id="debugging_output"
        style="width: 100%; border: 1px solid black;">
        <h1>Debugging Output</h1>
        <ol id="debugging_messages">
        </ol>
      </div>
    </body>
  </html>
```

Two events are logged by the page in Listing 5-3 — the `onLoad` event on the `body` element and the `onClick` event on the form's Submit button. Figure 5-8 shows a sample execution of the preceding code — a simpler logger display. Logging messages one and two in Figure 5-8 were event driven, while the third message was added via the textbox above.

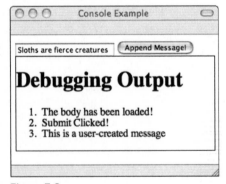

Figure 5-8

A Homework Assignment

You now have a (very simple) logging system. To make this logging system even easier to add and remove at production time, a developer could create code that allows the logging `div` to be added to the Web page dynamically. Such a feature would permit the developer to write RIA pages without worrying about the presence of a logger at all until it is necessary. When the logger is needed, a simple function call could be made to enable and attach the logger to the page. This feature is a great consolidation of the technologies presented thus far, and as such is left as an exercise for the reader to experiment with the skills learned in Part I of this book.

Here are some hints to get you started:

1. Extract the logging `div` and decide how to best load it from JavaScript (there are many ways you could do this).

2. Create a second function in `log.js` alongside `log` that either fetches this logging `div` from a separate document (via AJAX) or constructs it within JavaScript. Once you have this functionality, you are only a few lines of code away.

3. Write a third function, perhaps called `load_logger`, that takes the logger `div` and appends it as the very last child of the `body` DOM Element.

4. Finally, test your logger out with the following `body` tag:

```
<body onLoad="load_logger();">
```

If you need more help, return to Chapter 2 for DOM manipulation and a JavaScript primer, or Chapter 5 for AJAX and more in-depth examples of the technologies required. The solution and detailed documentation to this project are also available from the book's Web site.

Summary

In this chapter, you were introduced to some of the debugging tools available for RIA developers, and you learned some simple logging techniques that you can incorporate into your development methods. Future chapters expand on logging practices when JavaScript libraries are introduced. These library-based loggers offer advantages over the simple logger presented here.

Debugging tools and good logging practices are essential to the success of any sizable development project, and RIAs are no different. The tools provided in this chapter are valuable evidence gatherers when something unexpectedly goes wrong and the source of the problem is not clear. While debugging is often a reactive process, logging is a proactive step that you can take to make any problems that arise as easy to fix as possible.

This chapter also finishes Part I, in which you were given an introduction to the fundamental concepts and philosophies driving modern Web development as well as a brief introduction to the languages and technologies that will carry you through the rest of this book. Part II drills down further into ways that RIAs are actually implemented in the real world. It introduces Model-View-Controller-based development and several frameworks that make RIA development easy.

6

The Model-View-Controller (MVC) Pattern

There's a better way to do it. Find it.

— Thomas Edison

People think that computer science is the art of geniuses, but the actual reality is the opposite, just many people doing things that build on each other, like a wall of mini stones.

— Donald Knuth

This basic tenet ascribed to Edison, and the similar observation from Knuth, has been proven many times throughout the history of computer science. As with all areas of science, and engineering, no discovery is made without building upon the advancements made before it. In this chapter you learn the details of an architectural pattern that has evolved since the late 1970s and has been adapted to a variety of software applications. You learn what the Model-View-Controller architectural pattern is, how it was developed, and how is has been adapted to Web applications. You also learn how the Model-View-Controller pattern is used in three different languages — Java, Ruby, and Python — to develop Web applications.

The Model-View-Controller

This section delves into the details of the MVC architectural pattern and introduces you to MVC through a short exploration of its history. It then describes the details of the pattern, and how it has been adapted to Web applications. In addition, you will see some of the advantages and disadvantages of the pattern, in its various flavors.

When you understand the MVC concepts, you can easily describe a Web application (or really any application) that incorporates the approach without having to refer to it in the terms of any single programming language or framework. This ability is especially important in the Web development world, because the number and capabilities of languages and frameworks on both the client and server side is so rapidly evolving.

Later in the book, the examples are discussed explicitly in terms of the model, view, and controller. This is intended to enable you to follow along with each example, even when you're not particularly familiar with the framework of the language being used. If you're feeling really adventurous, you can use the distinction between model, view, and controller to implement any of the examples in the language, and framework, of your choice.

Origins: The Thing-Model-View-Editor

Like many great ideas in the computer industry, it all started in California, in the late 1970s at Xerox Parc. In May of 1979, Trygve Reenskaug, a Norwegian computer scientist at Xerox Parc and a visiting scientist in the Smalltalk group, drafted a technical note entitled "THING-MODEL-VIEW-EDITOR: an Example from a planning system" [sic]. This note outlined the underlying concept that makes up much of what the Model-View-Controller pattern is today. It outlined the concept of a *Thing* as real-world entity. A *Model* is defined as a software representation of a Thing. A *View* presents a visual representation of a model. There can be multiple views of a single model. An *Editor* acts as the bridge between a user and the possible views. The Thing would eventually disappear from the specification as it is less relevant to the core concept, while the Editor would later become the controller. This was discussed in a subsequent technical note "Models-Views-Controllers" in December of that year.

The concept was first implemented as a core design principle of Smalltalk, the first object-oriented programming language; and later, it was more formally articulated in Smalltalk in the document "Applications programming in Smalltalk-80(TM): How to use Model-View-Controller (MVC)," by Steve Burbeck. The document described the paradigm to Smalltalk developers, and showed how they could utilize it when developing their own applications within the Smalltalk window system.

The following roles were defined for the main components as implemented in Smalltalk:

❑ **View** — Manages the *output* to the display (graphical or textual). This consists of the logic necessary to create the user interface components and use the model to load data into the components.

❑ **Controller** — Manages keyboard and mouse *inputs* from the user. The control examines and interprets the inputs provided. Based on the inputs, it then forwards commands on to the model, and/or view.

❑ **Model** — Manages domain *data and processing*. This includes establishing a representation for the domain data, and operations that can be performed on the data.

Constrained relationships between each of the objects were also articulated:

❑ The view and controller should to have a direct one-to-one correspondence. Every view should have a reference to a controller, and vice versa.

❑ The relationship between the view and model, and the controller and model, was less direct. A notification protocol should be used whereby a view or controller is registered as being interested in a set of models. When a model changes its internal state, it should notify the set of all of its interested controllers and views. A model should never directly interact with a controller or view.

Since these humble origins as a technical note, architectures and frameworks incorporating aspects of the MVC concept have appeared in a multitude of applications to solve problems that require any nontrivial presentation layer. The toolkits and frameworks that are used to develop the majority of rich-client applications for Windows, Mac, and Linux/Unix platforms incorporate the MVC concept in some way. It has also been found that you can successfully apply variations on the concept to both traditional Web applications and RIAs also. Many common variations of the concept have been defined, and approaches to applying MVC to a variety of problems have been documented in both a language-specific and language-neutral way.

Frank Buschmann, Regine Meunier, Hans Rohnert, Peter Sommerlad, and Michael Stal provide a more general discussion of this in their book Pattern-Oriented Software Architecture, published by John Wiley and Sons. In this book, the concept is articulated as a general architectural pattern and is not directly related to any specific language. It also discusses the pattern independent of a particular application architecture (i.e., rich client, distributed, or Web application).

The Model-View-Controller Pattern in Detail

Since its origins, the concept of the MVC pattern hasn't changed all that much. Its motivation is still to separate these three core aspects of the system from each other, and provide a set of rules that govern the way they interact. The three original main components exist and interact in much the same way as originally outlined. Figure 6-1, which shows the traditional Model-View-Controller pattern, establishes the main components of MVC, and their primary interactions.

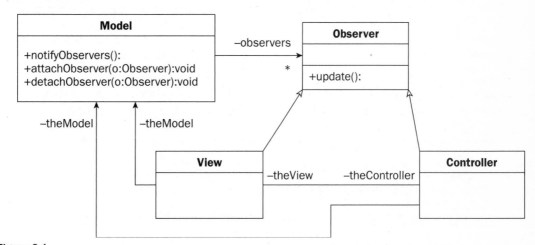

Figure 6-1

Notice that the diagram includes an `Observer` class in addition to the three main components. This class serves as the base for both the `Controller` and `View`, and enables the `Controller` and `View` to observe the state of the `Model`. It also enables the `Model` to notify all interested observers of changes, without knowing if the observer is a `View` or `Model`.

It may be easiest to explore the responsibilities of each component while considering a specific example. Suppose you're developing an application that allows a person to track their health history (e.g., height, weight, blood pressure). The application provides several functions that users can perform to view and record their health history. If you applied the MVC pattern to this type of application, you would develop three distinct and separate components. You might have a model object that represents a user's health details at a given point in time. You might also have one or more views that enable the user to view and edit their health information at a given time, and another that shows the history over time. Finally, you might have one or more controllers for the health information. See Figure 6-2 for the high-level class diagram of the basic application.

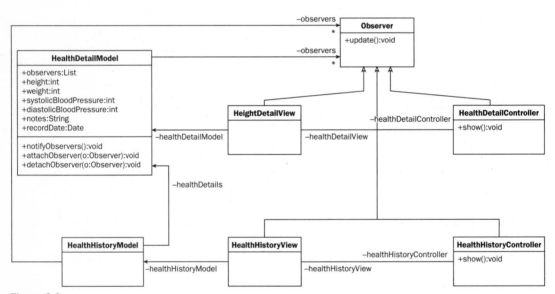

Figure 6-2

When you closely examine Figure 6-2, which shows a class diagram of the health and history application, you can outline the following responsibilities for the different components represented in the model:

The following is a list of view responsibilities (e.g., `HealthDetailView` or `HealthHistoryView`):

❑ Maintain a direct reference to a single model.

❑ Maintain a direct reference to a single controller.

❑ Attach itself as an observer of the model, on creation and association with a model (i.e., `attachObserver`).

❏ Use data defined in the model to create a visual depiction of the model.

❏ Update, or otherwise modify, the visual depiction based on requests from the controller (these may indirectly be user requests).

❏ Update, or otherwise modify, the visual depiction to reflect the changes, based on model notifications.

The following is a list of controller responsibilities (e.g., `HealthDetailController` or `HealthHistoryController`):

❏ Maintain a direct reference to a single model.

❏ Maintain a direct reference to a single view.

❏ Attach itself as an observer of the model, on creation and association with a model (i.e., `attachObserver`).

❏ Parse user inputs.

❏ Invoke functions that accomplish some business process on the model, or update the state of the model based on inputs.

❏ Invoke functions in the view that effect the presentation of the model based on inputs.

The following is a list of model responsibilities (e.g., `HealthDetailModel` or `HealthHistoryModel`):

❏ Maintain no direct reference to any specific model or controller.

❏ Maintain a set of multiple observers.

❏ Define data structures necessary to represent a real-world concept.

❏ Define the logic necessary to perform business operations with real-world objects.

❏ Notify all observers when its state has been updated.

Of course, many variations on the MVC pattern have been developed for different applications (e.g., Web applications or rich-client GUI frameworks). These responsibilities are not incorporated exactly as described above in every variation of the MVC pattern, and may be used to lesser or greater extent depending on the needs addressed in the variation. You see an example of this in the variation of the pattern frequently used when it is applied to Web applications. See the sidebar "The Controversial Controller" for more detail on a debate surrounding two particular flavors of the pattern.

MVC in Web Applications

The MVC pattern just described is quite useful when developing a rich-client application, but when you are adapting the MVC pattern to Web applications there's generally one significant design difference. In Figures 6-1 and 6-2, the `Controller` and `View` are shown as observers of the `Model`. This means that when the `Model` changes for any reason, all observing `View` and `Controller` objects are notified of the change. This is not a practical approach given the disconnected nature of Web applications. Not only does it introduce significant additional complexity, but this type of close synchronization is typically not required of a Web application. Figure 6-3, a variation on the MVC pattern, shows the relationships between the `Model`, `View`, and `Controller` in a typical Web application. Notice that the `Model` is completely independent of the `View` and `Controller` and can't notify any observers when it is updated.

This places an additional responsibility on the `View` and `Controller` to look for changes in the `Model` when necessary. Depending on the requirements of the application developed, you can typically employ one of two approaches to refresh the `View` based on updated `Model` data. One option, which you can frequently use when the `Model` is unlikely to get stale, is to look for an updated `Model` as the user interacts with the page. For example, look for updates when the user moves to a new page in the application, or clicks a button on the page. The other alternative, which you generally use when the `Model` frequently changes, is to periodically look for changes in the `Model` with JavaScript. When using AJAX in the Web application, it is simple to make an asynchronous request to look for an updated `Model` every time a timeout expires.

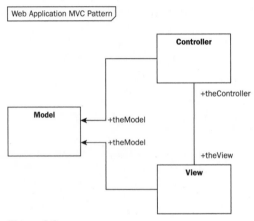

Figure 6-3

MVC Advantages

The advantages to using the MVC pattern are possible due to the separation of the three types of logic:

❑ The views or even the entire the UI can be replaced without rewriting business rules, due to the separation of presentation (view) from domain logic (model).

❑ You can define multiple views for the same model. This is also possible because of the view-model separation.

❑ The view only maintains details about rendering the data. Logic for parsing users' requests or selecting the next view is maintained separately. The separation of presentation (view) from control logic (controller) ensures this.

❑ You can easily use the same view in multiple places in the application flow. This is facilitated by the separation of view and controller.

❑ The view and controller are aware of model changes, but the model is not dependent on the controller or view. This is enabled through the specification of the view and controller as Observers.

MVC Disadvantages

Although the MVC pattern is quite useful in many applications, you have to consider its disadvantages when deciding whether or not to apply it. These include the following:

❑   Additional complexity is introduced into the system. This may be overkill for simple applications.

❑   Changes to the model are difficult to incorporate, as they may require modification to one or more views and controllers. This is due to the dependence of the view and controller on the model.

The Controversial Controller

Since the origins of MVC, there have been many interpretations of the pattern. The concept has been adapted and applied in very different ways to a wide variety of systems and architectures. This has led to a great deal of controversy and debate within the software engineering community as to the real intent of the concept, resulting in two quite distinct interpretations of the pattern.

The primary difference between the two interpretations focuses on the intent and responsibility of the controller and its relationship to the view. In one interpretation, each view has a separate controller, which is responsible for interpreting *only* the inputs relevant to its specific view. This interpretation of the concept most closely parallels the approach originally implemented in Smalltalk. When this approach is applied, the objective system will have a large number of very tiny controllers, each only capable of performing the processing of inputs relevant to a specific view.

The other interpretation, frequently discussed in the Java Enterprise world, establishes a single controller for all views. Generally, this controller (based on the Front Controller pattern) performs some top-level processing and validation, and delegates the processing for each view. Some say that rather than follow the MVC pattern at all, it more closely matches a different architectural pattern altogether (the presentation-abstraction-control pattern). This is discussed in more detail in the following section on MVC implementations in Java.

Although the merits and limitations of each approach are debated, the result in a Web application is usually similar. When you have many controllers, a framework generally uses some form of inheritance to allow any necessary common processing to be performed. Because the real work is typically delegated to another object when using a single controller, the controller doesn't become an unwieldy object of overwhelming complexity.

Regardless of the controversy, as with most aspects of software engineering, each interpretation has trade-offs. You should ultimately select the approach for any single application based on the requirements of the system under development. Note, however, that in the Web application programming world, the different frameworks available may support only one interpretation of the concept. This means that the way that MVC is applied in your Web application may be imposed on you when you select a particular framework.

Other MVC Strengths and Weaknesses

Of course, just as many flavors of the MVC pattern exist, they each have their own strengths and weaknesses, and you need to consider this. For example, consider the implementation of the MVC pattern without an observer, as is done in the common Web application version of the pattern. Without some consideration, this can easily lead to views composed of stale data. On the other hand, without an observer pattern, the complexity is reduced slightly, and there is no requirement to implement a notification method in the view or controller.

Using MVC in Java

MVC is applied in a variety of places in Java—for example, in the core language, as a part of the Swing toolkit. In the Web application programming world, you can implement MVC in a variety of ways. The book *Designing Enterprise Applications with the J2EE Platform, Second Edition* (java.sun.com/ blueprints/guidelines/designing_enterprise_applications_2e/) defines the terms *Model 1* and *Model 2* as two alternate architectures for Web applications using JSP pages.

The more basic architecture is Model 1, which is not considered to be a true application of the MVC pattern because it lacks the concept of the controller. In Model 1, the Web page (i.e., the presentation logic) directly accesses the JavaBeans (i.e., the model). Each Web page includes the logic necessary to select the next view, resulting in a decentralized approach. This architecture is quite simple, but generally isn't appropriate for more complex Web applications.

Conversely, the Model 2 architecture fully incorporates the MVC pattern. The following sections explore this in a bit more detail before examining some MVC frameworks that help reduce the effort required to implement a Java Web application that conforms to this model. Figure 6-4 shows a class diagram of the MVC pattern as implemented in Java's Model 2 architecture. Each of these components is explored in more detail in the following sections.

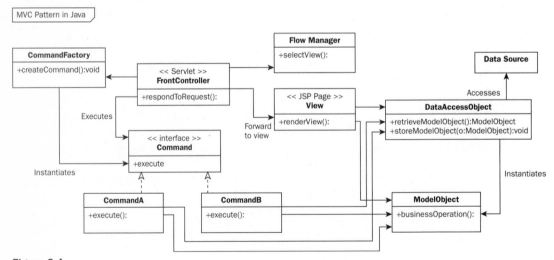

Figure 6-4

The Model 2 Architecture

Before jumping into the roles and their implementation in Java in any detail, it is important to note that you should use three different types of J2EE components to represent the model view and controller. You typically create the views with JSP pages. Because JSP pages are focused on HTML and are presentation driven, they are especially well suited to developing views. The controller logic is most easily encoded as a Servlet. A JSP page is not appropriate for the controller because it is focused on control logic, rather than logic for creating views. You usually define the models as JavaBeans, because this facilitates the incorporation of model data into the views.

The Controller in Model 2

See the sidebar "The Controversial Controller" for a high-level discussion of the responsibility of the controller in Java in comparison to other languages. Note, however, that the controller has a different role in a Java Web application than in architectures that incorporate the more traditional MVC pattern. Rather than have a separate controller for each view, the Java Web application approach uses a single controller that follows the Front Controller pattern.

> As noted earlier in the chapter, the MVC pattern is actually an aggregate pattern, and as such is composed of smaller patterns. For a very thorough examination of design patterns for J2EE applications, see the book Core J2EE Patterns: Best Practices and Design Strategies by Deepak Alur, John Crupi, and Dan Malks (Prentice Hall, 2003). In addition, see the catalog of patterns described at www.corej2eepatterns.com/Patterns2ndEd/index.htm.

The effect of using a single controller is that every view returns to the same controller, and the controller then applies any common logic required (for example, verifies that the user is logged in), handles the request, and finally selects and forwards to the next view. Of course, because every call comes into the same Java Servlet, it is necessary to delegate the majority of the work to other classes. Otherwise, the controller would quickly become unwieldy. The Java approach is to perform the global processing of the incoming request and use the command pattern to delegate any work specific to a particular view to a command object. The command object is then responsible for interacting with the model to perform some business processing. The controller then takes the result of the command and selects the next view, or feeds it into a Flow Manager responsible for selecting the next view for display. See the sequence diagram in Figure 6-5, which shows a front controller execution in Java, for an example interaction.

Note that there are alternative approaches to solving the concerns addressed in Java with the Front Controller, Flow Manager, and Command patterns. Other languages and frameworks (such as Ruby on Rails or TurboGears, described below) address this concern through some type of filtering logic, or through inheritance. Filtering logic allows multiple controllers to be triggered through a single request. You can use inheritance to establish a controller base class that includes logic to perform any common behaviors required. See the discussions of TurboGears and Ruby on Rails later in the chapter for more detail on these approaches.

The View in Model 2

As described earlier, the view is typically implemented as a JSP page in Java. If warranted, the Web application may use some form of a template service. This type of component is based on the Composition pattern, or, more specifically, the Composite View pattern, in J2EE applications. This pattern establishes a service capable of composing a view based upon the multiple independent subviews. The second notable aspect of the view in Java is its incorporation of custom tag libraries to simplify interaction with server-side code.

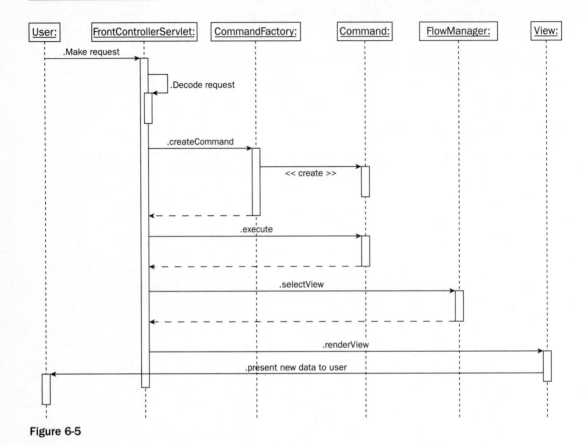

Figure 6-5

The Model in Model 2

The final aspect of the Model 2 architecture is the definition of the model. Three different approaches are commonly used when defining model classes in Java:

❑ If you're developing a full-blown J2EE application with a large client base, you may want to implement your model objects as EJBs. This enables them to run in the application server and make use of the many application server benefits, such as transaction management and work-load distribution.

❑ In other situations, if you're developing a very simple Web application, with very limited model object interactions, then it may be sufficient to define a set of basic model objects directly in the Web tier.

❑ A third approach, based on patterns, also exists for when you require a division between the tiers of your Web application but don't require the overhead of an application server. Depending on the requirements of the system, you can incorporate Data Access Objects (DAOs) that separate the data retrieval logic into a data layer that is distinct from the simple Java Bean style model objects. The sequence diagram in Figure 6-6 shows the interaction between the command and a DAO for data access.

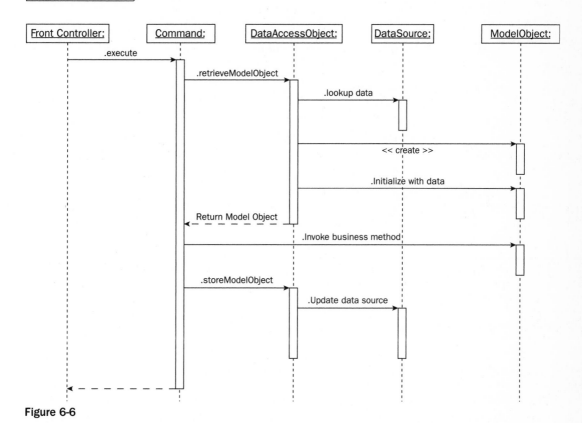

Figure 6-6

The Design of Health History in Java

Consider the example of the Health History application described earlier to gain a better insight into the differences between the Java Web application MVC and the general approach. Figure 6-7 shows a class diagram capturing the design of the example in Java. There are a few things to note here.

The first aspect to note is that the Observable pattern is not implemented, and the controller and view classes do not extend Observer. Also note that, assuming the Model 2 architecture is used, there is only a single controller, FrontControllerServlet, implemented as a Java Servlet that creates a Command with the CommandFactory and delegates all processing to it.

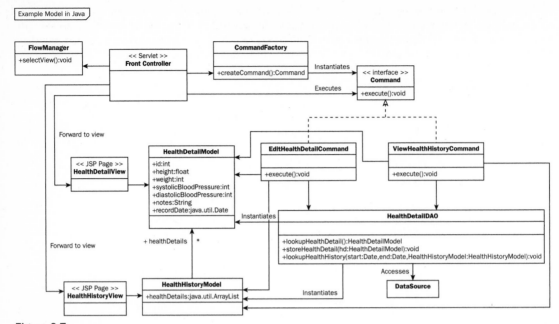

Figure 6-7

There are two command implementations. The `EditHealthDetailCommand` object can be used for viewing and editing a single health detail element, while the `ViewHealthHistoryCommand` object is used to view the history. The command execution when viewing health detail or health history is quite similar even though there are two different commands. The DAO is used to retrieve the appropriate model object, which is added to the HTTP session. Both editing an existing health detail entry and creating a new entry consist of similar processing performed by the `EditHealthDetailCommand` object. It retrieves the detail information from the HTTP request, creates a new `HealthDetailModel` object, and invokes the method `storeHealthDetail` on the `HealthDetailDAO`.

There are separate views for the health detail and health history. In Java, however, these would be JSP pages, and include Java code that retrieves the model object from the HTTP session and calls the various get methods on the model object to retrieve the data for display.

Separate model objects exist as well, and are defined as simple Java Beans. In this design, there is a single DAO that knows how to retrieve `HealthDetailModel` and `HealthHistoryModel` objects from the `DataSource`.

> *A common alternative implementation of the DAO is to have two separate DAOs (one for health detail and another for health history).*

MVC Frameworks for Java

As shown earlier, there are many commonalities when developing a standard Web application that incorporates MVC. This has led to the development of a wealth of frameworks that you can use when developing a Java based Web application. There are a few different categories of frameworks in J2EE, but they most typically focus on a single tier of a Java Web application. Frameworks may address the following:

- **Web tier frameworks (e.g., JavaServer Faces)** — Some may address one aspect of the Web tier, but these typically include some infrastructure for defining Model 2 controller and view components. Infrastructure for defining the view generally includes some form of template service for view composition and a tag library. The infrastructure for the controller usually includes a mechanism for incorporating a Front Controller Servlet, a Flow Manager, and Command objects (aka Actions).

- **Middle tier frameworks (e.g., Spring Framework)** — These frameworks address the business objects maintained on the middle tier, and focus on reducing business object dependency. They usually include some mechanism for assembling and configuring objects at runtime.

- **Integration tier frameworks (e.g, Hibernate)** — These typically introduce a layer of abstraction between a database or another data source, and the middle tier. For example, Hibernate facilitates the translation between data in a relational database and Java objects.

- **Web application frameworks (e.g., trails)** — The introduction of Ruby on Rails, described later in the chapter, established a new paradigm for Web application frameworks that addresses all aspects of Web application development. These frameworks provide mechanisms that attempt to facilitate the development of each tier, from presentation through the data layer.

The incorporation of a framework for any or all tiers can greatly reduce the complexity of a Web application and aid in integration with other commonly required third-party components. Depending on the framework, you can also greatly enhance the versatility of the Web application, and greatly simplify integration with other frameworks. Some of the more commonly used frameworks include the following:

- **Hibernate (**`www.hibernate.org`**)** — This is an integration tier framework that facilitates database independence. It provides mechanisms to automate and aid the development of Java objects from a database, or vice versa, and reduces the complexity required to translate between the database tables and Java objects.

- **The Spring Framework (**`www.springframework.org`**)** — A newer open-source Java application framework that includes an MVC framework. The architectural underpinnings of the framework are discussed in great detail in the book *Expert One-on-One J2EE Design and Development* by Rod Johnson (Wiley, 2002), and the code from the book actually served as the basis for the open-source project. As an all-encompassing framework, it covers all aspects of Java Web applications, but is known primarily for its capabilities on the middle tier. It includes several features that simplify management and assembly of business objects, and easily integrates with a large number of frameworks used for data access, such as Hibernate. It's so general, in fact, that it has a subproject dedicated to providing Spring on rich-client applications.

- **JavaServer Faces (JSF) (**`http://java.sun.com/javaee/javaserverfaces`**)** — Rather than being a framework implementation, like the other frameworks discussed here, this is a Java standard being developed through the Java Community Process. This Web tier specification is focused on the view and controller, and its application to UI development. It includes a lot of support for linking UI components to server-side objects, but lacks the middle tier support provided by the Spring Framework. Of course, you can integrate it with Spring or another framework to provide this support. In addition to being the Java-approved standard, several tools support JSF development, including Sun Java Studio Creator, J2EE 1.4 SDK.

❑ **Jakarta Struts 1** (`struts.apache.org`) — Developed as an Apache project, this is one of the original MVC frameworks developed for Web applications. This is a Web tier framework that's focused even more specifically on providing a controller mechanism. Similar to JSF, it includes no middle tier capabilities, but supports integration with the Spring Framework. It's widely popular, and has a huge community of users. It may, however, fall out of favor somewhat as newer, more all-encompassing Java Web tier frameworks, such as Struts 2 and Shale, are developed and gain maturity.

❑ **Jakarta Struts 2** (`struts.apache.org`) — The next generation of the Struts project, this is the result of a merger of Struts 1 and WebWork, another Web tier framework. Available soon, it is supposed to include better JavaServer Faces support and several AJAX-specific features, including an AJAX theme. Again, this is easily integrated with the Spring Framework for the middle tier.

❑ **Shale Framework** (`shale.apache.org`) — Another Web tier framework that conforms to the JSF specification. This originally started as a subproject of Struts 1, but has since become a top-level Apache project.

❑ **Tapestry** (`tapestry.apache.org/`) — Another approach to a Web tier framework, inspired by Apple WebObjects. This framework looks a bit different from more traditional frameworks, and comes with a slightly higher learning curve. It typically uses HTML with "Tapestry" attributes, rather than JSP pages. It seems to have a growing community of support.

Note that these frameworks exist to aid the development of the Web application, and are not appropriate for all Web applications. When deciding whether or not to use a framework, and selecting the framework to use, you should carefully weigh the advantages and limitations of each. Ultimately, the decision should depend on the needs of the application being developed. For simple projects, it's probably overkill to incorporate a full-blown MVC pattern. Other Web applications may have specific use cases that may make more effective use of alternative design patterns to be included.

Web Application Frameworks

Recently, a lot of work has been done to develop frameworks that are intended to address and ease all aspects of Web application development. MVC is commonly used as the underlying architectural pattern for the frameworks, which can be used to very rapidly produce a full-featured MVC Web application. They do impose several limitations, though, and the utility and applicability of any framework ultimately depends on the requirements of the system being developed. One significant advantage to using a framework is that you're required to write only a minimal amount of code to get up and running from scratch. The architecture of your Web application also benefits because, by using MVC, you follow a commonly used, powerful, and well-vetted pattern. A main disadvantage is that you're generally tied tightly to the framework, and must architect your application to conform to the framework. This may cause difficulty incorporating third-party components or nonstandard libraries. A framework can also make integration with existing databases difficult, if not impossible.

Most Web application frameworks provide the following capabilities:

❑ **JavaScript library** — Although most frameworks support the incorporation of any JavaScript library, they generally already include a JavaScript library off the shelf. Ruby on Rails, for example, includes Script.aculo.us, while TurboGears comes with MochiKit. See Chapter 8 for a closer examination of the capabilities of these JavaScript libraries.

❏ **View specification language** — A language for defining views based on server-side processing is included in any framework. This usually consists of an extension to standard HTML, and/or XML that enables you to embed code into the page in the language of the framework. For example, Rails represents a view as an RHTML document, an HTML document that can contain embedded Ruby.

❏ **Database to model object integration** — All frameworks include some mechanism to translate between model objects and database tables. The implementation may vary between frameworks, but generally one component, either database table or model object, is derived based on the other. Regardless of approach, the fully automated translation is only practical when you're starting with a new Web application and don't have an existing database. Most frameworks do provide a mechanism to map model objects to an existing database in case you're not starting from scratch. The offerings of the framework should be explored fully before a selection is made, though, because the level of support for this, and efficiency of these tools, varies greatly between frameworks.

❏ **Database interaction abstraction** — Frameworks generally include some form of abstraction for interactions as well. This alleviates Web application developers from writing SQL in their Web applications. One huge additional advantage of this is that the Web application isn't tied to any particular dialect of SQL or database. This means that you can change from one database implementation to another without worrying about updating all the SQL in your Web application.

❏ **Controller framework** — A fundamental aspect of most frameworks is a standard mechanism for defining controllers. This usually includes a base controller object that handles a lot of the lower-level details of HTTP requests and responses.

❏ **URL routing and controller-view association** — One main aspect included in most frameworks is a mechanism to ease URL routing, and the association of controllers and views. Simple conventions are frequently employed to allow URLs to be transparently translated to specific controllers, or controller functions. In addition, controller names or function names are generally mapped automatically to associated views.

❏ **View composition, controller routing, and controller inheritance** — Common functions such as user login must be performed in almost all Web applications, and views frequently share the same components (e.g., headers or footers). Frameworks enable these types of common behavior through several mechanisms. Typically, the view specification language includes a mechanism that enables the composition a view from a set of subviews. In a similar fashion, common application behavior is usually enabled through a combination of controller inheritance and some form of URL routing utility.

❏ **Model validation framework** — Another convenience provided by a lot of frameworks is the inherent support for validation of data. Validating data specified by a user is a common issue in Web applications (see Chapter 10) that can be greatly simplified through the incorporation of standard validation logic.

❏ **Test framework** — The Web application and software engineering community has widely adopted the practice of writing and automating unit tests, and many frameworks have been developed to support testing in a variety of languages. Most frameworks include mechanisms to aid you when developing and running unit tests.

❑ **Web server** — Traditionally, even the deployment of a Web application for testing is a nontrivial activity. You may need to package a set of files, relocate to a Web server deployment directory, and restart the server. Frameworks usually simplify this process by embedding a Web server into the framework. You're usually only required to execute a single command to start the Web sever and deploy your test application. You don't need to restart the server as you make changes to your Web application either, because they are usually configured to automatically detect and load changes to the Web application.

❑ **Console** — For interpreted languages, a console may be included. When you start the console within a particular project, it is initialized to the configuration of the project. This allows you to use it as a preconfigured sandbox in which you can interactively test or otherwise interact with your new objects, the project database, and other project scripts.

❑ **Standardized project directory structure** — All projects developed with the framework conform to the same directory structure. This usually consists of locations for third-party component configuration (e.g., database or Web server), source code divided into model, view, and controller modules, unit test files, and so on. Utilities are commonly provided to create the shell of a project to which you can add application logic.

❑ **Community tools** — Apart from the core framework capabilities and tools, many frameworks have additional tools that you can download separately. These tools are usually developed within the user community, are freely available, and are intended to make users more productive when using the framework. For example, RadRails is an Eclipse-based IDE for Ruby on Rails.

Ruby on Rails: a Ruby-based MVC Framework

The granddaddy of the all-encompassing Web application frameworks is Ruby on Rails, which was created by David Heinemeier Hanson at 37signals, and has been undergoing development since 2003.

Installation instructions and many detailed tutorials are accessible via the Ruby on Rails Web site (www.rubyonrails.org) or associated wiki (wiki.rubyonrails.org). These will walk you through the steps to develop a simple Hello World application. If you're new to this framework, we suggest you experiment with some of these before focusing on the MVC paradigm as implemented in Rails and outlined in this section. For the discussion here, it's assumed that you have already installed Rails. The authors are using Rails v1.1.2.

The framework follows a standard project directory structure, and provides a series of Ruby scripts useful for configuring projects and creating elements for your Web application. As a refresher, you can create a new project with the `rails` command. For example, you can create the health history project for the example Web application by executing the following from a command prompt:

```
c:\workspace>rails healthhistory
```

Database configuration is maintained in the file `<projecthome>/config/database.yml` (e.g., `c:\workspace\healthhistory\config\database.yml`). Also note the set of scripts under the `scripts` subdirectory. This framework even includes a script to start the test Web server. It's as simple as calling the following:

```
c:\workspace\healthhistory>ruby server
```

MVC Architecture in Ruby on Rails

The Rails framework fully embraces the MVC architecture, and outlines three basic types of objects to capture these concepts:

❑ **Action View** — Corresponds to the view, and is maintained under `<projecthome>/app/views` (e.g., `c:\workspace\healthhistory\app\views`). This is the Rails version of a view. These generally take the form of an RHTML file (similar to a JSP page).

❑ **Action Controller** — Corresponds to a controller object and is located under `<projecthome>/app/controller` (e.g., `c:\workspace\healthhistory\app\controller`). This contains the logic necessary to select the next view, instantiate the model class from database data, or store model objects to the database. Note that you can use a script to create the required shell for a new controller object with the following command:

```
c:\workspace\healthhistory>ruby generate controller healthdetail
```

The only additional modification required to implement a very simple vanilla controller is to add a single line that incorporates the scaffold to enable viewing, adding, editing, and deleting model objects, as follows:

```
class HealthdetailController < ApplicationController
   scaffold :healthdetail
end
```

The scaffold provides default views, and handling of operations to view the table, as well as to add, delete, and edit rows in the table. In practice, note that you generally need to replace the scaffold behavior with a controller that provides different operations, and references tailored views.

❑ **Active Record** — Corresponds to the model, and is defined in `<projecthome>/app/controller` (e.g., `C:\workspace\healthhistory\app\controller`). This is the Rails equivalent of a model object. There is a significant amount of infrastructure in Rails to facilitate the storage and retrieval of records. If you're using the default relationship between the database and the Active Record, you're not even required to add the table columns to the record as attributes, as you would in Java. You simply create an empty object that conforms to the table structure automatically as a part of the framework. Note that the generate script also works for models. For example, you can create a health detail object with the following:

```
c:\workspace\healthhistory>ruby generate model healthdetail
```

Note here, however, that an Active Record automatically assumes a table with the plural version of the same name to be defined in the database. For instance, the example assumes there's a table defined in the database with the name `healthdetails`.

Design of Health History in Ruby on Rails

Figure 6-8 shows the object model for the health detail example implemented in Rails. The entire implementation of the HealthDetail model object is provided by the framework. Also note, with the exception of including the scaffold above, that the controller implementation is empty as well. The majority of content not included by the framework is on the database, and presentation ends. The framework assumes that a table exists in the database that is mapped to the model object (e.g., the HealthDetails table). On the presentation side, the framework automatically provides default view implementations for listing and editing the model as a part of the scaffold, but in practice these are frequently overridden with user-defined views (e.g., `edit.rhtml` and `list.rhtml`).

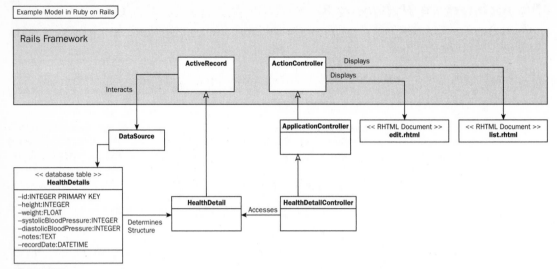

Figure 6-8

Differences between Java and Rails Designs

Note several significant differences between a design developed when following the Model 2 approach and the design developed using the concepts incorporated in Ruby on Rails. Ignoring the differences between Java and Ruby, and focusing on the design, you'll notice the following major differences:

❑ **Distributed control of application flow** — In Java, the flow through the application is managed by a centralized component called the Flow Manager. This is a bit different from Rails, where the flow of the application is encoded within each separate controller. A controller establishes only the views that it is capable of rendering, and the URL of the request determines which view should be rendered.

❑ **Controller filtering** — Note the ApplicationController object in Figure 6-8. All controllers inherit from this basic controller in the application. This enables you to specify common methods, but it also serves another purpose. The framework, however, provides the capability to define filters that are executed before the controller action is executed. You define common aspects of the Web application, such as the user login, in a single location in the ApplicationController, rather than in each implementation. This takes the place of the Front Controller Servlet concept in Java, which performs any top-level processing necessary for all requests.

❑ **Data definition, access, and storage details are hidden** — In Java, above, the DAO was necessary to abstract the details of the database access from the model specification. Rails uses a different approach. As noted above, the model implementation is generally empty, and a standard set of data access and storage routines are automatically provided by the Active Record.

❑ **Single model object and command** — The framework provides an implementation for a range of basic tasks on a model object. This includes the ability to show the list of all rows in the database for a particular model object, and to add, delete, view, and modify a single row in the database. This is all accomplished with a single model object and command. In the Java design of the example, an additional command and model object are used.

TurboGears: A Python-based Alternative to Rails

Similar to the Ruby on Rails framework is the TurboGears framework in Python.

You can explore installation instructions and several informative tutorials from the TurboGears Web site (www.turbogears.org). As with the Rails discussion above, we assume you already have TurboGears installed here. The authors are using TurboGears v1.0.

The main distinction between the two frameworks, apart from the obvious difference in languages, is that Rails was developed from the ground up, whereas TurboGears was developed by assembling a collection of existing tools into a single all-encompassing framework. The underlying technologies that served as the basis for TurboGears include the following:

❑ **Mochikit** — A JavaScript library that includes components such as Logging, Drag and Drop, and other visual effects that are common to many libraries. The site www.mochikit.com contains documentation and downloads of the library for use without TurboGears, which is discussed in Chapter 8.

❑ **Kid** — Template language that enables you to include embedded Python in an XHTML page. You either embed Python code explicitly with a `python` tag, or use an included set of attributes such as loops and conditionals to define dynamic content. You can download, or get detailed documentation on, Kid at www.kid-templating.org.

❑ **CherryPy** — An object-oriented framework that enables you to develop Web applications in Python. CherryPy includes mechanisms to do Web-centric operations such as simple URL mapping, server control, and request filtering. For more information on CherryPy, or to download the standalone version, see cherrypy.org/.

❑ **SQLObject** — Automatically maps between Python classes and database tables. SQLObject includes a mechanism for mapping Python objects to a relational database. It also includes a Python-based abstraction of standard SQL mechanisms that enables developers to interact with databases from a Python script or shell. Further information and downloads can be retrieved at www.sqlobject.org/.

Much like Rails, the TurboGears framework follows a standard directory structure, and includes utilities useful in management of a TurboGears project. A new project is created in TurboGears with the `tg-admin` command. A small difference from the Rails project creation process is that you are prompted for a project name and a default project package. The healthhistory project, for example, can be created in TurboGears with the following command:

```
c:\workspace>tg-admin quickstart
Enter project name: healthhistory
Enter package name [healthhistory]:
creating directory healthhistory
...
c:\workspace>
```

Also like Rails, a database configuration file and a test Web server are included. In TurboGears the database configuration file is `<projecthome>/dev.cfg` (e.g., c:\workspace\healthhistory\dev.cfg). The test Web server is started with a Python script, `<projecthome>/<project-name>-start.py`. Simply run this script as follows to start the Web server:

```
c:\workspace\healthhistory>python healthhistory-start.py
```

181

TurboGears also comes with an interactive shell configured for your project that you can start from the home directory of the project as follows:

```
c:\workspace\healthhistory>tg-admin shell
```

You can use this to easily load test data into the database or perform interactive tests of your application objects.

Finally, a utility called `Toolbox` is included as of the 0.9 version of TurboGears. This utility includes a set of Web-based tools for TurboGears. Most notably, this includes WebConsole, a Python interpreter, ModelDesigner, a tool to aid in designing and generating code for SQLObjects, and CakeWalk, a tool for modification of your SQLObject instances. The toolbox utility can be started with a command similar to the following:

```
c:\workspace\healthhistory>tg-admin toolbox
```

MVC Architecture in TurboGears

The TurboGears framework incorporates the MVC architecture in a way quite similar to that of Ruby on Rails. The TurboGears components that correspond to the MVC components are as follows:

❑ **Kid templates** — The TurboGears representation of a view. This is similar to other view representations such as JSP and RHTML, and consists of an extension to standard HTML that enables you to include embedded Python. For a given Web application, all Kid templates are generally located under `<projecthome>/<packagename>/templates` (e.g., `c:\workspace\ healthhistory\healthhistory\templates`).

❑ **Root controller classes** — Corresponds to a controller object in TurboGears, and is located in the file `<projecthome>/<packagename>/controller.py`. (e.g., `c:\workspace\healthhistory\ healthhistory\controller.py`). Several classes may be defined in this file. The main object in the file should be `Root`, which inherits from the `controllers.Root` object and is bound to the root of the project's URI (i.e., `/`). This object should hold a direct reference to any specific controllers that may be defined in the same file. The effect of defining a specific controller (e.g., `HealthHistoryController`) is the creation of another path (e.g., `/healthhistory`). Similar to controllers in Ruby, these contain the logic to look up database data and select a Kid template to display, given a requested URL.

❑ **SQLObjects** — These model objects are located in the file `<projecthome>/<packagename>/ models.py` (e.g., `c:\workspace\heathhistory\healthhistory\model.py`) in TurboGears. Similar to the convention in Rails, each object usually corresponds to a database table or view. Unlike Rails, however, these objects typically include the specification of the column details, and are frequently used to construct the database. SQLObjects defined in the `model.py` file generally require a table to be defined in your project database. TurboGears includes a mechanism for creating or deleting the database tables automatically with `tg-admin` when a `sql` argument is provided as follows:

```
tg-admin sql create
tg-admin sql drop
```

The command `tg-admin sql` is simply a wrapper for the SQLObjects command `sql-admin`, which you can use to add data to a table and execute arbitrary SQL, among several other useful functions. Detailed documentation is available at `www.sqlobject.org/sqlobject-admin.html`. The effect of running the `create` command as shown above is to create a table in the project database for each of your SQLObject model objects.

The Design of Health History in TurboGears

Figure 6-9 shows the health detail example discussed above as it may be implemented in TurboGears. The HealthDetail model object contains all the attributes necessary to represent health details for a user. Note that the data types for these attributes are instances of classes defined in the SQLObject library (see the SQLObject documentation for an exhaustive list). The base object SQLObject includes any functions necessary to store and load HealthDetail objects from the database. The Root controller inherits from a base controllers.Root object, and simply exposes the default view of the Web application and references a HealthDetailsController object. The HealthDetailsController looks up HealthDetails objects from the data source and exposes additional Kid pages for editing health detail and displaying a list of health detail. The other effect of this is to establish a path under the root for the health details (e.g., the path for editing health detail would be /healthdetail/edit). The framework provides a few basic Kid files, but these should not be confused with the scaffold provided by Rails. You cannot use them to provide any simple table list or editing capabilities. To perform any operation that is based on a model object in your project, you must define a Kid file that includes the mechanism to perform the editing.

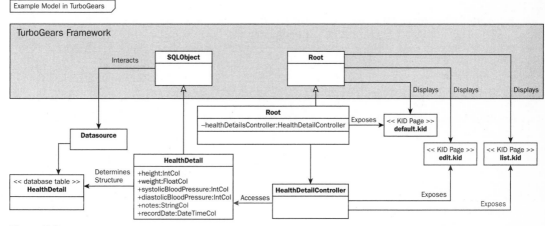

Figure 6-9

Differences between Rails and TurboGears

At first glance, the object model looks quite similar to Rails, and both frameworks appear to result in very similar application designs. However, ignoring the differences between the languages and tools provided, there are some primary differences between the approaches incorporated in the Ruby on Rails framework versus that in TurboGears:

❑ **Controller and view scaffold** — Rails provides a scaffold that significantly reduces the amount of code required to get a project up and running. It includes default implementations of views and controller application flow control. TurboGears, on the other hand, requires you to define the application flow by explicitly exposing your controller methods. You also need to define Kid files for each of the views. This requires you to do a bit more coding to get a simple project up and running, but in practice you'll want to tailor most, if not all, of your views anyway.

❑ **Model and database table relationship** — The data structure in the database is determined by the model object in TurboGears. In Rails, the database table determines the structure of the model object. This means you're required to look in the database to see the data structures in Rails, whereas in TurboGears you look at the model object.

MVC Implementation Quick Reference

The preceding differences between MVC patterns as implemented in Java, Ruby on Rails, and TurboGears are summarized in Table 6-1.

Table 6-1: Components Used to Implement MVC

	Model	View	Controller
Java	Java Beans (Java Objects)	JSP pages	Front Controller (Java Servlet)
			Flow Manager
	Data Access Objects		Command Factory
			Commands
Ruby on Rails	Active Record	RHTML documents	Action Controller
			Application Controller (for project)
			Application Controller (subclass for a specific model)
TurboGears	SQL Object	Kid documents	controllers.Root
			project.Root
			Python Object (controller for a specific model object, uses controllers.Root)

Summary

In this chapter, you've explored the Model-View-Controller architectural pattern in great detail. You've learned of its history, intent, and adaptation to Web applications. You've seen how a variety of frameworks for Web application development are based inherently on this concept, and you are now familiar with what these Web application frameworks have to offer. Through the discussion of the health history example, you've seen how the MVC pattern is incorporated in a Java Model 2 architecture application, as well as applications using the Ruby on Rails and TurboGears frameworks. Throughout the remainder of this book, the components of each example are defined as a part of the model, view, or controller. This enables you, with a little ingenuity, to implement any of the examples in the language and framework of your choice regardless of the reference language.

7

JavaScript Library Survey

There are only two kinds of programming languages: those people always bitch about and those nobody uses.

— Bjarne Stroustrup

For better or worse, JavaScript is one of those languages that people always complain about but are required to use. In the beginning of Web pages and simple Web applications, the dependence on JavaScript was minimal. It was used to perform relatively simple tasks on the fringe of the page such as animate a menu on the side or add a "hits" counter. People who worked with JavaScript always complained about it, but didn't feel too much pain. They usually didn't have to do anything very complex, and the capability probably wasn't essential. This made it less critical to ensure that the script worked in every browser and to include additional code to account for browser differences.

As Web applications became increasingly complex, the role of JavaScript was radically increased. It became necessary to write large amounts of JavaScript for a single Web application. This generally included a lot of repetitive code to perform the simplest of tasks, such as analyzing or manipulating a DOM document. To address this, the community started sharing snippets of commonly required JavaScript on forums and in script repositories. The problem with this was that the code snippets had no quality control. They varied vastly in how well they worked, how well they were written, and how easy they were to use. Another issue was that they usually defined global functions or variables that frequently conflicted when integrating with other scripts.

This has led to the development of larger JavaScript *libraries* that attempt to collect solutions to problems commonly faced in Web applications. The libraries are typically designed to allow easy integration and reuse across applications. Instead of the uncertain nature of code snippets, a library is typically developed according to a plan and includes documentation, unit tests, and a way to get support.

In this chapter you are introduced to the JavaScript library. A couple simple code samples show you how the use of a JavaScript library can significantly reduce the amount of duplicate and boilerplate code that a Web application developer is required to write. After learning about the capabilities that a JavaScript library commonly provides, you are introduced to four of the more popular open-source JavaScript libraries available, and you will see how they provide the capabilities discussed earlier.

JavaScript Library Basics

Before getting into the details of each JavaScript library, let's take a look at basics. In this section, you get to see the advantage to using JavaScript libraries through a simple example. You are also introduced to all of the libraries and can compare the basic statistics of each library side by side. Then you will explore capabilities common to many libraries, which will provide a basis for exploring each library in detail later in the chapter.

Why Use JavaScript Libraries?

The easiest way to see the effect of using a JavaScript library is through a simple example. In Chapter 5, you learned how to make asynchronous requests. If you recall from that example, you need to perform several steps to make a simple request. You need to create the XMLHttpRequest object, set up the method and URI of the request, and define the callback before you can finally send the request. In setting up the callback, you need to verify that the readyState of the request is 4 (or data transfer is completed) before getting into the details of the implementation. Of course, in the introductory chapter, you didn't get into the details of how to develop a request that can handle both Internet Explorer and other types of browsers. This requires a few additional steps. You also need to include some additional code for error handling not described in Chapter 5. This is because older browser implementations such as Netscape don't support the XMLHttpRequests. The following code gives an example of asynchronous request creation and calling that includes these necessary aspects:

```
var xmlRequest;
if (window.XMLHttpRequest) {
  xmlRequest = new XMLHttpRequest();
} else if (window.ActiveXObject) {
  try {
    xmlRequest = new ActiveXObject("Msxml2.XMLHTTP");
  } catch (e) {
    try {
      xmlRequest = new ActiveXObject("Microsoft.XMLHTTP");
    } catch (e) {}
  }
}
if (!xmlRequest) {
  return false; // return failure when request not created
}
```

```
...
xmlRequest.open("GET", aUrl, true);
xmlRequest.onreadystatechange = aCallback;
xmlRequest.send(null);
...
function aCallback() {
  if (xmlRequest.readyState == 4) {
    // handle requests
  }
}
```

Notice this includes many lines of JavaScript that are required anytime you want to create a request. In fact, the majority of requests created in the majority of Web applications should use a similar set of steps. This has led many libraries to provide a simplification of the asynchronous request mechanism. For example, consider the alternative code required when you use the Dojo JavaScript library's request function `dojo.io.bind`. All of the preceding code is boiled down into a single, easily understandable function call:

```
...
dojo.io.bind({
  url: aUrl,
  load: aCallback
});
...
function aCallback(type, data, evt) {
    // handle request
}
```

Notice that the majority of the boilerplate code is hidden, and the developer can focus on the details of the request. The same call is just as simple when using Script.aculo.us, another open-source JavaScript library:

```
...
new Ajax.Request(aUrl, {onSuccess:aCallback});
...
function handlerFunc(t) {
  // handle request
}
```

Both the Dojo and Script.aculo.us calls include all the capabilities of the standalone implementation. The functions can handle IE and other types of browsers, and the error handling is performed, but all of these details are hidden. The advantage of this, beyond avoiding severe finger cramps, is that now you can focus on the request being made, rather than write repetitive code to ensure that the object handles a variety of environments. You're also saved from defining a separate library of functions that performs common tasks. This is already done, and maintained, for you. All you need to do is download and use it. Because the library is intended to be reused, and maintained separately, it is likely to be more extensible, maintainable, and reusable anyway.

The asynchronous request is just a simple example of a rather small convenience function that serves to make the code more readable, and saves the developer from a few lines of repetition. You can further see the power of libraries if you consider more complex capabilities such as drag and drop. This is a highly complex function of a Web application that requires a significant amount of code. To give you some idea, consider the fact that the JavaScript file that defines the drag and drop component for Script.aculo.us v1.6.4 (i.e., `dragdrop.js`) is almost 1,000 lines of code. This doesn't even factor in the amount of code the file uses from other scripts in the library. When you use the library, you can make an element draggable with a single line of JavaScript:

```
new Draggable(elementId, {});
```

The alternative is to define and maintain a mass of JavaScript that is capable of performing the required operation. Although libraries are frequently critical to the success of a Web application, bear in mind that a JavaScript library is a tool and not a silver bullet. You need to consider some trade-offs when deciding to incorporate a library, including the cost to learn the library, the fact that the fixes to the library are performed outside of the project or company of the developer. This means that the developer likely has very little input as to when and how a bug is fixed, or how a needed enhancement is to be made, although this may be mitigated somewhat by the fact that the libraries examined here are open source.

The selection of a library is also critical, because the different libraries provide a wide variety of capabilities, and offer varying amounts of documentation, training, quality, and support. With that in mind, the next couple of sections discuss the various libraries and their characteristics.

The Various Libraries

This chapter provides a brief introduction to four JavaScript libraries and the capabilities that they offer. The following libraries are standard open-source libraries that have been adopted on a wide variety of projects:

❑ **Dojo** — Available at `dojotoolkit.org`. One of the larger and more mature of the libraries examined. Dojo has a wide range of capabilities, including a large set of user interface components (i.e., Dojo widgets), and a large user base.

❑ **MochiKit** — Available at `www.mochikit.com`. A medium-size library that focuses on simplifying JavaScript and providing extensible enhancements such as a framework for defining and handling events. MochiKit is included in the TurboGears Web application framework (see Chapter 6), and has a clear leaning toward Python developers.

❑ **Script.aculo.us** — Available at `Script.aculo.us`. This small library is bundled with Ruby on Rails and has a leaning toward Ruby developers. Note that Script.aculo.us is built on top of Prototype, a very small JavaScript framework that includes several extensions to basic JavaScript classes. The library focuses on visual utilities and includes a powerful mechanism for defining effects and performing drag and drop. The Prototype component focuses on providing enhancements to basic JavaScript.

❑ **Yahoo! User Interface (YUI)** — Available at `developer.yahoo.com/yui`. A large library developed by Yahoo!, but released under a BSD license. This library is more similar to Dojo, although it hasn't been around as long. It includes a wide variety of capabilities, including a large set of user interface components (i.e., YUI controls) such as a Calendar, Tree View, and Slider.

Note that although particular languages and Web application frameworks influenced MochiKit and Script.aculo.us, they are by no means restricted to use with only those languages. Above all, they are JavaScript frameworks, and are made up entirely of client-side JavaScript. Web applications written for any server-side language can use any of the libraries just described. For example, a Java Web application can use Script.aculo.us as its client-side JavaScript library.

Library Properties

Before getting into the details of each library, it may be useful to get a feel for the maturity, size, and availability of each library. This is captured in Table 7-1, which includes basic information such as version number and download and base script size for each of the four libraries. The base script size is the size of the script that you must send to the client to use the components and functions defined in the library. All of this should be taken into account when you're selecting a language to use in a Web application.

Table 7-1: Comparison of Basic Library Details

	Dojo	MochiKit	Script.aculo.us	YUI
Version	0.3.1	1.3.1	1.6.4	0.11.3
Download size	3.5Mb	292Kb	150Kb	3.645Mb
Base script size	127Kb	111Kb	50Kb	Depends on module used
License	Academic Free License, or BSD License	Academic Free License ,or MIT License	MIT License	BSD License
Bundled with framework (if any)	None	TurboGears	Ruby on Rails	None
Documentation	Very Limited	Good	Limited	Good

Frequently Provided Library Capabilities

Although the philosophy and intent of each JavaScript library differs widely, you should consider a set of possible capabilities when selecting a library for use in a Web application. Note that no library supports all the capabilities described below to the fullest possible extent, and more capabilities are not always better. Complex libraries such as Dojo and YUI have two main limitations in addition to all their advantages: They both have a much higher learning curve and frequently require more data to be sent to the client to use these additional capabilities. One consideration when selecting a library should be the size of the script that must be sent to the client (although increasingly ubiquitous high-speed connectivity may make this less of a concern). A large "include everything but the kitchen sink" library may be overkill when a more basic set of capabilities is desired. Given the widely different capabilities of each library, when deciding which library to use, you must also consider the requirements of the system you develop. If a less complex library is sufficient for the needs of the system, then it may be a better choice. On the other hand, if you expect that you will need the additional capabilities in the future, the initial investment in a more complex library may be desirable.

The following are some capabilities frequently provided in a JavaScript library:

❑   **Namespace support** — Most libraries understand the need to modularize code, and avoid potential for collision with other (sometimes preexisting) libraries. The mechanism typically used to avoid this issue is to define the library in a namespace. All Dojo components, for example, appear under the `dojo` namespace. To reference a component in Dojo, you need to reference the namespace first (e.g., `dojo.debug`).

❑ **JavaScript usability enhancements** — Several basic usability enhancements are included in most libraries. These can vary widely depending on the concerns of the library user community, but some common issues addressed are looping and shortcuts for commonly executed sets of operations, such as retrieval of a form field value by a string identifier.

❑ **Logging and debugging capabilities** — A very painful aspect of the JavaScript language is that it doesn't automatically include a mechanism to print out a message to a log. The only possibility is to use the `alert` command. See Chapter 5 for a detailed discussion of the necessity and some approaches for logging and debugging in Web applications. Rather than require you to write your own logging capability, a library generally includes at least some simple log capability.

❑ **User interface components** — Some libraries include a variety of additional user interface components. Some enhance existing elements such as drop-down lists, or provide completely new behavior, such as combo boxes or calendar components.

❑ **Drag and drop components** — This is simply a complex user interface component, but a very powerful aspect of a library. When included in a Web application, you can dramatically increase the user interactivity of the application. The capability is too complex to implement from scratch, but when you use a predefined library, the effort is almost trivial. See Chapter 12 for a detailed discussion of drag and drop.

Note that all four libraries examined have similar implementations. You can define elements as draggable (meaning users can drag the element around the window), or droppable (meaning users can place dragged items within the element). You can configure aspects of the drag and drop such as the delay when picking up a draggable object, and capture events on the elements, such as an event triggered when the user starts to drag the object. In addition, all four libraries provide a specialized mechanism to ease the use of drag and drop for the sorting of lists.

❑ **Visual effects and animations** — You can add visual effects and animations to Web page elements to increase the visual appeal of the Web application. These enable you to fade in/out, shake, grow/shrink, or move a page element. When applied judiciously, effects can greatly enhance a Web application. Of course, when they're overused or used inappropriately, the Web application can become frustrating or bothersome. See Chapter 13 for an examination of effects and how to use them to increase Web application usability.

❑ **Element style manipulation** — Cascading Style Sheets are an efficient representation for the style of a Web page, but are not without limitations. It is typically difficult to analyze or modify the style of an element on the page from within JavaScript. Several libraries include routines that make the style of elements easier to deal with.

❑ **AJAX support** — When a library is not used, several lines of code are required to define and respond to an AJAX call. In most cases, the interaction is quite similar; the user wants to make an asynchronous request and define a callback for execution after the data finishes loading. Most libraries include some mechanism to reduce the amount of code required to make these standard AJAX calls.

❑ **DOM support** — The DOM API is a very general-purpose API, which makes it quite powerful. Unfortunately, this also makes it quite difficult to use in JavaScript. Libraries frequently include convenience functions to reduce the complexity of analyzing and manipulating a document.

❑ **Event-handling enhancements** — Several libraries have extended the basic JavaScript event handling mechanism significantly, enabling you to define your own events, manage event listeners, and define event handlers.

❑ **Unit test framework** — The advent and increasing acceptance of Agile methodologies that focus on automation and integration has brought about the need for automated unit test frameworks that support a variety of systems and languages. JavaScript should be no different. As the complexity of JavaScript code increases, developers need mechanisms to automatically test this code. Libraries may include functions that enable you to unit test your JavaScript by defining test cases and making assertions about system state.

JavaScript Libraries in Detail

In this section, you learn the basics of the four up-and-coming JavaScript libraries, including a bit about their origins, intent, and maturity. You see how much support each library has for the capabilities discussed above. Through this section, you can begin to see the many similarities and vast differences between the philosophy, intent, and capability of each of the libraries. It is important to bear in mind that each library has its own advantages and limitations.

Dojo

As noted above, Dojo is one of the largest of the libraries examined, started in 2004 as a collaboration between a group of developers (Alex Russell, Dylan Schiemann, and David Schontzler) at Informatica who needed a portable JavaScript library. Their initial goal was to develop a library that could be reused across environments, and that included the best approaches to solving common problems in Web applications. This origin greatly explains the breadth of capabilities included in Dojo.

Dojo is currently maintained by the Dojo Foundation (headed by Alex Russell), and a core set of committers make enhancements.

> Because Dojo is such a large library, it is available for download in a variety of "Editions." For example, there is a Widget edition and an AJAX edition. Each edition contains a subset of the overall functionality of Dojo, and reduces the overall footprint required to include Dojo in your Web application.

Dojo Capabilities

Dojo has a wide variety of capabilities that address nearly all of the areas mentioned above, with the exception of a unit test framework:

❑ **Namespace support** — The breadth of Dojo and the effort to create a library that is reusable across a variety of environments led its developers to include one of the more sophisticated namespace and packaging systems available in an open-source JavaScript library. All Dojo code is broken up into modules and packages that must be explicitly included in your JavaScript with the `dojo.requires` function. This helps reduce the total amount of code that must be sent to the client with the page.

❑ **JavaScript usability enhancements** — Dojo includes a variety of usability enhancements, from simple shortcuts such as *for loop* enhancements to more complex components, including a `collections` module with classes such as `Stacks`, `Queues`, and `Dictionaries`. Given the use of a namespace in Dojo, however, shortcuts tend to be slightly more verbose than in certain other languages.

❑ **Logging and debugging capabilities** — Dojo has the capability to write log messages and turn logging on or off. It can display log statements at the bottom of the Web page or in an internal configurable frame. This frame can be resized, deleted, and removed. Unfortunately, there is no support for logging different messages at different levels that can be toggled on and off, as provided by some other libraries. Figure 7-1 shows the Dojo logger console.

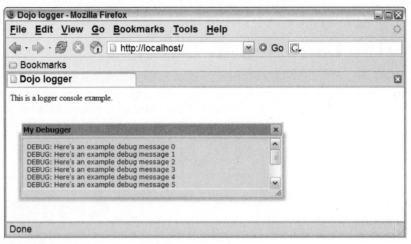

Figure 7-1

❑ **User interface components** — Dojo includes a vast array of user interface components, known as *widgets* in Dojo. You can even define your own widgets by extending base widget classes. You can programmatically specify widgets with JavaScript, or define them inline in HTML using a special element attribute dojoType. Figure 7-2 shows an example of a Web application developed with Dojo widgets. You can also see a live version of this example on the main Dojo site at dojotoolkit.org/dojo/demos/widget/Mail.html. The types of widgets in Dojo include the following:

   ❑ Widgets to replace or enhance standard HTML form fields such as check boxes, select fields, and combo boxes. Dojo even includes a rich text editor and spreadsheet widgets that you can define with a single line!

   ❑ Widgets such as windows and dialog boxes that aid page layout

   ❑ General-purpose widgets such as trees, fisheyes, and charts

❑ A set of widgets that validate form data. For example, you can use a validation widget to confirm that a text field contains a valid phone number. See Chapter 10 for a more detailed exploration of validation with Dojo widgets.

❑ **Drag and drop components** — As noted above, this is supported in a similar fashion in all libraries examined.

❑ **Visual effects and animations** — Dojo has a fairly large set of effects, including moving a page element, fading in and out, and shrinking or growing a page element.

❑ **Element style manipulation** — Dojo provides a large set of style analysis and manipulation routines. There are several functions for analyzing and modifying element size and position, and a few for modifying other aspects of style such as opacity and color. Finally, there is a collection of functions to manipulate the CSS rules applied, such as insert new CSS files, and insert and remove specific CSS rules.

❑ **AJAX support** — Ajax is supported in Dojo with a set of objects that simplify the `XMLHttpRequest` mechanism. The most common function is the `dojo.io.bind` utility, which you can use to create an asynchronous request. You can use the related `dojo.io.FormBind` function to make an asynchronous request that is automatically populated with data from a form.

❑ **DOM support** — Dojo provides a wide variety of functions for performing DOM analysis and manipulation. This includes functions for inserting, deleting, copying, moving, and analyzing DOM nodes.

❑ **Event-handling enhancements** — Dojo includes one of the more sophisticated event-handling implementations in an open-source JavaScript library. You can use the implementation, inspired by aspect-oriented programming concepts, to define complex interactions between components in a Web application. Rather than be restricted to DOM events, or even user-defined custom events, Dojo enables you to look at any function call, such as an event, and set up listeners for it.

❑ **Unit test framework** — None

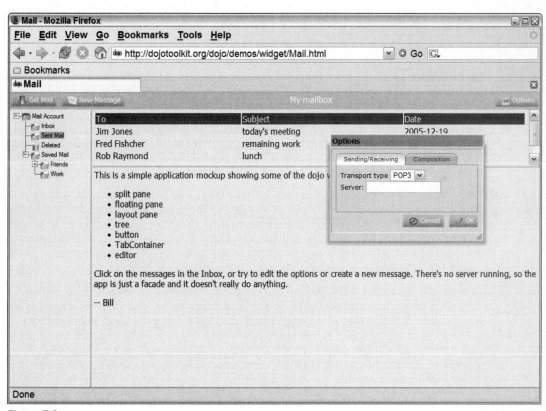

Figure 7-2

Dojo Advantages

The primary advantages of the Dojo library include the following:

❑ **A rich set of features** — Dojo components address a wide variety of issues common in Web applications, from user interface components to event handling. This means you don't have to rewrite common components, or collect several different JavaScript libraries that each provide a subset of the overall functionality required.

❑ **It's not tied to a particular framework, language, or user community** — This focuses development on components that are applicable regardless of any particular languages and frameworks. Other libraries may be driven more by the developers of a particular user community. For example, Ruby on Rails developers primarily drive Script.aculo.us development. Of course, if you're using a Web application framework like Ruby on Rails, this may be a disadvantage if you use Dojo.

❑ **It doesn't modify the global namespace** — Because all the classes and functions appear under the dojo module, you can easily drop Dojo into Web applications with preexisting JavaScript, or use other JavaScript libraries without concern for conflicting objects. Libraries that write global classes may cause naming conflicts when integrating.

Dojo Disadvantages

There are also several disadvantages to using the Dojo library:

❑ **More difficult to learn** — As you add more capabilities to Dojo, it becomes more difficult to learn to use all the functionality. When you initially download and learn the library, understanding the many different modules and functions available can be a bit overwhelming.

❑ **Limited documentation** — This is the case with many rapidly evolving, community-developed open-source efforts, but when paired with the complexity of the library itself, the learning curve is further exasperated. Dojo developers acknowledge this issue, and they are making an effort to enhance the current documentation.

❑ **Larger footprint** — You can see this by examining the size of the library on disk, as well as the amount of JavaScript sent to the client. Note that you can reduce the size on disk, to a certain extent, by removing various script files for use in a particular application. Dojo's use of modules, packages, and the `require` function helps reduce the amount of unused JavaScript sent to the client, and wisely selecting an appropriate Dojo edition can help reduce the size of the base JavaScript file sent to the client as well.

❑ **Less concise** — The fact that Dojo doesn't define global functions or classes is not only an advantage in certain ways, but also a limitation. Dojo cannot be as concise as some of the other libraries that do define functions and classes globally. For example, one of the most-loved aspects of the Prototype framework (on which Script.aculo.us is built) is the `$()` construct. This function is simply shorthand for the DOM function `document.getElementById`. Dojo has a similar construct `dojo.byId`, but it isn't nearly as concise because Dojo doesn't define any global functions or variables.

MochiKit

Bob Ippolito started the MochiKit library, and initially released it in July of 2005. The primary goal was to provide a well-documented and tested library that doesn't interfere with normal JavaScript. The library is heavily influenced by Python, and adds functional programming capabilities to JavaScript. It incorporates many ideas from Twisted and other Python-related frameworks and libraries. MochiKit currently comes bundled with TurboGears, a Python-based Web application framework.

Unlike other libraries, MochiKit is focused more on establishing an extensible library that helps developers deal with the need to write increasingly complex applications in JavaScript, rather than user interface components or effects. The result is that aspects of the library that provide user interface enhancements (e.g., drag and drop) are generally less mature and less capable than other aspects of the library (e.g., event handling). On the other hand, the library includes several quite powerful and extensible additions to JavaScript, such as AJAX support and the event-handling utility.

MochiKit Capabilities

You can think of MochiKit as the middle ground between large, broadly ranging libraries such as Dojo, and more minimal libraries such as Script.aculo.us. MochiKit provides a highly reusable and extensible set of components. The following list outlines the set of capabilities in MochiKit:

❑   **Namespace support** — MochiKit takes a unique and effective approach to namespace support. All components are defined in the MochiKit namespace, but the inclusion of the MochiKit namespace is optional. If the following script is specified before including the MochiKit script in your page, you can turn compatibility mode on:

```
<script type="text/javascript">MochiKit = {__compat__: true};</script>
```

When compatibility mode is on, you are required to use the fully qualified name for any MochiKit function. For example, the `compare` function is executed with `MochiKit.Base.compare(x, y)`. When compatibility mode is turned off, you aren't required to include the namespace. The compare function is simplified to `compare(x, y)`.

❑   **JavaScript usability enhancements** — There are several enhancements, including functions for manipulating dates and times, a wide variety of array operations and iteration mechanisms, and a variety of string formatting and manipulation functions.

❑   **Logging and debugging capabilities** — MochiKit has a great logging utility that includes several useful features. You can write a message to the log at a specified level (e.g., debug, warn). This log can be captured in the browser's native JavaScript console (depending on browser version), a MochiKit console at the bottom of the browser window, or in a MochiKit console in a separate window. The MochiKit console also enables you to filter by log level or regular expression. See Figure 7-3 for the inline logging pane in MochiKit. You can also experiment with this online at `www.mochikit.com/examples/logging_pane/index.html`.

❑   **User interface components** — None apart from drag and drop, and the Logging console.

❑   **Drag and drop components** — As noted previously, this is supported in a similar fashion in all the libraries examined. Note that the support in MochiKit is less complete and much less mature than other libraries such as Dojo or Script.aculo.us.

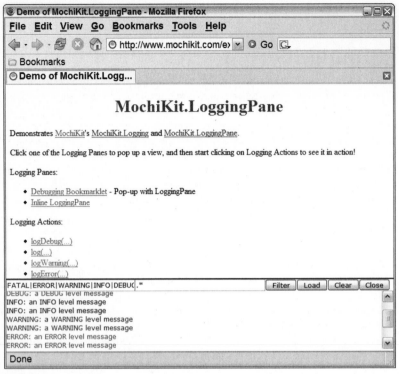

Figure 7-3

❑ **Visual effects and animations** — MochiKit currently has quite limited support for effects, and no animation support. Apart from the functions described under Element style manipulation, the library enables you to round the corners of an element. Figure 7-4 shows an example page that makes use of the rounded corners functions. You can view an online version at www .mochikit.com/examples/rounded_corners/index.html.

❑ **Element style manipulation** — MochiKit includes a small set of functions that enable you to analyze and modify an element's style. For example, you can reposition, show, or hide elements. It also provides a set of functions for creating and manipulating colors. This includes mechanisms to translate colors to and from a variety of formats (e.g., RGB, HSL), analyze a document to ascertain its colors, and retrieve standard colors.

❑ **AJAX support** — The inspiration for MochiKit's AJAX support was the Twisted event-driven networking framework in Python. The core of this implementation is the concept of a `Deferred` object as an abstraction for any asynchronous operation in Javascript. You can create deferred objects that correspond to asynchronous requests, and assign a collection of callback functions to be executed on successful or failed execution. It also provides a useful function `loadJSONDoc`, which enables you to make an `XMLHttpRequest` and get the response as a JSON document.

❑ **DOM support** — MochiKit includes a large set of functions for DOM manipulation, including functions for adding, replacing, or swapping out DOM nodes, elements, and attributes. Similar to Script.aculo.us, it includes `$()` as a concise and useful encapsulation of the `getElementById` function. It takes a functional approach to the construction of documents that is also quite powerful.

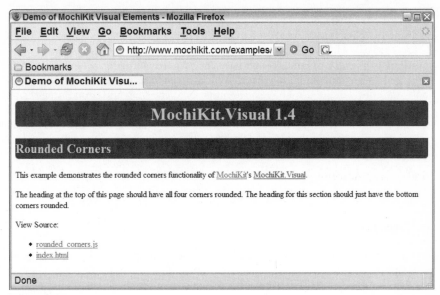

Figure 7-4

❑ **Event-handling enhancements** — MochiKit provides a powerful event-handling system. This includes a replacement for the base event API to handle events such as `onmouseover` or `onkeypress`. It also enables you to define and broadcast custom events.

❑ **Unit test framework** — None, although MochiKit does emphasize and make use of automated unit tests.

MochiKit Advantages

The following list describes some of the advantages to using MochiKit over other libraries:

❑ **Extensive documentation and unit tests** — Two key areas of focus in MochiKit development are documentation and unit tests. All functions and packages have complete documentation when compared to languages such as Dojo. Both serve to help users quickly learn the ins and outs of MochiKit.

❑ **Unobtrusive namespace support** — Because you can turn namespaces on or off, you're not required to use namespaces, but you can benefit from them when needed. When you don't use namespaces, MochiKit is more concise than libraries like Dojo that require namespaces. For example, you can use a construct such as `$()` as a shortcut for the `getElementById()` function. As noted above, Dojo provides a similar shortcut, `dojo.byId`, that is much less concise. On the other hand, if you are integrating with existing JavaScript and are concerned about conflicts, you can turn namespaces on. This enables you to prevent MochiKit from defining global functions or variables.

❑ **Minor modifications to the global namespace** — MochiKit maintains a high interoperability capability with other JavaScript libraries by significantly limiting modifications to the global namespace. This ensures you can easily integrate the library with other libraries such as Dojo.

❑ **Extensible components** — The design focus on extensible components ensures that the library is reusable and adaptable to a particular Web application. It was designed with the intent that Web developers would extend the base objects with their own behaviors.

197

MochiKit Disadvantages

Following are some of the disadvantages to using MochiKit:

❑ **Limited user interface enhancements** — The primary limitation when using MochiKit is its lack of robust user interface enhancements. It doesn't include any user interface components, has only one effect, and doesn't have any animations. The drag and drop implementation was ported from script.aculo.us, is relatively new, and is currently quite buggy. MochiKit is not a good choice for a Web application that requires extensive UI components. Note, however, that minor modifications to the global namespace described above means that you can integrate MochiKit easily with other libraries that provide UI capabilities when necessary.

❑ **Small user community** — In comparison to other libraries such as Script.aculo.us or Dojo, MochiKit currently has a much smaller user community.

Script.aculo.us

Script.aculo.us, created in June 2005 by Thomas Fuchs, was initially intended as an effects add-on to Prototype. Script.aculo.us is one of the smaller libraries, built on top of Prototype, a very small JavaScript framework that includes several extensions to basic JavaScript classes. Note that several of the features discussed in this section are actually features of the underlying Prototype library.

Given the library's origins as an effects add-on to Prototype, its most powerful components deal with the user experience. Script.aculo.us provides a wide variety of animations and effects, as well as one of the most powerful drag and drop implementations. Prototype, on the other hand, has a very narrow focus in that it is intended to simplify JavaScript development. It provides a handful of objects and functions that help reduce the amount of code required for common tasks, including, for example, functions to simplify creation of an AJAX request and to manipulate DOM elements.

Prototype grew out of the Ruby on Rails framework, and this heavily influences its development, but like all the other libraries explored here, it isn't tied to any particular language or framework.

Script.aculo.us Capabilities

Script.aculo.us provides a subset of the capabilities of other libraries, but what is provided is generally concise and powerful:

❑ **Namespace support** — None

❑ **JavaScript usability enhancements** — Script.aculo.us is based on the Prototype library, which is focused on enhancements to JavaScript usability, so this area has excellent support. Because namespaces aren't used, the library can extend existing JavaScript objects with additional functionality. For example, the `string` class has been extended to include a `stripTags` function. This function removes all HTML tags from the string.

❑ **Logging and debugging capabilities** — None

❑ **User interface components** — Script.aculo.us provides limited user interface components. This includes an autocompleter, a simple slider, and an in-place editor. The in-place editor looks like a normal label, but when clicked it becomes an editable text field or text area. The autocompleter and in-place editor both include AJAX and non-AJAX-based versions. See Figure 7-5 for an example of the autocompleter, also viewable at `demo.Script.aculo.us/ajax/ autocompleter_customized`.

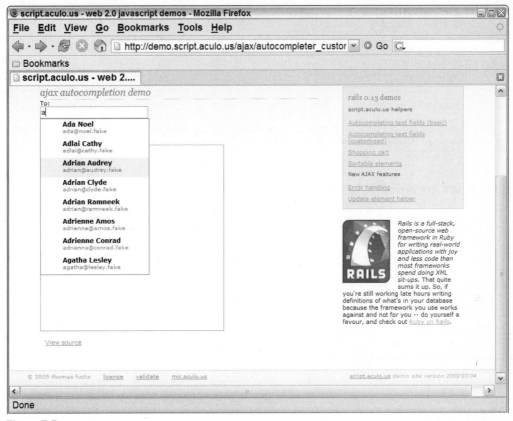

Figure 7-5

❏ **Drag and drop components** — As noted above, this is supported in a similar fashion in all libraries examined.

❏ **Visual effects and animations** — Script.aculo.us provides powerful representation for effects and animations. The effects are separated into five core effects and an extensible set of combination effects, which are based on the core effects. You can explore an excellent demonstration of some of the possible combination effects at `wiki.Script.aculo.us/scriptaculous/show/ CombinationEffectsDemo`.

❏ **Element style manipulation** — The Prototype component of script.aculo.us provides some support for manipulation of style. It includes functions for manipulating and analyzing an element's CSS classes, and some other functions for reading and potentially modifying specific aspects of an element's style, such as visibility or height.

❏ **AJAX support** — Script.aculo.us has AJAX support that includes objects for making a few different types of asynchronous requests, such as periodic requests. It includes an `Ajax.Responders` object that enables you to define functions that should execute in response to any AJAX request regardless of origin. Finally, it provides a set of objects and functions such as the `Ajax .Autocompleter`, which incorporate AJAX into user interface components.

❑ **DOM support** — Script.aculo.us provides a simple utility class `Builder` that you can use to create DOM elements. It also includes some simple DOM analysis and manipulation functions that come with Prototype. This includes the quite popular dollar ($) function, which encapsulates the DOM function `getElementById`, among several others.

❑ **Event-handling enhancements** — The support for events is limited in script.aculo.us, and builds on the standard browser event system. It includes the ability to add and remove an observer of a browser event.

❑ **Unit test framework** — Script.aculo.us includes a complete unit test framework that follows the standard unit test framework conventions. The framework includes classes that define a test unit, test case, runner, and assertions.

Script.aculo.us Advantages

The following are some of the advantages to using Script.aculo.us:

❑ **Concision** — Script.aculo.us is probably one of the most concise libraries, given the focus of Prototype on reducing the code required for common tasks, and the lack of namespaces.

❑ **Small footprint** — The footprint of script.aculo.us is one of the smaller footprints in the libraries surveyed. This is possible because there aren't a lot of objects defined that support the infrastructure alone.

❑ **Powerful effects, animations, and drag and drop capabilities** — Another significant advantage is that it includes a set of animations and effects that rivals Dojo and far exceeds MochiKit. The one lacking aspect is the limited support for other user interface components such as windows. Dojo's capabilities far exceed Script.aculo.us in this respect.

❑ **Large user community** — With users like Apple and Gucci, it's no wonder that script.aculo.us has a large user community. The fact that it's the de facto library for Ruby on Rails users doesn't hurt either.

Script.aculo.us Disadvantages

The disadvantages to using script.aculo.us include the following:

❑ **Modifies the global namespace** — A significant concern with script.aculo.us is the fact that it makes extensive modifications to the global namespace. It has several objects that directly extend and modify the behaviors of standard JavaScript objects.

❑ **Difficult to integrate** — This is related to the issues with global namespace modification described above. This can cause some unexpected results and problems when integrating with existing code sets, or attempting to integrate additional libraries.

❑ **Lack of extensibility** — Given the focus of script.aculo.us and Prototype on direct usability enhancements to standard JavaScript, it may be difficult to build on the library with your own extensions. Several of the other libraries explored here are designed with a greater focus on developer extensions. You can see an example of this with the event-handling extensions in script.aculo.us. These extensions are built directly on the DOM event-handling mechanism, and they do not allow you to define your own types of events. The other libraries examined here all provide some mechanism to define and trigger your own types of events.

❑ **Lack of documentation** — Although not quite as limited as Dojo, the documentation for script.aculo.us and Prototype is not nearly complete as the other libraries. This causes Web developers to face a higher initial investment when learning the libraries.

Yahoo! UI Library

The newest kid on the block is the Yahoo! UI (YUI) library, developed by Yahoo! and initially released in June of 2006. It is also one of the broader libraries because it addresses most capabilities offered by JavaScript libraries. The components in the library are divided into two primary groups. The Utilities group contains components for simplifying development, and includes modules that address areas such as scripting animation, drag and drop, asynchronous call creation, and events. The Controls group consists of a variety of UI components such as trees and containers.

YUI Capabilities

A wide variety of capabilities in many areas are included in the YUI, except for general usability enhancements and unit testing:

❑ **Namespace support** — YUI supports namespaces by defining all objects and functions within a global object YAHOO. This object defines the global namespace. It includes a mechanism that allows developers to define new namespaces for their applications and extensions, such as user interface components, built on the YUI.

❑ **JavaScript usability enhancements** — None

❑ **Logging and debugging capabilities** — YUI includes the most powerful logging utilities of the set. Like MochiKit, it enables you to log messages and filter to a specific level. In addition, you can define new message types and filter based on these new types. It can also write to the browser's native JavaScript console or an internal console panel. Finally, you can customize the log that's produced based upon the source of the message.

❑ **User interface components** — Although not quite as vast as the library provided in Dojo, YUI provides a large set of user interface components, called Controls in YUI. This includes an AJAX or local AutoCompleter, Slider, Menu, and Tree. It also includes containers for creating windows such as dialog boxes. Figure 7-6 shows an example AutoCompleter that also shows the YUI logger. An operational version of this example is available online at developer.yahoo.com/ yui/examples/logger/autocomplete.html.

❑ **Drag and drop components** — As noted above, this is supported in a similar fashion in all libraries examined.

❑ **Visual effects and animations** — YUI provides a powerful animation utility that enables you to script animations that you can use to perform common tricks such as fading in/out, fading into a color, and moving elements. For simple animations, you just specify the element you want to change, the attribute to change (e.g., border width, height, or opacity), and the degree of change. More complex animations, such as the animation of a scrollbar or moving an object, have specific animation objects defined. You can also add callbacks for events that are triggered on animation start or end, or on each frame of the animation.

❑ **Element style manipulation** — YUI also includes a set of functions in the DOM namespace that enable you to analyze and modify element positions, style attributes, and CSS classes.

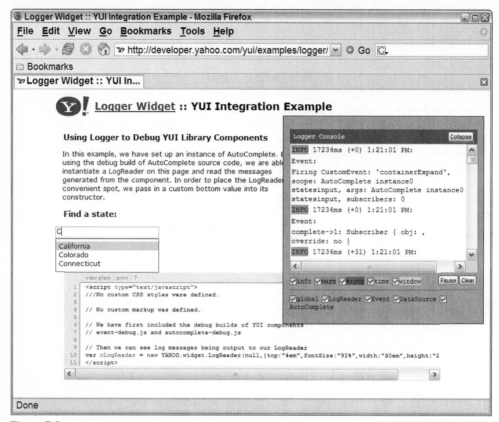

Figure 7-6

❏ **AJAX support**—YUI uses a Connection Manager to abstract the details of AJAX calls. The `asyncRequest` function creates the asynchronous request (called a *transaction* in YUI). It also includes a utility (`setForm`) that you can use in conjunction with the `asyncRequest` function to asynchronously submit form data, similar to `dojo.io.FormBind`.

❏ **DOM support**—YUI DOM extensions are currently fairly limited, and are focused mostly on the use of the DOM to modify an element's attributes. It does provide `getElementsBy` and `getElementsByClassName`, useful functions that search for elements that match a user-defined test function or have the specified CSS class.

❏ **Event-handling enhancements**—YUI event handling is similar to MochiKit. You can add or remove event listeners for DOM events. It provides an additional function, `onAvailable`, that enables you to specify a function to execute as soon as an indicated element is detected in the DOM. Also, as in MochiKit, you can define and listen for custom events.

❏ **Unit test framework**—None

YUI Advantages

There are several advantages to using this up-and-coming library:

❑ **Provides a rich set of features** — Similar to Dojo, the YUI library attempts to address the majority of capabilities desired in a JavaScript library. The capabilities include significant user interface capabilities, as well as a wide range of powerful language extensions such as event handling.

❑ **Does not modify the global namespace** — Like most other libraries examined, except script .aculo.us, all extensions appear under a single namespace. The ultimate effect is easier integration with existing code and other third-party JavaScript libraries.

❑ **Includes good documentation** — Even though YUI is released as an open-source library, Yahoo! maintains it. This means a variety of support is set up to assist developers in getting up-to-speed with the library. There are cheat sheets, detailed documentation, demos, and overviews for each of the modules.

YUI Disadvantages

The disadvantages to YUI are primarily associated with the fact that it covers such a broad area. These disadvantages include the following:

❑ **Less mature and has a small user community** — Note that this is the newest library, and it has a smaller user community when compared to more established libraries such as script.aculo.us or Dojo.

❑ **More difficult to learn** — Like any other large JavaScript library, when using YUI, the developer must invest more time initially to learn its capabilities, although the focus on documentation helps reduce this learning curve somewhat.

❑ **Less concise** — Because YUI uses a namespace like Dojo and MochiKit, the library cannot use the concise commands available to script.aculo.us. You must insert the name of the module before object and function names. For example, when retrieving the CSS style of an element, you need to use the fully qualified path to the function, e.g., YAHOO.util.Dom.getStyle.

❑ **Larger footprint** — A limitation common to larger libraries is the larger footprint incurred. Not only does the library take up much more disk space on the server, but it may also require additional data to be transferred to the server, depending on the capabilities utilized.

JavaScript Library Quick Reference

Table 7-2 shows the level of support provided by each of the JavaScript libraries examined. Empty cells indicate no support provided, an X in the table represents support, and a hyphen (-) means limited support is provided.

Table 7-2: Basic Capabilities of the Libraries Compared

	Dojo	MochiKit	Script.aculo.us	YUI
Namespace Support	X	X		X
JavaScript Usability Enhancements	X	X	X	
Logging and Debugging Capabilities	-	X		X
User Interface Components	X		-	X
Drag and Drop Components	X	-	X	X
Visual Effects and Animations	X	-	X	X
Element Style Manipulation	X	X	X	X
AJAX Support	X	X	X	X
DOM Support	X	X	X	-
Event Handling Enhancements	X	X	-	X
Unit Test Framework			X	

Summary

In this chapter you've seen why off-the-shelf JavaScript libraries have become such a critical component of a Web developer's toolbox. You've learned about the capabilities that JavaScript libraries frequently provide, and you have seen an example of how the amount of code required for an application can be drastically reduced when using a library. Finally, you were introduced to four common JavaScript libraries that are available. You've seen a bit of their intent, capabilities, advantages, and limitations. All of the libraries explored here are quite effective and useful in a variety of situations, but no library applies to all Web applications. Before selecting a library for a particular Web application, you should always consider the requirements of the application being developed. You'll build on this introduction in several chapters in Part III, where you'll get more closely acquainted with several of these libraries.

Compiling to JavaScript

8

Simplicity is prerequisite for reliability.

— **Edsger Dijkstra**

The JavaScript libraries compared in Chapter 7 greatly simplify the work (and pain) of developing a full-featured application in JavaScript, but sometimes developers just don't want to make the plunge into JavaScript development. Whether the reason is personal taste in computer languages, existing expertise in another environment, or the lack of time-tested development tools for JavaScript, you are not alone. This chapter examines two compiled-to-JavaScript solutions that enable developers to code in either Ruby or Java and then "compile" their code into JavaScript code for remote client execution.

The desire to migrate toward a higher-level language is not unlike the movement away from the C language. Unchallenged in its ability to produce exceedingly fast computer programs, C is as close to assembly language as high-level computer languages get. Programming in C can be like driving a sports car from inside the hood, directly tuning the engine as you go, but the real-world development costs are great. C contains all of the necessary primitives, but none of the real-world abstractions. It leaves the programmer prone to introducing catastrophic errors; and as application size grows, C code becomes unmanageable. With hardware as fast as it is, most developers would rather use a language such as Python, which can be essentially compiled to C during execution. The productivity gains during development are far worth the performance penalty during execution.

While the comparison of JavaScript to C is laughable in some respects, they share some similarities. JavaScript, like C, is the low-level king of its target environment, which in its case is the Web browser instead of the physical computer. JavaScript takes care of all of the primitives necessary to manipulate the DOM and the browser, but like C it lacks any of the abstractions that make everyday tasks simple and elegant. Like C, JavaScript can be used for programs of any size, but it becomes virtually unmanageable once the code reaches a certain amount. Many JavaScript libraries have emerged to make up for JavaScript's simplicity, much like various libraries for C, but some are arguing that the time has come to move to a higher-level language that is "compiled" to JavaScript.

One final advantage of a compiled-to-JavaScript approach is that the compiler handles the task of smoothing over the differences between the many different browsers on the market. One of the most painful aspects of developing with JavaScript (or CSS, for that matter) is that each version of each browser type has its own set of bugs, unsupported features, and special cases. Fine-tuning a page so that it appears and functions exactly the same in every browser can be a painstaking process. With compiled-to-JavaScript environments, the adjustments necessary to make code work across all browsers only need to be done once (by the group that writes the compiler), and it is done by developers who are experts in that particular area.

Enter the First Contenders

The compiled-to-JavaScript approach is new to the Web development camp, so its effectiveness in serious development settings is relatively untested. Given the year or so of initial reactions and critiques of this first wave of compiled-to-JavaScript tools, however, it looks like this method will become increasingly accepted as a viable option for mainstream RIA development.

This chapter takes an initial look at compiled-to-JavaScript offerings from both Google and the Ruby on Rails team. Google's solution, the Google Web Toolkit (GWT), is Java-based; the Rails offering, Ruby JavaScript (RJS), is Ruby-based. While both of these frameworks are similar in that they provide JavaScript alternatives, their overall goals and approaches are completely different, making direct comparison between the two difficult.

Google's approach is to trade the development environment of HTML, CSS, and JavaScript for the environment of Java, replacing the benefits and problems of the former with those of the latter. By recasting the task of Web development as that of programming a Java application, Google has managed to tame many aspects of Web development, such as debugging, that formerly made RIA programming so hard.

The Rails approach with RJS does not seek to eliminate HTML and CSS development, but rather to create a clean way for JavaScript to fit into the Model-View-Controller paradigm that Rails enforces. Whereas normal XHTML views describe the way that a RIA page is structured, RJS provides a type of view that describes how an existing XHTML view should *change* structure. This new type of view just happens to coincide with a Ruby-ized version of the DOM API.

Both of these approaches are interesting developments for RIA development. Though their different intentions mean they are not really competitors *per se*, their basic concepts, strengths, and weaknesses are examined in this chapter.

The Google Web Toolkit (GWT)

Google's approach to the GWT focuses on leveraging the existing success and productivity of the Java programming language to create tools for the Web. As Google's introduction to the toolkit states:

Java technologies offer a productive development platform, and with GWT, they can instantly become the basis of your AJAX development platform as well.

Their documentation goes on to list a wide number of productivity-enhancing tools available for Java developers—from development IDEs, such as Eclipse, to static type checking and code completion. These, combined with the existing pool of experienced Java developers, have prompted Google to take the position that the best way to deal with the new arena of JavaScript development is to redefine it in terms of the mature and established Java environment.

As such, the language that GWT developers use not only looks and feels like Java, it actually *is* Java. By creating a set of libraries that looks and functions almost exactly like those in Java's core, GWT is able to integrate seamlessly into the Java development environment. A Google-written compiler is further able to take a supported subset of the Java language and transform it into a mixture of HTML and JavaScript. Also included is a Tomcat-based test harness that uses a closed-source interpreter to transform the Java code directly into HTML and JavaScript at runtime, enabling debugging applications to step through the Web application line by line.

GWT Benefits

GWT offers an intriguing set of benefits to the RIA developer. Not surprisingly, many of these benefits derive from the fact that Google has managed to present a Web development environment that is almost completely Java-based. Among GWT's strengths are the following:

- ❑ **Debugging** — Debugging is the one area of RIA development that really sets it back when compared to traditional application development. GWT overcomes this problem completely by enabling both client-side and server-side debugging of a live application while in development mode. Because both are written in pure Java, you can even use your favorite debugging tool, such as Eclipse. Even if GWT had no other features, this alone would make it worth a look.

- ❑ **Java** — Many developers far prefer developing in Java to developing in JavaScript. From the breadth of development tools that exist to the richness of Sun's (and GWT's) libraries, Java presents a more evolved and object-oriented alternative to JavaScript. While GWT has yet to stand the test of time as a RIA development environment, if it becomes a huge success, its choice of Java as a language will be one of the most prominent reasons why.

- ❑ **Widgets** — While developers from a Web background will miss designing RIA interfaces in terms of a DOM tree, the Swing-style UI construction in GWT is a nice touch for the enormous number of developers with Java experience but little or no HTML experience. Layout managers make positioning and repositioning a snap, and widgets make constructs such as calendars (traditionally hard to do in HTML) easy to insert into a GWT application.

- ❑ **Cross-browser compatibility** — Google Web Toolkit's ability to produce code that will work for every browser is superb, thus eliminating what can be one of the biggest headaches of Web design. GWT automatically handles any special cases or fixes for a particular browser.

- ❑ **Seamless serialization** — GWT serializes objects like a dream. With no effort on the part of the developer, you can exchange objects between the client and the server. Because both the client and server portions of the code are developed in Java, you can use even the same object definition at development time.

GWT Drawbacks

Before jumping on the GWT bandwagon as an early adopter, some serious drawbacks should be considered. Adding Java into the RIA development mix doesn't alleviate 100% of the JavaScript headaches, and it adds some entirely new Java-specific problems in with the mix. Following are some of the chief concerns that should be considered before adopting GWT:

❑   **Bland user interfaces** — By exchanging HTML, CSS, and JavaScript for Java, Google has freed developers from a great many headaches, but this approach replaces the problems of HTML and CSS with the problems of Java and Java Swing. Anyone familiar with Java development knows that while Swing produces very functional interfaces, its interfaces are not very attractive. User interfaces built with GWT also suffer from this Spartan, boxlike approach to interface building, and there is only limited capability to modify the default appearance.

❑   **GWT lock-in** — Migrating a project from one framework to another is always a large task, but GWT makes migration virtually impossible. GWT easily integrates with existing JavaScript files, so it is easy to port code *to* GWT, but once a developer begins coding in GWT's Java syntax there is no turning back. Recovering JavaScript from the compiled GWT output is impossible, and translating the Java code by hand will require a complete rewrite.

❑   **Obfuscated code** — The flip side to GWT's ability to machine-generate JavaScript is that its compiler output is completely illegible. As long as your application is running smoothly and no customizations beyond what Google's compiler provides are needed, this might not be a problem. But don't expect to be able to peek under the JavaScript hood and understand what is going on.

❑   **Lack of gracefully degrading code** — This criticism might not be fair if the argument is made that GWT is for "hard-core" RIAs only. Other development frameworks are HTML-centric first and JavaScript-centric second, meaning that functionally limited HTML-only versions of the RIA are easy to produce for users with less advanced browsers. GWT treats both HTML and JavaScript as equally required capabilities on a browser, so applications using this framework are harder to adapt for browsers not with the times.

❑   **Artsy folks need not apply** — Many Web sites have two development teams: one technical, to handle the RIA plumbing, and another nontechnical, to ensure that the site looks good and is filled with content. GWT makes it difficult to provide nontechnical contributors with the access to design elements that they need because it replaces XHTML and CSS (easy for any non-techie to learn) with Java and Swing-style widgets (very hard for non-technical people to learn).

Developing with GWT

The Google Web Toolkit is available as a free download from Google's Web page at `code.google.com/webtoolkit`. The current version at the time of writing is 1.1.10. The development package includes the GWT compiler, a hosted interpreter, a set of examples, and several scripts to automate the task of project creation. The most recent version of GWT has support for all major platforms, whether Windows, Macintosh, or Linux.

GWT projects can be created via a script, similar to Web frameworks such as Ruby on Rails and TurboGears. The `applicationCreator` command builds the directory structure and template files necessary for a properly configured, empty GWT application. With an extra `-eclipse` argument, it will even configure your new application as an Eclipse project:

```
applicationCreator -eclipse MyProject com.ideastax.client.HelloWorld
```

Because GWT is Java, GWT projects are organized into packages in the same manner as traditional Java projects. Google suggests that GWT developers split their packages up into `server`, `client`, and `public` subpackages. The `client` package contains all of the code that is translated into JavaScript code for the client, the `server` package contains Java code that can be executed on the server, and the `public` package contains static files such as CSS and image files. Figure 8-1 shows an example representative directory tree for a GWT project.

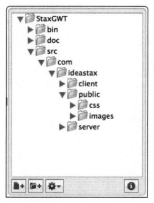

Figure 8-1

At the root package of a particular GWT application is a *module* definition. A module file is an XML document similar in purpose to the routes file in Ruby on Rails or the `web.xml` file in Tomcat. It configures which areas of the project should be treated as code, and contains bindings from various URL patterns to entry paths in the Java code. An example module for a Hello World application might appear as the one shown in Listing 8-1. When a user sends the request to the server, GWT knows that the default entry point for the GWT application is the `com.ideastax.hello.client` package.

Listing 8-1: An example module file

XML
```xml
<module>
  <inherits name="com.google.gwt.user.User"/>
  <entry-point class="com.ideastax.hello.client"/>
</module>
```

Most Web frameworks are organized around the idea that developers create XHTML Web pages and then use JavaScript to spruce them up. The result of this are the types of XHTML pages that you are used to seeing if you view the source of most pages on the Web today — medium-size XHTML documents with a series of JavaScript includes in the `head` section. GWT takes a completely different approach that enables the developer to start with an empty HTML page and populate it using machine-generated JavaScript. While page loading does not have to be done this way, it has the potential to make GWT source documents look strikingly different from what HTML developers might expect.

GWT pages start out as regular HTML documents, complete with all of the elements that the developer wishes to write by hand. This might be static header and footer elements, for example, or it could be nothing at all. Anything not provided in the static HTML page is bootstrapped into life via a small JavaScript file containing code that executes immediately on load and contacts your RIA server for further content. The server replies via AJAX and supplies the JavaScript and HTML fragments necessary to fill in the remaining parts of the RIA page. Therefore, initial page loads in GWT take a minimum of two round-trips to the server. Listing 8-2 shows an example GWT bootstrapping page for a Hello World application.

Listing 8-2: Example GWT page

XHTML
```
<html>
  <head>
    <!-- A module is an XML file which specifies the RIA configuration -->
    <meta name='gwt:module' content='com.ideastax.hello.Hello'>
    <title>Simple Hello World Application</title>
  </head>
  <body>
    <!-- This will cause our RIA page to load -->
    <script language="javascript" src="gwt.js"></script>

    <!-- This frame lets GWT provide history support for more advanced apps-->
    <iframe id="__gwt_historyFrame" style="width:0;height:0;border:0"></iframe>
  </body>
</html>
```

In the example in Listing 8-2, the body is left completely empty; it will be entirely defined by Java code in a separate part of the project. When loaded, the gwt.js file executes immediately and loads the content of the Hello World application via AJAX. For developers who never want to encounter HTML, Listing 8-2 can be as much HTML as you will ever see when developing in GWT. Most developers, however, probably prefer a more middle-of-the-road approach, which blends Java-defined page elements and HTML code.

Figure 8-2 shows an end-to-end time line of a GWT application running. The process begins with the user downloading a relatively empty HTML page. This page contains a fragment of JavaScript, which opens an AJAX connection to download the bulk of the RIA, which has been precompiled from a Java representation client package of the development project. This code, executed by the browser on receipt, constructs the RIA page inside the barren <body> tag. Sprinkled among this code might be AJAX callbacks to the server, which are handled and answered by a regular Java-compatible Web application server (such as Tomcat) running with the server package of the RIA project.

Developer Tools

GWT offers a few development tools that make RIA debugging in GWT light years ahead of any other framework. Because GWT applications are written in 100% Java, they cannot be used as a Web application without some sort of translation and compilation step that turns the Java into a set of Web documents. Google provides two tools for this translation: one to use for production and another to use for development.

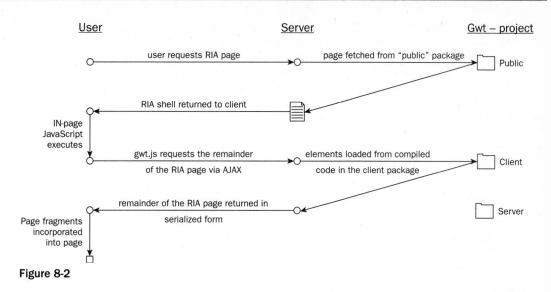

Figure 8-2

The production compiler is a closed-source, Java-based tool. Because it is Java-based, it can be easily scripted using Ant, making integration into a larger development environment a straightforward process. Even though the output of the compiler is HTML and JavaScript, don't expect to understand any of it. Google's compiler strips the names of variables and often writes cryptic JavaScript and HTML code. The good news is that your application will work across browsers and will be almost impossible to reverse engineer (try reverse engineering Gmail to see an example of obfuscated JavaScript). The bad news is that you cannot easily fix any bugs in the post-compilation code by hand or even locate their cause in the code. The following code is a representative snippet of the type of JavaScript code that one can expect GWT to produce:

```
function wy(BMb,CMb){if(!gc(CMb,15))return false;return FLb(BMb,CMb);}
function zcb(DMb){return cMb(DMb);}
_ = String.prototype;_.qf = iMb;_.k = kMb;_.Fgb = mMb;_.d = oMb;_.pf = pMb;_.rf =
rMb;_.lf = uMb;_.ad = vMb;_.tf = xMb;_.j = AMb;_.c = 'java.lang.String';_.l =
115;fMb = null;function EMb(FMb){var aNb=this.js.length - 1;var
bNb=this.js[aNb].length;if(this.length > bNb * bNb){this.js[aNb] = this.js[aNb] +
FMb;}else{this.js.push(FMb);}this.length += FMb.length;return this;}
```

The difficulty of understanding GWT's compiler output is a serious weakness. Efficiency and intellectual property benefits aside, it puts developers at the mercy of Google, leaving developers helpless if their compiler isn't capable of producing a particular feature necessary for a particular RIA feature. Google has a history of producing solid code, for sure, but no Web development framework should back a developer into a corner of obfuscated confusion to this extent.

GWT's illegible JavaScript output might be a deal-breaking weakness were it not for GWT's hosted mode. This is the second way in which GWT can translate Java into JavaScript, and it enables the developer to interpret the Java code at runtime. This allows developers to use the great breadth of Java debugging tools to step through the RIA code line by line while using it through a specially-hosted Web browser. Figure 8-3 shows both the hosted server and the hosted browser that can be easily invoked from a shell script.

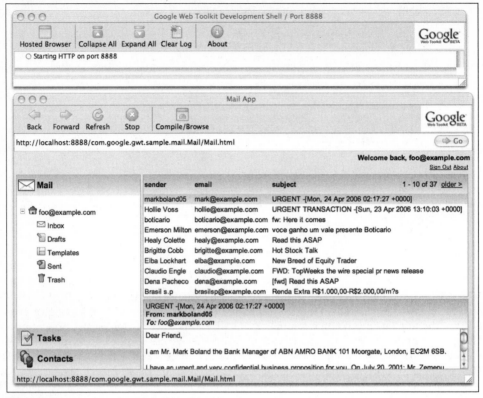

Figure 8-3

Recall from Chapter 5 how difficult it is to trace through a Web application while it is in use. You must tackle the client-side code using a tool such as Mozilla's Venkman, and almost no solutions exist that allow a user to step through the live server code. Google's hosted mode provides an unprecedented capability to monitor and debug an application during development time.

Look and Feel of GWT

Java Swing developers will feel immediately at home with the set of classes GWT provides to construct a RIA interface. Listing 8-3 shows a trivial Hello World application that renders an empty page and, upon load, display a pop-up that says "Hello, World!"

The Hello class implements the EntryPoint interface, making it a candidate for bootstrapping a just loaded RIA page. When the gwt.js file executes, it calls the code defined by the onModuleLoad () function:

```
package com.ideastax.hello.client;

import com.google.gwt.core.client.EntryPoint;
```

```
import com.google.gwt.user.client.Window;

public class Hello implements EntryPoint {
  public void onModuleLoad() {
        Window.alert("Hello, World!");
  }
}
```

GWT completely replaces the need to specify layout via XHTML structure through a set of Swing-style layout managers. While all other Web frameworks are DOM-tree and document-centric in their approach to Web design, GWT provides a layout and widget-centric option. Using what is essentially a Google-provided version of the Java's Swing toolkit, developers use a series of layout managers and panels to accomplish their design. While these layout managers ultimately translate into CSS and JavaScript for the sake of the remote browser, this happens behind the scenes and without any work on the part of the developer.

A telling example of the difference between XHTML-based development and Swing-style development is the required steps to implement the most popular Web layout: a three-column page with a header and footer. Most Web developers have encountered this layout so often that they can hammer out an XHTML template with accompanying CSS in a few minutes. With GWT, you do not need previous experience to make this layout work—just instantiate a DockPanel layout manager.

According to its documentation, DockPanel "lays its child widgets out 'docked' at its outer edges, and allows its last widget to take up the remaining space in its center." Figure 8-4 shows visually how the DockPanel layout is essentially a more flexible version of the three-column layout desired.

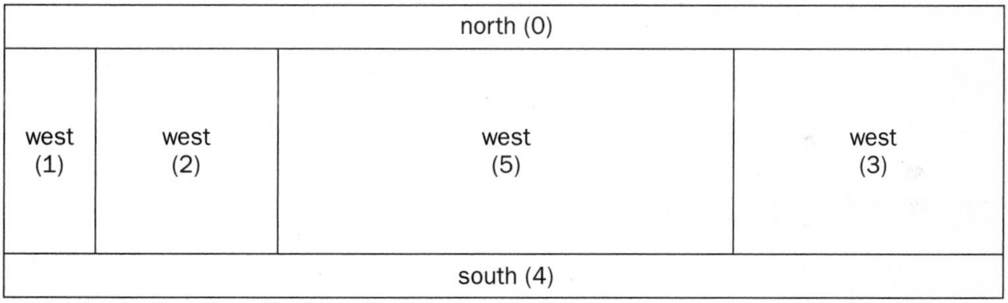

north (0)			
west (1)	west (2)	west (5)	west (3)
south (4)			

Figure 8-4

With this layout manager, creating a flexible three-column layout does not require pages of CSS and a well thought out DOM structure. Instead, just a few lines of Swing-style code suffice:

```
DockPanel dockPanel = new DockPanel();
dockPanel.add(headerPane, DockPanel.NORTH);
dockPanel.add(footerPane, DockPanel.SOUTH);
dockPanel.add(sidebar, DockPanel.WEST);
dockPanel.add(content, DockPanel.CENTER);
```

The GWT layout managers do take away some of a developer's ability to make minute adjustments to the styling of a layout, but they also provide great flexibility and ease as long as a developer's required layouts are within the layout manager's capabilities. Adding a right-hand column at runtime to the layout in the preceding example would normally be a complicated task, but it is a simple one-liner in the Java-style syntax of GWT.

The objects that are placed inside of layouts are not raw text but rather derivatives of the Widget class. A fragment of text is not contained in a <p> element, but instead perhaps in a Label widget. Or an area of the RIA might be defined by a Panel widget instead of a <div> element, for example. Looking at the com.google.gwt.user.client.ui package, Swing developers will feel familiar with everything available. Standard elements such as Button, HTML, Panel and Grid are there, as well as more complex elements such as Tree and MenuBar. While this approach will feel odd to developers with an HTML background, the ease with which complex UIs can be constructed can be very nice to work with.

Take, for example, the task of creating a table. In HTML, this requires enumeration of every <tr>, <th>, and <td> tag that is to appear in the table. Using a framework such as PHP or Rails, you can compress this code slightly with loops that output these tags alongside data from an array. GWT hides away the HTML table elements and allows developers to deal with the more intuitive Grid widget. The following example shows a function that you might use to set up a table at the beginning of a page load. It accepts a Grid object, an array of column names, and the desired number of data rows. It then resizes the grid and places the column names in the first row of the grid:

```
private void setupTable(Grid grid, String[] columnNames, int numberRows) {
grid.resize(numberRows+1, columnNames.length);
    for (int i = 0; i < columnNames.length; i++) {
      grid.setText(0, i, columnNames[i]);
    }
}
```

Adding this grid to a RIA page is as simple as adding it to a layout manager that is managing the display for a region of the page. When the Java code is compiled, the right combination of HTML and JavaScript is saved to provide the RIA with a dynamic table initialization.

Automatic Serialization

One feature of GWT that really deserves high praise is its ability to transparently serialize and deserialize objects written in Java. Some frameworks, such as Ruby on Rails, encourage the assembly of in-page fragments on the server side, and then these fragments are sent to the client as preformed HTML. The smooth serialization capabilities of GWT mean that it is more suited for sending full serialized objects to the remote client and then assembling an XHTML representation of the objects on the client side. Neither approach is better than the other across the board, but the GWT approach allows for some flexible possibilities for client-side caching and load-sharing.

To take advantage of GWT's serialization, all you need to do is implement the com.google.gwt.user .client.rpc.IsSerializable interface, which, like Java's Serializable interface, does not require extra code to implement. A photo album RIA might use a model object called Photo to store photo data for its users. If this model object also extends the IsSerializable interface, then Photo instances can seamlessly be sent to the client-side browser for any number of operations. Listing 8-3 contains a hypothetical serializable Photo object.

Listing 8-3: A serializable object

Java

```java
import com.google.gwt.user.client.rpc.IsSerializable;

public abstract class Photo implements IsSerializable {
private String name = "";
  private String imageUrl = "";

  public Photo() {
  }

  public String getName() {
    return name;
  }

  public String getImageUrl() {
    return imageUrl;
  }

  public void setName(String name) {
    this.name = name;
  }

  public void setImageUrl(String url) {
    this.imageUrl = url;
  }

}
```

The code in the client package can use a received array of Photo objects to display an album, but it can also store this array in the browser's memory to use later for some other task. Perhaps the user will want to view a slide show or print a checklist of photos to print, or will want auto-completion for photo names. With seamless serialization of Java objects, the potential of the client Web browser to share the load of work becomes much greater. Many Web development frameworks treat the browser as a place where only view code exists, but GWT encourages it as a place where both Model and Controller have a place too.

Ruby JavaScript (RJS)

The Ruby on Rails team has taken a different approach with RJS than Google did with GWT. Whereas GWT effectively eliminates XHTML, CSS, and JavaScript programming in favor of Java development, RJS embraces existing XHTML and CSS development techniques, opting instead to just replace JavaScript with a Ruby-based equivalent. An alternative, Ruby-based DOM API is provided, and calls to this API are transformed at runtime into JavaScript code sent to the browser. For Java developers who want to take their skill set to the Web, this approach might not be as familiar as GWT, but for existing Web developers, it requires little adaptation. RJS retains many of the advantages of current Web development techniques while attempting to minimize the aches and pains.

RJS continues the Rails built-in support for the Prototype and script.aculo.us libraries, so developers familiar with those will find it easy to transition from the `Effect`, `Draggable`, `Droppable`, and `Sortable` classes in JavaScript to the RJS shorthand for the same. While integration with these two libraries is a big plus, by far the biggest advantage of developing with RJS is the ability to use Ruby-style code blocks to affect the state of a RIA page.

Ruby can be a strange-looking language to developers who have not encountered it, but with a bit of practice, its concise syntax can lead to both rapid and readable development. Take the following example, which could be used to italicize all unsaved list items on a RIA page:

```
page.select("li.unsaved").each do |item|
    item.set_style :fontStyle => "italic"
end
```

RJS Benefits

RJS carries with it considerable benefits to developers who want to continue developing with XHTML and CSS but prefer Ruby over JavaScript. If your development platform is already Ruby on Rails, then you can take advantage of these benefits at virtually no cost:

- ❑ **Seamless Ruby on Rails integration** — RJS is a seamless component of the Ruby on Rails framework. This provides direct access to all of the reusable components of the Rails frameworks, including helpers, partials, and views. Because the code is interpreted at runtime, RJS files are able to reference both client-side and server-side variables, eliminating the need to serialize objects and transmit them over an AJAX connection.

- ❑ **Continues established Web development techniques** — Unlike GWT, RJS fits right in to the established trio of technologies (XHTML, CSS, JavaScript) that are common knowledge to all Web developers. This means that existing Rails applications are easy to adapt to RJS, and RJS-based applications are easy to adapt to other frameworks.

- ❑ **Fits nicely into the MVC paradigm** — Like the rest of Ruby on Rails, RJS has been designed to fit right in to the Model-View-Controller paradigm. Defining RJS files as a special type of active view helps organize code into a structure easily understood by anyone familiar with MVC concepts.

- ❑ **Built-in script.aculo.us and Prototype support** — RJS contains built-in shortcuts for all of the script.aculo.us and Prototype features, furthering the integration of these two libraries into the Rails framework.

RJS Drawbacks

Though RJS is a powerful tool, it too has some drawbacks, of which the most important are as follows:

- ❑ **Ruby on Rails dependence** — As with GWT, using RJS requires buying in to a larger overall framework. Although the output of the RJS interpreter is infinitely more readable than GWT's compiler, using RJS to generate client-side JavaScript files effectively requires the use of Ruby on Rails on the server side. GWT places no requirements on the server technology required to host the server side as long as it supports Java.

❑ **Hard to Debug** — Debugging in RJS is a mixed bag. On the one hand, its Ruby-style syntax greatly reduces the complexity of many common JavaScript tasks, meaning less chance for typos. On the other hand, because RJS is translated into JavaScript during runtime, errors that do occur are hard to debug.

Developing with RJS

As of Rails 1.1, RJS comes as a packaged component of the Ruby on Rails framework, so no additional downloads or configuration is necessary apart from having the Rails environment present on your system. This, combined with the fact that RJS generates JavaScript at runtime rather than development time, means that in order to take advantage of RJS, you must have already chosen to use the Rails framework.

The best way to picture how RJS fits into the overall Rails framework is as a special type of view code in the traditional Model-View-Controller paradigm. Whereas normal views describe how a page looks (using XHTML), RJS-based views describe how the look of a page changes (using JavaScript). This way of looking at things resolves the elephant-in-the-corner oddity of Web development in which developers pretend JavaScript does not exist when discussing MVC concepts. RJS answers that JavaScript does have a place in the MVC paradigm: it is a spunky type of view. Of course, this doesn't mean that RJS or JavaScript have to be used just for the view — as GWT's blurring of the client-server programming lines demonstrates — it is just a (strong) suggestion.

Within the Rails framework, RJS is made a part of the flow in the same way that a view normally would be. A request (in this case, almost always via AJAX) comes in from the client and is routed to a Controller. The Controller performs whatever work is needed to tender the request using application logic and Model objects, and then passes a set of variables to the RJS file, which specifies a JavaScript-based view. Rails processes the RJS view as regular Ruby code with a special set of objects and macros designed to Ruby-ize the expression of tasks relevant to DOM manipulation and page effects. Figure 8-5 shows this end-to-end flow.

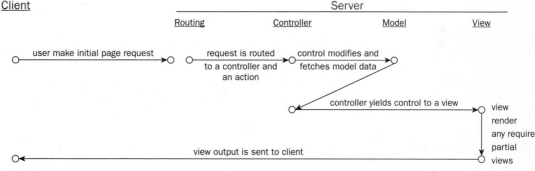

Figure 8-5

To cite a specific example, consider the task of allowing users to comment on a particular article or blog post. Most sites, commercial and personal, offer this feature without AJAX, requiring each comment post to trigger an entirely new page load. The remote user fills in a form and presses the Submit button to send an HTTP POST request to the remote server, after which the server's controller code adds the comment to a model object and rerenders the entire Web page with this new comment attached. This sequence is shown in Figure 8-6.

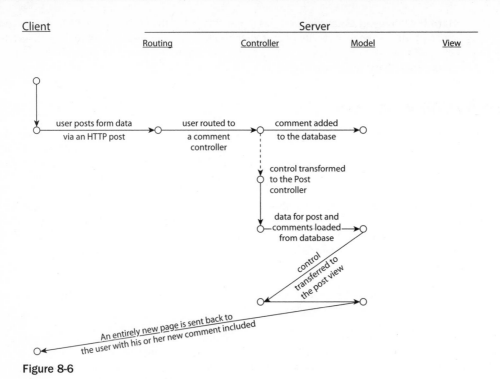

Figure 8-6

The AJAX-enabled version of such a comment form looks almost exactly the same. The user still enters information into the form and still sends it to the server via an HTTP POST operation. The controller still takes care of adding the comment and redirecting to the view. The only differences are as follows:

1. The HTTP POST occurs asynchronously behind the scenes via AJAX.

2. The view code returned by the server does not represent a completely new Web page, but rather instructions for how to update the existing Web page to represent its new post-comment state.

This new type of view is exactly what RJS was designed to represent, seamlessly integrating JavaScript into the MVC paradigm and replacing it with a more readable Ruby syntax. Figure 8-7 illustrates the RJS version of the comment submission.

Look and Feel of RJS

RJS looks and feels a lot like a Ruby adaptation of the JavaScript DOM API. Remember that JavaScript is a generalized scripting language not necessarily tied to the World Wide Web at all—it just happens to be the language that ended up being built into every browser in the world. JavaScript's ability to manipulate the DOM of Web pages is not an inherent feature; it is made possible by an API provided to it by the hosting Web browser. Differences in the way different browsers offer the API are the cause of many Web developer cross-browser compatibility woes. In many ways, RJS is just a Ruby-to-JavaScript compiler coupled with a Ruby adaptation of the DOM API, script.aculo.us API, and Prototype API.

In the tradition of renaming perfectly good concepts when adapting an existing process, RJS replaces the `document` object central to JavaScript with its RJS equivalent, named `page`. The `page` object represents the remote user's Web page and contains method calls for a variety of common manipulations. You can find complete documentation for this object at `rubyonrails.org/api/` under the `JavaScriptGenerator` class, but a few examples here provide an idea of how this object can be used.

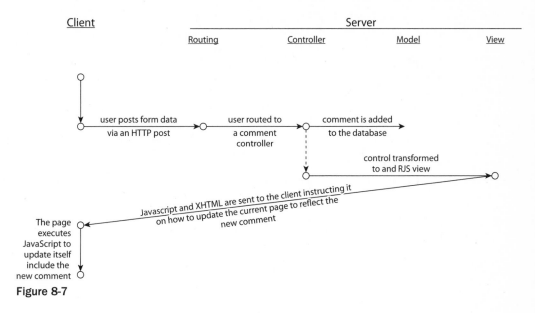

Figure 8-7

One of the most common operations needed by JavaScript views returned by AJAX is to replace one region of the DOM with another. Perhaps a `div` element named `error_message` sits waiting and empty at the top of a form so that real-time, server-side validation can be performed. The RJS view to fill this `div` with an error message might look like this:

```
page.replace_html 'error_message', 'You must fill in your first name!'
```

As an integrated element of the Rails framework, RJS also knows how to handle references to the views and partials that exist elsewhere in the Rails project. When a user logs in to a site via Ajax, for example, a developer might want to replace the user's sidebar with a "members only" variant. This can be accomplished dynamically with RJS code that uses the `page.replace_html` command in conjunction with an RHTML `partial`:

```
page.replace_html 'sidebar', :partial => 'members_only_sidebar'
```

RJS also has access to the variables defined by whichever controller invoked the RJS view. Perhaps a particular action on a RIA page allows the user to asynchronously add items to a to-do list. If the item just added is the first item on the list, then the RJS template should make the new to-do list visible to the user. If there is more than one item on the list, then it is assumed that the list is already visible, and the border of the list should be highlighted to call attention to the fact that the new item has been successfully added. This code assumes the `@todo` variable was prepared by the controller and contains the current to-do list items:

```
page[:todolist].visual_effect(@todo.size > 1 ? :highlight : :appear)
```

The preceding example contains a line that references both an in-page variable (page[:todolist]) and a server-side variable (@todo), so in a very different way than GWT, RJS enables developers to write client-side code that references server-side objects. In the case of GWT, these objects are serialized and sent to the server for conversion to XHTML. RJS expands the code and inserts the referenced object values at runtime, just prior to sending the response to the remote client.

While Ruby offers seamless weaving of client and server references in the same piece of code, it does not afford the debugging benefits that GWT does. As a loosely typed interpreted language, Ruby is not capable of the static type-checking that Java provides. Further, the server has no way of knowing if referenced client-side variables will exist when the code is executed inside within the browser. It can only trust the developer's word and blindly translate the RJS code into JavaScript. Any errors that arise will have to be caught on the client side.

One final aspect of the look and feel of RJS is its ability to use Ruby-style iteration and code blocks. These allow for a long string of statements to be combined for a very quick and concise description of certain concepts. You can use code blocks to cleverly nest concepts, such as actions to take after a delay, for example. Returning to the to-do list, the following code causes the browser to wait for three seconds, after which it highlights every unsaved item in the to-do list and notifies the user that there are unsaved items on the page:

```
page.delay(3) do
  page.select("li.unsaved").each do |item|
    item.set_style :fontStyle => "italic"
  end
  page.replace_html 'notice', 'You must save your work!'
end
```

Summary

Google Web Toolkit and Ruby JavaScript are two completely different approaches to rich Web development with one theme in common: replacing JavaScript with a more developer-friendly language.

GWT attempts to draw on the depth and breadth of existing Java experience by translating the task of RIA development into a form that Java developers already know how to work with. Using GWT, developers gain access to the rich world of Java development environments, debuggers, and testing suites. GWT projects can be written in nearly 100% Java with a set of UI classes that mimic Java's Swing toolkit. These "Widgets" make the production of Google-style applications as easy as adding Swing widgets to a layout manager.

RJS attempts to preserve the Ruby on Rails-style of MVC Web development while eliminating the need to write JavaScript. It presents itself as a special type of view that modifies views that already exist instead of providing a new one. In addition to providing a Ruby version of the DOM API, RJS provides shortcut utility methods to access the functionality of both the Prototype and script.aculo.us libraries. For developers who are considering or have already chosen Ruby on Rails as their development platform, RJS should definitely be considered as a technology to use alongside Rails for its ease of development and seamless integration.

9

An Introduction to ideaStax

---

*In corporate and government bureaucracies, the standard method for making a pre-
sentation is to talk about a list of points organized onto slides projected up on the
wall. For many years, overhead projectors lit up transparencies, and slide projectors
showed high-resolution 35mm slides. Now "slideware" computer programs for presentations are nearly everywhere. Early in the 21st century, several hundred million
copies of Microsoft PowerPoint were turning out trillions of slides each year.*

—Edward Tufte, in *The Cognitive Style of PowerPoint*

In the preceding quote, Edward Tufte, a renown expert on the presentation of ideas, rails against the
growth of slideware in business. In this chapter, you will have the opportunity to build something
different and possibly better — an idea generation and presentation tool that capitalizes on the
Web 2.0 philosophy of enhanced searchability, ubiquitous availability, and, as you shall see in
Chapter 15, greater social and collaborative capability. The application you create is called *ideaStax*,
and in addition to being a fun application, it serves an additional purpose, as discussed next.

Although numerous partial applications are shown throughout the chapters, it is useful to have a
complete application to demonstrate the point of this book, which is that the illustrated techniques
and frameworks can create a full and useful application. This chapter introduces ideaStax, an
application that organizes your thoughts on cards and arranges those cards into a presentation for
others to see.

Because of its comprehensive scope, ideaStax yields an understanding of application control flow,
data modeling, application effects, and user experience. You should examine ideaStax from the
standard perspectives of the user experience (view), the data model, and server-side and in-browser
controls. Given the numerous frameworks discussed in Part II, you had a wide variety of possibilities.
As discussed Chapter 5, Ruby on Rails (Rails for short) seems to do an excellent job of separating
MVC aspects, thus the authors decided to use Rails as an appropriate application framework for
demonstrating a complete application. As the application and the code is discussed, you may
notice the expressiveness and succinctness of Rails. Concepts such as Rails control flow, drag and

drop, page effects, and tagging and searching with variants of ideaStax will be illustrated, and you can play with a version of ideaStax online at `http://RIABook.ideastax.com:3000`. The code for ideaStax is available as a single zip file from `http://RIABook.ideastax.com/Chapter09.zip`.

ideaStax Concept of Operation

IdeaStax is a presentation centric application, a bit like a Web 2.0–style PowerPoint. Similar to PowerPoint, a user uses slides (called Cards in ideaStax) to present ideas, but unlike PowerPoint, IdeaStax allows a user to separate ideas from the slides they appear on, so that they can be separately searched and remixed into new Cards, and Cards can be remixed into many different presentations, or *timelines*, as we call them. Figure 9-1 shows this hierarchy visually.

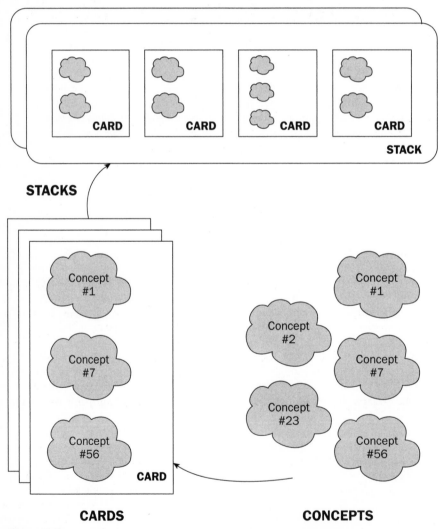

Figure 9-1

IdeaStax has three levels of hierarchy. Concepts aggregate into Cards. Cards aggregate to Stacks. Owing to this containment, the object models are naturally one-to-many in an upward direction. A Card can have many Concepts, and a Stack can have many Cards. A user can start using ideaStax at any point in the hierarchy, by creating a Stack and later adding Cards, or by creating Concepts, and later adding them to Cards, and so on.

Figure 9-2 shows a typical user experience presented by ideaStax. The rightmost column has thumbnail views representing previously created Concepts, and the leftmost contains thumbnail views of Cards. The horizontal spanner at the top of the RIAPage is a list of previously created Stacks. Clicking on the name of a Stack reveals the Stack and its collection of Cards in the span just below it. A Concept or Card can be previewed or edited in the large middle area by clicking the link below the image on the Concept thumbnail or the name of the Card. The view shown in the middle area, either in preview or update mode, is rich text, potentially containing images, links, and prose. Note that there are no objects in the system shown Figure 9-2, and this is the way you should expect to see ideaStax after downloading the code and following the setup instructions that follow.

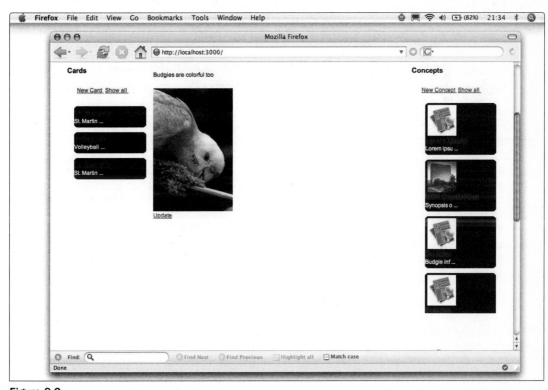

Figure 9-2

Creating a New Stack, Card, or Concept

To continue exploring ideaStax, create a new Stack, Card, or Concept in any order. Figure 9-3 shows the creation of a new Concept. The editor has the look and feel of the standard "scaffold" editor, which is constructed for you as a part of using the scaffold modifier on the declaration of the model. You can create a simple editor with which you can interact with a specific data model by including it in the declaration of the controller. For example, in the controller for Concepts, given the model name "concept," you could simply declare the following:

```
class ConceptController < ApplicationController
  scaffold :concept
... more methods
end
```

This gives you a decent interactive editor, which you could invoke directly from the URL address bar as

```
http//localhost:3000/concept/create
```

and Rails would understand this URL to mean the following:

❏   Route this request to the Concept controller. Look for a method called create.

❏   Then, if there is a scaffold for the model, use that HTML as a template to render a form with the fields from the Concept model.

❏   Give it an update, and destroy links that will then route back to the Concept controller and the appropriate method (which, by default, should have the same name as the link).

Although a scaffold provides a simple interface to the model and a default method of creating new objects in the data model, as well as editing and deleting existing object, it has limitations on the types of fields it can handle — namely, strings (as HTML textfields) multi-line entries (as HTML textareas), and dates or times, for which Rails generates customer form fixtures.

Because the desire is to illustrate methods for including a more full-featured JavaScript editor that enables rich text inputs, the authors opted not to implement the scaffold support. You can see the Concept creator and editor in Figure 9-3, which shows text and picture input.

Once you create a Concept, the interface's right column (see Figure 9-4, for example) fills with thumbnails of Concepts. The concern wasn't with scalability and other user experience issues, so if you create Concepts, they will simply scroll on forever. Notice that the column headers for both Cards and Concepts tell the user that there are no tags for the either.

Chapters 14 and 15 shows you how to design content filtering based on tagging, and that deals with scalability, but for now, you'll keep the design and code a little simpler.

Figure 9-3

Figure 9-4

Creating Cards

Once Concepts exist, an end user can mix and match them into Cards, rather like with PowerPoint except that Concepts are reusable and searchable in a way that objects on a PowerPoint slide have never been. Figure 9-5 shows an example of a newly created Card.

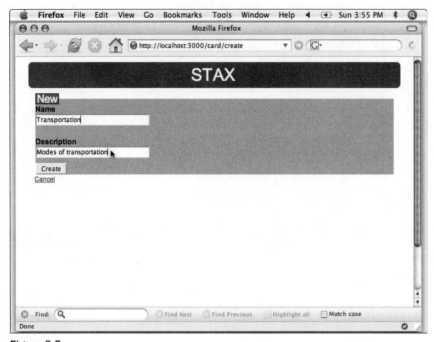

Figure 9-5

The created Concept showed a steam locomotive, so the examples that follow will create Cards to hold Concepts about modes of transportation. Here, you can use the interface much more like a typical Rails scaffold view, except of course that you want to have a consistent style sheet applied. The example in this and succeeding chapters uses a style that you can find in istax.css. As is normal in Web programming, as long as you declare a style sheet and name your DOM elements (divs and spans, for example) accordingly, the style is rendered.

After you save the new Card, the RIAPage updates with a thumbnail of the Card visible in the leftmost pane (see Figure 9-6).

Now that you have a Card in place, you can add a Concept (right now the only Concept) to it. A simple editor for a Card doesn't need to do much, certainly nothing as rich as the Concept editor. Because a Card in this application is simply a sequence of Concepts, a user just needs to get a Card into a Concept. A drag and drop model is appropriate. Figure 9-7 shows a Concept being dragged, and Figure 9-8 shows the Card, after updating, with the Concept. If you had more Concepts, you could continue to include them as well.

Chapter 12 explains the implementation of the ideaStax drag and drop model, but the model elements are included with the code available online. Note the AJAX visual effect of the Card growing to encompass the Concept. Chapter 13 covers user interaction, effects, and animation.

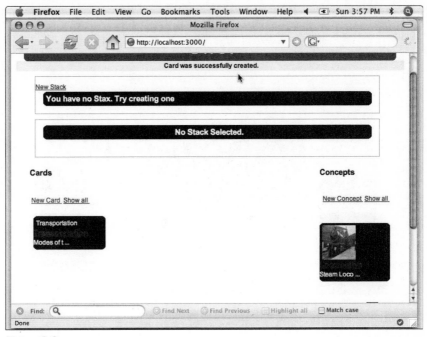

Figure 9-6

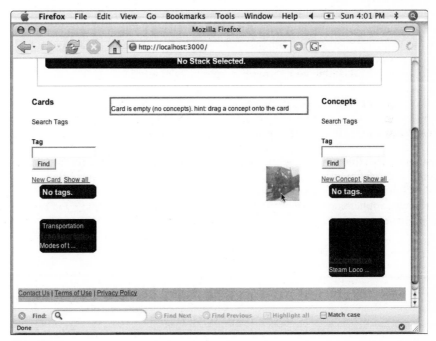

Figure 9-7

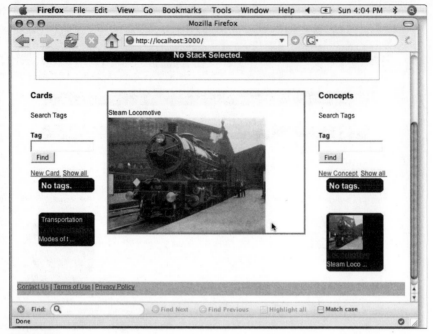

Figure 9-8

The user experience of drag and drop is seamless because of Rails' strong built-in support for AJAX. As you'll see shortly during the discussion of the control flow, Rails hides most of the implementation detail of the XMLHttpRequest and response handling, seen previously in Chapter 1, for example, and consumes a good deal of programmer energy and attention. The Ruby JavaScript (RJS) framework eliminates much of the hand coding you normally would have to write.

The creation of a Stack and the population of a Stack with a sequence of Cards both closely resemble the same operations you saw earlier for creating Cards and adding Concepts to a Card. Figure 9-9 shows the creation of a Stack, and Figure 9-10 shows an index page with a Stack, a Card, and a Concept.

This, in a nutshell, is the capstone application. You are now going turn to putting together the necessary ingredients to create the infrastructure for this application. This is useful not only in constructing this application, but also in a broader sense for creating a general RIA development capability. Then you will deconstruct this application, again useful in its own right, but also in helping you broaden your understanding of Rails in particular.

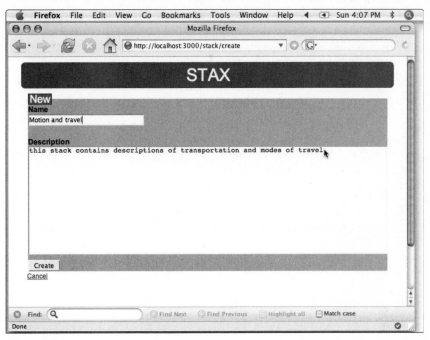

Figure 9-9

Figure 9-10

Getting Started: the Essential Elements

To get started, you need to download some elements. This section discusses how to download Stax, as well as MySQL and Ruby on Rails.

ideaStax

To get started, you will need a baseline version of the Stax code, which you can download from `http://riabook.ideastax.com/ideaStaxChapter09.zip`. Unzip this into the folder that you intend to use as the base directory for this application. You can also download it from the Wrox Web site at `www.wrox.com`.

The version of Stax from the zipped snapshot functions as documented earlier in the section "ideaStax Concept of Operation." The authors bundled the widgEditor from `www.themaninblue.com/experiment/widgEditor/` with the code, because of its small size and ease of integration with Rails and the Stax application in general. widgEditor is used because it provides basic rich font formatting such as bold, italics, links, and lists; and (some limited) font sizing. Additionally, it also supports inline images and headings, and generates XHTML.

In the Preview area of ideaStax, this is consumed as page formatting directives and produces properly formatted output, as you saw in Figures 9-3 and 9-8. Although it is open source and included in the bundle you download from Subversion (described next), should you ever want to reinstall it — for example, to get a newer version — it's relatively painless to (re)install:

1. Download widgEditor to a convenient folder and unzip it. Your ideaStax root should be somewhere else on disk. This chapter refers to this as <application-root>.

2. Copy the `widgEditor.js` file into the `<application-root>/public/javascripts` folder. You can configure the buttons that appear in it by changing widgToolbarItems in this file.

3. Copy the `widgEditor.css` file into your application's `<application-root>/public/stylesheets` folder.

4. Copy all the button images from the unzipped distribution to your `<application-root>/public/images` folder.

5. Include the JavaScript and .css files in your layout file. For Stax, the authors used a single layout file, which according to Rails convention is called `default.rhtml` (see Listing 9-1) and resides in `<application-root>/app/views/layouts/default.rhtml`. It is good practice to list the WidgEditor's style sheet last in the chain, as shown in the following listing.

Listing 9-1: Stax Rails layout default.rhtml

RHTML

```
<html xmlns="http://www.w3.org/1999/xhtml" xml:lang="en" lang="en">
<head>
<meta http-equiv="Content-Type" content="text/html; charset=UTF-8" />
  <%= stylesheet_link_tag 'main' %>
  <%= stylesheet_link_tag 'columns3'%>
  <%= stylesheet_link_tag 'istax'%>
  <%= stylesheet_link_tag 'scaffold'%>
  <%= stylesheet_link_tag 'info'%>
```

```
<%= stylesheet_link_tag 'widgEditor'%>
<%= javascript_include_tag :defaults %>
<%= javascript_include_tag "widgEditor" %>

</head>
<body>
    <div id="header">
    <%= render :partial => 'shared/header' %>
    </div>
    <div id="notifications">
    <%= render :partial => 'shared/notifications' %>
    </div>
      <div id="main-container">
            <%= yield %>
      </div>
      <div id="footer">
    <%= render :partial => 'shared/footer' %>
</body>
</html>
```

The additional stylesheets give ideaStax its multipanel look and feel and supply the normal Rails appearance (for example, to enable easy creation of model manipulation via scaffolds).

6. With WidgEditor installed, usage is simple; any text field you want to have rich text editing capabilities should be identified with a class attribute of widgEditor. A snippet of the Concept editor (see app/views/concept/_form.rhtml) in ideaStax shows an example of this usage:

```
<%= start_form_tag :action => 'update', :id => @concept %>
...
<%= text_area 'concept', 'html', "cols" => "10", "rows"=>"12",
"class"=>"widgEditor" %>
</div>
<%= end_form_tag %>c
```

MySQL

Although Rails is quite happy to work with a number of backing databases, here the authors set up things to use MySQL, always a good bet for its simplicity, availability, and ease of administration.

Several prebuilt bundles are available from mysql.org. If you have something else installed (for example, SQLite has grown very popular), you must adapt the code shown here and in Chapter 14, in particular, Tagger.cgi, and DBLookup.py, and the model creation, and photo and tag loaders (described in TableCreator.py and PhotoLoader.py). Post installation, you can check to ensure that all is well with MySQL (for example, that the executable was added to your PATH by the installer) by invoking MySQL from the command line (typically, mysql -u username -p).

A discussion on the specific setup of the ideaStax database and tables is in the next section, "Ruby on Rails Setup."

Whenever your database access does not seem to be working properly, remember to either configure MySQL on install to autostart on reboot, use one of the third-party MySql control panels, or keep the System Preference panel (OS/X) or the System Settings panel (Windows) in mind.

Ruby on Rails Setup

Rails is available from www.rubyonrails.org. For Windows, there's a self-executing installer; for OS/X (10.4) follow the installation instructions available at developer.apple.com/tools/rubyonrails .html or hivelogic.com/articles/2005/12/01/ruby_rails_lighttpd_mysql_tiger. To align the ideaStax code you've already downloaded with the Rails release, follow these steps. First, edit <application-root>/config/environment.rb.

1. Find the line specifying the Rails version similar to this one:

```
RAILS_GEM_VERSION = '1.1.6'
```

2. Adjust it to agree with the version you downloaded from the Rails site. Additionally, because it will be useful to modify subsequent dumps of the database schema to output in Ruby rather than SQL, find the following line in the file

```
# config.active_record.schema_format = :sql
```

and modify it accordingly:

```
config.active_record.schema_format = :ruby
```

3. Now edit <application-root>/config/database.yml to reflect your database choices. The following example shows a database configuration file set up for mysql. Depending on what database choices you have made, you will have to adjust the configuration accordingly.

```
development:
   adapter: mysql
   database: istax_development
   username: ria
   password: ria
   host: localhost
test:
   development
production:
   development
```

4. You will also need to create a database and authorize the username and password for the chosen data store. Typically, you need to perform steps such as the following (exemplified for MySQL). Assuming that the username and password are both 'ria':

```
$ mysql -u root -p
> create database istax_development;
> use istax_development;
> grant all privileges on *.* to ria@localhost identified by 'ria';
```

5. Now that you've created a database and a user, you can use

```
rake db_schema_import
```

from a terminal to create the supporting tables for the application by translating a Ruby definition of the schema (already supplied as an artifact of the Subversion check out) in SQL statements for your chosen database. The tables will exist after this step, but be empty of content. The output should resemble the following:

```
(in /Users/area51/ideaStax)
-- create_table("cards", {:force=>true})
   -> 0.0088s
-- create_table("cardships", {:force=>true})
   -> 0.0101s
-- create_table("concepts", {:force=>true})
   -> 0.0115s
-- create_table("stacks", {:force=>true})
   -> 0.0822s
-- create_table("stackships", {:force=>true})
   -> 0.0149s
-- initialize_schema_information()
   -> 0.0164s
-- columns("schema_info")
   -> 0.0069s
```

This step uses the models (expressed as Rails code) from `<application-root>/db/migrate` to create the tables used in the application. You can either create models by hand using direct SQL commands on the database or let Rails do most of the work for you by using Rails' migration capability. A Rails migration has an `up` method to create a table, and a `down` method to drop the table. You can use migrations to roll a database forward (say, to add a field) or back to an earlier incarnation. In Listing 9-2, the `up` method creates the Concept table with the fields rendered in the Concept creation form shown in Figure 9-3.

Listing 9-2: create_concepts.rb

RUBY
```ruby
class CreateConcepts < ActiveRecord::Migration
  def self.up
    create_table :concepts do |t|
      t.column "name", :string
      t.column "description", :string
      t.column "image", :string
      t.column "html", :text
      t.column "updated_at", :datetime
    end
  end

  def self.down
    drop_table :concepts
  end
end
```

Although this chapter does elaborate migrations further than this, you can find a more complete discussion at rubyonrails.org.

Now you have Rails and Stax set up to operate correctly aligned with the code. You will apply a similar strategy for any new projects you design.

ideaStax: the Implementation Detail

It's time to turn to an examination of the code base, and to start you'll look at the model. The data flow in a Rails application tends to bounce around a lot, and ideaStax is no exception. The graphic shown at the end of the chapter (Figure 9-12) depicts the flow of a Rails archetype. As you follow the flow through ideaStax, you actually may find it useful to sit with paper and pencil and trace the path through the program execution.

Deconstructing Concept, Card, and Stack

As you begin to deconstruct ideaStax, you should start with the simplest element of the implementation, the data model. In addition to the basic elements of the data model created manually by you or by using Rails migrations, Rails looks for supporting code (constraints, relational data) for the basic model in `<application-root>/app/models`, by convention, modules are named for the model element they support. The supporting model for representing Concepts is shown in Listing 9-3.

Listing 9-3: concept.rb

```RUBY
class Concept < ActiveRecord::Base
  # validations
  validates_presence_of :name
  validates_presence_of :description
  # Relationships to Join Tables
  has_many :cardships
end
```

The Concept model reflects the fact that Concepts exist on the "many" side of a "one-to-many" relationship with Cards — a Card can contain many Concepts, and the *cardships* model is cited as the join table for this relationship. As you will see from examining `card_controller.rb`, the `add_concept` method handles setting up the relationship between Cards and Concepts. Note, too, that you can specify validation checks that will be performed before a new record will be created or modified in the underlying model. The Rails SDK has over a dozen types of possible validations that you can perform on specific fields — and you can specify multiple validators. In this case, `validates_presence_of` requires that name and description be non-null. To observe this in action, try creating a new Concept with an empty name or description and attempt to save it (see Listing 9-4). You will see graphically that Rails notifies the users visually.

Listing 9-4: card.rb

```RUBY
class Card < ActiveRecord::Base
# validations
  validates_presence_of :name
  validates_presence_of :description
  # Relationships to Join Tables
  has_many :stackships
  has_many :cardships
  # Relationships to Entities via Through-Associations
  has_many :concepts, :through => :cardship
end
```

Cards have similar validation requirements for the name and description fields. In addition, join tables are specified for Concepts and Stacks. Notice that because Cards can contain multiple Concepts, the model specifies how the one-to-many relationship is maintained (via the statement has_many :concepts, :through => :cardship).

The Stack model implementation is similar to that of Card, whereby the Stack can contain many Cards, as shown in Listing 9-5.

Listing 9-5: stack.rb

RUBY

```ruby
class Stack < ActiveRecord::Base
  # Relationships to Join Tables
      has_many :stackships
  # Relationships to Entities via Through-Associations
  has_many :cards, :through => :stackships
end
```

The relational join tables are as one might expect them to be. Listing 9-6 shows the cardships model.

Listing 9-6: cardship.rb

RUBY

```ruby
class Cardship < ActiveRecord::Base
  belongs_to :card
  belongs_to :concept
end
```

Verifying Concepts, Cards, and Stacks

Now use the console to verify the Concepts, Cards, and the Stack you created earlier in the chapter. You can use the Rails development console to interact with the model or exercise controller methods. Invoke it like this from the application-root folder:

```
script/console
Loading development environment.
```

You can find all Cards by using a method on the Card class:

```
>> cards = Card. find(:all)
>> [#<Card:0x2571784 @attributes={"name"=>"Transportation", "id"=>"1",
"description"=>"Modes of transportation"}>]
```

You can find a specific card by using its unique id. This is the card you created in Figure 9-5:

```
>> card = Card.find_by_id(1)
>> #<Card:0x2549e00 @attributes={"name"=>"Transportation", "id"=>"1",
"description"=>"Modes of transportation"}>
```

And this is the Concept you created in Figure 9-3:

```
>> concept = Concept.find_by_id(1)
>> #<Concept:0x252eb50 @attributes={"html"=>"<p>Steam Locomotive</p><img
alt=\"Locomotive\"
src=\"http://upload.wikimedia.org/wikipedia/en/thumb/d/d8/Steam_Locomotive.jpg/300p
x-Steam_Locomotive.jpg\" />", "name"=>"Locomotive", "updated_at"=>"2006-10-08
15:50:18", "id"=>"1", "description"=>"Steam Locomotive ", "image"=>"<img alt=
\"Stax Concept\" src=\"http://upload.wikimedia.org/wikipedia/en/thumb/d/d8/
Steam_Locomotive.jpg/300px-Steam_Locomotive.jpg\" width=\"64\" height=\"64\"/>"}>
```

Remember from Listings 9-3 and 9-4 that Cards and their contents are related through the cardships relational table. As is typical for relational tables, the join is achieved via the system-assigned unique ids for both Cards and Concepts. Listing 9-7 shows the migration that sets up the cardships relation.

Listing 9-7: create_cardship.rb

RUBY

```ruby
class CreateCardships < ActiveRecord::Migration
  def self.up
    create_table :cardships do |t|
      # t.column :name, :string
      t.column :concept_id, :integer
      t.column :card_id, :integer
      t.column :position, :integer
    end
  end

  def self.down
    drop_table :cardships
  end
end
```

Again, you use the console to invoke the `find` method on the `Cardship` class to take a look at cardships:

```
>> cardships = Cardship.find(:all)
>> [#<Cardship:0x2525dd4 @attributes={"concept_id"=>"1", "card_id"=>"1", "id"=>"1",
"position"=>nil}>]
```

Finally, remember from Figure 9-9 that you created a new Stack as well. You can find all Stacks this way:

```
>> stacks = Stack.find(:all)
>> [#<Stack:0x250a958 @attributes={"name"=>"Motion and travel", "id"=>"1",
"description"=>"this stack contains descriptions of transportation and modes of
travel"}>]
```

And find a single Stack this way:

```
>> stack = Stack.find_by_id(1)
=> #<Stack:0x2500c8c @attributes={"name"=>"Motion and travel", "id"=>"1",
"description"=>"this stack contains descriptions of transportation and modes of
travel"}>
>>
```

Implementing the Views

The basic look and feel on the ideaStax RIAPage is implemented in `index.rhtml`, shown in Listing 9-8. A Rails RHTML file is a template for use by Rails to create and manage a RIAPage.

Listing 9-8: index.rhtml

RHTML

```
1 <div class="topper"></div>
2 <div class="staxlist">
3     <%= link_to  "New Stack", :controller => 'stack',
     :action => 'create'  %>
4     <% if ((@stacks == nil) || @stacks.empty?) %>
5         <%= render :partial => 'shared/voidspace',
    :locals => { :displaytext => "You have no  Stax. Try creating one" } %>
6     <% else %>
7         <%= render :partial => 'stack/stacklist',
    :locals => {:stacks => @stacks} %>
8     <% end %>
9 </div>
10
11 <div class="topper"></div>
12 <div id="timeline" class="timeline">
<!-- contains cards in this timeline -->
13     <% if ((@stack == nil) || @stack.empty?) %>
14         <%= render :partial => 'shared/voidspace',
    :locals => { :displaytext => "No Stack Selected." } %>
15     <% else %>
16         <%= render :partial => 'stack/stack',
    :locals => { :stack => @stack } %>
17     <% end %>
18 </div>
19
20 <div id="mainleft" >
21     <div class="spacer"></div>
22     <h3>Cards</h3>
23     <%= link_to "New Card ",:controller => 'card',
    :action => 'create'  %>
24     <%= link_to_remote  "Show all ",
    :update => "cardlist", :url => {:controller => "card",
    :action => "listcards"} %>
25     <div id="cardlist">
26         <%= render :partial => 'card/cardlist',
    :locals => {:cards => @cards}%>
27     </div>
28 </div>
29
30 <div id="maincenter" >
31     <div id="maincontent" style="display: none;" >
32     </div>
33 </div>
34
35 <div id="mainright" >
36   <div class="spacer"></div> <h3>Concepts</h3>
```

(continued)

Listing 9-8: *(continued)*

```
37      <%= link_to "New Concept ", :controller => 'concept', ↵
 :action => 'create' %>
38      <%= link_to_remote "Show all ", :update => "conceptlist", ↵
 :url => {:controller => "concept", :action => "listconcepts"} %>
39      <div id="conceptlist">
40          <%= render :partial => 'concept/conceptlist', ↵
 :locals => {:concepts => @concepts} %>
41      </div>
42 </div> <!-- End of rightcontent div -->
```

Note the following about Listing 9-8:

❑   Lines 2–9 create the Stack management area shown at the top of Figure 9-2. The Rails `link_to` embedded on line 3 specifies the transfer of control to the Stack controller (`stack_controller .rb`) and the create method. The Rails page interpreter tests to see whether there are any Stacks in the database. If not, then the empty Stack message at the top of Figure 9-2 is rendered, or else the Stack list shown in Figure 9-10 is rendered. Note that each of the renderers is a "partial" renderer.

❑   The point of a partial renderer is to refresh only part of a page. The control path always routes first to the controller. If there is a method by the same name (stacklist, in this case), then the method is executed. If not, then a view component is invoked. By convention, a partial renderer name starts with an underscore character. Thus, to find the stacklist logic, look for the file `<application-root>/app/views/stack/_stacklist.rhmtl`. Note that stacklist is passed an array of Stacks and consists of a single line of code (`<%= render :partial => 'stack/ thumbnail', :collection => stacks %>`). It also calls a partial renderer (`thumbnail.rhtml`). Note the collection syntax. When Rails encounters a collection, it implements an iterator that passes each member of the collection to the specified partial renderer.

❑   A similar logic is employed in the `<div>` declared in lines 11–18. When a Stack is created, it is rendered into the stacklist DIV above via the `_thumbnail.rhtml` with the Stack name as a link (see Figure 9-10). When the link is clicked, the list is rendered in the timeline `<div>`. The thumbnail partial renders each Stack name as a `link_to_remote`, which uses an `XMLHttpRequest` to route to the controller. The result of that request replaces the content of the timeline `<div>` (see `stack_controller.rb` and `load_stack.rjs`).

❑   The `mainleft` `<div>` (lines 20–29) is the area containing card thumbnails. It has the same implementation strategy you saw earlier for Stack. You have excised some line of code having to do with the implementation of tags and tagging. You won't need to be concerned about that until Chapter 15.

❑   The `maincenter` `<div>` (lines 30–34) is initially empty. You will see from inspecting the code that this area is constantly being replaced with new content depending on the operation the user selects — for example, previewing a Card with Concepts as shown in Figure 9-7. Updating a current Concept renders the Concept form shown in Figure 9-3 in this area as well. Think of the `maincenter` `<div>` as the main action area for all ideaStax activities, i.e., previews and updates.

❑   The `mainright` `<div>` (lines 35–42) contains existing Concepts and links to create new Concepts. It operates with the same design and implementation as that for Cards and Stacks.

Note that line numbers shown here may not match perfectly with the code you download from
`http://RIABook.ideastax.com/ideastax.zip` *for a couple reasons. First, the code download has additional capabilities (for example, tagging as implemented in Chapter 14). Second, the code is open source, and the authors and readers of the book will likely contribute new capabilities to the open-source code base over time.*

You can now look at the round-trip routing from the New Concept link to the appearance of the Concept's thumbnail in the `mainright <div>` and then a subsequent click of the thumbnail to preview a Concept in the `maincenter` area as a way of introducing the controller discussion in the section to follow.

Implementing the Controllers

Controllers are the final essential ingredient of the Model-View-Controller triad. In this section, the controller code and design is presented.

When a user clicks the New Concept link, there is a transfer of control explicitly stated in the tag (line 37)

```
<%= link_to "New Concept ",
      :controller => 'concept',
      :action => 'create'  %>
```

to the `concept_controller.create` method, in `<application-root>/app/controllers/concept_controller`. A snippet of this controller is shown in Listing 9-9.

Listing 9-9: concept_controller.rb (partial)

RUBY on Rails

```
60   def create
61     # Multiplex based on request type
62     if request.post?
63       @concept = Concept.new(params[:concept])
64       # User is posting data for a new one
65       if @concept.save
66         flash[:notice] = 'Concept was successfully created.'
67         redirect_to editor_url
68       else
69         # Do nothing.. fall through to the form
70         flash[:notice] = 'Concept was not created.'
71       end
72     else
73       # Fall through to the form after loading initial data
74       @concept = Concept.new
75       @concept.html = "Create a <em>new concept</em>"
76       @concept.image = "<img alt=\"Stax Concept\" ↲
   src=\"../images/stax.png\" width=\"64\" height=\"64\"/>"
77     end
78   end
```

Creating Tests for HTTP POST or GET

You can start by creating tests for a POST or a GET. When the HTTP Request is a GET, from the link_to, a prototype Concept (with fields helpfully pre-populated) is created (lines 72–77). Control is then transferred to a full-page renderer. You could have made it a partial renderer; examine the code in <application-root>/app/views/concept/load_concept.rjs (which is discussed a bit later and shown in Listing 9-12). The full-page renderer, shown in Listing 9-10, renders the form, including a Submit button. The rendered form is contained in <application-root>/app/views/concept/_form.hmtl, which isn't shown but which you can examine in the download. The Submit button form is shown in Figure 9-3. Now, when a user submits the form, the control flow turns right around and does a HttpRequest POST of the form data to concept_controller's create method. Now create executes lines 62–71. As a result, the index page is refreshed and because there are now Concepts, they become visible in the rightmost SPAN (here, exactly one Concept is shown).

Listing 9-10: create.rhtml

RUBY on Rails

```
1 <div class="spacer"></div>
2 <fieldset class="formfs">
3 <legend class="legend">New</legend>
4 <%= start_form_tag :action => 'create' %>
5   <%= render :partial => 'concept/form' %>
6   <%= submit_tag "Create" %>
7 <%= end_form_tag %>
8 </fieldset>
9 <%= link_to 'Back', editor_url %>
```

Using the Ruby JavaScript Construct as a Partial Renderer

You have seen some model code, some controller code, and some RHTML view templates and how they fit together. However, the Rails helper and its role in the architecture, as well as the Ruby JavaScript (RJS) construct, hasn't been covered. The helper category is covered in Chapter 15. Let's go one step further with Concepts and look at how you can use RJS as a partial renderer as well as an RHTML file.

When the Concept thumbnail is rendered (see Listing 9-8, line 40), control is transferred via the _conceptlist.rtml partial renderer, shown here in its entirety, to another partial renderer contained in _thumbnail.rhtml, shown in Listing 9-11:

```
<div class="spacer"></div>
<%= render :partial => 'concept/thumbnail', :collection => concepts %>
```

Listing 9-11: _thumbnail.rhtml

RHTML

```
1 <% if thumbnail != nil %>
2 <div class="darkbluecontainer">
3   <b class="dkbrtop"><b class="r1"></b> <b class="r2"></b> @ta
  <b class="r3"></b> <b class="r4"></b></b>
```

```
 4    <div class="nicelyspaced">
 5        <% name = "conceptImage_"+thumbnail.id.to_s %>
 6        <div id="conceptImage_<%= thumbnail.id.to_s %>" @ta
   class='conceptThumbnail'>
 7          <%= thumbnail.image %>
 8        </div>
 9    </div>
10      <% if (thumbnail != nil) %>
11    <H3>
12 <%=  link_to_remote thumbnail.name, :url => { :controller => "concept",@ta
   :action => "load_concept", :id => thumbnail.id }%>
13
14    </H3>
15
16      <% if ((thumbnail.description != nil) && @ta
   (thumbnail.description.length> 10)) %>
17        <%= thumbnail.description[0,10]+" ..." %>
18    <% else %>
19        <%= thumbnail.description %>
20    <% end %>
21    <% end %>
22    <b class="dkbrbottom"><b class="r4"></b> <b class="r3"></b>@ta
  <b class="r2"></b> <b class="r1"></b></b>
23 </div>
24 <div class="spacer"></div>
25
26 <%= draggable_element(name, :revert => true) %>
27 <% end %>
```

Both of these are contained in the `<application-root>/app/views/concept` folder. Most of the code specifies the formatting of the thumbnail image and the description of a Concept, and it's worthwhile reading simply as an illustration of how conditionals are handled in an RHTML template (for example, lines 16–20, where the description is elided if the string is longer than 10 characters), or how regular XHTML formatting is intermingled with embedded Rails directives.

For this examination of RJS, though, focus on line 12 and follow the control flow. Line 12 contains a `link_to_remote` tag. This tag, as opposed to a `link_to` tag, discussed above, is intended to kick off an `XMLHttpRequest` whereby the results replace a part of the page asynchronously, in typical AJAX fashion. Where RJS comes into play is that, instead of your having to generate the JavaScript to coordinate the AJAX action and event handling, Rails does it for you.

When a user clicks the Locomotive link shown in Figure 9-4, control transfers first to a controller method (`concept_controller.load_concept`) along with the database unique id of the record (`thumbnail.id`). Listing 9-12 shows what `load_concept` does in response.

Listing 9-12: load_concept.rjs

RJS
```
def load_concept
  @concept = Concept.find(params[:id]) rescue @concept = nil
end
```

Load_concept finds the right record and loads it into a variable. Rails then looks for something in the <application-root>/app/views/concept folder (either a view template beginning with an underscore, or an RJS file) and uses that as a renderer. In this case, it finds load_concept.rjs, partially shown here:

```
page["maincontent"].hide
page["maincontent"].replace_html :partial => 'concept/concept', @ta
 :locals => {:concepts => @concept }
page.visual_effect :grow, 'maincontent'
page.show   :maincontent
```

The AJAX action happens just as stated above. The maincontent <div> contents are "erased." A partial renderer is invoked. Its name is _concept.rhtml, and it's found in the same folder just mentioned. It's a partial renderer because it only replaces the maincontent <div>. The Concept held in @concept is passed to the _concept.rhtml renderer. Then a special effect (the script.aculo.us "grow" effect) is applied and the maincontent <div> is made visible again.

The _concept.rhtml partial renderer is pretty simple. It contains just the HTML field from the Concept record along with a link_to_remote tag labeled "Update":

```
<%= concept.html %>
<%= link_to_remote "Update", :url => { :controller => "concept", :action =>
"update_concept", :id => concept.id }%>
```

The effect of the partial render is shown in Figure 9-11.

Figure 9-11

242

As you would imagine, the "Update" link_to_remote transfers control back to concept_controller, and there finds a method called update_concept, as specified in the code snippet. As an exercise, open concept_controller.rb in Radrails, TextMate, or your favorite editor and trace the control flow through to the next step, assuming that a user clicked the Update link shown in Figure 9-11.

Rails Control Flow

Certainly it seems as though there is a good deal of routing going on in this implementation, but once again it follows the general flow control model for any typical Rails application, as shown in Figure 9-12.

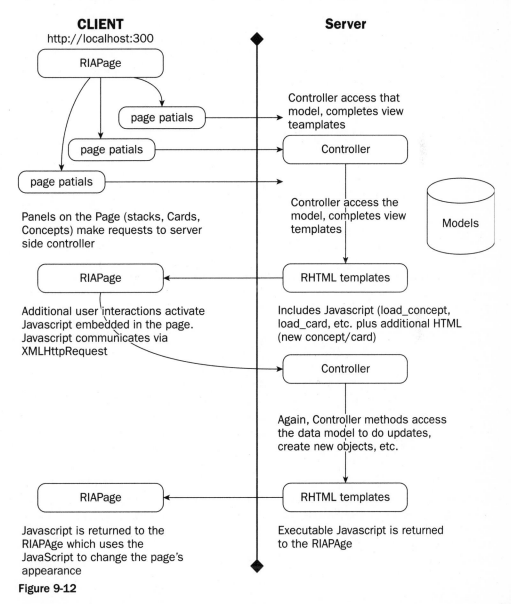

Figure 9-12

It takes a considerable amount of time to become comfortable with all the bouncing from one control point to the next; and in our opinion, developing in Rails simply does not have the same "feel" as developing in another of the frameworks previously discussed. One thing we constantly found ourselves asking was, "What does the next control point have to be, and how do we express the action required?" It differs considerably in syntax depending on whether the control point is an RHTML template, controller code, or an RJS module.

Another point to remember is that in the Rails worldview, subfolders are meaningful, as Table 9-1 shows.

Table 9-1: Rails Subfolders

Subfolder	Meaning
models	All data models should appear in .rb files in the app/models folder. Models are the classes that model and wrap the data stored in your application's database. Rails models allow the application developer relative independence from caring deeply about the underlying database implementation.
controllers	All controllers should appear in .rb files of the app/controllers folder. Rails maps HTTP requests (both GET and POST) to controllers and methods within the controller. The form_remote_tag and link_to_remote (both of which are used in Stax) are good examples of how Rails resolves tags embedded in the RHTML page into controller methods. Look at the implementation of the search form in the _searchtags .rhtml partial renderer, or the link_to_remote in the _thumbnail.rhtml that renders Concepts and Cards into the middle column of the main page, for example.
views	All views and partial views should appear in .rhtml (Ruby-embedded HTML) and .rjs (Ruby JavaScript) files in the app/views folder. RHTML files in the views subfolder are named to correspond with controllers or controller methods, and represent the display templates that are filled in with data from the application's controllers. Once filled in properly, Rails converts them to HTML, and returns the result (full pages or <div>/<span> elements) to the user's browser. RJS files generate JavaScript to be rendered in a RIAPage and what makes a page come to life. A good example in Stax of RJS interactivity is load_concept.rjs, which expands a thumbnail into the preview area by doing a partial HTML rendering, and produces the special "grow" effect.
helpers	All helpers should appear in .rb files of the app/helpers folder. Helpers are employed for a variety of miscellaneous uses, but primarily to rid controller code of clutter. Helpers most often perform some manipulation that is orthogonal to the primary mission of the controller. Accordingly, writing the right helper seems just the right approach for creating our tag clouds. Although you haven't seen helpers being used yet, whenever you create a new Rails application, a set of empty helpers is generated for you.

Notice the strict conformance to this structure in the code you've downloaded. Going outside this folder hierarchy is strongly discouraged and in fact may break your application.

Summary

This chapter laid out the capstone application and described the design and implementation. Subsequent chapters cover specific elements in greater detail:

❑   Chapter 10 expands the coverage to include autocompletion and in-browser validation.

❑   Chapter 11 discusses usability and other design elements that are implicitly a part of the capstone and any other modern RIAPage, but which aren't covered in this chapter.

❑   Chapter 12 takes on the topic of implementing drag and drop within a RIAPage. In this chapter, drag and drop was used as the editor technique for both Cards and Stacks, but wasn't expanded upon.

❑   If you were wondering what line 26 of Listing 9-11 does or how to perform the drag and drop shown in Figure 9-7, Chapter 12 is the place to jump in. Moreover, if you are exercising the code download and are wondering how to do the visual effect shown in the code snippet from load_concept.rjs, then Chapter 13 is the place for you.

❑   If you were curious about those places in Figure 9-2 that say "No Tags," read on to Chapter 14 and 15 to learn more about adding social aspects to your RIAPage.

Part III

RIA Development in Depth

10

Form Validation

A common mistake that people make when trying to design something completely foolproof is to underestimate the ingenuity of complete fools.

—**Douglas Adams,** *Mostly Harmless*

In order to explore the various patterns that you can apply when developing a Web application, this chapter examines a very common and frequently troublesome area of Web application development and design: the form. Since the dawn of HTML, forms have proven to be a thorn in the side of Web developers and Web users alike. The user invariably makes at least one mistake when filling out a form of any complexity. As is the case in any system, even rich-client platform systems, it is necessary to ensure that the data coming into the system conforms to the expected formatting and constraints.

The Web developer, well aware of the frequency of user mistakes, is required to incorporate validation capabilities into the system, but faces additional complexity. As is the case with all other aspects of Web programming, the Web developer must account for the disconnect between client and server when designing the validation capabilities of the system.

Incorporating Form Validation into Your System

There are many approaches to validating data in a Web application; a couple of quite useful, additional approaches are available when using AJAX. Some of the frequently used approaches to validation include the following:

- ❑ Server-side validation of the entire form, which includes the following two types:
  - ❑ Synchronous
  - ❑ Asynchronous
- ❑ Client-side validation with JavaScript
- ❑ Asynchronous server-side validation of a single form element

After exploring each of these approaches in more depth, you'll get some hands-on experience with each approach. Throughout the remainder of the chapter, you'll apply each of the approaches within a single form that captures the creation of a new user for a Web application. You'll create an unchecked form initially, and then add some client validation with Dojo. Next, you'll develop a server-side component capable of performing validation of the entire form on asynchronous submission. Finally, this foundation will be extended to include asynchronous server-side validation of a single field.

Server-Side Validation of the Entire Form

The simplest approach is to validate all data on the server when the form is submitted. This is also the safest approach, and you should always include it regardless of the additional approaches taken to enhance user interactivity. This is because the data is validated right before it is consumed. If a problem occurs, it is reported to the user, the user first fixes and then submits the correct fields, and the form is validated once again. As long as the data is validated and used at the same time, the system can't attempt to use invalid data. Other approaches cannot make this guarantee.

The primary disadvantage to this approach is that users end up perceiving a very disconnected process. They fill out a long form, submit it, receive notification of a whole handful of errors, and have to correct them all and try again. This is where the alternative approaches come in. Generally, they attempt to provide a more interactive experience by validating each field as it is filled out, rather than separately.

Validation on the server side can be performed in two ways, via synchronous or asynchronous request. Both approaches have basically the same effect, but the use of an asynchronous request has a significant advantage over the synchronous approach.

Synchronous Server-Side Validation of the Entire Form

Submitting a form synchronously forces the user to leave the page when submitting the form for validation. If the validation fails, the user is then returned to the original page, but, of course, the state on the original page has been lost. The Web developer has to include additional JavaScript code to manually repopulate the form in this case.

Asynchronous Server-Side Validation of the Entire Form

When using an asynchronous request, this step is not required because the user always remains on the same page. The page is simply updated to display the validation errors. The disadvantage to using an asynchronous request for this submission is that if the user has JavaScript disabled, then the request cannot be made, and some graceful form of degradation should generally be implemented.

Client-Side Validation with JavaScript

Because validating only on the server provides the user with such a disconnected experience, many Web sites include a simple validation of the form on the client using JavaScript. This provides a much more pleasant and interactive experience for the user. As the user types each key, or moves off each field, the field is validated. The user has an immediate response regarding the validity of the input. However, this approach doesn't release the developer from having to validate on the server, for a couple of reasons. The most obvious is that the user may have JavaScript disabled, in which case you need the server-side validation as the last line of defense.

Although the validation on the client side does provide a more pleasant user experience, it isn't always a viable approach. It works fine for situations when you can establish simple validation rules that JavaScript can execute without access to the server. For example, consider the validation of a phone number. It's most likely sufficient to ensure that it has the correct number of digits, a task that you can easily accomplish in client-side JavaScript with regular expressions. Consider as an alternative an online store form that processes some type of order. It's likely that the user must enter a part number that corresponds to a piece of inventory in the store. With server validation, the validation process is straightforward. The user types in a part number, and a database is checked to determine whether the part is available. Of course, this type of validation on the client is not possible without providing the list of all parts embedded in the form. Imagine sending one million valid part numbers with each part order form. It's hardly a feasible approach. The other limitation to client-side validation is that it requires the specification of validation logic in two separate places.

Asynchronous Server-Side Validation of a Single Form Element

The third alternative is to asynchronously validate a single field as the user tabs off it. This provides some benefit of both the preceding approaches, with minimal limitations. You use the full power of the server to access a database or incorporate other complex business logic, while gaining the enhanced interactivity by validating as the user enters each form field. An advantage to this approach is that it only requires the specification of the validation logic in a single place. Of course, this approach isn't without limitations itself. It requires much more server interaction, because a new server request is made when the user leaves each field.

It is generally neither practical nor desirable to use server-side validation of each field separately for every field on the form. This should be considered another approach, albeit a very powerful approach, when developing a more comprehensive scheme of client and server-side validation. The most effective schemes typically use asynchronous server-side validation of fields that are difficult to validate on the client and likely to be wrong, such as a username, in conjunction with client-side validation of simple fields, such as dates and numbers, and a final validation of the form on submission.

Capturing User Information

Now that you know the main concerns associated with validating form data and the common approaches taken on both server and client, this section begins with an example that explores a very common requirement of Web sites and applications: the construction of a user information form. Web sites and applications, which vary greatly in complexity, share the common need to collect data about the site's users. Sites requiring user data may range from those that provide mostly static information, but would benefit from a guestbook, to highly complex Web applications. Consider Web-based e-mail services such as gmail.google.com that require user information to associate with e-mail addresses, allow user preferences, and establish necessary security. Regardless of the reason, most sites of any complexity require users to provide some level of personal detail, and frequently create a personalized login to perform certain activities. This can be useful for a variety of reasons:

❑ **Preference capture** — Sites such as my.yahoo.com or www.google.com allow users to personalize the Web site content, and "look and feel" to provide a more effective user experience.

❑ **Subscription services** — Sites such as www.nytimes.com and www.ebay.com require a user to log in, and pay for premium services. For example, NYTimes requires a user to pay a monthly service fee to access premium services, including additional articles, e-mail alerts, and a preview function. eBay requires users to pay for each item they list for sale.

❑ **Access control** — Sites may need to identify users to allow them access to content they generated. Consider www.writely.com, a Web-based document editor. Users must be uniquely identified to determine which files are accessible and/or modifiable. It wouldn't be a very useful Web application if it allowed any Web site viewer to look at or modify any file on its server.

❑ **User tracking** — Sites also frequently find it useful to capture statistics about users for marketing purposes. Sites such as www.amazon.com frequently capture sales statistics for use in marketing to users.

The Unchecked User Form

This section gets you started by exploring a simple user input form that doesn't include any validation. You will build on this in the following sections to include client and server-side validation, and finally add on AJAX-based validation.

> *This example assumes that you are using Jakarta Tomcat v5.5 (see* tomcat.apache.org*) installed under* c:\Tomcat. *You should initially have an empty directory,* c:\Tomcat\webapps\ UserManager, *that will hold the user management Web application.*

For this example, start by creating a simple HTML page, UserFormv1.html, under your Web application root, that will create the new user form. Listing 10-1 contains the initial version of UserInputv1.html.

Listing 10-1: The nonvalidating UserInputv1.html

```
1  <html>
2   <title>Enter User Details</title>
3   <head>
4    <link rel="stylesheet" type="text/css" href="layout.css" />
5   </head>
```

```
6   <body>
7   <div class="titlebar">Stax</div>
8   <div class="functionbar">Enter User Details</div>
9   <div id="status" class="statusbar"></div>
10   <fieldset class="formfs">
11    <legend class="forml">User Detail</legend>
12    <form id="user_detail">
13     <table class="formelt">
14      <tr>
15       <td><label>Desired username</label></td>
16       <td><input name="username" id="username"/></td>
17       <td><label id="username-label">
18       </label></td>
19      </tr>
20      <tr>
21       <td><label>First name</label></td>
22       <td><input name="firstname" id="firstname"/></td>
23       <td><label id="firstname-label">
24       </lable></td>
25      </tr>
26      <tr>
27       <td><label>Last name</label></td>
28       <td><input name="lastname" id="lastname"/></td>
29       <td><label id="lastname-label">
30       </label></td>
31      </tr>
32      <tr>
33       <td><label>Birthday</label>
34         <label class="formnote">(e.g.,03/10/1974)</td>
35       <td><input name="birthday" id="birthday"/></td>
36       <td><label id="birthday-label">
37       </label></td>
38      </tr>
39      <tr>
40       <td><label>Email address</label>
41         <label class="formnote">(e.g., foo@bar.org)</label></td>
42       <td><input name="emailaddr" id="emailaddr" size="30"/></td>
43       <td><label id="emailaddr-label">
44       </label></td>
45      </tr>
46      <tr>
47       <td><label>Phone</label>
48         <label class="formnote">(e.g., 123-456-7890)</label></td>
49       <td><input name="phone" id="phone" size="14"/></td>
50       <td><label id="phone-label">
51         </label></td>
52      </tr>
53      <tr>
54       <td><label>Address1</label></td>
55       <td><input name="addr1" id="addr1" size="50"/></td>
56       <td><label id="addr1-label">
57       </label></td>
58      </tr>
59      <tr>
```

(continued)

Listing 10-1: *(continued)*

```
 60        <td><label>Address2</label>
 61          <label class="formnote">(optional)</label></td>
 62        <td><input name="addr2" id="addr2" size="50"/></td>
 63        <td><label id="addr2-label">
 64        </label></td>
 65      </tr>
 66      <tr>
 67        <td><label>City</label></td>
 68        <td>
 69        <input name="city" id="city"/>
 70        <label id="city-label">
 71        </label>
 72      </tr>
 73      <tr>
 74        <td><label>State</label></td>
 75        <td><select style="width: 200px" value="AL" class="userselect"
 76          name="state" id="state">
 77          <option id="AL" value="AL">AL - ALABAMA</option>
 78          <option id="AK" value="AK">AK - ALASKA</option>
 79          <option id="AZ" value="AZ">AZ - ARIZONA</option>
 80          <option id="AR" value="AR">AR - ARKANSAS</option>
 81          <option id="CA" value="CA">CA - CALIFORNIA</option>
 82          <option id="CO" value="CO">CO - COLORADO</option>
 83          <option id="CT" value="CT">CT - CONNECTICUT</option>
 84          <option id="DE" value="DE">DE - DELAWARE</option>
 85          <option id="DC" value="DC">DC - WASHINGTON, DC</option>
 86          <option id="FL" value="FL">FL - FLORIDA</option>
 87          <option id="GA" value="GA">GA - GEORGIA</option>
 88          <option id="HI" value="HI">HI - HAWAII</option>
 89          <option id="ID" value="ID">ID - IDAHO</option>
 90          <option id="IL" value="IL">IL - ILLINOIS</option>
 91          <option id="IN" value="IN">IN - INDIANA</option>
 92          <option id="IA" value="IA">IA - IOWA</option>
 93          <option id="KS" value="KS">KS - KANSAS</option>
 94          <option id="KY" value="KY">KY - KENTUCKY</option>
 95          <option id="LA" value="LA">LA - LOUISIANA</option>
 96          <option id="ME" value="ME">ME - MAINE</option>
 97          <option id="MD" value="MD">MD - MARYLAND</option>
 98          <option id="MA" value="MA">MA - MASSACHUSETTS</option>
 99          <option id="MI" value="MI">MI - MICHIGAN</option>
100          <option id="MN" value="MN">MN - MINNESOTA</option>
101          <option id="MS" value="MS">MS - MISSISSIPPI</option>
102          <option id="MO" value="MO">MO - MISSOURI</option>
103          <option id="MT" value="MT">MT - MONTANA</option>
104          <option id="NE" value="NE">NE - NEBRASKA</option>
105          <option id="NV" value="NV">NV - NEVADA</option>
106          <option id="NH" value="NH">NH - NEW HAMPSHIRE</option>
107          <option id="NJ" value="NJ">NJ - NEW JERSEY</option>
108          <option id="NM" value="NM">NM - NEW MEXICO</option>
109          <option id="NY" value="NY">NY - NEW YORK</option>
110          <option id="NC" value="NC">NC - NORTH CAROLINA</option>
111          <option id="ND" value="ND">ND - NORTH DAKOTA</option>
```

```
112          <option id="OH" value="OH">OH - OHIO</option>
113          <option id="OK" value="OK">OK - OKLAHOMA</option>
114          <option id="OR" value="OR">OR - OREGON</option>
115          <option id="PA" value="PA">PA - PENNSYLVANIA</option>
116          <option id="RI" value="RI">RI - RHODE ISLAND</option>
117          <option id="SC" value="SC">SC - SOUTH CAROLINA</option>
118          <option id="SD" value="SD">SD - SOUTH DAKOTA</option>
119          <option id="TN" value="TN">TN - TENNESSEE</option>
120          <option id="TX" value="TX">TX - TEXAS</option>
121          <option id="UT" value="UT">UT - UTAH</option>
122          <option id="VT" value="VT">VT - VERMONT</option>
123          <option id="VA" value="VA">VA - VIRGINIA</option>
124          <option id="WA" value="WA">WA - WASHINGTON</option>
125          <option id="WV" value="WV">WV - WEST VIRGINIA</option>
126          <option id="WI" value="WI">WI - WISCONSIN</option>
127          <option id="WY" value="WY">WY - WYOMING</option>
128        </select></td>
129      <td><label id="state-label"></label></td>
130    </tr>
131    <tr>
132     <td><label>Zip</label></td>
133     <td><input name="zip" id="zip" size="5" maxsize="5"/></td>
134     <td><label id="zip-label"></label></td>
135    </tr>
136    <tr>
137     <td></td>
138     <td></td>
139     <td><input type="submit" class="userbutton"
140       value="Create user"/></td>
141    </tr>
142    </table>
143   </form>
144  </fieldset>
145  </body>
146 </html>
```

Rather than rely on the plain, standard HTML formatting for the page, a reference is included to a cascading style sheet on line 4 of Listing 10-1. The definition of the CSS, "layout.css", is shown in Listing 10-2. You should also create and save this file under your Web application root (i.e., c:\Tomcat\webapps\ UserManager).

Listing 10-2: The referenced cascading stylesheet layout.css

```
1 body {
2     margin:          0px;  /* No Margin Outside the Object */
3     padding:         0px;  /* No Padding Inside the Object */
4     font-family:     Veranda, Arial, Tahoma, sans-serif;
5 }
6
7 .titlebar {
8     width:           100%; * Stretch to the container width */
9     height:          75px;
10    margin:          0px 0px 0px 0px;
```

(continued)

Listing 10-2: *(continued)*

```
11      background-color:    #444444;
12      color:              #FFFFFF;
13      text-align:         center;
14      font-size:          30pt;
15 }
16
17 .functionbar {
18      width:              100%; /* Stretch to the container width */
19      height:             50px;
20      margin:             0px 0px 0px 0px;
21      background-color:    #000044;
22      color:              #FFFFFF;
23      text-align:         center;
24      font-size:          20pt;
25 }
26 .statusbar {
27      width:              100%; /* Stretch to the container width */
28      height:             30px;
29      margin:             0px 0px 10px 0px;
30      background-color:    #CCCCFF;
31      color:              #000000;
32      text-align:         center;
33      font-size:          16pt;
34 }
35
36 .formfs {
37      background-color:    #9999FF;
38      font-size:          14px;
39 }
40
41 .forml {
42      font-size:          20px;
43      background-color:    #555599;
44      color:              #FFFFFF;
45      border:             solid thin black;
46 }
47
48 .formelt {
49      font-size:          12px;
50      font-weight:        bold;
51      margin:             5px 5px 10px 20px;
52 }
53
54 .formnote {
55      font-style:         italic;
56 }
57
58 input {
59      font-size:          12px;
60      vertical-align:     middle;
61 }
62
```

```
63 .userselect {
64     font-size:        12px;
65 }
66 .userbutton {
67     font-size:        14px;
68 }
```

After you save the new files, start your Web server and point a browser to `http://localhost:8080/`
`UserManager/UserInputv1.html`. You should get a page similar to the one shown in Figure 10-1,
which shows a nonvalidating user form. It includes a variety of form elements necessary to capture relevant user details, such as name, e-mail address, phone number, and address:

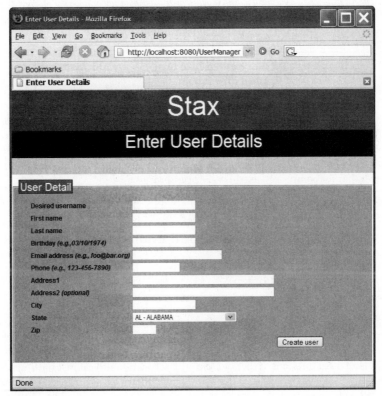

Figure 10-1

❑   The box surrounding the form fields is created with the `fieldset` tag (Listing 10-1, line 10), and
    the descriptive text "User Detail" in the top-left corner is created with the `legend` tag.

❑   The layout is produced by adding all elements of the form to a table with three columns. The left
    column holds the field label, the middle contains the form fields, and a final column is initially
    empty. You will populate this last field with the results of our server-side validation attempts later.

❑   At this point there is no client-side validation of the form. The user can specify any value for
    any element on the field and submit it to the server with the Create User button. Currently, this
    has no effect, and simply returns to the same page.

Validation in Practice: Client-Side Validation with Dojo

Now you're almost ready to start adding the validation. This requires significantly enhancing the existing static page, which includes the addition of JavaScript to perform client-side validation of the form fields, as well as constructing a variety of asynchronous requests necessary to validate the form elements on the server. Rather than manually produce the extensive amounts of JavaScript required for your Web application, it is much more efficient to incorporate a JavaScript library.

> *As described in Chapter 8, using JavaScript libraries in a Web application can greatly increase developer productivity, enhance code readability, and significantly reduce the complexity of Web applications. Rather than reinvent the wheel, it can be greatly effective to apply common solutions when developing several components necessary for many types of Web applications.*

As stated previously, you first want to analyze the needs of the Web application being developed before selecting a JavaScript library. After analysis, the Dojo Toolkit (http://dojotoolkit.org/) was selected for the user form in this section, for several reasons:

❑ Dojo provides a comprehensive framework for client-side form validation. Of the libraries surveyed throughout this book, Dojo provides the most complete and user-friendly library of form validation components. The validation library includes form elements that automatically capture and handle field events that require validation. This feature is a differentiator when compared to several other commonly used JavaScript libraries.

❑ Dojo provides an efficient mechanism for creating asynchronous calls. This mechanism includes a variety of hooks for error handling, and support for inclusion of form data.

❑ Dojo includes a combo box widget capable of dynamically loading server-side data via an asynchronous request.

❑ Dojo gives you a simple yet effective approach to debugging.

❑ Dojo has several functions to simplify DOM interactions and manipulation.

❑ Dojo provides functions to simplify searching for an element by id, similar to the Prototype library's concise $() operator.

Of course, this isn't a comprehensive list of Dojo's total functionality; it just outlines those aspects of Dojo of particular usefulness in terms of the user form Web application. Now that you've seen why Dojo was selected, the following sections demonstrate how to incorporate the Dojo Toolkit into your application. You learn how to install Dojo, and use the debug capabilities and client-side validation functions. You also see how to incorporate widgets in your application. To begin, you add the Debug Console widget, and finally make use of the variety of Dojo validation widgets.

Installing the Dojo Toolkit

After selecting Dojo as the JavaScript library, you simply need to download and install it. Because of its size, you may not want to include all aspects of Dojo in your Web application. To allow for this, Dojo is available in a variety of editions, each with different elements of the full Dojo Toolkit included. The authors are using the AJAX edition of Dojo version 0.3.1 available at http://download.dojotoolkit.org/

`release-0.3.1/dojo-0.3.1-ajax.zip`. Installation is as simple as extracting the downloaded zip file. For this example, you should unzip Dojo under `c:\Tomcat\webapps\UserManager\Javascript`. For more detail on the capabilities of Dojo, see Chapter 7.

Getting Started with Dojo

Before getting into the details of using Dojo for client-side validation, you need to include Dojo in your Web application. You initially need to add three scripts to the `head` element (directly following the `link` element) in `UserInputv2.html`:

1. The first script to enter sets up the Dojo configuration:

```
<script type="text/javascript">
 djConfig = {isDebug: true};
</script>
```

You must specify this script before you include the Dojo JavaScript (which is shown in step 2). `djConfig` is a global variable that defines common configuration options for Dojo. The preceding script turns on Dojo's debug output by setting the `isDebug` flag to `true`.

2. Include the Dojo script by adding the following below the first script:

```
<script type="text/javascript" src="Javascript/dojo-0.3.1-ajax/dojo.js">
</script>
```

3. Import the library required for validation as follows:

```
<script>
 dojo.debug("Using Dojo version: ", dojo.version.toString());
 dojo.require("dojo.widget.validate");
</script>
```

Note that the first line of the script in step 3 shows you how to use the `debug` function in Dojo. This is a very useful feature of Dojo that can greatly aid the Web developer in analyzing JavaScript execution. As the name implies, the `debug` function simply writes the given string, or set of strings, to the bottom of the browser window. As shown in the debug statement, you separate multiple strings with a comma. The debug statement displays the version of Dojo used.

The second line of the script in step 3 loads the `dojo.widget.validate` module into the environment. Dojo is organized into modules that may consist of many functions or classes in a related area — for example, the set of functions capable of validating a string are in the `dojo.validate` module. These modules are loaded dynamically with the `require` function, similar to Java's `import` directive.

Using Client-Side Validation Functions

Now that you've installed and set up Dojo, you're ready to add client-side validation of the username field. As indicated earlier, Dojo is one of the few JavaScript libraries that includes validation components. Two modules deal with validation in Dojo: `dojo.validate` and `dojo.widget.validate`. The `dojo.validate` module contains a set of functions that are useful when validating general components. Any of these validation functions can be invoked anywhere in standard JavaScript. For example, the `dojo.validate` module defines a function that validates an integer. This function returns `true` when you provide an integer argument, or when the argument is a string that can be converted into an integer. To see this function in action, replace the "Using dojo.widget.validate" debug statement in `UserInputv2` `.html` with the following calls to `isInteger`:

```
dojo.debug("Validation of \"32\" returns ",
  dojo.validate.isInteger("32"));
dojo.debug("Validation of 32 returns ",
  dojo.validate.isInteger(32));
dojo.debug("Validation of \"No\" returns ",
  dojo.validate.isInteger("No"));
var aDate = new Date();
dojo.debug("Validation of a date returns ",
  dojo.validate.isInteger(aDate));
```

As you can see, these functions are very handy when you need to verify that a data element is formatted as you expect. You can use the validation module to verify that strings conform to a variety of simple and complex formats such as integers, dates, URLs, and e-mail addresses. Most validation functions can also accept an optional set of flags. For example, the `isInteger` function accepts a `signed` flag that indicates whether or not the integer can must start with a plus (+) or minus (–) character. The function also takes an optional `separator` flag that establishes whether a thousands separator is allowed and if so, what character you should use. For example, the following call to the `isInteger` validation function indicates that validation will only return `true` if the integer is be signed, and thousands are either separated with a dot (.) or no thousands separator is present:

```
dojo.validate.isInteger("+32", {signed: true, separator: ["", "."]});
```

Note that you should define all flags between curly braces, i.e.,`{}`. The specified flag name is followed by a colon (`:`), which should be followed by the value you want to assign to the flag. You may assign multiple values to the flag if they're included in an array (established with square brackets, i.e., `[]`). See the multiple acceptable values "" and "." for the `separator` flag above. Refer to Appendix A for more details about the various validation functions in Dojo. All functions return `true` or `false` depending on the test.

Using Dojo Validation Widgets

A *widget* is a reusable component in the Dojo library that provides an enhancement to more simplistic HTML. Dojo includes a huge set of predefined widgets and is easily extensible, so you can even define your own widgets. Widgets enhance the user experience in many areas of a Web application — from helping the developer lay out a page to improving the look and feel of form elements or other page components. For example, there are widgets for trees, buttons, moveable internal panels, and combo boxes. There's even a fully interactive rich text editor widget that you can define in a single line! The following sections focus on the set of widgets that help validate form fields, and Chapter 11 examines in detail a server-backed combo box widget that has auto-complete capabilities. But before getting into the validation widgets, the following section examines another widget that's very useful for Web programmers: the Debug Console widget.

Adding the Debug Console Widget

In the previous section, we added various Dojo debug statements that are displayed in the same frame as the Web page. This is fine for performing simple debugging of small Web applications, but isn't very scalable for large asynchronous Web applications. When displaying debug statements in the same page, you interact with the Web application, and the page continues to grow with additional debug statements.

The fact that you're most likely making asynchronous calls more frequently than loading new pages in the AJAX-enabled Web application only complicates the problem. You ultimately end up with a Web application that has a long tail of debugging output at the bottom of the page, which forces you to continuously scroll to the bottom of the page, look at the output, and then scroll up to the top to interact with the page.

Dojo includes the Debug Console widget to help alleviate this problem. You can use this widget to redirect all debugging output to a separate floating internal panel. You can drag the panel around the page, close it, or resize it. The widget also includes an internal scrollbar, so that as debugging statements are added, the console gets a scrollbar rather than the Web page itself.

To add a debug console to `UserInputv3.html`, load the correct module by adding the following:

```
dojo.require("dojo.widget.DebugConsole");
```

This should be added to the head after the first `dojo.require` line that causes the `dojo.widget.validation` module to be loaded.

Then define your new widget by adding a new `div` specification near the bottom of the body of your current page. Add the following after the closing `fieldset` element, but before the closing `body` tag:

```
<div dojoType="DebugConsole" id="debugContainer" name="debugContainer"
    title="My Debugger" constrainToContainer="false" hasShadow="true"
    style="width: 500px; height: 200px; left: 50px;
    resizable="true" displayCloseAction="true"></div>
```

The preceding code defines a `div` with a few additional attributes that cause the Dojo widget to be created. The `dojoType` attribute specifies the type of attribute to create. This should correspond to a widget class such as `TitlePane`, `Checkbox`, or `DebugConsole`. A set of attributes specific to the type of widget that you're trying to create is also defined, including the following:

❑ A `title` attribute applicable when creating any type of floating pane. This enables you to specify a title to appear at the top of the panel.

❑ The `constrainToContainer` flag specifies whether the panel can be positioned outside of the normal Web application boundaries. If you position the pane at the bottom of the page when this is set to `false`, a scrollbar appears. When set to `true`, you cannot drag the frame past the bottom of the page.

❑ The `hasShadow` flag gives the panel a more three-dimensional appearance.

❑ The `style` attribute is the normal `css` attribute. In the preceding code, you use it to outline the dimensions and initial position of the panel.

❑ The `resizable` flag indicates whether or not the pane can be made larger or smaller.

❑ The `displayCloseAction` attribute indicates whether or not the frame can be closed.

That's all that's required to include a new widget in your page! The only additional change required to link up the `DebugConsole` is to modify your `djConfig` array to send debug messages to the new panel. The new value for the array should be the following:

```
djConfig = {isDebug: true, debugContainerId : "debugContainer" };
```

Finally, you may want to include a larger set of debug statements for experimentation by adding the following loop after your `dojo.require` statements:

```
for (var idx = 0; idx < 10; idx++) {
  dojo.debug("Here's debug message " + idx);
}
```

If you redeploy and reload, you get a new floating panel containing all your debug messages, as shown in Figure 10-2. You can drag the panel around the page, resize it, and even close it if you want.

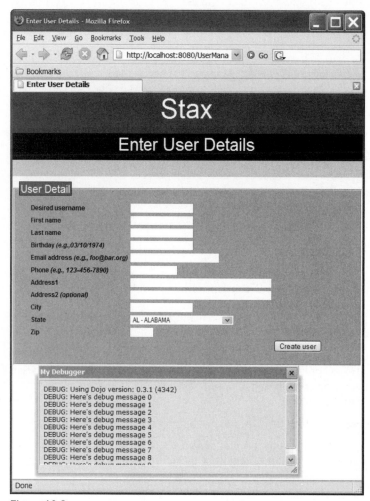

Figure 10-2

Adding the Username Field Validation Widget

Now that you've set up your debugger, you're ready to replace your standard HTML form elements with Dojo widgets that will perform the validation for you. To get started, create `UserInputv4.html` and modify the `username` form element to include a `dojoType` and some additional supporting attributes as follows:

```
<input name="username" id="username" dojoType="ValidationTextbox"
  required="true" missingMessage="* Username is required!"
  invalidMessage="* Invalid username!"/>
```

Setting the type to `ValidationTextbox` causes the form field to be replaced with the Dojo widget that includes validation capabilities. The remaining attributes tailor the behavior of the validation. The `required` flag indicates whether the field must be filled in. This is set to `false` by default. You can also optionally display tailored messages when a field element is invalid or missing with `missingMessage` and `invalidMessage` attributes. That's all that's required to validate your textbox. You may, however, want to tailor the appearance of your missing and invalid messages. You can do this by modifying the stylesheet to include an entry for `invalid` and `missing` as follows:

```
.invalid, .missing{
  font-size:   12px;
  font-weight:   bold;
  color:     #F00000;
}
```

If you redeploy and reload at this point, you'll get a new page with a username field that performs validation, as shown in Figure 10-3. As you type in a name the field is validated, an error message may display, and the field itself will appear either red or green depending on whether it's valid. The page on the left of Figure 10-3 shows the form before any username is specified. Note the field failed validation and is displaying an error message "Username is required!" On the right, the user has input a username that passed validation. The error message is gone (and the field has turned light green, although that can't be seen in the screenshot).

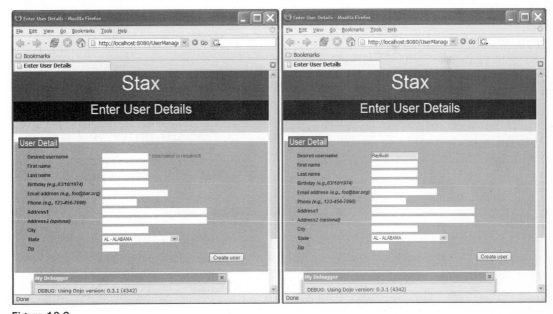

Figure 10-3

Dojo Validation Widget Reference

When using the validation textbox widget, any value entered into the field is considered valid. There are many other widgets capable of performing validation of a form field, as shown in Table 10-1. Each uses a different validation function, or multiple functions, described in detail in Appendix A, and can take any of the flags defined for the widget's associated validation function as element attributes. For example, you can define a validation widget for a shoe size input field that requires an integer between 1 and 20 with the following input element specification:

```
<input name="shoesize" id="shoesize"dojoType="IntegerTextbox"
  min="1" max="20" rangeMessage="* Shoesize must be between 1 and 20"></input>
```

Table 10-1: Dojo Validation Widgets

Widget	Validation Function (see Appendix A)	Test
ValidationTextbox	None	Accepts any value containing at least one non-whitespace character
IntegerTextbox	isInteger, isInRange	Accepts integer values, optionally within a range specified by max and min attributes
RealNumberTextbox	isRealNumber, isInRange attributes	Accepts real number values, optionally within a range specified by max and min
CurrencyTextbox	isInCurrency, isInRange	Accepts data formatted as currency (by default U.S. currency, i.e., $3.00), optionally within a range specified with max and min attributes
IpAddressTextbox	isIpAddress	Accepts values formatted as IP addresses
UrlTextbox	isUrl	Accepts values formatted as URLs
EmailTextbox	isEmailAddress	Accepts values formatted as e-mail addresses
EmailListTextbox	isEmailAddressList	Accepts values that define lists of e-mail addresses
DateTextbox	isValidDate	Accepts values that are formatted as dates (default is MM/DD/YYYY).
TimeTextbox	isValidTime	Accepts values that are formatted as a time (default is 12-hour, for example: h:mm:ss t).
UsStateTextbox	isState (US)	Accepts values that are two-letter U.S. state abbreviations
UsZipTextbox	isZipcode (US)	Accepts values formatted as zip codes
UsSocialSecurityNumber	isSocialSecurityNumber (US)	Accepts values formatted as social security numbers
UsPhoneNumberTextbox	isPhoneNumber (US)	Accepts values formatted as phone numbers, with optional extension

Dojo Validation Widget Attribute Reference

The shoesize widget defined in the preceding example code only includes a subset of the complete set of possible attributes that can be defined for a validation widget. Table 10-2 shows the set of attributes that you can define for a validation widget. You can define any of these attributes for any type of validation widget. Note that the standard HTML attributes (e.g., id or value) are not included. Also note that several of the optional attributes can cause the field value to be automatically modified to conform to a required standard (such as trimmed, or all lowercase or all uppercase).

Table 10-2: Dojo Validation Widget Attributes

Attribute	Default Value	Meaning
Trim	false	Removes leading and trailing white space
Lowercase	false	Converts all characters to lowercase
Uppercase	false	Converts all characters to uppercase
ucFirst	false	Converts the first character of each word to uppercase
Digit	false	Removes all non-digit characters
validColor	#cfc (e.g., green)	The color to assign to the field when it passes the validation test
invalidColor	#ffc (e.g., red)	The color to assign to the field when it fails the validation test
invalidClass	invalid	The name of the CSS class to assign to the field when it fails the validation test
invalidMessage	* The value entered is not valid.	The message to display when the field fails the validation test
missingClass	missing	The name of the CSS class to assign to the field when it is required but left blank
missingMessage	* This value is required.	The message to display when the field is required but left blank
rangeClass	range	The name of the CSS class to assign to the field when the value is out of range
RangeMessage	* This value is out of range.	The message to display when the field value is out of range
listenOnKeyress	true	When true, test the field on each key press; otherwise, test the field on blur.

Adding the Remaining Field Validation Widgets

At this point, you're ready to modify all the form fields to use Dojo widgets. Listing 10-3 shows an updated version of UserInputv5.html that performs required client-side validation.

Listing 10-3: UserInputv5.html updated to perform client side validation

```
1  <html>
2   <title>Enter User Details</title>
3   <head>
4    <link rel="stylesheet" type="text/css" href="layout.css" />
5    <script type="text/javascript">
6     djConfig = {isDebug: true, debugContainerId : "debugContainer" };
7    </script>
8    <script type="text/javascript" src="Javascript/dojo-0.3.1-ajax/dojo.js">
9    </script>
10   <script>
11    dojo.debug("Using Dojo version: ", dojo.version.toString());
12    dojo.require("dojo.widget.validate");
13    dojo.require("dojo.widget.DebugConsole");
14   </script>
15  </head>
16  <body>
17   <div class="titlebar">Stax</div>
18   <div class="functionbar">Enter User Details</div>
19   <div id="status" class="statusbar"></div>
20   <fieldset class="formfs">
21    <legend class="forml">User Detail</legend>
22    <form id="user_detail">
23     <table class="formelt">
24      <tr>
25       <td><label>Desired username</label></td>
26       <td><input name="username" id="username"
27        dojoType="ValidationTextbox" required="true"
28        missingMessage="* Username is required!"
29        invalidMessage="* Invalid username!"/></td>
30       <td><label id="username-label">
31       </label></td>
32      </tr>
33      <tr>
34       <td><label>First name</label></td>
35       <td><input name="firstname" id="firstname"
36        dojoType="ValidationTextBox" required="true"
37        missingMessage="* First name is required!"
38        invalidMessage="* Invalid first name!"/></td>
39       <td><label id="firstname-label">
40       </label></td>
41      </tr>
42      <tr>
43       <td><label>Last name</label></td>
44       <td><input name="lastname" id="lastname"
45        dojoType="ValidationTextBox" required="true"
46        missingMessage="* Last name is required!"
47        invalidMessage="* Invalid last name!"/></td>
48       <td><label id="lastname-label">
49       </label></td>
50      </tr>
51      <tr>
52       <td><label>Birthday</label>
```

```
 53       <label class="formnote">(e.g.,03/10/1974)</label></td>
 54     <td><input name="birthday" id="birthday" dojoType="DateTextbox"
 55      required="true" missingMessgae="* Birthday is required!"
 56      invalidMessage="* Invalid Birthday!"/></td>
 57     <td><label id="birthday-label">
 58     </label></td>
 59    </tr>
 60    <tr>
 61     <td><label>Email address</label>
 62     <label class="formnote">(e.g.,  foo@bar.org)</label></td>
 63     <td><input name="emailaddr" id="emailaddr" size="30"
 64      dojoType="EmailTextbox" required="true"
 65      missingMessage="* Email address is required!"
 66      invalidMessage="* Invalid email address!"/></td>
 67     <td><label id="emailaddr-label">
 68     </label></td>
 69    </tr>
 70    <tr>
 71     <td><label>Phone</label>
 72        <label class="formnote">(e.g., 123-456-7890)</label></td>
 73     <td><input name="phone" id="phone" size="14"
 74      dojoType="UsPhoneNumberTextbox"
 75      required="true" missingMessage="* Phone number is required!"
 76      invalidMessage="Phone number should be nnn-nnn-nnnn!"/></td>
 77     <td><label id="phone-label">
 78     </label></td>
 79    </tr>
 80    <tr>
 81     <td><label>Address1</label></td>
 82     <td><input name="addr1" id="addr1" size="50"
 83      dojoType="ValidationTextBox" required="true"
 84      missingMessage="* Address is required"
 85      invalidMessage="* Invalid address!"/></td>
 86     <td><label id="addr1-label">
 87     </label></td>
 88    </tr>
 89    <tr>
 90     <td><label>Address2</label>
 91        <label class="formnote">(optional)</label></td>
 92     <td><input name="addr2" id="addr2" size="50"
 93      dojoType="ValidationTextBox" required="false"
 94      invalidMessage="* Invalid Address!"/></td>
 95     <td><label id="addr2-label">
 96     </label></td>
 97    </tr>
 98    <tr>
 99     <td><label>City</label></td>
100     <td>
101     <input name="city" id="city"/>
102     <label id="city-label">
103     </label>
104     </td>
105    </tr>
106    <tr>
107     <td><label>State</label></td>
```

(continued)

Listing 10-3: *(continued)*

```
108        <td><select style="width: 200px" value="AL" class="userselect"
109          name="state" id="state">
110          <option id="AL" value="AL">AL - ALABAMA</option>
111          <!-- Remainder of State options -->
161          </select></td>
162          <td><label id="state-label"></label></td>
163        </tr>
164        <tr>
165         <td><label>Zip</label></td>
166         <td><input name="zip" id="zip" size="5" maxsize="5"
167          dojoType="UsZipTextbox" required="true"
168          invalidMessage="* Zipcode is invalid!"
169          missingMessage="* Zipcode is required!"></input></td>
170         <td><label id="zip-label"></label></td>
171        </tr>
172        <tr>
173         <td></td>
174         <td></td>
175         <td><input type="submit" class="userbutton"
176            value="Create user"/></td>
177        </tr>
178       </table>
179      </form>
180    </fieldset>
181    <div dojoType="DebugConsole" id="debugContainer" name="debugContainer"
182     title="My Debugger" constrainToContainer="false" hasShadow="true"
183     style="width: 500px; height: 200px; left: 50px;"
184     resizable="true" displayCloseAction="true"></div>
185    </body>
186  </html>
```

Notice in Listing 10-3 that each input field from the original HTML page has been extended to include several attributes necessary to define the Dojo widget, with two exceptions: the city and state fields. Leave these unchanged for now. These fields are examined in more detail in Chapter 11.

Adding Submission of Valid Forms Only

The last step in enhancing the form to do client-side validation is to block form submission until a completely valid form is defined. This requires the addition of a couple of JavaScript functions. To keep the HTML file page from becoming too cluttered, define the functions in a separate file. To do this, you must first create a new JavaScript file under the JavaScript directory named userform-helperv1.js. Move the code from the last script in the head of UserInputv5.html, i.e., the dojo.require statements, into your new file. Replace this last script definition with a new script in UserInputv6.html that is simply a reference to the new external JavaScript — for example:

```
<script type="text/javascript" src="Javascript/userform-helper.js">
</script>
```

Now you can write the validation function in `userform-helperv1.js`. First, create a function that validates any given field in the form. You will call this method with the name of each form field (i.e., username, lastname, etc.). Define a new `validateField` function as follows:

```
1  function validateField(fieldName) {
2    var fieldElt = dojo.widget.byId(fieldName);
3    if (fieldName.match("^city$")) {
4      // for now always assume the city is valid.
5      return true;
6    } else if (fieldName.match("^state$")) {
7      // not strictly necessary to validate the state because we're using
8      // a select. It should always be valid.
9      fieldElt = dojo.byId(fieldName);
10     var valid = dojo.validate.us.isState(fieldElt.value);
11     return valid;
12   } else {
13     var fieldElt = dojo.widget.byId(fieldName);
14     return ((fieldElt.isValid())&&(!fieldElt.isMissing()));
15   }
16 }
```

Note the use of a couple of very useful functions included with Dojo. Line 9 contains a call to the `dojo.byId` function. This is similar to the Prototype function `$()`, and serves simply as shorthand for `document.getElementById`. Note this returns a DOM node. A similar, yet different function, `dojo.widget.byId`, is called on line 2. This function returns a reference to a Dojo widget. You don't have to worry too much about the differences between the two right now; just bear in mind that you should generally use `dojo.widget.byId` when you want to retrieve a Dojo widget. Otherwise, use `dojo.byId`.

This function is basically separated into a conditional statement that handles three different situations. First, when dealing with the city field, always return `true`. Note that the city currently isn't a Dojo widget. You'll make further modifications to this in Chapter 11, so for now skip any validation, and always return `true`.

The portion of the conditional statement that handles the state element is defined from lines 6–11. Again, this is a special case. The state isn't a Dojo widget so it must be validated separately. Actually, you don't strictly need to validate it at all because it's a select element and has a limited set of options. It's just a good excuse to see the validation of a state in action. The element is initially retrieved on line 9, and has its value tested with the us locale-specific `isState` function on line 10.

The final section on lines 12–15 define the final clause of the conditional, and handle any of the other form fields, all of which are Dojo validation widgets and quite simple to check for validity. Because the validation method is maintained in the element, you can just call two functions: `isMissing` and `isValid`. The `isMissing` function of a validation widget returns `true` if the widget has no value specified and has its required flag set to `true`. The `isValid` function returns `true` if the value specified for the component passes the `isValid` test of the associated validation functions in the `dojo.validation` module. The element is simply checked to ensure that it is both valid and not missing (line 14).

After completing the validation function, you need to call the `validateField` function for each of your form elements by first defining an array of each of the element names in your form. You should define this near the beginning of your script file, after the last `dojo.require` statement, as follows:

```
var fieldNames = ["username", "firstname", "lastname", "birthday",
  "emailaddr", "phone", "addr1", "addr2", "city", "state", "zip"];
```

Next, define a new function `handleSubmit`, as shown in the code that follows. You'll see later that you can modify the form to call this function before the form submission occurs.

```
 1 function handleSubmit() {
 2   var statusElt = dojo.byId("status");
 3   statusElt.innerHTML = "Validating Data...";
 4
 5   var valid = true;
 6   dojo.lang.forEach(fieldNames, function(fieldName) {
 7     if (!validateField(fieldName)) {
 8       valid = false;
 9     }
10   }, true);
11   if (!valid) {
12     statusElt.innerHTML = "Can not create user! Fields below have errors";
13   } else {
14     statusElt.innerHTML = "Creating User...";
15   }
16   return valid;
17 }
```

This function has two primary duties. First, it updates the status div with the status of processing as the fields are validated (line 3), or the request to create the user is made (line 14). The function may alternatively update the status to indicate that the user cannot be created due to errors (line 12). Second, it's responsible for validating each form field (lines 5–0), returning `true` or `false` depending on whether or not all fields on the form are valid (line 16).

On line 6, you use another Dojo-specific construct, the `dojo.lang.forEach` function. This is quite useful for iterating over an array. It takes three arguments: the array that should be iterated over (i.e., `fieldNames`), the function to execute on each element in the array, and a Boolean that indicates whether or not the length of the array is constant throughout the duration of function execution. Because the array does not change during this function, the third argument on line 10 is `true`. This last argument simply enhances performance when the length of the array is static. Note that the function defined on line 6 takes a single argument, which corresponds to the object in the array being visited. This particular use of `forEach` loops over the list of all the field names on the form (defined in the `fieldNames` array).

Because you're writing a Web application with AJAX capabilities, you have the luxury of submitting the form asynchronously. The last function in the new JavaScript file is a very simple callback that is invoked after the form is handled on the server. Initially, you just update the status of the document to indicate that the form was submitted. Use the following to define the callback:

```
function submitCallback(data) {
  dojo.byId('status').innerHTML = "Submit Complete!";
}
```

The final step in adding the client-side validation is to modify the form submission process so that an asynchronous request is made when the form is submitted. You can also add the final form validation at this point. Add the following script to the bottom of UserInputv6.html, before the </body> tag:

```
1   <script>
2   dojo.addOnLoad(function(){
3    var fb = new dojo.io.FormBind({
4        formNode: "user_detail",
5        mimetype: "text/xml",
6        load: function(load, data, e) {
7          submitCallback(data);
8        }
9     });
10    fb.onSubmit = function(form) {
11      return handleSubmit();
12    }
13   });
14   </script>
```

This is a very interesting inline script that shows some other conveniences of using an off-the-shelf JavaScript library such as Dojo. First, line 3 has a call to a Dojo function addOnLoad that causes a new anonymous function to be called when the page is loaded. Note that Dojo modifies the normal way a page loads and unloads. To include code that is executed when the page is loaded, you *must* use the addOnLoad function instead of using the window.onload or defining an onload attribute for the body tag.

At this point, turn your attention to the new function that you've defined: Apart from debugging, it adds the new asynchronous form submission handling by creating a new FormBind object from the dojo.io module on lines 3–9. This object modifies the way the form is submitted to use an asynchronous call. You should create and initialize FormBind on page load to ensure that all the required libraries loaded and that all the necessary components have been created. There are several arguments to this constructor defined in an array, including formNode, mimetype, and load. The formNode argument should be the name of the form to which you're binding the asynchronous request. The mimetype should be "text/xml" if you're expecting an XML result; and the load should be the callback function. This is an inline function that simply calls your submitCallback function with the data returned from the asynchronous request.

The final portion of the onload function is to link in the final form validation prior to submission. To do this you need to define an onSubmit function for the FormBind (lines 10–11). This function takes the form that is being validated as an argument, and should return true or false. When true is returned, the submit action is allowed to proceed; otherwise, the form cannot be submitted and no call is made to the server.

That's all that's necessary to set up an asynchronous request and associate it with a form in Dojo! At this point, you're ready to redeploy and experiment with the user form. Notice you cannot submit the form until the user form is successfully validated. Also notice that the status div is updated with an indication of whether or not the form is correctly validated, or has been submitted. Figure 10-4 shows an example of both an unsuccessful (left) and successful (right) submission. The form on the left failed due to an invalid birthday.

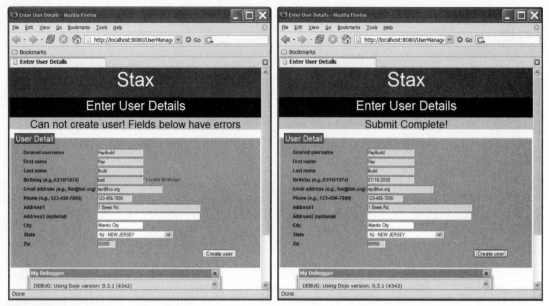

Figure 10-4

Validation in Practice: Server-Side Validation of the Completed Form

Now that you've added the client-side validation, you're ready to include the server-side validation of the entire form. Remember that although you are validating on the client side, you still need to keep the server as the last line of defense against invalid data. A Servlet and a helper class will perform the server validation, after which the Servlet will either create an object that holds the new user's details or report a detailed error message to the client.

In this section you begin by validating only the username on the server when the form is submitted. You will implement the server side by defining a model object that maintains information about the system's users, and a controller, as a Servlet, that can respond to a client request to create a user. You then learn to encode the validation as a helper object that is used by the controller Servlet. Next, you turn back to the client and extend the view to make use of the controller.

After implementing the validation of the username on the server, it's a simple step to extend the controller to validate the remaining form fields when the form is submitted. This is addressed in the remaining part of this section.

Implementing the Server Side

We begin by defining the three main components that make up the server-side aspect of form validation:

1. Define a model object that represents the user.

2. Implement a controller object that responds to a request to create a user by validating the user-name and creating the user when validation succeeds.

3. Create a helper class that is used by the Servlet to validate the username field and create a new user.

Defining the Model

Before getting into the details of the classes necessary for performing the validation, you need to take a closer look at the user details coming into the system, and what the requirements are for each piece of data. Table 10-3 shows the detail we intend to maintain about our user. The table includes each element that you need to maintain, the type of the expected data, whether the element is required, and a description of the criteria that should be used when validating the field. Notice in the table that several of the fields have slightly different validation requirements than on the client side. For example, the username field passes validation on the client side as long as any value is provided in the username field. The server component, conversely, does not validate a username that has any whitespace characters.

Table 10-3: Fields Necessary to Describe the System's Users

Field	Type	Validation Criteria
User Name	String	Any combination of letters or numbers. No whitespace is allowed.
First Name	String	Any value
Last Name	String	Any value
Email Address	String	Any combination of letters, numbers, dot (.), underscore (_), or plus (+), with the at (@) symbol somewhere in the address
Phone Number	Long	Any string containing 10 digits
Birthday	Date	A date in the format month/day/year, e.g., 12/31/1945
Address Line 1	String	Any value
Address Line 2	String	Any value
City	String	Any value
State	String	One of the 52 two-character state abbreviations, e.g., PA for Pennsylvania
Zip Code	Int	Any five-digit number

To get started on the server side, you should define a simple model object in the stax.model package to hold the data for a user. Define this class in a new file, User.java, under c:\Tomcat\webapps\ UserManager\WEB-INF\classes\stax\model. The new class is based on the first two columns of Table 10-3 and is shown in Listing 10-4. It simply holds the various pieces of user data required and provides mechanisms to get and set each field.

Listing 10-4: The user model object User.java

```
1 package stax.model;
2
3 import java.util.Date;
4
5 public class User {
6
7  private String username;
8  private String firstname;
9  private String lastname;
10  private String email;
11  private long phone;
12  private Date birthday;
13  private String addr1;
14  private String addr2;
15  private String city;
16  private String state;
17  private int zip;
18
19  public void setUsername(String username) {
20   this.username = username;
21  }
22  public String getUsername() {
23   return username;
24  }
25  public void setFirstname(String firstname) {
26   this.firstname = firstname;
27  }
28  public String getFirstname() {
29   return firstname;
30  }
31  public void setLastname(String lastname) {
32   this.lastname = lastname;
33  }
34  public String getLastname() {
35   return lastname;
36  }
37  public void setEmail(String email) {
38   this.email = email;
39  }
40  public String getEmail() {
41   return email;
42  }
43  public void setPhone(long phone) {
44   this.phone = phone;
45  }
46  public long getPhone() {
47   return phone;
48  }
```

```
49  public void setAddr1(String addr1) {
50    this.addr1 = addr1;
51  }
52  public String getAddr1() {
53    return addr1;
54  }
55  public void setAddr2(String addr2) {
56    this.addr2 = addr2;
57  }
58  public String getAddr2() {
59    return addr2;
60  }
61  public void setCity(String city) {
62    this.city = city;
63  }
64  public String getCity() {
65    return city;
66  }
67  public void setState(String state) {
68    this.state = state;
69  }
70  public String getState() {
71    return state;
72  }
73  public void setZip(int zip) {
74    this.zip = zip;
75  }
76  public int getZip() {
77    return zip;
78  }
79  public void setBirthday(Date birthday) {
80    this.birthday = birthday;
81  }
82  public Date getBirthday() {
83    return birthday;
84  }
85
86  public String toXMLString() {
87    return "<user>\n  <username>" + getUsername() + "</username>\n" +
88    "  <firstname>" + getFirstname() + "</firstname>\n" +
89    "  <lastname>" + getLastname() + "</lastname>\n" +
90    "  <birthday>" + getBirthday() + "</birthday>\n" +
91    "  <email>" + getEmail() + "</email>\n" +
92    "  <phone>" + getPhone() + "</phone>\n" +
93    "  <addr1>" + getAddr1() + "</addr1>\n" +
94    "  <addr2>" + getAddr2() + "</addr2>\n" +
95    "  <city>" + getCity() + "</city>\n" +
96    "  <state>" + getState() + "</state>\n" +
97    "  <zip>" + getZip() + "</zip>\n</user>";
98  }
99 }
```

Defining the Controller

Now that you've defined your model class that will hold the user data, you need to handle the incoming request. For this step, you must create a simple Java Servlet to receive the submitted form data. If you're new to working with Servlets, see Chapter 4 for a more explicit example. The new Servlet, `UserManagerServletv1.java`, is described in Listing 10-5; and you should create it under `c:\Tomcat\webapps\UserManager\WEB-INF\classes\stax\ui`. The Servlet has three basic responsibilities:

1. **Receive the request from the client and extract the user details**. See line 17. This sets the value of the `params` Map to the details provided for the user, such as username, first name, and birthday, as a part of the request.

2. **Use a helper class to validate the data and create a new `User` object when the data is valid.** You create and initialize this helper object with the user details on line 18. You then use it on line 19 to validate the data. Finally, if the validation is successful, then you use this object to create a new `User` object on line 22.

3. **Generate a response indicating success or failure.** See lines 25–39. After validation, a response is generated, which includes whether the user was valid, wrapped in a `valid` tag. In the case of an invalid set of input data, the response includes any errors encountered. The actual generation of these errors is explored in more detail shortly.

Listing 10-5: The Servlet UserManagerServletv1.java

```
1 package stax.ui;
2
3 import java.io.*;
4 import java.util.Iterator;
5 import java.util.Map;
6
7 import javax.servlet.*;
8 import javax.servlet.http.*;
9
10 import stax.model.User;
11 import stax.ui.helpers.UserDataHelperv1;
12
13 public class UserManagerServletv1 extends HttpServlet {
14
15   public void doGet(HttpServletRequest req, HttpServletResponse resp)
16   throws IOException, ServletException {
17    Map params = req.getParameterMap();
18    UserDataHelperv1 userHelper = new UserDataHelperv1(params);
19    boolean success = userHelper.validateParameters();
20    if (success) {
21     // Process user here
22     User theUser = userHelper.createUser();
23    }
24
25    resp.setContentType("text/xml");
26    resp.setHeader("Cache-Control", "no-cache");
```

```
27   resp.getWriter().write("<?xml version='1.0' encoding='UTF-8'?>\n");
28   resp.getWriter().write("<response>\n");
29   resp.getWriter().write(" <valid>" + success + "</valid>");
30   if (!success) {
31    Map errors = userHelper.getErrorsMap();
32    for (Iterator iter = errors.keySet().iterator(); iter.hasNext();) {
33     String key = iter.next().toString();
34     Object value = errors.get(key);
35     resp.getWriter().write(" <error>\n  <name>" + key + "</name>" +
36       "\n  <value>" + value + "</value>\n </error>\n");
37    }
38   }
39   resp.getWriter().write("</response>\n");
40  }
```

After creating the Servlet you need to define the `web.xml` file for the Web application. Listing 10-6 shows the contents of your `web.xml` file. It should be created under `c:\Tomcat\webapps\UserManager\WEB-INF`.

Listing 10-6: The Web application's web.xml file

```
 1 <?xml version="1.0" encoding="UTF-8"?>
 2 <web-app id="WebApp_ID" version="2.4"
 3 xmlns="http://java.sun.com/xml/ns/j2ee"
 4 xmlns:xsi="http://www.w3.org/2001/XMLSchema-instance"
 5 xsi:schemaLocation="http://java.sun.com/xml/ns/j2ee @ta
http://java.sun.com/xml/ns/j2ee/web-app_2_4.xsd">
 6 <servlet>
 7  <servlet-name>UserManagerServletv1</servlet-name>
 8  <servlet-class>stax.ui.UserManagerServletv1</servlet-class>
 9 </servlet>
10 <servlet-mapping>
11  <servlet-name>UserManagerServletv1</servlet-name>
12  <url-pattern>/user-managerv1</url-pattern>
13 </servlet-mapping>
14 </web-app>
```

Defining the Helper Class

This section describes how to perform the server-side validation with regular expressions and define a helper class that validates the username and creates a new user.

Validating with Regular Expressions

As shown above, the Servlet delegates all of the actual validation to a helper class. Before getting into the details of this class, you need to revisit the validation criteria column of Table 10-3. Note that because you're dealing with an HTTP request, the data for each field is sent as a string. This forces you to validate several fields before translating them into more efficient data types. For example, the fields for phone, birthday, and zip code are most efficiently represented as a `long`, `java.util.Date`, and an `int`.

The remaining criteria are necessary to ensure that string data is in the correct format. For example, the state must correspond to a valid U.S. state code. Because the data is initially provided as a string, the simplest mechanism for validation of most fields is to use regular expressions. You can express the validation criteria for each piece of user data as a regular expression, and you can test each parameter against the regular expression before converting it into the data type required by `User.java`. See Table 10-4 for the regular expression that corresponds to each data validation criteria specified in Table 10-3. This table also includes an indicator of whether or not the data field is required.

> *As would be expected, regular expressions are used within Dojo, along with many other client and server-side validation components as well.*

The single exception to this is the Birthday field. Java provides a class that assists in translating strings in a variety of formats into `java.util.Date` objects. This class, `java.text.SimpleDateFormat`, will be used to validate the Birthday field.

Table 10-4: Regular Expressions for Each Field

Field	Rqd	Regular Expression
User Name	Yes	^\w*$
First Name	Yes	^.*$
Last Name	Yes	^.*$
Email Address	Yes	^[a-zA-Z0-9-._+]+@[a-zA-Z0-9.-_.+]*$
Phone Number	Yes	^(.*[0-9].*){10}$
Birthday	Yes	None
Address Line 1	Yes	^.*$
Address Line 2	No	Not validated
City	Yes	^.*$
State	Yes	^AL|AK|AZ|AR|CA|CO|CT|DE|DC|FL|GA|HI|ID|IL|IN|IA|KS|KY|LA|ME|MD|MA|MI|MN|MS|MO|MT|NE|NV|NH|NJ|NM|NY|NC|ND|OH|OK|OR|PA|RI|SC|SD|TN|TX|UT|VT|VA|WA|WV|WI|WY$
Zipcode	Yes	^[0-9]{5}$

Implementing UserDataHelper

Now that you've outlined the validation mechanism for each field in the form, you're ready to define the helper class. Create a new class, `UserDataHelperv1.java`, under `c:\Tomcat\webapps\UserManager\WEB-INF\classes\stax\ui\helpers`. This simple helper class has two primary responsibilities: It performs the validation of the user data and creates user model objects.

A Regular Expression Review

A regular expression is a highly concise way of describing a pattern that may exist in a string. Here's a quick refresher on regular expressions and what some of the characters mean. For much more detailed information on using regular expressions in Java, see http://java.sun.com/docs/books/tutorial/extra/regex/index.html.

Let's look at the regular expression in Java that satisfies the validation criteria described above. The regular expression should match any string consisting of exactly five digits. The string cannot have any additional characters. Here's the regular expression that matches any valid zip code:

```
^[0-9]{5}$
```

Note a few special characters. The carat (^) matches the beginning of a line. The dollar sign ($) matches the end of a line. These are used above to ensure that the string doesn't include any additional characters before or after the 5 required digits.

A string matches any single character from a set of characters enclosed in brackets ([]), and a dash (-) is used to identify a range. In the preceding example, any single digit, e.g., 1 or 2, matches with the character class or character set [0–9].

A number enclosed in brackets identifies repetition. The example includes {5} to ensure that the character class [0–9] is repeated exactly five times. Other convenient indicators of repetition are the star/asterisk (*), which indicates 0 or more, the plus (+), which indicates 1 or more, or the question mark (?), which indicates 0 or 1.

Taken together, the preceding expression matches any string consisting of exactly five digits.

Defining the Attributes

A `UserDataHelper` has two primary attributes: the map that holds the parameters provided as a part of the HTTP request, and a map that holds any error messages encountered during validation. Start by creating these attributes and some methods for setting and retrieving the values:

```
private Map parameterMap;
private Map errorsMap;

public UserDataHelperv1(Map pMap) {
  parameterMap = pMap;
}

public Map getErrorsMap() {
  return errorsMap;
}
```

The format of the data maintained in the parameter map should be noted at this point:

❑　　Note on lines 17 and 18 from Listing 10-5 that the parameter map provided by the Servlet is the parameter map included as a part of the incoming `HttpServletRequest`. The keys in this map are string objects that correspond to the parameter names, and the values are string arrays that consist of each value provided for the key. In this example, you only have a single value provided for each key, so the string arrays will always have one element. An example key value pair is (`"username"`, {`"raybudd"`}).

❏ Because you know you're not providing multiple values for any parameter, you can write a simple convenience method to access the value in this map. This method takes a parameter name string like "username" as an argument. It looks up the value provided for the key in the `parameterMap` attribute and converts in into a single string object (e.g., "raybudd"). If the parameter doesn't exist, or the value is undefined or empty, it returns null. Include the code for this method to your class:

```
private String getArgumentValue(String argName) {
  Object arg = parameterMap.get(argName);
  if ((arg == null) || (((String[]) arg).length < 1)
    || (((String[]) arg)[0].trim().length() < 1)) {
   return null;
  }
  return((String[])arg)[0];
}
```

Defining the Method That Validates a Single Field

At this point, you're ready to define a method that can validate a given field. Recall from the preceding discussion that most fields can be validated by simply testing against a regular expression. To account for these fields, add the following method that validates a field given a regular expression:

```
public boolean validateField(String field, String regex,
  String errorMsg, boolean required) {
  String value = getArgumentValue(field);
  if ((required)&&(value == null)) {
   errorsMap.put(field, "The field " + field + " is required.");
   return false;
  }
  if ((value != null)&&(!value.matches(regex))) {
   errorsMap.put(field, "Invalid field " + field + ". " + errorMsg);
   return false;
  }
  return true;
}
```

Please note the following about this method:

❏ The `validateField` method has four arguments: `field` is the name of the field being validated (e.g., "username"); `regex` is the regular expression to use when validating the field (e.g., `^\w*$`); `errorMsg` is the message to be displayed when the regular expression fails; and `required` is a flag that indicates whether or not validation should fail if the field is empty or null. When `true`, the field must be provided or validation fails.

❏ The method returns a Boolean depending on whether the value provided for the field is valid. It may also update `errorsMap` to include the details of errors encountered. Error map holds key value pairs, where the key is a string that consists of the field name, and the value is a string describing the error. You'll see later how to return this to the client and incorporate it into the client display (e.g., "The field username is required.").

❏ This method starts off by getting the value for the field from the parameter map. Initially it performs some validation based on the existence of the parameter. If the field is required, and no value was extracted from the parameter map, then an error is added to the error map and validation fails. If the required validation passes, the value is tested against the regular expression. If the test fails, then the error map is updated with the field-specific error message provided as a method argument, and false is returned. Finally, `true` is returned if both the required and regular expression validations pass.

Defining Constant Attributes

Next, define two new constant attributes in the class: one that establishes the regular expression that should be use in the validation, and one containing the error message to display when the validation fails:

```
public static final String USERNAME_RE = new String("^\\w*$");
public static final String USERNAME_ERR =
  "Can not contain whitespace or special characters";
```

Defining the Method That Validates All Parameters

Now you're ready to define the validation method that uses the `validateField` method to validate all the parameters included in the HTTP request. Note from Listing 10-5 that the Servlet delegates all validation to the helper class in a single method call `validateParameters`. The following is an initial implementation of that method, which simply validates the username:

```
public boolean validateParameters() {
  errorsMap = new HashMap();
  boolean success = true;
  if (!validateField("username", USERNAME_RE, USERNAME_ERR, true)) {
   success = false;
  }
  return success;
}
```

This method simply reinitializes the `errorsMap` to ensure that no old errors are retained, and creates a local variable `success` that is initially `true`. Each field should then be validated, one at a time, and if any field fails validation, the value of success should be set to `false`. For example, in the preceding code, the username field is validated with the `validateField` method, and success is set to `false` if the username is not valid for any reason.

Defining the Method That Creates a New User Object

The final responsibility of the helper class is to create a new `user` object and initialize it with the provided input parameters. Initially the method only sets the username, but this is extended later. Define a new `createUser` method as follows:

```
public User createUser() {
  User theUser = new User();
  theUser.setUsername(getArgumentValue("username"));
  return theUser;
}
```

Compiling and Running the Servlet

At this point you've defined all the server-side pieces required to do the validation of the username. You're now ready to compile the Web application with a command similar to the following:

```
C:\Tomcat\webapps\UserManager\WEB-INF\classes>javac -classpath
"C:\Tomcat\webapps\UserManager\WEB-INF\classes;c:\tomcat\common\lib\servlet-
api.jar" stax\model\User.java stax\ui\helpers\UserDataHelperv1.java
stax\ui\UserManagerServletv1.java
```

Before you run the Web application, you need to make a client-side enhancement to perform the validation and make use of the results. At this point, it may be useful to revisit the way the `UserManagerServlet` validates the input data, and look a little closer at how it uses the validation results. As described above, if the validation is successful, the `user` object is created, and an XML response is created. This response looks similar to the following:

```
<?xml version='1.0' encoding='UTF-8'?>
<response>
 <valid>true</valid>
</response>
```

Handling unsuccessful validation is slightly different. On failure, the Servlet gets the error map constructed by the helper class, and creates an XML document containing each field name with an error, and the associated error. For example, when the username and phone parameters fail validation, the following XML is generated:

```
<?xml version='1.0' encoding='UTF-8'?>
<response>
 <valid>false</valid>
 <error>
  <name>username</name>
  <value>The field username is required.</value>
 </error>
 <error>
  <name>phone</name>
  <value>Invalid field phone. Ten digits required</value>
 </error>
</response>
```

Implementing the Client-Side by Enhancing the View

Three small extensions to the view, outlined next, are required to incorporate the use-manager Servlet in the user form. You need to extend the user form HTML page to call the user-manager Servlet when the form is submitted, define a function that looks at the validation result for success or failure, and extend the callback to make use of the Servlet response.

Calling the Servlet from UserFormv7.html

The first step to make use of the new Servlet on the client side is to modify `UserFormv7.html` to go to the `UserManagerServlet` when the form is submitted. This is done by modifying the form specification to include an action as follows:

```
<form id="user_detail" action="user-manager">
```

Defining a Function to Check the Validation Result

Next, you need to write a simple function to check your response to determine whether the validation on the server succeeded or failed. This function just looks at the value of the valid element, and returns a true Boolean if the value is the string true, otherwise, false is returned. Add the following isSuccessResponse function to userform-helper.js:

```
function isSuccessResponse(data) {
  var validElt = data.getElementsByTagName("valid")[0];
  var validVal = validElt.childNodes[0].nodeValue;
  dojo.debug("Got valid result from server: ", validVal);
  return validVal == "true";
}
```

Extending the Callback Function

Now you're ready to make use of the success or error response generated by the UserManagerServlet as above, under "Compiling and Running the Web Application." To do this, you enhance the callback script that you originally defined in userform-helper.js. The following is a new implementation of the submitCallback function that is invoked after the server has completed processing of the request:

```
1 function submitCallback(data) {
2   // clear out the old errors.
3   dojo.lang.forEach(fieldNames, function(fieldName) {
4     dojo.byId(fieldName + "-label").innerHTML = "";
5   }, true);
6
7   if (isSuccessResponse(data)) {
8     dojo.byId('status').innerHTML = "Successfully Created User!";
9   } else {
10    dojo.byId('status').innerHTML = "Could not create user! See below";
11    var errorElts = data.getElementsByTagName("error");
12    dojo.lang.forEach(errorElts, function(errorElt) {
13      var errNameElt = errorElt.getElementsByTagName("name")[0];
14      var errNameTxt = errNameElt.childNodes[0].nodeValue;
15      var errValueElt = errorElt.getElementsByTagName("value")[0];
16      var errValueTxt = errValueElt.childNodes[0].nodeValue;
17      var errLabel = dojo.byId(errNameTxt + "-label");
18      errLabel.innerHTML = errValueTxt;
19    }, true);
20  }
21 }
```

Notice the following about this function:

❑   Initially the new implementation has some handling to remove any old error messages. On line 3, notice the use of the dojo.lang.forEach function to loop over each form field name. For each name in the formFields array, the associated label is retrieved from the document with dojo .byId on line 4. Note that the name is constructed by taking the name of the field and adding the suffix "-label". For example, the username field has a corresponding label username-label that is cleared within this loop.

❑ The status updates depending on whether the server validation succeeded (line 8) or failed (line 10). If the validation failed, all the error elements are retrieved from the DOM (line 11) and looped over with the `dojo.lang.forEach` function on line 12.

❑ Now take a closer look at the actual function that is executed on each of the error elements (lines 13–19). This function gets the value of the name element (lines 13–14) and the value of the value element (lines 15–16). Notice that on line 17 the name value is used to retrieve the (now empty) label defined in `UserInputv7.html` that corresponds to each form field. Again the suffix `"-label"` is applied to the field name (for example, `username` becomes `username-label`). This label is updated on line 18 to contain the error message.

Compiling and Running the Web Application

At this point, if you rebuild and redeploy your Web application, you receive server-side validation of the username field. If you start your Web server and browse to `http://localhost:8080/UserManager/UserInputv7.html` again, you initially get a page that looks similar to the previous versions. In this version, however, when you specify an invalid username like "Bad Name" and submit the form, the page is updated to contain the an error message, as shown in the left side of Figure 10-5. When you correct the username and resubmit, the error is removed and you are notified that the user was created successfully, as shown in the right side of Figure 10-5.

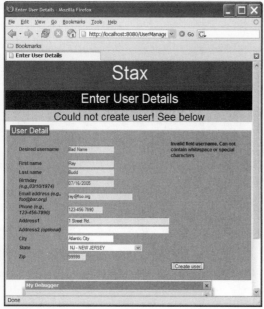
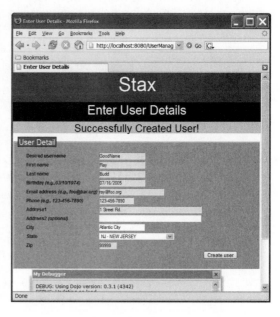

Figure 10-5

Enhancing the Helper by Adding Validation of the Other Form Fields

You're now ready to add the validation of the rest of the form fields. Because the infrastructure is already in place, you only need to modify the validation class to add the additional fields. See Listing 10-7 for an updated version of `UserDataHelperv2.java`, which validates all of the user forms. This version has several enhancements to the original class:

1. Several new constants are defined for the additional regular expressions and error messages.

2. The `validateParameters` method is updated to validate each of the remaining form fields (i.e., `firstname`).

3. The `createUser` method is updated to call a mutator (i.e., `setFirstname`) method on the user for each of the remaining form fields (i.e., `firstname`). Note that additional processing is performed on the phone number to strip out any non-digit characters and translate it into a `long`. Several other field elements are also translated into different Java types.

4. A method, `validateBirthday`, performs the validation of the Birthday field. This is necessary because the birthday validation doesn't use regular expressions. Instead, the validation method attempts to convert the date string into a date object with the `parse` method of the `SimpleDateFormat` class. If there's an error in the date string format, an exception is thrown. The exception handling then records an error message and returns a failed validation result. This simplifies the handling of the date because it easily captures date strings with values that are out of range—for example, an invalid date of 18/10/2006, which contains an invalid month.

In order to use the new version, `UserDataHelperv2.java`, *you need to create a new version of the controller* `UserManagerServletv2.java`, *which references the new version. You also need to update your* `web.xml` *file to include a specification for the new Servlet. Finally, you need to create a new version of the HTML file* `UserInputv8.html`, *which references the new Servlet. This is all shown in the source code downloadable from the Web site.*

Listing 10-7: UserDataHelperv2.java updated to validate all form fields

```
1 package stax.ui.helpers;
2
3 import java.text.ParseException;
4 import java.text.SimpleDateFormat;
5 import java.util.Date;
6 import java.util.HashMap;
7 import java.util.Map;
8
9 import stax.model.User;
10
11 public class UserDataHelperv2 {
12   public static final String AVALUE_ERR =
13     "Must contain at least one non-whitespace character";
14   public static final String USERNAME_ERR =
15    "Can not contain whitespace or special characters";
16   public static final String EMAIL_ERR = "Must match be in the form: " +
17    "username@domain.com";
18   public static final String PHONE_ERR = "Ten digits required";
19   public static final String STATE_ERR = "State code not recognized.";
20   public static final String ZIP_ERR = "Five digits required";
21
22   public static final String ANYVALUE_RE = new String("^.*$");
23   public static final String USERNAME_RE = new String("^\\w*$");
```

(continued)

Listing 10-7: *(continued)*

```
24  public static final String EMAIL_RE =
25    new String("^[a-zA-Z0-9-._+]+@[a-zA-Z0-9.-_.+]*$");
26  public static final String US_PHONE_NUMBER_RE =
27    new String("^(.*[0-9].*){10}$");
28  public static final String US_STATE_RE = new String(
29      "^AL|AK|AZ|AR|CA|CO|CT|DE|DC|FL|GA|HI|ID|IL|IN|IA|KS|KY|" +
30      "LA|ME|MD|MA|MI|MN|MS|MO|MT|NE|NV|NH|NJ|NM|NY|NC|ND|OH|" +
31      "OK|OR|PA|RI|SC|SD|TN|TX|UT|VT|VA|WA|WV|WI|WY$");
32
33  public static final String US_ZIP_RE = new String("^[0-9]{5}$");
34
35  private Map parameterMap;
36  private Map errorsMap;
37  private SimpleDateFormat dateformat;
38
39  public UserDataHelperv2(Map pMap) {
40    parameterMap = pMap;
41    dateformat = new SimpleDateFormat("MM/dd/yyyy");
42    dateformat.setLenient(false);
43  }
44
45  public Map getErrorsMap() {
46    return errorsMap;
47  }
48
49  public boolean validateParameters() {
50    errorsMap = new HashMap();
51    boolean success = true;
52    if (!validateField("username", USERNAME_RE, USERNAME_ERR, true)) {
53      success = false;
54    }
55    if (!validateField("firstname", ANYVALUE_RE, AVALUE_ERR, true)) {
56      success = false;
57    }
58    if (!validateField("lastname", ANYVALUE_RE, AVALUE_ERR, true)) {
59      success = false;
60    }
61    if (!validateField("emailaddr", EMAIL_RE, EMAIL_ERR, true)) {
62      success = false;
63    }
64    if (!validateField("phone", US_PHONE_NUMBER_RE, PHONE_ERR, true)) {
65      success = false;
66    }
67    if (!validateBirthday()) {
68      success = false;
69    }
70    if (!validateField("addr1", ANYVALUE_RE, AVALUE_ERR, true)) {
71      success = false;
72    }
73    // ADDR2 doesn't require any validation because any value is acceptable
74    if (!validateField("city", ANYVALUE_RE, AVALUE_ERR, true)) {
75      success = false;
```

```
 76   }
 77   if (!validateField("state", US_STATE_RE, STATE_ERR, true)) {
 78    success = false;
 79   }
 80   if (!validateField("zip", US_ZIP_RE, ZIP_ERR, true)) {
 81    success = false;
 82   }
 83   return success;
 84  }
 85
 86  public User createUser() {
 87   User theUser = new User();
 88   theUser.setUsername(getArgumentValue("username"));
 89   theUser.setFirstname(getArgumentValue("firstname"));
 90   theUser.setLastname(getArgumentValue("lastname"));
 91   try {
 92    Date bday = dateformat.parse(getArgumentValue("birthday"));
 93    theUser.setBirthday(bday);
 94   } catch(ParseException ex) {
 95    ex.printStackTrace();
 96   }
 97   theUser.setEmail(getArgumentValue("emailaddr"));
 98   String phoneDigitsS = getArgumentValue("phone").replaceAll("\\D", "");
 99   long phoneL = Long.parseLong(phoneDigitsS);
100   theUser.setPhone(phoneL);
101   theUser.setAddr1(getArgumentValue("addr1"));
102   theUser.setAddr2(getArgumentValue("addr2"));
103   theUser.setCity(getArgumentValue("city"));
104   theUser.setState(getArgumentValue("state"));
105   int zipI = Integer.parseInt(getArgumentValue("zip"));
106   theUser.setZip(zipI);
107   return theUser;
108  }
109
110  /**
111   * @return The error message, or null.
112   */
113  public boolean validateField(String field, String regex,
114    String errorMsg, boolean required) {
115   String value = getArgumentValue(field);
116   if ((required)&&(value == null)) {
117    errorsMap.put(field, "The field " + field + " is required.");
118    return false;
119   }
120   if ((value != null)&&(!value.matches(regex))) {
121    errorsMap.put(field, "Invalid field " + field + ". " + errorMsg);
122    return false;
123   }
124   return true;
125  }
126
127  private boolean validateBirthday() {
128   String birthday = getArgumentValue("birthday");
```

(continued)

Listing 10-7: *(continued)*

```
129   if (birthday == null) {
130    errorsMap.put("birthday", "Required field must be specified!");
131    return false;
132   }
133   try {
134    Date result = dateformat.parse(birthday);
135   } catch(Exception ex) {
136    errorsMap.put("birthday",
137    "The date must be of the form: mm/dd/yyyy");
138    return false;
139   }
140   return true;
141  }
142
143  private String getArgumentValue(String argName) {
144   Object arg = parameterMap.get(argName);
145   if ((arg == null) || (((String[]) arg).length < 1)
146    || (((String[]) arg)[0].trim().length() < 1)) {
147    return null;
148   }
149   return((String[])arg)[0];
150  }
151 }
```

Validation in Practice: Server-Side Validation of the Username

So far, the example you've been working through has used an asynchronous request to enable server-side validation of the entire form. This is useful because when you use a synchronous request, you need to ensure that form fields aren't blanked out if the form fails validation. This isn't the only advantage to using asynchronous requests, though. An asynchronous request also enables you to validate a single form field on the server while the user is busy interacting with other parts of the form. For example, you can verify that a zip code is valid, or that a phone number exists, while the user is filling out other parts of the form.

Of course, this approach, although very powerful, isn't applicable in every situation and should be used judiciously. It's initially tempting to overuse this in places where you shouldn't necessarily apply it. For example, you have no need to perform server-side validation that verifies a phone number includes all 10 digits. You should only use server-side validation when you need server-side processing. Bear in mind the following advantages and limitations when you consider using this approach:

❑   **Enables the use of server resources** — The primary advantage to this approach is that you can validate fields using server resources that aren't directly available to the client. For example, when validating a username, you can check the username database to ensure that the name doesn't already exist. Attempting this on the client side requires you to send every username with the form!

❑ **Instant feedback is provided to the user** — When you use an asynchronous request, users can keep filling in other form elements. They may not even know that a request was ever made!

❑ **Avoids the need to define validation logic twice** — When you validate with client-side JavaScript, you frequently need to duplicate logic on the client and server side, although frameworks such as Jakarta Struts can help resolve this issue. The use of an asynchronous request to validate a single field on the server solves the problem quite cleanly by localizing the execution of the validation to the server. You don't need to an adopt additional framework or infrastructure to avoid duplicating code.

❑ **Server-side validation is still required** — Unfortunately, you're still required to validate the entire form on the server when it's submitted. If the user has disabled JavaScript, no validation is performed! If the user submits the form before the asynchronous validation is received, an invalid element may be included.

❑ **Client-side validation is fast** — Generally, it's more effective to continue to use client-side JavaScript or other client-side approaches to validating many fields. This saves you from making extra unnecessary requests to the server.

After factoring in all of the preceding trade-offs, it becomes apparent that some fields on the user form don't require server-side validation; but other fields, such as the username, do benefit from such an approach. As described above, the username is one common type of form field that typically benefits from server-side validation because there's no realistic way to verify that a username doesn't exist on the client. Now you're ready to modify your user form to perform asynchronous server-side validation of the username field.

In the following example, the username is validated using a regular expression, to avoid introducing any additional complexity into the example. In most real-world applications, the validation function would look in a database to verify that the username doesn't already exist. Although this is out of the scope of this example, you're strongly encouraged to explore making this extension to the example code on your own.

Enhancing the View

In this section you add asynchronous validation of the username to the view by defining and calling a new function that makes an asynchronous request to validate the username each time a new username is specified.

1. Modify the username field in your `UserFormv9.html` to call a new validation function. This should be bound to the `onblur` event, so that each time the user removes focus from the username field, the function is called. You should define the new username field as follows:

```
<input name="username" id="username" dojoType="ValidationTextbox" required="true"
 missingMessage="* Username is required!" invalidMessage="* Invalid username!"
 onblur="validateUsername(this)"/>
```

2. Write the new `validateUsername` function, but first you need to add a new global variable that will hold the most recent value of the username field. Modify `userform-helperv3.js` to include the following variable defined after the `fieldNames` variable:

```
var lastUsername;
```

3. Add the new validation function `validateUsername` to the end of the `userform-helperv3.js` file as follows:

```
1  function validateUsername(usernameField) {
2   if ((lastUsername == usernameField.getValue())||
3     (!usernameField.isValid())||(usernameField.isEmpty())) {
4    return;
5   }
6   lastUsername = usernameField.getValue();
7   dojo.byId('status').innerHTML = "Validating Username";
8   dojo.io.bind({
9    url: "user-manager",
10    content: { validateusername: usernameField.getValue()},
11    load: function(type, data, evt) { validateUsernameCallback(data); },
12    mimetype: "text/xml"});
13  }
```

This function makes the asynchronous request using the `dojo.io.bind` function, which takes a single argument consisting of a series of key value pairs, which establish the details of the request. Commonly used properties specified for `dojo.io.bind` include the following:

- ❑ **url** — The URL that should be requested. You're simply going to the `/user-manager` Servlet.

- ❑ **content** — The parameters to include as a part of the request. This should be represented as a set of key value pairs. In the example above, a URL is created that contains a `validateusername` parameter as follows: `http://localhost:8080/UserManager/user-manager?validateusername=val`

- ❑ **mimetype** — Set to `plain/text` by default. This is the expected mime type of the response.

- ❑ **method** — Set to GET by default. This is the HTTP method to use for the request, either GET or POST.

- ❑ **load** — The callback function. This function is executed after the ready state of the asynchronous request is set to 4, i.e., after all the response data is loaded. This is set to a new callback function `validateUsernameCallback`, which you're going to write next.

The other interesting aspect of the `validateUsername` function is that it doesn't always make a request to the server. The initial `if` statement in the function includes the standard client-side validation on line 3 of the validation function (step 3 above). Of course, if the username doesn't pass client-side validation, or isn't even defined, there's no need to go to the server to figure this out. The statement also verifies on line 2 that the value of the username has actually been changed, by examining, and later updating (see line 6), the `lastUsername` variable. Again, there's no need to go to the server if the value being validated hasn't changed since the last validation attempt.

4. Define the callback function to be invoked after the username is validated. This is a simple callback similar to the full form callback, submitCallback, implemented above. The only difference is that only the username field is checked. The following shows the callback validateUsernameCallback:

```
function validateUsernameCallback(data) {
 var unameLbl = dojo.byId("username-label");
 var statusLbl = dojo.byId("status");
 if (isSuccessResponse(data)) {
  statusLbl.innerHTML = "Username is valid";
  unameLbl.innerHTML = "";
 } else {
  var errValueElt = data.getElementsByTagName("value")[0];
  var errValueTxt = errValueElt.childNodes[0].nodeValue;
  statusLbl.innerHTML = "Username is not valid!";
  unameLbl.innerHTML = errValueTxt;
 }
}
```

Enhancing the Controller

Now you're ready to move to the server side and enhance the controller so that is responds to the new types of requests. You first update the data helper UserDataHelperv3.java to include two additional methods that can perform the validation. Then, all that remains is to make use of these new functions from the Servlet:

1. The validateUsername method validates the username field as follows. Note that this method validates a single field, validateusername, provided as part of the request:

```
public boolean validateUsername() {
 errorsMap = new HashMap();
 return validateField("validateusername", USERNAME_RE, USERNAME_ERR, true);
}
```

2. The next new method determines whether the request is one for a username validation or validation of the full form. This is accomplished by looking at the parameter names. When the validateusername parameter is present, the validation of only the username is assumed. Define the new isUsernameValidation function:

```
public boolean isUsernameValidation() {
 return (getArgumentValue("validateusername") != null);
}
```

3. To make use of the new functions from the Servlet, change the doGet method in UserManagerServletv3.java to perform the appropriate validation, depending on the parameters, as follows:

```
public void doGet(HttpServletRequest req, HttpServletResponse resp)
  throws IOException, ServletException {
 Map params = req.getParameterMap();
 UserDataHelperv3 userHelper = new UserDataHelperv3(params);
```

```
    boolean success;

    if (userHelper.isUsernameValidation()) {
     success = userHelper.validateUsername();
    } else {
     success = userHelper.validateParameters();
     if (success) {
      // Process user here
      User theUser = userHelper.createUser();
     }
    }

    resp.setContentType("text/xml");
    // The remainder of the function is unchanged
   }
```

At this point you're ready to redeploy and try out the new form. Note that the username field is validated by the server as you tab off of it. Figure 10-6 shows a version of the user form that performs server-side validation of the username when you tab off of the field.

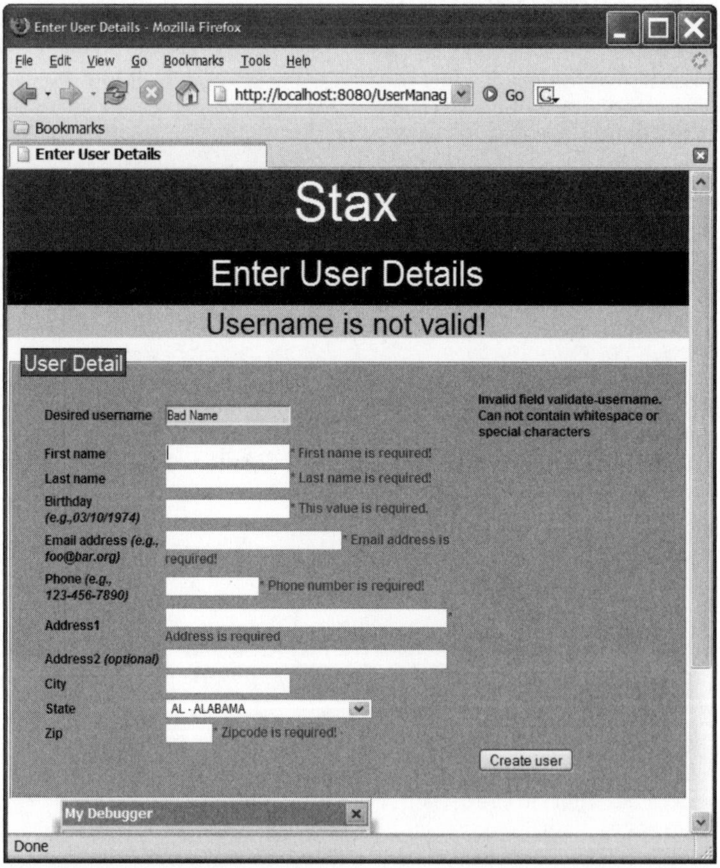

Figure 10-6

Summary

In this chapter you've explored the approaches to validation of a user form. You've seen the inclusion of three complimentary approaches in a single example:

- ❏ Client-side validation using Dojo widgets

- ❏ Asynchronous server-side validation of all form fields when the form is submitted.

- ❏ Asynchronous server-side validation of a single form field when the field is changed.

Through this example, you've also gained familiarity with Dojo, and have seen the convenience of using off-the-shelf JavaScript libraries. Next, you'll build on this example to explore the use of AJAX and Dojo to enhance the usability of your user form.

11

Form Usability

The designer or architect of Web applications, much like the architect of buildings, is required to deal with the two competing concerns of utility and beauty. Frequently, additional functionality in a Web application comes at the cost of simplicity and clarity. Although this is prevalent throughout all aspects of a Web application, it's more easily seen in the areas that require more user interaction, such as the form.

The temptation in form design is to focus on the user data you must collect, rather than on the user experience of filling out the form. Increasing the required user data is also likely to create a cluttered and confused form. Requiring more server interaction to process the data may split logically similar elements on the same form across two pages to facilitate the server processing.

The result is an unpleasant user experience. The user looks at a complex form, quickly becomes frustrated, and immediately makes a subconscious, or sometimes even conscious, decision about the cost versus benefit he gets from filling out the form. Of course, if the Web application provides a unique service, such as ticket payment, or other DMV service, a good user experience may not be important, but it is critical for applications that provide competitive services, such as online stores. A store with confusing, complex forms may lose a lot of money to more user-friendly stores.

Of course, rich client applications in a competitive market face similar issues, but it's less pronounced. This is due to the speed at which a user traverses the Web. The Web developer is constantly pressed to maintain a user's attention to keep the user at the site. With limitless nooks and crannies on the Web to crawl through, most users look through several different places at one time. If a Web site loses a user's interest, he or she can quickly replace it with another more appealing alternative.

Overview

Chapter 10 looked at form usability by exploring the issue of form validation. It introduced the Dojo library, and showed how to use it with AJAX to enable less invasive validation of user data. It then showed a series of examples involving a user detail input form that included the addition of client-side validation, batch validation of the form on the server side, and asynchronous server-side validation of single form fields.

This chapter builds on Chapter 10 and expands on form usability:

❑ It builds on your introduction to Dojo by exploring more aspects of this remarkable library. Alex Russell, the project lead for the Dojo Toolkit, gives you some insight into the motivation and future direction of the Dojo Toolkit in a sidebar at the end of the chapter.

❑ It dives into the general issue of form usability in a bit more detail, examining two questions. What limitations does the traditional Web paradigm impose that typically force you to design forms that cause user inconvenience and frustration? How can you incorporate AJAX in your forms to enhance both the beauty and utility of your forms, and reduce user frustration?

To answer the second question, the chapter introduces two examples that provide approaches to decrease the aggravation that users commonly experience when dealing with forms:

❑ In the first example, you extend your user form to populate the city and state fields when a zip code is provided.

❑ In the second example, you enhance the Web application to populate a combo box with a list of candidate cities when a state is selected. The combo box will also have auto-complete capabilities and tailor a drop-down list of cities based on text that the user types.

Because this chapter builds on the example constructed in Chapter 10, it's probably easiest for you to explore the examples there first, but not absolutely required. If you're already comfortable with Dojo and form validation approaches, you can start with this chapter. Just be sure to familiarize yourself a bit with the code from the previous chapter, because you'll be extending it in this chapter's examples.

Approaches to the Usable Form

Form usability issues have their origins, as do most issues in the Web development world, in the traditionally disconnected nature of Web interactions. For example, consider the user and server interactions when you do not use AJAX in a form. The browser loads the form. The user interacts with the form and submits it. The server processes the form and returns a new page. In this model users are disconnected from the processing power available on the server as they fill in the form.

Limitations to Synchronous JavaScript in Forms

Client-side JavaScript can be a great benefit because it increases the page's interactivity and streamlines the form's appearance, but without AJAX this paradigm is quite limited, for several reasons:

❑ **You must include all data that may be processed on the client in the page sent to the client.** This immediately removes the possibility of any operation that requires access to large amounts of data. It also frequently requires the inclusion of unnecessary data in an attempt to handle actions that the user may or may not actually perform. As more data is sent to the client, the ultimate effect for the user is a longer delay during the data transfer.

❑ **You must include any JavaScript that may be executed in the page sent to the client.** This immediately removes the possibility of any operation that requires access to very complex JavaScript. As Web applications and Web sites become increasingly complex, they require more and more JavaScript. Similar to the previous issue, as the size of JavaScript libraries increases, the ultimate effect is a longer user delay during data transmission.

❑ **Server software resources are unavailable while processing on the client.** Client-side scripts have no access to databases, the file system, third-party libraries, or software. The inability to access a database is especially limiting because it means that it's impossible to look up any data based on a user's input into a form without leaving the page. For example, if users select a classification of an item in a store (e.g., clothing), they must be forwarded to a new page before the types of the item can be looked up.

❑ **Server hardware resources are not available on the client.** This obvious issue is related to the last concern, and has a huge significance. Because all the JavaScript executes on the client, the client hardware constrains the Web application. This imposes more and more hardware requirements on the client as Web applications become more complex. The processing capabilities of increasingly powerful server configurations are wasted as you delegate more and more logic to the client.

The ultimate effect of using only synchronous requests in a Web application is that the developer is forced to design forms that cannot react to a user's selections in any meaningful way. As mentioned earlier, the user can't specify the class of product or pick a particular item without going to a new page. The developer cannot delegate complex operations to an existing third-party application or a language more suited to the task required without loading a new page.

Advantages to AJAX and JavaScript Effects in Forms

Of course, with AJAX, none of the above limitations exist. You can use an asynchronous call to retrieve data from the server behind the scenes as it is required based on the user's selections in the form. Your JavaScript may be dynamically fetched from the server with an asynchronous call only when required by the client. If the client requires access to resources on the server, they can be used without reloading the form. For example, you can retrieve a list of items of a given category from a database on the server and display them in a drop-down list. In general, designers can separate logic more cleanly. Processing that is better suited to a server can be moved to the server, without inhibiting user interactivity. JavaScript libraries can remain focused on user interface issues. It becomes easier to design and implement forms that are simple, yet quite usable. In particular, you can incorporate AJAX and common client-side JavaScript libraries into a form's design to increase the utility and interactivity of the form in the following ways:

❑ **Asynchronously load a JavaScript library** — As JavaScript libraries grow, it becomes impractical to load them fully with every page load. By loading each JavaScript component as it is required, you can significantly reduce the amount of data you initially transfer.

❑ **Populate a field with server data based on another field value** — In many cases, you can infer one field, based on one or more other input fields. One common example shown later in the chapter is the city, state, and zip code fields. All three are required to create a mailing address, but you can use the zip code to uniquely identify the city and state.

❑ **Populate a drop-down list with server data based on another field value**—Consider the example of a shopping site. You're now free to include a drop-down list containing the different types of items in the store. On the same form, and in the same page, you can have an updating drop-down list that contains the available items for a selected item type, as the user selects that item type. You can see examples of this later in the chapter as well.

❑ **Validate a field on the server**—The general topic of validation is covered in much greater detail in Chapter 10, but AJAX allows you to perform server validation without submitting the form. For example, you can validate a username field on the server by looking in the database to ensure that the name isn't already in use.

❑ **Show or hide parts of the form based on a user selection**—You greatly enhance a form's interactivity when you make only relevant form elements appear. Note that this isn't technically an advantage to using AJAX, but a capability provided by many JavaScript libraries. It is discussed in greater detail in Chapter 13.

Note, however, that it's easy to fall into the trap of overusing AJAX and JavaScript effects. Your overall goal should always be to simplify the form for the user, and thus reduce the amount of required work. You must consider the various use cases of the Web application when designing the form and deciding which elements should rely on AJAX or JavaScript effects. It's easy to design a form that looks flashy but doesn't enhance the user's experience. Overuse of AJAX or effects may even hinder performance and increase user frustration—for example, consider a form that is constantly updated with the result of asynchronous calls.

The remainder of the chapter consists of examples that put two of these approaches into practice in the user form. First, you see the population of a field based on an asynchronous server-side lookup. After this, you populate a drop-down list.

Form Usability in Practice: Populating a Field with Server Data

To get started with the examples, consider the user input form you developed in Chapter 10. One obvious usability issue in the user form is that it requires the user to specify redundant information. The format of a mailing address requires the user to specify a city, a state, and a separate zip code. Of course, you only really need to specify the zip code because it uniquely identifies both the city and state. As described earlier in "Limitations to Synchronous JavaScript in Forms," when using only synchronous JavaScript it's frequently impractical to update one form field based on another because you need to send vast amounts of data to the client in anticipation of what the user may enter. The city and state lookup example requires you to include 42,000 zip codes defined in the United States, as well as every corresponding city and state pair!

From the user's perspective, however, it is quite convenient to have this type of lookup performed, especially for people who live in Saint Mary of the Woods, Indiana, because they usually have to type in their entire city name when five digits would suffice. With AJAX, however, you can perform the lookup on the server asynchronously, as the zip code changes. You don't have to bog down the system with extraneous data in anticipation of what the user may enter, and the user isn't kept waiting while the lookup is performed. This section enhances the form to perform the remote call and update the city and state when the user tabs off of the form.

Implementing the Server Side

The first step is to extend the server side developed in Chapter 10 to perform a city and state lookup given a zip code. To accomplish this, you need to add a few new components your Web application:

1. Set up a database to hold the zip code table.

2. Define the model:

   ❑ An AddressLocale model object to represent the zip code, city, state triple

   ❑ A ZipCodeAnalyzer model object that holds the business logic necessary to populate the triple from a single zip code

3. Implement a controller object that invokes your new model object on a user request.

For a thorough description of the setup required for the Web application, see Chapter 10. See the book's Web site for the code from Chapter 10, which is used as a starting point for the example.

Setting Up the Database

The first step is to create a database that can hold the details of the zip code. Although you can use any database server, the authors are using a vanilla installation of MySQL version 4.0.26, available for download at http://dev.mysql.com.

After installing the database server, you need a dataset to populate a zip code table. A .csv file containing this data (zip_codes.csv) is available with all the code for this example on the book's Web site. It includes all the information that must be known about a zip code, such as the zip code, city, state, county, and geographic location. After retrieving the data file, you should download or write a simple batch script, an SQL script that creates the database and zip code table, and loads data into the zip code table. See Listing 11-1 for an example script that creates the table and loads the data on a Windows machine, and Listing 11-2 for the batch file that creates the database in MySQL.

This creates a database named stax that contains a single table named zipcode. These scripts assume that the default "root" user exists and has no password assigned. If you're using a different user or password, you need to modify the load-db.bat script to reflect this.

Listing 11-1: The MySQL script, zip_codes.sql, that loads the zip code data

```
drop table if exists zipcodes;

create table zipcode (
        id INTEGER NOT NULL AUTO_INCREMENT PRIMARY KEY,
        zip INTEGER,
        latitude FLOAT,
        longitude FLOAT ,
        city varchar(50),
        state varchar(2),
        county varchar(50),
        zipclass varchar(50)
);

LOAD DATA LOCAL INFILE 'zip_codes.csv'
```

(continued)

Listing 11-1: *(continued)*

```
        INTO TABLE zipcode
        FIELDS
                TERMINATED BY ','
                OPTIONALLY ENCLOSED BY '"'
        LINES TERMINATED BY '\n'
        IGNORE 1 LINES
        (zip, latitude, longitude, city, state, county, zipclass);
```

Listing 11-2: The batch script, load-db.bat, that creates the database and loads the zip codes

```
@echo off
set DBNAME=stax
set UNAME=root

mysqladmin -u%UNAME% -f drop %DBNAME%
mysqladmin -u%UNAME% -f create %DBNAME%
mysql -u%UNAME% %DBNAME% < ZIP_CODES.sql
```

Defining the Model

After setting up the database, you're ready to define your model. There are two main components, as described above. You must create a simple value object in the package `stax.model`, which represents a city, state, and zip code triple. See Listing 11-3 for the specification of the `AddressLocale` class. This class uses strings for the city and state and an integer for the zip code.

Listing 11-3: AddressLocale.java, the value object for city, state, zip code triples

```
 1 package stax.model;
 2
 3 public class AddressLocale {
 4   private String city;
 5   private String state;
 6   private int zip;
 7
 8   public AddressLocale(String aCity, String aState, int aZip) {
 9     this.setCity(aCity);
10     this.setState(aState);
11     this.setZip(aZip);
12   }
13
14   public void setCity(String city)   {  this.city = city; }
15   public String getCity()            { return city; }
16   public void setState(String state) { this.state = state; }
17   public String getState()           { return state; }
18   public void setZip(int zip)        { this.zip = zip; }
19   public int getZip()                { return zip; }
20 }
```

Now that you've defined a database table to hold the data, and created a model class that holds the triples, you can define the bridge between the two. The ZipCodeAnalyzer class, described in Listing 11-4, contains the logic necessary to look up the city and state from the zip code. This class, which you should define in a new package, stax.model.businesslogic, uses JDBC to connect to the database and look up the data.

Listing 11-4: Initial version of ZipCodeAnalyzerv1.java that looks up the database

```
1 package stax.model.businesslogic;
2
3 import java.sql.Connection;
4 import java.sql.DriverManager;
5 import java.sql.ResultSet;
6 import java.sql.SQLException;
7 import java.sql.Statement;
8 import java.util.ArrayList;
9
10 import stax.model.AddressLocale;
11
12 public class ZipCodeAnalyzerv1 {
13
14   public static final String DB_USER="root";
15   public static final String DB_PASS="";
16   public static final String DB_NAME="stax";
17
18   public ZipCodeAnalyzerv1() {
19     try {
20       Class.forName("com.mysql.jdbc.Driver").newInstance();
21     } catch(Exception ex) {
22       System.err.println("Could not register driver!");
23     }
24   }
25
26   public Connection getConnection() {
27     try {
28       Connection conn =
29         DriverManager.getConnection("jdbc:mysql://localhost/" + DB_NAME +
30             "?user="+ DB_USER + "&password=" + DB_PASS);
31       return conn;
32
33     } catch (SQLException ex) {
34       ex.printStackTrace();
35       return null;
36     }
37   }
38
39   public AddressLocale lookupCityStateZip(int zip) {
40     Connection conn = null;
41     try {
42       conn = getConnection();
43       Statement stmt = conn.createStatement();
```

(continued)

301

Listing 11-4: *(continued)*

```
44        ResultSet rs = stmt.executeQuery("SELECT zip, city, state " +
45            "FROM zipcode where zip='" + zip + "'");
46        ArrayList result = convertResultSet(rs);
47        if (!result.isEmpty()) {
48          return (AddressLocale)result.get(0);
49        }
50
51    } catch(SQLException sqlEx) {
52        sqlEx.printStackTrace();
53    } finally {
54        if (conn != null) {
55          try {
56            conn.close();
57          } catch(SQLException ex) {}
58        }
59    }
60    return null;
61  }
62
63  private ArrayList convertResultSet(ResultSet rs) throws SQLException {
64    ArrayList result = new ArrayList();
65    if (rs == null) {
66      return result;
67    }
68
69    while (rs.next()) {
70      int rZip = rs.getInt("zip");
71      String rCity = rs.getString("city");
72      String rState = rs.getString("state");
73      result.add(new AddressLocale(rCity, rState, rZip));
74    }
75    return result;
76  }
77 }
```

Note the following about this code:

❑ As with the preceding bat file, this class assumes you have a database named "stax" with a user "root" that has no password. You may need to tailor the DB_USER, DB_PASS, and DB_NAME attributes if you're using a different configuration.

❑ The constructor and getConnection method handle the steps necessary to load the JDBC driver and get a connection to the database.

❑ convertResultSet is a generic method that translates a result set containing rows of zip code, city, and state data into an AddressLocale object.

❑ The most interesting method, lookupCityStateZip, looks up the city and state in the database from a provided zip code. The zip code is used when performing a database lookup on line 44. The rows returned are translated into an AddressLocale object on line 46. The result of calling this method with a zip code is a single AddressLocale object that contains the triple. If the zip code provided is invalid, a null is returned.

Note that before running this class, you need to ensure that you have a JDBC library available to your runtime. If you're using MySQL, you can download and install the MySQL Connector/J (we're using version 3.1.13) from `http://www.mysql.com/products/connector/j/`. *You must then add this to your Tomcat installation so that you can run JDBC operations on the Web server. For example, the authors have placed a copy of the unpacked binary jarfile (`mysql-connector-java-3.1.13-bin.jar`) to the shared library directory of our Tomcat installation* `c:\Tomcat\shared\lib`.

After creating your new model files, you should recompile everything with a command similar to the following:

```
C:\Tomcat\webapps\UserManager\WEB-INF\classes>javac -classpath ⤸
"c:\tomcat\common\lib\servlet-api.jar" stax\model\*.java ⤸
stax\model\businesslogic\*.java stax\ui\*.java stax\ui\helpers\*.java
```

You may also want to test your configuration prior to running in a Web server. You can do this by adding a simple `main` function to `ZipCodeAnalyzerv1` that calls the `lookupCityStateZip` function, as follows:

```
public static void main(String[] args) {
   ZipCodeAnalyzer zca = new ZipCodeAnalyzer();
   System.out.println("Doing lookup");
   AddressLocale csz = zca.lookupCityStateZip(15001);
   System.out.println("Done! Result for " + csz.getZip() + " is: " +
       csz.getCity() + ", " + csz.getState());
   csz = zca.lookupCityStateZip(22209);
   System.out.println("Done! Result for " + csz.getZip() + " is: " +
       csz.getCity() + ", " + csz.getState());
}
```

You can then run with a command similar to the following:

```
C:\Tomcat\webapps\UserManager\WEB-INF\classes>java -classpath ⤸
C:\Tomcat\shared\lib\mysql-connector-java-3.1.13-bin.jar ⤸
stax.model.businesslogic.ZipCodeAnalyzerv1
```

If everything's working, you'll get a result such as this:

```
Doing lookup
Done! Result for 15001 is: ALIQUIPPA, PA
Done! Result for 22209 is: ARLINGTON, VA
```

Defining the Controller

At this point you've completed the required additions to the model. You're ready to set up your controller to manage zip code related activities. In the example Web application, you simply define a new Servlet responsible for the management of operations that deal with zip codes. Of course, you probably wouldn't want to do this in a typical Java Web application of any complexity that follows the MVC paradigm because it would lead to a confusing Web of many potentially competing controllers. A Java Web application generally lends itself nicely to the use of a single centralized controller that acts as the interface between the client and server sides. See Chapter 6 for a detailed discussion of this approach in Java. Create a new Servlet, `ZipManagerServletv1.java`, under the `stax.ui` package, as described in Listing 11-5.

Listing 11-5: ZipManagerServletv1.java, the controller for zip code operations

```java
 1 package stax.ui;
 2
 3 import java.io.*;
 4 import javax.servlet.*;
 5 import javax.servlet.http.*;
 6 import stax.model.businesslogic.ZipCodeAnalyzerv1;
 7 import stax.model.AddressLocale;
 8
 9 public class ZipManagerServletv1 extends HttpServlet {
10
11   private static ZipCodeAnalyzerv1 zipAnalyzer = null;
12
13   public void doGet(HttpServletRequest req, HttpServletResponse resp)
14     throws IOException, ServletException {
15     if (zipAnalyzer == null) {
16       zipAnalyzer = new ZipCodeAnalyzerv1();
17     }
18
19     String zipS = req.getParameter("zip");
20     String respData = "";
21
22     if (zipS != null) {
23       respData = getCityStateElements(zipS);
24     }
25
26     resp.setContentType("text/xml");
27     resp.setHeader("Cache-Control", "no-cache");
28     resp.getWriter().write("<?xml version='1.0' encoding='UTF-8'?>\n");
29     resp.getWriter().write("<response>\n");
30     resp.getWriter().write(respData);
31     resp.getWriter().write("</response>\n");
32   }
33
34   private String getCityStateElements(String zipS) {
35     int zip = Integer.parseInt(zipS);
36     AddressLocale loc = zipAnalyzer.lookupCityStateZip(zip);
37     String response = "";
38
39     if (loc != null) {
40       response = new String(
41         "   <state>" + loc.getState()  + "</state>\n" +
42         "   <city>" + loc.getCity() + "</city>\n");
43     }
44     return response;
45   }
46 }
```

As you can see, the controller is pretty simple initially. It creates and uses the `ZipcodeAnalyzerv1` that you defined earlier to perform the real work. The controller has three main responsibilities:

1. Instantiate and maintain the zip code analyzer (line 16) and invoke it when necessary (line 36).

2. Analyze the incoming parameters to get the zip code (line 19).

3. Generate the response. This includes setting up the response header (lines 26–27), formatting the zip code lookup result as valid XML (lines 40–42), and writing the response (line 30).

Rebuild and add your new Servlet to the Web application's `web.xml` file with the following:

```
<!-- servlet section of web.xml -->
<servlet>
  <servlet-name>ZipManagerServletv1</servlet-name>
  <servlet-class>stax.ui.ZipManagerServletv1</servlet-class>
</servlet>
<!-- servlet-mapping section of web.xml -->
<servlet-mapping>
  <servlet-name>ZipManagerServletv1</servlet-name>
  <url-pattern>/zip-managerv1</url-pattern>
 </servlet-mapping>
```

You can see your new controller in action by browsing to `http://localhost:8080/UserManager/zip-managerv1?zip=12010`, which should provide a response like the following:

```
<?xml version='1.0' encoding='UTF-8'?>
<response>
   <state>NY</state>
   <city>AMSTERDAM</city>
</response>
```

Implementing the Client Side by Enhancing the View

Now all that's left is to update the view:

1. Add a new event handler function that makes an asynchronous request to your new controller when the zip code is modified.

2. Define a callback and helper function that handles the server's response by updating the city and state fields.

3. Modify `UserInputv1.html` to make use of the new event handler function by invoking it when an `onblur` event is triggered for the zip code input field.

Defining the Event Handler Function

The first step is enhancing the controller to respond to a modification to the zip code by making an asynchronous request. To do this, add the following new function to your JavaScript file, `userform-helperv1.js`:

```
1 function handleZipChange(zipElt) {
2   var zipcode = zipElt.getValue();
3   if (dojo.validate.us.isZipCode(zipcode)) {
4     dojo.io.bind({
5       url:"zip-managerv1?zip=" + zipcode,
6       load: function(type, data, evt)
7         { zipChangeCallback(type, data, evt); },
8       mimetype: "text/xml"});
9   } else {
```

```
10     dojo.debug("Zipcode is not valid");
11  }
12 }
```

Notice this function begins by calling the `getValue` function (line 2) to retrieve the value of the zip code form field. Recall from the previous chapter that the zip code is a Dojo widget, rather than a vanilla form field. This means that the `value` property doesn't exist on the widget directly as it does on the form field, so calling `zipElt.value` won't work. This is true for most Dojo widgets that have underlying form fields (such as validation widgets or ComboBox widgets). These widgets provide two functions, `getValue` and `setValue`, that you should use instead. In certain situations, however, you may need to access the form fields to do more than just set the value. On these occasions, you can generally access the underlying form field by referring to the property that holds the field. Returning to the preceding example, you could retrieve or modify the text field that contains the zip code value by accessing the textbox property of the `zipElt` widget (i.e., `zipElt.textbox`).

After retrieving the zip code value, it should be validated one final time (line 3). Recall from Chapter 10 that you can directly call validation functions from JavaScript (rather than use the Dojo widget). The validation function is called one final time to ensure that an unnecessary server call isn't made with an invalid zip code.

Once it is determined that a reasonable value was provided for the zip code, you're ready to make the asynchronous call. Note that the `url` is the URL of your new zip code controller, and it includes a parameter with the value of the zip code.

Defining the Callback Function

Now you're ready to define the callback and a simple helper function as follows:

```
 1 function zipChangeCallback(type, data, evt) {
 2   var stateElts = data.getElementsByTagName("state");
 3
 4   if ((stateElts == null)||(stateElts.length == 0)) {
 5     dojo.debug("No response!");
 6     return;
 7   }
 8   var stateTxt = dojo.dom.textContent(stateElts.item(0));
 9   var cityElts = data.getElementsByTagName("city");
10   var cityTxt = dojo.dom.textContent(cityElts.item(0));
11   updateCityState(stateTxt, cityTxt);
12 }
13
14 function updateCityState(stateVal, cityVal) {
15   var stateElt = dojo.byId("state");
16   var cityElt = dojo.byId("city");
17   cityElt.value = unescape(cityVal);
18   stateElt.value = unescape(stateVal);
19 }
```

The `zipChangeCallback` takes the XML-formatted response generated by the zip-manager Servlet and retrieves the state and city. Some error checking (lines 4–6) is necessary to handle situations when no zip code can be found. To explore this a little more closely, consider the scenario in which a user types in 00000 for a zip code. Recall from the previous chapter that validation in Dojo is performed using regular expressions. Of course, it's impractical to define a regular expression that can handle every possible zip code and reject all invalid values, so any five-digit number passes validation. Actually, the validation even handles other zip code formats, such as the nine-digit zip code (e.g., 20010-3936), but this example only deals with five-digit zip codes. The only realistic way to truly verify that the zip code exists is through a database lookup on the server. An asynchronous server-side validation of the zip code when the user tabs off of the field is an ideal use of AJAX. It's left to you to explore the details of the implementation of this feature in the Web application on your own.

> *Although the server-side validation of a zip code* onblur *event is an interesting application of AJAX to explore, it is most likely an unwise use of AJAX in a real-world Web application. As a Web designer you must seriously consider the requirements of the system under development, and weigh both the pros and cons of implementing such features. In many Web applications it is sufficient to correct the zip code later (e.g., when an order is shipped) or not at all if the data is just for reference.*

Turning back to the new functions, after ensuring that the zip code lookup returned a valid result, the city and state text values are retrieved from the XML document. This is accomplished by using a DOM function, dojo.dom.textContent, available in Dojo. The dojo.dom package contains a wide variety of useful functions for analyzing or manipulating a DOM object. Table 11-1 provides an overview of the basic capabilities provided by the dojo.dom package. This particular function takes a DOM node and an optional text string as arguments and can be used to get or set the text value of the node. Here you're getting the text value of the city and state. Using the example zip-manager response from above would result in stateText and cityText being set to the strings "NY" and "AMSTERDAM", respectively.

Table 11-1: Overview of dojo.dom Functions

Function Type	Functions
Functions that assist in the analysis of a DOM node	isNode, isTag, isDescendantOf, hasParent, getTagName,innerXML, textContent
Functions that simplify searching within a document. These functions help you retrieve elements in relation to a particular node or tag.	firstElement, lastElement, nextElement, prevElement, getAncestors, getAncestorsByTag, getFirstAncestorByTag
Functions to ease the modification of a document's structure. These functions help you manipulate nodes, in relation to a particular node.	moveChildren, copyChildren, removeChildren, replaceChildren, prependChild, removeNode, insertBefore, insertAfter, insertAtPosition, insertAtIndex
Functions to reduce the complexity of creating a new document	createDocument, createDocumentFromText
Other functions	collectionToArray, getUniqueId

The final step in the callback function is to update the form fields to contain the new values, which is performed by the second function, updateCityState. This function simply looks up the form fields with dojo.byId and sets the value of these fields to the provided arguments. Note that the city and state fields are *not* Dojo widgets, so you can directly manipulate the value property, rather than use the Dojo widget functions for manipulating the value of a widget (i.e., setValue and getValue).

Invoking the Event Handler on Zip Code Change

Now that you've added the new JavaScript functions capable of handling the zip code changes, all that's left is to enhance `UserInputv1.html` to invoke the scripts when necessary. You can easily do this by calling `handleZipChange` when the user tabs off of the form field. Attach the function to the `onblur` event of the zip code by changing the field to the following:

```
<input name="zip" id="zip" size="5" maxsize="5" dojoType="UsZipTextbox"
    required="true" invalidMessage="* Zipcode is invalid!"
    missingMessage="* Zipcode is required!" onblur="handleZipChange(this)"></input>
```

At this point, you've completed all the changes necessary to enable your Web application to asynchronously update the city and state! If you redeploy your Web application, you should get the behavior shown in Figure 11-1. The zip code field is initially empty as shown on the left. When you type in a new zip code, an asynchronous request is made to the zip-manager Servlet. The zip-manager Servlet looks in the database for the city and state that corresponds to the zip code provided in the request, and returns them in an XML-formatted document. The form is then updated to contain the results of the lookup as shown on the right side of the figure.

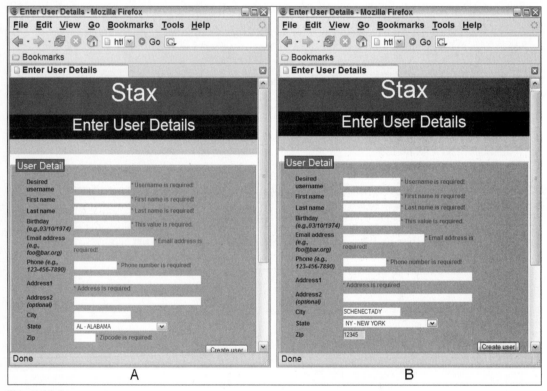

Figure 11-1

Form Usability in Practice: Using a Server Backed Combo Box

Another form usability enhancement being incorporated in many Web applications is a combo box backed by an asynchronous server-side data lookup based on another field. Almost all of the off-the-shelf JavaScript libraries that have a widget library include some form of combo box, a cross between a text field and a drop-down list (i.e., a select element). As the user types in text, the options in the list are narrowed until only one remains. Many JavaScript libraries even add an auto-complete capability, which fully populates the text field with the name of the first element in the list. The incorporation of this type of field in place of a standard select can greatly enhance the look and feel of a form, even when it isn't backed by a server-side lookup. Adding in the auto-complete capability can save the user considerable time, especially when typing long names, and help to reduce the potential for a typo.

An Auto-Complete Combo Box Example: Car Make

Consider the example of a Web application that allows a search based upon the make of a car. There's a pretty large set of possible car makes, but not so large that you wouldn't want to send the possible set of makes to the client for use in a select field, or a combo box. The only unfortunate aspect of using a select for this purpose is that a user who owns a Volvo must scroll through many pages to ultimately find the Volvo entry. With a combo box, as the user starts typing in "V" followed by "o," and so on, the number of options in the list is reduced to a much more manageable set, as shown in Figure 11-2. If you use an auto-complete feature, the user would only need to fill in the first four letters "volv," assuming that Volkswagon is the only other make of car starting with V.

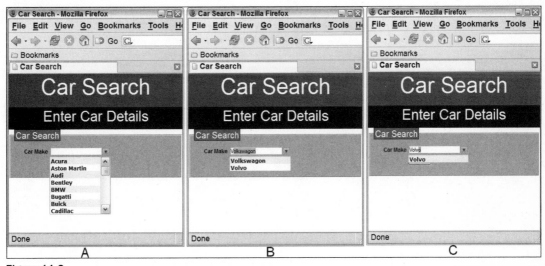

Figure 11-2

A Server-Populated Combo Box Example: Car Model

Of course, the utility of this component becomes magnified even more when you add the population of this field with a server-side lookup. Consider the car selection example. It may be a nice extension to also allow the user to search on the model as well as the make of the car. Unfortunately, including all models and all makes of cars in a single request is quite impractical, and wasteful. The dataset sent from the server would be quite large, and the majority of the models would never be required, as most users will generally select at most a few different car makes.

This situation is ideal for applying AJAX to select only the models associated with a single make of car in each request. Each time the user changes the value of the make combo box, the set of models for the selected make are asynchronously retrieved from the server and the model combo box is updated with the result. For example, when the user selects Volvo, and moves off the Make combo box, a behind-the-scenes asynchronous request returns only the set of Volvo models. The Model combo box is then updated to hold the set of Volvo models. If the user goes back and selects the Audi make, another asynchronous request retrieves the set of Audi models, and the combo box again updates with the new set (see the sequence diagram in Figure 11-3 for an example interaction). Depending on the application, you can even cache the old models for faster lookup if the same make is selected multiple times.

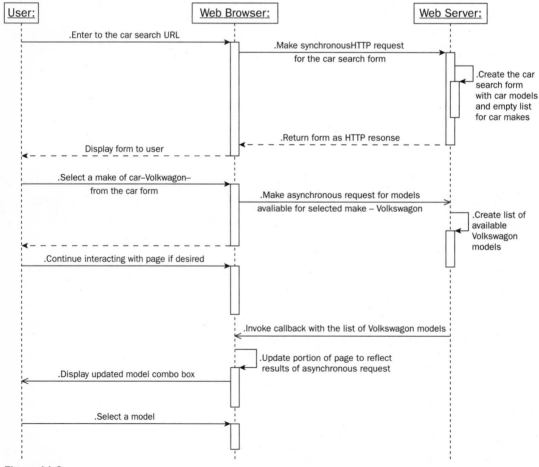

Figure 11-3

Now that you've explored the concept in more detail, you can take a closer look at how this is actually implemented by turning back to the user manager example. One place in the user form that would benefit from a server-backed combo box is the City field. Currently this field is simply a text field, and users must type in the entire name of their city. Providing an auto-complete capability for the city is desirable because city names are often long, and it takes less time than typing out the full name. It also reduces the possibility of specifying a city in a different state, or incorrectly spelling the name of a city. Of course, the dataset of all or even the main cities in the United States is quite large. You can easily see just how large by opening the MySQL command line, connecting to the stax database, and running a query like the following:

```
select count(distinct city) from zipcode;
```

The result returned indicates that there are almost 19,000 unique city names that have associated zip codes. Of course, it's impractical to send this full set of cities to the server with the user input page, but it's possible to greatly reduce the number of cities that make up the options in the city combo box by using the currently selected state. You can look at the number of cities for each state in the zip code table by running a query similar to the following:

```
select count(distinct city) as num_cities_in_state, state
    from zipcode group by state order by num_cities_in_state;
```

The average state has fewer than 500 cities, a much more manageable number than 19,000!

The rest of this section walks you through the steps necessary to implement the city field as a Dojo combo box widget and populate it when the user chooses a state with an asynchronous request.

Implementing the Server Side

As in the previous example, you start by extending the server side. First, you extend the model to look up the list of all cities in a given state from the database. After that, you update the controller to handle the requests for a city list.

Defining the Model

To populate a combo box with the list of possible cities given a state, you must be able to look up this information from the database, or calculate it in some other way. This capability falls into the business logic section of the model, and is quite similar to the zip code analysis performed in the previous example. You're accessing the same database table and generating a similar type of data, so this new functionality most logically fits in the `ZipCodeAnalyzer`. To add this new functionality, you simply need to extend the `ZipCodeAnalyzerv2` class to include a new method that performs the required database lookup. Create the new `lookupCities` method as follows:

```
1    public ArrayList lookupCities(String state) {
2      Connection conn = null;
3
4      try {
5        conn = getConnection();
6        if (conn == null) {
7          return new ArrayList();
8        }
9
10       Statement stmt = conn.createStatement();
```

```
11        ResultSet rs = stmt.executeQuery("SELECT distinct city " +
12            "FROM zipcode where state='" + state + "'");
13        ArrayList result = new ArrayList();
14        while(rs.next()) {
15           result.add(rs.getString("city"));
16        }
17        return result;
18
19      } catch(SQLException sqlEx) {
20        sqlEx.printStackTrace();
21      } finally {
22        if (conn != null) {
23          try {
24            conn.close();
25          } catch(SQLException ex) {}
26        }
27      }
28      return new ArrayList();
29   }
```

This method takes a string argument for the state code (e.g., PA, or MI) and returns a list of cities in the state as a `java.util.ArrayList` of `String` objects. Notice that this method is largely boilerplate, and follows the pattern of the `lookupCityStateZip` method in the same class.

Note that in a larger, more sophisticated system, this would most likely be refactored in some way, accessed via a Java object-to-database mapping service such as hibernate, or abstracted behind a data access object (DAO). This example retains the redundancy for simplicity and clarity.

The most interesting sections are on lines 11 and 12, where the database query is created. The query selects distinct cities that are in the state provided. For example, when PA is provided as the state argument, the query is as follows:

```
SELECT distinct city FROM zipcode where state='PA'
```

The other interesting difference is on lines 14–16, where each row in the result set is visited, and the city returned in the row is added to the array list to be returned. That's all that's required to extend your model to provide the new capability!

Defining the Controller

Now you're ready to enhance your controller to respond to the request for a state's cities by invoking the model and building an XML document with the model result. Because you're already using the zip analyzer model object to perform the city lookup, it makes sense to make the zip manager controller object responsible for responding to city list requests also. Of course, in a real-world application, you would probably use a more sophisticated controller approach, as mentioned earlier. Listing 11-6 shows an updated version of `ZipManagerServletv2`.

Listing 11-6: ZipManagerServletv2.java, updated to respond to city list requests

```
1 package stax.ui;
2
3 import java.io.*;
```

```
 4 import java.util.ArrayList;
 5 import java.util.Iterator;
 6
 7 import javax.servlet.*;
 8 import javax.servlet.http.*;
 9
10 import stax.model.businesslogic.ZipCodeAnalyzerv2;
11 import stax.model.AddressLocale;
12
13 public class ZipManagerServletv2 extends HttpServlet {
14
15   private static ZipCodeAnalyzerv2 zipAnalyzer = null;
16
17   public void doGet(HttpServletRequest req, HttpServletResponse resp)
18   throws IOException, ServletException {
19     if (zipAnalyzer == null) {
20       zipAnalyzer = new ZipCodeAnalyzerv2();
21     }
22
23     String zipS = req.getParameter("zip");
24     String stateS = req.getParameter("state");
25     String respData = "";
26
27     if (zipS != null) {
28       respData = getCityStateElements(zipS);
29     } else if (stateS != null) {
30       respData = getCityElements(stateS);
31     }
32
33     resp.setContentType("text/xml");
34     resp.setHeader("Cache-Control", "no-cache");
35
36     resp.getWriter().write("<?xml version='1.0' encoding='UTF-8'?>\n");
37     resp.getWriter().write("<response>\n");
38     resp.getWriter().write(respData);
39     resp.getWriter().write("</response>\n");
40   }
41
42   private String getCityStateElements(String zipS) {
43     // code unchanged
54   }
55
56   private String getCityElements(String stateS) {
57     ArrayList cities = zipAnalyzer.lookupCities(stateS);
58     StringBuffer response = new StringBuffer();
59     for (Iterator iter = cities.iterator(); iter.hasNext();) {
60       String city = (String)iter.next();
61       response.append("   <city>" + city + "</city>\n");
62     }
63     return response.toString();
64   }
65 }
```

The primary addition to this class is a new method that is capable of performing the city lookup given a state (lines 56–64). This method invokes the `lookupCities` method of the `zipAnalyzer` to get the list of cities associated with the state. The method then proceeds to create a snippet of XML that contains an element for each city in the state.

The only other modification required is a small extension to the `doGet` method. This must be updated to look for a new state parameter (line 34) and a handle to this parameter by invoking the `getCityElements` method (lines 29–31). At this point you can either call the Servlet with a zip code or a state. When the zip code is provided, the city and state are retrieved. When the state is provided, a list of cities in the state is returned.

Now you're ready to try out the new capability of your zip-manager Servlet. After adding it to the `web.xml` file, you can directly access the Servlet and look up, for example, the state of Rhode Island by entering a URL similar to the following one in your browser:

```
http://localhost:8080/UserManager/zip-managerv2?state=RI
```

The result is an XML document containing the list of cities for Rhode Island, formatted as follows:

```
<?xml version='1.0' encoding='UTF-8'?>
<response>
    <city>ADAMSVILLE</city>
    <city>ALBION</city>
    <!-- Etc. -->
    <city>SMITHFIELD</city>
    <city>JOHNSTON</city>
</response>
```

Implementing the Client Side by Enhancing the View

At this point you're ready to update your view to include the new city combo box as follows:

❑ Define a new Dojo combo box widget for the city text field in the `UserInputv2.html` page.

❑ Update the select element for the state field to invoke an event handler when the state is changed.

❑ Add the event handler, `handleStateChange`, to `userform-helperv2.js`, which is called when the state changes. This function will make an asynchronous request for the zip manager Servlet to retrieve the cities for the new state.

❑ Specify the callback function, `stateChangeCallback`, to `userform-helperv2.js`, which acts as the callback handler for the request created in the `handleStateChange` function. This function updates the dataset for the combo box to contain the new list of cities for the state.

❑ Update the `onload` function of `UserInputv2.html` to load the initial set of cities into the city combo box when the page loads.

Dojo Combo Boxes

Before getting into all the details of implementing the city combo box from the example Web application, it may be easiest to overview the capabilities provided in the Dojo combo box. This section explores some possible combo box specifications for the car "make" field discussed earlier in this chapter, and outlines other combo box properties.

Combo Boxes with Options Specified Inline

The following is a very simple example specification of a combo box for car makes:

```
<select dojoType="ComboBox" name="make" id="make">
  <option value="makea1">Acura</option>
  <!-- other makes -->
  <option value="makev2">Volvo</option>
</select>
```

Notice the following about this code:

❑ This specification is quite similar to a normal select. It includes the select element, with a set of options that represent each element in the drop-down list. The only difference in the select element is the appearance of the dojoType attribute. Recall from the previous chapter that this attribute establishes the type of widget that should be created, in this case a ComboBox.

❑ The option is the standard option specification in HTML that includes a value attribute. This value is sent as the parameter value if the option is selected (e.g., when Acura is selected, the request generated on form submission contains the parameter "make=makea1"). The text of the element is the text displayed in the drop-down list (e.g., the first element in the drop-down list is Acura).

Combo Boxes with Options Specified Remotely

This isn't the only way to specify the data that makes up the drop-down list for a combo box, though. There's an alternative approach in which the data to be displayed in the list is based on the result returned by a separate URL. The following code shows the same combo box specification with a new attribute, dataURL, that denotes the URL to use when retrieving the data:

```
<select dojoType="ComboBox" name="make" id="make" dataURL="carmakes.js">
</select>
```

Notice that the select element doesn't contain any option child elements to define the list contents. Instead, the dataURL attribute is used to create an asynchronous request after the page loads. The response to this request should be the data necessary to populate the contents of the drop-down list. Of course, in this example you must define a separate JavaScript file, carmakes.js, which defines the car makes as follows:

```
[["Acura", "makea1"], ["Aston Martin","makea2"], ..., ["Volvo","makev2"]]
```

Each inner array should have two elements: the display value and the option value. The first value of the inner array is the value that appears in the drop-down list of the combo box, such as the text data of the option element. The second value is the value of the option that is sent with the request parameter when the item is selected in the list. This is similar to the value attribute of the option element. You should also be aware that Dojo sends two parameters for each Combo Box field when the form is submitted. In the preceding example, if Acura is selected when the form is submitted, two parameters are created and initialized as follows:

```
make=Acura&make_selected=makea1
```

The first parameter, make, is the value typed into the combo box text field, while the make_selected parameter is the value selected from the drop-down. Generally these will be the display value and the option value, respectively, but this isn't necessarily the case. Depending on the value of the `force ValidOption` property, described next, the `make` value may correspond to a user-entered string that isn't in the drop-down list.

Other Combo Box Properties

Several other optional properties affect the behavior of the combo box, as shown in Table 11-2. You can add most of these properties as additional attributes of the `select` element, with two glaring exceptions. The last two properties in the table are actually properties of the data provider used to get the data for the combo box, rather than the combo box itself. To override the default behavior of either the `searchType` or `caseSensitive` property, you must set the property on the data provider, rather than the combo box. The effect of this is that you can't specify them as attributes of the combo box element, as you can for most other properties, such as `autoComplete` in Dojo. Instead, you must write a bit of JavaScript that is executed when the file loads. Returning to the example of the car makes, adding the following to the bottom of the HTML page turns case sensitivity on in the data provider:

```
<script>
  dojo.addOnLoad(function(){
    var cb = dojo.widget.byId("make");
    cb.dataProvider.caseSensitive=true;
  });
</script>
```

Table 11-2: Optional Properties of the ComboBox Widget

Property	Default Value	Meaning
mode	local	Either local or remote. This establishes the type of search to perform .When set to remote, the data for the combo box drop-down list is retrieved using an asynchronous call to the server, rather than with client-side JavaScript. As the user types into the field, asynchronous calls are made to the server to retrieve the updated drop-down list. When set to local, the set of data in the drop-down list is trimmed on the client side.
maxListLength	8	The maximum number of entries to appear in the drop-down list. If more entries are in the dataset, a scrollbar is used.
fadeTime	200ms	The drop-down list appears using a fade-in effect. This governs the amount of time (in ms) it takes to fade in the list.
forceValidOption	false	When `true`, the text field can contain only strings that already appear in the backing dataset. When `false`, the user can type any desired value into the text field. In the car make example, if the user enters Peugeot and this attribute is `true`, the field is set to the empty string when the user exits. The only accepted car makes are those that already appear in the data list.

Property	Default Value	Meaning
autoComplete	true	When true, the text field updates with the full name of the top element. When false, the text field only contains the typed letters. In the car make example, when this attribute is true, as the user types **Vol,** the text field updates to contain the string Volkswagon. When the user adds the "v" to the string, making "Volv," the text field value changes to Volvo.
dataProvider property: searchType	STARTSTRING	This should be one the following: STARTSTRING, STARTWORD, or SUBSTRING (you must specify these in all uppercase characters). This denotes the type of search that should be performed when narrowing the drop-down list options. STARTSTRING matches only options that begin with the search string. STARTWORD matches options containing words that begin with the search string. SUBSTRING matches options that contain the search string anywhere.
dataProvider property: caseSensitive	false	Indicates whether or not to perform a case-sensitive search

Defining the Dojo Combo Box

Turning back to the example, you need to first prepare for the new city combo box by updating your JavaScript file to include the correct package that defines the combo box widget. To do this, open userform-helperv2.js and add the following dojo.require statement after the dojo.require statement that is used to include the Debug Console:

```
dojo.require("dojo.widget.ComboBox");
```

Now you're ready to update UserInputv2.html to create the city combo box. First, change the original city specification from the standard input field

```
<input name="city" id="city"/>
```

to a Dojo ComboBox widget:

```
<select dojoType="ComboBox" dataUrl=""
  style="width: 200px" name="city" id="city" maxListLength="15"></select>
```

The specification of this combo box is very similar to the specification above. The dojoType attribute is set to ComboBox. The style, name, and id attributes are the same as in standard HTML. The dataUrl attribute, as described above, establishes the URL that is accessed when retrieving the dataset for the drop-down list. Notice that this field is empty in the preceding example. This is because you're going to be populating the drop-down list based on the selected state, rather than a static and predetermined URL.

Updating the Select Element

If you were to rerun the Web application now, you would have a combo box with an empty drop-down list. Before you can get a populated drop-down list, you need to add a new JavaScript function capable of responding to a state change by updating the data in the drop-down list. Update UserInputv2.html to respond to the onblur event of the state form field. This is done by changing the state select element specification to the following:

```
<select style="width: 200px" value="AL" class="userselect"
  name="state" id="state" onchange="handleStateChange(this)">
```

Adding the Event Handler

Now you can define your new state onchange event handler. Open userform-helperv2.js and add the following global variable to the beginning of the file after the lastUsername variable:

```
var lastState = "Unset";
```

In the onchange handler, you use this variable to cache the last state selected by the user. This cached state ensures that you don't make unnecessary calls to the server when the user tabs off the state field but doesn't actually change the value. Next, add the following function that responds to the state onblur events:

```
 1 function handleStateChange(stateElt) {
 2   var state = stateElt.value;
 3   if (lastState == state) {
 4     dojo.debug("Ignoring unchanged state: " + state);
 5     return;
 6   }
 7   lastState = state;
 8   if (dojo.validate.us.isState(state)) {
 9     dojo.io.bind({
10       url:"zip-managerv2?state=" + state,
11       load: function(type, data, evt)
12         { stateChangeCallback(type, data, evt); },
13       mimetype: "text/xml"});
14   } else {
15     dojo.debug("State is not valid");
16   }
17 }
```

Notice the following about this code:

❑   This method gets the value of the state (line 2) and returns early when the state is the same as the most recently cached state (lines 3–5).

❑   On line 8, a final client-side validation of the state is performed. Note that this step isn't strictly necessary because the state field is a read-only drop-down list, and there really isn't any easy way to provide an invalid state. In general, though, it's good practice to validate the input on the client side prior to making the asynchronous request. This saves the client from making extra requests that contain invalid data.

❑   If the state is valid, an asynchronous request is made to the zip-manager controller with the state argument on lines 9–13. The callback stateChangeCallback is invoked after the server response data loads.

Specifying the Callback Function

Now you're ready to create the callback. Add the implementation of the callback function to `userform-helperv2.js` as follows:

```
 1 function stateChangeCallback(type, data, evt) {
 2   var cityElts = data.getElementsByTagName("city");
 3   var cityField = dojo.widget.byId("city");
 4   var cbOptions = [];
 5
 6   for (var idx = 0; idx < cityElts.length; idx++) {
 7     var city = dojo.dom.textContent(cityElts.item(idx));
 8     cbOptions.push([city, city]);
 9   }
10   cityField.dataProvider.setData(cbOptions);
11 }
```

The preceding callback function handles the response from the server by updating the contents of the city combo box to contain the new list of cities:

❑ An array of DOM nodes that correspond to the candidate city elements returned from the server is retrieved on line 2.

❑ The city combo box is retrieved on line 3 with the `dojo.widget.byId` function. Recall the discussion of the differences between `dojo.byId` and `dojo.widget.byId` from Chapter 11. In this case, you must use the widget version of the function instead of `dojo.byId` because the city field is now a Dojo widget, rather than a standard form field.

❑ An array `cbOptions` is created on line 4, populated with the list of cities returned from the server on lines 6–9.

❑ Note another use of the `dojo.dom.textContent` function on line 7. Recall from the previous example that you can use this function to extract the text (in this case, the city name, e.g., SMITHFIELD) from a DOM node (in this case, a city element, e.g., <city>SMITHFIELD</city>).

❑ The city is then added to the `cbOptions` array (on line 8), following the same convention explored in the car make example earlier. Specifically, the city is added to a new two-element array, which is in turn added to the `cbOptions` array.

❑ Finally, on line 10, the `cbOptions` array is established as the set of values to be used when populating the drop-down list. This is accomplished by calling the `setData` function on the data provider for the combo box, and providing the array of option arrays. Two additional functions on the data provider are useful for dealing with the data in the drop-down list of the combo box. The `getData` function retrieves the set of data currently used for the drop-down list. The `addData` function adds a single element, provided as an array argument, to the options of the drop-down list. This array should contain two elements and follow the conventions outlined above.

One final step is to update some old references to the city field in the `updateCityState` function in `userform-helperv2.js`. As noted above, widgets should be retrieved with the function `dojo.widget.byId`. In the previous example you created a function, `updateCityState`, that updates the city and state given a city and state value. This function is currently set to look the city up with the `dojo.byId` function, and should be updated to use the function for widgets.

In addition, the same function directly sets the value of the city element on the line

```
cityElt.value = unescape(cityVal);
```

Recall from the first example that the value of a Dojo widget cannot be accessed or modified with the `value` property. You must use the two functions `getValue` and `setValue` provided for the widgets instead. Update the preceding line to use the widget function as follows:

```
cityElt.setValue(unescape(cityVal));
```

At this point, you can deploy and run the Web application. Notice that when you change the state, the names of cities in the city drop-down list is updated! Figure 11-4 shows the city combo box.

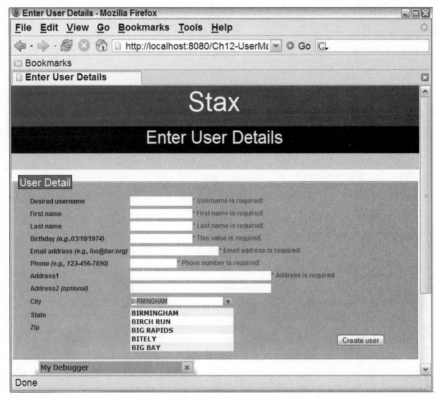

Figure 11-4

Updating the onload Function

One final extension is required for this example. Notice that when you initially load the page, the drop-down list is empty. Because the state is set to Alabama by default, you should also pre-load the drop-down list with the list of cites in Alabama. You can easily accomplish this by calling the new `handleStateChange` function after the page loads. In Chapter 11, you added a script to the end of `UserInputv2.html` that caused the form to be submitted asynchronously and validated prior to submission. You should now extend this script to include a lookup of the state element, and call the `handleStateChange` function after the form is loaded. Following is an updated `on load` function to be to be included at the end of `UserFormv2.html`:

```
<script>
  dojo.addOnLoad(function(){
      // set's city combo box from first selected state
      var itlState = dojo.byId("state");
      handleStateChange(itlState);

      var fb = new dojo.io.FormBind({
          formNode: "user_detail",
          mimetype: "text/xml",
          load: function(load, data, e) {
              submitCallback(data);
          }
        });
      fb.onSubmit = function(form) {
        return handleSubmit();
      }
  });
</script>
```

After this modification, when you redeploy and reload the Web application, the city field should be initially populated with the cities for Alabama.

Summary

This chapter has explored issues in form usability. You've seen a couple of examples that demonstrate how to use AJAX and Dojo to significantly increase the usability and interactivity in a User Form. Remember that although Java and Dojo were used in developing the examples in this chapter, the concepts are applicable to any server-side technology, from Python to PHP. In addition, using Dojo isn't required to implement these enhancements. Many client-side libraries, such as script.aculo.us, include some form of combo box. The key point is that regardless of the particular implementation, you can easily extend your Web application to include a variety of usability enhancements previously unavailable without asynchronous calls. The use of such enhancements can greatly improve the user experience, and reduce or eliminate their frustration.

Interview with Industry Leaders: Alex Russell, project lead for the Dojo Toolkit

On the Dojo Foundation, Collaboration, and His Role

Q: *How did the Dojo foundation come about?*

Alex: We did the foundation because we didn't know any better — we didn't know how much hard work it was going to be. When we started working on Dojo two and a half years ago, no one could care less about JavaScript. We looked at approaching Apache or one of the other foundations that didn't really have a language affinity to JavaScript. Because it was really rough, we said, "We'll do a paper tiger of a foundation." Later on, it did something that we didn't really expect, which was give companies who know how to deal with other legal entities someone to talk to.

Q: *Do you still do any of the day-to-day coding, or are you migrating to being the chief architect or advocate?*

Alex: I still hack. I do find myself pressed for the long blocks of time that it takes to sit down and figure something out and hack on it to make it work. Luckily, my job now as director of R&D lets me focus on stuff like that.

Q: *You have a pretty large and diverse group of collaborators. How do you keep the project organized?*

A: We have a weekly meeting every Wednesday at 3:00 P.M. (PT) on an IRC channel, and all the committers try to show up. We have an agenda that we work up before that meeting. That's our one chance a week to catch up on the issues of the day. Then we have the interest mailing list, which is a fire hose. We have the private committers' mailing list. We get a lot of stuff hashed out in those because more formal organization is not as necessary. It has problems like any open-source project does. People are volunteers; you can't fire who you didn't hire.

On Dojo History and Design

Q: *How did Dojo get its start, and how did the toolkit evolve?*

Alex: I was working with Dylan Schiemann and David Schontzler at Informatica one summer. We were faced with a project that had some pretty serious requirements. We were trying to hire some folks and wound up in contact with a bunch of people that we had known "back in the day" in the DHTML community, back when there had been such a thing, and [we] said, "Even if you're not interested in coming to work with us, how about joining up on a mailing list?" We got lucky in that we got all the right people on the mailing list. That mailing list is now the Dojo contributors' mailing list. It originally started out as a discussion about "what do we need next?" Everyone agreed that it would be great if we pooled our stuff because life was draining out of the community. We got some economical solutions to a bunch of the problems; we had all reinvented the wheel to be in everyone's best interest. We started off, and eight months or a year later, the AJAX thing happened, and the rocket took off. We weren't prescient; we were just lucky and desperate.

Q: *So the Dojo library is so broad because it was needs driven?*

Alex: Yeah, we had collectively built a bunch of reasonably sophisticated, high-end DHTML apps, and unlike our previous attempts, we were actually bringing some real-world experience to bear on the problem, looking back on what we'd done and saying, "Which of these things are salvageable?" and learning from our mistakes.

Q: *When you decided to pull these components together, did you pull them together with minimal redesign, did you do an initial complete top-down redesign, or refactor them from the bottom up?*

Alex: We laid out some of the things that had been missing. Mark Anderson wrote a packaging system for us because we recognized that we needed one. Then once we had the packaging system, we started importing things from other libraries, and making them feel like Dojo. In a lot of cases, we would look at what we already had and determine whether the API was right, and then go see what was workable. Like, the I/O system — we sat down and said, "What's the right API for this?" and fiddled around with what we had. That case wound up being a ground-up rewrite.

On Other JavaScript Libraries

Q: *Dojo is frequently compared with other JavaScript libraries, in articles like InfoWorld's "Surveying Open-Source AJAX Toolkits" by Peter Wayner. How do you think you stack up against other libraries such as MochiKit, script.aculo.us, or Protoype?*

Alex: One of the things he touched on as a reason for liking Dojo was the breadth of it. He did cover Rico, which is one of the things that's built on top of Prototype. The MochiKit guys are very tightly constrained to specific issues, and insofar as it goes, it's excellent code. There's no denying that. I think YUI is going to grow to Dojo-ish proportions at some point. It's all about the scope that you're going for. When we were working with Dojo we decided that we wanted to build a toolkit that's good for the folks on this list and then grow it out. Over time, we want to hit different audiences. At first you have a core, which is really only useful with people who know what problem they're trying to solve. Then you get to things like the widgets, where you have a library of pre-built widgets. You start to appeal to an incredibly different set of developers, folks who want to plug something in and make it go. I think that's part of the problem with trying to compare all libraries. He might not have included MochiKit because he wanted to do an evaluation of things that you could play with and drop in easily. You can't really do that with MochiKit. Yet.

Q: *You mention it's possible that YUI could grow to Dojo-ish proportions. Could you explain how or why?*

Alex: I kind of expected Yahoo! to keep making it go as far as they needed to for their product. The difference between us, and one of the only reasons we've been able to achieve acceptance, is that we represent a level playing field where there's nobody in control. The only differentiators between us and the YUI is that someone like AOL or IBM or Sun can come to the table, and if they contribute patches they can get a seat. That's the difference between it being an open-source community and having code that's yours. I've talked to the YUI guys. They're a great team and they're doing excellent work, and I think maybe they seem to be doing better work in some areas than we are. At the same time, what Yahoo! is building is a great solution for Yahoo!. I hope someday they open the process up, so other people can start to contribute. I think they deserve all the success they get, because they're doing really great work. The community process is a little bit more chaotic, maybe, than being in control.

On CometD

Q: *We've read your blog posts on CometD. Can you elaborate on this?*

Alex: CometD is an implementation of a JSON-based publish/subscribe event notification protocol that we're calling Bayeux. The protocol itself is a way for a browser and a specialized Web server to negotiate how they want to deal with publish/subscribe event notification delivery. CometD is a set of implementations of that. We've got a client implementation in Dojo subversion; we've got two server implementations. The hope is that we'll have this easy-to-implement, very straightforward JSON protocol for doing this.

Q: *So, with CometD, the pipe is open the whole time?*

Alex: Yeah, and the difference between Bayeux, the protocol, and the things that have come before it is that we have this negotiation step, where in some of the transports that it could negotiate to use, it might keep the connection open all the time, and some of them might not.

On the Future of Dojo

Q: *What's in store for Dojo in the future?*

Alex: We keep a road map document in subversion. It's more or less accurate with regard to the next version out. It's somewhat more speculative past that. The "big brass rings" for 1.0 are a couple of things that we're just starting to get, like some really good 2-D vector graphics stuff that'll work across every browser, data binding, internationalization, localization, and accessibility.

12

Drag and Drop

The Macintosh uses an experimental pointing device called a mouse. There is no evidence that people want to use these things.

—**John C. Dvorak,** *San Francisco Examiner,* **February 1984**

The mouse is so much more than a device for clicking links, and RIAs can take advantage of the full range of actions that it can communicate. This chapter demonstrates how to create some of the various mouse-centric RIA interaction patterns: draggable objects, drop-receiving containers, and sortable lists. These three behavior types are the core mouse operations for desktop systems, but for years they were ignored in the Web browser.

Mouse events are one of many classes of page events that can be captured by the browser and communicated to JavaScript callbacks. Although it's entirely possible to implement a custom solution for any of the patterns that this chapter demonstrates, nearly all available JavaScript libraries contain ready-made abstractions to provide these capabilities for you. For this reason, few circumstances require a developer to implement a custom solution.

This chapter begins with the basic concepts of dragging, dropping, and the sortable list in the context of script.aculo.us, one popular JavaScript library in use today. It then demonstrates these concepts as part of a useful interface that you can use as a base for a slide show editor in our capstone application, ideaStax. First a client-side-only version is demonstrated, which uses nothing but JavaScript, XHTML, and CSS. This kind of a solution is excellent for the sake of explanation, but is incomplete without the concluding section: a rewrite of the ideaStax Editor using a server framework to serve and persist the slide and slide-show data. By the end of this chapter, you should be familiar with a number of techniques and technologies, including drag, drop, and sortable list creation using script.aculo.us and basic Web development using the Ruby on Rails framework. Chapter 13, "User Interactions, Effects, and Animation," extends the material presented here to further enrich the developed interface.

Introducing Prototype and script.aculo.us

The JavaScript library that demonstrates the drag and drop functionality for this chapter is one of the front-running JavaScript libraries, and is actually a pair of independently developed libraries that complement each other's abilities: Prototype and script.aculo.us. Script.aculo.us was chosen because it provides simple and primitive graphics operations within a RIA page. Introducing the Ruby on Rails framework is another objective of this chapter, and Rails comes with built-in support for Prototype and script.aculo.us — another reason for the choice.

Understanding Prototype and script.aculo.us Capabilities

Prototype is a lightweight JavaScript library that, according to its Web site, "aims to ease development of dynamic Web applications." Put another way, what differentiates Prototype from many of the other JavaScript libraries on the Web is that it doesn't recreate the desktop on the Web, but rather makes JavaScript programming easier. It features the following:

- ❑ A number of handy shortcuts for common operations, such as abbreviating `document.getElementById(element)` with just `$(element)`

- ❑ A rock-solid set of AJAX helpers

- ❑ A lightweight, low-level, and narrow focus, which makes this a popular library to use as a springboard for other libraries. Script.aculo.us and Rico are two libraries that use Prototype as a base.

Script.aculo.us is an open-source project that provides many simple user-interface-related features for RIA programming. It falls short of the breadth and complexity of widgets offered by toolkits such as Dojo and MochiKit, but its simple interface make it easy for developers familiar with JavaScript to use and extend. Among script.aculo.us' main features are the following:

- ❑ Drag and drop handling

- ❑ Visual effects

- ❑ Auto-complete form elements

- ❑ A handy DOM Builder class that this chapter will introduce later

Both Prototype and script.aculo.us are built into the Ruby on Rails framework, complete with helper functions that automate frequently used operations.

By now you have surely realized that the variety of technologies, frameworks, and toolkits at your disposal in creating a RIA is vast. This book attempts to cover as many different technologies as possible to stress this diversity. The hope is that the keen reader can transfer skills demonstrated in one language or framework easily to the next. The script.aculo.us drag and drop techniques in this chapter are certainly transferable to other frameworks, as the basic concerns and development strategies transcend the particular implementation of the pattern.

Obtaining Prototype and script.aculo.us

Both Prototype and script.aculo.us are open source and available free of charge. You may find them at the sites listed below. Using them is no different than using any other piece of JavaScript code — simply place them in a directory within your Web root and include them in the `head` tag of the Web pages in which you want to use them.

Prototype	http://prototype.conio.net/
script.aculo.us	http://script.aculo.us/

DOM Elements in the Physical World

Before getting started with drag and drop, it's important to first take a few moments to review how a tree-based structure of information (your XHTML document) is translated into two-dimensional objects that can move around, overlap, and collide with each other. Understanding the properties behind this translation will enable you to think in a way that makes your RIA programming more flexible and creative.

Recall how XML is a fundamentally order-insensitive language for describing the structure of data. An XML parser does not care which element among a set of brethren comes first because it is the relationship between elements that matters. While an XHTML processor does pay attention to element order insofar as it displays elements in the order in which they were parsed as the default formatting rule, there are really few ways to derive any sort of physical structure from a modern XHTML document. Instead, CSS instructions position elements throughout the page, and while the position often makes use of the DOM tree structure, it needn't have any link whatsoever.

Cascading Style Sheets, therefore, are the primary source from which DOM elements are given the physical properties that allow them to be manipulated with the mouse as objects on the screen:

- ❑ The `top` and `left` properties position the element on the screen, either absolute to the top-left corner of the browser canvas or relative to the top-left corner of the containing DOM element.

- ❑ The `height` and `width` properties give the element a presence in two-dimensional space.

- ❑ The `z-index` provides a primitive third dimension that allows elements to specify in which "layer" of the Web page they exist. It gives JavaScript and the browser a way to resolve conflicts when multiple objects exist in the same physical space. In the case of the browser, this determines which element displays in front of other elements, possibly concealing them. In the case of drag and drop, the `z-index` could determine which of multiple drop zones gets dibs on an element being dropped. Figure 12-1 demonstrates the important CSS properties that pertain to drag and drop operations.

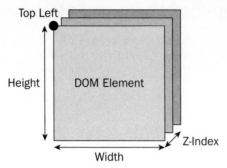

Figure 12-1

Making the jump from these properties to manipulating two-dimensional objects is not hard, but sometimes you need to take care when considering what happens after you drop an element somewhere else. After all, XHTML is a language of containment — every element exists within another element, all the way up to the html element, whether or not those elements have two-dimensional physical representations on the Web page. Thus, to drop an element on top of another is to drop it on top of every single element up the containment lineage of that element. Because this can grow confusing very rapidly, drag and drop behaviors are implemented by "blessing" particular objects to either exhibit the ability to be dragged or the ability to receive a drop. These objects, and only these objects, will subsequently respond to the appropriate events on the page.

Draggables

Draggable is a class in script.aculo.us that enables you to give a DOM element the ability to be dragged around within the Web page. Draggables respond to Mouse Down events inside their boundaries by following the mouse arrow as it moves until a Mouse Up event occurs. You can only move Draggables within the canvas of the browser window, of course.

There are several cases in which Draggable elements can enrich the RIA experience:

❑   Drag-enabled shopping carts allow users to drag items on top of the cart to add them for purchase. You can see an example on the script.aculo.us Web page.

❑   Web-based file storage applications might allow draggable file operations, such as dragging a file to the trash or to another folder.

❑   Increasingly, Web pages allow users to arrange widgets — such as RSS feeds, calendars, or weather reports — on member home pages. Each widget is generally of rectangular shape, and users can rearrange the columns and rows that contain them.

❑   The slideshow editor built in this chapter is, of course, a fourth example of draggable behavior.

Considering Draggable Requirements

Implementing a RIA with Draggable objects is not just as easy as creating the object and letting users drag at will. A number of considerations require careful thought before arriving at the implementation stage. Luckily, all of the behavioral considerations in the following list are included as pre-implemented features of almost every drag-capable JavaScript library. Here are some important options for contemplation before deciding how to utilize drag behavior in a RIA:

- ❑ **Drag appearance** — Should the appearance of the element when it's being dragged be different from when it's at rest? Changing the object's appearance during a drag action greatly improves the RIA interface's usability because it gives users a subtle cue that they are performing an action. A common effect to apply to dragged elements is to lower the element's opacity so that it appears ghostly above the Web page it is being dragged across.

- ❑ **Release behavior** — What happens to the dragged element when the user lets go of the mouse button? Should the element "snap back" to its original position or remain in the last recorded position before the mouse button is released? You usually treat this issue separately of any action that occurs after the element is dropped (these are handled by the Droppable object). If the Draggable object references a dialog box or widget on the screen, then it should probably stay at its new location after a drop, but if the Draggable object is a product dropped on a shopping cart, then it likely should return to its original spot on the page as the shopping cart updates the quantity.

- ❑ **Drag constraints** — Can the element move anywhere on the Web page or should it be constrained to a particular region? In cases where the release behavior is to snap back to the starting position (while a Droppable region responds with some other action), you do not need to place a drag constraint on the object; but in instances where the dragged object remains where the mouse was released (such as clip art within a slide), it's useful to constrain Draggable elements to only those locations where it makes sense to leave it.

- ❑ **Movement grid** — Should the element move freely, with ultra-smooth granularity, or should the element's movements snap to tick marks on a grid-style coordinate system? In the former case, every movement of the mouse should trigger an equal repositioning of the dragged element, whereas in the latter case the dragged element should only respond when the mouse moves a certain predefined number of pixels in one of the primary directions.

These are just some of the questions that you should ask before jumping into the implementation of Draggable user interaction patterns on a RIA page. Deciding precisely how the drag should occur minimizes the number of unexpected runtime glitches later in development.

Defining a Draggable

Script.aculo.us makes defining a Draggable element fantastically simple. The developer need only instantiate a new Draggable object somewhere in the XHTML page after the DOM element that is to be given Draggable behavior has already been defined. The signature of the Draggable constructor is as follows:

```
new Draggable(element_name, { options_hash });
```

The options hash accepts various options passed in as key value pairs. These options alter the way in which the Draggable object affects the element that it points to. Table 12-1 lists some of these options. Other options exist, and new ones are always being created by the script.aculo.us developers. For further information about any option not covered in detail here, visit the script.aculo.us wiki at http://wiki.script.aculo.us/.

Table 12-1: Script.aculo.us Draggable Options

Option Name	Description
handle	Specifies a given region that serves as the drag handle. The value can be either an element reference, an element ID, or a CSS class.
revert	Either a Boolean value that specifies whether the element should snap back to its starting position after the end of the drag or a function reference that is called when the drag ends
snap	Specifies a snap-to function that only allows the dragged element to assume certain positions on the page
zindex	The z-index that the item should take on while being dragged
constraint	Constrains the element to only being moved vertically or horizontally
ghosting	If set to true, a clone of the Draggable element is dragged instead of the original element itself. Once the element is dropped, the original replaces the clone.
starteffect	Defines an effect that is applied when dragging starts
endeffect	Defines an effect that is applied when dragging ends
reverteffect	Defines an effect that is applied when an element reverts back to the starting position

Droppables

Droppable is an active word that describes a passive behavior. It is also the class in script.aculo.us that enables a DOM element to react to Draggable elements that are dragged and then released on top of it. While the Draggable pattern allows Web users to interact with and move objects within a Web application, the Droppable pattern defines the reaction the Web application has to objects once they are released.

Considering Droppable Requirements

As with Draggable objects, developers must consider several variations on Droppable behavior:

❑ **XY drop criteria** — What are the requirements for being considered inside the Droppable region? CSS positions elements according to their top-left corner, width, and height, resulting in various interpretations of the definition of "within." While the default behavior of drag and drop libraries is likely fine for most developers, some applications require a developer to rewrite the code that determines when a dragged element is inside the boundary of a Droppable object.

❑ **Z-Index drop criteria** — Does this Droppable region override other Droppable regions that might occupy the same XY space? Some RIAs contain a deep layering of elements that may overlap each other. In the event that two Droppable elements overlap, a rule for deciding which element deserves the Draggable element is necessary; it might be the frontmost object, the backmost, or perhaps all elements.

❑ **Selective drop areas** — Can you drop any `Draggable` here or just certain ones? Perhaps a Web page has several different types of `Draggable` objects and `Droppable` areas. In such a case, limiting a `Droppable` element so that it only accepts certain `Draggable` elements is important. Two common ways of defining an acceptable `Droppable` area "guest list" are specifying a list of permissible CSS classes or specifying a parent element whose `Draggable` children are permitted.

❑ **Hover** — What should the `Droppable` object look like when an accepted `Draggable` element is hovering over it? Just as it helps to have an effect applied to a `Draggable` object when it is being dragged, providing an additional effect to show that the `Draggable` object has entered a `Droppable` region guides users to perform the correct actions on the RIA page without instructions. This is often accomplished by creating a CSS class that is applied to the `Droppable` element when a valid `Draggable` is overhead. The class might highlight the `Droppable` element's border or cause its background to adopt a different color or shade.

Defining a Droppable

Defining a `Droppable` element in script.aculo.us is just as easy as defining a `Draggable`. Simply instantiate a new `Droppable` object for each DOM element on the page that you want to have the capability to receive drops. As with the `Draggable` element, you should make the `Droppable` instantiation after the DOM element it references has already been defined:

```
Droppables.add(dom_element_id, { options_hash });
```

Just as with the `Draggable` object, the `Droppable` constructor allows for a hash that can contain many options to fine-tune the way the `Droppable` region performs. Table 12-2 lists the available options; and you can find more information at `http://wiki.script.aculo.us/`.

Table 12-2: Script.aculo.us Droppable Options

Option Name	Description
accept	Specifies a selective `Droppable` area based on a CSS class. Only elements with one of the specified CSS classes trigger a drop event.
containment	Specifies a selective `Droppable` area based on the parent element of the dragged object. Only elements with one of the specified parent elements trigger a drop event.
hoverclass	Specifies an additional CSS class that is applied to the `Droppable` region when a valid `Draggable` hovers over it
overlap	Specifies that the dragged element must be more than half-way inside the `Droppable` region before it is considered "inside"
greedy	Makes this `Droppable` region block other `Droppable` regions if more than one exist atop each other
onHover	A callback that executes when a `Draggable` object enters the region of a `Droppable` object
onDrop	A callback that executes when a `Draggable` object is dropped inside the `Droppable` object

Sortable Lists

Sortable lists are the third and final interaction pattern presented in this chapter. A sortable list builds off of the Draggable and Droppable patterns to create a container in which users can rearrange content with the mouse. The elements of a sortable list follow a linear order, but they may overflow to fill multiple columns or rows to express that order. Sortable lists are useful in many possible capacities within a RIA. For example, a user might want to organize photos in a slide show, or informational blocks in a sidebar.

Defining a sortable list is simple. The following code presents its constructor:

```
Sortable.create(contailer_element_id, { options_hash } );
```

The container_element_id is the ID of the container that is to contain the sortable items. The options hash can be populated with the options described in Table 12-3.

Table 12-3: Sortable List Options

Option Name	Description
tag	Sets the name of the outermost tag for each of the sortable elements
only	Restricts the sortable elements to elements of type tag (see above) with a specific CSS class or one of an array of specific CSS classes, defined by only
overlap	Specifies the basic direction of the list, either vertical or horizontal
containment	Specifies multiple sortable list containers that can accept the elements of this container
dropOnEmpty	Makes the sortable list container into a Droppable region that can accept Draggable valid elements from elsewhere on the page even when it is empty
scroll	If the CSS overflow property of the sortable list container is set to scroll, this property causes the list to scroll as the user drags a list item past the end of the visible list
onChange	Sets a callback that is called whenever the order of the sortable list changes while the user is dragging an element from one place to another
onUpdate	Sets a callback that is called whenever the user drops a list item into a new position that changes the sort order of the list

In addition to the options listed in Table 12-3, you can apply many of the options for the Draggable object to a Sortable. You can use the options constraint, handle, hoverclass, and ghosting in the same way that they are applied to the Draggable object and they will affect elements in the sortable list when they are being dragged.

Drag and Drop in Context:
The ideaStax Editor

By the end of this chapter, you'll have completed an end-to-end RIA page that makes use of the
`Draggable`, `Droppable`, and `Sortable` classes. This interface, developed in this chapter and the next,
illustrates the beginning of the main component of the book's capstone RIA, ideaStax. The ideaStax
Editor shown over the next two chapters enables users to organize photos from a library into slide
shows, and to preview each slide. Later in the book, text slides, tagging, and searching will be added as
capabilities. The different elaborations on the ideaStax concept used in the following chapters are hosted
on this book's Web site and are available for download and inspection. A more full-featured version
intended to illustrate the lessons of this book as a whole is also provided on `www.ideastax.com` for
downloading and community contribution.

Basic Design

The interface to the ideaStax Editor contains three main parts: the Library, the Timeline, and the Editor:

❑ The Library contains photos owned by the ideaStax user that you can turn into Slides. You can
   search and tag (to be implemented in Chapter 15) the Library, which loads dynamically after
   starting the Editor. You can drag photos from the library into the Timeline, where they are
   added to the Timeline without being removed from the Library.

❑ Once in the Timeline, a Photo becomes a Slide object, enabling it to be rearranged and ordered
   in a sortable list with other Slides.

❑ You can drag both slides and photos into the Editor, which in this chapter just displays a large
   version of the dragged item. Figure 12-2 contains a mock-up of the desired editor — the ideaStax
   Editor.

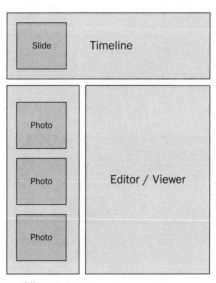

Library

Figure 12-2

You can easily implement this template with the XHTML body shown in Listing 12-1. Other than CSS and JavaScript included in the `head` element, the code in Figure 12-1 represents the entirety of the required starting code for this interface — everything else will be created and loaded dynamically through JavaScript. The CSS code that you need to provide layout and stylistic guidelines for this structure is left out as an exercise for the reader, but all of the code (including somewhat attractive CSS) is available on the book's Web site at www.wrox.com.

Listing 12-1: XHTML

```
<!DOCTYPE html PUBLIC "-//W3C//DTD XHTML 1.0 Strict//EN"
  "http://www.w3.org/TR/xhtml1/DTD/xhtml1-strict.dtd">
<html xmlns="http://www.w3.org/1999/xhtml">
<head>
 <link href="/css/main.css" rel="Stylesheet" type="text/css" />
  <link href="/css/slide.css" rel="Stylesheet" type="text/css" />
  <link href="/css/large_slide.css" rel="Stylesheet" type="text/css" />
  <script src="/script/prototype.js" type="text/javascript"></script>
  <script src="/script/effects.js" type="text/javascript"></script>
  <script src="/script/dragdrop.js" type="text/javascript"></script>
  <script src="/script/builder.js" type="text/javascript"></script>
  <script src="/script/stax.js" type="text/javascript"></script>
 <title>ideaStax Editor</title>
</head>

<body onload="">
 <div id="slideshow_timeline"></div>

<div id="library" class="imagelist">
</div>

<div id="main_panel">
 <div id="viewer"></div>
</div>
</body>
</html>
```

The only other design required before diving into the Prototype and script.aculo.us parts of the ideaStax Editor is the structure of a slide. The Editor will use the same XML structure to display a photo or a slide — the only difference is an extra CSS class applied to the slide element. The slide consists of two parts: a face and a caption. The face will display the image that the slide represents and the caption will contain a concise title for the image for browsing and searching purposes (implemented later in this book). Figure 12-3 shows an example slide view.

Figure 12-3

The chosen structure for a slide is shown in Listing 12-2. For simple JavaScript (and script.aculo.us) programming later, this design relies heavily on predictable element IDs. In the example shown in Listing 12-2, the pound symbol (#) in the element ID is meant to stand for the key that references the slide in the server-side database. Throughout this chapter, the keys are somewhat arbitrarily assigned because there is not yet a server implementation to provide slides to remote clients.

Listing 12-2: The slide structure

```
<div id="slide_#" class="slide">
    <div id="slide_#_face" class="slide_face">
        <img id="slide_#_image" src="hikone.jpg" />
    </div>
    <div id="slide_#_caption" class="slide_caption">
        <h1 id="slide_#_caption_text">Hikone Canal</h1>
    </div>
</div>
```

As with the overall page layout, the required CSS that provides this structured data with some character is left to the reader's imagination, but an example implementation is available online. In our implementation, the visual characteristics (such as size) of the slide structure vary depending on whether the slide is in the Library, the Timeline, or the Editor. You can easily do this using class-based CSS styles that depend on the element's DOM tree lineage and allow the XHTML representing slide objects to remain simple and uniform throughout the RIA page.

Planning for Drag and Drop

Planning which areas should receive certain JavaScript capabilities is always a good idea before coding. Each of the three areas of the ideaStax Editor behave differently with respect to the photos and slides that are dragged around, and it turns out that each uses a different script.aculo.us class to accomplish these behaviors:

❑   **The Library** — The Library `div` itself is just a container for a list of photos (which are identical to slides — the difference becomes clear when you develop a model for the ideaStax Editor later in the chapter). Photos in the Library don't require any special rearranging capability, but they do need to be able to be dragged onto the Editor (for preview) or into the Timeline (for addition). Therefore, you should give each photo structure in the Library div a `Draggable` instance.

❑   **The Editor** — The Editor does not contain anything by default, but is the recipient of dragged photos or slides for editing purposes. Thus, you need not take any special actions for the Editor's contents, but you must make the Editor `div` itself a `Droppable` region, able to accept photos from the Library and slides from the Timeline.

❑   **The Timeline** — The Timeline is the most complex of the three areas in the ideaStax Editor because it must accept incoming photos from the Library, copy them, and add them to itself. It also needs to provide sortable list functionality for the photos contained within it so that once you add photos to the Timeline, the Slides that contain them can be sorted and rearranged into new orders. To handle all of these requirements, the Timeline `div` is given a `Sortable` instance, and the `dropOnEmpty` parameter is turned on so that the container can define a callback to execute when new items are dropped upon it.

Implementation Plan

The rest of this chapter steps through the implementation of the drag and drop features of the ideaStax Editor twice. The Editor is implemented twice to demonstrate different aspects of drag and drop in the real world:

❑ The first implementation is an all-client, all-JavaScript implementation that you can run out of a set of files in a folder from your desktop. This implementation demonstrates how to use `Draggables`, `Droppables`, `Sortables`, as well as the script.aculo.us Builder class, from a JavaScript-only environment.

❑ The second implementation involves rewriting the Editor for a real production system with a server backend. This chapter uses Ruby on Rails because of its built-in Prototype and script.aculo.us support, and because the full-blown ideaStax implementation online is written with the Rails framework. The server-backed version of the ideaStax Editor demonstrates how drag and drop operations are made to communicate via AJAX to a remote server and trigger data manipulation events that create and save a user's work without the user having to reload the Web page.

A Client-Only ideaStax Editor

The client-only ideaStax Editor can be treated as an extended example of Prototype and script.aculo.us use. Implementing the features in the "Planning for Drag and Drop" section earlier is about all that you need in order to take the shell of the already developed Editor and turn it into a canvas for ordering and interacting with slides. One extra step is necessary, though: creating the slide objects. In the server-backed version this is an easy, XHTML-centric task, but to get exposure to the script.aculo.us Builder class, the client-only version will construct slides the hard way — using JavaScript.

While the second implementation is organized more traditionally according to the Model, View, and Controller necessary to achieve the ideaStax Editor, the client version lacks a Model and Controller; existing only in the Web browser makes it nothing more than a JavaScript-intensive view (but an instructive one, nonetheless!). As such, this implementation is organized around the different major components of the design. It begins with the prerequisite — creating a Slide construct on the page — and then continues to the Library, the Editor, and the Timeline, in that order.

Creating Slides Dynamically with script.aculo.us' Builder

At various points during usage of the ideaStax Editor, you need to create new slide constructs in XHTML so that you can either add slides to the page or duplicate an existing slide elsewhere on the page. As you will see with subsequent examples in this book and further experience developing RIAs in real life, you can take two basic approaches to the asynchronous construction of dynamic content on a RIA page. Neither of the following two methods is categorically better than the other, but they certainly have different characteristics:

❑ **Pre-construct XHTML structures on the server side to transmit to the client for direct insertion into the DOM tree of the current Web page.** This is often easier to code and maintain because preparing the XHTML takes place during the pre-processing stage of the Web server, which means that the coding effort is often 90% XHTML and 10% JavaScript. The downside to this approach is that it can require many more AJAX requests to the browser than the serialized object approach, described next.

❑ **Transmit serialized objects (in JSON or XML, for example) to the client and then have the client transform them using JavaScript into components on the current page's DOM tree.** Assuming you implement this skillfully, it can require many fewer round-trips to the browser, but at the cost of having to write large pieces of JavaScript code to interpret the result and modify the `document` object that represents the DOM tree accordingly.

Because each approach suits different developers at different times, this chapter uses the function of slide creation to compare and contrast the two approaches to building content to be dynamically added to a RIA page. The client-only version of the ideaStax Editor will use a JavaScript-only approach, and the server-backed version will pre-form the XHTML for each slide on the server and transmit it for injection at the client.

Script.aculo.us provides a handy cool called `Builder` that you can use to concisely prepare new DOM structures from within JavaScript. The `Builder` interface for creating a new node is straightforward:

```
Builder.node(tagType, { attributes }, [ children ]
```

The arguments required for building a new node are the DOM element tag type, a hash table of options, and an array of child nodes. You can completely omit either of the latter two arguments and the Builder will respond appropriately.

Using this function and the built-in DOM tree functions described in Chapter 2, creating the structure for a slide as laid out in Listing 12-2 is a straightforward task. If read out loud, the JavaScript code to do so reads much like what one's inner monologue might be while writing the XHTML code by hand.

1. Because the goal is a reusable function to create slide objects, you start with an empty function that accepts variables for the pieces of information that might change from slide to slide:

```
function createSlide(elementID, image, caption) {
}
```

2. For this example, you build the slide object from the inside out, so you create a text node to hold the caption text for the slide being created. Use the `document.createTextNode` function introduced in Chapter 2:

```
captionText = document.createTextNode(caption);
```

3. The Builder is introduced to enclose the `captionText` node inside an `h1` element with an ID of `#_caption_text`, where the pound symbol is a stand-in for the `elementID` passed in through the arguments of the function. Next, the `h1` element (stored in the variable `caption`) is added as the only child of a `div` element with class name `slide_caption`:

```
// Create the caption H1
caption = Builder.node(
        'h1',
        {id:elementID + '_caption_text'},
        [captionText]
);

// Add the H1 to a DIV element
slideCaption = Builder.node(
 'div',
 {id:elementID + '_caption', className:'slide_caption'},
 [caption]
);
```

Assuming that `elementID` was set to "slide_1" and `caption` was set to "Hikone," the `slideCaption` object now reflects the following XML:

```
<div id="slide_1_caption" class="slide_caption">
   <h1 id="slide_1_caption_text">Hikone</h1>
</div>
```

5. The slide is now half complete. Constructing a `div` element to contain the slide's Photo is a similar process:

```
// Create an image that references the provided image link
face = Builder.node(
 'img',
 {id:elementID + '_image', src:image}
);

// Create a div element to hold the image
slideFace = Builder.node(
 'div',
 {id:elementID + '_face', className:'slide_face'},
 [face]
);
```

6. Finally, create the last `div` element to contain the entire slide and add the `face` and `caption` structures as children using the Builder's argument list. Notice that this code gives the slide `div` a class name of `photo`. This is used later as a trick to distinguish Timeline slides (photos) from Library slides:

```
slide = Builder.node(
 'div',
 {id:elementID, className:'photo'},
 [slideFace, slideCaption]
);
```

The complete JavaScript function to create an XHTML representation of a slide is provided in Listing 12-3.

Listing 12-3: Creating a slide object from JavaScript

JavaScript
```
function createSlide(elementID, image, caption) {
 //logDebug("Creating Slide '" + caption + "'");
 // Create the caption portion
 captionText = document.createTextNode(caption);
 caption = Builder.node(
        'h1',
        {id:elementID + '_caption_text'},
        [captionText]
 );
 slideCaption = Builder.node(
        'div',
        {id:elementID + '_caption', className:'slide_caption'},
```

```
                [caption]
        );

        // Create the face portion
        face = Builder.node(
                'img',
                {id:elementID + '_image', src:image}
        );

        slideFace = Builder.node(
                'div',
                {id:elementID + '_face', className:'slide_face'},
                [face]
        );

        // Assemble and return the final slide
        slide = Builder.node(
                'div',
                {id:elementID, className:'photo'},
                [slideFace, slideCaption]
        );
        return slide;
    }
```

As you can see, creating elements for insertion to a RIA page using JavaScript is a conceptually straight-forward process, and one that guarantees that dynamic behaviors do not require connecting to a remote server. The only problem is that it somewhat awkwardly ties the structure of the XHTML document to a series of JavaScript code statements. If you use this technique extensively throughout a RIA, then updating the JavaScript to reflect new XHTML structures can be an arduous task. It also prevents nondevelopers from making improvements on a RIA's design.

Populating the Library with Draggable Slides

Now that a facility exists to construct slides programmatically, you can create a second function to seed the photo library with a few starter images. The images in this example, of course, are pre-cropped and placed in a subdirectory of the root development folder so that they are available to the Web browser. This function needs to perform three steps: create a set of slides, add these slides to the Library, and then create a Draggable object for each slide so that you can drag them elsewhere in the ideaStax Editor:

1. Because the client-only version of the ideaStax Editor has no model or database to provide data, you must hard-code the slide data into the JavaScript file.

Although this is not an ideal way to store this information, it is quick and concise, and therefore suffi-cient to accomplish a side detail that is not the focus of this chapter.

The following code creates an array of hash tables to store some sample slide data. This array is then iterated over to populate the Library:

```
// An array of sample data for easy adds/removals
slides = [
{name:"slide_1", image:"/images/hikone.png", description:"Canal In Hikone"},
{name:"slide_2", image:"/images/wedding.png", description:"Wedding"},
```

```
{name:"slide_3", image:"/images/flower.png", description:"A Flower"},
{name:"slide_4", image:"/images/sthelens.png", description:"Mt. St. Helens"},
{name:"slide_5", image:"/images/monticello.png", description:"Monticello"}
]
```

While experimenting with the client-only ideaStax Editor, you can easily add or remove slides from the Library by including or excluding them from this array.

2. Transform these array items into XHTML slide objects; but before doing that, you must load a reference to the library and clear the Library's contents. Fetch a reference to the library using Prototype's $() function and then wipe its children clean with the following code:

```
// Get a reference to the slide library
library = $('library');

// Remove all of the child nodes of the library
while (library.firstChild) {
  library.removeChild(library.firstChild);
}
```

3. Now you can use a `for` loop to iterate over the `slides` array, call the `createSlide` function for each slide, and then append the slide as a child to the location in the DOM tree referenced by the `library` variable.

4. As a final step, create a `Draggable` object for each new slide added to the Library. Listing 12-4 contains the complete code for the complete function, `loadSlideLibrary()`.

Listing 12-4: Loading Draggable slides into the Library

JavaScript
```
function loadSlideLibrary() {

  // Create an array of our sample data so that we can easily add or remove items
  slides = [
  {name:"slide_1", image:"/images/hikone.png", description:"Canal In Hikone"},
  {name:"slide_2", image:"/images/wedding.png", description:"Wedding"},
  {name:"slide_3", image:"/images/flower.png", description:"A Flower"},
  {name:"slide_4", image:"/images/sthelens.png", description:"Mt. St. Helens"},
  {name:"slide_5", image:"/images/monticello.png", description:"Monticello"}
  ]

  library = $('library');

  // Remove all of the child nodes of the library
  while (library.firstChild) {
    library.removeChild(library.firstChild);
  }


  // Create a slide for each item in the sample data array
  for (var i=0; i<slides.length; i++) {
    slide = createSlide(
      slides[i]['name'],
```

```
      slides[i]['image'],
      slides[i]['description']
   );
   library.appendChild(slide);
  new Draggable(
     slide.id,
     {
       revert:true,
       ghosting:true
     }
   );
  }
}
```

The Library code for this example RIA page is complete. The only requirement is for the
`loadSlideLibrary()` function to be called from somewhere on the page. A quick modification to
the original template from Listing 12-1 adds a hyperlink inside of the Library that will cause Library's
contents to load:

```
<div id="library" class="imagelist">
  <p><a href="#" onclick="loadSlideLibrary()">Load Library</a></p>
</div>
```

Try out this new functionality by loading the ideaStax Editor in a Web browser and clicking the link.
Figures 12-4 and 12-5 show the ideaStax Library before and after loading photos, respectively, and
Figure 12-5 demonstrates one of the newly created slides being dragged out of the Library.

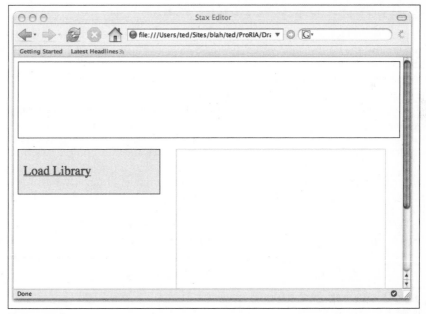

Figure 12-4

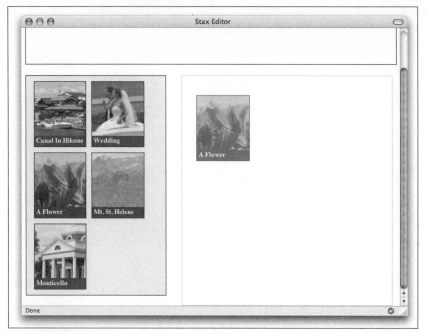

Figure 12-5

Creating a Droppable the Editor Pane

The Editor pane within the ideaStax Editor lets you see how a `Droppable` object is used in the context of a real RIA. For now, the Editor pane within the ideaStax Editor just displays a large view of whatever was dropped into it. In the open-source version of ideaStax available on the Web site, this pane allows the user to edit the contents of the slide after it is dropped in.

The bulk of the work in implementing `Droppable` behavior is often determining what happens once the `Draggable` object is dropped. In the case of the Editor, you want to copy the dropped slide object and add that copy as the sole child of the Editor pane `div` element. To accomplish this post-drop behavior, you create two functions, `copySlide()` and `loadSlideForEdit()`, which take care of these tasks in a reusable way.

The `copySlide()` function takes advantage of the rigid naming requirements that are placed upon the XHTML slide objects. The outer `div` element of the slide serves as the base element ID for the fields within. If the outer ID is `slide_4`, then you know that the image tag is named `slide_4_image`, for example. Therefore, if you have the handle on the outer slide ID, then grabbing the slide description and image filename is an easy lookup task. The code in Listing 12-5 takes a reference to the DOM element representing an XHTML slide, looks up the image location and caption text, and then uses the `createSlide` function from Listing 12-3 to build a copy.

Listing 12-5: Duplicating an XHTML slide

JavaScript

```
function copySlide(element) {
    droppedImage = $(element.id + "_image");
```

```
    droppedCaptionText = $(element.id + "_caption_text");

    image_location = droppedImage.getAttribute('src');
    caption_text = droppedCaptionText.innerHTML;

    newNode = createSlide(element.id + "_copy", image_location, caption_text);
    return newNode;
}
```

The `loadSlideForEdit` function is designed to accept a slide, copy it, and then add it as a child of the Editor `div`, replacing any children that were already there. The function additionally checks to ensure that the receiving `div` is the Viewer.

Finally, you create a `Droppable` object to provide the Viewer with a way of catching `Draggable` objects and calling the functions in Listings 12-5 and 12-6. Create a function `initializePage()` that is called from the `body` element's `onLoad` property. This function contains the code to set up both the Timeline and the Editor. Listing 12-7 contains the initialization function, with code to set up `Droppable` behavior for the Editor.

Listing 12-6: Adding a slide to the Viewer

JavaScript
```
function loadSlideForEdit(slide, destination) {
  slide_copy = copySlide(slide)
  if (destination.id == 'viewer') {
    while (destination.firstChild) {
      destination.removeChild(destination.firstChild);
    }
    destination.appendChild(slide_copy);
  }
}
```

Listing 12-7: Page initialization

JavaScript
```
function initializePage() {
  Droppables.add(
    'viewer', {
      accept: 'photo',
      onDrop:loadSlideForEdit
    }
  );
}
```

Notice that the `onDrop` property of the `Droppable` referenced the `loadSlideForEdit` function without any notations about its use. This is because the `onDrop` property of a `Droppable` requires a reference to a function with either of the two following signatures:

```
function onDropCompatibleFunction(draggedElement, droppableElement)
function onDropCompatibleFunction(draggedElement, droppableElement, event)
```

Because `loadSlideForEdit` implements the first of these two signatures, you only need to pass in the function's name for the `onDrop` property to work.

The Editor pane is now complete. Try reloading the page and dragging different slides into its boundaries. Figure 12-6 shows the incremental progress of the ideaStax Editor Panel.

Figure 12-6

Implementing the Sortable Timeline

Implementing the Timeline is the final step in the client-only ideaStax Editor and completes this extended example by demonstrating how you use the `Sortable` object. The Timeline needs to act in two different capacities — as a `Droppable` and as a `Sortable`. As a `Droppable`, the Timeline accepts `div` elements with the CSS class `photo` that have been dragged from the Library. As a `Sortable`, the Timeline permits `div` elements with the CSS class `slide`, to be rearranged using the mouse.

Implementing the Droppable Behavior

Because Timeline elements have to be present in order to sort them, the `Droppable` behavior should be implemented first. Re-open the file containing the `initializePage()` function created to initialize the Editor's `Droppable` instance and append a new `Droppable` instantiation to the function. Listing 12-8 contains the updated `initializePage()` function. It ties the `Droppable` instance to the Timeline `div`, and only accepts elements with a CSS class of `photo` that originate from the Library's `div` element.

Listing 12-8: Updated initializePage Function

JavaScript
```
function initializePage() {
  Droppables.add(
        'viewer', {
        accept: 'photo',
        onDrop:loadSlideForEdit
        }
  );

  Droppables.add(
        'timeline', {
        accept: 'photo',
        containment: 'library',
        onDrop:addSlideToTimeline
        }
  );
}
```

The `onDrop` property of the new `Droppable` requires that you create a new function, `addSlideToTimeline`, to take care of copying and adding a new XHTML slide to the Timeline div. This function behaves a lot like the `loadSlideForEdit` function, but with some important extra features, and in fact it is the place where the `Sortable` behavior is created.

Implementing the Sortable Behavior

When a `Sortable` object is instantiated for a particular container, both the container and the contained elements are transformed as a result of the new object. The container is given special `Droppable` capabilities, and the contained elements are given special `Draggable` capabilities. This means that when you introduce a new element to a list that has already been made `Sortable` (such as in the Timeline), you have to take steps to add the new element to the list of objects that compose the sortable list. The easiest way to do this is to destroy the `Sortable` object that existed before and create a new one in its place. The pseudo-code for this is as follows:

```
destroySortable
addObject
createSortable
```

Listing 12-9 contains the JavaScript implementation of this pattern to complete the function `addSlideToTimeline`. The code first checks to ensure that the `timeline` variable actually contains a reference to the Timeline. Then it destroys the `Sortable` object that referenced the Timeline, creates and adds a new slide to the Timeline, and recreates a `Sortable` object.

Earlier in the chapter it was mentioned that slides from the Library have the CSS class `photo`, and slides within the Timeline have both class `photo` and `slide`. Notice how the code in Listing 12-9 takes advantage of this by limiting the `Sortable` objects to only those that have the class of `slide`. Think of this as a rudimentary form of type-checking for our RIA page—if something goes wrong and somehow a Library photo is moved into the Timeline in the wrong way, the photo will refuse to rearrange itself like the rest of the slides, letting you know that you've copied it incorrectly.

Listing 12-9: The addSlideToTimeline Function

```
function addSlideToTimeline(slide, timeline) {
  if (timeline.id == 'timeline') {
    Sortable.destroy('timeline');

    slide_copy = copySlide(slide);
    timeline.appendChild(slide_copy);
    Element.addClassName(slide_copy, 'slide');

    Sortable.create(
      'timeline', {
        tag: 'div',
        only: 'slide',
        constraint: 'horizontal'
      }
    );
  }
}
```

The client-only version of the ideaStax Editor is now complete! Reload the page in your Web browser to try out the new Editor. Try loading the slide library dynamically, previewing a slide in the Editor panel, adding a few slides to the Timeline, and then rearranging them. Figure 12-7 shows slides being rearranged in the completed ideaStax Editor.

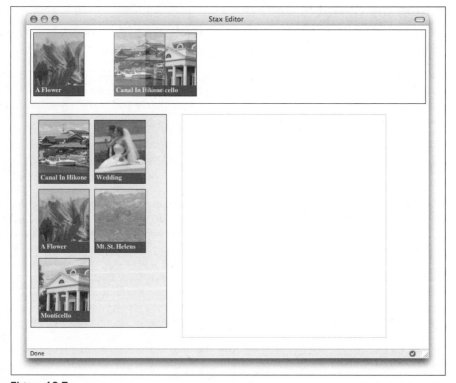

Figure 12-7

Client-Only Implementation Summary

You have now seen the full implementation of an example drag and drop interface using just JavaScript, XHTML, and a bit of CSS. Rolling everything by hand (instead of using helper functions as you will soon see with Ruby on Rails) is a wonderful way to gain confidence with a new set of technologies, and the resulting implementation is one that can easily function in a variety of environments in which no server is present. What client-only implementation lacks, however, is any connection to a greater pool of resources—a community-wide image library or slide repository—and any way to save a Timeline so that users can share and come back to it later. The remainder of this chapter refactors the ideaStax Editor just developed into an end-to-end Ruby on Rails application that makes use of a backend server and database so that these important features can be realized.

A Server-Backed ideaStax Editor

The client-only version of the ideaStax Editor just demonstrated provides a good reference example for the script.aculo.us `Draggable`, `Droppable`, and `Sortable` objects, but it leaves out the very important part of the server. In most real RIAs, objects such as `Droppable` and `Sortable` have callbacks hooked into AJAX calls that contact the remote server to notify it of the event. Figure 12-8 depicts the common pattern of operations for such RIA objects. Each action triggers a request to the remote server whose contents describes the action that just took place. The server, not client-side JavaScript, then decides how to update the RIA page and sends back an appropriate update, which the client inserts into a predefined spot in the DOM tree.

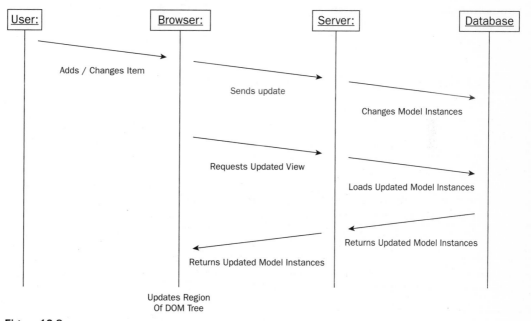

Figure 12-8

Contrast the underlying pattern described here with creating an all-JavaScript or XML+JavaScript solution. It likely requires more AJAX requests, and thus more server resources, but it often simplifies the creation and maintenance of *partials* on the server side. A *partial* is the word coined by the Ruby on Rails team to refer to a small, atomic chunk of View (as in MVC View) code that can be reused. The XHTML slide from the ideaStax Editor is the perfect example of a partial — it is small, self-contained, reusable, and is only used as a building block for a greater page.

Recall how the previous implementation required you to design the slide partial in XHTML first, but then rewrite it as a set of script.aculo.us Builder and JavaScript commands so that new slides could be created in the client. With the style of RIA programming in the server-backed implementation, partials can remain in their XHTML states on the server side; no JavaScript is needed.

The server-backed ideaStax Editor has a number of other differences. Photos load from a database query instead of a hard-coded JavaScript array. Script.aculo.us objects are told of URLs to which they can make AJAX requests. Finally, one of the additional goals of this part of the chapter is to introduce the Ruby on Rails framework. This involves a good deal of quickly introduced new syntax and terminology, but the core concepts of Model, View, and Controller remain the same, so it should be easy to acclimate. Ruby on Rails (or just "Rails," as it is often called) enforces that code be strictly organized into Models, Views, and Controllers, so the organization of this chapter follows that paradigm instead of a feature-by-feature organization.

Getting Started with Rails

This chapter assumes that your computer already has Ruby, the Ruby on Rails framework, and the MySQL database installed and ready to use. Because this is the first chapter that uses Ruby on Rails, a few extra steps are shown to help you set up the Rails project. If you do not yet have Ruby on Rails, visit its Web site at www.rubyonrails.com to download a copy; its only prerequisite is the Ruby programming language, available free at www.ruby-lang.org/.

First generate a new Rails project with the rails command. Navigate to the folder in which you want to begin your project and type the following:

```
rails stax
```

This creates a new folder titled stax that contains the entire environment necessary to build your Rails application.

Only one more configuration step is necessary before launching back into the ideaStax Editor implementation, and that is letting Rails know how to connect to your local database. Rails stores this information in the config directory inside a file named database.yml. Upon opening this file, you see what appear to be three different database definitions: development, test, and production. Although this example does not use this feature, Rails allows your application to be loaded in any one of several user-defined environments. This helps demarcate the differences between the development and production settings, for example, and can be a great risk reducer for production projects that are also under active development.

The ideaStax Editor only uses the development database for now. Modify the development settings so that they look like Listing 12-10. You must provide your own username and password, of course. This example assumes that you have already created an empty database in MySQL named stax.

Listing 12-10: Rails database settings

```
development:
  adapter: mysql
  database: stax
  username: <your database username>
  password: <your database password>
  host: localhost
```

The Rails environment is now configured and ready for development. You can even boot up the included Web server and leave it on for the rest of the chapter — Rails does not require any server restarts as long as the environmental configuration does not change. In a console window, navigate back to the root of the project and type the following:

```
ruby script/server webrick
```

Figure 12-9 shows the result you should see in your console when you run the WEBrick server.

If you open a Web browser and direct it to `http://localhost:3000`, then you will see the default welcome page for your Rails application. A hint for the following pages: Open a second console while the WEBrick Web server is running in the current one. You need it to execute several generation scripts included in the Rails framework.

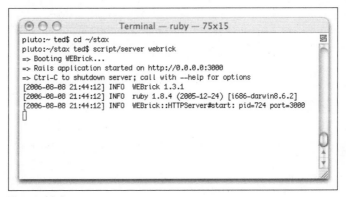

Figure 12-9

Creating the Model

The Model is one of the most important differences between an in-place (client-only) RIApage and a server-backed one. Every user action on the page that contains meaning eventually needs to be converted into some formal representation and sent to the server to be persisted. When users return to the site, the model is called upon to help reconstruct where they left off. In the world of Web development, creating a Model often has two steps:

1. Define a database schema. The schema lists the database table structure so that the database knows in what format it will receive and provide information.

2. Define objects that map to the database schema and possibly contain information about how they relate to each other.

As you will see, the process in Rails follows exactly these steps, and in fact the Rails framework does most of the hard work for you.

Rails contains a handy script called `generate` that can produce stubbed-out code for many common entities that RIA programmers need. You will make use of the generate script to begin defining three models. The server-backed version of the ideaStax Editor uses three basic models to persist user data: the `Photo`, the `Slide`, and the `Timeline`. The `Photo` model stores instance data for photos in the Library. The `Slide` model contains data for slides that are added to the Timeline object, and the `Timeline` model contains data for different arrangements users have made in the Timeline sortable list.

From the root directory of the Rails project, type the following three commands to generate the models:

```
ruby script/generate model photo
ruby script/generate model slide
ruby script/generate model timeline
```

Each of these commands generates a series of empty model files and text fixtures for editing. As the first step, edit the schema definitions so that you can define the fields of data that each object should contain. Rails automatically makes any field in the database schema available through getters and setters on Model instances.

Defining the Schema

Schema definitions are stored in the `db/migrate` directory in a format known as *ActiveRecord Migrations*. Migrations are a powerful way to specify a database schema as a series of incremental changes. During testing, you can move the schema forward and backward between versions to test different stages of the development. Notice that three files exist in this directory

```
001_create_photos.rb
002_create_slides.rb
003_create_timelines.rb
```

These files correspond to the three steps of schema migration that the `generate` commands have implied will occur. Open the first file, `001_create_photos.rb`, for editing and fill it in to look like Listing 12-11.

Listing 12-11: Photo schema definition

```
class CreatePhotos < ActiveRecord::Migration
 def self.up
  create_table :photos do |t|
   t.column :name, :string
   t.column :caption, :string
   t.column :image, :string
  end
 end

 def self.down
  drop_table :photos
 end
end
```

Rails migrations require that we define two steps, self.up and self.down, that tell the framework how to perform a migration step and undo a migration step, respectively. In the case of a Photo object, the self.up step defines three strings — name, caption, and image — to add to the model; and the self.down step simply removes the Photo table from whatever database you specified in the databases.yml file. Next, open the 002_create_slides.rb file and edit it to match Listing 12-12.

Listing 12-12: Slide schema definition

```
class CreateSlides < ActiveRecord::Migration
  def self.up
    create_table :slides do |t|
      t.column :photo_id, :integer
      t.column :timeline_id, :integer
      t.column :position, :integer
    end
  end

  def self.down
    drop_table :slides
  end
end
```

Listing 12-12 shows three fields on the Slide model: photo_id, timeline_id, and position. All three store an integer value. Notice that an id field is nowhere to be found on either this table or the one that came before. Because almost every table in a Web application has an ID field, Rails always takes care of defining one for you (you can prevent this automatic behavior if you want, but such a situation rarely arises). The photo_id field and timeline_id field represent the Photo and Timeline associated with this slide. The position field eventually holds the position of this slide in its particular Timeline.

Oddly enough, the Timeline table does not need to store any data other than Timeline IDs. In a full-blown RIA, all sorts of tagging and ownership data would likely appear on all of these tables, but this chapter's example requires none of that. Because Rails automatically defines an ID field for each table, no further changes are needed on top of the empty template that the generate command provided.

The real work for the Timeline Model appears when you define relationships between the two objects. The ideaStax Editor must save the order of slides in a stack when the user changes it, so Rails must be told of the relationship between Timeline instances and Slide instances and how to read the order of Slides in a particular Timeline. You already paved a bit of the way by adding position and stack_id fields in the Slide object; now Model implementations tells Rails how to use those fields.

Implementing the Model Objects

Model implementations in Rails describe how different Models are related to each other. Rails automatically creates getters and setters for all of the columns in the schema, so no code is necessary to map Model objects to their underlying schema implementations for simple Models. Models are stored to the app/model directory of the Rails application, so navigate to that directory and look at the files that the generate command has created:

```
photo.rb
slide.rb
timeline.rb
```

Open `photo.rb` and fill it in with the code in Listing 12-13.

Listing 12-13: Photo Model implementation

```
class Photo < ActiveRecord::Base
  has_many :slides
end
```

The `Photo` Model only needs to contain one line to link it to the `Slide` model. It seems odd to think of the `Photo` as "having" `Slides` — the other way around seems more appropriate in the real world — but the `has_many` relationship in Rails describes the side of a Model relationship that does not contain the foreign key. In other words, you may have many `Slides` that all contain the same `Photo` by reference through the `photo_id` field in the schema; therefore, `Photo has_many Slides`.

Open `slide.rb` and fill it in to look like Listing 12-14. Observe from the Listing 12-14 that the `Slide` model defines a `belongs_to` relationship. This is the other half of the `has_many` relationship.

Listing 12-14: Slide Model implementation

```
class Slide < ActiveRecord::Base
  belongs_to :photo
  belongs_to :timeline
  acts_as_list :scope => :timeline
end
```

The `belongs_to` commands tell Rails that each instance of the `Slide` model always explicitly references exactly one `Photo` instance and one `Stack` instance. The `belongs_to` command causes Rails to look inside the `Slide` schema for the foreign key of the `belongs_to` object. Unless more clarifying parameters are provided, Rails assumes that the field containing the foreign key is the lowercase, singular version of the Model name with the suffix "id," attached, so `Timeline` defaults to `timeline_id` and `Photo` defaults to `photo_id`, just as you named them in the schema definition. This is one of many examples where Rails makes assumptions about Model, View, and Controller names if you provide no explicit instruction.

The third command in the `Slide` model, `acts_as_list`, tells Rails that the `Slide` objects for a particular `Timeline` should be loaded as a Ruby list that can be manipulated just as any other list in Ruby. The `scope` parameter lets Ruby know that the list behavior should be scoped by the Slide relationship so that each list of `Slides` is only composed of `Slides` instances owned by the same `Timeline`. This enables many `Slides` to have a list position of 1 if they are owned by different `Timelines`. The position field on the `Slide` model, incidentally, is another assumption that Rails makes when you use the `acts_as_list` command.

Finally, open the `timtline.rb` file and edit it to look like Listing 12-15.

Listing 12-15: Timeline Model implementation

```
class Timeline < ActiveRecord::Base
  has_many :slides, :order => :position
end
```

Just as a Photo has many Slides, so does a Timeline have many Slides. This relationship is expressed with the has_many command. The order parameter tells Rails that the Slides in each Timeline have a stated order, and this order is stored in the position field in the Slide model. Notice that the word slides is pluralized as :slides in the parameters. This is a hotly debated topic among developers, and Ruby on Rails actually requires programmers to properly pluralize Model names according to English standards. It may take a while for you to get used to this feature, and you can turn it off if you really hate it, but most users find it very easy on the eyes.

You have now completed all of the model code required for the server-backed version of the ideaStax Editor. Next, you load up your database with some test data and rewrite the Editor to use remote instead of local data.

Populating the Photo Model with Sample Data

The Rails framework contains extensive support for testing, and one of the key objects in the Rails test environment is called a *fixture*. Fixtures are sets of data that populate a database during testing so that models have data to drive them, but you can also load fixtures into the database at any time. In this section, a fixture is developed to populate the Photo model with instance data in the same way that an array of values provides data for the Library photos in the server-only version. The fixture serves as half of the replacement for the loadSlideLibrary() function from the serverless version of the ideaStax Editor.

Ruby permits you to define fixtures in one of two different formats: YAML and CSV. YAML (a recursive acronym for *YAML Ain't Markup Language*) is certainly the more human-readable of the two (you used YAML when setting the database configuration), but CSV is often far more useful and is universally understood among programmers. You'll use CSV for your Slide fixture, so the first step is to rename the Photo fixture for CSV format. Navigate through your project to the test/fixtures/ directory and rename the photos.yml file to photos.csv. Then open the file and replace the contents with the CSV file in Listing 12-16.

Listing 12-16: Photo fixture

```
id,name,image
1,Canal In Hikone,/images/hikone.png
2,Lee and Lauren,/images/wedding.png
3,Flower,/images/flower.png
4,Mt. St. Helens,/images/sthelens.png
5,Monticello,/images/monticello.png
```

The format of this file is familiar to anyone who has worked with CSV files before. The first line lists the column names for which the file contains data. Each subsequent line has values for those properties, separated by commas. Notice that any mention of the description column defined in the Photo schema is omitted — Rails does not require a complete record in fixtures.

Raking the Database

With the schemas, Models, and fixtures prepared for the ideaStax Editor, you can update the database to the current version. Rails has defined scripts that perform these tasks for you, and you can access them via the rake command. The Rake framework packaged with Rails is exactly equivalent to the Ant framework that is often packaged with Java projects. Just like Ant, Rake is a tool for scripting configuration, compilation, testing, and deployment tasks related to a development project.

The first Rake task that you need to run is called `migrate`. This brings the database schema up to the current version as defined by the files in the `db/migrate` directory. The following command executes the migrations to create the database tables that hold `Photo`, `Slide`, and `Timeline` instance data:

```
rake migrate
```

Next, load the fixtures into the database with this Rake task:

```
rake db:fixtures:load
```

Output for these two commands is shown in Figure 12-10.

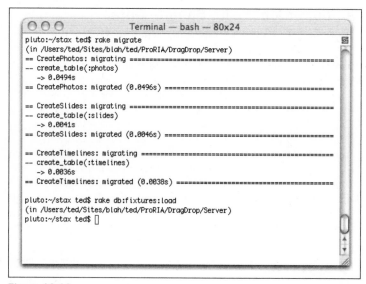

```
pluto:~/stax ted$ rake migrate
(in /Users/ted/Sites/blah/ted/ProRIA/DragDrop/Server)
== CreatePhotos: migrating ====================================================
-- create_table(:photos)
   -> 0.0494s
== CreatePhotos: migrated (0.0496s) ===========================================

== CreateSlides: migrating ====================================================
-- create_table(:slides)
   -> 0.0041s
== CreateSlides: migrated (0.0046s) ===========================================

== CreateTimelines: migrating =================================================
-- create_table(:timelines)
   -> 0.0036s
== CreateTimelines: migrated (0.0038s) ========================================

pluto:~/stax ted$ rake db:fixtures:load
(in /Users/ted/Sites/blah/ted/ProRIA/DragDrop/Server)
pluto:~/stax ted$ []
```

Figure 12-10

Having run both rake tasks, the MySQL database becomes populated with both tables and sample data. If you have a database viewer available (many free ones are available online if you do not), open it and examine the schema that the ActiveRecord Migrations framework built for you. Figure 12-11 shows a snapshot of the Photos table, as an example. If you have experience with Web development and the concept of Migrations piques your interest, try the framework out a little more by switching between different versions of your schema. Run the `rake migrate` command with the argument `VERSION=#` after the word migrate. Different version numbers cause the schema to roll forward or backward, creating and destroying tables and data.

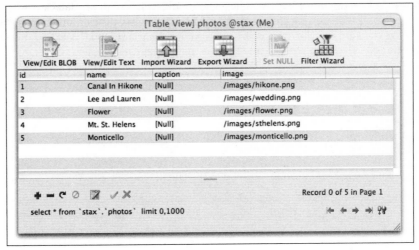

Figure 12-11

ActiveRecord Migrations provide a nice reusable and portable alternative to creating a database manually using SQL commands. In Chapter 14, you are shown how information similar to this can be loaded into a database using the command-line `mysql` client, which anyone with MySQL already has installed.

Creating the View

With the Model complete, it is time to turn our attention to the View. Views in Ruby on Rails fall into three categories: layouts, views, and partials.

❑ Layouts are XHTML shells that wrap around page-specific content. Usually a layout defines the `head` element (thus including any necessary CSS or JavaScript files) and opens and closes the `body` tag but marks a spot inside the `body` for individual pages to fill in.

❑ Views represent the XHTML code necessary to display one complete Web page. Views may require that a layout wrap around them, and they may also be composed of partials.

❑ Partials, as you know from the beginning of the server-backed section, are small atomic chunks of XHTML that completely describe one component of a Web page.

All three types of View code are written in RHTML, which looks just like XHTML but allows for Ruby commands to intermingle with the XHTML document. These commands are enclosed within a special tag that is familiar to developers with PHP or ASP experience:

```
<%
   // Ruby code goes here!
%>
```

Using these tags, you can implement layouts, views, and partials with placeholders for variables that are passed into them. It is the responsibility of the invoker of the view to ensure that any local variables defined by the view are set. The `<%= ... %>` tag is a special variant of the `<% %>` tag that outputs whatever value the code block evaluates to into the Web page where the element occurs. As an example, the RHTML

```
<% a = 1
   5.times do %>
<p>This is time <%= a %></p>
<% a += 1
  end %>
```

results in the following XHTML code returned to the client:

```
<p>This is time 1</p>
<p>This is time 2</p>
<p>This is time 3</p>
<p>This is time 4</p>
<p>This is time 5</p>
```

Variables can be initialized either inside the View or inside a Controller that transfers control to the View. In most cases, the Controller populates several variables with data from the database. When it calls the View (or *renders* the View, in Rails parlance), the View verifies the existence of, and then makes use of, these variables.

Constructing the Layout

Rails provides a location for you to store layouts so that Controllers and Views know where to find them. Navigate to the `app/views/layouts` directory and create a new file called `editor.rhtml`. Fill it with the code from Listing 12-17.

Listing 12-17: ideaStax Editor layout

```
<!DOCTYPE html PUBLIC "-//W3C//DTD XHTML 1.0 Strict//EN"
"http://www.w3.org/TR/xhtml1/DTD/xhtml1-strict.dtd">

<html xmlns="http://www.w3.org/1999/xhtml">
<head>
 <%= stylesheet_link_tag 'stax' %>
<%= javascript_include_tag :defaults %>
 <title>ideaStax Editor</title>
</head>
<body>
 <%= yield %>
</body>
</html>
```

Notice how some of the elements in the `head` are replaced with Rails functions surrounded by `<%= %>` tags. Rails provides many functions that act as shorthand for frequently sought patterns. These helper functions all return String objects that you can output to the RIA page with the `<%= %>` construct. The `stylesheet_link_tag` command creates an XHTML link to a CSS file in the `public/stylesheets` directory. You have to change this command to match your CSS filename.

The `javascript_include_tag` performs a similar reference but for JavaScript files in the `public/javascripts` directory. The `:defaults` argument tells Rails to import Prototype and script.aculo.us, the preferred libraries in Rails development. Finally, the `yield` command in the body tag tells Rails where individual pages that use this template will insert their contents.

With the layout in Listing 12-7 in place, you can implement the remaining views and partials as if they already exist inside the `body` tag. This is both a time-saver and a good development practice, because any changes you need to make to the `head` elements of pages in the ideaStax Editor can be made in a central place.

Constructing the Photo Partial

Loading the slide library in the server-backed ideaStax Editor still occurs dynamically, but instead of building the XHTML for each slide from a JavaScript file, the server prepares the slides and sends them via AJAX to the `Library div` element. Listing 12-18 shows the XHTML slide defined as a partial in the manner illustrated above. Place this code in the directory `app/views/photo` (you may have to create this) and name it `photo.rhtml`. Be sure to prefix the filename with an underscore character — that tells the Rails framework that this is a partial.

Listing 12-18: Photo partial

```
<div id="<%= id %>" class="photo <%= extraclass rescue '' %>">
<div class="slide_face">
        <img src="<%= photo.image %>" />
</div>
<div class="slide_caption">
        <h1><%= photo.name %></h1>
</div>
</div>
```

Notice that the partial expects an instance of the `Photo` model named `photo` to be present, because in several places the instance variables defined in the `Photo` schema are retrieved from the `photo` object. Later, you will see how to pass the `photo` variable into this partial as a local variable. With the `photo` partial in hand, you never need to write the XHTML to represent a `Photo` again. It is maintained here and referenced as required.

Constructing the Library Partial

The next partial you need is one to represent the contents of the ideaStax Library. This partial is responsible for accepting a list of `Photo Model` instances, iterating over that list, and displaying the `photo` partial for each one. Additionally, it has to assign `Draggable` behavior to each `photo` that it displays, so as part of the iteration loop, a script.aculo.us helper function will be employed.

Create a partial called `list.rhtml` in the `app/views/photo` directory. You may have to create this directory because you have not yet generated Controllers with the generate script. The name `list` was chosen instead of `library` because the partial does not actually define the Library `div` itself — it only lists the contents. Fill in the partial with the code in Listing 12-19.

Listing 12-19: Library _list partial

```
<% @photos.each do |photo|
  name = "photo_" + photo.id.to_s %>
  <%= render :partial => 'photo/photo',
                      :locals => { :photo => photo, :id => name } %>
  <%= draggable_element(name, :revert => true) %>
<% end %>
```

This partial looks a lot like the photo partial except for two new items. Inside of the each loop, the list partial invokes another partial, the photo partial, with the current photo object. The photo partial expects two variables, and an optional third: photo, id, and extraclass. These variables are passed in during the partial rendering command through a hash table called locals. The format of this argument is as follows:

```
:locals => {  :local_variable1 => value_1,
             :local_variable2 => value_2,
             :local_variable3 => value_3 }
```

In this way, bits of information that the partial requires are made available to it.

The second new item in this partial is a script.aculo.us helper function for the Draggable object. This function looks very similar to the JavaScript code from the client-only version except it has been Ruby-ized. The command

```
<%= draggable_element(name, :revert => true) %>
```

produces the JavaScript code

```
<script type="text/javascript">
//<![CDATA[
new Draggable(name, {revert:true})
//]]>
</script>
```

Constructing the Timeline Partial

Finally, you need to create a partial for the Timeline to list its contents in a fashion similar to that of the Library. The partial in Listing 12-20 is also named list.rhtml, but it goes in the app/views/timeline directory.

Listing 12-20: Timeline _list Partial

```
<% if (! timeline.nil?)
  timeline.slides.each do |slide|
  name = "slide_" + slide.id.to_s %>
  <%= render :partial => 'photo/photo',
                      :locals => { :photo => slide.photo, :id => name, ⮐
:extraclass => 'slide' } %>
  <% end
  end
%>
<%= sortable_element(
```

```
           'timeline',
           :tag => 'div',
           :constraint => 'horizontal',
           :only => 'slide',
           :update => 'timeline', :url => {:controller => 'timeline', :action => ⤴
    :sort}
           )
    %>
```

The code in Listing 12-20 first confirms that the local variable `timeline` is not empty. `Timeline` is assumed to be an instance of the Timeline Model, so through the `has_many` association on the Model, each Slide instance attached to a Timeline is available through the `Timeline.slides` method. Like Listing 12-19, the code iterates over a set of objects — this time slides — and invokes the `photo` partial on the `photo` associated with each slide. The Timeline chooses to fill in the `extraclass` variable for the `photo` partial so that the XHTML objects have the additional class of `slide` in the same way that they did in the client-only version.

Finally, the partial creates a sortable element using a helper to make the slides within the Timeline exhibit the Sortable behavior. A new property is used in this version of the ideaStax Editor: `update`. The `update` property takes two arguments: a `div` ID and a URL. When a sort action has occurred, script.aculo.us uses Prototype to visit the URL over an AJAX connection and updates the contents of the specified `div` element with the server response.

Constructing the Editor View

So far, you've created a layout to contain the larger page and partials to provide building blocks. The only remaining View component is to implement a view for the Editor itself. This view looks almost identical to the `body` element contents originally laid out in Listing 12-1. Create a new file called `view.rhtml` under the `app/views/editor` directory. Again, you may have to create this directory. Complete the file so that it resembles Listing 12-21.

Listing 12-21: The Editor View

```
<div id="timeline">
<%= render :partial => 'timeline/list', :locals => {:timeline => @timeline} %>
</div>

<div id="library" class="imagelist">
<%= link_to_remote 'Load',
         :url => {:controller => 'library', :action => 'library'},
         :update => 'library'
%>
</div>

<div id="main_panel">
 <div id="viewer"></div>
</div>

<%= drop_receiving_element('timeline',
         :containment => "'library'",
         :accept => 'photo',
         :update => 'timeline',
         :url => { :controller => "timeline", :action => "add", :timeline =>
@timeline.id }) %>
```

Notice how similar the XHTML structure is to Listing 12-1. Within the `timeline`, the `timeline/list` partial is rendered, with the local variable `timeline` taking on the global variable `@timeline` that may exist. The Library starts out just as it did before — with a link that initiates the Library loading process.

The `link_to_remote` command is a helper function to the Prototype library, which constructs a hyperlink that, when clicked, executes an AJAX request and optionally uses the result to replace a portion of the DOM tree, among other things. The formed link in this view updates the contents of the library `div` to replace (by default) its children with whatever is returned from the Controller named `library` and the Action on that controller also named `library`.

Finally, just as in the `initializePage` function of the client-only version, the Timeline `div` is made a drop-receiving element that only accepts elements that are from the `library` div and have the CSS class 'photo.' In this instance, the `update` property is set so that every drop action results in an AJAX request to the `add` Action on the `timeline` Controller.

Views Summary

You have now created a layout to contain pages for the ideaStax Editor, several partials with which to build a page, and the main Editor view to bring them all together. Perhaps by now you have found that constructing View code with an MVC-centric framework greatly simplifies the way in which you translate concepts directly into code. It keeps concerns concise and separate and facilitates reuse of components. With both the Model and View code in hand, you only need a few Controllers to bridge the requests, the data, and the presentation and complete the RIApage.

Creating the Controller

Controllers in Rails serve as the coordinators, objects that accept incoming HTTP requests, perform any actions that may be required, gather any data necessary to provide a response, and then designate a View object as the appropriate response item. Several Controllers have, by necessity, already been referenced from the View code already presented; completing the server-backed ideaStax Editor is just a matter of filling in the implementation of these controllers.

To get started, create four Controllers in the same way that Models were created earlier:

```
ruby script/generate controller photo
ruby script/generate controller editor
ruby script/generate controller library
ruby script/generate controller timeline
```

For each of the preceding Controllers, this generates not only code in the `app/controllers` directory, but also the `app/views` directory. Notice that you have created one controller for every item that has a View implemented. Normally, the step of creating Controllers comes before implementing the Views, and the directories under `app/views` that you had to create in the last step are pre-made by the `generate` script. This chapter switches the order in which they are usually implemented in hopes that creating the Controller glue code is made easier when the destination Views are fully understood.

One topic in Rails that has not yet been explained is the concept of *Routes* — patterns for taking a URL and interpreting it as an invocation of a Controller action and accompanying arguments. These are left untouched for now, other than to say that by default, the Ruby on Rails framework interprets URLs as follows:

```
http://HOST:PORT/Controller/Action/ID
```

For example, without any customization, the URL `http://localhost:3000/editor/view/3` causes Rails to invoke the method (called an Action) named `view` on the Controller named `editor`. Additionally, a variable named `id` is set to the value 3 in a special hash table of parameters made available to the Controller. This bit of knowledge helps explain later both where Controller variables come from and how you can programmatically express URLs through property hashes instead of explicit strings.

Building the Editor Controller

The Editor Controller is the only component in the server-backed ideaStax Editor that has absolutely no parallel in the client-only version. When a user visits the main Editor page, the Controller is responsible for either creating a new editing session or retrieving a saved session for that user. This is handled through an optional Timeline ID variable passed in through the URL:

1. Open the `Editor` controller and note that it is just an empty class definition with no logic:

```
class EditorController < ApplicationController
end
```

2. Define a new Action on this Controller called `view`:

```
class EditorController < ApplicationController
  def view
  end
end
```

By default, an Action will redirect to the view of the same name, so visiting the `http://localhost:3000/editor/view` URL now causes Rails to return to the browser the contents of the `editor/view.rhtml` page wrapped in the `layouts/editor.rhtml` layout. Knowing that the view Action can detect whether an ID was passed in to the URL, you need to exhibit the following conditional behavior:

❑ If the user included a Timeline ID in the URL, then that Timeline instance should be loaded and displayed to the user.

❑ If the provided Timeline ID refers to something that does not exist in the database, then the server should respond with an error message.

❑ If the user provided no ID at all, a new Timeline instance should be created and the user should be redirected to a URL that corresponds to that Timeline instance.

Fill in the view Action so that it matches Listing 12-22, which implements the behavior just described.

Listing 12-22: The Editor Controller

```
class EditorController < ApplicationController
  def view
    if params[:id].nil? or params[:id].empty?
      @timeline = Timeline.create
      redirect_to :action => 'view', :id => @timeline.id
    else
      begin
        @timeline = Timeline.find(params[:id])
      rescue
```

(continued)

Listing 12-22: *(continued)*

```
      render :text => "Bad Timeline ID."
    end
   end
  end
 end
```

This Controller code should look strange to just about anyone who has developed in a non-Web-based environment before — it does not look like it does much of anything at all! Remember, though, that the task of the Controller is just to set up the variables required by the View, which then is returned to the user, so Controllers' implementations are often little more than initializing a few variables:

❑ The `view` action first determines whether any data was passed into the controller in a parameter called `id`. If not, the controller creates a new instance of the `Timeline` model using the `Timeline.create` method (automatically present on all Rails Models) and redirects the user to a URL that explicitly specifies this ID. The first time the ideaStax Editor is ever viewed, for example, the user is redirected from the path `/editor/view` to `/editor/view/1` because a new Timeline instance is created and implicitly saved to the database for editing.

❑ The next case in the preceding `view` Action determines whether there is an `id` parameter provided by the caller. If so, then the code attempts to load the instance into a view-accessible variable named `@timeline` using the `.find(id)` method on the Timeline model, also provided automatically on all Rails Models. If locating this record succeeds, then no further actions need be taken; the control flow in the `view` Action ends and the Rails framework redirects the context to the `editor/view.rhtml` file with the loaded `@timeline` variable (variables passed from Controller to View should be preceded with an @ symbol to make them global).

❑ If the Timeline lookup fails, an exception is thrown. Just as the `catch` keyword provides an exception-handling block in Java, the `rescue` keyword allows for exception handling in Ruby. The rescue block provided in Listing 12-21 simply renders a raw error message to the screen. In a real RIA, the error handling would be much more elegant, but the `render_text` command gets the job done for this example.

Building the Library Controller

The Library Controller need only provide one Action — the library action that is called from the `app/views/editor/view.rhtml` file. Listing 12-19 already defines a partial to fill in the contents of the library, and the main Editor view already defines the outer structure of the library. All that you need for the `library` Action is to set up the `@photos` variable required by the `library/list` partial.

Listing 12-23 shows the Library Action. You should place this code in the `app/controllers/library _controller.rb` file. It loads all Photo Model instances in the database using the `.find_all` command available to all Rails Model objects. It then bypasses the default view (which is `views/library/library.rhtml`) and renders instead the partial `views/library/library.rhtml`, passing through the global variable `@photos` to the partial's local variable `photos`.

Listing 12-23: The Library Controller

```
class LibraryController < ApplicationController
 def library
  @photos = Photo.find_all
```

```
    render :partial => 'library', :locals => { :photos => @photos }
  end
end
```

Building the Timeline Controller

Not quite the keystone of the application, but close enough to be the last piece to fall into place, the Timeline Controller is the most complex of the three Controllers and provides actions to view, add to, and change Timelines. The add Action handles asynchronous adds to the Timeline when a drop event occurs from the Library to the Timeline. The list Action lists the Timeline's slide contents in the same manner as the Library's list action. Finally, the sort Action updates the position fields on slides within a timeline when they are rearranged. To see how these actions are called, return to the definitions of Droppables and Sortables in the View code in Listing 12-20 and Listing 12-21 and observe how each of these Actions is referenced in the callbacks of their events.

Listing 12-24 contains the complete Timeline Controller class, which you should place in app/controllers/timeline_controller.rb. By now, many of the patterns shown in the Controller should be familiar. The list Action, for example, loads a Timeline Model instance using a lookup parameter passed into the HTTP request, and redirects to the Timeline list partial that knows how to display a Timeline's contents. This pattern is the case for the list Action on almost any Controller.

Listing 12-24: The Timeline Controller

```
class TimelineController < ApplicationController
  def add
    @timeline = Timeline.find(params[:timeline])
    if (params[:id].split("_")[0] == 'photo')
      photo = Photo.find(params[:id].split("_")[1])
      slide = @timeline.slides.create
      slide.photo = photo
      slide.save
    end
    render :partial => 'timeline/list', :locals => {:timeline => @timeline}
  end

  def list
    @timeline = Timeline.find(params[:timeline])
    render :partial => 'timeline/list', :locals => {:timeline => @timeline}
  end

  def sort
    @timeline = nil
    params[:timeline].each_index do |i|
      slide = Slide.find(params[:timeline][i])
      slide.position = i
      slide.save
      @timeline = slide.timeline if @timeline.nil?
    end
    render :partial => 'timeline/list', :locals => {:timeline => @timeline}
  end

end
```

The add Action reads the parameter id, which contains the DOM element ID of the Photo to be added as a slide to the Timeline. It confirms that the ID of the element begins with "photo_" and then reads the number after the underscore to look up that particular Photo instance in the database. After loading the photo, it creates a new Slide instance on the Timeline referenced by the HTTP request and assigns the photo to that new slide. Finally, it returns to the user the updated version of the Timeline _list partial to display in the Timeline div.

The sort Action accepts the ordered list of Sortable element IDs that script.aculo.us passes back to the server on an update event and loops through them. For each ID, it locates the Slide instance in the database and sets its position field to the position in the array. As with the add Action, it finishes by rendering the Timeline list partial so that the browser can redisplay the new list, verifying for the user that the data was correctly updated on the server.

The End-to-End ideaStax Editor

The implementation of the Timeline Controller finishes the server-backed ideaStax Editor. Recall that Rails interprets paths on the URL by default as Controller/Action/Id. Try to load Timeline number 500 by directing your browser to http://localhost:3000/editor/view/500. (Hint: there is no Timeline number 500.) Lo and behold, the browser returns with the error message from the Editor Controller shown in Figure 12-12.

Figure 12-12

Try creating a slide by stripping the ID off of the URL and simply visiting http://localhost:3000/ editor/view. The Web browser immediately redirects to editor/view/1—the sign that a new Timeline was created and saved to the database. Drag some slides into the Timeline and move them around a bit and then refresh the page to ensure that the Timeline remains as it was before the reload. Now create two or three more Timelines by loading the page without an ID argument and drag more slides into those. Once you have at least two different saved Timelines, you can test the ideaStax Editor by attempting to load prior Timelines. Instead of the error message you saw before, you see each particular Timeline exactly as you left it!

Finally, open a database viewer if you have one handy and see how your use of the Web page has affected the instance data stored in the Timeline and Slide tables. Figure 12-13 shows the Slide table after a few experiments with the RIA page. As long as the database remains constant, the Timelines created on the RIA page never go away.

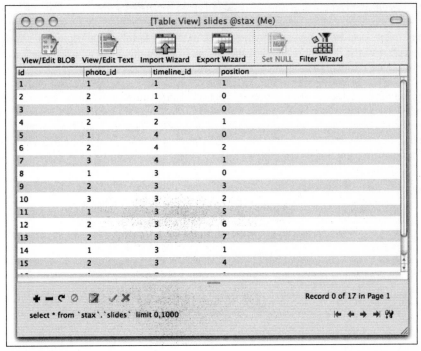

Figure 12-13

Summary

This chapter introduced some of the ways in which RIApages can take advantage of the mouse. Draggable objects, Droppable regions, and Sortable lists made possible by script.aculo.us were used as examples of objects that enable pages within a Web browser to emulate the interaction patterns that users expect from years of desktop use. The closer that Web applications can come to mimicking the types of interactions that desktop applications contain, the better chance RIA developers have of jumping into a rapidly growing market of Web-based replacements for existing desktop-centric powerhouse software.

This chapter also provided a side-by-side comparison of the exact same RIApage implemented with two entirely different strategies. The client-only version of the ideaStax Editor provided practice for JavaScript skills and the script.aculo.us objects and showed off the features of the script.aculo.us Builder. This strategy also showed how much of the burden for processing objects and updating a RIApage can be placed on the client, requiring less attention from the server. The server-backed version of the ideaStax Editor took the completely opposite approach, relying entirely on the server to process and update regions of the page as the user triggered events via script.aculo.us objects. This server reliance comes at a cost, but at the benefit of thinking in terms of partials and views. A server also allows for database persistence, a prerequisite to any RIA in the real world.

Finally, the server-backed version of the ideaStax Editor provided a forum in which to tour some of the features of the Ruby on Rails framework. Rails is a newcomer to the Web development game but it has quickly gained respect from developers and has a considerable following. Rails' easy integration with MVC concepts and the Prototype and script.aculo.us libraries make it a good choice for the open-source ideaStax implementation available on the book's Web site.

The next chapter introduces various special effects and animation techniques, continues the use of script.aculo.us, and introduces the various effects-oriented features it provides. Chapter 14's extended example guides you through the modification of the ideaStax Editor created in this chapter to provide more aesthetic user feedback and to create an "edit mode" in which the user can zoom in to edit a slide without distraction from the rest of the page.

13

User Interaction, Effects, and Animation

It's about the user interface, baby!

—script.aculo.us Web site

When users sit down at a computer, they make certain assumptions about the interface. Scrollbars appear on the bottom and right-hand side of a window, buttons appear as raised rectangles, dragging the title of a window causes the window to move—regardless of operating system these assumptions apply and within a particular operating system may become stricter. Assumptions users make about a system benefits both developers and users because they constitute a certain visual language through which the two can communicate. In desktop applications this visual language is so well defined that first-time users can generally sit down and be productive with a new program without any explanation.

The agreed upon visual lexicon for the World Wide Web is much smaller than the one for desktop applications. In fact, only the hyperlink, image, and form elements are officially in the XHTML specification. For simple Web pages in which the purpose is to replicate a document or form digitally (in other words, the "traditional" World Wide Web), these basic elements offer a level of instant recognition that enables the first-time site visitor to immediately become productive. For the types of rich Internet sites that you will construct, however, no universal visual language yet exists; and Web developers have the extra burden of creatively inventing how to best present material to minimize the necessary explanation.

Luckily for RIA developers, the void of standard user interface controls on the Web is rapidly being filled by a variety of JavaScript libraries and toolkits. Available offerings range from full-featured, desktop-style widgets (such as Dojo or GWT) to Web-specific patterns (such as script.aculo.us).

This chapter delves into the topic of creating and applying special effects with the script.aculo.us library, which produces effects ranging from timed notifications to slide-show-style transitions to simple motion animations. Clever application of these subtle effects provides visual cues that reinforce the user's understanding of what is going on and that hint at possible actions the user might take.

Effects Introduction: Hide and Seek

The most basic visual effect possible in any application is the hiding and showing of elements. In fact, most JavaScript effects that RIA developers apply are just extra eye candy on top of an element's appearance or disappearance. Showing or hiding an element in the DOM tree is useful in many different situations. Collapsible sidebars widgets are common on many sites, for example. Clicking the title of the widget causes its contents to disappear into a smaller, less cluttering view. Other times it is useful to pre-load a large amount of information but only reveal a small portion at a time. The ideaStax Editor developed in Chapter 13, for example, could have pre-loaded the photo library on page loading and kept it hidden instead of waiting for the user to click the Load Library link to fetch the Library's contents from the server. These are just two of many possible reasons why the capability to hide portions of the DOM tree is useful.

Prototype includes three built-in functions that make showing and hiding portions of the DOM tree a snap. These three functions are listed in Table 13-1.

Table 13-1: Showing and Hiding with Prototype

Function	Description
show	Makes an element visible if it was not already
hide	Makes an element invisible if it was not already
toggle	Toggles the visibility of an element

You just need to apply any of the three functions in Table 13-1 to any DOM element to have the corresponding effect. When one of these functions is called, the effect occurs on all children of the calling element as well.

To demonstrate these functions, you're going to provide a way to toggle the visibility of the contents of the ideaStax Library so that the page is less cluttered when the Library isn't in use. To follow the standard way in which this feature is usually implemented, you'll give the Library a title bar that will serve as the trigger for the visibility toggle.

First, you must update the XHTML representation of the Library from Chapter 13 a bit. Instead of the simple one-div approach taken before, use a two-layered version to differentiate the Library's title from its contents. To preserve backward compatibility with the element ID-specific portions of the code from Chapter 12, the contents of the Library remains in a div with ID contents, but this element now wraps in another div, library_container, that also includes space for the Library's title bar:

```
<div id="library_container">
    <div id="library_title">Asset Library</div>
```

```
            <div id="library" class="imagelist">
            </div>
    </div>
```

To add toggle functionality to the Library contents, set the `onClick` property of the `library_title` element so that it invokes a `toggle` command. The command `$('library').toggle()` will toggle the `div` with an ID of `library` between visibility and invisibility. Use the following code:

```
    <div id="library_title" onClick="$('library').toggle();">
```

Listing 13-1 contains the complete code for this example.

Listing 13-1: RHTML

```
    <div id="library_container">
      <div id="library_title" onClick="$('library').toggle();">Asset Library</div>
      <div id="library" class="imagelist">
    <%= link_to_remote 'Load',
            :url => {:controller => 'library', :action => 'library'},
            :update => 'library'
    %>
      </div>
    </div>
```

Try out the new Library by reloading the ideaStax Editor and loading the Library. Clicking on the title of the Library should toggle the Library contents between visibility and invisibility.

The script.aculo.us Effect Class

Script.aculo.us provides a wide range of visual effects that you can apply to elements through the `Effect` class. These effects are generally one-time transformations, very similar to slide transitions in presentation software: fade in, fade out, shake, and others. You can apply them to any DOM element and they affect the entire contents of that element and all of its children. Script.aculo.us makes the creation of these effects easy; just instantiate them and the Web browser's rendering engine takes care of the rest.

The effects provided by JavaScript libraries such as script.aculo.us are especially useful to apply when a fragment of XHTML has been asynchronously added or removed from a RIAPage. In a traditional Web application, each hyperlink click triggers a completely new page load. The visual experience of moving from one Web page to another clearly implies that new information is present, so users automatically scan the new page for new content. AJAX-driven RIAs, however, update themselves piece by piece without reloading the page. Because the line between viewing and refreshing the page is blurred, users might not always realize when an action they have taken has resulted in new page content. This portion of the chapter guides you through using the script.aculo.us `Effect` class to provide users with various visual clues that actions have taken place within the RIAPage.

Using Effects

You use the script.aculo.us `Effect` class in much the same way as a `Draggable` or `Droppable`. An effect is immediately triggered by instantiation, so just the act of creating an effect causes the user of a RIA to see its animation unfold on the page. Table 13-2 contains a list of script.aculo.us' bundled effects at time of writing.

Table 13-2: Script.aculo.us' Built-in Effects

Effect	Required Argument	Description
Appear	Element Reference	Fades in a hidden element
BlindDown	Element Reference	Slides the element down from the top like a window blind
BlindUp	Element Reference	Slides the element up from the bottom like a window blind
DropOut	Element Reference	Makes the element appear to drop out of place downward into non-existence
Fade	Element Reference	Fades the element to the end opacity (defaults to zero) and then removes it from display on the page
Fold	Element Reference	Folds the element, first by shrinking it vertically and then horizontally, giving it the appearance of folding into non-existence
Grow	Element Reference	Grows the element from non-existence to its full size
Highlight	Element Reference	Briefly changes the background color of an element and then fades it back into its starting color
Move	Element Reference	Moves the element from one location on the page to another
MoveBy	Element Reference, y, x	Moves an element smoothly by the stated x and y amounts. The element must have relative or absolute CSS positioning.
Opacity	Element Reference	Smoothly changes the element's opacity (using the common optional arguments to set from, to, and duration)
Parallel	Array of Effect References	Synchronizes several effects so that they occur at the same time
Puff	Element Reference	Enlarges the element as it drops in opacity, giving it the appearance of puffing away
Pulsate	Element Reference	Pulsates the object five times between visible and nonvisible

Effect	Required Argument	Description
Scale	Element Reference, percent	Changes the width and height of an element based on a percentage value of its current size
ScrollTo	Element Reference	Scrolls the page smoothly so that the referenced element is at the top of the viewing pane
Shake	Element Reference	Shakes the element back and forth horizontally
Shrink	Element Reference	Shrinks the element down into its bottom-center. Then it disappears.
SlideDown	Element Reference	Slides the element down from its top edge into visibility
SlideUp	Element Reference	Slides the element out of visibility through its top edge
Squish	Element Reference	Shrinks the element up into its top-left corner. Then it disappears.
SwitchOff	Element Reference	Removes the element from visibility as if it were a television switching off
Toggle	Element Reference	Combines either the appear, slide, or blind script.aculo.us effect with Prototype's toggle operation

All of the effects listed in Table 13-2 have a long list of optional arguments that can change the way in which the effect appears to the user. Some of these arguments are effect-specific, while others are common to all of the `Effect` classes in script.aculo.us. Table 13-3 contains a list of these common options, which can be provided in a hash table after the required arguments. The combination of packaged effects and the wide range of options that can be added provide a wide range of visual flair that you can add right out of the box. For more specific details about any of these arguments, or any of the effects, view the script.aculo.us wiki at `http://wiki.script.aculo.us/`.

Table 13-3: Options Shared By All script.aculo.us Effects

Optional Argument Name	Date Type	Default	Meaning
duration	Float	1.0	How long, in seconds, the effect should take from start to finish
fps	Integer	25	How many frames per second the effect should attempt to achieve. Cannot exceed 100.
transition	Effect.Transitions function	Effect.Transitions .sinusoidal	Sets a function that perturbs the animation by some amount between 0 and 1

Table continued on following page

Optional Argument Name	Date Type	Default	Meaning
from	Float	0.0	Sets the starting point of the transition
to	Float	1.0	Sets the ending point of the transition
sync	Boolean	False	Specifies whether the effect should render each frame automatically or should wait for some external process to call `render()`
queue	Hashtable	(none)	Sets queuing options for use with Effect.Queues
direction	String	"center"	The direction that the effect should proceed in. Can only be used with growth and shrinking effects.
beforeStart	Function Pointer	(none)	A function to be executed before the effect begins
beforeUpdate	Function Pointer	(none)	A function to be executed before redrawing each frame
afterUpdate	Function Pointer	(none)	A function to be executed after redrawing each frame
afterFinish	Function Pointer	(none)	A function to be executed after the effect ends

Example: Effects-Based Notifications

Sometimes a strictly visual cue isn't enough to convey the required information to a user, but the event you want to convey is still not important enough to warrant prime real estate on the Web page. In these cases, you can often employ *notifications* to deliver a message to the user near the top of the page. Notifications are short, one- or two-sentence messages sent from the Web server to a user to indicate that a particular event or problem occurred. In a way, they are similar to logging statements intended for the user.

If you've used sites such as Google's Gmail, then you are familiar with the notification concept. Figure 13-1 shows the top portion of Gmail's interface immediately after someone sends a message. The rest of the page looks exactly like the regular inbox view except for the rounded box with the message "Your message has been sent." A full confirmation page to inform users of sent mail would be overkill, so the information is packed into this tiny space. Notifications usually appear in exactly this manner: as a small addition to the top of the page, directly under the logo or navigation strip. They integrate into the page in such a seamless way that the rest of the page looks as though no notification framework were built into the RIA at all.

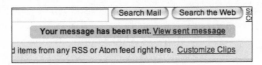

Figure 13-1

You can use script.aculo.us effects to flash a notification when an event occurs on the page:

1. First, you need an empty `div` element to contain notifications that arise on the page. This element should become a permanent part of the page layout and should be placed directly under the title portion of the page layout so that it gets immediate attention from the user when a change occurs within it:

```
<div id="notifications></div>
```

2. Now you need a `sendNotification` function so that JavaScript code throughout the RIA can easily send messages to the user. First, the code hides the notifications `div` (just in case) and clears its contents by looping over its children and removing them from the DOM tree. Next, it creates and adds the notification message as a paragraph element within the `div` using the script.aculo.us `Builder` class introduced in Chapter 13.

3. After adding text to the `notification div`, the `sendNotification` function shows the `div` element with the Prototype `show()` call and uses the script.aculo.us `Effect.toggle` class to begin a ten-second fadeout of the message.

Listing 13-2 shows the `sendNotfication` function.

Listing 13-2: The sendNotification function

JavaScript
```javascript
function sendNotification(message) {
 node = $('notifications')
 node.hide();
 while (node.hasChildNodes()) {
        node.removeChild(node.firstChild);
 }

 notificationText = document.createTextNode(message);

 notification = Builder.node(
        'p',
        {id:'user_notification'},
        [notificationText]
 );
 node.appendChild(notification);
 node.show();
 Effect.toggle(node,'appear', {duration: 4});
}
```

Because the Prototype and script.aculo.us commands operate on any HTML element regardless of its contents, you can make your notification `div` as fancy or as Spartan as you like without changing the JavaScript code. Figure 13-2 shows an image of what a notification using the preceding code might look like in ideaStax. The notification in the example is in the process of fading out.

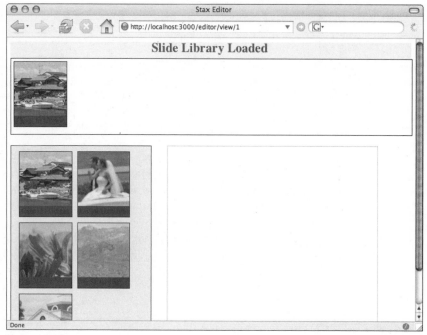

Figure 13-2

Binding Effects to Other script.aculo.us Actions

Most of the objects and patterns in the script.aculo.us library have been created with placeholders so that you can easily tie effects or other arbitrary JavaScript to events. Many AJAX-oriented Prototype functions also have hooks in which you can place JavaScript code (in this case, `Effect` calls). The next examples demonstrate how easily you can wire effect instantiations to events on objects in these two libraries.

Draggables, Droppables, and Sortables

Script.aculo.us provides several build hooks for `Draggables`, `Droppables`, and Sortables to define effects that modify the way they appear to the user. Tying effects to these classes gives them a considerable boost in aesthetics and perceived usability.

Draggables

Each instantiation of a `Draggable` class allows for the three optional properties shown in Table 13-4.

Table 13-4: Effect Bindings for the Draggable Class

Property	Default	Description
starteffect	Opacity	The effect you should apply to the Draggable element when the user starts dragging it
endeffect	Opacity	The effect that you should apply to the Draggable element when the user stops dragging it
reverteffect	Move	The effect that you should apply to the Draggable element while it reverts back to its starting location

As you can see from the values shown in Table 13-4, these properties are already used by default: the starteffect and endeffect apply the changes in opacity that occur when an element is dragged and the reverteffect animates the movement back to its starting position when the element is released.

However, just because these are the defaults (and admittedly, you will probably always want to use them) that does not mean you can't override them with your own Effect references. The following code causes the slides to shake back and forth as they are dragged out of the Library when applied to the Draggable definitions for the ideaStax Library:

```
new Draggable(
   slide.id,
   {
     revert:true,
     starteffect:Effect.Shake
   }
);
```

The Rails equivalent of this code is as follows:

```
<%= draggable_element(element_name,
                      :revert => true,
                      :starteffect => "Effect.Shake" )
%>
```

Alternatively, you can use an effect like Effect.Pulsate to make the element blink in and out of visibility. Most of the script.aculo.us effects that you can apply to a visible object leave the element invisible when the effect is finished, so it's odd, to perform them on the starteffect trigger. These element-disappearing effects could still be applicable when a Draggable element is dropped, however. Dropping a Draggable slide on a trash can icon, for example, should probably make that effect disappear with an Effect.Puff instead of the default Effect.Move back to the starting position.

Droppables

Instead of providing Effect-specific hooks, the Droppable class provides two callbacks that you have already seen: onHover and onDrop, as shown in Table 13-5. The onHover callback is executed whenever a valid Draggable object is dragged so that it is hovering over the Droppable element, and the onDrop callback is executed if this object is then dropped on the Droppable element.

Table 13-5: Callbacks on the Droppable Class

Event	Description
onDrop(function)	Executes the function when an element is dropped
onHover(function)	Executes when the Draggable element is dragged into the accepted region of the Droppable

For some nice visual feedback in the ideaStax Editor, you can modify the onDrop action of the Timeline Droppable so that it momentarily highlights itself every time you add a new element. This gives users an extra bit of reassurance that they have done something expected of them. In the client-only version of the ideaStax Editor, the Timeline Droppable has already been defined in Listing 13-8 (the server-backed version is defined in Listing 13-21):

```
Droppables.add(
  'timeline', {
  accept: 'photo',
  containment: 'library',
  onDrop:addSlideToTimeline
});
```

Because the addSlideToTimeline function is already tied to the onDrop event in the Timeline, adding the highlight effect is just a matter of placing it inside the addSlideToTimeline function. The following addition to the addSlideToTimeline function accomplishes this goal:

```
new Effect.Highlight('timeline');
```

When someone adds slides to the Library, the Library momentarily fills with light-yellow highlighting and then fades back into its regular white background.

You should add the highlight effect to the Ruby on Rails version of the ideaStax Editor a bit differently. Because Rails uses the onDrop event to trigger the AJAX operations, the complete event should be used instead to bind the effects code to the successful completion of the AJAX call. The highlighting that appears, then, not only represents that an element has been dropped, but also that the AJAX call that saves the element to the server's timeline model has completed successfully. The following option to the drop_receiving_element call from Listing 13-21 adds this effect:

```
:complete => "new Effect.Highlight('timeline');"
```

As you might have guessed, you can provide for a :fail option when the remote call returns a failed result. Attached to the original drop_receiving_element call, the final code looks as follows:

```
<%= drop_receiving_element('timeline',
            :containment => "'library'",
            :accept => 'photo',
            :update => 'timeline',
            :url => { :controller => "timeline", :action => "add", :timeline =>
@timeline.id },
            :complete => "new Effect.Highlight('timeline');") %>
```

Sortables

As with the `Droppable` object, `Sortable objects` provide a more generalized way to add visual effects into the mix. The `hoverclass` property, which you can pass in when you add the `Sortable` container, provides an extra class that is applied to `Droppable` objects when they are within the boundaries of the drop-receiving `Sortable` element. Further, `Sortable` containers contain two callbacks, `onChange` and `onUpdate`, which provide the opportunity to respond immediately when the state of your sortable list changes.

Combining Effects

The `Effect.Parallel` class in script.aculo.us enables you to combine multiple effects at the same time. Because element effects are exposed as regular JavaScript classes, the `Effect.Parallel` class can provide a flexible range of combination options through a simple interface. The combination of effects that it permits does not need to focus on just one element, so you can use this class both to compose effects simultaneously on one object and to synchronize effects in parallel across many objects.

The signature of the `Effect.Parallel` class is shown in the following snippet. Two arrays are passed into its constructor. The first array contains the `Effect` classes to be performed and the second contains an array of options that are shared across the effects in the first array:

```
new Effect.Parallel( [array of effects ], [ options common to all effects ] );
```

As an example of when this class might be useful, consider the fade-out effect that removes a notification from the page in the notifications example:

```
Effect.toggle(node,'appear', {duration: 4});
```

When the fade-out completes, the element disappears suddenly from the page, causing the entire page contents to jolt suddenly upwards in response. You can prevent this by providing a fixed, permanent notifications space via CSS, but you can also smooth it by combining the fade-out effect with another script.aculo.us effect to slowly slide the notification out of view.

The following code offers an equivalent to the `Effect.toggle` from the notifications example with one change: The notification block simultaneously fades out and smoothly slides up off of the page. The result is that the entire page slides slowly up to take its place instead of jolting up at the last moment:

```
new Effect.Parallel([
        new Effect.Opacity(node, {from: 1.0, to: 0.0, duration: 5}),
        new Effect.SlideUp(node, {duration: 5})
]);
```

Modal Windows and the ideaStax Previewer

The final example of this chapter brings together several effects in a more sophisticated way to create a *modal window*. A modal window is a child window of a larger application that users must close before they can return to the parent application. In desktop applications, modal windows almost always come in the form of dialog boxes for operations such as save, open, and print. In Rich Web Applications, you can use this type of window both for dialog box questions and full-screen document previews. Modal windows are an excellent example of a desktop concept that is made possible on the Web through use of JavaScript effects.

This section demonstrates how to integrate the shell of a modal preview window into the ideaStax Editor from Chapter 13. While a few bits of the code are ideaStax specific, the great majority of this code works out of the box in any RIA that uses Prototype and script.aculo.us. The requirements of the ideaStax Previewer are that it must provide a near full-screen space on top of the ideaStax application to preview various slides and photos at a larger size and without distraction from the rest of the RIA. When this preview mode is invoked, a `div` element containing the preview should appear as an overlay to the current screen. The rest of the application outside the preview `div` should darken in color and prevent the user from clicking anything. When the preview `div` is closed, the application lightens and returns to normal operation.

To create a modal window, such as the ideaStax Previewer, follow these steps:

1. Define the XHTML structure that represents the preview container. Filling in this preview container with content is outside the scope of this example, so only a simple structure is required. Listing 13-3 contains a simple structure that works for the purposes of this example. The listing contains references to a variable named `@photo`, but if you remove these references, the same XHTML structure works for any project's environment. To integrate this structure into the ideaStax application, you should add Listing 13-3 as a partial called `_preview.rhtml` in the `views/photo` directory.

Listing 13-3: The Preview Container

RHTML

```rhtml
<div id="preview">
    <div id="photo_<%= @photo.id %>_edit" class="edit">
      <div class="control">
          <h3>Editing "<%= @photo.name %>"</h3>
      </div>
      <div class="contents">
      </div>
    </div>
</div>
```

2. Add an action called `preview` on the `PhotoController` in ideaStax. This action takes an ID through the parameters hash as an argument and returns the preview for the photo referenced by that ID. This code responds to AJAX requests directed at `/photo/preview`:

```ruby
def preview
    respond_to do |type|
      type.js do
        @photo = Photo.find(params[:id])
          render :partial => 'preview', :locals => {:photo => @photo}
      end
    end
end
```

The `respond_to do` loop is a recent addition to Rails. It allows the handling of requests to differ based on the mechanism (such as AJAX) through which the request was made. Used properly, this structure leads to clean and concise code with little repetition — just one action can provide multiple variations on a response according to whether the request was from a user, an AJAX call, or from some other programmatic entity such as an RSS reader.

3. To integrate the preview partial in Listing 13-3 into another (non-Rails) environment, just be sure to insert it into the project in such a way that it can be retrieved remotely through an URL. That URL will be used later by the code that initializes the preview mode.

Positioning the Preview Window

Next, you need some CSS definitions to give this structure a prominent display when you add it to the DOM tree. Listing 13-4 contains half of the display code necessary to give the Previewer the full-screen effect that is desired.

Listing 13-4: CSS Styling for the Preview Window

```css
CSS
#preview {
  background-color:  #EEEEEE;
  border: 5px solid blue;
  position:  absolute;
  z-index: 31;
}
```

Note the following about this code:

❑ The `border` and `background-color` attributes are solely for visual emphasis, but the `position` and `z-index` attributes are important for the correct functioning of the modal view. Absolute positioning ensures that any positioning is specified in absolute terms instead of terms relative to the parent container. The `z-index` is set to an arbitrarily large number that ensures that the window displays on top of the other elements on the page.

❑ The CSS in Listing 13-4 leaves out the instructions to specify the size and actual position of the preview element. Because the user may resize the browser window between when the page first loads and when the preview loads, you use JavaScript to provide the size and location of the preview partial on demand. This ensures that it properly reflects the size of the browser window at the time it is added.

❑ You can store the missing sizing code in a reusable function called `sizeToScreen` that takes an element and a percentage value as an argument. The function then resizes and positions that element so that it centers in the browser window and takes up the specified percentage of the total space available. Creating this function is the next step.

Unfortunately, fetching the size of the browser canvas from JavaScript differs from browser to browser, so the code to accomplish that includes a different implementation for each browser type. One of several ways to handle both Mozilla-based browsers and Internet Explorer is the following code:

```javascript
var windowWidth, windowHeight;

if(document.layers||(document.getElementById&&!document.all)){
  windowWidth=window.innerWidth;
  windowHeight=window.innerHeight;
}
else if(document.all){
  windowWidth=document.body.clientWidth;
  windowHeight=document.body.clientHeight;
}
```

This code uses other known differences between the two browser environments to determine which method of fetching the browser viewing area size is appropriate. The variables windowWidth and windowHeight contain the size of the viewing area within the browser window when this code is finished executing. Once these two values are known, the remaining code is the same across all browsers.

Calculating the desired width and height of the element passed into the sizeToScreen function is simply a matter of multiplying the screen width and height by the percentage value (between 0.0 and 1.0) provided as an argument to the function. An offset is needed too, so that the element can be correctly positioned in relation to the screen's edges. This offset is just one-half of the difference between the element size and the screen size.

Figure 13-3 shows a diagram of these layout calculations, and Listing 13-5 contains the JavaScript equivalent of the diagram.

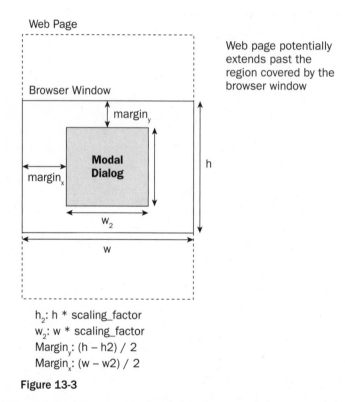

h_2: h * scaling_factor
w_2: w * scaling_factor
$Margin_y$: (h − h2) / 2
$Margin_x$: (w − w2) / 2

Figure 13-3

Listing 13-5: Layout Calculations for the Modal Window

```
newWidth = windowWidth * percent;
h_margin = (windowWidth - newWidth) / 2;

newHeight = windowHeight * percent;
v_margin = (windowHeight - newHeight) / 2;
```

Listing 13-6 contains the final `sizeToScreen` code that brings together the CSS styles from Listing 13-3 with the element sizing code just discussed. You apply the sizing properties to the provided element using the `Element.setStyle` function from the Prototype library. This function dynamically modifies the CSS properties of an element based on a hash table passed into it that maps the CSS properties to their desired values.

Listing 13-6: The sizeToScreen Function

JavaScript

```javascript
function sizeToScreen(element, percent) {
  var windowWidth, windowHeight;

  if(document.layers||(document.getElementById&&!document.all)){
      windowWidth=window.innerWidth;
      windowHeight=window.innerHeight;
  }else if(document.all){
      windowWidth=document.body.clientWidth;
      windowHeight=document.body.clientHeight;
  }

  newWidth = windowWidth * percent;
  h_margin = (windowWidth - newWidth) / 2;

  newHeight = windowHeight * percent;
  v_margin = (windowHeight - newHeight) / 2;

  Element.setStyle(element, {
          height: newHeight + 'px',
          width: newWidth +'px',
          left: h_margin + 'px',
          top: v_margin + 'px'
  });
}
```

Fetching the Preview Window

You're now ready to create the functions that enter and exit the preview mode. The XHTML fragment that contains the preview is addressable through the relative path /photo/preview/:id, where :id stands for an integer representing the ID of the photo that is to be previewed. The CSS styles set in Listing 13-4 causes this XHTML to display on top of the rest of the page, and a function called sizeToScreen resizes the preview element so that it takes a prominent position in the center of the page.

To tie these three preparations together, create a function called openPreviewMode(id) that accepts the integer ID of an asset to preview and uses AJAX to load the respective preview structure into the page. Listing 13-7 contains the openPreviewMode function. Note the following about the code:

❑   The URL /photo/preview/:id is generated and stored in the variable url to provide to the AJAX request object, which is instantiated with a number of options to customize it for the task at hand.

❑   The method property is set to 'get', which by convention should always be the HTTP method used when the purpose is just to fetch information.

❑ The `insertion` property tells Prototype that the response from the server should be appended at the bottom of the `body` element on the current page (which happens to have the ID `editor_body`—the first argument to the `Ajax.Updater`).

❑ The `evalScripts` property is set to `true`, which causes the browser to execute any JavaScript code contained in the remote response. This is important because the code that will call `sizeToScreen` will be returned as part of the AJAX response.

Listing 13-7: The openPreviewMode function >>

```
function openPreviewMode(id) {
  // Load the preview structure at the bottom of the body
  var url = '/photo/preview/' + id;
  var myAjax = new Ajax.Updater( 'editor_body' , url,
            {        method: 'get',
              insertion:Insertion.Bottom,
              evalScripts:true});
}
```

Following along in the ideaStax Editor prototype developed in Chapter 12, you add this function call as an `onClick` action on the titles of slide objects. In the `photo/_photo.rhtml` partial, just replace the fragment of XHTML that contains the photo's name with the following code:

```
<h1><a href="#" onClick="openPreviewMode(<%= photo.id %>);">
  <%= photo.name %>
</a></h1>
```

After making sure to include the new JavaScript functions in the `head` section of the ideaStax template, reload the ideaStax Editor and try clicking the titles of some of the slides. If you have inserted the preceding code correctly, clicking a slide title should cause a small version of the preview structure to appear somewhere toward the bottom of the Web page (because of its insertion at the end of the `body` element). Figure 13-4 shows a picture of this. Completing the basic structure of the preview mode is now only a matter of writing the transitions in and out of preview mode.

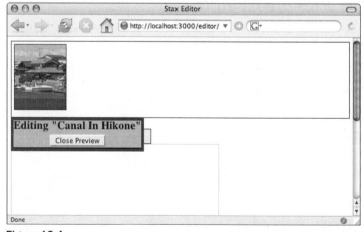

Figure 13-4

Transitioning In and Out of the Preview Window

To position the preview mode in its rightful place at the center of the screen and to dispose of the preview when the user is finished previewing, you need two new JavaScript functions: `zoomInPreview` and `closePreviewMode`. Both assume that the preview fragment has already been fetched and added to the XHTML document.

Zooming In to the Preview

Listing 13-8 contains the code to grow the preview pane until it takes up 80% of the Web browser's available space. The code first uses Prototype's $ function to fetch a reference to the preview element and then immediately hides it to prevent intermediate steps from being visible to the user. Next, the function uses the `sizeToScreen` function to center and size the element so that it fills 80% of the current browser window. Finally, the `Effect.Grow` class is used to make the preview pane appear to grow into existence from the center of the page.

Listing 13-8: The zoomInPreview function

JavaScript

```
function zoomInPreview() {
  // Resize it to take most of the screen
  previewNode = $('preview');
  previewNode.hide();
  sizeToScreen(previewNode, 0.8);
  new Effect.Grow(previewNode);
}
```

The function `zoomInPreview` in Listing 13-8 is called from the preview fragment as soon as it is loaded into the body of the Web page via AJAX. This code cannot rest inside of the `openPreviewMode` function because the AJAX call updates the DOM tree asynchronously; the preview element might not be added by the time the `zoomInPreview` code executes. Because this code is called from the returned partial, the required elements are guaranteed to be present at the time of execution, and the execution should happen quickly enough that the `previewNode.hide()` function takes effect before its presence is even rendered at the bottom of the `body` element in the RIAPage. Insert the following code at the end of the preview partial from Listing 13-3. This is executed because the `Ajax.Update` call from Listing 13-7 set the `evalScripts` option to `true`.

```
<script type="text/javascript" charset="utf-8">
zoomInPreview();
</script>
```

Save these modifications to the code and try clicking on the title of one of the slides again. This time, instead of a small update to the bottom of the Web page, the preview should appear from the center of the screen and grow to take over nearly the entire space.

Disposing the Preview

Removing the preview from the screen requires nearly the same process as displaying it. Define the following JavaScript function to "puff" the preview out of existence. This script.aculo.us effect gives the element the appearance of floating up into mist and disappearing:

```
function closePreviewMode() {
  new Effect.Puff($('preview'));
}
```

Attach this function to the preview window by adding a submit button with an `onClick` event to call it. The following code shows the definition of the submit button, and Listing 13-9 shows the completed preview partial after one last change is made to it in the next step:

```
<input type="submit" value="Close Preview" onClick="closePreviewMode()" />
```

Making the Preview Modal

The code up to this point has provided a simple facility to preview some fragment of XHTML in large size at the center of the screen and to then dismiss it so that it goes away. If the previewed fragment does not take up the whole screen, however, the user can still interact with elements on the edges of the page that the preview does not cover. To make this preview truly modal, you need to prevent the user from doing that.

Creating a Semi-Transparent "Screen"

To block access from the RIAPage while viewing the modal dialog, you must place a "screen" in between the preview `div` and the rest of the page. This screen should cover the entire span of the window and block any mouse events from reaching the elements beneath it. Ideally, the screen is semi-transparent so that users see the underlying RIAPage, but understand that they are intentionally being prevented from accessing it.

The CSS code in Listing 13-4 placed the preview `div` at a z-index of 31. A full-screen div that rests at a z-index of 30, then, can successfully divide the RIAPage into two, because the entire page except for the preview will be below this new element. Call this divider element `cover`, set the z-index to 30, and color it black with the following CSS:

```
#cover {
  position:  absolute;
  z-index: 30;
  background-color: #000000;
}
```

Luckily, the `sizeToScreen` functionality is generalized so that you can apply it to the `cover` element as well.

Sizing the Screen

The statement `sizeToScreen($('cover'), 1.0)` causes the DOM element with an ID of `"cover"` to take up the entire extent of the visible page. Before you can size it, though, you have to add it to the page, so add it to the preview partial that the AJAX call returns. It is important to add this `div` element *before* the JavaScript call to `zoomInPreview` because this function will soon be making references to it. The browser must have already processed the `cover` element in order to operate on it at the time `zoomInPreview` executes. Listing 13-9 shows the completed preview partial with the `cover` and `preview` XHTML fragments and the `zoomInPreview` function call.

Listing 13-9: Completed preview partial

RHTML
```
<div id="cover">
</div>
<div id="preview">
```

```
<div id="photo_<%= @photo.id %>_edit" class="edit">
    <div class="control">
        <h3>Editing "<%= @photo.name %>"</h3>
        <input type="submit" value="Close Preview" onClick="closePreviewMode()" />
    </div>
    <div class="contents">
    </div>
</div>
</div>
<script type="text/javascript" charset="utf-8">
zoomInPreview();
</script>
```

Amending the zoomInPreview and close PreviewMode Functions

Now amend the zoomInPreview and closePreviewMode functions so that they perform similar actions for the cover element as they do for the preview element. Listing 13-10 contains the final version of the zoomInPreview function. Notice that for every action taken on the preview element, a similar action is taken at the same time for the cover element. Additionally, because of the Effect.Opacity effect applied to the cover node, two additional steps must be taken to ensure that it is both transparent and visible at the time the effect takes place.

Listing 13-10: Completed zoomInPreview function

RHTML
```
function zoomInPreview() {
  // Resize it to take most of the screen
  previewNode = $('preview');
  coverNode = $('cover');

  previewNode.hide();
  coverNode.hide();

  sizeToScreen(previewNode, 0.8);
  sizeToScreen(coverNode, 1.0);

  coverNode.setOpacity(0);
  coverNode.show();

  new Effect.Opacity(coverNode,{from:0.0, to:0.8, duration:2.0});
  new Effect.Grow(previewNode);
}
```

Disposing the Screen Element

The final closePreviewMode function, shown in Listing 13-11, contains an additional effect to rid the screen of the cover element.

Listing 13-11: Completed closePreviewMode function

```
function closePreviewMode() {
  new Effect.Puff($('preview'));
  Effect.toggle($('cover'),'appear', {duration: 0.7});
}
```

A Completed Modal Preview

The addition of the `cover` element to shield the user from clicking on the background RIAPage completes this generalized modal element example. Figure 13-5 shows an image of the modal preview overlaying the ideaStax Editor, but what it cannot show is the animations script.aculo.us provides to usher this preview mode into and out of focus. Try this example on your own to find a sequence of effects that you and your users will find visually pleasing.

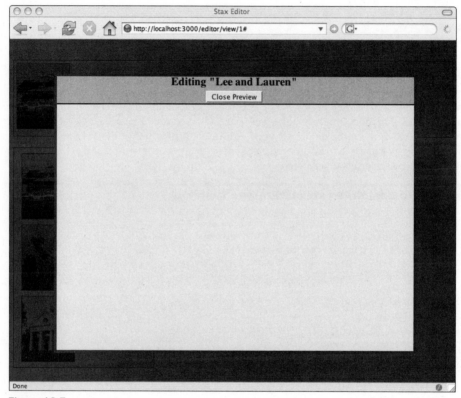

Figure 13-5

The example presented here was explained in the context of a preview feature, but you can generalize the exact same code and techniques of this chapter for use with elements of any shape or purpose. To extend and experiment with your understanding of the code presented here, search online to find out how to add a callback to the `resize` event on your browser of choice. Tie a function to this callback that resizes and recenters the `preview` and `cover` div elements when the window is resized.

Some work remains to be done to bring this example up to production quality. Better CSS styling is needed on the modal preview to make it appear more professional. More important, the sizing of the preview and screen elements is fixed once the `sizeToScreen` function is called: If the user scrolls or resizes the window, then both the preview and the blocking screen remain in their old position.

As another exercise, build upon the code here to create a generalized a modal dialog box in the style of a desktop application's quit confirmation. The box should be driven by a single function called `requestConfirmation` that accepts three arguments:

- ❑ A text string containing the confirmation question
- ❑ A function pointer that is executed if the user confirms the statement
- ❑ A function pointer that is executed if the user rejects the statement

Thinking of your development tasks in general terms like this leads to the development of a personal library of reusable components that make you a more effective developer. Functions such as zoomToScreen or requestConfirmation can slowly form the basis of your own personal JavaScript library, which can be included across all projects in which you participate, reducing development time and standardizing the look and feel of your RIAs.

Summary

This chapter demonstrated some of the ways that JavaScript effects can add to the usability of a RIAPage. Looks *do* matter when it comes to Web design—the nontext elements of a RIAPage can convey an enormous amount of feedback and information for users. JavaScript effects offer an easy and well-accepted way to convey small bits of feedback when a user has performed an action that does not warrant an entire page refresh.

The chapter presented the script.aculo.us Effects library as an easy way to introduce effects into a RIA with little development cost. The examples provided general scenarios in which RIA developers find effects useful, and highlighted some of the ways in which you can bind effects to events on other objects in the script.aculo.us library. Finally, the concept of modal dialogs was introduced, and an example implementation of a modal dialog was provided.

The next chapter delves into the task of creating a system around your backend model data that enables it to sort and search in a powerful yet simple way. You are shown how you can give both structured and unstructured data greater value by enabling users to classify it with tags.

14

Tagging and Rating (I): Creating an Infrastructure

The Web is moving from being a place where people access information to a place where people access other people in an information-rich environment

— Paul Saffo, Institute for the Future

. . . search is now the greatest applied computer science R&D problem in existence. It will drive the priorities of artificial intelligence and other sub-fields for decades to come . . .

—Dr. Gary Flake, Microsoft visionary

Finding something of interest on the Internet, in unstructured or semi-structured data, has long vexed knowledge engineers and information analysts. The conventional approach is to re-express data into structured data silos, most often relational databases. The original content is represented as a pointer to a binary object on a file system, and a lot of descriptive data is stowed away in a database. It is hoped that, given a sufficiently good set of descriptive terms, you can tease the desired "something" out from the larger mass of digital data. However, "restructuring" data can result in loss of the original context or additional, meaningful information, which means reconstructing the relationship of data to other data through data mining post facto.

This problem, serious enough in textual data, is exacerbated in the digital era, which is full of podcast and video blog publishers and consumers. For publishers, classifying content along all the useful dimensions that might maximize uptake became less likely. For consumers, "Find what I mean" searching hardly ever yielded solid results. For the average Internet user, finding anything digital in the growing mass of data from contributors across the globe is a serious problem.

Best current practice for creating searchable descriptive data (metadata) around Web content is to enlist the human energy and cognitive brainpower of Internet users to achieve a manual version of what algorithms do reasonably well for URLs and text, and rather less well for other kinds of data. One approach to creating a tagging infrastructure, using MySQL and server-side Python, is covered in this chapter. In the following chapter, tagging capability will be added to the capstone ideaStax application by adding a plug-in to the Ruby On Rails framework.

Understanding the Tagging Problem

At the dawning of the new century, DARPA and the W3C launched near simultaneous efforts (DAML — DARPA Agent Markup Language, and OWL — Ontological Web Language) to create a new markup language that describes Web items in an "unambiguous, computer-interpretable form." Theoretically, you can expand this language enough to describe "everything" about arbitrary content and its relationship to other content. Whether this was a success is still an open research question.

One problem in any line of universally extensible knowledge thinking is demonstrated in Figure 14-1, which shows that unstructured data requires metadata to provide post-capture search and classification.

Figure 14-1

Adding Folksonomy to Web Content

With the techniques discussed in this chapter and Chapter 15, your users can participate in creating an informal classification of the content of your RIA. An informal classification system created by content users has come to be known as a *folksonomy,* sort of a play on the word taxonomy, meaning a formal classification system. Wikipedia.com defines it as follows:

"A *folksonomy* is a collaboratively generated, open-ended labeling system that enables Internet users to categorize content such as Web pages, online photographs, and Web links. The freely chosen labels — called tags — help to improve a search engine's effectiveness because content is categorized using a familiar, accessible, and shared vocabulary. The labeling process is called *tagging.* Two widely cited examples of Web sites using folksonomic tagging are Flickr and Del.icio.us.

"Because folksonomies develop in Internet-mediated social environments, users can discover (generally) who created a given folksonomy tag, and see the other tags that this person created. In this way, folksonomy users often discover the tag sets of another user who tends to interpret and tag content in a way that makes sense to them. The result, often, is an immediate and rewarding gain in the user's capacity to find related content."

Search systems work at the keyword level, which is subjective. The photo's creator may title it "Lighted Palm." An automated feature extraction system might tag it with physically descriptive terms, such as "tree," "water," or "building." Other folks might think "holidays" or "beach," or even a location, such as "Villa Julia" or "French West Indies." But the user may become frustrated by entering the wrong "code" words (for example, "vacation villa") and not finding the photo. These relationships may languish undiscovered without the input of many "just plain folks" gathered around a Web presence promoting community participation (as opposed to a formal, highly structured knowledge-engineered information Web). When you architect and implement your RIA to enable user input regarding content, you create the social dimension of your RIA, which, as Chapter 1 pointed out, is a hallmark of modern RIAs. How do you add this dimension to your code? The rest of the chapter tells you how.

A Tagging Application

The RIAPage for the illustrative application for this chapter is shown in Figure 14-2. This figure illustrates a *tag cloud* — user tags for the content in a database on the server. Anytime a user selects one of the tags from the tag cloud, a DIV on the same page refreshes with the set of URLs for photographs corresponding to the tag. Whenever a photo's link is selected, the relevant photo is revealed. In this chapter, you create an infrastructure for tagging and reviewing, and in the next chapter, for adding comments in a useful way to the database. For now, we will concentrate on a generic application demonstrating a simple model view and controller for tagging a corpus of information and presenting tags in a way far more impactful than, for example, a table.

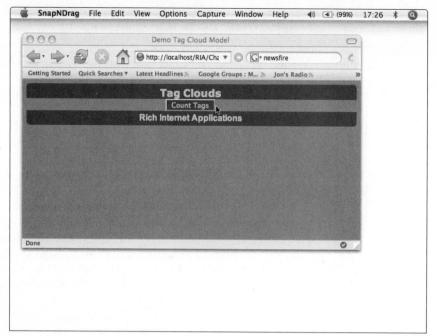

Figure 14-2

Listing 14-1 shows the deceptively simple RIAPage that corresponds to Figure 14-2; and the capabilities of the application are illustrated in Figures 14-3 through 14-5.

Listing 14-1: Tagging.html

HTML

```html
<!DOCTYPE html PUBLIC "-//W3C//DTD XHTML 1.0 Strict//EN"
"http://www.w3.org/TR/xhtml1/DTD/xhtml1-strict.dtd">
<html>
<head>
<title>Demo Tag Cloud Model</title>
<!-- stylesheets -- >
<link rel="StyleSheet" href="../../stylesheets/RIAStyle1.css" TYPE="text/css">
<link rel="stylesheet" href="../../stylesheets/tag_cloud.css" type="text/css" />
<link rel="stylesheet" href="../../stylesheets/rounded_corners.css"
        type="text/css" />

<!--JavaScript view and controller code -- >
<script type="text/javascript"
   src="../../../scripts/MochiKit/MochiKit.js">
</script>
<script type="text/javascript" src="Tagger.js" ></script>
<script type="text/javascript">
//<![CDATA[
  var roundedCornersOnLoad = function () {
    roundClass("h1", null, {corners: "top"});
```

```
        roundClass("h2", null, {corners: "bottom"});
  };
  addLoadEvent(roundedCornersOnLoad);
//]]>
</script>

</head>
        <body>
            <h1>Tag Clouds</h1>
            <center><button onclick="TagQuery()">Count Tags</button> </center>
            <h2>Rich Internet Applications</h2>
            <div class="tag_cloud" id="HERE">
            <span id="cloud"/>
            </div>
        </body>
</html>
```

In Listing 14-1, several style sheets are applied and allowed to cascade. An algorithm for showing a tag's popularity, shown in Listing 14-13, will apply the `tag_cloud.css` font sizing styles to produce the range of small to very large live tags shown in the tag cloud in Figure 14-3. The `RIAStyle1.css` has been shown previously (Chapter 4, for example) and produces the overall page look and feel.

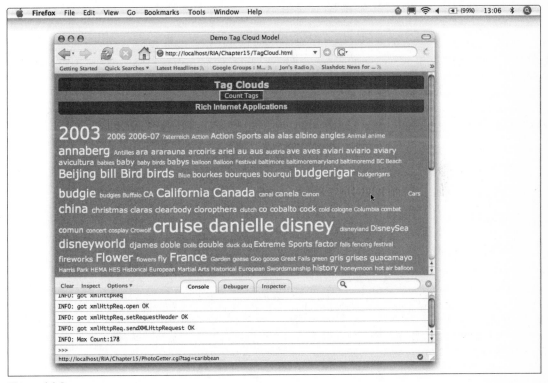

Figure 14-3

Note the following about Listing 14-1:

❏ The <H1> and <H2> tags have a special look applied to them (half rounding.) This is a visual effects accomplished by one of the libraries (MochiKit.Visual) packaged with MochiKit. By including MochiKit (src="../../../scripts/MochiKit/MochiKit.js"), the application can touch every library in the MochiKit namespace.

❏ Notice the addLoadEvent() function. Always use this instead of HTML tag attributes, such as the <body onLoad="DoSomeFunction()> style directive. Mixing and matching causes conflicts with MochiKit's DOM handling code implemented in MochiKit.DOM. When in doubt, include the MochiKit library, and then let MochiKit orchestrate the action, rather than use HTML markup attributes.

❏ There is one active DIV on the page, containing the SPAN "tagcloud", which will be replaced with the tags from the model when the Count Tags button is activated.

❏ In Figure 14-3, the tag cloud is populated with tags of various sizes, indicating the relative number references to the term compared with the rest of the tag population. Each of the tags is actually a link, which, when clicked, reveals the set of pictures referred to by the tag. Notice that the FireBug debugging pane in the lower part of the figure, which is a plug-in for Firefox (available from http://www.joehewitt.com/software/firebug/), is shown opened, and several debug messages from Tagger.js are logged. MochiKit offers standard logging output through the MochiKit.Logging library.

Finally, when a user clicks one of the tags in Figure 14-4, a new document shows the actual photograph source site, as shown in Figure 14-5. Rather than capture the JPEG content and incorporate it into the RIA, this is a case where your application probably ought to redirect to the actual site. This maintains the utility of the site producing the content you catalogue.

Figure 14-4

Figure 14-5

Getting Started: the Essential Elements

The capstone application in this chapter helps you determine how to organize a tagging infrastructure. It takes the shape of a typical distributed RIA, which, unfortunately, has a few "working parts" you must install. If there had been a simpler way to illustrate this chapter's essential points, the authors would have done so. The upside is that given the effort you make to work the code in the example, you receive a good understanding of tagging, and an application architecture and code that's fairly reusable. To work with this example, you will initially use Python, MochiKit, and MySQL. The architecture for the initial version of the implementation is shown in Figure 14-6.

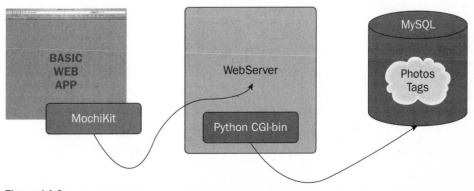

Figure 14-6

3

Application control flows from the RIAPage to Tagger.js, which coordinates the link to the Model containing both Photos and Tags. TagQuery makes an XHLHttpRequest to a server-side Python CGI module that accesses the database maintaining the model. The mechanism of both the Controller and Model access are covered later in the chapter. This RIA is typical in properly separating the application elements according to the MVC architecture, discussed in Chapter 6:

❑ The View is implemented in the browser-resident RIAPage

❑ The Model is implemented as a MySQL data store managed by server-side Python.

❑ The Controller is JavaScript leveraging MochiKit.

This example is rather simpler than previous examples, such as the capstone presented in Chapter 9, in that the initial pages and subsequent interactions are not dynamically generated and mediated by a framework (e.g., Django, Rails, or TurboGears). Instead, the initial page just invokes JavaScript in the browser, which in turn makes the XMLHttpRequest call to the Python CGI, which accesses the model via a MySQL library. It does generate a result page dynamically, which replaces the initial page, but it's primitive compared to applications you've already seen in the book.

Python

Install this for server-side CGI scripting. Already well known to you as an agile language for general application implementation, Python is also the most object-oriented member of the Perl/PHP/Python trinity of server-side agile languages. Most developers have Python installed already — for example, it comes as standard issue on modern Mac OS/X machines; but if you don't have it, go to python.org and download one of the pre-built kits. Versions 2.3 or 2.4 are fine for this chapter.

MySQL

Although there are a number of competitors in the "easy-to-setup, easy-to-admin" relational arena (e.g., PostgresSQL, SQLite), MySQL is probably the best known. Several pre-built bundles are available from mysql.org. If you have something else installed (e.g., SQLite has grown very popular), you have to adapt the code shown later in `Tagger.cgi` and `DBLookup.py`, and the model creation and Photo and Tag loaders described in `TableCreator.py` and `PhotoLoader.py`. Post installation, you can check to ensure that all is well with MySQL (for example, that the installer added the executable to your PATH) by invoking MySQL from the command line — typically, `mysql -u username`.

Remember to either configure MySQL on install to autostart on reboot, use one of the third-party MySQL control panels, or keep the System Preference panel (OS/X) or the System Settings panel (Windows) in mind whenever your database access seems not to work properly.

MySQLdb

MySQLdb is a Python library. You also need the Python API for MySQL (notice that in the application's Python server-side components, MySQLdb is imported):

1. The library is available at `http://dev.mysql.com/downloads/python.html`. Download `MySQL-python.exe-1.2.1_p2.win32-py2.4.exe` for Windows.

2. Download and unzip `MySQL-python-1.2.1_p2.tar.gz` for Mac OS/X and Linux.

3. After downloading, navigate to the download folder in the Windows Explorer or terminal window (Mac and Linux). For Windows, just double-click the .exe file and follow the dialog. For Mac and Linux, run

```
python setup.py install
```

in the download directory containing the package's setup.py. This installs the library in the site-packages folder relative to the Python home folder.

4. Again, if you intend to use SQLite, you need to pick up and install the pysqlite Python library from pysqlite.org and follow a similar install process.

Flickr Photo API

To illustrate the concept, you could conceive of several bodies of digital data to use as a corpus—and indeed several important open, social sites, such as del.icio.us, have. The problem is that you need to quickly and conveniently create an arbitrarily large corpus. Luckily, an enormous source of instantly available pre-tagged digital data is only a Python module away.

An easy choice for this chapter is flickr.com. It's a handy place to gather an information corpus to work with. Most important, however, it has a useful API that you can invoke via Python or the usual suspects in the agile language pantheon. You can find the complete documentation for the API at www.flickr.com/services/api/.

The server-side Python acts as a proxy to invoke the Flickr service APIs. Remember from Chapter 4 that modern browsers generally forbid cross-domain server call redirection. Hence, the server-side Python both acts both as proxy, and, through some clever method called signature manipulation, creates Flickr service invocations.

Apache Web Server

There are a couple of open-source competitors—for example, LigHTTPD. Again, most developers have Apache installed already—it comes as standard issue on modern Mac OS/X machines. If you don't have it, go to www.apache.org and download one of the pre-built kits. You may find it necessary to do some mild configuration tinkering to ensure that Apache recognizes Python (.py) files as legitimate CGI-bin executables:

1. After installing Apache, locate the httpd.conf file, edit it, and find the <Directory> </Directory> stanza. The following code shows an example setup (in this case, for Mac OS/X), but the setup is similar regardless of operating system. Remember that when you first install Apache, there may not be an httpd.conf file. If not, look for the httpd.conf-dist file and copy that into httpd.conf. This ensures that you have a handy backup should you misconfigure the working copy. Here's the section you want to change:

```
#
# This should be changed to whatever you set DocumentRoot to.
#
    <Directory "/Library/WebServer/Documents">
    ...
    #
        Options Indexes FollowSymLinks MultiViews ExecCGI
    </Directory>
```

397

2. Regardless of other options that you may set for other purposes, you definitely want to set "ExecCGI" to ensure that a connection is made to "wire in" server-side CGI-bin scripts and code. Additionally, you should name a directory for CGI-bin executables. This entails modifying another stanza. Locate a stanza in `httpd.conf` that looks like the following:

```
#
# ScriptAlias: This controls which directories contain server scripts.
# ScriptAliases are essentially the same as Aliases, except that
# documents in the realname directory are treated as applications and
# run by the server when requested rather than as documents sent to the client.
# The same rules about trailing "/" apply to ScriptAlias directives as to
# Alias.
#
```

Modify the `ScriptAlias` line to point to a directory relative your Web server's installation home base. Technically, `/cgi-bin/` need not be in the path of the Apache install, but it's a good idea from an administrative standpoint. Here, the example shows a Mac OS/X install, but the concept is similar for any operating system. The `/cgi-bin/` chosen is relative to the DocumentRoot shown (in this case `/Library/WebServer/`):

```
ScriptAlias /cgi-bin/ "/Library/WebServer/CGI-Executables/"
```

3. Additionally, you also want to look at a stanza that resembles the following, to ensure that the directory assignment is correct, and that you are allowing or restricting invocation from Web pages as appropriate. For development and testing purposes, this should not matter.

```
<Directory "/Library/WebServer/CGI-Executables">
        AllowOverride None
        Options None
        Order allow,deny
        Allow from all
</Directory>
#
# AddHandler allows you to map certain file extensions to "handlers",
# actions unrelated to filetype. These can be either built into the server
# or added with the Action command (see below)
#
        # If you want to use server side includes, or CGI outside
# ScriptAliased directories, uncomment the following lines.
#
# To use CGI scripts:
#
AddHandler cgi-script .cgi
AddHandler cgi-script .py
```

If you use an off-machine Web server — for example, through your low-price ISP — you may need special permission to perturb the stock Apache configuration.

MochiKit

The RIAPages in this chapter use the MochiKit JavaScript library (contained in `MochiKit.js`), which like other libraries and frameworks is documented as a part of the chapter's side mission to educate you about the popular tools available. You use MochiKit to facilitate both the remote procedure call and certain page effects and animations. You can download it from `mochikit.org` and install it relative to the Apache Document Root folder. In Figure 14-7, the DocumentRoot is the "Documents" folder.

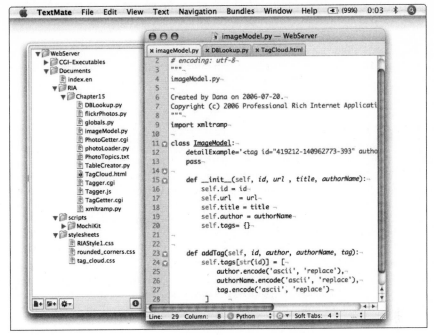

Figure 14-7

Assuming a running Apache server, invoking `http://localhost` yields the Web page `index.en`, and `http://localhost/RIA/Chapter14/TagCloud.html` yields Figure 14-2:

1. If you set up folders as shown, you should juxtapose the other critical files (such as Tagger.js and the cgi-bin script it invokes (`./PhotoGetter.cgi?tag=tag`) relative to the invoking `TagCloud.html` RIAPage.

2. If you reconfigure the parts of the Web server's installation hierarchy, remember to change references in the appropriate code files (principally `Tagger.js`).

3. Note too that you need to make the configuration modifications in `httpd.conf` as shown above so that files with .cgi extensions can exist wherever (relative to DocumentRoot) you want, rather than *only* in the cgi-bin folder.

4. Don't forget to make cgi-bin files executable on systems that enforce file permissions.

MochiKit is designed, as creator Bob Ippolito explains, to make JavaScript "suck less," which means JavaScript languished for a significant number of years in a disorganized state with no rigorous attempt to collect and categorize its various elements. As a result, prior to the Web 2.0 era, JavaScript had an air of casual messiness. MochiKit and other client-side libraries both organize and build broadly useful functions atop the raw JavaScript language in the browser. The complete library documentation is available in PyDoc/RubyDoc/JavaDoc form at `www.mochikit.com`.

In this chapter, you use a few of the many libraries in the MochiKit namespace:

❑ **MochiKit.DOM** — DOM manipulation API and functions

❑ **MochiKit.Logging** — Because, as the Web site remarks, "We're all tired of `alert()`."

399

❑ **MochiKit.Async** — Manages all asynchronous and deferred callback style tasks; in this application, you use it for creating and managing the XMLHttpRequest.

Now that your configuration elements are in place, you're ready to try the code and the application. You can find the code for the application in the chapter at `http://abraxas-soft.com/RIA/code/Chapter14.zip`.

Data Mining

The book's capstone application will contain a fairly small corpus to begin with, but that only becomes larger over time as users contribute content and tag content. This builds a valuable corpus of material and search metadata, which any tag cloud implementation you create needs to data mine. For this chapter, however, it's useful to mine an existing data corpus from the Web so that you can practice and become familiar with the concepts. One excellent source is the enormous set of photographic material contained in the Flickr photo repository at flickr.com.

Flickr holds photos contributed by the original photographer, and tags added by the photographer and others. Additionally, Flickr has a well-defined open API for several popular agile languages, including PHP, Perl, Ruby, and Python. The complete API is well documented at `www.flickr.com/services/api/`, and you can click through to practice using any of the service calls and observe the results.

Downloading Photo Metadata

In this chapter, you use Python both to interface the Flickr API and to store photo URLs and tags in a MySQL database. Listing 14-2 shows the XML returned from a call to fetch photo metadata via the Flickr REST API, where a typical call would resemble the following:

```
http://www.flickr.com/services/rest/?method=flickr.photos.getInfo&api_key=<key>
&photo_id=73592514
```

The basic download plan contains multiple steps:

1. Create an arbitrary set of tags to seed the model. The format of search terms used by `photoLoader.py` (shown in Listing 14-8) is simple: one word or term per line; ignore lines beginning with #.

2. Use Flickr's flexible search API to access photo metadata. The search API allows searches using a wide range of criteria, but in this case you are interested only in searching via tags. Thus, a search for photos with the seed tag "Annaberg ruins" (constructed in the Python code, Listing 14-2(b)) resembles the following:

```
http://www.flickr.com/services/rest/?method=flickr.photos.search&api_key=xxx&tags=
Annaberg+ruins
```

Flickr, like many of the services such as those covered in Chapter 3's exploration into mashups, will insist that you supply an API key. Obtaining a noncommercial API key (the kind we are using for experimentation) is easy. Visit `www.flickr.com/services/api/misc.api_keys.html`.

The result set from that query resembles the code shown in Listing 14-2(a).

Listing 14-2(a): Flickr photo search result XML

XML

```xml
<rsp stat="ok">
 <photos page="1" pages="1" perpage="100" total="1">
   <photo id="73592518" owner="11203358@N00" secret="7f0d31dd8d" server="20"
    title="AnnabergRuins" ispublic="1" isfriend="0" isfamily="0"/>
 </photos>
</rsp>
```

The API documentation further elaborates the meaning of some of the fields, but what you're interested in is the ID field for each publicly accessible photo found by your tag-based search.

Accessing Photo Metadata

Now that you have basic information, you want to use that ID to access the trove of additional metadata associated with the photo. In particular, you want the additional tags for the photo to augment your folksonomy. Remember that your own applications will be augmented from the comments and tags of your users. This step is a shortcut to gain tags much more rapidly.

You use the ID from the photo above to construct a call like this:

```
http://www.flickr.com/services/rest/?method=flickr.photos.getInfo&api_key=xxx&photo
_id=73592518
```

This mines the photo for additional tags (including of course, the original). This in turn yields the XML result set shown in Listing 14-2(b).

Listing 14-2(b): Flickr photo information XML

XML

```xml
<rsp stat="ok">
 <photo id="73592518" secret="7f0d31dd8d" server="20" dateuploaded="1134591948"
   isfavorite="0" license="0" rotation="0" originalformat="jpg">
   <owner nsid="11203358@N00" username="dana_virtual" realname="" location=""/>
   <title>AnnabergRuins</title>
   <description>
    The Annaberg ruins on St.Johns ...
   </description>
   <tags>
     <tag id="1783595-73592518-240565" raw="Annaberg">annaberg</tag>
     <tag id="1783595-73592518-194236" raw="USVI">usvi</tag>
     <tag id="1783595-73592518-11760"  raw="Virgin">virgin</tag>
     <tag id="1783595-73592518-2102" raw="Islands">islands</tag>
     <tag id="1783595-73592518-9960" raw="StJohn">stjohn</tag>
     <tag id="1783595-73592518-21714" raw="Caribbean">caribbean</tag>
     <tag id="1783595-73592518-3981177" raw="AnnaBergRuins">annabergruins</tag>
   </tags>
   <urls>
     <url type="photopage">
        http://www.flickr.com/photos/11203358@N00/73592518/
```

(continued)

Listing 14-2(b) *(continued)*

```
      </url>
    </urls>
  </photo>
</rsp>
```

Referring back to Figure 14-3, you can see some of these terms in the tag cloud shown there, and now you know where they originated (but not how to use them to construct the cloud — that comes a bit later). You will use this information, particularly the data highlighted in Listing 14-2(b), to populate a data model on the server backing the TagCloud RIAPage.

The relationship between Tags and Photos is represented in Figure 14-8.

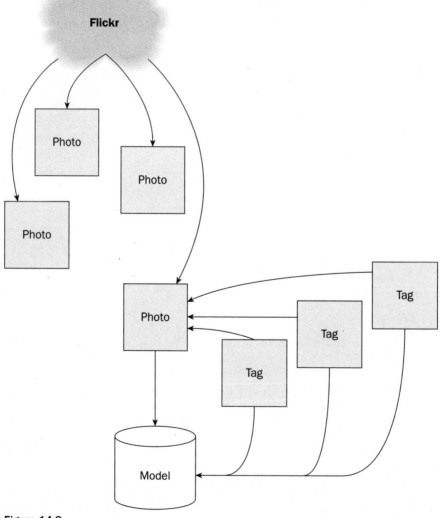

Figure 14-8

Next, you'll want to represent this data model on your server, and delve into the Python code to do the data mining.

Setting Up the Data Model

What constitutes a simple, but sufficient data model for representing both photographs and associated tags? You have three tables: one for holding photo data to be extracted from Flickr (but that could be from any source); one for holding tag metadata; and a linking table. Listing 14-3 shows the schema for all three tables. Note that they closely mirror the data representation scheme that Flickr uses, minus much of the additional data extraneous to the model you need to support in your application.

As Figure 14-9 shows, each Photo in the Photos table is uniquely identified by an ID, as are the (potentially) many Tags associated with each Photo, held in the Tags table. A linking table (Photos_Tags) joins the two tables and creates the "one Photo to many Tags" relationship. You create the databases and the tables.

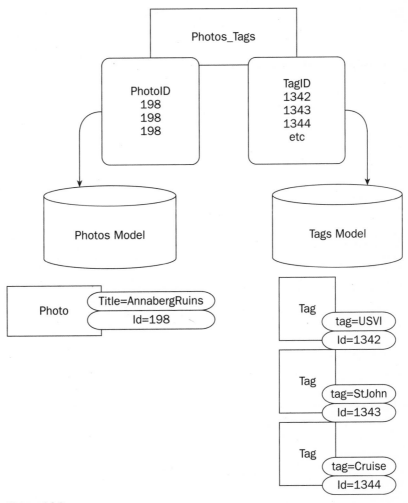

Figure 14-9

Setting Up the Data Tables

First, assuming you have installed MySQL, you need to create a MySQL database to contain the tables with the SQL CREATE DATABASE command. You may need to become the root MySQL user in order to accomplish administrative tasks. You will need to create a database and authorize the username and password for the chosen data store:

```
$ mysql -u root -p
> create database TAGGINGDB;
> use istax_ TAGGINGDB;
> grant all privileges on *.* to xyzzy identified by 'xyzzy';
```

You can replace the occurrences of 'xyzzy' with whatever username and password you prefer. The SQL grant privileges command ensures that your chosen username may operate on the tables in the taggingdb.

Your goal is to create the three required tables so that their schema is as shown in Listings 14-3, 14-4, and 14-5. The knowledge representation strategy is fairly simple and typical of representations whereby there is a one-to-many relationship between the Photos themselves (represented in the Photos table) and multiple tags (represented in the Tags table) referring to a given photo.

Listing 14-3: Photo tagging tables

SQL

```
mysql> show tables;
+--------------------+
| Tables_in_taggingdb |
+--------------------+
| Photos             |
| Photos_Tags        |
| Tags               |
+--------------------+
3 rows in set
```

Listing 14-4: Photos table schema

SQL

```
mysql> describe photos;
+---------+--------------+------+-----+---------+----------------+
| Field   | Type         | Null | Key | Default | Extra          |
+---------+--------------+------+-----+---------+----------------+
| id      | int(11)      |      | PRI | NULL    | auto_increment |
| photoID | varchar(16)  | YES  |     | NULL    |                |
| author  | varchar(255) | YES  |     | NULL    |                |
| title   | varchar(255) | YES  |     | NULL    |                |
| url     | varchar(255) | YES  |     | NULL    |                |
+---------+--------------+------+-----+---------+----------------+
5 rows in set (0.00 sec)
```

Thus, a typical selected row in the Photos table might contain the following:

```
id: 198
photoID: 73592518
author: dana_virtual
title: AnnabergRuins
url: http://www.flickr.com/photos/11203358@N00/73592518/
```

In the final composite application for the chapter, when your user selects a Tag, this and other information is returned.

Listing 14-5: Tags table schema

SQL

```
mysql> describe Tags;
+--------+--------------+------+-----+---------+----------------+
| Field  | Type         | Null | Key | Default | Extra          |
+--------+--------------+------+-----+---------+----------------+
| id     | int(11)      |      | PRI | NULL    | auto_increment |
| tag    | varchar(255) | YES  |     | NULL    |                |
+--------+--------------+------+-----+---------+----------------+
2 rows in set
```

Thus, in the final composite, a typical selected row in the Tags table might contain the following:

```
id: 1343
tag: USVI
```

Listing 14-6 shows the link table, whose contents are simply the primary keys of the Photos and Tags tables.

Listing 14-6: Photo tagging tables

SQL

```
mysql> describe Photos_Tags;
+---------+---------+------+-----+---------+-------+
| Field   | Type    | Null | Key | Default | Extra |
+---------+---------+------+-----+---------+-------+
| photoId | int(11) | YES  |     | NULL    |       |
| tagID   | int(11) | YES  |     | NULL    |       |
+---------+---------+------+-----+---------+-------+
```

Now that the data model structure is clearer, Listing 14-7 creates a small functional script to instantiate the requisite tables.

Listing 14-7: TableCreator.py

PYTHON

```python
 1 #!/usr/bin/env python
 2 # encoding: utf-8
 3 """
 4 TableCreator.py
 5
 6 Created by dana  on 2006-07-20.
 7 Copyright (c) 2006 Rich Internet Applications.
 8 """
 9
10 import sys
11 import os
12 import MySQLdb
13
14 class TableCreator (object):
15
16     def __init__(self, database):
17         self.database = database
18
19     def connectDB(self):
20         try:
21             self.connection =  MySQLdb.connect(host="localhost",
 user="xyzzy", passwd="xyzzy", db=str(self.database) )
22         except MySQLdb.OperationalError, message:
23             errorMessage = "Error %d:\n%s" % (message[ 0 ], message[ 1 ] )
24             self.connection =   None
25
26     def setCursor(self):
27         try:
28             self.cursor = self.connection.cursor()
29         except MySQLdb.OperationalError, message:
30             errorMessage = "Error %d:\n%s" % (message[ 0 ], message[ 1 ] )
31             self.cursor = None
32
33     def dropCursor(self):
34         self.cursor.close()
35
36     def dropConnection(self):
37         self.connection.close()
38     def dropTable(self, tableName):
39         try:
40             self.cursor.execute("DROP TABLE "+tableName)
41         except MySQLdb.OperationalError, message:
42             errorMessage = "Error %d:\n%s" % (message[ 0 ], message[ 1 ] )
43
44     def createTable(self, tableName, theTable):
45         sqlString = "CREATE TABLE "+tableName+"("
46         for i in theTable: sqlString += i+", "
47         sqlString = sqlString[:len(sqlString)-2]
48         sqlString += ")"
49         print sqlString
50         try:
51             self.cursor.execute( sqlString )
```

```
52              self.cursor.execute("commit")
53          except MySQLdb.OperationalError, message:
54              errorMessage = "Error %d:\n%s" % (message[ 0 ], message[ 1 ] )
55
56
57
58 def main():
59     photoTable = [
60     "id INT PRIMARY KEY NOT NULL AUTO_INCREMENT",
61     "photoID varchar(16)",
62     "author VARCHAR(255)",
63     "title VARCHAR(255)",
64     "url VARCHAR(255)"
65     ]
66
67     tagsTable = [
68     "id INT PRIMARY KEY NOT NULL AUTO_INCREMENT",
69     "tag VARCHAR(255)"
70     ]
71     photos_tagsTable = [
72     "photoId INT",
73     "tagID INT"
74     ]
75     tC = TableCreator("TaggingDB")
76     tC.connectDB()
77     tC.setCursor()
78     tC.dropTable("Photos")
79     tC.dropTable("Tags")
80     tC.dropTable("Photos_Tags")
81
82     tC.createTable("Photos", photoTable)
83     tC.createTable("Tags", tagsTable)
84     tC.createTable("Photos_Tags", photos_tagsTable)
85     tC.dropCursor()
86     tC.dropConnection()
87
88
89
90 if __name__ == '__main__':
91     main()
```

TableCreator is fairly simple:

1. You import the MySqldb Python-to-MySQL interface library (line 12) so that its methods are available to you.

2. There are functions for utility operations (lines 19–55) for connecting to and disconnecting from the database, setting a cursor, and so on.

3. Beginning at line 58, a list of the three table schemas conforming to the specifications shown in Listings 14-3 through 14-5 is made.

4. At line 75, the simple process of dropping the tables (if they exist) and recreating them begins.

An alternative way of performing the table recreation chore is to create the needed SQL statements and feed them as a script to the standard input stream of the mysql interpreter — for example:

mysql –u username < someTableCreator.sql

This is certainly a time-honored practice, and there are two small advantages to using a general-purpose programming language approach. First, once the operating system tells the command-line interpreter that files ending in .py are the same as .exe (Windows) or .app (OS/X) or a.out files (Linux), you gain a double clickable application that you can distribute. Second, you can build more robust error handling into a full-blown program than a simple MySql input script. Which method you choose is mostly a matter of personal preference.

Using TableCreator, you can experiment with designing and recreating the data model as many times as you want. Now, of course, you need to put some content into the pristine tables so you can show off your great tag cloud.

Populating the Pictures Database

In Listing 14-8, a `photoLoader.py` is used to extract tags and photo identifiers from Flickr. Using the Flickr Python API, the program reads the topical descriptions from an external file and then stores their content in a MySql database.

Listing 14-8: photoLoader.py

PYTHON

```
 1 #!/usr/bin/env python
 2 # encoding: utf-8
 3 """
 4 photoLoader.py
 5 """
 6
 7 import os,sys
 8 import xmltramp
 9 # === Global imports
10 from globals import *
11 # === Local imports
12 from flickrPhotos import *
13 from dbHandler import DBHandler
14 from imageModel import ImageModel
15
16
17 # === global modules ===
18 def suggestedTopics(topicFile):
19     photoList = []
20     F = file(topicFile,"r")
21     for line in F.read().split('\n'):
22         if line == "":
23             print "Skipping ", line
24             continue
25         if line[0] == '#':
26             print "Skipping ", line
27             continue
28         photoList.append(str(line))
```

```
29      F.close()
30      return photoList
31
32 def main(argv=None):
33      print "User Name:",sys.argv[1],"Search Result Upper
   Bound:",sys.argv[2], "Tag File:", sys.argv[3]
    # typically dana_virtual 25        0 PhotoTopics.txt
34      USER_NAME = sys.argv[1]
35      UPPERBOUND = int(sys.argv[2])
36      TERMFILE = sys.argv[3]
37      tagList = suggestedTopics(TERMFILE)
38      for tag in tagList:
39          if tag is "": tagList.remove(tag)
40      client = FlickrPhotos(API_KEY)
41      db = DBHandler()
42      me = client.flickr_people_findByUserName(username=USER_NAME)
43      if me is None:
44          print "Can't Continue"
45          sys.exit(-1)
46      print "ME:", me
47      myID = me('nsid')
48      person = client.flickr_people_getInfo(user_id=myID)
49      db.connectDB()
50      # get photos from tags
51      for tag in tagList:
52          print "Searching for photos with tag :", tag
53          photos = client.flickr_photos_search(tags=tag)
54          db.setCursor()
55          limit = 0
56          for photo in photos: # the result set from Flickr
57              limit += 1
58              if limit >= UPPERBOUND: break
59              photoInfo = client.flickr_photos_getInfo⤶
   (photo_id=photo('id'))
60              for url in photoInfo.urls: ⤶
    # just one URL will be fine for this application
61                  thisURL = url
62                  break
63              imageModel = ImageModel(photoInfo('id'),⤶
   thisURL,photoInfo.title, photoInfo.owner('username'))
64              #print "IMAGEMODEL:", imageModel.id, "url :", ⤶
   imageModel.url ,"title:", imageModel.title, imageModel.author
65
66              if not db.insertDataIntoPhotos(imageModel.id, ⤶
   imageModel.author, imageModel.title, imageModel.url ):
67                  print "skipping this Photo"
68                  continue;
69              # get the max(id) from the model;
70              photoID = db.getID("Photos")
71              print "photo id", photoID
72
73              for pTag in photoInfo.tags:⤶
    # add all the tags for this photo to the tag DB
```

(continued)

Listing 14-8 *(continued)*

```
74                    imageModel.addTag(pTag('id'), pTag('author'), "",⊃
      pTag('raw'))
75              for i in imageModel.tags.iterkeys():
76                  print imageModel.id+">>>", imageModel.tags[i][2]
77                  db.insertDataIntoTags(imageModel.tags[i][2])
78                  tagID = db.getID("Tags")
79                  db.insertJoinTable(photoID, tagID)
80          db.dropCursor()
81
82      sqlSelect = """
83      SELECT PHOTOS.URL FROM PHOTOS,PHOTOS_TAGS,TAGS ⊃
      WHERE PHOTOS.ID = PHOTOS_TAGS.PHOTOID AND TAGS.ID = PHOTOS_TAGS.TAGID ⊃
      AND TAG      S.TAG = 'wildlife'
84      """
85      selectTagCounts = """
86      select  distinct(tag), count(tag)  from tags group by tag;
87      """
88
89      db.dropConnection()
90
91
92 if __name__ == "__main__":
93     sys.exitmain())
```

Notice the following about the code for Listing 14-8 (`photoLoader.py`):

❑ A couple of useful global variables are held in `globals.py` (line 10), which you can see in Listing 14-10.

❑ The details of interacting with the digital data source are implemented in `flickrPhoto.py`, imported on line 12.

❑ Much of the tedious "heavy lifting" of interacting with the database mechanism underlying the data model is held in a different module, `dbHandler.py`, imported on line 13.

❑ Finally, an intermediate representation is implemented in `imageModel.py`, imported on line 14. Invoking `photoLoader` from the command line typically looks like

```
Python photoLoader.py <username> 250 PhotoTopics.txt
```

where the arguments are an upper bound, which you'll use to limit the depth of data mining for photos with the seed tag from the topics specified in the file specified as the second argument.

❑ The action starts on line 32, where the command-line arguments are checked.

❑ On line 37, a list of the seed topic tags is extracted from the text file (`tagList = suggestedTopics (TERMFILE)`) and used as the loop controller starting at line 37 (`for tag in tagList: `).

❑ On line 53 (`photos = client.flickr_photos_search(tags=tag)`), you get a collection of the photos. At this point, you're probably frantically looking ahead to the `flickrPhotos` class, shown next in Listing 14-9, to find a function called `flickr_photos_search`. Actually, there isn't one, nor is there a `flickr_photos_getInfo` function (line 59). That's easy to explain, but let's cover the remainder of the main code first.

- ❏ One more thing to notice about line 59 is that the `photoInfo` object that's returned from the function seems to be in a form directly useable as a Python object. This is an effect of using the `xmltramp` XML parser/handler, which translates XML structures into equivalent Python.

- ❏ Although it's unlikely, as shown in Listing 14-9, the query could potentially return multiple photo URLs, but our model doesn't support it, so at line 60, you select only the first URL in the list of URLs.

- ❏ Once the photo information is stored into the Photos table, you iterate through the rest of the `photoInfo` structure to pick up the array of tags, which are then inserted into the Tags table at line 73.

Setting Up the Flickr Photo Interface

As mentioned earlier, the module shown in Listing 14-9, `flickrPhotos.py`, is responsible for managing the interface to the content provider.

Listing 14-9: flickrPhotos.py

PYTHON

```
 1  #!/usr/bin/env python
 2  import sys
 3  import os
 4  import xmltramp
 5  import codecs
 6  from types import *
 7  from urllib import urlencode
 8  import MySQLdb
 9  # === Global imports
10  from globals import *
11  # === Local imports
12  from dbHandler import DBHandler
13  from imageModel import ImageModel
14
15  class FlickrError(Exception):
16      def __init__(self, code, message):
17          self.code = code
18          self.message = message
19
20      def __str__(self):
21          return 'Flickr Error %s: %s' % (self.code, self.message)
22
23  class FlickrPhotos:
24      def __init__(self, api_key):
25          self.api_key = api_key
26
27      def __getattr__(self, method):
28          def method(_self=self, _method=method, **params):
29              _method = _method.replace("_", ".")
30              url = HOST + PATH + "?method=%s&%s&api_key=%s" % \
31                  (_method, urlencode(params), self.api_key)
32              print "Calling URL:",    url
```

(continued)

Listing 14-9 *(continued)*

```
33              try:
34                      rsp = xmltramp.load(url)
35              except IOError, msg:
36                      print "EXCEPTION >>>" , msg
37                      return None
38              return _self._parseResponse(rsp)
39          return method
40
41      def _parseResponse(self, rsp):
42          if rsp('stat') == 'fail':
43              raise FlickrError(rsp.err('code'), rsp.err('msg'))
44          try:
45                  return rsp[0]
46          except:
47                  return None
```

For Listing 14-9, line 27 begins an interesting block of code that represents a creative use of Python's meta-class capability. The calls from the photoLoader into the FlickrPhotos class call *methods*, which, as you can see, do not exist. When an attribute (an instance variable or a method) is not found, program control is transferred to __getattr__, which is in effect a "last chance" handler. Here, it creates the missing method and converts the method signature (on line 29) to something that can subsequently be passed to the Flickr REST API. Thus, the function call to flickr_photos_getInfo (Listing 14-6, line 45) is converted into flickr.photos.getInfo by the replacement of all "_" characters with "." characters (line 29). It was rather accommodating of Flickr to create call signatures so amenable to such manipulation. On the next line, the _method string is concatenated with the HOST and PATH strings (from globals.py) and a complete URL is formed. This is loaded by xmltramps, and on completion of the call, the result is parsed and a useable Python object returned.

ImageModel.py (shown in Listing 14-10) does little useful beyond ASCII encoding of tag data, which, because Flickr is an internationally accessed site, can be in a range of Unicode representations.

Listing 14-10: imageModel.py

PYTHON

```
1 #!/usr/bin/env python
2 class ImageModel:
3     def __init__(self, id, url , title, authorName):
4         self.id = id
5         self.url  = url
6         self.title = title
7         self.author = authorName
8         self.tags= {}
9
10    def addTag(self, id, author, authorName, tag):
11        self.tags[str(id)] = [
12            author.encode('ascii', 'replace'),
13            authorName.encode('ascii', 'replace'),
14            tag.encode('ascii', 'replace')
15            ]
```

DBHandler.py (see Listing 14-11) deals with the particular requirements of interfacing the MySql data store.

Listing 14-11: dbHandler.py

PYTHON

```
1  #!/usr/bin/env python
2  # encoding: utf-8
3  """
4  dbHandler.py
5
6  Created by dana on 2006-07-20.
7  Copyright (c) 2006 Professional Rich Internet Applications.
8  """
9  import sys
10 import xmltramp
11 from types import *
12 import MySQLdb
13 from globals import *
14
15 class DBHandler:
16     def __init__(self):
17         self.data = None
18         self.fields = None
19         self.connection = None
20
21     def connectDB(self):
22         try:
23             self.connection =  MySQLdb.connect(host="localhost", ⤶
user=USER, passwd=PASSWORD, db="TaggingDB" )
24         except MySQLdb.OperationalError, message:
25             errorMessage = "Error %d:\n%s" % (message[ 0 ], message[ 1 ] )
26             self.connection =    None
27
28     def setCursor(self):
29         try:
30             self.cursor = self.connection.cursor()
31         except MySQLdb.OperationalError, message:
32             errorMessage = "Error %d:\n%s" % (message[ 0 ], message[ 1 ] )
33             self.cursor = None
34
35     def dropCursor(self):self.cursor.close()
36     def dropConnection(self):self.connection.close()
37
38     def execCursor(self, sqlStatement):
39         try:
40             self.cursor.execute( sqlStatement )
41         except MySQLdb.OperationalError, message:
42             errorMessage = "Error %d:\n%s" % (message[ 0 ], message[ 1 ] )
43             return None
44
45     def insertDataIntoPhotos(self, ID, author, title,  url ):
46         try:
```

(continued)

Listing 14-11 *(continued)*

```
47              author = str(author)
48              url = str(url )
49              url = url .replace("'", "\\'")
50              #sqlStatement = "insert into TaggingDB.Photos (PHOTOID, ⤸
AUTHOR, TITLE, URL) values(\'"+id+"\',\'" \
51              #   +author+"\',\'"+title+"\',\'"+url+"\')"
52              sqlStatement = 'insert into TaggingDB.Photos (PHOTOID, ⤸
AUTHOR, TITLE, URL) values(' + \
53              '"' + str(ID) + '",' + \
54              '"' + str(author) + '",' + \
55              '"' + str(title) + '",' + \
56              '"' + str(url) +'")'
57              print "INSERT PHOTOS Statement:" , sqlStatement
58              self.execCursor(sqlStatement)
59              return True
60          except MySQLdb.OperationalError, message:
61              errorMessage = "PHOTOS Error %d:\n%s" % (message[ 0 ], ⤸
message[ 1 ] )
62              print "Failed to inset TaggingDB.Photos record"
63              return False
64          except:
65              print "Failed to inset TaggingDB.Photos record"
66              return False
67
68      def insertDataIntoTags(self, tag):
69          try:
70              tag = str(tag)
71              tag = tag.replace("'", "\\'")
72              sqlStatement = "insert into TaggingDB.Tags (TAG) ⤸
values(\'"+tag+"\')"
73              print "INSERT Statement:" , sqlStatement
74              self.execCursor(sqlStatement)
75          except MySQLdb.OperationalError, message:
76              errorMessage = "TAGS Error %d:\n%s" % (message[ 0 ],⤸
 message[ 1 ] )
77              print "Failed to inset TaggingDB.Tags record"
78      def insertJoinTable(self, photoID, tagID):
79          photoID = str(photoID)
80          tagID = str(tagID)
81          sqlStatement = "insert into TaggingDB.PHOTOS_TAGS (PHOTOID, ⤸
TAGID) values(\'"+photoID+"\',\'"+tagID +"\')"
82          print "INSERT Statement:" , sqlStatement
83          try:
84              self.execCursor(sqlStatement)
85          except MySQLdb.OperationalError, message:
86              errorMessage = "PHOTOS_TAGS Error %d:\n%s" % ⤸
(message[ 0 ], message[ 1 ] )
87              print "Failed to inset TaggingDB.Tags record"
88
89      def getID(self, tableName):
90          self.cursor.execute("select cast(Max(id) as unsigned integer) ⤸
from "+tableName)
91          result_set = self.cursor.fetchall()
92          return result_set[0][0]
```

Because the requirements of most relational databases are fairly similar, it's easy to adapt to others such as SQLite. Certainly, the code could be refactored to reuse some of the insertion code, but in Listing 14-12, we opted for readability over cleverness.

Listing 14-12: globals.py

```python
PYTHON
HOST = 'http://flickr.com'
PATH = '/services/rest/'
USER = 'YOUR_USER_NAME_HERE'
PASSWORD = 'YOUR_PASSWORD_HERE'
API_KEY = 'YOUR_API_KEY_HERE'
```

Globals is a home for any useful global symbols.

Running `PhotoLoader` from the command line with some popular search terms should result in a reasonably well-stocked data model, which enables you to move onto the next steps.

Scoring Tags

Now that the database is populated with some good data, you can finally accomplish the Tag Cloud application.

Using Styles to Implement the Tag Cloud

`Tagger.js` is imported in the `TagCloud.html` (refer to Listing 14-1) and provides the vital control logic for the Tag Cloud, as shown in Listing 14-13.

Listing 14-13: Tagger.js

```javascript
JAVASCRIPT
 1 // globals
 2 var _i = null;
 3 var _choices = ["smallestTag", "smallTag", "mediumTag", "largeTag", ⤶
     "largestTag"];
 4 var _cFn = null;
 5 var _x = null;
 6 var _newDOM = "cloud";
 7 var _granularity = null;
 8 var _fontDivisions = null;
 9
10 var xmlHttpReq = false;
11 var gotMetadata = function (oData) {
12     var payload = evalJSONRequest( oData);
13     var payloadLen =  payload.what.Result.length;
14     var maxCount = 1;
15     var currentCount = 0;
16     var acceptableMin = 10;
17     var tagDivs = [];
```

(continued)

Listing 14-13 *(continued)*

```
18
19      for (var i = 0;i < payload.what.Result.length;i++){
20          currentCount = parseInt(payload.what.Result[i].count);
21          if (currentCount > maxCount){ maxCount = currentCount;
22      }
23
24      log("Max Count:"+maxCount);
25      var granularity = maxCount / _choices.length;
26      _fontDivisions = [granularity, granularity * 2, ⤵
            granularity * 3, granularity * 4,  maxCount];
27      var x = null;
28      for (var i = 0; i < payloadLen; i++){
29          var count = parseInt(payload.what.Result[i].count);
30          if (count < acceptableMin){
31              continue;
32          }
33          x = createSpan(payload.what.Result[i].tag, count);
34          tagDivs.push(x);
35      }
36
37      replaceChildNodes( "cloud", P( null, tagDivs)); //MochiKit
38 };
39
40 var createSpan = function (tag, count) {
41      var choice = null;
42      for (var i =0; i < _fontDivisions.length; i++){
43          if (count <= _fontDivisions[i]){
44              choice = _choices[i];
45              break;
46          }
47      }
48      theTag = A( {href: "./PhotoGetter.cgi?tag="+tag}, tag );
49      _x = SPAN ({"class": choice }, theTag,  " ");
50      return [_x];
51 };
52 var metadataFetchFailed = function (err) {
53    log( "The metadata for MochiKit.Async could not be fetched :"+err);
54 };
55
56 var TagQuery = function () {
57      xmlHttpReq = getXMLHttpRequest()
58      log("got xmlHttpReq ");  // uses MochiKit logger
59      xmlHttpReq.open( "GET", "Tagger.cgi", true);
60      log("got xmlHttpReq.open OK ");
61      xmlHttpReq.setRequestHeader('Content-Type', ⤵
            'application/x-www-form-urlencoded');
62      log("got xmlHttpReq.setRequestHeader OK ");
63      var d = sendXMLHttpRequest( xmlHttpReq);
64      d.addCallbacks(gotMetadata, metadataFetchFailed);
65      log("got xmlHttpReq.sendXMLHttpRequest OK ");
66 }
```

For Listing 14-13, note the following:

❑ TagQuery is called from TagCloud (Listing 14-1) whenever the user clicks the Count Tags button. On line 57, an XMLHttpRequest is created, using a function wrapper from MochiKit that does away with the inline platform/browser check.

❑ Lines 58, 60, 62, and 65 show the use of MochiKit's logging function, which you can see in Figure 14-3.

❑ On line 64, callbacks for the successful and failure cases of the XMLHttpRequest are specified.

The request is made to `Tagger.cgi` on the local server, and that will handle access to the data model. It accesses the database and then returns JSON, which is then parsed within `gotMetadata`. Note that `evalJSONRequest`, also part of MochiKit, is simply a wrapper for JavaScript `eval`, so the caution mentioned in Chapter 4 applies: You shouldn't use it for untrusted sites. In this case, however, the site is yours, so this won't be a problem.

JSON Data from the Tagger

The JSON you create in `Tagger.cgi` and return is structured like this:

```
{ "what":{
    "Result":[
        {"tag":"06","count":"5"},
        {"tag":"1-5-Fav","count":"1"},
        {"tag":"105mm f/2.8G VR Micro","count":"1"},
        {"tag":"10D","count":"6"},
        {"tag":"120","count":"2"},
        {"tag":"14 juillet","count":"2"},
...
        {"tag":"Zwieselalm","count":"3"}
    ]
  }
}
```

In the preceding code, what is the key for a dictionary object `Result`, which in turn contains a large array, with each slot in the array containing a dictionary of tags and tag counts. Thus, you can access the returned payload using operators such as `payload.what.Result[i].tag` to refer to a tag text, and `payload.what.Result[i].count`, the count of the pictures the tag points to; `payload.what.Result.length` is the length of the `Result` array.

In `gotMetaData`, you make two passes through the `Result` array. The first yields the maximum count value. The second (beginning on line 27) assigns a font size to each of the terms. You also toss out any "small fish" from the tag cloud. Anything less than the acceptable minimum is eliminated; otherwise, you create a SPAN DOM element, push it onto the `tagDivs` array, and then replace the `cloud` DOM element. In `createSpan`, you use functions from the MochiKit.DOM library to construct a HYPERLINK (A) tag (line 48), and use that in turn to create a SPAN tag (line 49). Note that the URL referred to in the A tag is composed of `PhotoGetter.cgi` plus the tag itself, which, by virtue of being appended to the URL in HTTP GET request fashion, becomes available to the `PhotoGetter` server-side module.

In the Tag Cloud application, the size of the tag's fonts represents the relative popularity of the tag in the total universe of tags. The code arbitrarily uses five gradations — from `"smallestTag"` to `"largestTag"` (line 3). Line 6, `newDom`, is the same name as the SPAN tag in `TagCloud.html`. This DOM element will be replaced on every refresh, which occurs in the `gotMetadata` callback on line 37 (`replaceChildNodes(` `"cloud", P( null, tagDivs));`)

Shown next in Listing 14-14, `Tagger.cgi` is invoked from `Tagger.js`. Its job is to produce the tag cloud array elements fetched as a ResultSet via the call to `getDistinctTags()`, shown on line 11. You described the format of the returned JSON above; and on line 20 you can see how it is created.

Listing 14-14: Tagger.cgi

PYTHON
```
1 #!/usr/local/bin/python
2
3 import sys
4 import os
5 import cgi
6 import cgitb
7 from DBLookup import TagLookup
8
9 returnString = ""
10 t = TagLookup()
11 returnV = t.getDistinctTags()
12 returnString = "\"Result\":[\n"
13
14
15 for i in returnV:
16     returnString +="{\"tag\":"+ "\""+   i[0] +"\","
17     returnString +="\"count\":"+ "\""+   str(i[1]) +"\"},\n"
18 returnString = returnString[:len(returnString)-2]
19 print  >> sys.stdout, "\n"
20 print  >> sys.stdout, '{ "what":{\n'+ returnString +']\n}\n}'
```

Database Lookups

Now that you have content classified in the TaggingDB database, you can use `DBLookup.py` (Listing 14-15) and its convenience functions, which abstract away some of the chores related to extracting tag data from the backing store. The function `getTagCount(self, tag)` returns the count of tags matching the query target input as the `tag` argument to the function. `GetPhotoSet(self, tag)` returns a result set consisting of the rows from the database matching the query term `tag` passed to the function. Finally, a call to `getDistinctTags()` will produce a result set consisting of the unique tags from the Tags table.

Listing 14-15: DBLookup.py

PYTHON
```
1 #!/usr/bin/env python
2 import os, sys
3 import time
4 import MySQLdb
5
6 class TagLookup (object):
```

```
 7      def getTagCount(self, tag):
 8          try:
 9              connection = MySQLdb.connect(host="localhost", ⊃
                user="dana", passwd="xyzzy", db="TaggingDB" )
10          except MySQLdb.OperationalError, message:
11              return "CONNECTION Error %d:\n%s" %(message[0], message[1])
12              connection =   None
13          if connection is not None:
14              try:
15                  cursor = connection.cursor()
16              except MySQLdb.OperationalError, message:
17                  return "CURSOR Error %d:\n%s" % (message[0], message[1])
18                  cursor = None
19          if cursor is not None:
20              try:
21                  selectStmt = @ta
                    "select count(tag) from Tags where tag like \""+ tag+"\""
22                  cursor.execute(selectStmt)
23                  result_set = cursor.fetchall()
24                  return "Count of tags like '%s' :%s"  % @ta
                    (tag, result_set[-1][0])
25              except MySQLdb.OperationalError, message:
26                  return "SELECT Error %d:\n%s" % (message[0], message[1])
27
28      def getPhotoSet(self, tag):
29          try:
30              connection = MySQLdb.connect(host="localhost", ⊃
                user="xyzzy", passwd="xyzzy", db="TaggingDB" )
31          except MySQLdb.OperationalError, message:
32              return "CONNECTION Error %d:\n%s" % (message[0], message[1])
33              connection =   None
34          if connection is not None:
35              try:
36                  cursor = connection.cursor()
37              except MySQLdb.OperationalError, message:
38                  return "CURSOR Error %d:\n%s" %(message[0], message[1])
39                  cursor = None
40          if cursor is not None:
41              try:
42                  selectStmt = "SELECT PHOTOS.URL, PHOTOS.TITLE FROM ⊃
                    PHOTOS,PHOTOS_TAGS,TAGS   "+ \
43                  "WHERE PHOTOS.ID = PHOTOS_TAGS.PHOTOID AND "+ \
44                  "TAGS.ID = PHOTOS_TAGS.TAGID AND TAGS.TAG like \""+ tag+"\""
45                  cursor.execute(selectStmt)
46                  result_set = cursor.fetchall()
47                  return result_set
48              except MySQLdb.OperationalError, message:
49                  return "SELECT Error %d:\n%s" % (message[0], message[1])
50
51      def getDistinctTags(self):
52          selectStmt = "SELECT  DISTINCT(TAG), COUNT(TAG) ⊃
            FROM TAGS GROUP BY TAG"
53          try:
54              connection = MySQLdb.connect(host="localhost", ⊃
```

(continued)

Listing 14-15 *(continued)*

```
                         user="xyzzy", passwd="xyzzy", db="TaggingDB" )
55           except MySQLdb.OperationalError, message:
56               return "CONNECTION Error %d:\n%s" % (message[0], message[1 ] )
57               connection =    None
58        if connection is not None:
59            try:
60                cursor = connection.cursor()
61            except MySQLdb.OperationalError, message:
62                return "CURSOR Error %d:\n%s" % (message[0], message[1])
63                cursor = None
64        if cursor is not None:
65            try:
66                cursor.execute(selectStmt)
67                result_set = cursor.fetchall()
68                return result_set
69            except MySQLdb.OperationalError, message:
70                return "SELECT Error %d:\n%s" % (message[0], message[1])
```

As mentioned above, `Tagger.cgi` uses the functions from the `TagLookup` class in `DBHandler.py` to get a count of the distinct (nonduplicated) Tags and their textual content from the Tags table. Then, when a user click on a tag, `PhotoGetter.cgi`, shown in Listing 14-16, is invoked as a server-side URL. Remember that each tag was created with this hyperlink specified in its A tag, containing the actual link to the photo.

Server-Side CGI for Getting a Tagged Photo

`PhotoGetter.cgi`, shown in Listing 14-16, is a server-side Pythoncomponent or finding and presenting a photo from Flickr with a specific tag. As shown in Figure 14-4, when a user clicks the tag `"Orient Bay"`, the hyperlink to which the browser is redirected is the actual Flickr page containing the photo, as shown in Figure 14-5. This is one case where a full-page replacement is necessary, as Flickr "owns" the actual content, a fact that ought not be obscured.

Listing 14-16: PhotoGetter.cgi

PYTHON
```
1 #!/usr/local/bin/python
2 import cgi
3 import sys
4 import os
5 import cgitb
6 from DBLookup import TagLookup
7
8 cgitb.enable()
9 kvPairs = {'result':'UNKNOWN RESULT'}
10
11 returnString = ""
12 if os.environ.has_key('QUERY_STRING') and os.environ['QUERY_STRING'] != '':
13     kvPairs = os.environ['QUERY_STRING']
14
15 kvPairs = cgi.parse_qs(kvPairs)
16
17 t = TagLookup()
```

```
18 returnObject = t.getPhotoSet(kvPairs['tag'][0])
19
20 returnString = "\"" + str(returnObject) +  "\""
21 headers=['<!DOCTYPE html PUBLIC "-//W3C//DTD XHTML 1.0 ⤶
      Transitional//EN" "http://www.w3.org/TR/xhtml1/DTD/ ⤶
      xhtml1-transitional.dtd">',
22 '<html xmlns="http://www.w3.org/1999/xhtml" xml:lang="en" lang="en">',
23 '<head>',
24 '<meta http-equiv="Content-Type" content="text/html; charset=utf-8" />',
25 '<TITLE>Photo Results</TITLE>',
26 '<link rel="StyleSheet" href="../../stylesheets/RIAStyle1.css" ⤶
      TYPE="text/css">',
27 '<link rel="stylesheet" href="../../stylesheets/tag_cloud.css" ⤶
      type="text/css" />',
28 '</HEAD>',
29 '<BODY> ',
30 '<DIV CLASS="tag_cloud" ID="HERE">']
31 footers = [
32 '</DIV>',
33 '<BODY>',
34 '</HTML>'
35 ]
36 print  >> sys.stdout,'Content-type: text/html\n\n'
37 for h in headers:
38     print >> sys.stdout, h+"\n"
39 for r in returnObject:
40     print >> sys.stdout, '<a href="'+str(r[0])+'">'+str(r[1])+"</a> "
41 for f in footers:
42     print >> sys.stdout, "\n"+f
43 print  >> sys.stdout,  "\n</DIV>\n<BODY></HTML>"
```

For Listing 14-16, notice the following:

❑   `PhotoGetter.cgi` looks up the tag (line 17) represented by the tag passed as an argument to this cgi-bin module.

❑   Lines 12–15 show the Pythonic method for pulling arguments from the URL. Remember that arguments are appended to the URL and chained together delimited by the '?' character in an HTTP GET call. In this application, the argument is in the format *?tag=tag-text*.

❑   On line 18, the call is made to `getPhotoSet`, and this is turned into a SQL `select` statement.

❑   Line 42 in `DBLookup.py` creates the following statement:

```
"SELECT PHOTOS.URL, PHOTOS.TITLE FROM PHOTOS,PHOTOS_TAGS,TAGS
WHERE PHOTOS.ID = PHOTOS_TAGS.PHOTOID AND TAGS.ID = PHOTOS_TAGS.TAGID
AND TAGS.TAG like <the tag passed as a part of the invocation>"
```

Because each tag text can point to a large number of photos, the URLs and titles of a number of photos are selected. These are used to create a page that replaces the tag cloud page. The method for constructing the page is somewhat familiar to anyone who has done dynamic HTML generation.

❑   Lines 37–43 print, in order, the HTML header elements, a set of ANCHOR tags, and the HTML closing elements. Because the transport layer for the invocation of the `PhotoGetter.cgi` is HTTP, printing to `sys.stdout` effectively writes a new HTML page across the HTTP transport and into the waiting browser.

The Dynamically Generated RIAPage

The source for a given page of photos produced by PhotoGetter will strongly resemble Listing 14-17. An example can be seen in Figure 14-4.

Listing 14-17: Typical PhotoGetter-produced Web page

```html
HTML
<!DOCTYPE html PUBLIC "-//W3C//DTD XHTML 1.0 Transitional//EN"
"http://www.w3.org/TR/xhtml1/DTD/xhtml1-transitional.dtd">
<html xmlns="http://www.w3.org/1999/xhtml" xml:lang="en" lang="en">
<head>
<meta http-equiv="Content-Type" content="text/html; charset=utf-8" />
<title>Photo Results</titla>
<link rel="StyleSheet" href="../../stylesheets/RIAStyle1.css" TYPE="text/css">
<link rel="stylesheet" href="../../stylesheets/tag_cloud.css"  type="text/css" />
</head>
<body>
<div CLASS="tag_cloud" id="HERE">
<a href="http://www.flickr.com/photos/amoraleda/206972277/">Natural Bridges at
Sunset</a> 
<a href="http://www.flickr.com/photos/amoraleda/206971835/">Rolling Waves</a> 
<a href="http://www.flickr.com/photos/bloritsch/206417510/">r12-Provia-
100-0036</a> 
<a href="http://www.flickr.com/photos/bloritsch/206417478/">r12-Provia-
100-0035</a> 
...
<a href="http://www.flickr.com/photos/77639420@N00/153676042/">Lovers at
sunset</a> 
<a href="http://www.flickr.com/photos/77639420@N00/112856886/">Old Court House
Phillipsburg</a> 
<a href="http://www.flickr.com/photos/liang_2005/206939158/">Flower</a> 
</div>
</body>
</html>
```

Clicking any of the photo's links on that page navigates back to the original content page. You can see an example Figure 14-4. That's it — a complete tagging application, from data acquisition and mining to the tag cloud view and back to the original digital content.

Summary

This chapter showed you techniques for creating the output (i.e., view only) side of social tagging, and created a robust infrastructure for representing tags. Unlike many didactic examples, you can easily adapt and apply the techniques from the chapter. You saw that MochiKit is a valuable client-side library organized along "Pythonic" coding principles.

Looking ahead to Chapter 15, you will learn how to tag the easy way (after doing it the hard way here) and learn how apply the technique to the capstone application for the book.

Tagging and Rating(II): Using Social Capability

Man — a being in search of meaning.

— **Plato**

In Chapter 14, you implemented a tagging system for online digital content and perhaps saw the utility in having a capability for linking to content via the concept to which it related. Chapter 14 also introduced a primitive weighting system for deciding the popularity (perhaps even the worth) of various tags, and showed you how to depict ranking visually. The authors, however, saved most of the really critical content for this chapter — namely, how to use integrate tagging capability regardless of the makeup of the application.

> *See this discussion of tagging at* `www.technologyreview.com/TR35/TR35.aspx?`
> `TRID=432.`

To illustrate those concepts, you move from hand-coding Python, as described in Chapter 14, to a comprehensive framework (namely, Ruby on Rails), and turn from the example photo tagging exercise from the last chapter back to the capstone Stax application.

Stax So Far

First, let's do a short review of the current operational baseline. Then you will learn how to move that baseline forward with a tagging and searching capability. When you last visited Stax in Chapter 13, you saw one variation on the Stax theme. This chapter shows another variant, one somewhat closer to the design intent — as depicted in Figure 15-1.

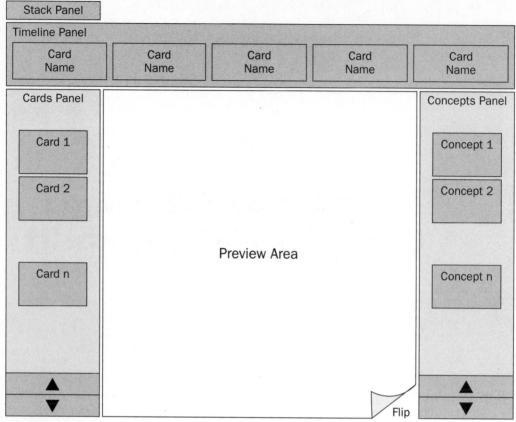

Figure 15-1

Stax Design Center

As Figure 15-1 shows, this Stax variant contains several rectilinear areas that comprise the RIAPage's application space. Remembering the Stax containment model, which specifies that a stack can have many cards, and a card can have many concepts, the visual model enables manipulation of all these elements. The example uses a three-column layout in which each column can expand as the window gracefully grows and shrinks as the window maximizes and minimizes. Columns are specified as consuming a fixed percentage of the browser's space.

Because much of the visual action takes place in the preview area, the example gives that space a greater share of the page (60%), and each of the other columns is allotted 20%. To illustrate tagging and searching without adding the complexity of the entire Stax application, the code for this variant deals only with the elements related to concepts and cards, ignoring stack and card composition. You can download the code for this version of Stax from `http://riabook.ideastax.com/Chapter09/ideaStax.zip` if you want to build along with the narrative in this chapter. A version complete with tagging can be downloaded from `http://riabook.ideastax.com/ideaStax.zip`. Figure 15-2 shows a screen shot of the actual application, the base Stax RIApage, in the form you'll start with in this chapter.

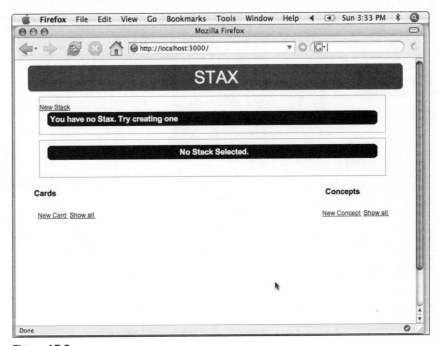

Figure 15-2

When you select a concept from the rightmost panel, the concept fills the preview area as rich data, just as it appears if you add it to a card. Similarly, a card selected from the leftmost panel displays in the preview area. An example of this interaction is shown in Figure 15-3. The user has selected a concept from the Concepts panel and it is expanded into the preview area.

Figure 15-3

The Edit button opens a rich text editor, and on updating the concept, the user is navigated back to the previous page. A user can also add a new concept; this navigates the user to the edit form reused from the edit and update capability. A field in the form is available for the user to specify a URL, which is used for a thumbnail picture to represent a concept visually; if one isn't supplied, the default Stax logo is used. The Editor panel interaction is shown in Figure 15-4. A similar preview and edit capability is available for a selected card. You create cards to contain a sequence of concepts, and you can later edit them by the addition or resequencing of concepts.

Retrieving Concepts and Cards

Thus far, absent any filtering, the Cards and Concepts panels list all possible cards and all possible concepts residing in the network cloud. Working with such overabundance is an obvious problem, as bad a problem as getting hundred or thousands of page hits from a search engine. Concepts and Cards panels would scroll on interminably. Ideally, Stax end users only want to view the collection of cards or concepts relevant to the themes of interest to them at any moment, and the collection should be retrievable using terms meaningful to them.

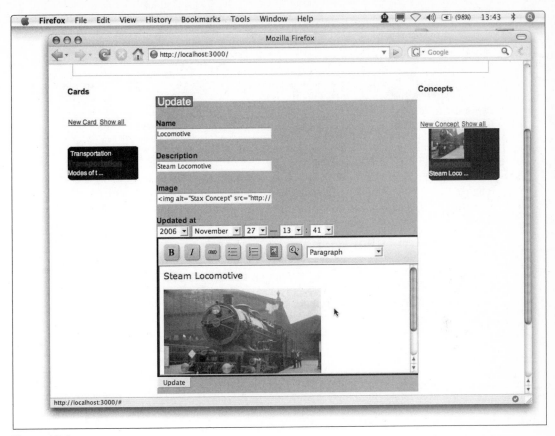

Figure 15-4

Retrieval results for digital content previously tagged via the collective "wisdom of crowds" should have a much higher yield than those that search engines supply. "Wisdom of crowds" tags employ similar concepts that are likely to be more consistent and coherent. It follows, then, that these tags are likely to yield very good search results; and in fact our experience on the open Web with sites such as del.icio.us support this assertion (see the sidebar "Serving the Collective Good: Tagging Folksonomy," in this section). Thus, the essence of social and collaborative capabilities in Web 2.0 is based on the ability to associate tags with content. That's the *why* of tagging and searching. In this chapter, you're about to turn Stax into a social and collaborative application by creating a filtering system that enables user-contributed tagging and later retrieval, and that's the *how*.

Getting Started: the Essential Elements

To get started, you need some essential elements. You need a baseline version of the Stax code, Ruby on Rails, and a relational database; the authors close MySQL for a variety of reasons, documented in various places in the book, but other options are possible with Rails. In the following sections, the essential ingredients are described.

Serving the Collective Good: Tagging Folksonomy

As del.icio.us innovator Joel Schachter explained in a 2006 interview with *MIT Technology Review*, attempting to improve future recall and retrieval of digital information (say, by making notes somewhere about what content "is" or "means" or by bookmarking sites) is based not on the fact that you or your RIA's user should do this, but because without a system such as you're going to implement in this chapter, the situation quickly gets out of hand. According to Schachter:

"You bookmark for one of two reasons: either you think you're going to need that page again somewhere down the road, or you don't have time to read it now, but you want to read it later. The challenge is, once you've got all these bookmarks, how do you manage them? The problem we're really dealing with is memory and recall, and using technology to make your memory more scalable." (For the full text of this interview, check out `www.technologyreview.com/TR35/TR35.aspx?TRID=432`).

Schachter also explains that "if you're trying to tag a page in a way that'll get you back there someday, you want to use *your* vocabulary, not someone else's." This applies to the digital content represented by concepts, cards, and stacks of cards in the book's capstone application. If multiple people in an enterprise environment, or a community of interest, act in their own (future) interests, they are willing to add tags in a way that is meaningful to each of them. In the aggregate, *all* the tags applied by *different* people yield a pretty good description to *anyone*, whether it is someone in the community intensely interested in the content or just a naïve searcher. By enabling a search with tagging, you enable both your own selfish goals (recalling something in words meaningful to you) as well as the broader — even altruistic — goals of supplying a potentially large number of descriptive terms that point to the same piece of digital content. To paraphrase Schachter, your goal is to design a system that "like a healthy market, turns individual self-interest into collective good."

Schachter also claims that the deep structure of the tagging system is largely irrelevant. For a counterpoint to his assertions, read the interview at the end of this chapter by semantic Web expert John Hebeler.

Stax

To begin, you need a baseline version of the Stax code, which you can download from `http://riabook.ideastax.com/ideaStax.zip`.

The version of Stax from the repository will function as documented in Chapter 9. This is the base to which you add tagging and search capabilities. As mentioned in Chapter 9, the widgEditor was bundled from `www.themaninblue.com/experiment/widgEditor/` with the code because of its small size and ease of integration with Rails and the Stax application in general. The authors like widgEditor because it provides basic rich font formatting such as bold, italics, links, and lists; and (some limited) font sizing. It also supports inline images and headings, and generates XHTML. In the preview areas of Stax, this is consumed as page formatting directives and produces properly formatted output. Although it is open source and included in the bundle you download from Subversion, should you ever want to re-install it (for example, to get a newer version), it's relatively painless to (re)install:

1. Download widgEditor from the URL cited above to a convenient folder and unzip it.

2. Your Stax root should be somewhere else on disk. This chapter uses `<application-root>`. Copy the `widgEditor.js` file into the `<application-root>/public/javascripts` folder. You can configure the buttons that appear in it by changing `widgToolbarItems` in this file.

3. Copy the `widgEditor.css` file into your application's `<application-root>/public/stylesheets` folder.

4. Copy all the button images from the unzipped distribution to your `<application-root>/public/images` folder.

5. Include the JavaScript and .css files in your layout file. For Stax, use a single layout file, which according to Rails convention is called `default.rhtml` and resides in `<application-root>/app/views/layouts/default.rhtml`. It is good practice to list the widgEditor's style sheet last in the chain, as shown in Listing 15-1.

Listing 15-1: Stax Rails layout default.rhtml

RHTML

```rhtml
<html xmlns="http://www.w3.org/1999/xhtml" xml:lang="en" lang="en">
<head>
<meta http-equiv="Content-Type" content="text/html; charset=UTF-8" />
  <%= stylesheet_link_tag 'main' %>
  <%= stylesheet_link_tag 'columns3'%>
  <%= stylesheet_link_tag 'istax'%>
  <%= stylesheet_link_tag 'scaffold'%>
  <%= stylesheet_link_tag 'info'%>
  <%= stylesheet_link_tag 'widgEditor'%>
  <%= javascript_include_tag :defaults %>
  <%= javascript_include_tag "widgEditor" %>

</head>
<body>
    <div id="header">
    <%= render :partial => 'shared/header' %>
    </div>
    <div id="notifications">
    <%= render :partial => 'shared/notifications' %>
    </div>
      <div id="main-container">
            <%= yield %>
      </div>
      <div id="footer">
    <%= render :partial => 'shared/footer' %>
</body>
</html>
```

The additional stylesheets give Stax its multipanel look and feel and supply the normal Rails appearance (for example, to enable easy creation of model manipulation via scaffolds).

6. With widgEditor installed, usage is simple; any text field you want to have rich text editing capabilities should be identified with a class attribute of `widgEditor`. A snippet of the Concept editor in Stax shows an example of this usage:

```
<%= start_form_tag :action => 'update', :id => @concept %>
...
<%= text_area 'concept', 'html', "cols" => "10", "rows"=>"12",
"class"=>"widgEditor" %>
</div>
<%= end_form_tag %>
```

Figure 15-5 shows the breakout of the Stax application into the canonical MVC elements. Rails favors (perhaps even demands) convention over configuration. This means that Rails will look for certain elements in explicit folder locations relative to your application root folder. As depicted in the figure, that snapshot of Stax you downloaded earlier in the chapter adheres to the Rails naming convention. Thus, all code for the concepts controller will be found in the folder `controllers` and in the file `concept_controller.rb`. Table 15-1, later in the chapter, describes Rails' folder conventions more formally.

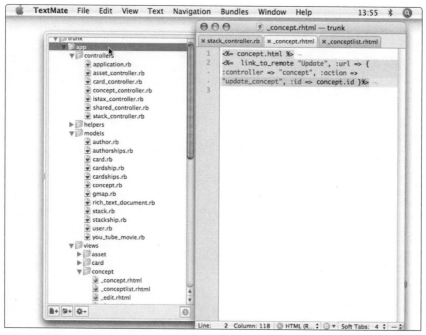

Figure 15-5

MySQL

The authors are extending the Stax code which was done in Chapter 10 in Rails. Although Rails is quite happy to work with a number of backing databases, Chapter 10 was set up to use MySQL, always a pretty good bet for its simplicity and ease of administration.

As stated in previous chapters, several pre-built bundles are available from mysql.org. If you have something else installed (for example, SQLite has grown very popular), you must adapt the code shown later in `Tagger.cgi` and `DBLookup.py`, and the model creation and photo and tag loaders described in

`TableCreator.py` and `PhotoLoader.py`. Post installation, you can check to assure that all is well with MySql, for example, that the executable was added to your PATH by the installer, by invoking MySQL from the command line (typically, `mysql -u username`).

Whenever your database access does not seem to work properly, remember the suggestions mentioned previously in Chapter 14: either configure MySQL on install to autostart on reboot, use one of the third-party MySql control panels, or keep the System Preference panel (OS/X) or the System Settings panel (Windows) in mind as possible causes.

Ruby on Rails

Rails is available from rubyonrails.org. For Windows, there's a self-executing installer; for OS/X (10.4), follow the installation instructions available at `http://developer.apple.com/tools/rubyonrails.html`, `http://hivelogic.com/articles/2005/12/01/ruby_rails_lighttpd_mysql_tiger developer.apple.com/tools/rubyonrails.html`, or `http://hivelogic.com/articles/2005/12/01/ruby_rails_lighttpd_mysql_tiger`. To align the Stax code you've already downloaded with the Rails release, you need to perform several tasks:

1. Edit `<application-root>/config/environment.rb`:

   ❑ Find the line similar to `RAILS_GEM_VERSION = '1.1.6'`, specifying the Rails version.

   ❑ Adjust it to agree with the version you downloaded from the Rails site.

   ❑ Additionally, because it is useful to modify subsequent dumps of the database schema to output in Ruby, rather than SQL, find the line `# config.active_record.schema_format = :sql in the file` and modify it to `config.active_record.schema_format = :ruby`.

2. Edit `<application-root>/config/database.yml` to reflect your database choices. The following code shows a database configuration file set up for mySQL. Depending on what database choices you make, you must adjust the configuration accordingly.

```
development:
  adapter: mysql
  database: istax_development
  username: ria
  password: ria
  host: localhost

# Warning: The database defined as 'test' will be erased and
# re-generated from your development database when you run 'rake'.
# Do not set this db to the same as development or production.
test:
  development
production:
  development
```

3. Create a database and authorize the username and password for the chosen data store. Typically, you follow steps such as these (exemplified for MySQL):

```
$ mysql -u root -p
> create database istax_development;
> use istax_development;
> grant all privileges on *.* to ria identified by 'ria';
```

4. Now that you've created a database and a user, you can use `rake db_schema_import` to create the supporting tables for the application by translating a Ruby definition of the schema (already supplied as an artifact of the Subversion check out) in SQL statements for your chosen database. The tables will exist after this step, but they will be empty of content.

Now you have Rails and Stax set up to operate as in Chapter 10. However, one additional step is required to add tagging capabilities.

Installing the acts_as_taggable plug-in

This is a Rails plug-in that you must install separately. You can do it once and it becomes part of your site's library. Install it after you've downloaded the Stax branch mentioned above from Subversion and installed it. Although the plug-in is already installed as a convenience to you, if you ever need to re-install it, you can do so by navigating to the root of your application using the following command-line script:

```
ruby script/plugin install acts_as_taggable
```

You'll see a number of statements written to stdout:

```
+ ./acts_as_taggable/init.rb
+ ./acts_as_taggable/lib/README
+ ./acts_as_taggable/lib/acts_as_taggable.rb
+ ./acts_as_taggable/lib/tag.rb
+ ./acts_as_taggable/lib/tagging.rb
+ ./acts_as_taggable/test/acts_as_taggable_test.rb
```

Next, you create models and table strategies to support tagging. In contrast to Chapter 9, where we created models for each new element of the application (concepts, cards, stacks), you should not generate the usual models for tags and taggings, the tables holding the tag text, and tag links to other tables, respectively. Rails knows the search path for models, and if you put in models of your own in the usual location (<application-root>/app/models), the actual model definitions installed above into <application-root>/vendor/plugins/lib are ignored.

You still need to create a migration with `script/generate migration <module name>`. It doesn't really matter what you call the migration module, but for the sake of this example, use something associated with the models you just generated. Therefore, in a terminal window, move to <application-root> and enter

```
./script/generate migration create_tags.
```

If you are using Windows, you will have to explicitly call the Ruby interpreter:

```
ruby ./script/generate migration create_tags
```

As a convenience, this has already been added to the zip file snapshot for the chapter's code, but it's beneficial for you to know how to accomplish it. It will generate a harmless error when you run it.

This writes something such as the following to stdout:

```
create db/010_create_tags.rb
```

Next, do a similar migration for taggings with `./script/generate migration create_taggings`. This yields a pair of files empty save for the method names `self.up`, which is used in this case for creating a new table, and `self.down`, which is used for dropping it. Modify `<version number>_create_tags.rb` to create a tags table with a single column, as shown in Listing 15-2. In the code snapshot package, this is contained in `<application-root>/db/migrate/006_create_tags.rb`.

Listing 15-2: create_tags.rb

RHTML
```rhtml
class CreateTags < ActiveRecord::Migration
  def self.up
    #Table for your Tags
    create_table :tags do |t|
      t.column :name, :string
    end
  end

  def self.down
    drop_table :tags
  end
end
```

Set up the taggings table migration as well, as shown in Listing 15-3. In the code snapshot package, this is contained in `<application-root>/db/migrate/010_create_taggings.rb`.

Listing 15-3: create_taggings.rb

RHTML
```rhtml
class CreateTaggings < ActiveRecord::Migration
  def self.up
    create_table :taggings do |t|
      t.column :tag_id, :integer
      #id of tagged object
      t.column :taggable_id, :integer
      #type of object tagged
      t.column :taggable_type, :string
    end
  end

  def self.down
    drop_table :taggings
  end
end
```

When we run the `rake migrate` command shortly, these tables are set up to support polymorphic tagging. Next, you must add a single line to every model you intend to use tags with. In this application, you want to tag all three elements in the hierarchy: Concepts, Cards, and Stacks. Listing 15-4 is an example of the concepts model in `concepts.rb`, post modification.

Listing 15-4: concept.rb

RUBY

```ruby
class Concept < ActiveRecord::Base
  # vaidations
  validates_presence_of :name
  validates_presence_of :description
  # Tagging
  acts_as_taggable

  # Relationships to Join Tables
  has_many :authorships, :as => :authorable
  has_many :cardships

  # Relationships to Entities via Through-Associations
  has_many :authors, :through => :authorships, :class_name => "User"
end
```

Validating Tagging via the console Command

This modification now permits you to associate tags with any arbitrary model. You can see this by opening the console and exercising a few methods defined in `acts_as_taggable.rb`. As depicted in Figure 15-6, we have created a few concepts, which we show using the graphical CocoaMySQL database tool.

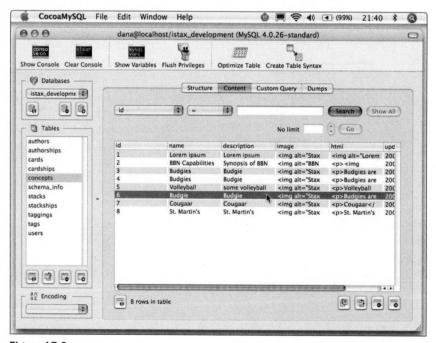

Figure 15-6

Now we'll use the console to choose any existing concept (in this case, concept 6) and tag it. If you have built and exercised the code in Chapter 9, you'll have existing concepts; otherwise, you'll want to run the application from `http://localhost:3000` and create a concept or two, in order to follow along with examining the output from `console` shown below, and to add tags to the concepts:

```
ruby script/console
Loading development environment.
>>  concept = Concept.find(6)
=> #<Concept:0x155016c @attributes={"html"=>"<p>Budgies are colorful too</p>",
"name"=>"Budgie Information", "updated_at"=>"2006-09-11 21:13:11", "id"=>"6",
"description"=>"Budgie information", "image"=>"<img alt=\"Stax Concept\"
src=\"../images/stax.png\" width=\"64\" height=\"64\"/>"}>
>> concept.tag_with("budgerigar, budgie, parakeet")
=> ["budgerigar", "budgie", "parakeet"]
```

The Concept class now has a `tag_with` method implemented through `acts_as_taggable`; next, you can reference the collection of associated tags by a tags method:

```
>> concept.tags.each do |t|
?>      puts t.name
>> end
==> budgerigar
==> budgie
==> parakeet
```

As you can see, the tags table now has three new entries, shown in Figure 15-7, and the relational join table taggings (shown in Figure 15-8) now link the row in the concepts table to the appropriate three rows in the tags table.

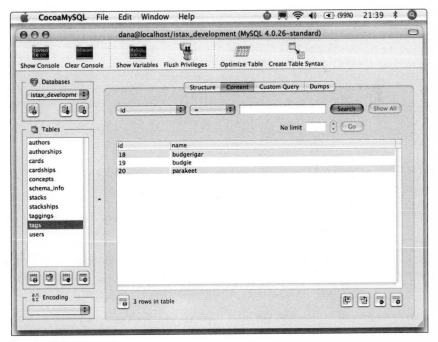

Figure 15-7

435

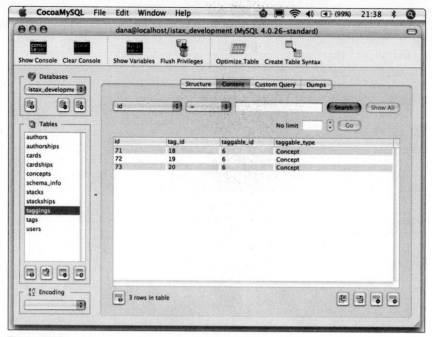

Figure 15-8

Further, the `concept` instance now has an associated array of tags:

```
>> concept
=> #<Concept:0x155016c @taggings=[], @tags=[#<Tag:0x2764d40
@attributes={"name"=>"budgerigar", "id"=>"18"}>, #<Tag:0x2764d04
@attributes={"name"=>"budgie", "id"=>"19"}>, #<Tag:0x2764cc8
@attributes={"name"=>"parakeet", "id"=>"20"}>], @attributes={"html"=>"<p>Budgies
are colorful too</p>", "name"=>"Budgie Information", "updated_at"=>"2006-09-11
21:13:11", "id"=>"6", "description"=>"Budgie information", "image"=>"<img
alt=\"Stax Concept\" src=\"../images/stax.png\" width=\"64\" height=\"64\"/>"}>
```

Finally, you can test the capability to find a set of objects by requesting it by tag, as shown here:

```
>> @cards = Card.find_tagged_with("Island")
=> [#<Card:0x152d1d0 @attributes={"name"=>"St. Martin's", "id"=>"5",
"description"=>"St. Martin's Information"}>]
```

This produces a result set with a single card in it. You use this capability later to implement the `searchtags` method added to the `card_controller` logic.

Note what Rails has done behind the scenes. For each base class you added to the mix in `acts_as_taggable`, it created the one-to-many relationships shown in Figures 15-7 and 15-8 with a couple of constructs (in `acts_as_taggable.rb`):

```
has_many :taggings, :as => :taggable, :dependent => true
has_many :tags, :through => :taggings
```

Notice that the `Tagging` class is smart enough to get the type of a tagged instance:

```
>> Tagging.tagged_class(concept)   #     => "Concept"
```

This is also shown in Figure 15-8. When you tagged the Concept, the Taggable class recorded that as well. The knowledge of which base class is tagged becomes useful, given that your goal is to tag all three major types of objects in Stax. As you can probably guess, the tag model definition declares

```
has_many :taggings
```

This means you can link a single tag to a number of concepts, card, or stacks—precisely the behavior you want. The `taggings` link tables' model declares (in `tagging.rb`) that it's on the "many" side of the one-to-many relationship with respect to both the Tags model and any class that mixes in the `taggable` attribute:

```
belongs_to :tag
belongs_to :taggable, :polymorphic => true
```

Implementing the Controllers and Views

Now that you have the supporting model, you need to learn how to add tag editing to the user experience and then how to use tagging to filter Cards and Concepts that appear in the left and right panels. The effect that you want to achieve in the editing user experience resembles Figure 15-9.

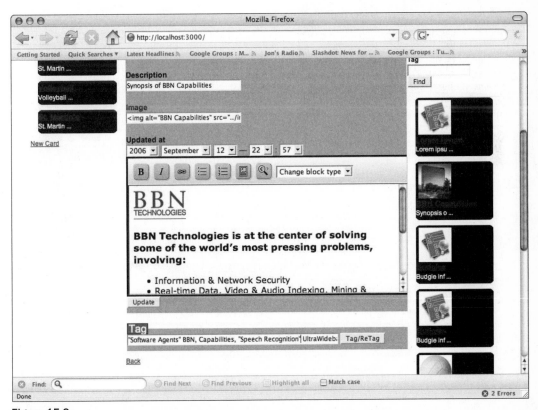

Figure 15-9

Whenever users create or update a card or a concept, they should also have the capability to add tags to the item. You can see a tag editing area at the bottom of the editing panel. When the user chooses Tag/Re-Tag, tags are posted to the model and the user can thereafter use them as a search mechanism. Using Search Tags to filter options of either Cards or Concepts is shown in Figure 15-10 (before a choice has been made) and Figure 15-11 (which shows Cards and Concept Filtered by User Tags).

In Figure 15-11 only the single Concept tagged "volleyball" (right panel, Tag text area) and the single Card tagged "island" (left panel, Tag text area) are now shown.

Implementation of the Controller and View Code

Let's examine how this is implemented from the controller and view code. Recall from Chapter 9 that you create the composite view through `index.rhtml`, and that the view has vertical panels: "mainleft" for Card thumbnails; "maincenter" for preview and edit; and "mainleft" for Concept thumbnails. To the "mainleft" <div> element, add a partial render, which you should call card/searchtags, as shown in Listing 15-5; and then do a similar operation for the "mainright" <div> element.

Figure 15-10

Figure 15-11

Listing 15-5: Index.rhtml (partial)

RHTML

```rhtml
<div id="mainleft" >
    <div class="spacer"></div>
    <h3>Cards</h3>
        <%= render :partial => 'card/searchtags' %>
      <div id="cardlist">
        <%= render :partial => 'card/cardlist', :locals => {:cards => @cards} %>
      </div>
</div>
```

and

```rhtml
<div id="mainright" >
    <div class="spacer"></div>
    <h3>Concepts</h3>
        <%= render :partial => 'concept/searchtags' %>
    <div id="conceptlist">
        <%= render :partial => 'concept/conceptlist', :locals => {:concepts =>
@concepts} %>
    </div>
</div>
```

Remember that partial renders are Rails' way to modularize view templates, which compose a piece of a larger page. The rendered form is shown in Figure 15-12.

Figure 15-12

Here, in both template stanzas, control is passed to `card_controller` or `concept_controller` as appropriate, which should contain a `searchtags` method. You will add one to `card_controller` now and a similar one to `concept_controller`. In `card_controller`, add the method `searchtags`. The method is shown in Listing 15-6.

Listing 15-6: card_controller.rb (partial)

RUBY

```
    class CardController < ApplicationController
 1  def searchtags
 2    # Multiplex based on request type
 3    respond_to do |type|
 4      type.html {}
 5      type.js do
 6        @cards = Card.find_tagged_with(params[:tag])
 7        render :partial => 'cardlist', :locals => {:cards => @cards}
 8      end
 9    end
10  end
```

Here, as documented in the comment, the code logic branches, depending on whether the request is an HTML request. If it is (line 4), then the logic just falls through and renders the search form (which you'll examine shortly), as shown in Figure 15-12. If it's a JavaScript AJAX request (line 5), then the logic branches to find the cards tagged with the contents of the text field ("Island"), shown in Figure 15-12.

On line 6 of the preceding code, a new cards collection smaller than the universe of all cards is created, and control is passed (line 7) to the HTML page where the `'cardlist'` <div> element is rerendered with the new set of cards. Remember that you exercised the `find_tagged_with` method of `taggable` when you looked at the various facets of the tagging implementation with the console above, and found that the query "Island" produced the one result, which is rendered (refer to Figure 15-12).

By looking at the source for the main page, you can see that pressing the submit ("Find") button does indeed create a new AJAX request, which is then routed by Rails to the proper controller by the script.aculo.us `Ajax.Updater` method:

```
<form action="/card/searchtags" method="post" onsubmit="new
Ajax.Updater('cardlist', '/card/searchtags', {asynchronous:true, evalScripts:true,
parameters:Form.serialize(this)}); return false;">
```

Implementing the Cardlist Renderer

You've seen the cardlist partial renderer before (in Chapter 10); a partial renderer, it calls another partial renderer (thumbnail), whose job it is to render each member of the collection of cards. Cardlist is both (initially) called to render thumbnails of all the cards in the data store, and again to render the list of tagged cards, as shown in Listing 15-7.

Listing 15-7: _cardlist.rhtml

RHTML

```
<div class="spacer"></div>
<%= render :partial => 'card/thumbnail', :collection => cards %>
<%= link_to "New Card", :controller => 'card', :action => 'create' %>
```

By convention, partial render names always begin with the underscore "_" character, which cues Rails as to their function. The highlighted RHTML directive above passes control to `_thumbnail.rhtml` for each member of the collection of cards that was just produced on line 7 of Listing 15-6.

Finally, the thumbnail rendering code shown in Listing 15-8 makes the pretty list of cards.

Listing 15-8: _thumbnail.rhtml

RHTML

```
1  <div class="darkbluecontainer">
2    <b class="dkbrtop"><b class="r1"></b> <b class="r2"></b>
     <b class="r3"></b> <b class="r4"></b></b>
3    <% if (thumbnail != nil) %>
4      <H3>
5         <%=  link_to_remote thumbnail.name,
6              :url => { :controller => "card",
7              :action => "load_card",
8              :id => thumbnail.id }
9         %>
10     </H3>
11
12     <% if((thumbnail.description != nil)&&
            (thumbnail.description.length> 10)) %>
13        <%= thumbnail.description[0,10]+" ..." %>
14     <% else %>
15        <%= thumbnail.description %>
16     <% end %>
17   <% end %>
18   <b class="dkbrbottom"><b class="r4"></b> <b class="r3"></b>
19   <b class="r2"></b> <b class="r1"></b></b>
20 </div>
21 <div class="spacer"></div>
```

This is primarily just display code with the exception of the `link_to_remote` tag beginning on line 5. The look and feel is dictated by the `istax.css` stylesheet. The `link_to_remote` directive creates an HTML <A> (link) tag to a remote action defined by `options[:url]` (using the `url_for` format) that's called in the background using XMLHttpRequest.

You can insert the result of that request into a DOM object whose id you can specify with `options[:update]`. Usually, the results are partially prepared by the controller with either `render_partial` or `render_partial_collection`. Typically, the tag produced in the HTML resembles

```
<a href="#" onclick="new Ajax.Request('/card/load_card/6', {asynchronous:true,
evalScripts:true}); return false;">Volleyball</a>
```

where the `/card/load_card/6` URL specified in the `Ajax.Request` method routes to a method called `load_card` in the `card_controller`, passing a parameter of '6'. Load_card looks like this:

```
def load_card
    @card = Card.find(params[:id]) rescue @card = nil
end
```

The card with id = 6 (the `params [:id]` argument to the `Card.find` class method) is yielded, and control is passed to a renderer also called `load_card`—in this case, implemented by `load_card.rjs`. Load_card replaces the `"maincontent"` <div> tag, the middle column, with the `concept.html` attribute of each concept contained within the card; remember from the card model that it maintains a one-to-many relationship with concepts:

```
class Card < ActiveRecord::Base
  # Tagging
  acts_as_taggable
  # Relationships to Join Tables
  has_many :stackships
  has_many :cardships
  has_many :authorships, :as => :authorable

  # Relationships to Entities via Through-Associations
  has_many :concepts, :through => :cardships
end
```

An identical implementation is created for the Concepts panel.

Certainly it seems as though there is a good deal of routing going on in this implementation, but once again it follows the general flow control model for any typical Rails application, as shown in Figure 15-13.

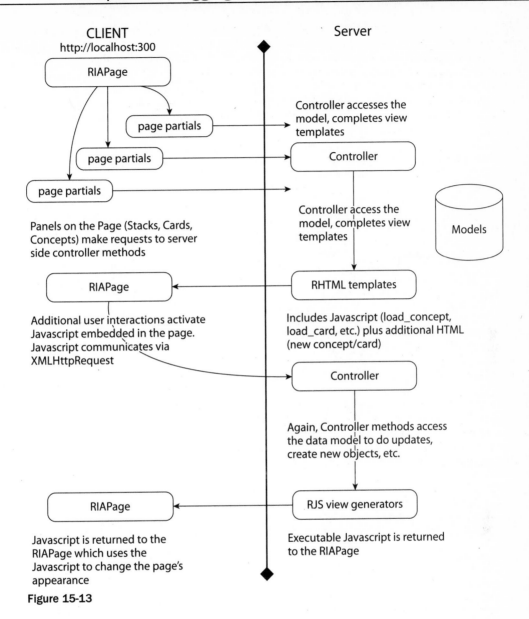

Figure 15-13

Adding a Tag Cloud

That's it — a complete tagging capability added to your Stax application. Suppose you wanted to add a tag cloud as shown in Chapter 14. While it's probably not as useful in this context, let's look at the design and implementation detail next.

As you may remember from Chapter 14, the technique you use to determine the size of fonts for tags in the tag cloud is to get a result set from the database that contained the tag and the number of times it was referenced. That's exactly what you do here, only this time in Rails, rather than Python. It would be nice if the `acts_as_taggable plugin` class had such a function because it's mixed into each of the object classes in the Stax application. Unfortunately, it doesn't implement such a method "out of the box." However, it's just a Ruby class, so you can certainly modify it to offer such a function. Find the `acts_as_taggable.rb` file and the open it with an editor. You want to modify the Singleton module to add the function shown in Listing 15-9.

Listing 15-9: acts_as_taggable.rb

RUBY

```ruby
module SingletonMethods ...
def tags_count(options)
    sql =  "SELECT  tags.id AS id, tags.name AS name, COUNT(*) AS count "
    sql << "FROM tags, taggings, #{table_name} "
    sql << "WHERE taggings.taggable_id = #{table_name}.#{primary_key} "
    sql << "AND taggings.tag_id = tags.id "
    sql << "AND #{sanitize_sql(options[:conditions])} " if options[:conditions]
    sql << "GROUP BY tags.name "
    sql << "HAVING count #{options[:count]} " if options[:count]
    sql << "ORDER BY #{options[:order]} " if options[:order]
    sql << "LIMIT #{options[:limit]} " if options[:limit]
    find_by_sql(sql)
end
end # module Singleton
```

The `acts_as_taggable` plug-in does a lot behind the scenes, but its major purpose is to implement all the complicated detail dealing with writing SQL against the actual underlying database implementation, converting from SQL result sets into a standard Rails model. After saving the file, you can test the method directly using the development console. Because it's a Singleton method, you want to invoke it through the class and not through an instance of a class:

```
$ script/console
>> @tags = Concept.tags_count :limit=> 100
>> @tags.each do |t|
?>   puts "Concept ID = #{t.name} count = #{t.count}\n"
>> end  ==>
Concept ID = 747 count = 1
Concept ID = Agents count = 1
Concept ID = BBN count = 1
Concept ID = Beach count = 1
Concept ID = budgerigar count = 3
Concept ID = budgie count = 3
... and so on
```

Now that you have the capability to get counts of tags, you can create the algorithm to size tags and link them to the subset of content (Stacks, Cards, or Concepts) to which they refer. To accomplish this most readily, you can use a Rails helper class method to implement the tag cloud itself. Remember that in the Rails worldview, subfolders are meaningful, as Table 15-1 reminds us. The folder containing these subfolders is (by Rail convention) <application-root>/app.

Table 15-1: Rails Folder Conventions

Subfolder	Description
models	All data models should appear in .rb files in the app/models folder.
	Models are the classes that model and wrap the data stored in our application's database. Rails models enable the application developer relative independence from caring deeply about the underlying database implementation.
controllers	All controllers should appear in .rb files of the app/controllers folder.
	Rails maps HTTP requests (both GET and POST) to controllers and methods within the controller. The form_remote_tag and link_to_remote (both of which are used in Stax) are good examples of how Rails resolves tags embedded in the RHTML page to controller methods. Look at the implementation of the search form in the _searchtags.rhtml partial renderer, or the link_to_remote in the _thumbnail.rhtml that renders Concepts and Cards into the middle column of the main page, for example.
views	All views and partial views should appear in .rhtml (Ruby embedded HTML) and .rjs (Ruby JavaScript) files in the app/views folder.
	RHTML files in the views subfolder are named to correspond with controllers or controller methods, and are the display templates that are filled in with data from the application's controllers. Once filled in properly, Rails converts them to HTML, and returns the result (full pages or <div>/<span> elements) to the user's browser. RJS files generate JavaScript to be rendered in a RIAPage and are what makes a page come to life. A good example in Stax of RJS interactivity is load_concept.rjs, which expands a thumbnail into the preview area by doing a partial HTML rendering, and achieves the special "grow" effect.
helpers	All helpers should appear in .rb files of the app/helpers folder.
	Helpers can be employed for a variety of miscellaneous uses, but they primarily are used to rid controller code of clutter. Helpers most often perform some manipulation that is orthogonal to the primary mission of the controller. Accordingly, writing the right helper seems just the right approach for creating our tag clouds. Although helpers haven't been used as yet, whenever you create a new Rails application, a set of empty helpers is generated for you.

Because the helper function is probably most appropriate to completing the RIAPage's main page (in the istax/index.rhtml file), you need to edit the istax helper file. Add the method shown in Listing 15-10 to the (previously empty) IstaxHelper class.

445

Listing 15-10: helpers/istaxHelper.rb

RUBY

```
 1 module IstaxHelper
 2   def tag_cloud(klazz, category_list)
 3     @tag_cloud = klazz.tags_count(:limit => 100)
 4     max = @tag_cloud[0].count.to_i
 5     min = @tag_cloud[0].count.to_i
 6
 7     # first pass
 8     @tag_cloud.each do |t|
 9       count = t.count.to_i
10       max = count  if count > max
11       min = count  if count < min
12     end
13     divisor = ((max - min) / category_list.size) + 1
14
15     # second pass
16     @tag_cloud.each do |t|
17       yield  t.name, category_list[t.count.to_i]
18     end
19   end
20 end
```

The helper algorithm is inspired by Tom Fakes at craz8.com, who suggested the following approach:

You want to pass in a class by name (e.g., Concept or Card), and a set of bins in which the tag should be slotted. This can take many forms; primarily it's used for returning a visual hint about how the tag should be rendered as HTML. The example (see Listing 15-11) renders each tag as a <SPAN> and uses the count returned by this `tag_cloud` helper to dictate the font size for the tag. You make a first pass to get `min` and `max` from the tag counts. This way, you know what the boundaries for the various categories are. You make a second pass to the co-routine shown in lines 16–18. This is where you return each pair (tag and count) back to the `index.rhtml` page.

You can see how the productions of the second pass are used in the page after you modify istax/ index.rhtml, next. Edit the file to modify the "mainright" <div>, adding the stanzas highlighted to what's already there (for this exercise, you'll just modify the Concepts panel).

Listing 15-11 istax/index.rhtml (revised)

RHTML

```
1 <div id="mainright" >
2     <div class="spacer"></div>
3     <h3>Concepts</h3>
4     <%= render :partial => 'concept/searchtags' %>
5     <%= link_to "New Concept", :controller => 'concept', :action =>
      'create'  %>
6     <br/>
7     <% tag_cloud(Concept, %w(x-small small medium large x-large))
      do |tag, font_size| %>
8     <span style="#{font_size}">
9     <%= link_to_remote  " #{tag} ",:update => "conceptlist", :url =>
      {:controller => "concept", :action => "searchtags", :tag => tag } %>
```

```
10      </span>
11        <% end %>
12      <br/>
13      <div id="conceptlist">
14      <%= render :partial => 'concept/conceptlist', :locals => {:concepts =>
@concepts} %>
15      </div>
16 </div> <!-- End of rightcontent div -->
```

What happens here?

❑   On line 7, you call the helper function as a part of a code block that passes the Concept class
     and a list of font sizes to tag_cloud, and then take its productions (Listing 15-10, lines 16–18)
     and use them to construct a <span> element.

❑   Within the <span>, you use the identical controller method you did in Listing 15-6, where the
     controller returns the reduced set of the class for rendering — only those objects that have been
     tagged with the tag in the tag cloud. Earlier in the chapter, you returned only those objects
     tagged with the search term entered into the search form, but the strategy is precisely the same.

Refreshing the browser demonstrates that the tag cloud is correctly implemented, as Figure 15-14 shows.

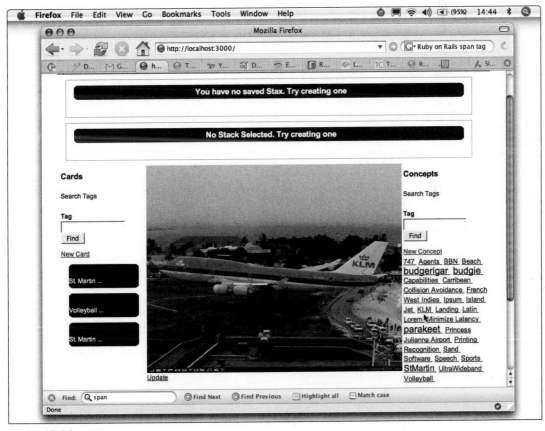

Figure 15-14

447

Part III: RIA Development in Depth

Notice from Figure 15-14 that when the total population of tagged objects is small (as it is here), the effect of adding another tag or so to the population appears more significant than it may really merit. In the tags shown, "budgie" is shown in a larger font than "747," but in the console session shown after Listing 15-9, the actual counts are 3 for "budgie" and 1 for "747"; not a very significant difference in fact. This reflects the simplicity of our algorithm.

Also notice that there is a possibility that stray tags may be left in the tags model, owing to the destructive algorithm used to store tags.

Summary

This chapter expanded on the principles learned in Chapter 14, attaching a tagging and searching capability to the capstone application. Additionally, you saw one strategy for adding a tag cloud as well, this time using Ruby on Rails instead of the Python in Chapter 14. Tagging is a critical aspect of Rich Internet Applications, and now you have code and two programming methods for achieving this important capability.

The Next Step — Semantic Tagging (Tags with Attitude)

What's the next step beyond "folkonomic tagging," tagging that uses simple unconnected words or phrases to describe digital content? This narrative by John Hebeler, Senior Scientist with BBN Technologies, who specializes in thinking about and building value using semantic Web and software agent technologies, previews the world beyond folkonomies.

Semantic tagging fills in the void between tags, the connections and relationships that change disjoint collections of words into thoughts and concepts.

Tagging, albeit wonderful, has some awful shortcomings. It depends on a direct hit of an ad hoc collection of letters (really just repeating symbols). The direct hit approach works fine when the collection of letters or tags is rare and your interest is broad. You will no doubt find *something* useful. However, the situation is quite the reverse when the collection of letters is common and your interest is specific. Here you need to shift through thousands of possibilities. Ten thousand responses is almost the same as zero — it just takes you longer to realize your failure.

Clearly, tags help us manage the ever-increasing digital mass that teases us with potential. The human-inserted tags are often quite accurate and appropriate. Popularity of tags helps converge to a true digital marker — a useful and credible pointer. However, the frustration can be quite palpable. You know the digital item is out there; if only you can construct the right tag combination to find it. You ask for yachts, but little comes back. Now, if only you had asked for boats. Did you ever ask for parts of boats — good luck. How about related forms of transportation? Oh, the weaknesses of tags go on.

What is missing? Simply tag dark matter. Tag dark matter represents the many relationships and connections between tags that are missing and then filled in by our brain when we process associated tags. Why was baseball and kindness tagged together? Oh, when you read it or see the picture you will get it. That's right, you will get it, but the unfortunately the tags do not. You are forced to wade through the actual responses searching for your concept that is hopefully connected to your chosen tag. There is no connection to the multiple tags describing an item except that they exist together. Why are they together? We figure that part out. What if those many connections were put into the tags — what if the tags related to themselves to form a real context that offers not just better explanations but also interesting paths to related information. Do that, and the tags have reached a new level — semantic tags.

Semantic tagging connects tags with each other in meaningful ways. Connections or links make the Internet. Now let us put that magic to work in producing useful information. An engine is connected to an automobile and to Google. Relationships separate the engines into two distinct concepts. This even extends beyond the chosen tag; an engine relates to power — the power of searching for Google and the horsepower for the automobile. However, with more connections, which engine becomes crystal clear.

Semantic tags move clouds to context structures. Connections fall into three major types: part of, type of, and peer. A mustang is a type of car and a type of horse, which are both, by the way, types of transportation. Finally, there is a catchall — peer relationships. Social networks are full of peer relationships. Here, as almost always, the relationship itself is important. I may have a relationship with Christi but what type of relationship? Is she my mother, my wife, my child, my enemy, my boss, and so on? Clearly, the relationships themselves are interesting and offer key digital markers to find our way through this ever-growing mess of possibilities. Semantic tags can also identify outliers — tags that do not seem to belong. This could indicate an error or truly something novel and exciting. Did you know that Jill won a Gold Medal at the Olympics? No, you don't add mustard to a car's engine.

Will this new semantic structure of relationships and links limit my freedom to search and tag? Well, truly structure is not a bad thing. Do you care about the structure of the building you're in? Do you care about the structure of this narrative? Do you care about the underlying structure of the universe? Well, maybe not. Structure usually gets the short end of the stick because it appears to threaten our precious freedoms. Actually, the opposite is true. Without structure, you would simply fall apart, as would this narrative. Structure enables freedom. And in this case, a semantic structure provides the freedom to find better information faster.

How do I use semantic tags? Semantic tags allow you to ask a question within a context. You don't simply supply keywords (although that would still work and may in many situations serve your purposes). You supply keywords properly related to other keywords to form a concept. For example, if I were searching for "John Smith," my friend, I could naively put the two keywords and then wade through thousands of responses, including ones that don't even refer to people. Now what if I provided a context tag that included John Smith friend of John Hebeler; works for BBN, etc. I would not have to provide too much context to find the exact John Smith. (Even easier in my case, because I have few friends). Interestingly enough, semantic responses also offer clear paths to related information — we get to explore our information to discover new stuff. How many friends does John have? Do I know any of them?

OK, so how do you create semantic tags? First, you start with some existing structure emanating from existing sources — you already know how much of this world fits together. How many ways can you assemble a Boeing 777? What are the symptoms of various diseases? How many relationships can you have with another human? Oh, there is lots of fuzziness in doing this, but you can't escape the truth in this. Many areas maintain well-known structures captured in formal ontologies. Ontologies are formal ways of relating concepts to one another through defined relationships and restrictions (see `www.w3.org/TR/owl-features`). Ontologies are a type of tagging with built-in relationships and restrictions — engines power automobiles, automobiles have four tires, etc. This existing structure maintains some heritage that I could choose to trust or not. I could combine various structures to establish my exact context. "I am looking for a doctor located in Africa with skills treating Lyme disease."

The challenge is mapping these well-known relationship or ontologies with the contributed tags to form semantic tags. Various initiatives are under way in both the academic and commercial worlds — so be on the look out for tags with attitude — semantic tags (and all your search dreams will come true)!

Part IV
Advanced Selected Topics

16

Providing an API

> *"The most profound technologies are those that disappear: they weave themselves into the fabric of everyday life until they are indistinguishable from it."*
>
> — **Mark Weiser**

In Chapter 3, you saw how easily you can create mashups to combine the strengths of several different services into a unified Web view. While the number of "power app" mashups are currently few (nearly all center on maps, photographs, or weather information), their utility is unquestionable. This chapter begins the final part of the book, which shows you how APIs can extend the reach of a RIA outside the Web and into applications on the desktop. Technologies such as widgets (Chapter 17) often provide desktops with a slice of a RIA's functionality with shortcuts to open the full Web view. Applications such as desktop blogging tools and RSS aggregators can use APIs to provide offline features. Digital immersive environments, too, such as Second Life (Chapter 18) are even beginning to support the features necessary to provide in-game representations of data pulled from a RIA's API. All of these examples of the new Web spreading across various media are examples of using a RIA's API.

An Application Programming Interface (API) is simply a well-defined contract stating how a particular service can be interacted with. It specifies a series of requests that can be made, the information required to accompany each request, and the promised results of the request if the preconditions are met. The results might be a status value representing the success of a remote action (such as saving a blog entry to the server-side database) or they may be a set of information for use by the API client (such as a list of photo URLs in a user's photo album).

Providing an API allows for greater integration of a RIA with other tools in ways that are both expected and unexpected. In either case, the result is often a positive one. It increases the usefulness of your service, increases the size of the audience, and provides mashup developers with a richer tool set from which to work.

This chapter briefly introduces common strategies for providing a developer API and preparing application logic for that API.

Choosing How to Expose Your Service

Fundamental to the task of providing an API is choosing how to make it available. There are a variety of methods over which a RIA might expose its functionality to third-party developers. Most Web applications today have APIs that sit atop the ubiquitous HyperText Transfer Protocol (HTTP) that drives the World Wide Web. In addition to using HTTP, there are a number of ways in which you can handle the format of requests and responses. In today's development environment, two alternatives reign supreme: home grown service definitions and Web Services.

The Home-Grown Solution

Home-grown solutions are the least complex and usually involve regular HTTP POST and GET requests to the Web server that mimic the way a Web browser would interact with it. The API server processes the incoming request just like any other and then returns some result, usually in the form of XML. This type of API is attractive for several reasons. It is simple to develop and understand because HTTP communication is built in to virtually all programming languages. Further, treating the API in this way enables it to be developed in the exact same way that the Web-facing portion of the API was developed, possibly even sharing Model and Controller code. This method of development is also the easiest to test because you can simulate API access using regular Web forms.

The home-grown method becomes problematic when considered in the greater context of RIA APIs. If every service defines its interface differently — the serialization protocols, the return values, the error codes — then API development on the Web might as well be back in the heydays of the mid-90s before standardizing languages such as XML were adopted. Every time a developer wants to use a new RIA API, that developer must build his or her own API access code from scratch, learning the new interface along the way. While this state of being certainly isn't ideal, you will soon see that in reality it is not as cumbersome as it may seem, and in fact is often more convenient than competing methods in reality.

The Web Service Solution

The primary competitor to the home-grown API strategy is the use of Web Services. The term *Web Services* generally refers to interactions governed according to the WS-* set of specifications published by the World Wide Web Consortium. Implementation of these specifications involves communicating procedure calls and their results via the Simple Object Access Protocol, or SOAP. The standardization of this XML-based serialization language allows for the creation of proxy objects on the client side so that developers can program as if a remote service is really just a local object. At runtime, invocation of the proxy object's methods triggers a behind-the-scenes SOAP request to the remote server to fetch the result.

Using Web Services and SOAP has a number of advantages. Serialization and deserialization of data is handled entirely by the SOAP library used to perform the communication. Many code-generation tools also exist to transform service descriptions (given in WSDL — the Web Services Description Language) into *stub code* that can be used to access the remote functionality. This means that developing with a RIA API can have all of the comforts of developing for a desktop environment: documentation, code auto-completion, and object-oriented style implementation encapsulation. While these are some powerful advantages, the setup cost of developing a Web Services-based API and setting up a client project to consume Web Services is often too great for developers to bear. For that reason, while they have taken hold in enterprise applications, they are seldom seen within the Web community.

Choosing Casual over Formal

Rich Internet Application APIs are one of the areas in which textbook knowledge runs slightly against empirical observation of the real world. Web Services are the most advanced and recent form of accessing remote functionality, so in the idealized world of print they are often held up as the modern-day standard for API development. In many senses this is true: Technologies such as SOAP, when they work, enable the automatic generation of proxy objects so that developers can make use of an external service with almost no knowledge that they are doing so. This, and a whole host of other features, prevents API users from having to learn a new API mechanism for every single RIA they wish to connect to.

In reality, though, nearly all RIAs on the Internet use just a set of regular HTTP requests to provide their API. This is partly because Web Services can be cumbersome to implement and partly because HTTP presents such a beautifully simple interface. Regardless of the reason, this book takes the empirically derived opinion that while Web Services can be an excellent choice for enterprise-level service development, rolling one's own HTTP-based API is a perfectly fine solution for most RIA developers.

In the end, the choice of which API implementation strategy to use is ultimately yours, and you should make it in the best interests of those who will be using it. The best way to understand what your users are up against is to sign up for developer accounts with several Web companies and experiment with *their* APIs. Learn what you like and don't like about how they expose their features, and incorporate these lessons into the implementation plan for your own API.

Exposing a Service over HTTP

The example Stax API that is presented later in this chapter follows the lead of most Web APIs today and makes use of the same types of HTTP calls that a Web browser makes. Exposing functionality in this way also happens to be the most simple of all possible choices in terms of implementation.

Because API calls come in the form of regular HTTP requests, no special application server (such as Tomcat) is needed, as it would be to host Web Services. Implementation of many API functions may be exactly the same as controller actions that already exist but with a different view returned. A good way to start out with such an API is to build an API controller that receives all requests to your domain under the subdirectory /api. As you add functions to the API, treat them as if you were developing for the Web face of your RIA and implement them as actions on the API controller. The views returned from these actions should be in some XML format defined by your API documentation.

Metering Access

One of the first questions that should enter any developer's mind when planning an API is "How do I control who uses this?" The need to control API access has nothing to do with greed or exclusivity (although it could), but rather with protecting the safety of your Web application. The Web-facing interface of a RIA is protected against denial-of-service attacks, intentional or unintentional, by a powerful limit: the users are human beings. When a user makes a mistake while using a RIA, it might mean traveling to the wrong page or clicking the wrong link. When an API developer makes a mistake, however, it may result in some remote computer accidentally making ten million rapid requests to your RIA's API. A *metered API* limits the possibility of such an accident causing damage.

Metering access also protects you or your company from the financial burden that can arise if your API becomes exceedingly popular. When the Web interface of your RIA becomes popular, you can offset any costs required to finance the increased traffic by adding revenue that these page views can generate. When an API becomes popular, however, there are few ways to turn this traffic into dollars; it is the API *users* who profit. If your API becomes so popular that its Web hosting fees begin to rise, metering access can become an essential safeguard against out-of-control hosting costs.

The word metering usually implies that some fee is associated with each use. In reality, most RIAs offer their API developers a generous number of free uses per day. If a Web site using the API becomes so popular that it hits the ceiling of the number of daily uses allowed by the API agreement, then the site's administrator can generally contact the provider of the API to negotiate an increase in the number of allowed daily uses, usually for a fee.

Web APIs are usually *stateless*, meaning that the only context the Web server can use in answering an API request is the data provided alongside the request itself. Because of this, the concept of "logging in" to an API account is impossible because the logged-in state is not transferred from one request to the next. The developer's credentials must instead be presented with every API request, so nearly all API metering schemes involve the use of API keys (or developer keys) that are a required argument of every exposed API method. Developers sign up for an individual key on the RIA's main Web site, and this key uniquely links them to their particular API account.

A key usually consists of a long semi-random string of characters, such as those that can be produced with a hashing algorithm such as MD5 or SHA. The key does not have to be short, like a regular password, because human beings are never supposed to use or memorize it; instead, it's stored as a constant in third-party code and provided by a user's Web applications at the time of request. Listing 16-1 shows one possible way of generating a developer key in Ruby.

Listing 16-1: Creating a Developer Key

Ruby

```ruby
def create_api_key(user_name)
  require "digest/sha2"
  developer_key = Digest::SHA256.hexdigest(Time.now.to_s + user_name)
end
```

Once you make developer keys available, some global policy should define how many requests per day (or some other unit of time) each developer should be allowed to make. The policy should be treated as global, but stored individually on each developer's database record to allow for individual adjustments to this limit in the future.

In the database layer of your Web application, create a table that stores the API key, developer information, and access information. Table 16-1 shows a simple example of what this table might look like.

Table 16-1: Table Structure for Metering Developer API Access

Field Name	Field Type	Field Description
api_user_id	Integer	A primary key for the table
email_address	String	A contact e-mail for this particular user
Name	String	The name of this API developer
api_key	String	The developer's API key
requests_today	Integer	The number of requests made by this developer today
last_request_date	Date	The date of the last request made. This determines when to reset the requests_today value.
max_allowed_requests_per_day	Integer	The maximum number of requests that this API user is allowed per day

The schema in Table 16-1 provides all the data needed to meter access based on a daily maximum:

❑   Each time a developer users an API method, the last_request_date is checked to determine whether it matches the current day. If it does not, the last_request_date updates to the current day and the requests_today field is set to zero.

❑   The requests_today field is checked against the max_allowed_requests_per_day value. If the former is greater than the latter, the request is denied. If the user has not reached his or her limit, the requests_today field is incremented and the record is saved to the database before responding to the API call.

Figure 16-1 shows a flowchart of the complete API authentication process. Armed with a database table as described by Table 16-1 and the authentication process shown in Figure 16-1, protecting your API is a simple task. Every API function begins by calling the authentication mechanism before attempting to proceed further. If the authentication is a success, the RIA processes and answers the API request. If the authentication is a failure, the RIA returns a predefined error code.

Depending on the type of RIA and the features in the API, developers might want to create a more secure authentication process in which a hash of the API key is stored instead of the key itself. This prevents a hacker who stealthily compromises the database data from being able to use the values within to access the API under the guise of other users.

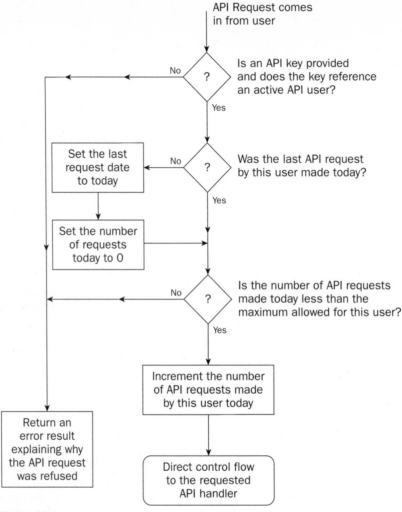

API Request comes
in from user

Is an API key provided
and does the key reference
an active API user?

No

Yes

Set the last
request date
to today

Was the last API request
by this user made today?

No

Yes

Set the number
of requests
today to 0

Is the number of API requests
made today less than the
maximum allowed for this user?

No

Yes

Increment the number
of API requests made
by this user today

Return an
error result
explaining why
the API request
was refused

Direct control flow
to the requested
API handler

Figure 16-1

Defining the Interface

When developing an API, the most important concern is not the model or the code; it is the API users. Because each API really has two users, the developer and the remote computer, a good interface definition is of great importance. Defining an API can take either a bottom-up or a top-down approach, depending on how the API is being exposed.

Developers who choose to use Web Services to provide an API to their Web application have the advantage of automatically generating a WSDL file from their API's controller code. WSDL, the Web Services Description Language, is a standard way of expressing the method calls available on a Web Service and the inputs and outputs that each expect. API users can download this file and use it to generate the proxy objects mentioned earlier in this chapter, completely eliminating the need to manually write any communication code. This method of service definition is usually a bottom-up approach, because the service definition is generated to reflect the code, instead of the other way around. Of course, the WSDL file should always be accompanied by clear human-readable documentation.

Developers who home-grow an HTTP-based service usually take a top-down approach to service description, starting out with documentation and then creating the implementation to match. Because there is no way to generate a formal service definition, the clarity and precision of your API description is of paramount importance. Clear descriptions of the required HTTP command, the style of argument encoding, enumerations of possible results, and the format in which results will be delivered are all required in order for users to properly interact with your service. It is advantageous to begin preliminary design sketches in a format that can be evolved into the official API documentation, solving two tasks at once.

An Example API for Stax

To continue with the Stax concept as a medium through which to provide examples, this section walks you through constructing a simple API that enables third-party software to upload images to the Stax library. Rather than just a simple image, the upload is a full-blown reusable "concept" within Stax. It has a name, description, tags, and an image file.

This section discusses the steps for writing documentation, and contains an example of the documentation you should write for the API. It then covers how to construct the API itself.

Writing Documentation

Because the Stax API is not Web Services–based, you use a top-down approach and begin by writing documentation:

1. Create a nicely typeset document that you can evolve into the official developer's guide.

2. Begin the document with a general description of how method calls should be made. Such a note isn't necessary if you use Web Services as the transport medium, because the name "Web Services" already implies a specific type of service definition and request-response behavior.

3. Once the manner in which API method calls should be made is clearly noted, create a Table of Contents that holds the method calls that might be available from Stax. Table 16-2 contains three possible API methods.

4. For each API method, create a small section that further describes the method, lists the required parameters to that method call, and describes the return result.

Documentation Sample

This section shows an example of what your API documentation should look like once you've followed the steps in the last section.

Making a Stax Method Call

Requests to the Stax API should be made with an HTTP POST connection to Stax. The URL for the request should be in the following form:

```
http://www.ideastax.com/api/{developer_key}/{command}
```

The variable {developer_key} should be substituted with your developer API key, and the variable {command} should be replaced with the particular API method you want to access.

Arguments for each command should be encoded in the regular format of HTTP POST variables. If one of the arguments is a file, the request should be sent as a multi-part post.

Results will always be returned in XML format specified by each particular API call. HTTP error codes will only be sent as a response in the event of an unforeseen server error and should be treated as a failed result.

Table 16-2: Methods Table of Contents

Command	Description
add_image_concept	Upload and add a new image concept to the Stax Library.
get_concept_html	Fetch the HTML rendering of an object in the Stax Library.
get_concepts_by_tag	Fetch a list of Stax Library objects that are tagged with the specified tag.

Method Details

add_image_concept

Upload and add a new image concept to the Stax Library.

Arguments

Name	Type	Description
Name	String	The short caption of the image
Description	String	A longer description of the image
Tags	String	A space-delineated list of tags that should be given to the image
File	MIME-encoded file	A file encoded in the same manner

Return Values

On success	`<result success="true" />`

On failure	`<result success="false" />`
	Or, if one or more reasons for the failure have been identified:
	`    <result success="false" >`
	`<reason>Reason for failure 1.</reason>`
	`<reason>Reason for failure 2....</reason>`
	`</result>`

get_concept_html

Fetch the HTML rendering of an object in the Stax Library.

Arguments

Name	Type	Description
id	Integer	The ID of the concept to fetch

Return Values

On success	`<div class="result success">`
	`<!-- The HTML for the concept would be here -->`
	`</div>`

On failure	`<div class="result failure">`
	`<p class="reason">An error message would go here.</p>`
	`</div>`

get_concepts_by_tag

Fetch a list of Stax Library objects that are tagged with the specified tag.

Arguments

Name	Type	Description
tag	String	The tag with which to look up a list of concepts

Return Values

On success	```<result success="true"> <concepts> <concept name="The Name" type="The Type" id="The ID" /> </concepts> </result>```

On failure	`<result success="false" />`
	Or, if one or more reasons for the failure have been identified:
	`<result success="false" >`
	`  <reason>Reason for failure 1.</reason>`
	`  <reason>Reason for failure 2....</reason>`
	`</result>`

Constructing the API

Finally, the following sections show an example implementation of the `add_image_concept` for the Stax API. The required duties of this API call are twofold: It must allow a user to upload an image to the Web server and it must create a new image concept in the Stax library that references that image. Because this API is provided over a regular HTTP connection, create the space to provide the functionality by generating a new Controller called the `ApiController`. Before creating the `add_image_concept` action, several helper functions must be built as private members on the `ApiController`.

Creating a New Image Concept

Listing 16-2 shows the private method on the API controller that creates a new image concept and saves it using ActiveRecord. This code assumes the existence of an ActiveRecord model called `Concept` that stores the name, description, and HTML depiction of a concept. The model also implements the `Taggable` interface so it can be tagged with the `tag_with` command.

Listing 16-2: add_concept function

Ruby

```ruby
def add_concept(name, description, tags, image_filename)
    concept = Concept.new
    concept.name = name
    concept.description = description
    concept.tag_with tags
    concept.image = ''
    concept.html = "<img src=\"/images/upload/#{image_filename}\"/>"
    return concept.save
end
```

Saving the Uploaded Image File

In order to use this function, the image first has to be saved in a location within the document root of the Web server. Listing 16-3 shows a `save_file` function that takes a multi-part encoded file from the post variables and the fully qualified path to the desired save location. After performing several checks to ensure that the file is of an acceptable size and type, it opens the destination file for writing and reads the uploaded file into it.

Listing 16-3: save_file function

Ruby

```ruby
def save_file(uploaded_file, desired_location)
  image_types =
    ["image/jpeg", "image/pjpeg", "image/gif", "image/png", "image/x-png"]
  max_file_size = 2097152

  # Make sure file is there
  if uploaded_file.blank?
    return false
  end

  # Make sure file isn't empty
  if (uploaded_file.size == 0)
    return false
  end

  # Make sure file is of correct type
  if (! image_types.include? uploaded_file.content_type.chomp)
    return false
  end

  # Make sure file isn't too big
  if (! (uploaded_file.size < max_file_size))
    return false
  end

  # Rewind the file
  file.rewind

  # Open the destination file and
  begin
    File.open(path_to_file(desired_location), "wb") {
      |f| f.write(uploaded_file.read)
    }
  rescue
    return false
  end

  return true
end
```

Adding the API Method

The actual `add_image_concept` action (see Listing 16-4) that is exposed to third-party developers via the `ApiController` will use the `add_concept` and `save_file` functions. This action loads the four fields required by the API description. It creates a new filename based on the original filename of the uploaded file using the `sanitize_filename` and `path_to_file` functions (shown in Listing 16-5), saves the uploaded image to a Web-accessible directory, and then records the concept in the database. Only if all three of these actions succeed does the function return a successful result.

Listing 16-4: The add_image_concept function

Ruby
```ruby
def add_image_concept

    name = params[:name]
    description = params[:description]
    tags = params[:tags]
    file = params[:file]

    # Make sure the name won't overwrite another.
    i=1
    new_name = sanitize_filename(file.original_filename)
    new_name = new_name+(i+=1).to_s while File.exists? (path_to_file (new_name))

    if (    save_file(file, new_name)
         && add_concept(name, description, tags, new_name))
      render :text => '<result success="true" />'
    else
      render :text => '<result success="false" />'
    end

end
```

No validation needs to be done on the posted form data because it is assumed that, in Rails fashion, validation rules are put on the ActiveRecord model object itself, so failing to provide a name or a description causes the `save_file(file, new_name)` function to return `false` because the `concept.save` function will return `false`.

The `sanitize_filename` function and the code that uses it are tricks that you can find on the Ruby on Rails wiki page. Used in combination with the `path_to_file` function, which provides the full path to the `upload` directory, the code in Listing 16-5 ensures that an incoming filename is valid by replacing non-alphanumeric characters with underscore characters.

Listing 16-5: The sanitize_filename and path_to_file functions

Ruby
```ruby
def sanitize_filename(name)
    File.basename(name.gsub('\\', '/')).gsub(/[^\w\.\-]/,'_')
  end

def path_to_file ( filename )
    RAILS_ROOT + "/public/images/upload/" + filename
  end
```

After the filename is sanitized, the following line appends numbers to the end of the filename until the name does not refer to a file already on the disk. This prevents two users with identically named files from overwriting each other's uploads.

```
new_name = new_name+(i+=1).to_s while File.exists? (path_to_file (new_name))
```

Adding Authentication

A developer key-based access control mechanism is not a part of this API, but adding it is simply a matter of integrating the logic from Figure 16-1 into the API controller so that it runs before control is directed to any of the actions on that controller. In Ruby on Rails, this type of catchall check can be done with what is called a *filter*. The following `before_filter` command causes the function `check_api_key` to execute before any controller action is called:

```
class ApiController < ApplicationController
  before_filter :check_api_key

  def add_image_concept
    # Implementation here...
  end

  ...
  ...

  def check_api_key
    # Check the developer's API key using the process in Figure 17-1
    # and possibly halt request with an error result. If the request is
    # valid, simply return with a value of "true"
  end
end
```

The `check_api_key` function then performs the logic outlined in Figure 16-1. If the developer key is valid and has not yet exceeded the number of daily uses, then the function simply returns without any control-changing result. If the developer key is not valid or has exceeded the daily limit, the `check_api_key` function renders an error response and halts execution of the controller code.

With the API controller and the `add_image_concept` action in place, any third-party application can post a new image concept to Stax by sending an HTTP POST request to `http://www.ideastax.com/api/add_image_concept` and providing the proper post variables.

Summary

Providing an API is becoming an essential part of every successful RIA and can lead to many positive benefits. API access enables a RIA's capabilities to extend outside of its main interface into other Web sites, desktop operating systems, and desktop applications. The results are increased use of and exposure to your RIA, and if you are lucky, unforeseen creative tools conjured up by API developers. Several strategies for exposing an API exist, but the two most common by far are HTTP and Web Services. HTTP tends to be the preferred method among RIA developers.

This chapter discussed one strategy for metering access to an API through the use of developer keys. Metering an API from the beginning is important so that you can maintain quality of service if the API becomes wildly popular. It also stressed the importance of providing good API documentation, and included an example developer's document for a portion of a potential Stax API. Finally, an implementation for one function of the Stax API was given in Ruby on Rails.

The last two chapters continue the API theme from the standpoint of the third-party developer. Chapter 17 demonstrates how to use desktop widgets to provide a tiny, always-on window into a RIA, and Chapter 18 explores ways in which Web APIs can extend all the way into three-dimensional virtual worlds.

17

RIA Widgets

The case for desktop Widgets (Dashboard Widgets on Mac OS X, Gadgets on Windows Vista, and Yahoo! Widgets on both platforms) may not seem to be exceptionally strong, given the amount of emphasis we have placed on moving applications into the network cloud, but there is a case for lightweight functionality resident on the desktop.

Consider that lightweight applications have been a part of desktop computing as far back as Borland Corporation's Sidekick on MS-DOS. These early expressions of handy utilities that were always "just there" invoked by some simple keyboard combination, needing no explicit launch, were called *terminate and stay resident (TSR)* programs. TSRs went out of fashion with the advent of Windows and true multi-tasking, whereby multiple programs could be launched and the cost of switching between them was (for the user) essentially nil. Perhaps more important, the very idea of manipulating the operating system's low-level interrupts seemed like tempting fate in the era of worms and viruses. With the disappearance of MS-DOS and the advent of more capable operating systems, the OS could now take care of swapping out application pages, and the user could have as many programs running apparently simultaneously as long as they had sufficient RAM and the attention span to handle multiple tasks.

Still, there was something annoying about going to the Start menu, finding the Accessories entry, selecting Calculator, and waiting for it to launch just to add up a column of numbers. Perhaps it derived from a mismatch in user expectations, in which there seemed to be multiple kinds of applications: certain ones that users commonly accessed for "office productivity" type activities, another one for simple tasks. At times, the dividing line between the two actually seemed to fairly blur, but like art or obscenity, you knew which was which when you experienced it.

Clearly, there are these things called *applications*. This class of multi-functional and expensive software is created by a large software company. A user knows them because they are sold in cardboard boxes and occupy shelf space in PC stores. Vendors fight to dominate shelf space and positioning in the brick and mortar retail world. A word processor performs a variety of functions, from layout and font specification to spell checking. To the user, it is OK for them to be complex, consume a lot of memory, and have huge menu systems and steep learning curves.

Then there was a second class of executable code. These were simpler in function, and their utility was patently obvious from their user interface. They shouldn't have to be "launched" in any way, and a user shouldn't have to go looking for them. A calculator simply dealt with a sequence of number transforms, a clock simply displayed time. These things seemed to be more like utility functions that are somehow "different" for users than an application, though perhaps not obviously so to a developer.

Thus, a need for this second type of application has always been a part of the end users' computing experience, and operating systems have always provided some method for invoking and using them. In this chapter, you explore a new way of creating handy, easily invoked utility functions that go a bit further than the previous generation's small applications, and you'll find out why *plus ça change, plus c'est la même chose* — the more a thing changes, the more it is the same.

Surveying the Field

First, consider the gross features of these desktop-resident micro applications. In general, three open API engines are used to produce and run them:

❑   **Google Desktop Gadgets** — Available for Microsoft Windows, this application logic may be either VBScript or JavaScript. The Gadget may interact with external URLs and on-platform ActiveX components.

❑   **Apple Dashboard Widgets** — This is Apple's approach to a Widget framework included in Mac's OS/X. A Widget definition is similar to a Web site, consisting of a combination of HTML, CSS, and JavaScript.

❑   **Yahoo Widgets** — The only open API toolkit and engine that can run on both Windows and Mac OS/X, this engine/runner is not built into the operating system, but exists as a standalone application. In order to achieve some semblance of seamless operation, the engine can be launched on startup either in Windows or on Mac OS/X.

Accordingly, we've decided to illustrate the concept using Yahoo's Widget set and engine. The simple project requires a little preparation, described in the next section.

Getting Started: the Essential Elements

Before getting into the structure and content of a Yahoo! Widget, you need to download and install a few basic components. Of course, you need a text editor such as GNU Emacs, and you may also want to install a graphics application such as Gimp or Photoshop. This won't be necessary to run the examples, but you'll soon see that the definition of a Widget generally requires the creation of a variety of images. The following Yahoo! Widget-specific components are also required:

❑ **Yahoo! Widget Engine** — Available for both Mac and Windows platforms at `http://widgets`
`.yahoo.com/download/`. The engine is the component that enables you to install and run the
Widgets that you download and develop. The engine currently comes with several Widgets that
you can try out and whose source code you can examine.

❑ **Yahoo! Widgets Developer SDK** — Available at `http://widgets.yahoo.com/workshop/`. The
developer SDK enables you to write your own Widgets on Windows. As it provides a variety of
utilities included in Mac OS/X, it's only required if you're running on a Windows machine.

❑ **Yahoo! Widget Engine Reference Guide** — Along with several other reference documents, this
is also available at `http://widgets.yahoo.com/workshop/`. This guide serves as the primary
reference for the JavaScript extensions available to Yahoo! Widgets, as well as the details of the
format and composition of Widget files.

❑ **Widget Converter Widget** — Available at `http://widgets.yahoo.com/gallery/view`
`.php?widget=40093`. This is a very handy Widget that isn't currently bundled with the
Developer SDK. It can be used to convert Widgets into a variety of formats.

See the specific Web sites for detailed documentation on installation. Note that for the examples in this
chapter, the authors are using a Windows XP version 3.1.4 of the Widget Engine, version 3.1.2 of the
Widget SDK, and version 2.0 of the Widget Converter.

Unpacking a Widget with the Widget Converter

You may have noticed when you installed the Widget Engine, a directory named `My Widgets` containing
a variety of `.widget` files was created under the `My Documents` folder. These files define a single packaged
Widget that is similar to a zip file. Each file simply contains all the JavaScript, Widget, and image files
needed to run a Widget.

One convenient aspect of the Yahoo! Widget Engine is that a wide variety of Widgets are included, and
you can download many more from the Widget gallery at `widgets.yahoo.com/gallery/`. In addition,
you can dissect and examine any of these Widgets in detail, giving the Widget developer a wide variety
of examples to explore.

When you install the Widget Engine, you get an informative tutorial that shows you how to load,
unload, and otherwise interact with Widgets. This isn't covered here, but is available online. If you miss
this during the installation, or want a refresher, see `http://widgets.yahoo.com/basics/`.

The first step to looking at the internals of a Widget is to unpack the contents of the Widget into a directory. The Widget Converter Widget, shown in Figure 17-1, makes this a simple drag and drop process.

Figure 17-1

To use the Widget Converter:

1. Drag a Widget from a desktop folder into the dark-gray bar with the text No File Selected near the top of the Widget. For example, you can extract the contents of the Widget Converter itself by dragging the `Widget_converter-win.` widget into the Widget.

2. Indicate the type of conversion to perform in the drop-down list. Although you can set this to one of three options depending on the input file or folder, set this to Folder so that you can view the source of the Widget. The options are as follows:

   ❑ **Flat File** — Translates a directory containing a Widget into a Widget file (e.g., `Calendar.widget`). You can use this to package all the pieces of your Widget together when you're ready to distribute it. Note that this is the recommended format for deploying your Widgets.

   ❑ **Folder** — Translates a Widget file (e.g., `Battery.widget`) into a directory so that you can view and manipulate each of its components.

   ❑ **Zipped** — Produces a Widget file (e.g., `Calendar.widget`) that is similar to a flat file, but compressed so that the download is smaller. This is not recommended for versions of the Widget Engine after version 3.0 because the compression causes significant performance issues.

3. Press the Convert button. That's all there is to it! After a brief delay, you'll be notified that your Widget was converted, as shown in Figure 17-2.

Figure 17-2

File Structure and Packaging

Once expanded, you're ready to take a look at the source of the Widget. Looking at the directories created by the Widget Converter shows several directories and files common to all Widgets, including the following:

```
Widget_Converter-win
 + Contents
   - Converter.kon
   + Resources
     - About.png
     - base.png
   ...
```

The top-level directory name corresponds to the name of the Widget, and contains a single subdirectory, Contents. This typically contains two main elements: a folder named Resources that contains a variety of images used by the Widget, and a file with a .kon extension. This file looks like a normal XML file and contains the specification of the Widget. More complex Widgets may also include separate JavaScript files for the code required by the Widget. The motivation for this is similar to the motivation for separating the JavaScript from an HTML page. It separates the specification of the Widget (or HTML page) from the processing logic.

Widget Specification File Overview

Opening and examining a Widget specification file (.kon files) reveals several aspects common to many Widget specifications. They are based on XML and start with the standard XML processing instruction:

```
<?xml version="1.0" encoding="UTF-8"?>
```

This is generally followed by a widget element that contains one or more window elements. The window element generally contains a collection of elements that defines the images, text fields, and text areas to include in the window. After the window specification, the Widget's actions are defined. An *action* is a bit of JavaScript code that is invoked when an associated triggering event occurs. The actions are typically followed by one or more preferences that enable a user to tailor aspects of the Widget, such as text font or color. Finally, an about-box element may be included. This element may contain several child elements that define a window containing information about the Widget and its developer. The following code shows the skeleton commonly seen in a Widget specification file:

```
<widget>
  <window>
    <!-- image and text elements in the window -->
    <text>...</text>
  </window>
  <window>...</window>
  <action trigger="onload">
    <![CDATA[
      // JavaScript code
    ]]>
  </action>
  <action>...</action>
  <preference>...</preference>
  <preference>...</preference>
  <about-box>
  </about-box>
</widget>
```

Before continuing on to the example presented in this chapter, you may want to use the converter to unpack other Widgets, and explore the similarities and differences in the specifications.

Defining Your First Widget: a Hello World Exercise

Now that you've seen the contents of a Widget, you're ready get into the details of Widgets, and define a simple Hello World example. In this first example, you'll get back to the basics and create a Widget that says "Hello World!" Later, you'll make some extensions to this that include responding to a user's interactions, making use of a user's preferences, and retrieving data from a remote server.

The Basic Hello World

The first step in creating a new Widget is to set up the Widget directory structure as shown earlier. Create the directories `HelloWorldvA\` and `HelloWorldvA\contents` to hold the Widget. Then create a new file, `HelloWorldvA.kon`, and define the simple Widget shown in Listing 17-1.

Listing 17-1: HelloWorldvA.kon: the initial version of the Hello World Widget

```
 1 <?xml version="1.0" encoding="UTF-8"?>
 2 <?konfabulator xml-strict="true"?>
 3 <widget debug="on">
 4   <window name="mainWindow" height="400" width="500"
 5     visible="true" opacity="255" title="HelloWorldvA">
 6     <textarea name="quoteLabel" editable="false" hOffset="75"
 7       vOffset="100" width="425" data="Hello World!" font="ariel"
 8       size="18" color="#CCFF00" bgColor="#3333CC" bgOpacity="255">
 9     </textarea>
10   </window>
11 </widget>
```

As noted above, a Widget specification is simply an XML file. Line 1 contains a processing instruction that tells the XML processor that it's dealing with an XML file, and line 2 is a processing instruction specifying that a strict interpretation of XML should be used when parsing the Widget. By default, the Widget parser doesn't require a Widget to conform to all aspects of the XML specification. For example, you can specify an attribute value that isn't surrounded by quotes. This can cause problems if the Widget must ever be parsed as an XML file, so it's generally better to set this flag to `true`.

The Hello World example includes three elements all nested within each other. The top-level element, a `Widget`, is defined on line 3. This Widget contains a single element, a `window`, defined on lines 4 and 5. The window element, in turn, contains a single `textarea` element (lines 6–8) that displays the Hello World message. Note that the specification of the text area as a child of the window element implies that the text area should be created within the container window.

Note that several attributes are defined for each of the elements. There is an optional `debug` attribute for a Widget that causes a debug console to be displayed when the Widget is created. This console captures log messages created with a `log` function that will be described later, and queries the Widget about the state of objects, among other features. To see more detailed information on the console capabilities, consult the reference guide or type **/help** into a console window.

The `window` element contains a set of attributes that primarily establish presentation details such as window size and location. The text area has similar presentation-oriented attributes, such as `width`, `hOffset`, and `vOffset`, which establish the horizontal width, and horizontal and vertical offset of the text area (assuming 0, 0 is the top-left corner of the container window). It also contains a variety of attributes that affect the way the area is presented. The `editable` attribute establishes whether or not the user can modify the text in the text area. The `color`, `font`, and, `size` attributes establish the look of the rendered text. Of course, a `data` attribute is needed to define the text string that should be created in the area. Of special note are the `bgColor` and `bgOpacity` attributes. These establish the color and opacity of the background, respectively. Note that you need to specify a non-zero `bgOpacity` value (valid values range from 0–255) to get a visible color. Because the default opacity is 0, specifying only a `bgColor` has no effect on the background color.

A Shift from Elements to Attributes

The Yahoo! Widget Engine is still under quite heavy development, and the format for a Widget specification is changing in significant ways. As of version 3.1.1 of the reference guide, examples are given primarily with the properties of a component (such as a window) specified as child elements, rather than attributes. Looking at the Hello World example in listing 17-1, according to v3.1.1 of the reference guide, the `bgColor` attribute of the `textarea` element should be defined as an element, rather than an attribute. The specification from lines 6-8 of listing 17-1 would therefore become the following:

```
<textarea name="quoteLabel">
  <editable>false</editable>
  <hOffset>75</hOffset>
  <vOffset>100</vOffset>
  <width>425</width>
  <data>Hello World!</data>
  <font>ariel</font>
  <size>18</size>
  <color>#CCFF00</color>
  <bgColor>#3333CC</bgColor>
  <bgOpacity>255</bgOpacity>
</textarea>
```

In future releases, however, there will be a shift from representing many component properties as elements to representing them as attributes. For example, the text area will be defined as shown in lines 6–8 of Listing 17-1. See the blog posting at `http:/widgets.yahoo.net/blog/?p=11` for more information on this change.

Fortunately, as of version 3.1.4 of the Widget Engine, you can specify many of the component properties as either attributes *or* elements. This enables you to adopt this change for many of the existing properties earlier rather than later. When possible, the examples in the book use attributes instead of elements to represent a component's properties.

As with most of the rapidly developing toolkits and libraries in this book, see the Web for the latest developments. Specifically, consult the Widget home page as well as the blog (`http://widgets.yahoo.net/blog`) for more information.

Now that you've defined your new Widget, you're ready to try it out. To test Widgets that aren't ready for deployment, it's not necessary to go through the process of packaging them into a Widget file. To test a Widget without packaging it first, right-click the Yahoo! Widget Engine icon and select the Open Widget button. This brings up an Open Widget dialog that you can use to browse to the folder containing the Widget and select the `HelloWorldvA.kon` file for opening. Once open, you should see something similar to that in Figure 17-3.

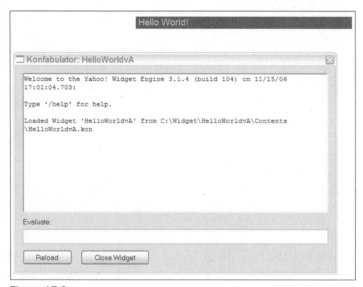

Figure 17-3

By default, a Widget behaves like most other windows. When any other window is brought into focus and dragged on top of the Widget, it covers the Widget. In experimenting with your Widget, you may want to alter the default behavior to keep the Widget on top of other windows. You can easily do this by right-clicking the Widget and selecting Widget Preferences from the menu that appears. A new dialog will appear that contains a variety of properties for the Widget. Setting the level of window property to the topmost option ensures that the Widget stays on top, even when other windows are dragged over it.

Packing the Widget with the Widget Converter

After you finish developing a Widget, you're ready to package it into a Widget file so that it can be easily distributed to Widget users. A good final step in preparing the Widget for packaging is to turn off the debug console if you're using it; note that Yahoo! requires this before you upload your Widget to their Widget gallery. After turning debugging off, you can package the Widget in a few easy steps:

1. Load the Widget Converter Widget into the Yahoo! Widget Engine again.

2. Open an Explorer window and browse to the directory that contains the base Widget directory.

3. Drag the base Widget (i.e., `HelloWorldvA`) directory and drop it on the dark-gray bar in the Widget Converter.

4. Select Flat File from the list of Convert to options.

5. Press the Convert button.

After the Widget is packaged, you get a successful completion message, as shown in Figure 17-4. Your new Widget file will be placed in the same directory containing the base Widget directory. At this point you can load your Widget into the Widget Engine as you would any other Widget.

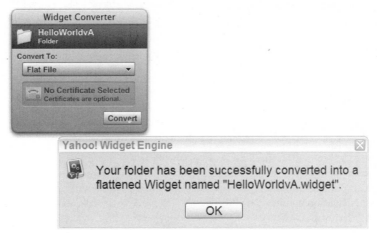

Figure 17-4

Extending Hello World

Now that the initial version of Hello World is working, you're ready to add some simple functionality. In this section, you extend the Widget with several additional capabilities:

❑ Replace the static text "Hello World!" with a random quote provided by a remote server.

❑ Have the Widget respond to double clicks by looking up and displaying a new quotation in the text area.

❑ Enable users to customize the Widget look and feel by defining a set of Widget preferences.

Replacing the "Hello World!" Message

The first step is to replace the message "Hello World!" by looking up a quote on a server when the Widget is loaded. To implement this part of the example, you need access to a server that will provide a quote when requested by a remote client. See http://RIABook.ideastax.com/phpscripts/quoter.php, which is a simple php script that returns a quote in response to an HTTP post. The post request takes a single argument, parameter1, which returns a random quote from a predefined set of quotes when the value random is provided.

To add the lookup of a quote from the server when the Widget is loaded, open the HelloWorld file and add a new action element to the end of the Widget specification:

```
1 <widget debug="on">
2   ...
3   <action trigger="onLoad">
4     <![CDATA[
5     function getQuote() {
```

```
 6          log("Looking up new quote");
 7          var quoteURL = new URL();
 8          quoteURL.location = "http://abraxas-soft.com/phpscripts/quoter.php";
 9          quoteURL.postData = "parameter1=random";
10          quoteURL.fetch();
11          quoteLabel.data = quoteURL.responseData;
12       }
13
14     getQuote();
15     ]]>
16   </action>
17 </widget>
```

Note the following about the preceding code:

❏ The `action` element defined on line 3 is similar to a standard JavaScript event handler. The content of the action element is a bit of JavaScript code that should be executed when the action is triggered. Notice that the JavaScript is defined in a CDATA section with `<![CDATA[ ... ]]>`. This specification ensures that the Widget Engine doesn't misinterpret greater than (>) and less than (<) symbols as parts of an XML element specification when it's parsing the Widget file.

❏ The triggering event is indicated with a `trigger` attribute on the `action` element. Notice that the triggers look quite similar to the events in a Web page. In this case, the trigger is the `onload` event that occurs when the Widget is loaded. Other examples of events that can trigger an action include `onMouseDown`, `onMouseUp`, or `onTimer`, which is an event triggered at a regular interval. (Refer to the *Yahoo! Widget Engine Reference Guide* for the full list of action triggers.)

❏ Looking inside the CDATA section to the JavaScript that is executed reveals several interesting aspects of a Widget. First, note that this action defines a single function, `getQuote`, on lines 5–12, and invokes the function once on Line 14. Also note that line 6 in the `getQuote` function shows a very useful extension to JavaScript provided by the Widget Engine. The global `log` function used here enables you to write debug information to the console loaded with a Widget when the Widget's debug attribute is set to `true`.

❏ Continuing on in the `getQuote` function shows an example use of the `URL` object, an extension to core JavaScript that is included with the Widget Engine. This object enables a Widget to easily interact with remote servers. On line 8, the `location` property of the object is set to the quote server's php script. Because the php script is expecting a `POST` rather than a `GET`, the `postData` property must also be set (line 9). This is only required when a post is being performed, and can be used to define the data to include in the request.

❏ The `fetch` function invoked on line 10 causes the request to the remote server to be made. This function takes an optional `location` argument that sets the location property and performs the fetch from the given location, but the argument isn't necessary in this case because the property is set manually on line 8. Note that an asynchronous request is also possible if the `fetchAsynch` function is used. This function takes a reference to the callback function to invoke when the request is finished. When you use an asynchronous request, you can use the function `cancel` to cancel the request, if necessary.

❏ After the fetch has been performed, the response information is available. This includes the `responseData` property, referenced on line 11, which contains the data returned from the server. Other properties available after the fetch is performed include `response`, which contains the response code (e.g., 200 or 404) of the request. You can also use the function `getResponseHeaders()` to get the header detail for the response.

❏ Line 11 shows another useful aspect of Widgets and JavaScript defined in a Widget. When you define an element in a Widget (such as a window or text area), and assign a name property to it, a global JavaScript variable of the given name is automatically created for the element. In the Hello World example above, you define a text area named `quoteLabel`. You can then directly reference the text area with the corresponding variable `quoteLabel` and change the data property, as shown on line 11.

That's all that's necessary to replace the hello world message with a quote provided by the server! If you reload the Hello World Widget at this point, you'll get a text area that contains a random quote. Each time you reload the Widget, you'll get a new quote.

Updating the Quote on Double-Click

Now that you've written a function to update the quote, it's a simple enhancement to react to user clicks on the text area. All you need to do is write a listener for mouse click events, and call the `getQuote` function. To add this new listener, add a new child element to the existing `textarea` element as follows:

```
<textarea name="quoteLabel" ...>
  <onMultiClick>
    <![CDATA[
      if (system.event.clickCount == 2) {
        getQuote();
      }
    ]]>
  </onMultiClick>
</textarea>
```

From the preceding code, note the following:

❏ A new `onMultiClick` event handler is defined as a child of the `textarea` element. This causes the JavaScript included in the CDATA section for the element to be executed anytime the user makes multiple clicks on the text area. If the user clicks a different area within the Widget, the code isn't executed.

❏ The `textarea` element isn't limited to including JavaScript for mouse click events only. You can define additional elements for any event relevant to a text area, such as `onKeyPress` or `onGainFocus`. Also note that the text area isn't unique in this capability; other elements such as `text` or `windows` can include specific event-handling elements.

❏ Looking at the code within the CDATA section shows a very simple function. An `if` statement analyzes the `system.event.clickCount` property that holds the number of mouse clicks. When two clicks are counted, the `getQuote` method is invoked and the quote is updated. This makes use of another JavaScript extension available for a Widget, the `system` object. You can use this object to retrieve information about the system on which the Widget is running, such as battery level (see `system.battery`) or CPU activity (see `system.cpu`). The `event` property of the `system` object is very important when writing event handlers for a Widget, as this property maintains information about the most recent event received by the Widget.

At this point, you've finished adding the code to update the quote when the user double-clicks the text area. After saving the .kon file and reloading the Widget, with each double-click on the quote, a new quote is retrieved from the server and displayed in the text area.

Allowing Customization with User Preferences

At this point, the enhancements to the Hello World example are almost finished! The current version of the Widget is limited because the look and feel of the Widget is quite static. The user cannot change the size of the text or the color of the Widget without modifying the values in the .kon file. The only aspects of the Widget that the user can change are some preferences regarding the window. These include the level of the window, the opacity, and whether the window position is locked; and these can be set from the preferences dialog of the Widget. To display this dialog, right-click the Widget and select Widget Preferences.

In a real-world Widget, most users would appreciate the opportunity to tailor its look and feel to suit their personal tastes. Fortunately, the Widget Engine provides an easy mechanism to capture user preferences for a wide variety of the Widget's aspects. A Widget can contain one or more child elements of type preference. These elements enable the Widget developer to add fields to the Widget preference dialog. Each preference can be assigned a name, type, and default value, as well as several other optional attributes, as shown in the following example:

```
<preference name="fontPref" title="Font" type="font"
  defaultValue="Ariel" description="Select the text font"/>
```

A key attribute to the preference element is the type attribute, which establishes the type of preference being captured, (i.e., color, font, or file). The Widget preference dialog then uses the specified type when deciding what type of control to use to capture the preference. For example, if the preference captured is a color, the preference Widget brings up a color palette that the user can choose from, rather than make the user type in a six-digit hexadecimal number for the color.

Finally, preferences can be separated into different groups by defining a preferenceGroup element as a child of the Widget, and including a reference to the preferenceGroup element in the preference element with the group attribute. Note that although at times it's useful, it's not always necessary to define a preference group for your Widget preferences. If you decide not to define your preferences within a specific group, they're automatically placed in a group named "General."

At this point, you're ready to define a preference group and a few user preferences for the Hello World Widget. Start by adding a new preferenceGroup element and four new preference elements to the bottom of the Widget defined in HelloWorldvA.kon:

```
<widget debug="on">
  ...
    <preferenceGroup name="Text" order="1" title="Text Attributes"/>
    <preference name="bgColorPref" title="Background Color" type="color"
      group="Text" defaultValue="#3333CC"
      description="Select the background color"/>
    <preference name="fgColorPref" title="Color" type="color" group="Text"
      defaultValue="#CCFF00" description="Select the text color"/>
    <preference name="fontPref" title="Font" type="font" group="Text"
      defaultValue="Ariel" description="Select the text font"/>
    <preference name="sizePref" title="Size" type="slider" group="Text"
      defaultValue="18" ticks="10" minLength="5" maxLength="35"
      description="Select the text size"/>
  </widget>
```

This causes fields to be created in the Widget preference dialog that can capture the desired background color for the text area, as well as the desired font, color, and size of the text from the user. If you reload the Widget at this point and bring up the Widget preferences dialog, you'll see the new set of preferences, as shown in Figure 17-5.

Figure 17-5

Of course, at this point, if you modify the preferences in the dialog and save them, nothing happens! That's because you've added the capability to capture the user's preferences, but still need to update the text area to reflect the selections. This requires you to add and invoke a new global function as a part of the onLoad action, as follows:

```
<action trigger="onLoad">
  <![CDATA[
  function updateFromPreferences() {
    quoteLabel.bgColor = preferences.bgColorPref.value;
    quoteLabel.color = preferences.fgColorPref.value;
    quoteLabel.font = preferences.fontPref.value;
    quoteLabel.size = preferences.sizePref.value;
  }

  function getQuote() {
  ...
  }

  updateFromPreferences();
  getQuote();
  ]]>
</action>
```

From the preceding code, note the following:

❑ The `updateFromPreferences` function updates the look of the text field based on the values provided by the user. If no value is provided, the default is automatically used. To accomplish this, the function accesses a global object, `preferences`, that is available to the Widget. The `preferences` object has a separate property for each preference defined for the Widget. Each preference object includes of a variety of properties that describe the preference, such as the `value` and `defaultValue`, among others.

❑ The Widget Engine manages the preferences objects, so they always reflect the user's most recent selections. The preferences are even automatically saved and reloaded when the machine is restarted or the Widget is reloaded.

❑ Because the preferences are saved and loaded automatically, there are two occasions when the preferences must be used to set the look of the text area: when the user changes a preference, and when the Widget is loaded. Above, a call to `updateFromPreferences` was added before the `getQuote` function invocation to ensure that the preferences are reloaded when the Widget is loaded. Handling user changes to a preference requires the addition of a new action as follows:

```
<action trigger="onPreferencesChanged">
    updateFromPreferences();
</action>
```

At this point, you've got a fully functional Widget that is updated based on a user's preferences. After reloading the Widget, the text area updates to reflect the user's preferences. Figure 17-6 shows the Hello World Widget, with colors tailored by the user.

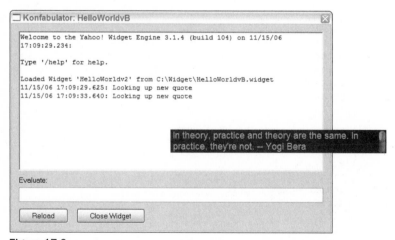

Figure 17-6

Listing 17-2 shows the final version of the Hello World Widget, with a remotely retrieved quotation on load and double-click, and the inclusion of a user's preferences.

Listing 17-2: HelloWorldvB.kon — the complete Hello World Widget

```
1  <?xml version="1.0" encoding="UTF-8"?>
2  <?konfabulator xml-strict="true"?>
3  <widget debug="on">
4    <window name="mainWindow" height="400" width="500"
5      visible="true" opacity="255" title="HelloWorldvB">
6      <textarea name="quoteLabel" editable="false" hOffset="75"
7        vOffset="100" width="425" data="Hello World!" font="ariel"
8        size="18" color="#CCFF00" bgColor="#3333CC" bgOpacity="255">
9        <onMultiClick>
10         <![CDATA[
11         if (system.event.clickCount == 2) {
12         getQuote();
13         }
14         ]]>
15         </onMultiClick>
16       </textarea>
17    </window>
18    <action trigger="onLoad">
19      <![CDATA[
20      function updateFromPreferences() {
21        quoteLabel.bgColor = preferences.bgColorPref.value;
22        quoteLabel.color = preferences.fgColorPref.value;
23        quoteLabel.font = preferences.fontPref.value;
24        quoteLabel.size = preferences.sizePref.value;
25      }
26
27      function getQuote() {
28        log("Looking up new quote");
29        var quoteURL = new URL();
30        quoteURL.location = "http://abraxas-soft.com/phpscripts/quoter.php";
31        quoteURL.postData = "parameter1=random";
32        quoteURL.fetch();
33        quoteLabel.data = quoteURL.responseData;
34      }
35
36      updateFromPreferences();
37      getQuote();
38      ]]>
39    </action>
40    <action trigger="onPreferencesChanged">
41      updateFromPreferences();
42    </action>
43    <preferenceGroup name="Text" order="1" title="Text Attributes"/>
44    <preference name="bgColorPref" title="Background Color" type="color"
45      group="Text" defaultValue="#3333CC"
46      description="Select the background color"/>
47    <preference name="fgColorPref" title="Color" type="color" group="Text"
48      defaultValue="#CCFF00" description="Select the text color"/>
49    <preference name="fontPref" title="Font" type="font" group="Text"
50      defaultValue="Ariel" description="Select the text font"/>
51    <preference name="sizePref" title="Size" type="slider" group="Text"
52      defaultValue="18" ticks="10" minLength="5" maxLength="35"
53      description="Select the text size"/>
54  </widget>
```

A More Useful Example: Incorporating the Stax API

Now that you've seen the basics, you're ready to look at a more complex Widget that serves as an add-on to the capabilities of a larger Rich Internet Application. In the last chapter, you extended the Stax application to include an API that enables you to programmatically upload images and define new concepts for use in Stax. In this section, you build on this work and make use of the API from a new Widget that enables you to create concepts on the client.

The advantage to using a Widget for this type of operation is that it can interact with the client system, thereby using any resources available only on the client. The Widget can make use of these resources because it's running on the client, as opposed to a Web application, or even a RIA, which ultimately runs on the server.

Some examples of the many client interactions that are possible with a Widget include the following:

❑   Client file system interactions such as reading or writing a file on the client system

❑   System analysis such as examining the amount of CPU or memory in use

❑   Interacting with iTunes or other applications running on the client system

❑   Examining the number and power level of any batteries connected to the client system

---

Widget Visualization: Backgrounds and Buttons through Images

One aspect of the Widget Engine that differs greatly from programming languages such as Java or Python, or a JavaScript library such as Dojo, is that the creation of visual components is done through images, rather than predefined library elements (similar to Web applications developed without using a JavaScript library such as Dojo). This means that there is no programmatic way to construct and present a window, panel, or frame to the user.

Instead, the developer is expected to include and reference image files from within the Widget to create the background and other visual elements of the Widget. Some elements such as text areas are displayed, and can include tailored aspects such as foreground and background colors (as shown in the previous example), but this is not sufficient for most real-world Widgets.

In the majority of cases, the developer has created tailored images for the Widget, which has the advantage of enabling a more unique and, in many cases, visually appealing appearance, but it has the drawback of a potentially higher development cost. As noted above, almost any non-experimental Widget development requires a graphics application such as Photoshop or Gimp.

The example Widget for the StaxConceptCreator uses a variety of images for the background, the button, and an upload icon. These can all be downloaded from the book's Web site. Of course, if you're feeling particularly creative or adventurous, you can develop your own tailored images to use in the Widget.

In the example that follows, you make use of the file system to enable the upload of the image to the server. You also take advantage of the fact that the Widget runs on the client system, which enables users to drag and drop the file to be uploaded, rather than require them to enter the file by name, or use the standard file browser component.

Make sure that you've gone through the previous chapter before working through this example, or have a working version of ideaStax downloaded from the book's Web site. You'll need this to invoke functions in the Stax API from your Widget.

Setting Up the Example

To get started, create a new folder named `StaxConceptCreatorvA`, and the standard `StaxConcept CreatorvA\contents` subfolder for the Widget. Because this Widget is a bit more complex, you also need to create a folder to hold the images used by the Widget (see the following sidebar for information about the use of images in a Widget). Although not required, images and other non-JavaScript resources for a Widget are frequently placed in a subfolder of the `contents` folder named `resources`.

Creating the Basic Widget

Now that the Widget directory structure is created, and the required images are available, you're ready to write a basic Widget specification in a new file, `StaxConceptCreatorvA.kon`, as shown in Listing 17-3. Save this under the `StaxConceptCreatorvA/contents` directory.

Listing 17-3: StaxConceptCreatorvA.kon — the initial version of the concept creator Widget

```
1  <?xml version="1.0" encoding="UTF-8"?>
2  <?konfabulator xml-strict="true"?>
3  <widget debug="on">
4    <window name="window" title="Stax Concept CreatorvA" height="300"
5      width="300" visible="true" shadow="false" opacity="255">
6      <image name="backgroundImg" src="Resources/background.png"
7        opacity="255"/>
8      <text name="titlebar" hOffset="75" vOffset="20"
9        data="Stax Concept Creator" font="ariel" size="18"/>
10
11     <image name="uploadImg" src="Resources/upload-icon.png"
12       hOffset="20" vOffset="50">
13       <tooltip>Drag an image into this area</tooltip>
14     </image>
15
16     <text name="imageLabel" hOffset="75" width="220" vOffset="70"
17       data="Upload Image" truncation="end" font="ariel" size="12"/>
18     <text name="imageName" hOffset="75" width="220" vOffset="90"
19       data="None" truncation="end" font="ariel" size="12"/>
20
21     <text name="nameLabel" hOffset="20" vOffset="125" font="ariel"
22       size="14" data="Concept Name"/>
23     <textarea name="nameField" color="#000000" bgColor="#FFFFFF"
24       bgOpacity="255" width="150" alignment="left" vOffset="130"
```

(continued)

Listing 17-3: *(continued)*

```
25          hOffset="30" data="a name" scrollbar="false" font="ariel"/>
26
27      <text name="descriptionLabel" hOffset="20" vOffset="160"
28          font="ariel" size="14" data="Concept Description"/>
29      <textarea name="descriptionField" color="#000000"
30          bgColor="#FFFFFF" bgOpacity="255" width="150" alignment="left"
31          vOffset="165" hOffset="30" data="" scrollbar="false"
32          font="ariel"/>
33
34      <text name="tagLabel" hOffset="20" vOffset="195" font="ariel"
35          size="14" data="Tags"/>
36      <textarea name="tagField" color="#000000" bgColor="#FFFFFF"
37          bgOpacity="255" width="150" alignment="left" vOffset="200"
38          hOffset="30" data="" scrollbar="false" font="ariel"/>
39
40      <text name="statusLabel" hOffset="40" vOffset="240" font="ariel"
41          size="14" data="Status: Waiting" color="#0000FF"/>
42
43      <image name="uploadButtonImg" src="Resources/upload-button.png"
44          hOffset="200" vOffset="250">
45          <onMouseDown>
46            <![CDATA[
47              uploadButtonImg.src = "Resources/upload-button-down.png";
48            ]]>
49          </onMouseDown>
50          <onMouseUp>
51            <![CDATA[
52              uploadButtonImg.src = "Resources/upload-button.png";
53            ]]>
54          </onMouseUp>
55      </image>
56    </window>
57 </widget>
```

Note the following about the preceding code:

❑   Looking at Listing 17-3 reveals a set of elements quite similar to those in the Hello World example. The first two lines contain the processing instructions, and lines 3–5 specify the details of the Widget and window.

❑   Lines 6–7, 11–14, and 43–55 are all examples of the image element that you can use to include an image such as a JPG, GIF, or PNG in a Widget. In all cases, you specify the source of the image with the src attribute, the name, and the position relative to the top-left corner of the Widget with hOffset and vOffset. The first image on lines 6–7 is a simple image that constitutes the background of the Widget.

❑   The image defined on lines 11–14 creates a small icon in the upper-left corner of the Widget. You'll see later how to use an event handler to capture the names of files that the user drags and drop on the icon. It also shows the use of the optional tooltip element, which defines a tip to be displayed when the user moves the mouse over the image. Lines 16–19 define two lines of text that will present the name of the file to be uploaded.

❑   The most complex image is the `uploadButtonImg`, which depicts a button users click when they want to upload a new image and concept. Creating the visual effect of pressing when the user clicks the button requires a bit more work. You actually use two images to create the button. The first image, `upload-button.png`, represents the button when the user is not clicking it. An alternate image, `upload-button-down.png`, loads when the user clicks the mouse on the button. This is accomplished by changing the source of the image element when the user presses the mouse while over the image, or releases the mouse while pressed over the image. On line 47, the `mouseDown` event handler sets the image to the pressed view of the button, while the `mouseUp` event handler changes it back to the normal unpressed state (line 52).

❑   Lines 21–38 simply define the text areas and text fields necessary to capture the details of the concept, such as the name, description, and tags that should be associated. Notice that the read-only fields on a single line are defined with a text element, while the user input fields are text area elements with the `editable` attribute set to `true`. In addition, note the use of a new `scrollbar` attribute in the text area specification. Setting the `scrollbar` attribute to `false` forces the text area to occupy only a single line. Otherwise, the text area automatically spans multiple lines and automatically creates a scrollbar, as in the Hello World example. The final text field on lines 40 and 41 are used to show the user the status of the concept creation requests.

If you save and load `StaxConceptCreatorvA.kon` in the Widget Engine, you see an image similar to that in Figure 17-7. When you press the Upload button, its appearance changes (but of course no upload is performed). When you hover the mouse over the icon in the upper-left corner, a tooltip appears. Now you're ready to add some drag and drop handling!

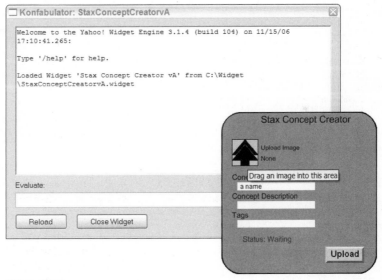

Figure 17-7

Adding File Drag and Drop

Now that you've got a basic version of the Widget defined, adding drag and drop handling is as simple as writing a new event handler for the `uploadImg` that is created in the upper-left corner of the Widget. A powerful event handler on the client side is the `onDragDrop` event handler, which can be defined as follows:

```
<image name="uploadImg" src="Resources/upload-icon.png"
  hOffset="20" vOffset="50">
  <tooltip>Drag an image into this area</tooltip>
  <onDragDrop>
    <![CDATA[
      if (system.event.data[0] == "filenames") {
        handleFileDrop(system.event.data[1]);
      }
    ]]>
  </onDragDrop>
</image>
```

The `onDragDrop` event automatically indicates that a filename is being dropped as a part of the event in the zero index of the `system.event.data` property. The event also maintains the absolute path of the file that was dropped in the first index (`system.event.data[1]`). This is passed as an argument to a new function, `handleFileDrop`. A new `onLoad` action that contains this new function should be defined after the closing window tag as follows:

```
1  ...
2  </window>
3    <action trigger="onload">
4      <![CDATA[
5        var uploadFile;
6        var uploadEnabled = false;
7
8        function handleFileDrop(longfilename) {
9          log("looking at file: " + longfilename);
10         uploadFile = longfilename;
11         var fidx = longfilename.lastIndexOf("/");
12         var shortFileName = longfilename.substring(fidx+1);
13         imageName.data=shortFileName;
14
15         if (validFile(shortFileName)) {
16           uploadImg.colorize="#00FF00";
17           uploadEnabled = true;
18         } else {
19           uploadImg.colorize="#FF0000";
20           uploadEnabled = false;
21         }
22       }
23
24       function validFile(filename) {
25         return filename.toLowerCase().match(".*\.(jpg|png|bmp|gif|tif)");
26       }
27
```

```
28     ]]>
29     </action>
29  </widget>
```

The `onload` action establishes two new global variables: `uploadFile` contains the fully qualified name of the file that is to be uploaded, and `uploadEnabled` is a Boolean value that indicates whether or not the user should be allowed to upload the file. Because the user is only allowed to upload images, the upload should only be possible when the images pass validation. It also contains the specification of two functions: `validFile`, on lines 24–26, is a helper function that ensures that the file dragged into the Widget is an image (by looking at its extension). This is used by `handleFileDrop`, the function responsible for performing the majority of the work.

`handleFileDrop` is responsible for accomplishing four tasks:

1. Update the global `uploadFile` variable with the name of the file dragged into the Widget (line 10).

2. Extract the name of the file from the fully qualified path, and display this value in a label on the Widget (lines 11–13).

3. Use the `validateFile` function to assess whether or not the file is valid (line 15), and enable or disable the upload (lines 17 and 20).

4. As a final visual trick, the color of the Upload button can be updated to either green or red depending on whether or not the upload file is valid. This is accomplished on lines 16 and 19 by using `colorize`, a property of an image that can be used to change its color.

Reload the Widget once again and you can drag files into the icon. As files are dropped on the Widget, it updates to reflect the dropped file, as shown in Figure 17-8.

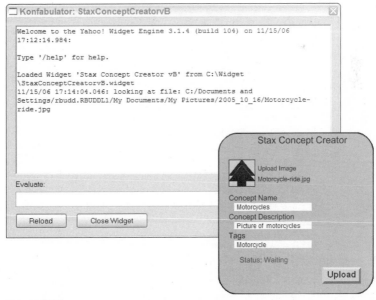

Figure 17-8

487

Uploading the Concept to the Stax Server

Now that you're capturing all the information required by Stax, you're ready to make the call to the Stax API. Recall from Chapter 16 that you defined an API that enabled you to upload a new image concept using a URL similar to the following:

```
http://localhost:3000/api/add_image_concept
```

Of course, in a production environment, you want to replace the localhost address with one that references the deployed RIA:

```
http://www.ideastax.com/api/add_image_concept
```

This URL takes four arguments: a name, a description, a collection tag, and the file to upload. It responds with a response element that contains a success attribute set to true or false depending on whether or not the operation succeeded. For example, on success, the following response is returned:

```
<response success="true"/>
```

Enhancing the Mouse Up Handler

Invoking the Stax API requires you to make some enhancements to the onMouseUp handler you previously defined as a child of the Upload button, uploadButtonImage. The implementation should be updated as follows:

```
1    <onMouseUp>
2      <![CDATA[
3        if (uploadEnabled) {
4          log("Uploading file" + uploadFile);
5          uploadButtonImg.src = "Resources/upload-button.png";
6          statusLabel.data="Status: Uploading ... ";
7          runCommandInBg("curl " +
8            "-F \"name=" + nameField.data + "\" " +
9            "-F \"description=" + descriptionField.data + "\" " +
10           "-F \"tags=" + tagField.data + "\" " +
11           "-F \"commit=Upload File\" " +
12           "-F \"file=@" + uploadFile + "\" " +
13           "http://localhost:3000/api/add_image_concept",
14           "uploadResponse");
15         uploadEnabled = false;
16       }
17     ]]>
18   </onMouseUp>
```

Looking at the code, note the following:

❑   The upload flag is now checked before anything else (line 3). This ensures that you can't upload a new image unless the user has dragged a valid image into the Widget.

❑   If the upload is possible, it is performed with the curl utility included with the Yahoo! Widget Engine. This utility is included because it's a bit more sophisticated than the simple URL object, and can be used to perform more complex Web interactions, such as the multi-part form post required.

❑ Curl is invoked with a global function, runCommandInBG, included by the Widget Engine. This function executes a command in the background, and notifies the Widget when the command has completed. This enables you to invoke external commands without making the Widget appear frozen. This function takes two arguments: the command to execute, defined as a string, and a string that denotes a tag. Don't worry too much about the tag for now; you'll learn more about that when you learn how to handle the completion of the command.

❑ The command includes a variety of arguments that define the concept to be created and are based on the user input fields (lines 8–10). It also takes an argument that references the name of the file to be uploaded (line 12), and the URL to use when uploading the file. An example invocation of curl for a tree image would be as follows:

```
curl -F "name=A Tree" -F "description=My tree out back" -F "tags=Trees" -F
"commit=Upload File" -F "file=@c:/photos/mytree.jpg"
http://localhost:3000/api/add_image_concept
```

❑ Note that the handler also updates the label that shows the status to indicate that an image is being uploaded (line 6), and disables the Upload button (line 15). This is necessary to ensure that users don't inadvertently upload the same image twice.

Enhancing the Mouse Down Handler

You should also update the onMouseDown handler for the uploadButtonImg at this point to make use of the new uploadEnabled variable. The Upload button image should only be modified when the upload is enabled. You accomplish this by adding the simple check as follows:

```
<onMouseDown>
  <![CDATA[
    if (uploadEnabled) {
      uploadButtonImg.src = "Resources/upload-button-down.png";
    }
  ]]>
</onMouseDown>
```

Incorporating the Response from the Server

In the previous section you saw how to invoke the curl command in the background with runCommandInBg. This section describes how to use the "uploadResponse" tag provided as a function argument to incorporate the output of the curl command.

To understand how to capture and analyze responses to the upload command, you need to understand a bit more about how onRunCommandInBg works. When any call to onRunCommandInBg completes an action, onRunCommandInBGComplete is triggered on the Widget. Recall from earlier examples of action specifications that the details for the most recent event are maintained in the system.event property, and are generally used by an action to analyze and handle the event.

Because you can have a variety of invocations of the runCommandInBg function from the same Widget, you need a way to distinguish the different onRunCommandInBG calls, which is where the "upload Response" tag comes into play. The value of the system.event.data property is set to the value of the "uploadResponse" tag, enabling you to disambiguate among the various invocations of runCommandInBg.

There is another use of the tag argument as well. Commands executed frequently produce some output data, which the Widget most likely must capture and use. When using `runCommandInBg`, a global variable with the same name as the tag should also be created. After the command finishes running, the variable holds the output from the execution.

To see an example of handling the completion of a command started with `runCommandInBg`, you should write a new action triggered by the `onRunCommandInBGComplete` event. Define this as a child of the Widget element, after the `onload` action:

```
<action trigger="onRunCommandInBGComplete">
  <![CDATA[
    if (system.event.data.match("uploadResponse")) {
      uploadEnabled = true;
      if (uploadResponse.match(".*<result success=\"true\"/>.*")) {
        statusLabel.data="Status: Upload Successful";
      } else {
        statusLabel.data="Status: Upload Failed";
      }
    }
  ]]>
</action>
```

The first step of the function is to verify that the command completed was the command tagged with `"uploadResponse"`, and when this is the case, enable the Upload button once again. This is followed by analyzing `uploadResponse`, which, as noted above, has been updated to hold the output of the command. Recall that the response has a `success` attribute set to `true` when the upload was successful:

```
<response success="true"/>
```

The second `if` statement looks for the preceding string and either updates the status label to indicate the success when found or otherwise updates the label to indicate a failure.

You'll also need to define the new variable with the same name as the tag to hold the response from the server. Add a new global variable, `uploadResponse`, to the `onload` action specification as follows:

```
<action trigger="onload">
  ...
  var uploadFile;
  var uploadResponse;
  ...
</action>
```

Adding User Preferences

Much like the Hello World application, you most likely want to include a set of preferences that the user can tailor. This Widget enables a user to tailor the text color and font of the status label, as well as the background color of the Widget. This last preference is similar to the text color, but is accomplished through the use of the colorize aspect of an image. As noted above, you can use the `colorize` property to change the color of an image. See Listing 17-4 for the final version of the StaxConceptCreator Widget, which includes drag and drop capability, upload of the image and concept information to the Stax server, and user preferences.

Listing 17-4: StaxConceptCreatorvB.kon — the final version of the concept creator Widget

```
1  <?xml version="1.0" encoding="UTF-8"?>
2  <?konfabulator xml-strict="true"?>
3  <widget debug="on">
4    <window name="window" title="Stax Concept Creator v2" height="300"
5      width="300" visible="true" shadow="false" opacity="255">
6    <image name="backgroundImg" src="Resources/background.png"
7      opacity="255"/>
8    <text name="titlebar" hOffset="75" vOffset="20"
9      data="Stax Concept Creator" font="ariel" size="18"/>
10
11   <image name="uploadImg" src="Resources/upload-icon.png"
12     hOffset="20" vOffset="50">
13     <tooltip>Drag an image into this area</tooltip>
14     <onDragDrop>
15       <![CDATA[
16         if (system.event.data[0] == "filenames") {
17           handleFileDrop(system.event.data[1]);
18         }
19       ]]>
20     </onDragDrop>
21   </image>
22
23   <text name="imageLabel" hOffset="75" width="220" vOffset="70"
24     data="Upload Image" truncation="end" font="ariel" size="12"/>
25   <text name="imageName" hOffset="75" width="220" vOffset="90"
26     data="None" truncation="end" font="ariel" size="12"/>
27
28   <text name="nameLabel" hOffset="20" vOffset="125" font="ariel"
29     size="14" data="Concept Name"/>
30   <textarea name="nameField" color="#000000" bgColor="#FFFFFF"
31     bgOpacity="255" width="150" alignment="left" vOffset="130"
32     hOffset="30" data="a name" scrollbar="false" font="ariel"/>
33
34   <text name="descriptionLabel" hOffset="20" vOffset="160"
35     font="ariel" size="14" data="Concept Description"/>
36   <textarea name="descriptionField" color="#000000"
37     bgColor="#FFFFFF" bgOpacity="255" width="150" alignment="left"
38     vOffset="165" hOffset="30" data="" scrollbar="false"
39     font="ariel"/>
40
41   <text name="tagLabel" hOffset="20" vOffset="195" font="ariel"
```

(continued)

Listing 17-4: *(continued)*

```
42          size="14" data="Tags"/>
43        <textarea name="tagField" color="#000000" bgColor="#FFFFFF"
44          bgOpacity="255" width="150" alignment="left" vOffset="200"
45          hOffset="30" data="" scrollbar="false" font="ariel"/>
46
47        <text name="statusLabel" hOffset="40" vOffset="240" font="ariel"
48          size="14" data="Status: Waiting" color="#0000FF"/>
49
50        <image name="uploadButtonImg" src="Resources/upload-button.png"
51          hOffset="200" vOffset="250">
52          <onMouseDown>
53            <![CDATA[
54              if (uploadEnabled) {
55                uploadButtonImg.src = "Resources/upload-button-down.png";
56              }
57
58            ]]>
59          </onMouseDown>
60          <onMouseUp>
61            <![CDATA[
62              if (uploadEnabled) {
63                log("Uploading file" + uploadFile);
64                uploadButtonImg.src = "Resources/upload-button.png";
65                statusLabel.data="Status: Uploading ... ";
66                runCommandInBg("curl " +
67                  "-F \"name=" + nameField.data + "\" " +
68                  "-F \"description=" + descriptionField.data + "\" " +
69                  "-F \"tags=" + tagField.data + "\" " +
70                  "-F \"commit=Upload File\" " +
71                  "-F \"file=@" + uploadFile + "\" " +
72                  "http://localhost:3000/api/add_image_concept",
73                  "uploadResponse");
74                uploadEnabled = false;
75              }
76            ]]>
77          </onMouseUp>
78        </image>
79      </window>
80      <action trigger="onload">
81        <![CDATA[
82          var uploadEnabled = false;
83          var uploadFile;
84          var uploadResponse;
85
86          function updateFromPreferences() {
87            statusLabel.font = preferences.statusTextFontPref.value;
88            statusLabel.color = preferences.statusTextColorPref.value;
```

```
 89          backgroundImg.colorize = preferences.backgroundColorPref.value;
 90        }
 91
 92      function handleFileDrop(longfilename) {
 93        log("looking at file: " + longfilename);
 94        var fidx = longfilename.lastIndexOf("/");
 95        uploadFile = longfilename;
 96        var shortFileName = longfilename.substring(fidx+1);
 97        if (validFile(shortFileName)) {
 98          imageName.data=shortFileName;
 99          uploadImg.colorize="#00FF00";
100          uploadEnabled = true
101        } else {
102          imageName.data=shortFileName;
103          uploadImg.colorize="#FF0000";
104          uploadEnabled = false;
105        }
106      }
107
108      function validFile(filename) {
109        return filename.toLowerCase().match(".*\.(jpg|png|bmp|gif|tif)");
110      }
111
112      updateFromPreferences();
113    ]]>
114  </action>
115  <action trigger="onRunCommandInBGComplete">
116    <![CDATA[
117      if (system.event.data.match("uploadResponse")) {
118        uploadEnabled = true;
119        if (uploadResponse.match(".*<result success=\"true\"/>.*")) {
120          statusLabel.data="Status: Upload Successful";
121        } else {
122          statusLabel.data="Status: Upload Failed";
123        }
124      }
125    ]]>
126  </action>
127
128  <action trigger="onPreferencesChanged">
129    updateFromPreferences();
130  </action>
131  <preference name="backgroundColorPref" title="Background Color:"
132    type="color" defaultValue="#AAAAAA"
133    description="Select window color."/>
134  <preference name="statusTextColorPref" title="Status Text Color:"
135    type="color" defaultValue="#0000FF"
136    description="Select the status text color."/>
137  <preference name="statusTextFontPref" title="Status Text Font:"
138    type="font" defaultValue="Ariel"
139    description="Select the status font."/>
140 </widget>
```

Note the following:

❑ The preference implementation is quite similar to that in the Hello World Widget. The preferences are defined on lines 131–139.

❑ The `onload` action has a new function definition for `updateFromPreferences` (lines 86–90).

❑ The `colorize` property of the background image is used on line 89.

❑ As in Hello World, the `updateFromPreferences` function is invoked once when the page is loaded (line 112), and as a part of the `onPreferencesChanged` function (lines 128–130).

Now you've finished the Stax Concept Creator Widget! All that remains is to package the Widget with the Widget Converter and make it available to any Stax users. See Figure 17-9 for an example of the Widget after a valid file has been uploaded.

After creating the new concept and uploading the image, Stax is updated with the new concept, as shown in Figure 17-10.

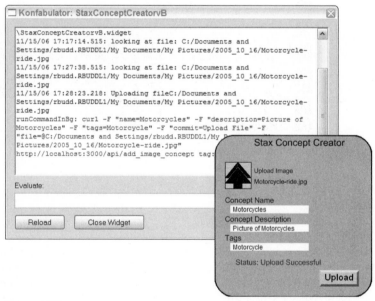

Figure 17-9

Figure 17-10

Summary

In this chapter, you've seen the basics of Widget creation using the Yahoo! Widget Engine, including how to set it up and how to use the Widget Converter to pack and unpack Widget files. Hello World explored the creation of a simple Widget that displays a hello world message, and gave an example of using a URL object to look up a quote from a remote server. Finally, a more realistic Widget was explored with the Stax concept creator Widget. You saw how to use the Stax API developed in the previous chapter to upload a new image to the server and create a new concept for the image.

18

Rich Immersive Environments

Hiro is approaching the Street. It is the Broadway, the Champs Elysees of the Metaverse. It is the brilliantly lit boulevard that can be seen, miniaturized and backward, reflected in the lenses of his goggles. It does not really exist. But right now, millions of people are walking up and down it.

—**Neal Stephenson,** *Snow Crash*

Like any place in Reality, the Street is subject to development. Developers can build their own small streets feeding off of the main one. They can build buildings, parks, signs, as well as things that do not exist in Reality, such as vast hovering overhead light shows and special neighborhoods where the rules of three-dimensional spacetime are ignored.

—**Neal Stephenson,** *Snow Crash*

You've come a significant distance in this book, from understanding and writing simple mashups to a complete and functional application. Now that you have a sense of your own power and of what it means to program applications above the platform level, let's look at what might lie ahead. In particular, let's ponder the question of what exists beyond Web 2.0 programming and ask the question, "If there's a Web 3.0, what is it and what does it look and feel like?" In writing this text, the authors thought a good bit about that question, and while we can offer no definitive answers, we can suggest a vision that may point toward this future.

One possibility for the next-generation Web is that it may be embodied as a rich and immersive environment, which instead of appearing to a user as a two-dimensional form in a browser will steep a user in a three-dimensional world filled with places to see, avenues to walk, people to interact with, objects and environments to play with, things to buy, and services to access. Applications grounded in such an environment will require a completely different style of manipulation by and interaction with the user. You, in turn, will need to reconsider what the concept of "interface" means, and how to engage a user with your creations.

In this chapter, you will gain a rudimentary mastery of the dominant *rich immersive environment* known as Second Life. Second Life has captured both mindshare and a considerable amount of actual commerce revenue for the participants and creators of virtual value. The code examples shown are fairly basic, but illustrate both adding behaviors to objects and communicating with external Web services.

Additionally, this chapter includes a very worthwhile interview you won't want to miss with Wagner James Au, embedded reporter for Second Life and chief blogger for New World Notes (nwn.blogs.com). His insights into the e-life and commercial vitality of Second Life are both instructive and entertaining.

Looking Back in Rich Immersion: The World of Magic Cap

To understand that vision, let's travel a bit back in time first. The idea of representing interaction with physical representations of people, places, and things is not a new one. Before there was the World Wide Web, before the browser, innovators were creating modes of interaction intended to support a user illusion of interacting with cartoonish representations of familiar things or visiting familiar places. Figure 18-1 shows a user running the Magic Cap interface on a small purpose built device (called a *communicator*) created especially to support the interface of local on-platform tasks and tasks distributed over a dial-up or radio network.

Figure 18-1

From the desktop, a user could make a voice telephone call (wireline), use e-mail, or do personal information management activities. Magic Cap offered a more realistic desktop portrayal than what Microsoft delivered in their Windows product line, but otherwise this part of the experience was a fairly sterile and solo pursuit. The most interesting thing about Magic Cap was that once the user left the desktop environment, they could "travel." Because Magic Cap maintained a "place" metaphor, users could move from their desktop into a hallway and visit other rooms in their virtual homes, doing things like playing simple single-user games. The hallway is shown in Figure 18-2.

Figure 18-2

Users could also travel out of their house to a place called *downtown*, which (for your purposes in understanding where this chapter will lead you) is where the interface became interesting. Users could install packages represented as building exteriors and simple interiors, which represented various services. One of the few screenshots that remain of such a service, a diner, is shown in Figure 18-3.

Figure 18-3

The experience of interacting with such a service was much like filling out a Web-based form might be in Web 1.0 or Web 2.0 today. Although the illusions of place, travel, and interaction with a cartoon representation of a storefront were maintained, the vision was essentially the same sterile, solitary interaction model of Web 1.0 collectively understood today.

General Magic launched in 1993, with the generous backing of the once powerful U.S. telephony giant AT&T, but was essentially sunk within a year due to the emerging World Wide Web, and the browser in a little over a year later. Even AT&T, not always the most forward-thinking company, could read the handwriting on the wall. Thus reality bit hard, and the Internet and consequent World Wide Web we got as a result were nothing like a parallel embodiment of the real world.

Forward in Time: The World of Snow Crash

Around the same time as the little remembered emergence and rapid demise of Magic Cap, Neal Stephenson's seminal work, *Snow Crash*, was published. As the quotes at the head of the chapter suggest, *Snow Crash* presented the concept of the *metaverse*, a vast world where action, adventure, community, and commerce all co-mingled to create life as we know it, only different. Back in the dimly remembered adolescence of the Internet, Stephenson encouraged users to think of "cyberspace" as though it had physicality, as though it were a "place" in some sense like London or Paris, but less bounded by the laws of time and space.

Books like *Snow Crash* convinced users that someday they would interact in such a way that real life and virtual life would co-exist as parallel and co-equal domains, that the facile among us would operate with equal capability in either realm; and that the things that might be possible to do, to feel, to buy, to experience in the physical realm would be equally possible (perhaps even more so) in the other. Many thinkers even suggested that experiencing existence in the unbounded virtual realm of the metaverse might be superior in some dimensions to real life. Indeed, though the action in the *Snow Crash* narrative takes place equally in real and virtual space, the protagonist's adventures in the metaverse are far more compelling than his existence in real life.

At the time *Snow Crash* was written (1992), the concept of the metaverse was a pipe dream, and pretty far off futurist stuff. Computers and networks simply could not support the seamless illusion of immersion in another place, in another embodiment. Some experts were fairly certain that eventually Moore's Law on the periodic doubling of compute power, the variously attributed law of network capacity doubling, and Metcalf's Law on the utility of networks might someday make the vision of an immersive experience, expressed in terms of time and place and interacting with other people, a reality.

And Now: The World of Second Life

In 2003, a barely noticed implementation of a metaverse did in fact spring to life. Called *Second Life*, by late 2006 it had became the most-hyped vision of the future of an interactive, shared, social, commercial framework since the emergence of HTML, HTTP, and the original NCSA Mosaic Web browser.

What is so compelling about Second Life and other emergent virtual (non-game worlds)? As a 2006 interview with Philip Rosedale, the chief executive of Linden Labs explains, entering Second Life, people's digital alter egos — known as *avatars* — can move around and do everything they do in the physical world, but without such bothers as the laws of physics. According to Rosedale, "When you are at Amazon.com [using current Web technology] you are actually there with 10,000 concurrent other people, but you cannot see them or talk to them," Rosedale said. "At Second Life, everything you experience is inherently experienced with others."

Think of what this would mean to a social site, such as that discussed in Chapter 2. Instead of posting entries and responses on a site such as slashdot.org or digg.com, and then reading them from a Web page or an RSS feed, imagine conversing, in real time, with actual peers on emerging stories from real Reuters or CNet news feeds. Imagine opening a storefront site for your next brilliant idea and having it literally be a storefront, where you could literally and in real time interact with your user base and potential customers. Imagine a world in which you could multi-task by first tending to personal activities from "home" and then turning attention to "work" and then breaking for lunch in an RPG (role-playing game) adventure or going to a virtual beach in the middle of the day. Figure 18-4 shows one of the authors relaxing on a (virtual) beach.

Figure 18-4

That's the promise that Second Life delivers; and in this chapter, you will master some of the programming paradigm to advance this vision. The authors caution that before you get carried away by these heady pronouncements, be aware that Second Life as it currently exists is a down payment on a future vision. Perhaps many of you reading this book will deliver the rest of the vision, taking it in directions that we can scarcely dream.

Remember that just before the advent of the PC era, the chairman of IBM famously told his board of directors, "There is a world market for only about five computers." A later IBM chairman mused, "What are all these people going to do with computers in their homes? Print out recipes?" We do not pretend to know where Second Life and its progeny will lead humanity, but we do know that there is room for more than five participants, and end users are doing far more than printing recipes. The following list suggests some reasons why metaverses, and especially *Second Life,* should be on your developer radar:

❑ **Commerce is built into Second Life** — It has a real economy fueled by a real currency. Although most of the goods and services in Second Life are virtual, the money is real, and the intellectual property you create is yours. Thus, the programming you do in this world is convertible to real revenue. Residents spent over USD $200 million in this virtual world in 2006.

❑ **Every object in Second Life is there because a software developer created it** — Currently, the Second Life incarnation of the metaverse is the open frontier, the wild west. No large players dominate the landscape; by mastering Linden Scripting Language (LSL), you are on even footing with any developer anywhere.

- ❑ **Potential customers are very loyal to the environment and the experience** — It is estimated that Second Life "residents" currently spend 40 hours a month in-world, a little more than 10% of the amount of time the average American spends watching television per month. Consider the positive impact for your company of that level of exposure to potential consumers.

- ❑ **Second Life is inherently a social experience, rather than a game-playing environment** — It has been estimated that slightly less than 50% of Second Life residents are female; this far exceeds female immersion in game-playing environments. Any Web-based business that can attract genders equally holds tremendous promise.

- ❑ **Your creations are potentially infinitely scalable** — For example, you can create shade-changing sunglasses or dirigibles and after you sell the first copy, you'll still have an infinite number left.

Second Life: The Programmer's View

The primary attraction for a software developer in using a platform like Second Life is the ability to create objects that have credible dynamism, even when compared to AJAX and Web browser–based applications. Virtually every one of the objects you encounter in Second Life (SL), from beach balls to shopping malls, has been created by a developer or a developer team. A short (and incomplete) description of SL is that it is a huge simulator running a potentially enormous number of finite state machines (FSMs). The scripting environment controlling the execution of every one of the FSMs — yours and others, is a C-like language called Linden Scripting Language (LSL).

The "Hello World" script, the one produced each time you either click the New Script button in the in-world object builder, or right-click New Script in your Inventory, looks like the code shown in Listing 18-1.

Listing 18-1: Default LSL script

LSL

```
default
{
    state_entry()
    {
        llSay(0, "Hello, Avatar!");
    }

    touch_start(integer total_number)
    {
        llSay(0, "Touched.");
    }
}
```

This script does two simple things. First, whenever the object is instantiated, and even before it is rendered, the object proclaims (by using the `llSay()` function), "Hello, Avatar!" on the open chat channel to anyone within earshot. Additionally, if a user touches the object to which the script is attached, the touch callback, `touch_start`, fires. You will find as you work with LSL scripting that flow control is fairly easy to comprehend, especially if you have any experience with event-driven programming

This should look sufficiently familiar to any C or Java programmer as to be relatively trivial, although there are some subtleties, described in the next couple of sections. For now, note some tantalizing clues. The preceding script is a complete state machine that you can attach to an arbitrary object. The identifiers 'default', 'state_entry', and 'touch_start' are not random terms, but rather one of several built-in callback names that can appear in the default FSM handler collection (called, conveniently enough, 'default'). While you, as a developer, can define your own state handler callbacks, and jump to them using the 'state' flow control statement, only the built-in states may occur within the confines of the default code block. Table 18-2 provides a complete listing of built-in states.

LSL Data Types

LSL uses a syntax that should be familiar to C or Java developers. It features the types shown in Table 18-1. Although some of these are obvious, others may surprise most developers. C programmers may be happy to see the explicit support for string operations, such as concatenate (via the + operator), and the usual operations supported for Java strings.

Table 18-1: LSL Data Types

Data Type	Usage
integer	Whole number in the range -2,147,483,648 to 2,147,483,647
float	Decimal number in the range 1.175494351E-38 to 3.402823466E+38
vector	Three floats in the form < x , y , z >. Usually a position, color, or Euler rotation. An example declaration is vector a = <1,2,3>;
rotation	Rotations consist of four floats, in the form < x , y , z , s >. The s term connotes an angular measurement.
key	A UUID (specialized string) used to identify something in SL, notably an agent, object, sound, texture, other inventory item, or dataserver request
string	A sequence of characters, limited only by the amount of free memory available to the script
list	A heterogeneous collection of other data types, (i.e., excluding list itself)

As Table 18-1 shows, in addition to C native types such as integer and float, LSL also explicitly supports the UTF-8 string type, which behaves just as you would expect it to (in Java, not C), and a key type for creating, manipulating, and representing globally unique identifiers (GUIDs). There are no user-defined constants, thus nothing like an enum exists.

LSL is event-driven, features states, and supports 3D variable types (vector and quaternion). As you might expect, LSL has built-in functions for manipulating physics and social interaction among avatars. LSL adds some interesting keywords, such as state, which is essentially a go to operator that forces a transition in a new state handler.

For representing collections, LSL seems somewhat impoverished, supporting only the `list` type. There are no arrays or dictionaries, and lists cannot contain other lists. Lists in LSL are sufficiently annoying that an expanded description of them is offered here:

❑ The `list` type may contain heterogeneous elements comprised of lists of other primitive data types. Lists are created via comma-separated values (CSVs) of the other data types, enclosed by square brackets: `["` and `"]`. A typical list declaration would resemble the following:

```
//a list with a two integers, a string, float, vector and rotation
list l = [42,0, "electric sheep",3.1416,<1.0,2,0>,<0,0,0,1>];
```

❑ Lists store not only type metadata about each list item, but also its type, accessed through list accessor primitives `llGetListEntryType` and `llCSV2List`. (A small annoyance with LSL is that every built-in function — and there are myriad — must begin with `ll`, as if developers needed a reminder as to whose scripting environment they were using.)

❑ Lists can only be read using accessor functions (rather than bracket notation). Thus, to retrieve the first element from the list declared above and cast it to a string, you might use the following:

```
string element;
element = llList2String(l,0);
```

❑ Elements fetched from lists are accessed and cast to type in a single operation; `llList2Float` retrieves an element and casts it to float, `llList2Integer` casts the element to integer, and so on.

❑ An interesting bit of extra fun is that the LSL compiler will only accept code with a maximum of 72 items in a list declaration (call it a "feature"). You can grow endless lists (up to the size of machine memory) by using concatenation thereafter. Even at the time of declaration, you can make a longer list of shorter compile-time defined lists via concatenation. For example, `longerList = listOne + listTwo;` will compile perfectly well.

❑ One additional shortcoming is that because lists cannot contain other lists, multi-dimensional arrays are difficult to create and manage. One way to get around both the lack of arrays and the lack of an explicit object model is to use *list striding*.

To create an internal structure in lists, you must use striding. A strided list is simply a list with items grouped together in a fixed and repeating layout. If, for example, you needed in-memory containment to record visitors to your store, such a list might contain the visitor name, the amount of Linden dollars spent, the item purchased, and the number of minutes spent on your premises. Although you would periodically persist this cache to a formal database, you might nonetheless want a short-term cache. In this case, you might use a strided list:

```
integer STRIDE = 4;
list patrons = ["Zeno Chambers", 500, "Magic Broomstick", "2006-10-31", "Biggie
Pike", 50, "Flagon of Pumpkin juice", "2006-10-31", "Mae Moriarity", 25, "Halloween
Hangover Kelper", "2006-11-01"];
```

Then you could use one of the strided list convenience functions to assist in managing the list. For example, to sort (ascending) a strided list, you would use the following:

```
patrons = llListSort(patrons, STRIDE, TRUE);
```

States

Although you can define callback listeners (or states) of your own, outside of the default block, Table 18-2 shows the only ones supported in the default block. Note that they can also appear outside the default block.

Table 18-2: LSL Built-in States

Event	Trigger
at_rot_target	Rotational target set when `llRotTarget` is reached
at_target	Target set when `llTarget` is reached
attach	Object attaches or detaches from agent
changed	Anytime external events applied to inventory, color, shape, scale, texture, link, or ownership change aspects of the object
collision	Fires while an object collides with another object
collision_end	Fires when an object stops colliding with another object or stops being penetrated while `llVolumeDetect` is set
collision_start	Fires when task starts colliding with another task or starts being penetrated while `llVolumeDetect` is set
control	Fires when one of the controls taken with `llTakeControls` is pressed/held/released
dataserver	Object receives asynchronous data
email	Object receives e-mail
http_response	Object receives response to request made with `llHTTPRequest`
land_collision	Object is colliding with land
land_collision_end	Object stops colliding with land
land_collision_start	Object starts colliding with land
link_message	Object receives a link message sent via `llMessageLinked`
listen	Object is within hearing range of chat matching the criteria set in `llListen`, usually a channel descriptor. Hearing range is fixed in Second Life to be 10 meters.
money	Fires when money is given to the object
moving_end	Object stops moving or when task exits a sim
moving_start	Object begins moving or when task enters a sim
no_sensor	Fires when a call to `llSensor` or `llSensorRepeat` results in no targets sensed
not_at_rot_target	Fires when a rotational target set with `llRotTarget` is not yet reached

Table continued on following page

Event	Trigger
not_at_target	Fires when a target set with llTarget is not yet reached
object_rez	Fires when object rezzes (instantiates) another task using llRezObject, and the object is rendered
on_rez	Fires when an object is rezzed (instantiated) and the object is rendered (from inventory or another task)
remote_data	Fires on any kind of XML-RPC communication
run_time_permissions	Fires when an agent grants runtime permissions to an object requested via llRequestPermissions
sensor	Fires as a result of llSensor or llSensorRepeat functions
state_entry	Any transition into the state and on startup
state_exit	Any state transition out of the state
timer	In intervals set by llSetTimerEvent, a float represents a fraction of a second
touch	While agent clicks on object
touch_start	When agent starts clicking on object
touch_end	When agent stops clicking on object

To illustrate states, code blocks, transitions, and helper functions, regard Listing 18-2, adapted from an example available from the LSL scripting wiki site (http://lslwiki.com/lslwiki/wakka.php?wakka=HomePage).

Listing 18-2: Multiple states and helper functions

LSL

```
1 integer g_whisper = 1;
2 integer g_loud = 2;
3
4 say(integer channel, string message, integer style )
5 {
6     if (style == g_loud){
7         llSay(message);
8     }
9     if (style == g_whisper){
10         llWhisper (channel, message);
11     }
12 }
13 default
14 {
15     state_entry()
16     {
17         say(0, "Now in default state. *yawn*", g_whisper );
18     }
19
20     touch_start( integer iTouched )
```

```
21      {
22          state funky;
23      }
24
25      state_exit()
26      {
27          say(0, "Hey... I feel a little funny... Strange...", g_whisper );
28      }
29 }
30 state funky
31 {
32      state_entry()
33      {
34          say(0, "I'm in a FuNkY state!", g_loud );
35      }
36
37      touch_start( integer iTouched )
38      {
39          state default;
40      }
41
42      state_exit()
43      {
44          say(0, "Aw, I'm starting to mellow, man...", g_loud );
45      }
46 }
```

Note the following about Listing 18-2:

❏ Lines 4–11 define a simply utility function that will restrict the range of the utterance to 10 meters (whisper) or 20 meters (loud), but will respond on the public channel (channel 0) so that anyone can read its output. As an exercise, try this script on an object you create: See if you can extend it to include a third message state (g_private_message, for example), and use the llOwnerSay(string message); function to privately message the owner of the object. Note that a user-defined function should not be used to switch states; rather, use functions within the default block.

❏ Lines 13–29 are the default block, which must be present in an object's script. Note the use of the say helper function on lines 17 and 27. Control transfers to the utility function and flow picks up inside the enclosing handler on its return. When the object is touched, control migrates to a separate FSM block beginning on line 30. Note that while the default FSM block does not need to be prefaced by the state keyword, other FSM blocks do. Also note the use of the state_exit function (lines 25–28). This function is not normally needed in the default block, but here it is useful because the object transitions from the default state to the funky state. In this trivial example, there is no transitional cleanup to perform, but in a more complex state machine, there almost certainly would be.

❏ Beginning at line 32, state_entry is the handler function that's immediately called when the funky state is entered. In LSL, state_entry is the place to do any initialization or additional construction needed to set up the operating conditions for the state. Figure 18-5 shows a large floating sphere that contains this script.

In Figure 18-5, which shows the LSL multi-state script in action, the object owner, ElectricSheep Expedition, has touched the sphere a number of times. The object executes its exit handler, whispering, "Hey . . . I feel a little funny . . . strange . . ." The next line of output shows that the sphere has now transitioned, as it announces to anyone in the normal 20-meter range, "I'm in a FuNkY state!" When ElectricSheep touches the sphere again, it executes the exit handler for the current state, outputting, "Aw, I'm starting to mellow, man . . . ," and then returns to the default state, beginning the cycle once again.

Figure 18-5

LSL Statements and Flow Control

An LSL statement is a line of code terminated by a semicolon. All statements in a program are separated from one another by semicolons (the compiler ignores whitespace). Groups of statements aggregate to functions as in C or Java, delimited by curly braces. As in Ruby and Python, LSL follows the "principle of least surprise" (at least if you're coming from a C-like programming worldview).

Flow control keywords (see Table 18-3) in LSL are very like C in their syntactic construction, and operate precisely as a C programmer might expect. One addition is the `jump` statement, which many of us have never seen; it's equivalent to the ancient "goto" statement and effects an immediate transfer of control to a label which is the object of the `jump` statement. Thus, a `jump label20;` statement will transfer control to a block of code beginning `label20:` and immediately begin executing there. The `state` keyword is similar in nature, but on execution it transfers flow control immediately to a state handler, as shown in Listing 18-2, line 22.

Table 18-3: LSL Flow Control

Keyword	Description
if-else	Executes the statement until the semicolon, or a block of statements within curly braces if the expression contained within parentheses is `true`
while	Executes some statements as long as an expression contained within parentheses is `true`
do-while	Executes some statements at least once and then as long as an expression contained within parentheses is `true`
for	Executes some statements a set number of times. Uses notation identical to C, C++, or Java.
jump	Jumps to another part of a function or event. Yes, folks, the "goto" has returned!
return	Exits a function or event (and may return a value)
state	Transitions from one script state to another. May transition to a user-defined state not in the `default` block.

You may also attach multiple scripts to the same object, enabling a style of small, single-function scripts to evolve. This leads to scripts that perform specific functions (e.g., hover) and allows scripts to be combined to form new behaviors. This ability to create Ruby-style *mixins* is very powerful, but remember that the SL engine is not multi-threaded, so in cases where an object inherits its behavior from multiple state machines, consider the effect that "dueling event handlers" might have on the externally observed actions of the object.

Because Second Life (through LSL) is essentially a finite state machine handler, scripts attached to objects (which may be avatars or any other created object in the Second Life world) are essentially all event-driven listener functions. You can generate events in one state machine block that queue that event and fire the handler for the event (eventually). We say "eventually" because LSL is not multi-threaded; thus, any events preceding the one you create in a given state are fired first. There is no guarantee of ordering.

The structure of an LSL script is fairly rigid, and roughly as described in Listing 18-2. There *must* be a stanza that is encapsulated by the identifier "default." Thus, for example, when you create an object, click the Content tab, and then click the New Script button, a script template called "New Script" is created, as shown in Figure 18-6.

Figure 18-6

Getting Started: The Essential Second Life Elements

First, you'll need to download the Second Life client for your platform. There are clients for Windows, Mac OS X, and Linux at www.secondlife.com. After installing, create an identity and an avatar for yourself. Those are easy and fun exercises, but can be distracting timesinks. Every Avatar carries with it an inventory of purchased or created objects. You need to create objects and then copy them to your inventory. If you buy and hold virtual land in Second Life, you can place whatever you want there and it will remain. This rule applies equally to items you purchase from others or items you create. Thus, for example, even though your library of objects may, by default, contain a number of interesting items, from a parrot to a log cabin, and although you may create artifacts, as illustrated in Listing 18-3, you will need to acquire land to give them a permanent home. This is how thousands of "residents" have created commercial revenue-producing sites that vend fashions, automobiles, and other virtual-only artifacts.

After going in-world, it's highly recommended that you teleport to one of the sandbox areas. You can build and test objects of your own creation in a sandbox and then copy them into your inventory.

> Note that all sandboxes are wiped twice a day, so be sure to copy your creations back into your inventory periodically (a rough equivalent of the dictum "save early, save often").

You can create an object using in-world building tools or import external constructs created via a variety of tools, from Google's Sketchup or Blender 3D (for creating structural models) to Avimator (for creating animations). In-world tools are acceptable for creating many types of objects, but because you may be more familiar with other tools, creating externally and importing may be a better choice. The same applies to IDEs and external editors. In script-building mode, you can access a syntax highlighting editor, but plug-ins exist for popular external text editors.

Connecting Second Life to Real Life

This script demonstrates both a typical finite state machine and some of Second Life's asynchronous communication capability. Second Life supports XML-RPC and HTTP Requests, and you can write handler methods capable of sending and receiving e-mail message traffic. This exercise demonstrates the e-mail interface. You create an object that exists in the virtual world, sitting apparently dormant, but reporting the ongoing chat to an e-mail address of your choice. To preclude the possibility of an e-mail flood, you set a short timer to shut off the object's listening capability.

Listing 18-3: Chat-Catcher LSL

```
LSL
 1 //This script forwards all surrounding chat to the via email
 2 string  g_Mail_Addr = "somename@somemail.com";
 3 integer g_email = FALSE;
 4 integer g_IM = FALSE;
 5 integer g_listen_channel = 0;
 6 integer g_command_channel = 2;
 7 float   g_maxtimeout = 180.0;
 8
 9
10 string g_emailStateOn = "Recording has been enabled!";
11 string g_emailStateOff = "Recording has been disabled!";
12 string g_IMStateOn = "IM relay has been enabled!";
13 string g_IMStateOff = "IM relay has been disabled!";
14
15 default
16 {
17     on_rez(integer param) {
18         llResetScript();
19     }//on_rez
20
21     // toggle state during the touch handler
22     state_entry(){
23         string owner = llGetOwner();
24         llGiveInventory(owner, ⤶
    llGetInventoryName(INVENTORY_OBJECT, 0));
25         llListen( g_command_channel, "", owner, "" );
26         llListen( g_listen_channel, "", NULL_KEY, "" );
27         llInstantMessage(owner, g_emailStateOff+" Type: 'IM!' ⤶
    to enable IM feedback.");
28         llInstantMessage(llGetOwner(), llDetectedName(0) + " touched me.");
```

(continued)

Listing 18-3: *(continued)*

```
29              llSetTimerEvent(g_maxtimeout);
30
31      }//state entry
32
33      listen( integer channel, string name, key id, string message ){
34          string owner = llGetOwner();
35          if (channel == g_command_channel){
36              list messageContent = llParseString2List(message, [" "], []);
37              integer len = llGetListLength(messageContent);
38              message = llList2String(messageContent,0);
39              if(message == "!hear"){
40                  g_email = FALSE;
41                  llInstantMessage(owner, g_emailStateOff);
42              }//disable email
43              if(message == "hear!"){
44                      if (len < 2){
45                          llInstantMessage(owner, "incomplete message: ⤷
    I need an email address too");
46                      } else {
47                          g_email = TRUE;
48                          g_Mail_Addr = llList2String(messageContent,1);
49                          llSetTimerEvent(g_maxtimeout);
50                          llInstantMessage(owner, g_emailStateOn+⤷
    " sending to "+g_Mail_Addr);
51                      }
52              }//enable email
53              if(message == "!IM"){   //default mode
54                  g_IM = FALSE;
55                  llInstantMessage(owner, g_IMStateOff);
56              }//disable IM
57              if(message == "IM!"){
58                  g_IM = TRUE;
59                  llInstantMessage(owner, g_IMStateOn);
60              }//enable IM
61          }
62          if(g_email){
63              if(g_IM){
64                  //send IM to owner of chat channel relay if on
65                  llInstantMessage(owner, message);
66              }
67              //send email to owner of chat channel relay
68              llEmail(g_Mail_Addr, "SL Listening", message);
69          }//end if(g_email)
70      }// end listen
71
72      timer(){ // on expire of timer, discontinue
73          g_email = FALSE;
74          g_IM = FALSE;
75      }
76
77 }//default
```

Note the following about this code:

❑ The first dozen or so lines declare and instantiate useful global variables. The `g_maxtimeout` is set to three minutes, but you may want to experiment with this. The general chat channel (`g_listen_channel`) is 0. A private channel (`g_command_channel`) is set aside for the object to listen to commands from its owner.

❑ On line 17, the script is reset using `llResetScript`. This is always a good idea, especially if the script is attached to an object intended for sale or transfer. On transfer to a new owner, any listens set to the owner are reset, and all pending events are cleared when the object is instantiated by its new owner. After a `llResetScript` invocation, control is transferred to the `default` block, and its `state_entry` is triggered. When writing and debugging the script, you can achieve the identical effect as specifying "reset" in the script editor.

❑ Lines 22–31 are the initializer for the default FSM block. The script transfers ownership of the object to which the script is attached to the new owner. Next, in lines 25–26, the object posts a listen on channels 0 and 2. Then the object issues two private message to the object owner, and sets the operational maximum time for the script to operate (lines 28–30).

❑ In the `listen` handler, whenever a message is received on channel 2, the object parses it (lines 35–52). The object is anticipating a message from the following set:

  ❑ **"/2 hear! emailname@email_address"** — This command forwards any conversation in the object's proximity to the e-mail address specified as the second argument.

  ❑ **"/2 !hear"** — This command cancels any listens on the public channel (channel 0).

  ❑ **"/2 IM!"** — This command will private message the general (channel 0) conversation to the object's owner, even if the owner is no longer in the proximity of the conversation (teleported to another place, for example).

  ❑ **"/2 !IM"** — This command cancels the forwarding of public messages as private messages to the object's owner.

❑ On line 36, the listener uses `llParseString2List` to break the input message into a list of strings. The command itself is the zero'th element of the list, and is pulled from the list on line 38. Note that the message channel designator (`"/2"`) is not a part of the message payload, and messages to the command channel must be prefaced with this command channel qualifier. Any messages, whether from the object owner or anyone else in proximity, will be heard on channel 0, and no channel designator is needed for public chat messages.

❑ If the "hear!" message is incomplete, this is checked in lines 44–46, and a private message is sent back to the object owner. If the message has an e-mail address, the e-mail address is teased from the message body (which by now has been parsed into a list). Line 38 splits the message body into a list, with whitespace as the separator. This code doesn't check the e-mail address for valid syntax, but that could be easily added by turning the string into a list with the "@" sign as the separator, and looking at the list length.

❑ Lines 53–66 complete command channel processing to turn private messaging on or off. On line 68, an e-mail message is sent to the e-mail address provided.

Try this out on an object you create. Note that some privately owned land in Second Life may not permit you to instantiate the object. Figure 18-7 shows an avatar creating the Chat Catcher Object. Figure 18-8 shows creating the Chat Catcher script shown in Listing 18-3.

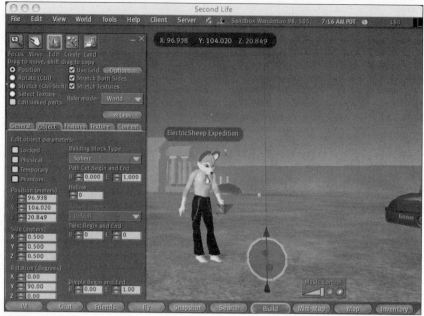

Figure 18-7

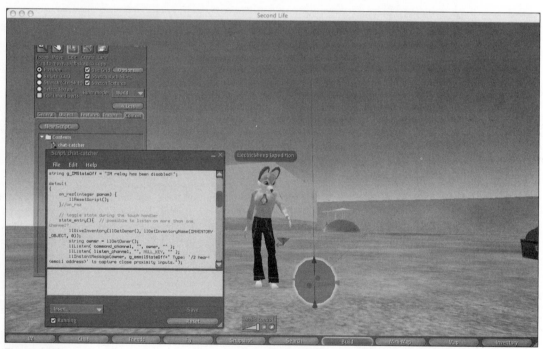

Figure 18-8

A Web 2.0 Demonstration of Second Life

Although Second Life is an extremely rich world, both users and content creators would suffer greatly if it were an entirely closed world, so many places in Second Life stream Internet content into the world and many objects are asynchronously refreshed from the Web. Just as in a browser-based application, a full page refresh would break the fluidity of the user experience. The simulation must continue seamlessly in Second Life. In Web 2.0 applications, the implementations you've seen and created remedy this situation by performing partial asynchronous page refreshes. In Second Life, the same result is accomplished by the event handler infrastructure. A specific event handler, http_response (see Table 18-2 for the entire list), responds to returned server data.

Client (Second Life)-Side Query Generator

An HTTP request can be made via the llHTTPRequest function from anywhere in the state machine or a helper function called from the state machine. Let's look at the strategy in Listing 18-4, which shows the client side of the interaction.

Listing 18-4: Quotation generator

LSL

```
1  // store my object's request; all scripts in object get the same replies
2  key gRequestid;
3
4  integer gCommandChannel = 2;
5  string gMyServer = "http://abraxas-soft.com/phpscripts/quoter.php";
6  string gOwner;
7  default
8  {
9      on_rez(integer param) {
10         llResetScript();
11     }
12     // toggle state during the touch handler
13     state_entry(){
14         llGiveInventory(llGetOwner(),
   llGetInventoryName(INVENTORY_OBJECT, 0));
15         gOwner = llGetOwner();
16         llListen( gCommandChannel, "", gOwner, "" );
17
18         llInstantMessage(gOwner, " Type: '/2 random!'
   to get a random quote of the day.");
19         llInstantMessage(gOwner," Type: '/2 quote! #'
   to get a specific quote by number.");
20
21     }
22     listen( integer channel, string name, key id, string message ){
23         // pick apart the command
24         if (channel != gCommandChannel) return;
25         list messageContent = llParseString2List(message, [" "], []);
26
27         integer len = llGetListLength(messageContent);
28         message=llList2String(messageContent,0);//either random! or quote!
```

(continued)

515

Listing 18-4: *(continued)*

```
29          if(message == "random!"){
30              gRequestid = llHTTPRequest(gMyServer,
31              [HTTP_METHOD, "POST",
32               HTTP_MIMETYPE, "application/x-www-form-urlencoded"],
33              "parameter1=random");
34          }else if(message == "quote!"){
35              if (len < 2){
36                  llInstantMessage(gOwner, "incomplete message: ⊃
   format is '/2 quote #'");
37                      return;
38              }
39              string which = llList2String(messageContent,1);
40
41              gRequestid = llHTTPRequest(gMyServer,
42              [HTTP_METHOD, "POST",
43               HTTP_MIMETYPE, "application/x-www-form-urlencoded"],
44              "parameter1=quote&parameter2="+which);
45          } else {
46              llInstantMessage(gOwner,"incorrect command.");
47          }
48      }
49      http_response(key request_id, integer status, list metadata, ⊃
   string body)
50      {
51          if (request_id == gRequestid)
52              llWhisper(0, "Quote of the day: " + body);
53      }
54 }
```

Note the following about Listing 18-4:

❑ Lines 1–5 declare some useful global variables. Although there are no hard-and-fast conventions for variable naming, adopting C conventions, such as prefacing globals with "g," is useful in aiding others to maintain your code. You need to modify the server URL to use your own. If you want to test against a target implementation, you may use the one mentioned on line 5. Like the example in Listing 18-3, a private command channel (2) is used to capture user input from the object's owner to the object. The object posts a listen on its private channel on line 16, and messages its owner via private message on lines 18 and 19.

❑ When the human owner tells the object either /2 random! or /2 quote <number>, the object responds through its listen handler (lines 22–48) by parsing the user's message and sending an outbound HTTP request, either line 30 or 41, depending on the request type. Notice the typical parsing technique used in LSL. First the message is split into a list through the llParseString2List method. Then the parser separates the elements of the string into a list based on the word delimiters array, argument two, and keeping with individual words any characters mentioned in the third argument.

❑ Typically, the individual list elements can be cast to an appropriate primitive type, as on line 28 or 39. Each string can be examined directly, and there are LSL conversion functions to convert strings to uppercase or lowercase and to select substrings.

Server-Side Quote of the Day Query Handler

The server side is almost as simple. Remember that a PHP array is always a dictionary type, but it can imitate the semantics of a list type. You need only specify a key for the first key/value pair, and subsequent entries, if specified as shown (without a key), will take on the next key value in sequence. Thus, the second member of the array may be accessed as `$arr[1]`, the third as `$arr[2]`, and so on, as if they were list indices. Listing 18-5 shows the quotation server code.

Listing 18-5: Quotation server

PHP

```php
<?
// Only works with PHP compiled as an Apache module
$arr = array(
0 =>"Welcome to the quote store",
"DRM 'manages access' in the same way that jail 'manages freedom.'",
"Give a man a fish, and he'll have fish for dinner. Teach him to fish, and you've
just blown away your entire $!&% marketbase.",          7 "I'm altering our deal ...
pray I do not alter it further. -- Darth Vader",
"Premature optimization is the root of all evil. - Donald Knuth" ,
"Aide-toi, le Ciel t'aidera - Help yourself, the Sky will help you - Jeanne
D'Arc.",
"In spite of everything, I still believe that people are really good at heart. -
Anne Frank",
"In theory, practice and theory are the same. In practice, they're not. -- Yogi
Bera",
// ... expand the array of quotes to taste ...
"When fascism comes to America it will be wrapped in a flag and carrying a cross.
",
"The opposite of love is not hate, it's indifference -- Jerry Seinfeld ",
"The terrorists hate our freedom, so by eliminating the freedom, we can stop the
terrorists from hating us "
);
// get things from $_POST[]
$parameter1    = $_POST["parameter1"];
$parameter2    = $_POST["parameter2"];

srand((double)microtime()*1000000);
if ($parameter1 == "quote") {
    echo $parameter1. "\n". "\n";
    if ($parameter2 > sizeof($arr) ) $parameter2 = 0;
    $quote =  $arr[$parameter2];
} elseif ($parameter1 == "random") {
    $random = (rand()%sizeof($arr));
    $quote =  $arr[$random];
} else {
    $quote =  $arr[0];
}
echo $quote . "\n";
?>
```

The parameters are picked from the POST request and read. If the first parameter requests a specific quote from the stack, then the second parameter is the specific quote number. If the first parameter matches "random", then a random quote is pulled off the stack. In either case, the quote is returned via the echo function. Figure 18-9 shows an avatar exercising the quote object and server.

Figure 18-9

Summary

We began this book by telling you that you are in the midst of an important change in the way that applications are conceived and delivered, and by suggesting that armed with the right knowledge you can be instrumental in being an important part of that change. Now, in the book's final chapter, we lay down some hints about what may be over the next horizon. Second Life looks quite different from the Rich Internet Applications we designed and you implemented throughout the book. It requires a client download, and the control mechanisms for interaction are more like operating in a game environment than like working with a form in a browser.

Although the delivery mechanism may look a bit different from the browser-as-application-container model, the important elements of application delivery we've shown you throughout the book will remain relevant. In this chapter, you were able to exercise asynchronous server invocations and client-side response handlers. Additionally, you saw evidence that using a scripting language and a support framework will likely continue to be the state-of-the-art methodology to rapidly create robust applications. Applications are going to become increasingly network-centric; they are going to involve accommodating user-created content; and the design and coding approach you employ will create value by iteration and user reaction, rather than complex up-front design.

Be assured, though, that whatever delivery mechanisms emerge in the foreseeable future, the techniques and design approaches you have mastered will remain valid and an important new part of your capabilities.

A Conversation with Second Life's Official "Embedded Reporter": Wagner James Au

To better understand the dynamics of Second Life, both for end users and developers, we interviewed Wagner James Au (whose avatar name "in-world" is Hamlet Au). After arriving in-world, our interview team was invited to Au's office, with a view of a virtual San Francisco, shown in Figure 18-10. Left to right, the participants are Wagner James Au, Ray Budd, and Dana Moore.

Figure 18-10

On the Differences between Second Life and Previous Online Environments

Q: Hamlet, how long have you been involved in online communities?

Hamlet Au: In various forms, since college in the early 90s, first messaging boards like Plato and then later the WELL, and gradually MMOs like Everquest, though I never really got deeply involved in those.

Q: What do think you derive from being an actual resident in what I would define as "real cyberspace"? I differentiate a place like Second Life as being real cyberspace, and World of Warcraft (WoW) and the like as being game sims, but maybe I am being arbitrary.

Hamlet Au: No, I think that's a fair distinction. Traditional MMOs like WoW only let you embody yourself and your real personality to a certain level, whereas in Second Life you can do that not only through your avatar and your behavior but by what you literally bring into the world. Like this view of San Francisco, which is taken from my real-life apartment where I'm sitting right now. Even something as subtle as that allows me to merge my avatar with who I really am offline.

On the Social and Community Aspects of Second Life

Q: Here, people seem to be able to adopt an avatar and no one asks, "So what do you do in real life?" Will we experience the kind of crossover-into-real life kind of experiences that we have seen develop from The WELL and IRC, or is the "world enough" this time around? In the early days of IRC and The WELL, the participants knew or sought to know each other in context of chat and in real life as well.

Hamlet Au: Yeah, that kind of crossover started happening very early on, to the point where there's already a name for it: *mixed reality event*, where, for example, a real-life party will incorporate a Second Life space so people who can't make the real-life party can attend and interact in the Second Life analogue. People started doing that as early as 2004, so the desire to merge both realities was there early on.

On Second Life Economics

Q: Your role in Second Life is to act as the official embedded reporter and you also write a blog?

Hamlet Au: Yes, I do. It's at nwn.blogs.com. I was Linden Labs' official "embedded journalist" from 2003 to early 2006, so over three years. I helped document Second Life's emergence as a real community, and tell its stories to the world. I still do that, just on an independent basis now.

Q: The concept of embedded journalist in a synthetic world is fascinating if perhaps a little weird.

Hamlet Au: Well, I lucked into it. It came as a suggestion of Robin Harper of Linden Labs, during a demo of Second Life, when I was just a straight-up civilian freelance writer for Salon, Wired, and such.

Q: A follow on economics question: Clearly a first generation of a micro-economy is emerging in Second Life. It's not likely to be a final form, though. Do you expect to see the emergence of real jobs and a revenue model sufficient to attract our book's readers? Although much has been made of a Second Life resident called Anshe Chung making real-world revenues from selling real estate in Second Life, there must be more economic diversity? Are there in-world jobs other than escort, model, or club bouncer?

Hamlet Au: There's actually a wide variety of jobs emerging in Second Life. I agree there's been significant emphasis on Anshe Chung and that economic model per se. Here are some other viable professions I've written about: private detective, aerospace engineer, weapons manufacturer, architect, public notary, journalist, filmmaker, tour guide, programmer, protection agency, car designer, interior decorator.

Q: And these are all jobs that to some degree depend on software development to create the illusion of an underlying reality?

Hamlet Au: Yes, and these are generally jobs where the person is something totally different in real life. Cubey Terra is the top aerospace engineer, for example, although it's not like he works for Northrop Grumman or whatever. Private detectives: Check out my story "Watching the Detectives."

On the Immersive Qualities of Second Life

Q: So how does Second Life square with your early notions of a synthetic world? Do you see SL as the meta-verse, and if not, what else does it need to become the metaverse, where metaverse was set out quite vividly in Snow Crash?

Hamlet Au: What drew me to Second Life and made me stay (because I started getting good game industry offers that tempted me to leave Linden Labs) was that Second Life did seem to be a realization of Stephenson's metaverse. (Hamlet Au offers us a chair.) This is a perfect example. I was feeling uncomfortable standing up talking so long, and it didn't feel hospitable to have you guys standing around either. No one told me to feel that way; it's just part of the embodied experience.

I enjoyed traditional MMOs, but they fell so far short of what you'd read about in *Snow Crash*, I couldn't get that deeply into them.

Q: Do you see Second Life as another place for a Web presence or is it something much more — perhaps a next incarnation of the Web?

Hamlet Au: A "3D MySpace" has been a cute high-concept description of Second Life, although probably a "3D YouTube" is even better nowadays.

Q: The direct use of an economic infrastructure?

Hamlet Au: I still think it shines most in the free build sandboxes, because you'll see all those things plus dynamic 3D building and scripting on-the-fly, so you can actually create objects and spaces as you interact with people, and collaborate with them in that building.

Q: One critic of Second Life remarks that "I can't help wondering what Marshall McCluhan would have made of it." In Understanding Media, he said that a new medium initially apes the form/content of older media. Thus, early movies were stage plays on film, until Sergei Eisenstein and D.W. Griffith came along and explored film's novel capabilities, like montage, multithreaded plots, etc. So here we have radio trying to emulate TV in a brave new virtual world. A world awaiting its Eisenstein. How do you react to his observation?

Hamlet Au: I'd say he hasn't been following the development of computer games or virtual worlds very closely. There have already been several developers who qualify for the Eisenstein role. Will Wright is the most obvious example, synthesizing some elements of traditional visual narrative with the interactivity only possible in the computerized medium. And I've been following the rise of people in Second Life who, while not on a par with someone like Will yet, are definitely starting to play with Second Life and who do demonstrate it as a distinct medium.

On What's Emerging in Second Life

Q: Clearly there are emergent aspects unique to this medium. I have read of the movement to create a self-sustaining ecology in Second Life, which begs a question: Can you conceive of a time when Second Life is more than a set of relatively static "sets" to support character interaction? This is a variant of the "If a tree falls and no one is there to hear it, does it really fall?" observation.

Hamlet Au: Yeah, we gotta see that — RIGHT NOW! We'll continue this interview on a cloud. I'll teleport you.

(We teleport from Au's office and wind up on the cloud shown in Figure 18-11)

Figure 18-11

Hamlet Au (shouting): Right-click on the cloud and hit Sit! So this is Svarga, the artificial ecosystem, with weather and growing plants and birds and this cloud, which moves according to the "natural" wind patterns and rains on the island, watering the plants. If you like, this is the *Battleship Potemkin* of virtual worlds, except without all those poor Russian women getting trampled on the stairs. It's . . . a scientific experiment and a self-contained environment-as-art installation and an educational tool and, well, you can see how far things can go from here.

Part V
Appendix

Appendix: Dojo Validation Functions and Flags

Appendix: Dojo Validation Functions and Flags

This appendix provides a brief reference to the validation functions and flags available in Dojo. It initially describes functions used to validate basic data types such as integers, dates, and times. Following that, Internet-related validation functions such as IP or e-mail addresses are outlined. Finally, local-specific validation routines are examined.

Basic Dojo Validation Functions and Flags

As noted in Chapter 11, Dojo provides functions that are very useful for verifying that basic data values, such as integers, dates, and times, are formatted as you expect. Most validation functions can accept an optional set of flags. For example, the isInteger function accepts a `signed` a flag that indicates whether or not the integer must start with a plus (+) or minus (–) character. The function also takes an optional `separator` flag that establishes whether a thousands separator is allowed and if so, what character you should use. For example, the following call to the isInteger validation function indicates that validation will only return `true` if the integer is be signed, and thousands are either separated with a dot (.) or no thousands separator is present:

```
dojo.validate.isInteger("+32", {signed: true, separator: ["", "."]});
```

Note the following about the validation functions shown in the preceding code:

❑   You should define all flags between curly braces, i.e., {}.

❑   The specified flag name is followed by a colon (:), which should be followed by the value you want to assign to the flag.

❑ You may assign multiple values to the flag if they're included in an array (established with square brackets, i.e., []). See the multiple acceptable values "", and "." for the `separator` flag above.

❑ All functions return `true` or `false` depending on the test.

The following sections describe the basic Dojo validation functions and flags.

isText

This tests the length of a text string. It returns `true` if the string is not empty and does not violate any flags provided.

Flag	Default Value	Meaning
Length	Not defined	The required accepted string length
Minlength	Not defined	The minimum accepted string length
Maxlength	Not defined	The maximum accepted string length

isInteger

This tests whether a string defines an integer. The string can only contain digits, an optional sign, and a thousands separator.

Flag	Default Value	Meaning
Signed	Sign is optional	`true`, `false`, or `[true, false]` identifies whether a +/- sign is required, not allowed, or optional
Separator	Comma (,) is optional	The thousands separator you should use

isRealNumber

This tests whether a string is a real value number. This includes the requirement for an optional sign and thousands separator as well as a required number of decimal places, use of exponential notation, and inclusion of a sign on the exponent.

Flag	Default Value	Meaning
Signed	Sign is optional	`true`, `false`, or `[true, false]` identifies whether a +/- sign is required, not allowed, or optional
Separator	Comma (,) is optional	The thousands separator you should use
Places	Optional, unlimited	The required number of decimal places
Decimal	Period (.)	The character to use for the decimal point

Flag	Default Value	Meaning
Exponent	Optional	`true`, `false`, or [`true`, `false`] identifies whether the use of exponential notation is required, not allowed, or optional
eSigned	Optional	`true`, `false`, or [`true`, `false`] identifies whether a +/- sign on the exponent is required, not allowed, or optional

isInRange

This tests whether a string is within the range defined by the `min` and `max`. This function accepts currency, real numbers, and integers.

Flag	Default Value	Meaning
Max	Infinity	A number identifying the maximum acceptable value for the number
Min	Infinity	A number identifying the minimum acceptable value for the number
Decimal	Period (.)	The character to use for the decimal point

isNumberFormat

This tests whether a string conforms to a set of number formats identified by the format flag.

Flag	Default Value	Meaning
Format	"###-###-####", for example: 123-456-7890	A string or array of strings that identify the acceptable formats for the number. The appearance of a pound sign (#) means a digit is required, and a question mark (?) means the digit is optional.

isCurrency

This tests whether a string is defined as required to identify a monetary value. This is a locale-independent test. Local-specific versions of this test are defined below.

Flag	Default Value	Meaning
Signed	sign is optional	`true`, `false`, or [`true`, `false`] identifies whether a +/- sign is required, not allowed, or optional
Symbol	dollar sign ($)	The symbol to use for the currency

Table continued on following page

Flag	Default Value	Meaning
Placement	before	`before` or `after` identifies whether the symbol should be before or after the value
Separator	comma (,) is required	The thousands separator that you should use
Cents	cents are optional	`true`, `false`, or `[true, false]` identifies whether the two digits that represent the cents must, cannot, or can optionally appear after the decimal place
Decimal	period (.)	The character to use for the decimal point

isValidTime

This tests whether a string conforms to a set of time formats that the format flag identifies. There are three flags:

❑ **format** — This has a default value of "h:mm:ss t." It is a string, or array of strings, that identifies the acceptable time formats. Using the following abbreviations:

Format	Units	Format	Units
h	Hour in day (0-12)	m	Minutes (0-60)
hh	Hour in day (00-12)	mm	Minutes (00-60)
H	Hour in day (0-23)	s	Seconds (0-60)
HH	Hour in day (00-24)	ss	Seconds (00-60)
t	amSymbol, or pmSymbol		

❑ **amSymbol** — The symbol you use for AM, this has a default value of "AM."

❑ **pmSymbol** — The symbol you use for PM, this has a default value of "PM."

is12HourTime

This is a convenience function that tests whether a string conforms to one of two common 12-hour time formats: "h:mm:ss t" or "h:mm t". No flags are allowed.

is24HourTime

This is a convenience function that tests whether a string conforms to one of two common 24-hour time formats: "HH:mm:ss" or "HH:mm". No flags are allowed.

isValidDate

This tests whether a string or array of strings conforms to a set of date formats identified by the format flag. The general format is "MM/DD/YYYY." You can use the following abbreviations:

Format	Units	Format	Units
YYYY	Four-digit year	DD	Day in month (01–31)
M	Month in year (1–12)	DDD	Day in year (1–366)
MM	Month in year (01–12)	ww	Week in year (1–53)
D	Day in month (1–31)	d	Day of the week 1–7

Dojo Internet Validation Functions and Flags

Dojo also provides a set of functions for validating constructs such as URLs, e-mail addresses, or IP addresses. The following sections provide a list of the Internet-related validation functions and flags.

isIpAddress

This tests whether a string conforms to standard IP address conventions. All flags should be `true` or `false`, and are `true` by default.

Flag	Meaning
allowDottedDecimal	Accepts period (.) separated decimal format, e.g., 127.0.0.1
allowDottedHex	Accepts period (.) separated hexadecimal format, e.g., 0x7F.0x00.0x00.0x01
allowDottedOctal	Accepts period (.) separated octal format, e.g., 0177.0000.0000.0001
allowDecimal	Accept an single decimal number between 0–4294967295
allowHex	Accepts a single hexadecimal number between 0x0–xFFFFFFFF.
allowIPv6	Allows IPv6 addresses. The format is eight groups of four hexadecimal digits, e.g., 2001:0db8:85a3:08d3:1319:8a2e:0370:7334
allowHybrid	Allows IPv4 mapped IPv6 address format. The format is five hexadecimal digits followed by the IPv4 address, e.g., ::ffff:192.0.2.128

isUrl

This tests whether a string conforms to URL formatting conventions. In addition to the flags in the table that follows, this handles any flag that `isIPAddress` handles. Unless noted, flags should be `true` or `false`, and are `true` by default.

Flag	Meaning
scheme	`true`, `false`, or [`true`, `false`] indicate require, do not accept, or accept the standard URL schemes, e.g., `http://` and `ftp://`. Optional by default.
allowCC	Allows a two-letter country code, e.g., .uk and .ie
allowGeneric	Allows generic domain names, e.g., .com and .edu
allowInfra	Allows infrastructure domains, e.g., .arpa

isEmailAddress

This tests whether a string conforms to e-ail address formatting conventions. In addition to the flags in the table that follows, this handles any flag that `isIPAddress` handles. Unless noted, flags should be `true` or `false`, and are `true` by default.

Flag	Meaning
allowCruft	Accepts a URL-formatted e-mail address, e.g., <mailto:foo@bar.com>
allowIP	Accepts an ipaddress instead of a hostname. The default value is `true`.
allowLocal	Accepts the localhost host name. The default value is `false`.
allowPort	Accepts a port as a part of the e-mail address. The default value is `true`.
allowCC	Allows a two-letter country code, e.g., .uk and .ie
allowGeneric	Allows generic domain names, e.g., .com and .edu
allowInfra	Allows infrastructure domains, e.g., .arpa

isEmailAddressList

This tests whether a string conforms to e-mail address formatting conventions. In addition to the flags in the following table, this handles any flag that `isEmailAddress` handles.

Flag	Meaning
listSeparator	The separator to use for each e-mail address. The default values accepted are ";", ",", "\n", or " ".

Locale-Specific Validation Functions in Dojo

There are specific modules under the `validate` module that deal with locale-specific validation of fields. When calling a locale-specific function, you should include the location, as shown in the following call to the `us` specific function `isState`:

```
dojo.validate.us.isState("OH")
```

In Dojo 0.3.1, locale-specific functions are defined in modules for the United States (`us`), Germany (`de`), and Japan (`jp`), as shown in the various sections that follow.

us.isCurrency

Verify that a string is defined as required to identify a monetary value in the United States. Valid patterns include a dollar sign. Cents are optional, e.g., $22.34.

us.isState

Verify that a string corresponds to a valid state abbreviation. There are two flags:

Flag	Meaning
allowTerritories	The default value is `true`. Identifies whether territories (e.g., Guam) are included.
allowMilitary	The default value is `true`. Identifies whether military areas are included.

us.isPhoneNumber

Verify that a string conforms to common U.S. phone number formats. Valid formats include the following:

###-###-####	(###) ###-####	###.###.#### x#???
(###) ### ####	### ### ####	### / ###-#### x#???
###.###.####	##########	(###) ### #### x#???
### / ###-####	###-###-#### x#???	### ### #### x#???
(###) ###-#### x#???		

us.isSocialSecurityNumber

Verify that a string conforms to common U.S. social security number formats. Valid formats include the following:

"###-##-####"	"### ## ####"	"#########"

us.isZipCode

Verify that a string conforms to standard U.S. zip code number formats. Valid formats include the following:

"#####-####"   "##### ####"   "#########"   "#####"

jp.isJapaneseCurrency

Verify that a string conforms to standard Japanese currency conventions. The yen symbol must be in front of the number and no cents are allowed, e.g., ¥500.

de.isGermanCurrency

Verify that a string conforms to standard Euro currency conventions. This requires the Euro symbol to follow the number. The separator character is a period (.) and the decimal character is a comma (,), e.g., €1.000,90.

Index

Index

F

Listings (continued)